ISBN 978-0-260-06402-8
PIBN 10925488

United States
Circuit Court of Appeals

For the Ninth Circuit.

CONTINENTAL LAND COMPANY, a corporation, JULIUS C. JOHNSON, MABLE JOHNSON, SAMUEL T. SEATON, MARY A. SEATON, EMMA RATHS, MARTHA RATHS BALDWIN, WARREN BALDWIN, HENRY RATHS, GEORGE RATHS, ALBERT RATHS, ARTHUR RATHS, ALMA RATHS CLARK, FRED CLARK, MARY RATHS MARNHART, CLARENCE MARNHART, MINNIE RATHS, FRED RATHS and MANITA RATHS,

Appellants.

vs.

UNITED STATES OF AMERICA,

Appellee.

Transcript of Record

Upon Appeal from the District Court of the United States for the Eastern District of Washington, Northern Division.

FILED

MAY 7 - 1936

PAUL P. O'BRIEN,

United States

Circuit Court of Appeals

For the Ninth Circuit.

CONTINENTAL LAND COMPANY, a corporation, JULIUS C. JOHNSON, MABLE JOHNSON, SAMUEL J. SEATON, MARY A. SEATON, EMMA RATHS, MARTHA RATHS BALDWIN, WARREN BALDWIN, HENRY RATHS, GEORGE RATHS, ALBERT RATHS, ARTHUR RATHS, ALMA RATHS CLARK, FRED CLARK, MARY RATHS MARNHART, CLARENCE MARNHART, MINNIE RATHS, FRED RATHS and MANITA RATHS,

Appellants.

vs.

UNITED STATES OF AMERICA,

Appellee.

Transcript of Record

Upon Appeal from the District Court of the United States for the Eastern District of Washington, Northern Division.

INDEX

[Clerk's Note: When deemed likely to be of an important nature, errors or doubtful matters appearing in the original certified record are printed literally in italic; and, likewise, cancelled matter appearing in the original certified record is printed and cancelled herein accordingly. When possible, an omission from the text is indicated by printing in italic the two words between which the omission seems to occur.]

Index

NAMES AND ADDRESSES OF ATTORNEYS
OF RECORD

J. M. SIMPSON,
 United States Attorney,
  Spokane, Washington

S. R. CLEGG,
 Assistant U. S. Attorney,
  Spokane, Washington

B. E. STOUTEMYER,
 District Counsel, Bureau of Reclamation,
 Portland, Oregon
  Attorneys for Plaintiff, and Appellee

PARKER W. KIMBALL,
 Old National Bank Bldg.
  Spokane, Washington

F. J. McKEVITT,
 Old National Bank Bldg.
  Spokane, Washington

I. K. LEWIS,
 Duluth, Minnesota

EDW. H. CHAVELLE,
 Lyon Bldg.
  Seattle, Washington

CHAS. A. ATEN,
 Wilbur, Washington
  Attorneys for Defendants, and
   Appellants

In the District Court of the United States for the Eastern District of Washington, Northern Division.

No. L-4760

UNITED STATES OF AMERICA,

Plaintiff,

vs.

CONTINENTAL LAND COMPANY, a corporation; JULIUS C. JOHNSON; MABEL JOHNSON; and GRANT COUNTY, A MUNICIPAL CORPORATION: (claimants of Tracts No. 1 and No. 2) SAMUEL J. SEATON; MARY A. SEATON; and OKANOGAN COUNTY, a municipal corporation; (claimants of Tract No. 3)
EMMA RATHS, widow; MARTHA RATHS BALDWIN and WARREN BALDWIN, her husband; HENRY RATHS, GEORGE RATHS; ALBERT RATHS and ARTHUR RATHS, bachelors; ALMA RATHS CLARK and FRED CLARK, her husband; MARY RATHS MARNHART and CLARENCE MARNHART, her husband; MINNIE RATHS, spinster; FRED RATHS and MANITA RATHS, his wife; and OKANOGAN COUNTY, a municipal corporation; (claimants of Tracts No. 4, No. 5 and No. 6),

Defendants.

SUMMONS

UNITED STATES OF AMERICA to CONTI-
NENTAL LAND COMPANY, a corporation;
JULIUS C. JOHNSON; MABLE JOHNSON;
and GRANT COUNTY, a municipal corporation; (claimants of Tracts No. 1 and No. 2)
SAMUEL J. SEATON; MARY A. SEATON;
and OKANOGAN COUNTY, a municipal cor-
poration; (claimants of Tract No. 3) EMMA
RATHS, widow; MARTHA RATHS BALD-
WIN and WARREN BALDWIN, her hus-
band; HENRY RATHS, GEORGE RATHS,
ALBERT RATHS and ARTHUR RATHS,
bachelors; ALMA RATHS CLARK and FRED
CLARK, her husband; MARY RATHS
MARNHART and CLARENCE MARNHART,
her husband; MINNIE RATHS, spinster;
FRED RATHS and MANITA RATHS, his
wife; and OKANOGAN COUNTY, a municipal corporation, (claimants of Tracts No. 4,
No. 5, and No. 6) defendants above named:

You are hereby summoned to appear within
twenty (20) days after the service of this summons,
exclusive of the day of service, and defend the
above entitled action in the Court aforesaid; **and
in case of your failure so to do, judgment will be
rendered against you according to the demand [1*]
of the complaint,** which has been filed with the
Clerk of said Court.

---

*Page numbering appearing at the foot of page of original certified
Transcript of Record.

WITNESS, the HONORABLE J. STANLEY
WEBSTER, United States District Judge, at Spokane, Washington this 28th day of December, 1933

A. A. LaFRANBOISE,

[Seal]   Clerk.

By...

Deputy Clerk.

ROY C. FOX
    United States Attorney
E. J. FARLEY
    Assistant United States Attorney
B. E. STOUTEMYER
    Attorneys for Plaintiff.
    Spokane, Washington.

[Endorsed]: Filed Feb. 7, 1934. [2]

[Title of Court and Cause.]

COMPLAINT

Comes now the plaintiff, United States of America, by the Undersigned attorneys acting under and
by direction of the Attorney General of the United
States, and for its cause of suit against the above
named defendants alleges:

I.

That the defendant Continental Land Company
is a corporation organized and existing under and
by virtue of the laws of the State of Washington
and having its principal place of business in the
City of Spokane. [3]

II.

That the defendants Julius C. Johnson and Mable Johnson (also known as Mabel Johnson) are husband and wife.

III.

That the defendants Samuel J. Seaton and Mary A. Seaton are husband and wife.

IV.

That the defendants Emma Raths, widow, Martha Raths Baldwin and Warren Baldwin, her husband, Henry Raths, George Raths, Albert Raths and Arthur Raths, bachelors, Alma Raths Clark and Fred Clark, her husband, Mary Raths Marnhart and Clarence Marnhart, her husband, Minnie Raths, spinster, and Fred Raths and Manita Raths, his wife, are heirs at law of William Raths, deceased.

V.

That the defendants Grant County and Okanogan County are municipal corporations existing pursuant to the laws of the State of Washington.

VI.

That pursuant to the acts of Congress of June 17, 1902 (32 Stat. 388) and of June 16, 1933 (48 Stat. 195), the Secretary of the Interior of the United States of America as such officer and as Federal Emergency Administrator of Public Works has caused surveys and investigations to be made of the Columbia Basin project on the Columbia River, a federal project having for its purposes: [4]

Regulation of the flow of said stream by storage reservoirs; and

Coordinated development and use of said stream for the various purposes for which it is adapted, including navigation, hydro-electric power, flood control and irrigation, including irrigation of public lands of the United States,

all in respect to the waters of the Columbia River and contemplating the construction of dams for storage of the waters thereof and means for the diversion thereof and the utilization of the power generated by such storage and diversion, all in pursuance of the Constitution and laws of the United States; that such surveys and investigations have been particularly directed to the immediate plans of construction of a dam across said Columbia River at or near the head of the Grand Coulee, which dam constitutes the first unit and an integral part of a larger Grand Coulee dam which will form a part of the complete Columbia Basin project and serve as the diversion dam therefor and also as the principal storage reservoir on said stream to regulate the flow of said stream for flood control and to serve the purposes of navigation and power development at all points on such stream below said Grand Coulee dam.

VII.

That under appropriations made for that purpose by Congress, the Corps of Engineers, United States Army, have conducted exhaustive investigations of the Columbia River for the purpose of determining the best use of said stream and its tributaries for the various purposes to which it is adapted and has adopted a comprehensive and coordinated plan for the development and use of said stream for navigation, flood control and irrigation and [5] for the development of electrical energy to pay the cost of the proposed construction and for irrigation, pumping and industrial and domestic use.

VIII.

That the said comprehensive plan for the coordinated development of the Columbia River for navigation, flood control, power, and irrigation includes the construction of a series of dams at various points on the Columbia River, the uppermost of which is the Grand Coulee Dam.

IX.

That the said Grand Coulee Dam is the key structure in the said comprehensive plan for the coordinated development of said stream, in that the said Grand Coulee Dam will provide the necessary storage capacity to store the peaks of the Columbia River floods and by storing the floods and releasing the stored water during the low water season will improve the flow of said stream for navigation, power development, and irrigation and will reduce the flood dangers on the lower part of the stream.

X.

That it is estimated that the storage to be made available behind the said Grand Coulee Dam will about double the amount of firm power which can be developed at each of the proposed dam sites be-

tween the Grand Coulee and the mouth of the Snake
River and will increase by about 50% the amount of
firm power that can be developed at each of the
several dam sites below the mouth of the Snake
and that the said increased amount of firm power
made possible at each of said [6] lower dams by
reason of the storage behind the Grand Coulee Dam
is an important factor in the feasibility of each of
said lower dams as a self-liquidating project.

XI.

That in pursuance of the provisions of the said
act of June 16, 1933 (48 Stat. 195) the Emergency
Public Works Board and the Emergency Public
Works Administrator under the authorization of the
President of the United States has allocated for
the construction of said first unit dam and appurtenant structures from the Emergency Public Works
Fund, available by reason of said last mentioned act,
a sum of money estimated as sufficient to construct
said dam and acquire the necessary rights of way
therefor; and in pursuance of said last mentioned
act, and the allocation made thereunder, the said
Secretary and Emergency Public Works Administrator has authorized the construction of said dam
and the reservoir to be formed thereby and the acquisition of the necessary rights of way therefor.

XII.

That the plaintiff intends in good faith to construct said dam and reservoir and that the same is
now in actual course of construction.

XIII.

That the following described tracts of land are necessary for the construction of said dam and appurtenant structures and the reservoir in connection therewith and are located within the Eastern District of Washington: [7]

Tract No. 1

Lots One (1), Two (2), Three (3) and Southwest quarter of Northwest quarter (SW¼ NW¼), Section 1, Township 28 North, Range 30 East, Willamette Meridian, in Grant County, Washington, containing 169.25 acres, more or less.

Tract No. 2

Lots Four (4) and Five (5); also Northwest quarter of Southwest quarter (NW¼ SW¼) and Southwest quarter of Southwest quarter (SW¼ SW¼), Section 1, Township 28 North, Range 30 East, Willamette Meridian, in Grant County, Washington, containing 164.50 acres, more or less.

Tract No. 3

Lots One (1) and Two (2), Section 31, Township 29 North, Range 31 East; Lots Five (5), Six (6), Seven (7), Section 36, Township 29 North, Range 30 East; Lots Six (6), Seven (7), Eight (8), Nine (9), Section 1, Township 28 North, Range 30 East, Willamette Meridian, in Okanogan County, Washington, containing 315.30 acres, more or less.

Tract No. 4

Lots Two (2), Three (3) and Four (4), Section 6, Township 28 North, Range 31 East, Willamette Meridian, in Okanogan County, Washington, containing 111.37 acres, more or less.

Tract No. 5

Lot Three (3), Section 31, Township 29 North, Range 31 East, Willamette Meridian, in Okanogan County, Washington, containing 39.89 acres, more or less.

Tract No. 6

Lot Four (4), Section 31, Township 29 North, Range 31 East, Willamette Meridian, in Okanogan County, Washington, containing 39.97 acres, more or less;

plate showing said lands being attached hereto as a part hereof. [8]

XIV.

That the fee simple title to the lands herein described as Tracts No. 1 and No. 2 stands on the records of Grant County in the name of the defendants Continental Land Company, Julius C. Johnson and Mable Johnson; that the said defendants are in possession of said lands and that the defendant Grant County claims some interest therein, the exact nature and amount whereof is unknown to the plaintiff.

XV.

That the fee simple title to that part of Tract No. 3 described as follows:

Tract No. 3-A

Lots Five (5), Six (6), Seven (7), Section 36, Township 29 North, Range 30 East; Lots Six (6), Seven (7), Eight (8), Nine (9), Section 1, Township 28 North, Range 30 East, containing 217.45 acres, more or less

stands on the records of Okanogan County in the name of the defendants Samuel J. Seaton and Mary A. Seaton; that the remainder of Tract No. 3 described as follows:

Tract No. 3-B

Lots One (1) and Two (2), Section 31, Township 29 North, Range 31 East, containing 97.85 acres, more or less,

is unpatented land in which the said defendants claim some right, title, interest or possessory right; that the said defendants are in possession of Tract No. 3; and that said defendant Okanogan County claims some interest therein, the exact nature and amount whereof is unknown to the plaintiff. **[9]**

XVI.

That the fee simple title to that part of Tract No. 4 described as follows:

Tract No. 4-A

Lots 2 and 3, Section 6, Township 28 North, Range 31 East, Willamette Meridian, containing 75.69 acres, more or less,

and all of Tracts No. 5 and No. 6 stand on the records of Okanogan County, Washington, in the name of William Raths but that the said William Raths is now dead and that defendants Emma Raths, Martha Raths Baldwin and Arthur Baldwin, her husband, Henry Raths, George Raths, Albert Raths, Arthur Raths, Alma Raths Clark and Fred Clark, her husband, Minnie Raths, Fred Raths and Manita Raths, his wife, are heirs at law of the said decedent. That the remainder of Tract No. 4, described as follows:

Tract No. 4-B

Lot 4, Section 6, Township 28 North, Range 31 East, Willamette Meridian, containing 35.68 ing 75.69 acres, more or less,

is unpatented lands in which the said defendants claim some right, title and interest or possessory right. That the said defendants are in possession of said lands and that the defendant Okanogan County claims a tax lien interest in said lands, the amount and extent of which lien is to the plaintiff unknown. [10]

XVII.

That the United States has in good faith undertaken to purchase said lands without avail, the plaintiff and defendants being now in disagreement as to the market value of the lands herein described, and the United States does now in good faith continue its offer of purchase aforesaid.

WHEREFORE, Plaintiff prays that it be adjudged that the public use requires the condemnation of the real property hereinbefore described, and that this Court proceed to determine the respective interests of the defendants herein, and that title in fee simple be decreed to the United States upon the

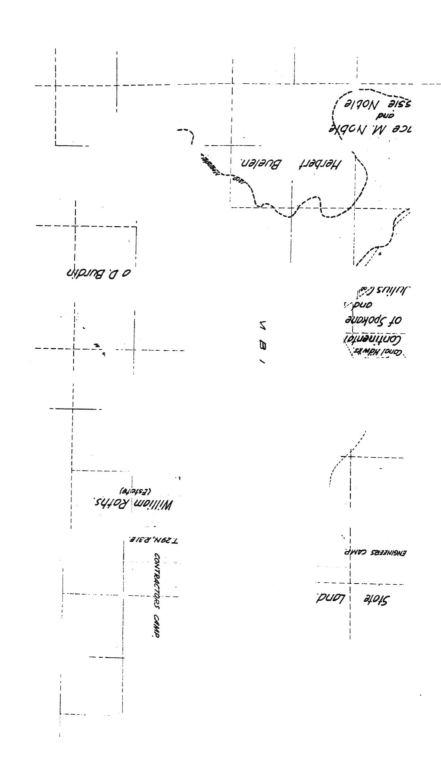

United States paying into Court, for defendants, the reasonable value of said property as ascertained by the Court.

ROY C. FOX

United States Attorney Eastern Dist. Wn.

B. E. STOUTEMYER

Attorneys for the Plaintiff,

Residing at Spokane, Washington and Portland, Oregon, respectively [11]

United States of America
State and District of Oregon
County of Multnomah—ss.

B. E. Stoutemyer, being first duly sworn, upon his oath says:

That he is District Counsel of the United States Bureau of Reclamation and as such officer is in possession of the facts to which the foregoing complaint pertains, and is duly authorized to make this verification for and on behalf of the plaintiff United States of America.

That he has read the foregoing complaint, knows the contents thereof, and believes the facts stated therein to be true.

B. E. STOUTEMYER

Subscribed and sworn to before me this 27th day of December, 1933.

[Seal]   EVA M. HARDIN

Notary Public for Oregon

My commission expires ....

Deputy Clerk, U. S. District Court,

Eastern District of Washington

[Endorsed]: Filed Dec. 27, 1933. [12]

[Title of Court and Cause.]

ORDER OF POSSESSION.

It appearing to the Court that in the above entitled cause the United States has filed a petition
for condemnation of the following described lands:

Lots 1, 2, 3 and SW¼ NW¼, Section 1, T. 28
N., R. 30 E., WM

Lots 4 and 5; also NW¼ SW¼, and SW¼
SW¼, Section 1, T. 28 N., R. 30 E., WM

Lots 1 and 2, Section 31, T. 29 N., R. 31 E.;
Lots 5, 6, 7, Section 36, T. 29 N., R. 30 E.; Lots
6, 7, 8, 9, Section 1 T. 28 N. R. 30 E., WM

Lots 2, 3, 4, Section 6, T. 28 N., R. 31 E., WM

Lot 3, Section 31, T. 29 N., R. 31 E. WM

Lot 4 Section 31, T. 29 N., R. 31 E, WM

and that pursuant to Chapter 307 of the Act of Congress [13] of February 26, 1931 (46 Stat. 1421),
entitled "An Act to expedite the construction of
public buildings and works outside the District of
Columbia by enabling possession and title of sites
to be taken in advance of final judgment in proceedings for the acquisition thereof under the power of
eminent domain," the Secretary of the Interior and
Emergency Administrator of Public Works has
signed and caused to be filed herein a declaration of
taking of said above described lands for the public
purposes named in the complaint herein;

And it further appearing to the Court that the
sum of money estimated by said acquiring authority to be just compensation for the land taken has
been deposited in this court to the use of the persons entitled thereto;

And it further appearing to the Court that under the provisions of the said Act of Congress and by reason of the acts and things aforesaid, the United States is now the owner in fee simple of the above described land and entitled to possession thereof;

It is hereby ORDERED that from and after the date of this order that the United States and its duly authorized officers and agents have immediate possession of the above described lands, provided that the defendants Samuel J. Seaton and Mary A. Seaton, his wife, may have the period of ten days from and after the service of this order in which to remove their household goods and other personal property from said above described premises.

And it is further provided that Emma Raths, and those persons residing with her, may have the period of thirty days from and after the service of this order in which [14] to remove their household goods and other personal property from said above described premises.

And it is further ORDERED that a copy of this order be served upon the defendants herein.

Dated this 27th day of December, 1933.

J. STANLEY WEBSTER
United States District Judge.

[Endorsed]: Filed Dec. 27, 1933. [15]

[Title of Court and Cause.]

ANSWER

Come now the defendants, Continental Land Company; a corporation; Julius C. Johnson and Mable

Johnson, his wife; Emma Raths, widow; Martha
Raths Baldwin and Warren Baldwin, her husband;
Henry Raths, George Raths, Albert Raths and
Arthur Raths, bachelors; Alma Raths Clark and
Fred Clark, her husband; Mary Raths Marnhart
and Clarence Marnhart, her husband; Minnie Raths,
spinster; and Fred Raths and Manita Raths, his
wife, and for answer to the complaint of the plaintiff, admit, deny and allege as follows:

I.

Admit paragraphs 1, 2, 3, 4, 5, 6, 7, 8, 9, 10, 11,
12, 13, 14, 15 and 16 to be true. [16]

II.

Answering paragraph 17, these defendants admit
that the United States has undertaken to purchase
said lands without avail, but specifically deny that
said undertaking on the part of the United States
was in good faith; admit that plaintiff and these
answering defendants are now in disagreement as
to the market value of the lands described in said
complaint, and allege the fact to be that the value
of the lands owned by these answering defendants
is far and away in excess of the offer of purchase
of the plaintiff, United States of America; deny
that the United States of America does now in
good faith continue its offer of purchase.

WHEREFORE, these answering defendants pray
that they be awarded compensation for their respective properties, the same to be estimated by reference to the uses for which said property is suitable, having regard to the existing business or wants

of the community or such as may be reasonably
expected in the immediate future and in accordance with the rules of law, practice and procedure
in such cases made and provided for.

> CANNON, McKEVITT & FRASER
> PARKER W. KIMBALL
> Spokane
> CHARLES A. ATEN, Wilbur, Wn.
> Attorneys for Defendants,
> Continental Land Company,
> Johnson and Raths. [17]

State of Washington
County of Spokane—ss

A. J. PRINS, being first duly sworn, upon oath
deposes and says:

That he is vice president of the Continental Land
Company, a corporation, one of the answering defendants herein; that as such official he has his office
and resides in the City and County of Spokane,
State of Washington; that he makes this verification for and on behalf of the said Continental Land
Company and the other answering defendants herein
and that he is authorized so to do; that he has
read the within and foregoing answer, knows the
contents thereof and that the same is true as he
verily believes.

> A. J. PRINS

Subscribed and sworn to before me this 15th day
of June, 1934.

[Seal]   GLADYS MYERS
Notary Public in and for the State of Washington
Residing at Spokane, Washington.

True copy of within instrument received this 15th day of June, 1934.

                    J. M. SIMPSON
                        Attorney for Plaintiff

[Endorsed]: Filed June 15, 1934. [18]

[Title of Court and Cause.]

VERDICT

WE, THE JURY IN THE ABOVE ENTITLED CAUSE, find for the defendant CONTINENTAL LAND COMPANY, a corporation, in the sum of $1260.63

                    W. H. LITTLE
                        Foreman.

[Endorsed]: Aug. 2, 1935. [19]

[Title of Court and Cause.]

VERDICT

WE, THE JURY IN THE ABOVE ENTITLED CAUSE, find for the defendants, JULIUS C. JOHNSON and MABEL JOHNSON, his wife, in the sum of $623.75.

                    W. H. LITTLE
                        Foreman.

[Endorsed]: Filed Aug. 2, 1935. [20]

[Title of Court and Cause.]

VERDICT.

WE, THE JURY IN THE ABOVE ENTITLED CAUSE, find for the defendants, EMMA RATHS, widow, et al. in the sum of $2506.67.

W. H. LITTLE
Foreman.

[Endorsed]: Filed Aug. 2, 1935. [21]

[Title of Court and Cause.]

VERDICT.

WE, THE JURY IN THE ABOVE ENTITLED CAUSE, find for the defendants, SAMUEL J. SEATON and MARY A. SEATON, his wife, in the sum of $8491.87.

W. H. LITTLE
Foreman

[Endorsed]: Filed Aug. 2, 1935. [22]

In the District Court of the United States for the Eastern District of Washington, Northern Division.

No. L-4760.

UNITED STATES OF AMERICA,

Plaintiff.

vs.

CONTINENTAL LAND COMPANY, a corporation; JULIUS C. JOHNSON; MABLE JOHNSON; and GRANT COUNTY, a municipal corporation; (claimants of Tracts No. 1 and No. 2)

SAMUEL J. SEATON; MARY A. SEATON; and OKANOGAN COUNTY, a municipal corporation; (claimants of Tract No. 3)

EMMA RATHS, widow; MARTHA RATHS BALDWIN and WARREN BALDWIN, her husband; HENRY RATHS, GEORGE RATHS, ALBERT RATHS and ARTHUR RATHS, bachelors; ALMA RATHS CLARK and FRED CLARK, her husband; MARY RATHS MARNHART and CLARENCE MARNHART, her husband; MINNIE RATHS, spinster; FRED RATHS and MANITA RATHS, his wife; and OKANOGAN COUNTY, a municipal corporation; (claimants of Tracts No. 4, No. 5, and No. 6),

Defendants.

D. L. UNDERWOOD, D. W. UNDERWOOD, CORA UNDERWOOD, PAULINE UNDERWOOD, ALAINE PETTIJOHN, EDWARD MICHALOWSKI, and H. E. PETTIJOHN,
Intervenors.

JUDGMENT.

This cause having come on for trial on the 15th day of July, 1935, and stipulation having been made in open court between counsel for the plaintiff and counsel for the defendants herein that the United States of America has the right to condemn the property described in the complaint herein for the purposes alleged in the complaint, [23] and the issues arising upon the complaint of the plaintiff and the answers on file herein, other than those disposed of by the said stipulation, having been duly tried before the Court and a jury, and the said jury having returned their verdict herein, in and by the terms of which the said jury made the following award to the several defendants herein, to wit:

For the tract commonly referred to as the Continental Land Company tract, more particularly described as Tract No. 1 in the complaint on file herein, and hereinafter more fully set out, the sum of $1260.63.

For the tract commonly referred to as the Johnson tract, more particularly described as Tract No. 2 in the complaint on file herein, and hereinafter more fully set out, the sum of $623.75.

For the tract commonly referred to as the Seaton tract, more particularly described as Tract No. 3 in the complaint on file herein, and hereinafter more fully set out, the sum of $8491.87.

For the tract commonly referred to as the Raths tract, more particularly described as Tracts No. 4, No. 5, and No. 6 in the complaint on file herein, and hereinafter more fully set out, the sum of $2506.67.

And it appearing during the trial of the said above entitled cause that counsel for the plaintiff herein offered to accept a judgment in the above entitled cause wherein it shall be expressly provided that there is excepted from the property condemned such mineral rights, if any, as the intervenors D. L. Underwood et al may have in that part of the Seaton tract within the boundaries of the so-called Sand Hill placer claim.

And it appearing to the Court from the records and files in the above entitled action that under date of December 27, 1933 a declaration of taking under the provisions of the Act of Congress of February 26, 1931 (46 Stat. [24] 1421, 1422), signed by the authority empowered by law to acquire the lands described in the complaint, to wit, the Secretary of the Interior, was filed in the above entitled cause of action and that with the said declaration of taking there was deposited into the registry of the court, to the use and for the benefit of the persons thereto entitled on the said 27th day of December, 1933, the sum of $11,267.92 as the estimated just compensation for the said premises described in the said complaint and in the said declaration of taking, to wit:

Continental Land Company Tract (Tract No. 1)—Lots One (1), Two (2), Three (3) and Southwest quarter of Northwest quarter (SW¼NW¼), Section 1, Township 28 North, Range 30 East, Willamette Meridian, in Grant County, Washington, containing 169.25 acres, more or less.

Johnson tract (Tract No. 2)—Lots Four (4) and Five (5), also Northwest quarter of Southwest quarter (NW¼SW¼) and Southwest quarter of Southwest quarter (SW¼SW¼), Section 1, Township 28 North, Range 30 East, Willamette Meridian, in Grant County, Washington, containing 164.50 acres, more or less.

Seaton tract (Tract No. 3)—Lots One (1) and Two (2), Section 31, Township 29 North, Range 31 East; Lots Five (5), Six (6), Seven (7), Section 36, Township 29 North, Range 30 East; Lots Six (6), Seven (7), Eight (8), Nine (9), Section 1, Township 28 North, Range 30 East, Willamette Meridian, in Okanogan County, Washington, containing 315.30 acres, more or less.

Raths tract—(Tract No. 4) Lots Two (2), Three (3), and Four (4), Section 6, Township 28 North, Range 31 East, Willamette Meridian, in Okanogan County, Washington, containing 111.37 acres, more or less.

(Tract No. 5) Lot Three (3), Section 31, Township 29 North, Range 31 East, Willamette Meridian, in Okanogan County, Washington, containing 39.89 acres, more or less.

(Tract No. 6) Lot Four (4), Section 31, Township 29 North, Range 31 East, Willamette Meridian, in Okanogan County, Washington, containing 39.97 acres, more or less. **[25]**

and thereupon title in fee simple absolute vested in the United States of America and the same was deemed to be condemned and taken for the use of the United States of America and at the same time the right of just compensation vested in the persons entitled thereto, to wit, the defendants herein.

And it appearing to the Court that under the provisions of the said act of February 26, 1931 (46 Stat. 1421, 1422) the said defendants became entitled to interest at the rate of 6% per annum on the amount finally awarded as the value of the property, from the date of taking until the date of payment except that interest shall not be allowed on so much thereof as shall have been paid into court, and it appearing to the Court that the excess of the said award over the amount so paid into court is the sum of $1615.00 on which sum the defendants are entitled to interest at the rate of 6% per annum from said date of taking, to wit, December 27, 1933, until the balance of the said award is paid into court for the defendants, the said interest to be paid into court and to be thereafter distributed to the several defendants on a pro rata basis as the court may direct.

NOW, THEREFORE, IT IS HEREBY OR-
DERED, ADJUDGED AND DECREED that the
award of the said jury to the defendants, together
with interest at the rate of 6% per annum on the
sum of $1615.00 from the said 27th day of Decem-
ber, 1933, the date of taking, until the balance of
the said award is paid into court herein, is the just
and reasonable compensation to be allowed to the
said defendants, and that the defendants shall have
judgment against the United States of America
for the said sum of Twelve thousand eight hundred
eighty-two dollars and ninety-two cents [26] ($12,-
882.92) plus interest on the said sum of Sixteen
hundred fifteen dollars ($1615.00) at the rate of six
per cent (6%) per annum from the said date of
taking, December 27, 1933, until the balance of the
said award is paid into court for the defendants,
the said interest payment to be prorated to the
said defendants as the court may direct and the said
award when paid into court to be distributed to
the defendants as ordered by the court as their
interests shall appear.

AND IT IS FURTHER ORDERED, AD-
JUDGED AND DECREED that the above de-
scribed property is condemned and that fee simple
title thereto has vested in the United States of
America, expressly excepting therefrom, however,
such mineral rights, if any as the intervenors D. L.
Underwood et al may have in that part of the
Seaton tract within the boundaries of the so-called
Sand Hill placer claim, the rights of the said in-

tervenors (if any rights they have) to remain entirely unaffected by this suit, entirely unaffected by this judgment, and entirely unaffected by any order, decree or declaration of taking filed in this action.

DONE this 23d day of September, 1935.

J. STANLEY WEBSTER

Judge

[Endorsed]: Filed Sept. 23, 1935. [27]

[Title of Court and Cause.]

AMENDED PETITION FOR NEW TRIAL.

Come now the defendants, Continental Land Company, a corporation; Julius C. Johnson and Mable Johnson, his wife; Samuel J. Seaton and Mary A. Seaton, his wife; Emma Raths, widow; Martha Raths Baldwin and Warren Baldwin, her husband; Henry Raths, George Raths, Albert Raths and Arthur Raths, bachelors; Alma Raths Clark and Fred Clark, her husband; Mary Raths Marnhart and Clarence Marnhart, her husband; Minnie Raths, spinster; and Fred Raths and Manita Raths, his wife, and move the Court for a new trial herein for the reasons and upon the grounds following:

I.

Irregularity in the proceedings of the Court, by which defendants were prevented from having a fair trial. [28]

II.

Accident or surprise which ordinary prudence could not have guarded against.

III.

Inadequate damages appearing to have been given under the influence of passion or prejudice.

IV.

Error in the assessment of the amount of recovery.

V.

Insufficiency of the evidence to justify the verdict or the decision, or that it is against law.

VI.

Errors in law occurring at the trial and excepted to at the time by said defendants, which said errors of law consisted of the following:

(a) Error of the Court sustaining the objection made by the plaintiff to testimony introduced by said defendants by the witnesses Thompson, Thomas, Duffy, Batchellor, Creager and Chase for the purpose of establishing the fact that the property being taken by the plaintiff was valuable for damsite purposes and that it had a market value for such purposes.

(b) Error of the Court striking all the testimony introduced by said defendants and by the witnesses above mentioned for the purpose of establishing the facts above stated.

(c) Error of the Court in withdrawing such testimony and evidence from consideration by the jury and instructing the jury not to consider any of the evidence above mentioned for the purposes above stated.

(d) Error of the Court in denying the motion of said defendants to be permitted to open their case for the purpose of introducing evidence by the witnesses above mentioned to establish the fact that the lands of these defendants being condemned [29] by the plaintiff all lie above the mean highwater level of the Columbia River.

(e) Error of the Court in refusing the offer made by said defendants to introduce testimony to show that the lands being taken by the plaintiff all lie above the mean highwater level of the Columbia River.

(f) Error of the Court in refusing to submit to the jury the question of the availability of the lands of said defendants for use as a damsite and to submit to the jury the market value of the lands of said defendants for damsite purposes.

VII.

Error in law arising out of instructions given by the Court to the jury and failure of the Court to give requested instructions of defendants.

PARKER W. KIMBALL
CANNON, McKEVITT & FRASER
I. K. LEWIS
EDWARD H. CHAVELLE
CHARLES ATEN
        Attorneys for Defendants

Service of the within motion is hereby admitted this 9th day of August, 1935.

S. R. CLEGG
    Asst. U. S. Atty
J. M. SIMPSON
    Attorneys for Plaintiff

[Endorsed]: Filed Aug. 9, 1935. [30]

———

September 1935 Term—14th day.

Monday, September 23, 1935.

COURT CONVENED PURSUANT TO ADJOURNMENT, at 10 A. M.

PRESENT: Honorable J. Stanley Webster, Judge, A. A. LaFramboise, Clerk, J. M. Simpson, U. S. Attorney, S. R. Clegg, Assistant U. S. Attorney, R. R. Isaacs, Deputy U. S. Marshal.

PROCEEDINGS.

[Title of Cause.]

Defendant's amended motion for new trial argued by I. K. Lewis for defendants, and denied.

*   *   *   *   *   *

Thereupon Court adjourned until Thursday, September 26th, at 2:00 P. M.

J. STANLEY WEBSTER,
                District Judge. [31]

[Title of Court and Cause.]

ASSIGNMENTS OF ERROR.

Come now the Defendants in the above entitled cause and file the following Assignments of Error upon which they will rely upon the prosecution of the appeal of the above entitled cause from the judgment entered herein, dated September 23, 1935 and filed on September 25, 1935.

I.

That the United States District Court for the Eastern District of Washington, Northern Division, erred in granting Plantiff's motion to "strike from the record all testimony in regard to the market value of the lands in question for dam site purposes." [32]

II.

That the Court erred in refusing to grant Defendants' request No. 9 for instructions to the jury, which request was as follows:

"It is not necessary for defendants in order to establish a market value for the lands in question as of December, 1933, or within a reasonable time thereafter, to prove that at said time there were actual sales of lands of similar character. If you find from the evidence that said lands were inherently adapted for dam site or other purposes you are entitled to consider such adaptability in determining what, if any, market value said lands possessed at said time."

III.

That the Court erred in refusing to Grant Defendants' request No. 10 for instructions to the jury,
which request was as follows:

"If you find from all the evidence that any
of the tracts of land involved in this action, or
any portion of any such tract, was especially
suited or adapted for use as a dam site, in
December, 1933, and that, at that time, or within a reasonable time after December 1933, any
such tract or parcel of land could have been
sold for such use to any purchaser other than
the United States Government, then you are
instructed that you should return a verdict in
favor of the owner of any such tract or parcel
of land for the amount of many which you find
from all the evidence, such tract or parcel of
land could be sold for, in December 1933, or
within a reasonable time thereafter, considering its adaptability for use as a dam site as
well as all other uses for which the tract or
parcel was adapted."

IV.

The Court erred in instructing the jury, as follows:

"When in the course of my instructions I
said to you that it was your function to ascertain the reasonable and practical adaptability
of the property in question you, of course, will
understand that I did not intend to include its
value or claimed value as a dam site. That

question is withdrawn from the consideration
of the jury and the adaptability and availability of the property in question which you
will consider will be those adaptabilities or uses
disassociated from any claimed use for a dam
site.'' [33]

V.

The Court erred in denying Defendants' motion
for a new trial.

VI.

The Court erred in entering judgment in favor
of Defendants and against Plaintiff, the United
States of America, ''for the said sum of $12,882.92
plus interest on the said sum of $1615.00 at the rate
of 6% per annum from said date of taking, December 27, 1933, until the balance of the said award is
paid into Court for the Defendants,'' for the reason
that said judgment deprived Defendants of their
legal right to recover the fair market value of their
lands for all uses for which said lands are reasonably adaptable, including their use and adaptability
as a dam site; and deprived Defendants of their
right to just compensation for their said lands guaranteed by the Constitution of the United States of
America and the Constitution of the State of Washington.

WHEREFORE, the said Continental Land Com-
pany, Julius C. Johnson, Mable Johnson, Samuel J.
Seaton, Mary A. Seaton, Emma Raths, Martha
Raths Baldwin and Warren Baldwin, her husband,
Henry Raths, George Raths, Albert Raths and
Arthur Raths, bachelors; Alma Raths Clark and

Fred Clark, her husband; Mary Raths Marnhart and Clarence Marnhart, her husband, Minnie Raths, spinster; Fred Raths and Manita Raths, his wife; the Defendants and Plaintiffs In Error, pray that the judgment of the District Court of the United States for the Eastern District of Washington, Northern Division be reversed, and that the said District Court be directed to grant Defendants a new trial in said action.

Dated Nov. 20, 1935.

> PARKER W. KIMBALL
> F. J. McKEVITT
> I. K. LEWIS
> EDWARD H. CHAVELLE
> CHARLES ATEN
> By PARKER W. KIMBALL
> > Attorneys for Defendants

Copy rec'd this 29th day of November, 1935.

J. M. SIMPSON

> United States District Attorney

B. E. STOUTEMYER

> Counsel U. S. Bureau of Reclamation

[Endorsed]: Filed Nov. 29, 1935. [34]

[Title of Court and Cause.]

PETITION FOR AN ORDER ALLOWING AN APPEAL.

The Defendants in the above entitled cause feeling themselves aggrieved by the rulings of the Court and the judgment entered herein dated September 23rd, 1935 and filed September 25th, 1935, complain of the record and proceedings had in said cause, and also the rendition of the judgment in the above entitled cause in the United States District Court, for the Eastern District of Washington, Northern Division, against said defendants, dated September 23rd, 1935 and filed September 25th, 1935; that grievous error hath appeared to the great damage of said defendants, petitioners pray for an order allowing said defendants to prosecute [35] an appeal from the United States District Court, in and for the Eastern District of Washington, Northern Division, to the United States Circuit Court of Appeals, for the Ninth Circuit, under and according to the laws of the United States in that behalf made and provided; and also that an order be made fixing the amount of the security which the Defendants shall give and furnish upon said appeal, and the time within which said bond shall be furnished, and that upon giving of such security all further proceedings of this Court be suspended and stayed until the determination of the appeal by the United States Circuit Court of Appeals, for the Ninth Circuit, and your petitioners will ever pray.

Dated this 20th day of November, 1935.

> PARKER W. KIMBALL,
>
> F. J. McKEVITT,
>
> I. K. LEWIS,
>
> EDWARD H. CHAVELLE,
>
> CHARLES ATEN,
>
> Attorneys for Defendants.

Copy rec'd this 29th day of November, 1935.

> J. M. SIMPSON,
>
> United States District Attorney.
>
> B. E. STOUTEMEYER,
>
> Counsel U. S. Bureau of Reclamation.

[Endorsed]: Filed Nov. 29, 1935. [36]

[Title of Court and Cause.]

ORDER ALLOWING APPEAL

On motion of Parker W. Kimball, one of the attorneys for the Defendants, and upon filing a petition for an order allowing an appeal and assignments of error,

IT IS ORDERED: That the petition be and the same is hereby granted, and said Defendants are hereby allowed to make an appeal to the United States Circuit Court of Appeals for the Ninth Circuit, to have reviewed in the United States Circuit Court of Appeals for the Ninth Circuit the rulings of the Court and the judgment heretofore entered herein; and that the amount of bond on appeal be and hereby is fixed in the sum of $1000.00 to be executed by Defendants, as principal, and by such surety or sureties as shall be approved by the Court, and which bond shall [37] operate as a cost bond, such bond to be filed on or before the 5th day of December, 1935.

Dated Nov. 29th, 1935.

J. STANLEY WEBSTER
U. S. District Judge for the Eastern District of Washington, Northern Division.

[Endorsed]: Filed Nov. 29, 1935. [38]

[Title of Court and Cause.]

BOND ON APPEAL

KNOW ALL MEN BY THESE PRESENTS:

That we, Continental Land Company, a corporation, Julius C. Johnson, Mable Johnson, Samuel J. Seaton, Mary A. Seaton, Emma Raths, Martha Raths Baldwin and Warren Baldwin, her husband, Henry Raths, George Raths, Albert Raths and Arthur Raths, bachelors, Alma Raths Clark and Fred Clark, her husband, Mary Raths Marnhart and Clarence Marnhart, her husband, Minnie Raths, Fred [39] Raths and Manita Raths, his wife, as principals, and United States Fidelity and Guaranty Company, a corporation, as surety, are held and firmly bound unto United States of America, the above named plaintiff, in the sum of One Thousand Dollars, ($1,000.00), to be paid to said United States of America, plaintiff, for the payment of which sum, well and truly to be made, we bind ourselves, our heirs, administrators, successors and assigns, jointly and severally, by these presents.

Signed and dated this 29th day of November, 1935.

The condition of the foregoing obligation is such that:

WHEREAS, at a regular term of the District Court of the United States, for the Eastern District of Washington, Northern Division, sitting at Spokane in said District, in the above mentioned suit pending in said Court, being cause No. L-4760, final judgment was rendered in said action under date of September 23, 1935, the reference to which is had for the particulars thereof, and

WHEREAS, the above named principals have filed a petition for an order allowing an appeal from said judgment to the Circuit Court of Appeals, in and for the Ninth Circuit, and an order has been entered allowing said appeal and fixing the cost bond in the sum of One Thousand Dollars, ($1,000.00), to be furnished by said appellants,

NOW, THEREFORE, if the above named principals (appellants above named) shall prosecute said appeal to effect and pay all costs if they fail to make their plea good, then this oblig- [40] ation shall be null and void, otherwise to remain in full force and effect.

> CONTINENTAL LAND COMPANY, JULIUS C. JOHNSON, MABLE JOHNSON, SAMUEL J. SEATON, MARY A. SEATON, EMMA RATHS, MARTHA RATHS BALDWIN and WARREN BALDWIN, HENRY RATHS, GEORGE RATHS, ALBERT RATHS and ARTHUR RATHS, ALMA RATHS CLARK and FRED CLARK, MARY RATHS MARNHART and CLARENCE MARNHART, MINNIE RATHS, FRED RATHS and MANITA RATHS, Principals,

> By PARKER W. KIMBALL,
> > One of their Attorneys.

> UNITED STATES FIDELITY AND GUARANTY COMPANY

[Seal] By WILL A. KOMMERS
> > Attorney-in-Fact

O.K. as to form.

> J. M. SIMPSON
> > U. S. Atty.

The above bond approved November 30, 1935.

> J. STANLEY WEBSTER
> > District Judge.

[Endorsed]: Filed Nov. 30, 1935. [41]

[Title of Court and Cause.]

CITATION.

THE PRESIDENT OF THE UNITED STATES,
to: The United States of America, and to B. E.
Stoutemyer and J. M. Simpson, its attorneys,
GREETINGS:

You are hereby notified that in a certain cause in
the United States District Court, in and for the
Eastern District of Washington, Northern Division,
wherein the United States of America is plaintiff
and Continental Land Company, a corporation,
Julius C. Johnson, Mable Johnson, Samuel J. Seaton, Mary A. Seaton, Emma Raths, Martha Raths
Baldwin, and Warren Baldwin, Henry Raths,
George Raths, Albert Raths and Arthur Raths,
Alma Raths Clark and Fred Clark, Mary Raths
Marnhart and Clarence Marnhart, Minnie Raths,
Fred Raths and Manita Raths, are defendants, an
appeal has been allowed the defendants and plaintiff
in error therein to the United States Circuit Court
of Appeals for the Ninth Circuit. You are hereby
cited and admonished to be and appear in said
Court at San Francisco, California, thirty days
after the date of this citation to show cause, if any
there be, why the judgment appealed from, and the
rulings of the Court from which appeal is taken,
should not be corrected and speedy justice done the
parties in that behalf.

WITNESS, the Hon. CHARLES EVANS
HUGHES, Chief Justice of the Supreme Court of

the United States of America, this 30th day of Nov., 1935.

J. STANLEY WEBSTER
U. S. District Judge for the Eastern District
of Washington, Northern Division.

Copy rec'd this 11-30-35.
J. M. SIMPSON,
U. S. Atty.

[Endorsed]: Filed Nov. 30, 1935. [42]

———

[Title of Court and Cause.]

STIPULATION FOR TRANSMISSION
OF ORIGINAL EXHIBITS

IT IS HEREBY STIPULATED AND AGREED, by and between the attorneys for the parties in the above entitled action, that all of the original exhibits and all exhibits offered and refused by the Court now on file with the Clerk of the above entitled Court be forwarded to the Clerk of the United States Circuit Court of Appeals for the Ninth Circuit at San Francisco, California, as a part of the record in the above entitled cause.

Dated at Spokane, Washington, this 23d day of March, 1936.

J. M. SIMPSON
B. E. STOUTEMYER
Attorneys for Plaintiff
PARKER W. KIMBALL
F. J. McKEVITT
I. K. LEWIS
Attorneys for Defendants

[Endorsed]: Filed Mar. 25, 1936. [43]

[Title of Court and Cause.]

BILL OF EXCEPTIONS INCLUDING CORRECTIONS AND ADDITIONS REQUESTED BY PLAINTIFF

Be it remembered that on this 15th day of July, 1935, the above entitled cause came regularly on for trial before the Hon. J. Stanley Webster, and a jury impaneled and sworn to try the issues presented on the pleadings heretofore filed herein, the same being an action in condemnation to determine the fair market value of real estate acquired by the Government in condemnation proceedings at Grand Coulee on the Columbia River in the State of Washington.

The plaintiff appeared by its duly authorized represent- [44] atives and attorneys, Mr. B. E. Stoutemyer, District Counsel of the United States Bureau of Reclamation, and Mr. J. M. Simpson, United States District Attorney for the Eastern District of Washington. Defendants appeared in person and by each and several of their legal representatives and attorneys, Mr. I. K. Lewis, Mr. Parker W. Kimball, Mr. F. J. McKevitt, Mr. Edward H. Chavelle, and Mr. Charles Aten.

A motion was made by Mr. Edward H. Chavelle, attorney for Samuel J. Seaton and Mary A. Seaton, to withdraw the answer filed by said defendants, and said motion granted.

By agreement, Plaintiff's action against the several defendants was tried as one cause, on one record, for all purposes. Whereupon the following proceedings were had, testimony taken and exhibits introduced:

An opening statement was made to the jury on behalf of plaintiff by Mr. Stoutemyer and the following oral stipulation was made in open Court:

Mr. STOUTEMYER: The plaintiff and all the defendants have agreed that the government has a right to condemn the property described in the complaint in this case and that the only issue for trial is the value of the property.

To this stipulation the attorneys for defendants assented and the court then ordered:

Judge WEBSTER: Let the record so show.

Thereupon the following proceedings were had:

The following written stipulation, which was duly signed by the attorneys for the plaintiff and the attorneys for all the defendants and was filed with the clerk of the court, was offered and received in evidence herein, the said written stipulation being in words and figures as follows: [45]

"IT IS HEREBY STIPULATED by the undersigned counsel for the respective parties in the above entitled action, that, in the event that the Court shall rule that defendants are permitted to introduce evidence tending to prove the special adaptability and availability of their lands for a damsite, or for other special uses, and to introduce evidence of value and damage based thereon, so much of the text, tables, statistics, maps and other information as may be used and relied upon by witnesses for any of the parties, and contained in documents and publications included on the 'List of official publications on Columbia River and Columbia Basin Project,' hereunto attached and consisting of 29 numbers, numbered from 1 to 29 inclusive, may be received in evidence if and to the extent that the same are found to be relevant and material and may be used by the witnesses on behalf of all parties to said action as a basis and foundation for expert evidence, all parties, however, reserving the right to object to the same as irrelevant and immaterial. ·

"IT IS FURTHER STIPULATED that the said excerpts, tables, maps, statistics and data may be taken from copies of said records, documents and publications and may be received in evidence without objection, except that objection may be urged that the same is irrelevant and immaterial, and without authentication or foundation being laid;

"In the event that the court shall rule that defendants are not permitted to introduce evidence of special adaptability or of value or damage based thereon, then the foregoing part of this stipulation shall be of no effect.

"IT IS FURTHER STIPULATED AND AGREED that the backwater from the Grand Coulee dam now under construction (the low dam) will flood about eighteen thousand acres of privately owned land divided into six hundred tracts in different ownerships, also some public lands of the United States and lands of the Colville and Spokane Indian Reservations including both tribal and allotted lands. That prior to the date of the filing of the complaint

in the above entitled cause of action, the Columbia Basin Commission filed upon and secured a permit to appropriate under the state
law 100,000 second-feet of the water of the
Columbia River for use in connection with the
Columbia Basin project, and stands ready to
assign such water filings to the United States
for the purposes of the said project. That the
lands which will be flooded by the backwaters
from the said dam also include state lands of
the State of Washington, both uplands and
riparian lands, and lands in the bed of the
stream. That under date of January 4, [46]
1934 the Secretary of the Interior filed with
the State Commissioner of Public Lands of
the State of Washington the notice copy of
which is hereto attached as Exhibit A and the
list of lands attached thereto, which shows the
various tracts of state lands to be used in whole
or in part for the purposes of the said project.
That the Colville Indian Reservation borders
the Columbia River for a number of miles immediately above the said Grand Coulee damsite
and that any power dam constructed at such
site would necessarily flood some of such Indian
reservation lands, including both allotted and
tribal Indian Lands.

"IT IS FURTHER STIPULATED that any
party may prove the ownership, description
and location of any land, which may be material in this action, by offering in evidence a
list of such lands signed and certified by the
Auditor of the County in which any such lands

are located. Such list or lists shall recite the name of the owners, and his or their addresses, if known, the legal description of the land involved and the approximate number of acres which shall be flooded by the contemplated improvement of the Columbia River. IT IS STIPULATED that no party shall be required to produce certified abstracts of title, or the original record books, in order to prove the description and ownership of such lands.

"IT IS ALSO STIPULATED that copies of any maps, reports, records, or statistics compiled or published under authority of state or national government, or of any board, commission, or tribunal thereof, may be received in evidence without objection except as to their competency and materiality. The right to object to the admission in evidence of said lists of lands, maps, reports, records, or statistics on the ground of incompetency or immateriality is expressly reserved.

"Dated April 27th, 1935.

      "J. M. SIMPSON
      B. E. STOUTEMYER
          Attorneys for Plaintiff
      PARKER W. KIMBALL
      GUY O. SHUMATE
      S. J. McKEVITT
      EDWARD M. CHAVELLE
      I. K. LEWIS
          Attorneys for Defendants

Attorneys for Intervenor [47]

"EXHIBIT A.

Feb. 16, 1934

"State Commissioner of Public Lands
        and
Division of Hydraulics,
    State Department of Conservation and Development,
        Olympia, Washington.
Dear Sirs:

Reference is made to my letter of January 4 to the State Commissioner of Public Lands, and to his letter to me of January 10, in which he points out a few errors in the land descriptions attached to the notice. To correct these errors the notice of January 4, 1934 is reissued, nunc pro tunc.

Please take notice, therefore, that pursuant to the Act of Congress of June 17, 1902 (32 Stat. 388) and acts amendatory thereof or supplementary thereto, the United States intends to make examinations and surveys for the utilization of the waters of Columbia River and its tributaries in the development of the proposed Columbia Basin Project.

The foregoing notice is given pursuant to Section 3378 of Pierce's Code (1929).

Please take further notice that attached hereto, identified as 'Exhibit A' and made a part hereof is a list of lands owned by the State of Washington, over and upon which the United States requires rights of way for canals, ditches, laterals and sites for reservoirs and structures appurtenant thereto; and such additional rights of way and quantities of land as may be required for the operation and maintenance of the completed works for the said proposed Columbia Basin Project. Please file this notice, together with the attached list, in your office, as a reservation from sale or other disposition of such lands, so described, by the State of Washington.

The notice last herein given is in pursuance of Section 3380 of Pierce's Code (1929).

Very truly yours,

(Sgd) T. A. WALTERS

First Assistant Secretary

Inc. 336129. [48]

"BED AND SHORE LANDS OF WASHINGTON STATE AFFECTED BY COLUMBIA BASIN PROJECT

Bed and Shore Lands of	Range East	Township North	Section
Columbia River	30	28	Whole Twp.
,,　　,,	30	29	36, only
,,　　,,	31	28	Whole Twp.
,,　　,,	32	28	,,　　,,
Sanpoil River	33	28	8 and SE¼ of 5
Columbia River	33	28	Whole Twp.
,,　　,,	34	27	,,　　,,
,,　　,,	34	28	,,　　,,
,,	35	27	
,,　　,,	35	28	
Spokane River	35	28	,,　　,,
Columbia River	35	29	
,,　　,,	35	30	
,,　　,,	36	28	,,　　,,
Spokane River	36	28	
Columbia River	36	29	
,,　　,,	36	30	
,,　　,,	36	31	
,,	36	33	
	36	34	,,　　,,

"BED AND SHORE LANDS OF WASHINGTON STATE AFFECTED BY COLUMBIA BASIN PROJECT

Bed and Shore Lands of	Range East	Township North	Section
Spokane River	37	27	Whole Twp.
,, ,,	37	28	,, ,,
Columbia River	37	30	,, ,,
,, ,,	37	31	
,, ,,	37	32	
,, ,,	37	33	,, ,,
	37	34	
	37	35	,, ,,
,, ,,	37	36	
,, ,,	37	37	,, ,,
Slough	37	37	22, 23, 26, 27
Columbia River	37	38	Whole Twp.
Spokane River	38	27	,, ,,
Columbia River	38	37	,, ,,
,, ,,	38	38	,, ,,
,, ,,	38	39	,, ,,
Spokane River	39	27	19 and 20
Columbia River	39	38	Whole Twp.
,, ,,	39	39	,, ,,
,, ,,	39	40	,, ,,
,, ,,	40	39	
,, ,,	40	40	,, ,,
,, ,,	41	40	9, 16, 17, 19, 20 and part of 4

[49]

"UPLANDS OF WASHINGTON STATE AFFECTED BY COLUMBIA BASIN PROJECT

UPLANDS

Range East	Township North	Section	Subdivision
30	28	16	NW¼NW¼, S½NW¼, SW¼NE¼, SE¼, SW
30	29	36	Lots 1, 2, 3, 4, SE¼NW¼, NE¼SW¼, S½SW¼
31	28	16	N½NW¼, SE¼NW¼ except small tract deeded to school district for schoolhouse grounds
32	28	16	SW¼NW¼, W½S½, SE¼SE¼, Lots 1, 2, 3
33	28	16	N½NW¼, SW¼NW¼, NW¼NE¼, SE¼NE¼, Lot 1
34	28	16	Lot 1
34	28	36	SE¼SE¼, Lots 1, 2, 3, 4, 5
35	27	16	Lots 1, 2
36	28	16	Lots 1, 2, 3, 4, 5, 6, 7
36	29	2	SE¼NW¼
36	29	6	NE¼SW¼, NW¼SE¼, Lots 1, 2, 3, 4, 5
36	30	36	E½NW¼, NW¼SW¼, Lots 1 and 2
37	27	36	N½SE¼, Lots 1, 2, 3
37	31	4	Lot 4
37	33	5	E½SE¼, Lots 5, 6
37	33	16	NE¼SW¼, NE¼, NE¼NW¼ (except school site), NE¼SE¼, SE¼SW¼
37	36	36	NW¼NW¼, SE¼NW¼, S½NE¼, N½SE¼, NE¼SW¼, NW¼SW¼, SW¼NW¼
37	37	16	W½NE¼, SW¼SW¼, Lots 3, 4, 5, 6, 7, 8, SW¼SE¼
37	38	36	Lot 4
38	37	16	Lots 1, 2, 3, 4, S½SE¼NE¼, NE¼SE¼, NW¼NE¼
38	37	31	Lots 3, 4, and 5, Block 23, Original Town of Marcus
38	38	10	SE¼SW¼
38	38	15	W½SE¼, E½NW¼
38	39	36	Lots 1, 2, 3, 4
39	39	16	Lots 1, 3, 4, 5
41	40	16	Lots 1, 2, 3, 4, 5

"LIST OF OFFICIAL PUBLICATIONS ON COLUMBIA
RIVER AND COLUMBIA BASIN PROJECT
INTENDED FOR STIPULATION

1. The Columbia Basin Irrigation Project, A
Report by Columbia Basin Survey Commission, State of Washington, Copyright
1920.   June, 1920

2. Consulting Engineers (D. C. Henny, James
Munn and C. T. Pease) Report to the
U. S. Bureau of Reclamation, reviewing
report mentioned in No. 1.   Dec., 1920

3. Report on Columbia River Pumping and
Power Project by Willis T. Batcheller,
made to the Department of Conservation
and Development, State of Washington.   Feb., 1922

4. Columbia Basin Irrigation Project, State of
Washington, a Report by George W.
Goethals and Company, Inc., to the Department of Conservation and Development, Copyright 1922.   Mar., 1922

5. Report to the Federal Power Commission on
the Uses of the Upper Columbia River,
by Board of Engineers, Washington Government Printing Office, 1923.   June, 1922

6. Report by Homer J. Gault, Engineer, Bureau of Reclamation, Department of the
Interior, including Land Classification,
by A. T. Strahorn, Soil Scientist, Bureau
of Soils, Department of Agriculture.   Mar., 1924

7. Report by Board of Engineers (A. J.
Wiley, James Munn, J. L. Savage) to
the U. S. Bureau of Reclamation, reviewing report by Homer J. Gault, mentioned
in No. 6.   April, 1924

"LIST OF OFFICIAL PUBLICATIONS ON COLUMBIA
RIVER AND COLUMBIA BASIN PROJECT
INTENDED FOR STIPULATION

8. Report by Columbia Basin Board of Engineers, (Louis C. Hill, Joseph Jacobs, Charles R. Locher, Richard R. Lyman, Arthur J. Turner, and O. L. Waller) to the U. S. Bureau of Reclamation, Department of the Interior.   Feb., 1925

9. Columbia Basin Reclamation Project Hearings before the Committee on Irrigation and Reclamation of the United States Senate, Seventieth Congress, on S. 1462, United States Government Printing Office.   Jan., 1928

10. The Columbia Basin Project Hearings before the Committee on Irrigation and Reclamation of the House of Representatives, Seventieth Congress, on H. R. 7029, United States Government Printing Office.   Jan., 1928

11. Columbia River and Minor Tributaries, report by United States Army Engineers, War Department, to 73rd Congress, 1st Session, House Document No. 103, Volumes I and II, United States Government Printing Office, 1933.   1934

[51]

12. The Columbia Basin Project Hearings before the Committee on Irrigation and Reclamation of the House of Representatives, Seventy-Second Congress, First Session on the Bill H. R. 7446, United States Government Printing Office, 1932.   June, 1932

13. U. S. Department of the Interior, Bureau of Reclamation Reports, Specifications and Drawings, Grand Coulee Dam and Power Plant, Railroad, Construction Camp, and appurtenances, Specifications No. 570 et al.   1934

"LIST OF OFFICIAL PUBLICATIONS ON COLUMBIA
RIVER AND COLUMBIA BASIN PROJECT
INTENDED FOR STIPULATION

14. U. S. Geological Survey Water Supply Papers Nos. 492, 512, 532, 552, 572, 592, 612, 632, 652, 672, 692, 707, 722, also unpublished records for the succeeding years 1932, 1933 and 1934, for the Columbia River and its tributaries.

15. Dominion Water Power and Hydrometric Bureau Water Resources Papers for British Columbia, Nos. 14, 18, 21, 23, 25, 30, 39, 43, 47, 51, 53, 59, 61, 65, also unpublished records for the years 1929 to 1934 inclusive, for the Columbia River and its tributaries.

16. Bulletin No. 78, Hydroelectric Power in Washington, Part III, A Brief on Proposed Grand Coulee Dams, by C. E. Magnusson, Director of Engineering Experiment Station, University of Washington. Feb., 1935

17. Annual Reports of the Commissioner of Réclamation to the Secretary of the Interior for the Fiscal Years ended June 30, 1920 to 1934 Inclusive.

18. Annual Reports of the present Columbia Basin Commission, State of Washington, for the years 1933 and 1934

19. Water Supply Paper No. 579, Power Capacity and Production in the United States, by C. R. Dougherty, A. H. Horton and R. W. Davenport, U. S. Govt. Printing Office 1928

20. Census of the Electrical Industry, Central Electric Light and Power Stations for the years 1922, 1927 and 1932.

21. Annual Reports of the Seattle Lighting Department 1922 to 1934 incl.

"LIST OF OFFICIAL PUBLICATIONS ON COLUMBIA
RIVER AND COLUMBIA BASIN PROJECT
INTENDED FOR STIPULATION

22. Annual Reports of the Tacoma Light Department 1920 to
1934 incl.

[52]

23. U. S. Geological Survey Annual Summaries of Production
of Electricity for Public Use and Consumption of Fuels
in Generating Electricity for Public Use for the years
1919 to 1934 inclusive.

24. Electrical World Supplement—Data on Output and Peak
Load of Largest Generating and Distributing Companies
in the United States and Canada for the years 1916 to
1934 inclusive.

25. Department of Public Works, State of Washington, records
of power production and distribution, report for 1934.

26. U. S. Geological Survey and U. S. Army Engineers Topo-
graphic Sheets A to H inclusive, for the Columbia River
from the International Boundary to Priest Rapids.

27. U. S. Geological Survey and U. S. Army Engineers Topo-
graphic Sheets 1, 2, 3 and 4, inclusive, for Grand Coulee,
Grant County, Washington.

28. Hydroelectric Handbook by Wm. P. Creager and Joel D.
Justin, with the assistance of nine contributors, pub-
lished by John Wiley & Sons, Inc., New York, Chaplin
& Hall Limited, London, Copyright 1927.

29. Design and Construction of Dams, including Masonry, Arch,
Rock Fill, Timber and Steel Structures, also the princi-
pal types of movable dams, by Edward Wegmann, C. E.,
M. Am. Soc. C. E., Consulting Engineer, New York, with
a mathematical discussion and description of multiple
arch dams by Fred A. Noetzli, D. Sc., M. Am. Soc. C. E.,
Los Angeles, 8th Edition, 1927, by John Wiley & Sons,
Inc., New York, Chaplin & Hall Limited, London."

[53]

F. A. BANKS

being duly sworn as a witness on behalf of the plaintiff, testified as follows:

Direct Examination

I have had the following educational qualifications and experience in engineering work. I was graduated from the University of Maine in 1906, with the degree of Bachelor of Science in Civil Engineering. In September, 1906 I was appointed as engineering aid with the Bureau of Reclamation and have been employed in that organization ever since and am still so employed. Between 1909 and 1913 I was chief designing engineer at Boise. I prepared the preliminary plans for the Arrowrock Dam, which at that time was the largest in the world. In 1913 to 1916, inclusive, I was construction engineer of the Jackson Lake Dam, which I had previously designed, $800,000 structure. In 1917 to 1919, inclusive, I was construction engineer of the Minidoka project; from 1920 to 1926, inclusive, construction engineer on the American Falls dam ($8,000,000 structure); from 1927 to August 1, 1933, construction engineer on the Owyhee project, including the Owyhee dam, which at that time was also the highest dam in the world and costing $6,000,000, together with the Owyhee tunnels that cost about $4,000,000, and $2,000,000 worth of canal structures; beginning August 1, 1933, I was assigned to the Coulee Dam project as construction engineer on the Grand Coulee Dam and am so employed at the present time.

(Testimony of F. A. Banks.)

Mr. Stoutemyer then offered for identification an aerial photographic map of the property sought to be condemned, the map was marked for identification as Plaintiff's Exhibit B and tied on the blackboard for use of the witness. [54]

, Mr. Stoutemyer: We will now offer in evidence the map which is marked Plaintiff's Exhibit B.

Mr. Lewis: No objection.

Whereupon plaintiff's identification No. B was admitted in evidence and became identified with the record as PLAINTIFF'S EXHIBIT B.

Mr. Banks (continuing): Some of the light spots appearing on the photograph are tracts which have been cleared of sagebrush; other light spots are merely outcroppings of sand. The growth on the darker colored land is sagebrush. [55]

The proposed dam which is under construction at this time will serve the purposes of a diversion dam for the Columbia Basin project, improvement of navigation by creating a lake 150 miles long running from the dam to the Canadian boundary and, by regulation of the low flow of the river and increasing it, will improve navigation all the way from the dam site to the coast.

There is a fluctuation of about 50 feet in the water surface between high water and low water and the depth to bed rock below low water is about 150 feet, making about 200 feet altogether from the high water down to the lowest part of the foundation. It will be necessary to build a dam 200 feet high before you get to a point where you are above the

(Testimony of F. A. Banks.)
natural flow water mark or surface of the river.
That foundation, including construction of 200 feet
below the high water line of the river, is necessary
before any head can be secured for power development purposes. The cost of putting in the foundation up to the point before any head is secured for
power development purposes is about $60,000,000.

There are over 600 separate tracts of private land
in different ownerships which will be flooded by the
low dam. There are about 900 different owners of
the various tracts of private lands which will be
flooded by the low dam. The number of separate
ownerships of private land which will be flooded by
the high dam is about twice as many as flooded by
the low dam.

The nearest tribal lands of the Colville Indian
Reservation are located just a little over half a mile
above the dam, as shown on the photograph Plaintiff's Exhibit B. The Indian reservation extends
along that side of the river for over 100 miles, about
120 miles, [56] above the dam. It would not be
possible to construct any dam at that site without
flooding both the allotted lands and the tribal lands
of the Colville Indian Reservation. Another Indian
reservation which will be flooded by the back waters
from the dam is the Spokane Indian Reservation.

A map showing the location of the Indian reservation lands and the reservoir site was admitted in
evidence as PLAINTIFF'S EXHIBIT C.

Mr. Banks (continuing): This map, Plaintiff's
Exhibit C, was prepared under my direction and

(Testimony of F. A. Banks.)

shows the flow line for the dam called the Grand Coulee high dam and in single cross-hatching are shown the Indian lands and in double cross-hatching are shown the lands that are public lands withdrawn under the first form from all forms of entry. The double cross-hatched lands have been withdrawn for power site purposes and they were so withdrawn prior to the time these suits were filed.

The lands described in the complaint are needed for the purpose for which they are being condemned. These lands are located about 22 to 24 miles from the nearest railroad station. The Continental Land Company lands and the Johnson lands are on the same side of the river as the railroad and the Seaton, Raths and Burdin property on the opposite side. The bridge across the Columbia River nearest to these lands is at Brewster about 50 miles away. There was a ferry crossing the river at this point.

The purpose for which the land has been used was mostly grazing, with a little attempt at dry farming. The dry farming has not been successful as indicated by the stubble or lack of stubble and other evidence of [57] cultivation. The average rainfall in that section is about 8 inches per annum.

As far up the river as Hunters there are about 14,000 acres of Indian lands that will be flooded and some beyond that that we do not have a record of.

(Testimony of F. A. Banks.)

Cross Examination

The witness being asked on cross examination as to the value of defendants' lands for use as a dam-site, the following objection was urged:

"Mr. STOUTEMYER: We object to that. That question raises the principal issue in this case which is a legal question. If your Honor thinks so we might argue that in the absence of the jury."

"Judge WEBSTER: Yes, we might as well dispose of it now. That runs thru the case like a thread, and we might as well dispose of it once and for all."

Following an extended argument by Mr. Stoutemyer, not in the presence of the jury, the court stated:

"Judge WEBSTER: Now, I have some views with respect to this question of evidence we are considering, and I will state them, then if Counsel for the other side wish to argue against these views I will hear them.

"On the question of the proper measure of damages in a condemnation case the authorities are practically at one. The land owner is entitled to the present fair market value of the property taken—'present' referring to the time of the act of taking, and the fair market value of the property at that time is to be determined by taking into account the highest and best use or uses to which the property in question is reasonably and practically adapted.

(Testimony of F. A. Banks.)

"The property owner is entitled to no benefit because of the construction of the improvement in contemplation by the taker. Nor is he entitled to have an added value to his land because of the necessity of the taker in acquiring it. He is entitled to its present fair market value in the light of the highest and best use to which it is reasonably and practically adapted. The reasonableness and practicability of the uses of the property must not be speculative; they must be real [58] and actual, and they must be so reasonable and so practicable as to reflect themselves in the present market value of the land. The mere fact that a piece of property is being condemned by the taker for a particular purposes does not deprive the owner of the land of the right to show its special adaptability for that purpose for, otherwise, he would be deprived of the highest and best use of his property. If this property is sought to be condemned for a reservoir, for instance, but in its construction its dam site feasibility, if it has any, would be destroyed, and the owner would be able to show this property's market value is enhanced because it had a special adaptability for its use as a dam site, no one would contend the property owner is deprived of the right to show the special adaptability of his property for a dam site, even though it is being condemned for a reservoir by the Government. Let us assume the Government is undertaking

(Testimony of F. A. Banks.)

to condemn it for a dam site, and it has a special value as a dam site, the owner is entitled to have that element of value taken into account in determining what he has been deprived of.

"Now whether or not the claimed special use or adaptability of a particular piece of property is reasonable or practical, that is to say, is so removed from the realm of speculation, is so real and actual in the light of the circumstances in the particular case it would increase the present fair market value of the property to any one in the market to purchase it, that would be a fact to be determined in the light of the circumstances of the particular case.

"Now, it may be in this case, because of the magnitude of this enterprise, the large number of ownerships that would be affected by the construction of this dam, the tremendous cost of the improvement, and all of the physical and legal difficulties that would be in the path of any one acquiring this piece of property for a dam site, is of course, competent evidence because it would tend to show that the claimed special adaptability of this particular piece of land did not enhance its present market value. But the right of the owner of the property to show, if he is able to, that his property has a particular use or adapted to a particular purpose cannot be lost to the property owner merely because the taking party is taking it for that purpose.

(Testimony of F. A. Banks.)

"Now, the question in this case is, in the light of the fact this property is adjacent to a navigable stream over which the Government has authority and control; the fact that the construction of the dam at that point would interfere with the areas constituting Indian Reservations, or lands withdrawn from entry, or would involve the flooding of lands of many proprietors holding property in separate ownerships, is, of course, all proper to be shown for the purpose of establishing that the [59] land —that the claimed special adaptability of the property does not increase its market value— that no one would be willing to give any more for it on the market with that adaptability than if it did not have any such adaptability. But the fact the Government is taking it for a dam site does not deprive the owner of showing, if he is able to, that it has a special value for a dam site.

"Now, do any of you gentlemen wish to present an argument against those views?

"Mr. LEWIS: I am glad to say, your Honor, that what preparation we have been able to make in this matter accords entirely with the views expressed by the Court.

"Question read: 'Have you considered the possibility of their being useful as a site for a dam crossing the Columbia river, or part of a dam?'

(Testimony of F. A. Banks.)

"Mr. STOUTEMYER: We renew our objection.

"Judge WEBSTER: And the objection will be overruled.

"Mr. STOUTEMYER: We take an exception.

"Judge WEBSTER: Exception allowed. Proceed with your cross examination."

Mr. Banks further testified that there is a dam site at Grand Coulee which is suitable for the construction of a dam; that the United States Army Engineers, which is a branch of the Government particularly charged with explorations and investigations of that character, made an investigation and exploration of the Columbia River for the purpose of selecting a suitable dam site; that the Engineers' investigation covered the Columbia River from about two hundred miles below Grand Coulee to a distance of about one hundred twenty-five miles above, or northerly from Grand Coulee; that they explored the bed of the river from the mouth of the Snake River, which is about two hundred miles below, or south, of Grand Coulee up to Kettle Falls, which is about one hundred and twenty-five miles to the north of Grand Coulee, making a total stretch of river explored of about three hundred and twenty-five miles. **[60]**

That said exploration disclosed that the Grand Coulee dam site is the most feasible one for all purposes as a combination for irrigation, navigation, power and flood control.

(Testimony of F. A. Banks.)

The Grand Coulee site was particularly adaptable for irrigation because of the fact that the Grand Coulee itself, situated at this point, invites the pumping of water out of the river, at a relatively low lift, and storing it in the coulee for irrigation purposes.

Grand Coulee is located near defendants' lands and is one of the largest examples of erosion that there is existing today. It was caused by glacial action causing the Columbia River to erode a new channel though the lava beds, and is a natural storage reservoir.

At this point Government counsel interposed the following objection and motion:

"Mr. STOUTEMYER: Before we go any farther we wish to make our record by moving to strike out all of this testimony and object to this line of testimony in regard to the alleged adaptability for dam site purposes for the reason that under the facts stipulated in the record it is impossible for any private party to use this dam site for dam or reservoir purposes, and, therefore—

"Judge WEBSTER: Counsel will bear in mind that the Court has no stipulation before him, and the motion to strike will be denied.

"Mr. STOUTEMYER: The stipulation is filed in the record. A written stipulation filed by the Clerk."

(Testimony of F. A. Banks.)

The channel or Grand Coulee extends southerly from the present dam site for a distance of about fifty miles down to Soap Lake; there is a dam to be constructed at each end of the Coulee some twenty-four to twenty-five miles apart, so that the Coulee will be used as a storage and regulating reser- [61] voir.

The average depth of the water in Grand Coulee when the coulee is used as a regulating and storage reservoir will be about thirty-five feet and the average width of the reservoir in the coulee will be about a mile or more, so that there will be in the Grand Coulee a lake some twenty-four or twenty-five miles long averaging a mile or more in width, with a depth of about thirty-five feet.

The water for irrigation purposes will be taken from the lower or southerly end of the lake. The dam at Grand Coulee, by raising the level of the river, will greatly lessen the pumping lift and the cost of pumping the water from the river into the reservoir. The physical structure of the river bed adjoining defendants' lands is a granite formation, a good foundation for a dam, entirely suitable for any dam. The banks of the river likewise have a perfectly suitable granite formation. The top of the high dam when complete will be about thirty-four hundred feet long. It is definitely decided that the high dam will be completed.

The high dam will raise the water about 355 feet above ordinary low water mark of the river. At

(Testimony of F. A. Banks.)

ordinary low water the river is about 50 feet deep, so that the surface of the water will be about four hundred or four hundred and five feet above the dirt bed of the river.

The location for the pump to pump the water into Grand Coulee is on Julius Johnson's property.

The river at high water is about 1800 feet wide, and the top of the dam is 4200 feet wide. From the point reached by the river at ordinary high water to the point reached by the top of the dam, there will be a distance of about 1800 feet or 1900 feet on each side of the river; that is, about 1800 or 1900 feet of the dam, at each end, [62] extends over on and rests upon defendants' lands involved in this action.

The top line of the dam was drawn by the witness in the form of a red line extending across the river from east to west on Plaintiff's Exhibit B.

Considering the physical structure at this point, there are some good features about it and some not so good, the good features being granite foundation for the dam. Some of the unfavorable features are that the granite out in the middle of the river is located a long way down in the water and you have to go from 150 feet to 300 feet below the water to get the foundation. The great difficulty is the excavation you have to make in getting a footing. The foundation is suitable for a dam when you get to it. The banks of the stream are

(Testimony of F. A. Banks.)

not closer together at Grand Coulee than in most places. There are a number of places where the banks come closer together and where the foundation is much closer to the surface of the river than here. It would be difficult to state whether the conditions at this point make the best physical foundation for a dam site.

The water will be raised by the high dam to elevation 1289 sea level datum. The sea level datum at the International Boundary is considerably above that.

Redirect Examination

On redirect examination the witness testified that the total estimated cost of the Columbia Basin project, including the irrigation features of the project, is about $400,000,000; the $400,000,000 estimate does not include any allowance for interest on the irrigation features of the project. The estimated cost of the dam [63] and power plant is about $175,000,000 and the rest of the $400,000,000 is the cost of the irrigation project, the estimate being exclusive of interest on the $225,000,000 irrigation cost. If interest were added during the construction period of ten years, the cost would be nearly double. I do not consider the Columbia Basin irrigation project a feasible project for private development. There would not be any chance for profit to any private investor who might built that project. It would not be possible for a private investor to break even on the project, without

(Testimony of F. A. Banks.)

making any profit. This is not the most economical site on the Columbia River for power purposes. Kettle Falls, Foster Creek and Priest Rapids are all cheaper sites to develop, cheaper per kilowatt hour of power development, and they would also require less total investment, which would be an advantage for private development. This large development would not be desirable for private development because it requires too much investment in the first place and the carrying charge would be too great during the development period. The site has no value to anybody except the Government. It is necessary for the Government to forego interest on its investment in the irrigation development in order to keep the price of the irrigated lands within limits which it would be possible for settlers to pay. **[64]**

W. R. PROWELL,

being duly sworn as a witness on behalf of the plaintiff, testified as follows:

Direct Examination

My name is W. R. Prowell. I live in Wenatchee, Washington and have lived there for 44 years. Practically during all the period since 1891 I have bought and developed and sold real estate in the Columbia River Valley and territory adjacent thereto. These lands which I have been selling and buying include grazing and dry-farming lands in

(Testimony of W. R. Prowell.)

a residence on this land at the time of the appraisal which I valued at $75, but I do not believe it was there at the time of taking by the Government. In my opinion the reasonable market value of the Johnson lands in December 1933 was $623.75. That includes all the value which contributed to the market value of the land and included the building which would be deducted if it has been removed.

The Continental Land Company lands are in lots 1, 2 and 3 and the SW¼NW¼ of Section 1, T. 28 N., R. 30 E., a total of 169.25 acres. Five acres are fairly low and could be irrigated easily; 10 acres are at a little bit higher lift and 154.25 acres are fair pasture land. There was a log cabin on the land worth $75 and wire fencing worth $100. In my opinion the reasonable market value of the Continental Land Company lands for all the purposes to which they could be adapted in December 1933 was $1210.63 including the improvements.

Re-Direct Examination.

Leaving out of consideration the Government project, there was no value to the lands involved in this case for damsite purposes. There is no market for damsites in that territory. [67]

THOMAS F. RODDY,

being duly sworn as a witness on behalf of the plaintiff, testified as follows:

Direct Examination.

My name is Thomas F. Roddy and I live in Wenatchee. I have lived there something over 25 years.

(Testimony of Thomas F. Roddy.)

I have been in the orchard business and in the real-estate business buying and selling and owning and operating various kinds of land on the Columbia River and its tributaries. For the past ten years I have been exclusively in the real estate business and own land bordering on the Columbia River at the present time. I have had experience in appraising land for others than the Government. Between December 18 and 27, 1933 I examined and was over all the lands involved in this suit.

My individual segregation on the Seaton tract was as follows: 4½ acres of cultivated land on which I placed a valuation of $50 per acre; 27 acres of tillable land—not broken—on which I placed a valuation of $40 per acre; 8 acres of cultivated land on which I placed a valuation of $35 an acre; 73 acres of land classed as tillable land but not broken on which I placed a valuation of $30 per acre; 182 acres of grazing land on which I placed a valuation of $5 per acre; 5.9 acres occupied by roads on which I placed no valuation; 14.9 acres poor grade grazing land on which I placed a valuation of $2 per acre; being a total of 315.3 acres on which N placed a valuation of $4714.80 not including improvements. In my opinion the reasonable market value of the Seaton lands in December, 1933 for all purposes for which they were available for which there was any market value, leaving out of consideration the government project, was $7254.80 including improvements. The lands on the Seaton place are

(Testimony of Thomas F. Roddy.)

best adapted for the operation of stock ranch. I do
not recall that there was any extensive [68] amount
of the Seaton tract that had been farmed. The average rainfall in this section is 8 to 10 inches. Al-
mira would be the closest and best way to a railroad
station from the Seaton tract at the present time.
Seaton's land is on the opposite side of the river
from the railroad. The closest bridge would be at
Brewster, 40 or 50 miles away. The improvements
on the Seaton property consisted of an 8-room frame
dwelling house, barn, concrete reservoir or well, garage, chicken house, some sheds, corrals and other
small outbuildings. The first story of the house was
made up of about 12x12 timbers and they looked
like timbers that might have been salvaged from
the river. In making my appraisal on that property I took into consideration every element of
value, exclusive of the Government project, which
contributed to the market value. I gave the property
the full market value it had for any and all purposes. I do not think the property has any value
for damsite purposes. I have been trying to sell
lands of my own located on another one of the Army
Engineers' proposed damsites. I have not been very
successful and have not had any offer on it. I have
a one-half interest in that land. I do not think
there is any market demand for damsites of the
magnitude of the Grand Coulee damsite.

Referring to the Raths tract, it lies on a higher
bench above the Seaton property—between that and

(Testimony of Thomas F. Roddy.)

the mountain. There was some land that had been cultivated the year I saw the property and some had not been cleared. Some was on the mountainside—fair grazing land and some was just plain rock. The cultivated area showed, from the indication of the stubble, that it had been a very poor crop. According to my segregation on the Raths [69] tract there were 26.63 acres of cultivated land, 37.5 acres of tillable land, 32.86 acres of fairly good pasture land and 94.24 acres rocky or poor grazing land. There was a small house 18 feet square with a small addition to it; a barn 16x24 feet; a chicken house 12x12 feet; a pretty good stock corral; and there was an outside cellar with stone walls 10x14 feet. Leaving out of consideration the government project, in my opinion the reasonable market value of the Raths tract, for cash, for any and all purposes adapted, is $2086.18, including the improvements. I do not believe there is any market value for the lands in the Raths tract for damsite purposes.

Referring to the Johnson tract, designated as lots 4, 5 and the NW¼SW¼, SW¼SW¼ of Section 1, T. 28 N., R. 30 E., there was one acre of good tillable land; about 15 acres of land on the high bench that is tillable but covered with sagebrush; 148.5 acres of grazing land, most of it on a very steep slope. I visited the land on the 21, 22 and 26 of December, 1933. Leaving out of consideration the government project and taking into consideration every element of value and every use to which this land

(Testimony of Thomas F. Roddy.)

could be put, the reasonable value of the land in the Johnson tract in December 1933 was $620.50 including the fencing. There is no market value for the land for damsite purposes.

Referring to the Continental Land Company tract, that land is very similar to the Julius Johnson land. It is on the west bank of the river and lies from water level up to an elevation of probably 1600 feet. A great deal of it is quite steep and has rock on the surface of it. There is about 150 acres that is better grazing land than on the Julius Johnson tract adjoining. There [70] are 15 acres that might be adapted for truck gardening if it had water, and the rest is best adapted for grazing land for which purpose it has been used. Leaving out of consideration the government project and taking into consideration every element of value which the land had and the best use and most valuable use to which it was adapted and every use for which it had a market value, the reasonable market value of the lands of the Continental Land Company tract in December 1933 was $1137.75 including the improvements.

Re-Direct Examination.

The discussion about the Grand Coulee project during recent years has been a discussion with reference to the attempt to get the government interested in building that project and there never has been any private enterprise ever contemplated, to my knowledge, in all of this time.

W. R. COOLEY,

being duly sworn as a witness on behalf of the plaintiff, testified as follows:

Direct Examination

My full name is W. R. Cooley and I live in Spokane. I have lived there for 35 years. The last 25 years I have been in the general real estate business which has included handling of land all through eastern Washington. I have done appraisal work on many occasions for the government and for clients of my own. I have owned lands myself, mainly farming and grazing lands and irrigated tracts. I have owned lands in Okanogan, Lincoln and Grant counties and I own some in Grant county now. I first saw the lands in this suit in 1930 and on several occasions I went over these lands in 1933. [71]

In the Seaton tract I found a strip of land containing about 315 acres, and classified the land as follows: 4½ acres of cultivated land and some attempt made at irrigation; 27 acres tillable land not broken; 8 acres of cultivated land on the second bench and 73 acres tillable but not broken; 182 acres of fair pasture land and about 5.9 acres used for road; 14 acres of poor pasture; about 3 miles of fencing. The improvements consisted of an 8-room dwelling, barn, private spring, well, garage, hen house and sheds. The improvements are the same as shown on the photograph introduced in evidence. I established the value of the orchard shown on plaintiff's Exhibit "D" at about $10 per tree. My appraisal of the barn is $250; the value of the house

(Testimony of W. R. Cooley.)
is $1700. The lands in these several tracts are best
adapted for grazing purposes. The lands are about
26 miles from the nearest railroad station. The annual rainfall in that section is about 8 inches. Leaving out of consideration the government project
and any development arising therefrom and taking
into consideration every other possible use and every
market demand there may be for any of these lands,
for any and all purposes other than a government
purpose, in my opinion the reasonable market value
for cash of the Seaton tract in December 1933,
including improvements, was $5758.

Referring to the Raths Tract, there are about 26
acres of cultivated land; about 38 acres tillable; 32
acres of pasture, fairly level; 61 acres of poor pasture; about 33 acres of very mountainous, rocky
land. Leaving out of consideration the government
project and any development in connection therewith, and taking into consideration every other
element of possible use and [72] market demand
for any and all purposes for which there is a market or use, in my opinion the reasonable market
value of the Raths' land for cash in December,
1933 was $1435 including improvements.

The Johnson tract consisted of about 1 acre of
level land practically at the river level; about 15
acres of second bench land which when cleared
would be tillable; about 140 acres of rocky, steep
pasture land. There were no improvements on that
land at the time I viewed it. There was no evidence
of cultivation. Leaving out of consideration the gov-

(Testimony of W. R. Cooley.)

ernment project and any demand arising from the government project, and taking into consideration every other possible use for which this land is adaptable and considering all uses for which it may have a market value and giving it the greatest market value which it had for any use, other than the use of the government, in my opinion the reasonable market value of the Johnson lands for cash in December, 1933 was $600.

The Continental Land Company lands contained 15 acres sloping up gradually from the river bank and giving evidence of being capable of profitable cultivation if irrigated; the balance of the land is steep, rocky pasture land covered with sage brush, and on the upper portion of it above the more rocky portion the land flattens out a little and probably could be regarded as a better grade of pasture than some of the Johnson land. There is no evidence of cultivation of the Continental Land Company's tract. Leaving out of consideration the government project and taking into consideration every other possible use and every demand for which there is a market value and giving to the property the greatest market value that it [73] had for any purpose for which there is a demand for the property, in my opinion the reasonable cash market value of the Continental Land Company's land in December, 1933 was $1092.92. Considering the distance from the nearest railroad station, the lack of a bridge crossing the river, the lack of power facilities and all the other conditions applicable to these lands, there is no better or more profitable use to which

(Testimony of W. R. Cooley.)

they could be put *then* the grazing and farming purposes for which they had been used previously.

None of the lands involved in this suit had any market value in December, 1933 for damsite or reservoir purposes. There was no market demand for a damsite of such size as this at this location that I know of.

G. H. SELLAR,

being duly sworn as a witness on behalf of the plaintiff, testified as follows:

Direct Examination

My full name is George H. Sellar. I reside in east Wenatchee, across the river from the city of Wenatchee. I have lived there for 13½ years. I have been in the business of orchard growing, buying and selling of real estate and in the real estate business as a broker. I have owned lands, developed orchards, operated them, been President of the Real Estate Board and Chairman of the Appraisal Committee. I have had experience in appraising lands for cities, counties, banks, trust companies and loan associations and individuals. I examined the land involved in this case between December 18 and 28, 1933. In my opinion, the present use, that is for grazing and stock raising, is the best use that the land could be put to. There is some [74] evidence of dry farming. The rainfall is from 8 to 10 inches per annum.

(Testimony of G. H. Sellar.)

Leaving out of consideration any value for government project and taking into consideration every other possible use or value, and taking into consideration every element of value which contributed to any market value the lands might have, in my opinion the Seaton tract was worth $6616.88 in December, 1933, including improvements. On the same basis and as of December, 1933, the Raths tract with improvements was valued at $1937.85; the Julius Johnson tract, which has no improvements, at $611.88; the Continental Land Company tract with improvements at $1135.63. These lands are about 26 miles from the nearest railroad station. There was no bridge across the Columbia River in that vicinity in December, 1933. The only means available for crossing the river was a cable ferry; there were no power lines available in that vicinity at that time. None of the lands to which I have referred had any market value for a damsite or reservoir purposes in December, 1933. [75]

BARRY DIBBLE

was called as witness for the plaintiff and having been duly sworn testified as follows:

I am a consulting engineer and have been employed in that profession about 11 years. I have been in civil engineering work since my graduation from college in 1903, that work including largely electrical, mechanical and irrigation engineering. I

(Testimony of Barry Dibble.)

graduated from the University of Minnesota in 1903 with degree of electrical engineer and since that time have been employed in the following engineering work—the Shawnigan Water & Power Company in the Province of Quebec, the Twin Cities Rapid Transit Company in Minneapolis, in 1909 I entered the Reclamation Service as office engineer in the office of the chief electrical and mechanical engineer and from that time until the end of 1924 I was employed by the Reclamation Service. For 5 years I was on the development of the power system of the Minidoka project in Idaho; for 8 years more I was manager of that project, during which time I initiated the construction of the American Falls dam; from there I was transferred to the Denver office of the Bureau of Reclamation as chief electrical and mechanical engineer; from that position I resigned about the end of 1924 and was appointed consulting engineer to the Bureau of Reclamation and later consulting engineer in the Indian Irrigation Service. I was consultant on the construction of power dam at the Coolidge dam in Arizona for the Indian Service and have done some other work for the Indian Service. I was consultant for the National Irrigation Commission of the Government of Mexico on power developments in connection with irrigation dams which were under consideration. There have [76] been a number of other employments of similar character.

(Testimony of Barry Dibble.)

I was also employed by the Army Engineers in connection with their report of the proposed development on the Columbia River. I was consultant generally on the power market features of the Army Engineers' report and handled the detail work of the power market survey. I prepared the data in that report in regard to power markets. In that connection I made an investigation of the markets in the region which might be reached from these developments. My work in connection with the power feature of the Army Engineers' report was done during the years 1930 and 1931 and the report completed about the first of August, 1931. In that report it was assumed the market for power would probably continue to increase but that the rate of increase would gradually decline so that in a period of 30 years it would be about half of what it had been prior to 1929. The rate of increase which was assumed would occur between 1930 and 1933 was the initial rate of increase of $9\frac{1}{2}\%$ per annum but the assumed increase has not been realized. The actual experience with reference to the power market during that period has been that the actual power production during the years up to 1934 actually decreased and instead of having $9\frac{1}{2}\%$ increase each year we actually experienced some decrease between those years. In 1934 the power production was about the same as in 1930. The total installed electrical power capacity within the area which was estimated might be reached from the dam

(Testimony of Barry Dibble.)

at Grand Coulee was about 1,300,000 kilowatts generated capacity—that was approximately the amount available in December 1933. That available capacity is about 50% more than necessary to serve the market at the present time. [77]

The Bonneville dam was authorized prior to December 1933 but I do not know whether it was actually under construction prior to that time. The additional capacity that will be provided from the Bonneville dam is about 430,000 kilowatts. In addition to the surplus capacity already installed and the capacity being provided at the Bonneville dam, there is additional capacity of about 700,000 kilowatts that can be installed in plants or developments partially developed at the present time. The total capacity in the plants now developed plus the Bonneville capacity plus the partially developed capacity at other sites is about 2,400,000 kilowatts, of which about 1,500,000 kilowatts is more than the present load requires or about 1,500,000 kilowatts excess capacity. The load requirement in that region on or about December 1933 were somewhat less than they are at the present time—about 1,500,000 kilowatts less than these plants can supply. It is my opinion that the present equipment and the equipment that can be installed in the plants already partially completed will take care of the power requirements of the territory tributary to the Grand Coulee dam until about 1945.

(Testimony of Barry Dibble.)

The estimated cost of the Grand Coulee plant is about equal to the total capitalization of all the electrical utilities in that region. The cost of putting in the foundation for the Grand Coulee dam up to high water line is fully equal, if not greater than the cost of the Foster Creek development. The Foster Creek development can produce power far more cheaply than the one at Grand Coulee. The amount of the investment required at Foster Creek would not be nearly as large as at Grand Coulee. The proposed Foster Creek development [78] would be preferable for power development for any private power or utility company because of the lower initial investment which would be required at Foster Creek which would make the fixed charges much lower to be added to the cost of production of power. The initial cost of the foundation of the Grand Coulee dam up to high water would be more than the cost of the full development of the project at Priest Rapids. The Priest Rapids development would cost less than one-third of the total Grand Coulee cost. The Grand Coulee project is not one which would lend itself to unit developments, starting with a small unit to supply early demands and increasing later on. The large amount of the cost which is required to build the dam at Grand Coulee would make it prohibitive to develop it on a small scale.

The principal market for power in the northwestern section of the United States, particularly

(Testimony of Barry Dibble.)

the states of Washington and Oregon, is in the vicinity of Puget Sound. Another large power market is in the vicinity of Spokane, including the mining sections of northern Idaho. There is another center in the vicinity of Portland. From my experience in engineering and electrical work and my investigation of the power market and knowledge of the cost of the Grand Coulee dam development, it is my opinion that it is not a feasible site for a private or utility company development for the following reasons. It's largely a matter of the cost of the initial development and hydraulic development of the site, partly because of the very deep foundation—the fact that the dam has to be relatively long means the dam itself creates a very large cost [79] and as the power market grows gradually it would not be able to absorb rapidly the total available power at the dam site. Smaller sites would have cheaper initial hydraulic development and would be economically more profitable. The Foster Creek site can be developed with about 40% of the power that can be developed at Grand Coulee and the smaller development at Foster Creek would be at less cost per unit per kilowatt hour than the larger one at Grand Coulee. The Foster Creek site would have the advantage of small initial cost as well as the advantage of smaller unit price. Taking into consideration the probable growth of power demand which might be expected from past experience and assuming the money for a private or

(Testimony of Barry Dibble.)
utility company investment at Grand Coulee would
cost 6% per annum, such private development would
not show a profit. I have made an estimate and
calculation as to what the results of such an investment will be year by year in future years in case
that should be undertaken. My estimate is based
on the assumption that money was borrowed at 6%
for the construction, that the power market expands, that the power is available in 1940, that the
market from that time on is available along a curve
so that it is some 60% or 70% larger than at the
present time, and that continues to increase but at
a decreasing rate. The power it is assumed is sold
at the plant at 2¼ mills per kilowatt hour. On
that assumption the deficit or loss in 1941 would be
$11,000,000. The loss or deficit gradually increases
until about 1947 it reaches $11,500,000. From that
time on it decreases somewhat with expanding market but at the end of 1958 or in the year 1958 it [80]
is still over $9,000,000 and the accumulated deficit
or loss has become $115,000,000 by 1958. From this
time on the power is assumed to be entirely mar-
keted and the deficit continues to grow because it
is not possible to increase the sales. In this estimate the deficit of each year is added to the capital,
assuming that it is necessary for the owner of the
power plant to pay the interest on the bonds if he
continues to own the plant and therefore the accumulated deficit increases the capital and deficit
on which the interest is charged. I carried out that

Continental Land Company

(Testimony of Barry Dibble.)
calculation until the year 1960 by which time the
actual deficit or loss shown by that calculation would
be $215,000,000. That is in addition to the original
investment, which is about $197,000,000 including
interest during construction. I do not know of any
utility company operating in this section with sufficient financial resources to finance such a large
development as the one at Grand Coulee dam. The
condition as to availability of private capital for
utility development in the fall and early winter of
1933 was that there was practically no money available for investment in that sort of an undertaking.

Re-Direct Examination.

With reference to the possibility of using power
in future years for aluminum production—taking
into consideration the principal deposits of ores for
that kind of development—the plants for such purpose would naturally go to some tidewater location,
either Bonneville or some such place as that. The
curve of the power demand shown [81] in my diagram and that shown in the Army Engineers' report made some years earlier are identical up to
1930 but between 1930 and 1934 the predicted increase of $9\frac{1}{2}\%$ did not occur, therefore beginning
in 1934 I took the conditions that actually existed
instead of the prediction that proved incorrect. The
average load in 1934 was about 106,000 kilowatts
less than was estimated in making the Army report.
In my estimate I am assuming that in future years

(Testimony of Barry Dibble.)

the 9½% annual increase would be realized—beginning at 9½% but tapering off gradually. The difference of over 100,000 kilowatts between the prediction for 1934 and the realization of the actual use at that date has a tremendous influence on the result of the computation—taking into consideration the 9½% increase per year and this difference in the base. That is one of the reasons why there is a difference in my estimates of results and the predictions assumed in the Army report. The rate of interest also has a very great effect. There is also another difference between the tables to which counsel has referred and the one which I have made. The item of taxes was necessarily set up in connection with private development but the table to which Mr. Lewis referred (in the Army report) was for public development and omits taxes. He was referring to a table which assumed the public development would get money at 4% and pay no taxes. A private company would have to pay at least 6% and have to pay taxes. In the table to which I have referred as applying to private development I have assumed taxes at the rate of 1½% on the actual investment. The difference between a 4% rate of interest and no taxes and a 6% rate of interest and 1½% taxes compounded in the form of [82] deficits over a period of years, together with the difference resulting from my correction of estimated demand to actual demand, are the factors which account for the difference between the tables to

(Testimony of Barry Dibble.)
which counsel has referred in the Army report and
my table in which I have computed heavy annual
loss. In view of these differences between the costs
of public development and private development, it
is not feasible for any private concern to develop
the Grand Coulee dam site for power development
purposes.

Referring to counsel's references to predictions
as to growth in power demand as set out in a certain report of the Federal Power Commission attributed to the prediction of the power companies,
a reference was made showing probable increase of
20% some time in the future over the load in 1929
—that figure appears here in the estimate to be
20.7% and applies to the United States as a whole.
The expected increase on the same basis for the
Pacific Northwest is given as 15.4%. The report
doesn't say definitely how many years are included
in the period during which the predicted increase
of 15% was to take place but states on page 15
that these figures are estimated to conform to the
power companies' estimates for 1937. Those figures, then, are comparatively the figures for 1929
and cover the change which is estimated to occur
over a period of 8 years. What that amounts to
in the rate of increase per year for the period referred to is about 2% per year—it would be less
than that probably. The rate of increase which I
predicted in my computations started with an estimate of 9½% beginning with the base year. [83]

(Testimony of Barry Dibble.)

In regard to the value of the storage back of the
Grand Coulee dam, the witness testified:

The cost of the five million acre feet of storage
at the Grand Coulee dam obtained by adding 80
feet to the dam for use for draw-down purposes
is more expensive than the cost of obtaining the
same amount of storage in lakes or reservoir sites
higher up the river and its tributaries—about six
times more expensive than the cost of obtaining the
same storage at the upstream sites. At the time the
Army Engineers' report was made, the lower river
sites were included but the estimates were based
upon the assumption that only one plant would be
brought into service at a time and that the second
plant would not be started until it was needed to
carry the increase in load. Any power made available from Grand Coulee under conditions as they
existed in the fall of 1933, after Bonneville was
started, would have to compete with the large additional power development at Bonneville and the
market would have to be divided between the two.
I estimate that it will take until 1945 to absorb the
surplus power now available, including Bonneville
and also including the power capacity for which
provision was already made in plants that are partially completed— plants that have been built, such
as Rock Island, with part of the generators installed but not all. It was estimated that about
700,000 kilowatts of additional capacity may be installed in plants that are thus partially completed

(Testimony of Barry Dibble.)

and an additional 430,000 kilowatts may be installed at Bonneville. These additional plants with the present installed capacity are estimated to be sufficient to carry the load until 1945.

The storage referred to in the Army Engineers' report [84] as "upstream storage" includes reservoirs known as Hungry Horse located in Montana, Flathead Lake located in Montana, Priest and Pend O'Reille lakes located in Idaho, Kootenai and Couer d'Alene lakes in Idaho, and Kootenay lake in Canada. The same reservoir sites are regarded as upstream storage both in the case of Grand Coulee and the Foster Creek site. The expression "upstream storage" in connection with the Foster Creek site does not have anything to do with storage at Grand Coulee. The fact that upstream storage referred to in the Army Engineers' report is considered in connection with both of these sites does not in any way affect the comparison of the cost per kilowatt by which it appears that the Foster Creek development would produce power at considerably lower cost per kilowatt than the Grand Coulee development. The fact that in the Army Engineers' report the Grand Coulee site is considered on the assumption of having upstream storage at these reservoirs available gives a more favorable view to this site than it really is, because of the fact it makes available without cost the benefits of upstream storage in increasing the minimum flow of the Columbia River. With reference to the large

(Testimony of Barry Dibble.)
proposed dam and power plant at The Dalles to
which I have referred as being larger than Grand
Coulee and comparable as to cost per kilowatt hour,
would say that the location of that dam and power
plant would be at the head of slack water from the
Bonneville dam. The slack water would enable ocean
vessels to proceed up the river from Bonneville to
The Dalles—that is, vessels as large as can go
through the locks at Bonneville. That fact would
be an advantage particularly with reference to any
industries manufacturing metals — chemicals and
especially those requiring import of foreign ores.
The [85] proposed large dam at The Dalles would
provide slack water for navigation up to Pasco on
the Columbia River and up the Snake River a long
way.

A. F. DARLAND,

being duly sworn as a witness on behalf of the
plaintiff, testified as follows:

Direct Examination.

My full name is A. F. Darland. My profession is
hydroelectric engineer. I graduated from the University of Washington Engineering College in 1914
with a degree of bachelor of science and electrical
engineer. From 1914-1915 I was employed by the
light department of the city of Tacoma, as an electrical mechanic on distribution and maintenance

(Testimony of A. F. Darland.)

work. In 1915-1916 I was employed by the General
Electric Company at Schenectady, New York, and
Pittsfield, Mass., in the engineering department; in
1917 I was re-employed by the city of Tacoma as
engineer in the study of power sites and electric
rate investigations. From 1918-1922 I was electrical superintendent for the Todd Ship-Building
Company, engaged in the design and construction
of their plant and in the electrical construction of
numerous merchant ships and three scout cruisers
for the U. S. Navy. Beginning in 1923 and continuing on until April, 1934, I was superintendent
of electrical design and construction for the city
of Tacoma engaged in the construction of two hydro-
electric plants including dams, powerhouses, transmission lines, substations—one hydro-electric plant
being of 50,000 h.p., a second of 75,000 h.p.—and a
steam electric station of 33,000 h.p., at an aggregate
cost of about $15,000,000. From the latter part of
September, 1930 until I left the service of the city
of Tacoma, I was also consulting engineer for [86]
the Columbia Basin Commission. Since April, 1934
I have been employed as engineer. reporting to Mr.
Banks on the Columbia Basin project.

I collaborated with Mr. Dibble in the study he
made of the development of Grand Coulee dam and
power plant by private enterprise, assuming money
would cost 6% and assuming the growth of the
power market to which he has referred. I have
made a study of the power market and growth

(Testimony of A. F. Darland.)

thereof in this section in connection with my work for the state of Washington. Referring to Defendants' Exhibit "3", the diagram correctly shows the actual amount of power development and use in the Northwest section and the growth or falling off in such demand up to and including 1934. The curve shows the average load and kws and is an historical record beginning in 1907 up to and including 1934. That compilation includes all the territory within a radius of 300 miles of Grand Coulee project and the entire state of Oregon is included. The rate of increase of growth prediction beginning in 1934 and continuing is based upon a study made by the Bureau of Reclamation and reported in one of the documents that has been admitted by stipulation, beginning at the rate in 1934 of 9½% and gradually reducing the rate of increase to 4¾% after three years and down to zero in 60 years. There are about 400,000 kws of additional generating capacity that is already available in existing plants in the northwestern district for load increase. Full development at Bonneville will amount to 430,000 kw, and there will be brought in from plants now under construction or partially constructed but not completed in this territory slightly over 700,000 kw. At the rate of increase which I have assumed, about ten years will elapse before the surplus already available plus the surplus from Bonneville and [87] partially erected plants will be used up. On the basis of the assumed increase in load

(Testimony of A. F. Darland.)
and in power demand in future years and on the
assumption that private companies would have to
pay at least 6% interest and taxes, my study has
shown development of the project would not be
feasible by private enterprise—it would earn a perpetual deficit. My figures as to those deficits are
the same as Mr. Dibble's.

The estimated growth of power demand in the
United States generally and in the Northwest particularly, appearing in a certain report of the
Federal Power Commission that has been referred
to in this case, does not assume on the average the
same regarding rate of increased demand from year
to year as Mr. Dibble and I have assumed in our
calculation. The effect upon the results of our cal-
culations as to the losses from a private development would be, if we were to use the report of the
Federal Power Commission, that the losses would
be heavier than we have shown.

The cost of the high Grand Coulee dam and
power plant completed is about equal to the capitalization of all the private operating facilities in
this state. From the study I have made of this
subject and from my experience in the electrical
business and in the light of the costs involved and
the markets which can or may be anticipated, I do
not think the Grand Coulee power site is a feasible
site for development of private interests.

PLAINTIFF RESTS. [88]

There was an opening statement to the jury on behalf of Defendants.

WILLIS T. BATCHELLOR,

sworn as a witness for defendants, testified:

That he is a hydraulic, electrical engineer, graduated from the University of Washington in 1911 and was given his master's degree in electrical engineering in 1915 from the University of Washington; that he has been employed by the Puget Sound Power & Light Company and in the Seattle municipal power plant; that he has had an extended and varied experience in the designing and construction of power projects and in determining the suitability and appraising the value of damsites.

That he made investigations, engineering studies and cost estimates of all of the larger dam sites and power sites in the Puget Sound region, investigating about twenty such sites. As a result of such studies, the city of Seattle undertook to develop the Skagit River power project, capable of developing more than a million horse power, at a cost of one hundred million dollars; that he made the original preliminary engineering studies on which the present development of the Skagit project is based. That he prepared the water power applications for both the State and Federal rights to develop the Skagit River.

(Testimony of Willis T. Batchellor.)

That he was employed by the state of Washington to make engineering studies and to report to the Director of Conservation and Development on the feasibility of developing the Grand Coulee project with particular reference to irrigation and power. This exploration and report were made in 1921 and 1922. He also made an investigation of the principal power sites in north British Columbia and southeast Alaska. Since entering private practice, he has had experience in [89] financing the development of hydro-electric power projects and has had opportunity to investigate many of the largest water power projects in the United States, including Carolina, Michigan, California, Oregon, Washington, British Columbia and Alaska. Since 1928 he has served as Chief Engineer of the Quincy Valley Irrigation District.

He had prepared a map, Defendants' Exhibit 6, which was received in evidence, showing the area affected by the Grand Coulee development and the various points of interest within said area. The dam is to be built about a half mile down stream from the northerly end of Grand Coulee. At ordinary water level the Columbia River at this point is about twelve hundred feet wide, with a stream flow of an average of 110,000 cubic feet per second. The bed of the old gorge or Grand Coulee is about six hundred feet above the ordinary level of the river.

(Testimony of Willis T. Batchellor.)

Owing to the physical characteristics of the area through which the Columbia River flows, it would be physically and financially impracticable to use the Columbia River for irrigation reclamation purposes, except by using Grand Coulee as a storage reservoir. Grand Coulee is peculiarly adapted for use as a storage reservoir for irrigation because there are native rock walls on both sides and a glacial silt deposit covering the bed of the canyon, making it comparatively watertight. There are about 410,000 acres of fertile land in the Quincy Valley District which can be economically reclaimed and irrigated by the use of Grand Coulee as a storage reservoir, and there are approximately 1,200,-000 acres in the Columbia Basin which can be reclaimed and irrigated from Grand Coulee. The Grand Coulee reservoir will have an area of about 25,000 acres, and can economically store about half a million acre feet of the water. The only construction necessary [90] to convert Grand Coulee into such a storage reservoir is the construction of a small dam at each end of the coulee to prevent the water from running out.

Sufficient water can be pumped out of the Columbia River to supply the entire Quincy District without in any way depleting the water necessary to supply the power plant at Grand Coulee.

After the construction of the dam there will be a pumping lift of about 285 feet from the level of the water in the Columbia River to the Grand Coulee

(Testimony of Willis T. Batchellor.)

reservoir. This is a perfectly practicable and economical lift. If the two hundred foot dam, or the low dam, were to be built, it would be entirely economical and practicable to pump the water into the Grand Coulee reservoir by using two pumps, each lifting the water one-half the distance. They are pumping water a distance of five hundred feet in Seattle at present by a similar arrangement.

At this point the Court allowed an exception to all adverse rulings, without a specific request in each instance; subject, however, to possible disapproval of the Appellate Court.

The witness continued: If the Grand Coulee reservoir were filled during the season of high water, there would be ample water with no further pumping to take care of the total irrigation requirements of the first unit of the Quincy District for about one-half of the irrigation season.

At this point, the witness being asked his opinion as to the special adaptability of Grand Coulee for use in reclaiming and irrigating the Quincy District, Mr. Stoutemyer objected: [91]

"We object to that as I have objected to all questions with regard to availability and adaptability, or with regard to its value for dam site purposes, and move to strike out all the testimony along that line for the following reasons: that under the state of facts as shown in this case by the stipulation of the parties, the facts judicially known to the Court and,

(Testimony of Willis T. Batchellor.)

particularly, the fact that this is a navigable stream—that there are over six hundred separate ownerships in private ownerships in the small, or low dam, reservoir, and twice that number in the area flooded by the high dam; the fact of the flooding of Indian Reservation land; the fact of flooding reserved Government land, withdrawn for power sites and reclamation purposes; the water appropriated; the necessity for using state lands which are not available for that purpose, and under all the conditions and facts which appear and have been agreed upon by stipulation in so far as they are not already in the record by admission of the allegations of the complaint, creates a situation where, aside from the size of the project, it is for legal reasons a project which can be developed only by the Government and, therefore, it is not a proper measure of damages or a proper inquiry as to the value of a tract of land at such a location for alleged dam site purposes.

"Judge Webster: And the objection will be overruled.

"Mr. Stoutemyer: May we have an exception.

"Judge Webster: Yes."

The witness further testified: That the site of which Defendants' lands form a part is especially

(Testimony of Willis T. Batchellor.)

adapted to the creation and development of the Quincy Irrigation District, and that he knows of no other area in the United States which so well lends itself to the development of an irrigation project. Public attention and public interest have been centered on Grand Coulee ever since the witness' report on that project was filed in 1922, and from that time there has been increasing interest and discussion by public bodies.

Owing to the granite formation on Defendants' lands, which extends across the river and serves as a solid foundation for a dam, there is no site as suitable for a dam, and there is no other site on the Columbia River where a [92] dam can be built, at any cost, which will serve the purposes served by the Grand Coulee site. Defendants' lands are most suitable for a dam site.

In the development of water power three elements are important: 1, the volume of water; 2, the fall or head; and, 3, uniformity of flow resulting from storage.

No stream flows uniformly the year round; there is a high water period and a low water period in every stream; uniformity of flow is accomplished by storing water during high water periods and releasing it during periods of low water. The most important element is the fall or head; then flow and storage are of about equal importance.

There is no fall or head on the Columbia River from which any water power can be developed for

(Testimony of Willis T. Batchellor.)

a distance of one hundred ten miles upstream from Grand Coulee, and a distance of seventy-five miles downstream. The average slope or fall in the Columbia River during that entire distance of one hundred eighty-five miles is about two feet to the mile, which is insufficient to create any power. The entire head or fall at Grand Coulee is created and furnished by the dam which can not be built without using Defendants' lands. There is no other site on the Columbia River within this area of one hundred eighty-five miles upon which it would be possible to build a dam two hundred feet in height. The witness stated that he has carefully investigated the Columbia River from the Canadian boundary to the ocean. Between the mouth of the Spokane River and Foster Creek, the Grand Coulee dam site is the only dam site of commercial proportions. There is only one other dam site within the entire area of one hundred eighty-five miles, and that one would be limited to about forty feet in height. [93]

The peculiar fitness of the Grand Coulee dam site lies primarily in the fact that there is a granite dike which has been cut by the Columbia River to a depth of six hundred feet. A dam six hundred feet high could be built, from the standpoint of engineering. In other possible sites on the river, this condition does not exist. Elsewhere, granite is not found on both sides of the river. At Foster Creek there is granite on the south bank, but there is a

(Testimony of Willis T. Batchellor.)
glacial fill on the north bank; and there is no granite
to be found further down the river. A high dam
wouldn't be a safe engineering structure at the
lower sites. In the entire stretch of the Columbia
River from the International Boundary to the mouth
of the Snake River, there is no place where there
is a natural fall or head sufficient to generate any
commercial power.

The dam, built on Defendants' lands, creates and
contributes the fall or head amounting to three hundred fifty feet, which is a little more than twice the
fall at Niagara Falls. The dam also creates a
storage reservoir to store water upstream, which
regulates the stream flow. Every foot of the fall
or head is produced at the dam. There is no natural fall at the Grand Coulee dam site, or in that
vicinity. The site on which the dam is built, therefore, becomes of primary importance and is indispensible to the development of power. The reservoir created behind the dam will increase the uniform flow of the Columbia River from 18,800 cubic
feet per second to 41,500 cubic feet per second, an
increase of approximately two and one-half times.
There is no site further down the Columbia River
capable of creating any storage. Therefore, any
other site would be less valuable. Development of
the Grand Coulee dam site will greatly increase the
power which can be de- [94] veloped at the power
sites lower down the river, due to the fact that the
Grand Coulee dam will equalize the stream flow

(Testimony of Willis T. Batchellor.)

down as far as the mouth of the Snake River, and will more than double the useful flow. Below the mouth of the Snake River the minimum flow of the Columbia River will be increased about fifty per cent (50%).

The Grand Coulee dam will increase the power output of the Columbia River about sixty per cent (60%) during ninety per cent (90%) of the time, and under the rules of the Federal Power Commission, the Grand Coulee dam would be entitled to receive substantial payments from the future development of sites lower down the river, based on the benefit which they will obtain from the Grand Coulee storage.

The granite formation on Defendants' land and in the river bed extends about six hundred feet above the river on either side. "It is very prominent and you just couldn't miss it." There is no other place on the river that has such characteristics. That formation is important in building a dam, because it is necessary to have a solid foundation and a water-tight reservoir.

Defendants' lands at Grand Coulee form the only site on the entire Columbia River suitable for such a dam, having in mind the granite formation. The witness recommended the Grand Coulee dam site for development in his report back in 1921 and 1922.

The granite is continuous from the high projection on the east side of the river across the bed of

(Testimony of Willis T. Batchellor.)
the stream to and forming a part of the granite
projection on the west side of the river. It would
not be practicable to construct a dam any considerable distance either upstream or downstream
from the dam site recommended in 1921. The
granite nose [95] or projection on the east side of
the river extends but a short distance, and the dam
would have to abut against it. On the west side of
the river, conditions are quite similar. It would
not be possible to move this dam more than one or
two hundred feet on the east side, or possibly five
or six hundred feet on the west side of the river.

At this point the witness presented Defendants'
Exhibit 10, showing the position of the five tracts
of land involved in this action in relation to the
damsite described in his testimony.

It would be physically impossible to construct a
dam without using Defendants' lands, taken in this
proceeding "no matter how much money you wanted
to spend."

Mr. Batchellor further testified that in determining whether private capital would undertake
such a development as is contemplated for Grand
Coulee the controlling considerations would be, first,
the physical characteristics of the dam site. Having
determined that the dam site is suitable from physical considerations, the two remaining questions
which private capital would need to answer would
be: secondly, whether there is a market for the
power, and, thirdly, whether such market could be

(Testimony of Willis T. Batchellor.)
supplied, at a profit, from power produced at the particular site.

The witness then detailed the study which he had made of those questions, and stated that in his opinion, based upon such studies, there is, and will be, as the years go by, a market for all electric power which can be generated at Grand Coulee, and that private capital would be justified in acquiring and developing the project. Mr. Batchellor testified that the Grand Coulee project could and would be financed by private capital at a profit. That private capital "is always ready for a proposition of that kind [96] which will show a profit, and would, therefore, at this time, or any time under consideration, have been interested in any investment such as I propose." That private capital would first build an initial unit with a dam two hundred feet high, and add to it as the market required.

At this point Mr. Batchellor produced a chart, Defendants' Exhibit 13, which shows graphically the estimated growth of the power market in the area tributary to Grand Coulee, and testified that other power sites beside Grand Coulee must be developed, because the entire electrical output of Grand Coulee, together with the capacity of all other developed sites, will not be able to supply the estimated market. That his studies, as shown by the chart, indicate that by 1950 it will be necessary to have a billion kilowatt hours from other power plants. That by 1941 there will be an actual de-

(Testimony of Willis T. Batchellor.)

mand in the market for the block of power from
the initial unit at Grand Coulee, and that without
the Grand Coulee power there will be an actual
shortage of power necessary to supply this area;
that if Grand Coulee is not developed, this block of
power will have to be supplied from some other
site.

Following 1941, the low dam, or the initial unit,
proposed to be built by private capital, will not
produce enough power to supply the market; accordingly, private capital would proceed to add to
the height of the dam and to install additional power units. By 1947 the dam will be built to its full
height of twelve hundred and eighty feet, and by
adding turbines and generators the development
will supply the requirements of the power market
until 1949.

Private capital, in the development of Grand
Coulee, would be able to determine the approximate
amount and increase in the business available, and
would build a plant [97] which was commensurate
with that amount of business and add to it as the
market required. "In this way the plant would be
financially successful. That is the way power plants
are generally built by private capital."

> "Q. That is, build the plant to suit the mar-
> ket, then increase it as the market increases?
> "A. That's true."

Mr. Batchellor testified that the type of development and construction to which he had testified is

(Testimony of Willis T. Batchellor.)
generally recognized as proper, standard engineering construction, and that it was the original plan of the Government first to build a low dam and then to add to it later on. The cost of the first development, or the initial unit, would be $75,000,000.00 The operation will show a small surplus by the end of the second year.

Mr. Batchellor testified that the complete development of the Grand Coulee project will involve a total investment of $231,000,000.00, and that the project would show a surplus in 1952 of $15,000,-000.00. That beginning in 1960 the sum of $5,000,-000.00 annually would be set aside in an amortization fund so that by 1985, the end of the license period, the Grand Coulee project would have an amortization fund of $231,000,000.00, the amount of the total investment; and that in addition to this amortization fund the Grand Coulee project will develop a surplus of $13,000,000.00 annually.

"Q. Now then, Mr. Batchellor, with such results from the operation of the Grand Coulee plant, which you say is practicable to design, by private capital, what would you say as to whether private capital would be in the market to purchase the Grand Coulee dam site in the year 1933?

(After objection made and overruled.)

"A. Private capital would be interested in this project as outlined. [98]

"Q. In the fall or the winter of 1933?

"A. Yes sir—or at any time.

"Q. Now, then, coming to the question of what would be a fair, market value of these five tracts of land in the fall and winter of 1933 —in that connection, Mr. Batchellor, it is our understanding that you are entitled to take into consideration all the uses to which these several tracts of land are reasonably adaptable. You are not permitted to take into consideration any value which may be contributed to any one of these tracts of land by the Government operations, that is, by anything that is being done by the Government, but you are permitted to take into account all uses or purposes to which these lands are reasonably adaptable to the extent only that such uses have actually affected market value. Have you, at my request, made a study of the question of fair market value of those lands in December, 1933, with this definition and limitation in mind which I have just recited to you?

"A. I have.

"Q. I will ask you to have in mind that the fair market value as it is understood in questions of this kind is that price at which the property could be sold on the open market if a willing and informed buyer were negotiating and dealing with a willing and informed seller, each willing to complete the negotiations, but being under no compulsion to do so. With that

(Testimony of Willis T. Batchellor.)

definition and limitation in mind have you formed an opinion as to what would be a fair market value of those five tracts of land in December, 1933?

"Mr. Stoutemyer: We object to that question for the reasons previously stated, and for the further reason this witness has not qualified himself as to market value.

"Judge Webster: And the objection will be overruled.

To which ruling Plaintiff excepts.

"A. I have."

Mr. Batchellor testified that in December, 1933, the fair market value of the several tracts of land belonging to Defendants was: the Rath tract, $500,-000.00; the Seaton tract, $2,000,000.00; the Continental Land Company and Julius C. Johnson tracts, $2,000,000.00.

Mr. Batchellor testified that he had studied other available sites for power development and that [99]

"there is no other single site on the Columbia River, or elsewhere, where a similar block of power could be developed at any price."

There are several sites on the Columbia River where smaller blocks of power may be developed. Foster Creek, Chelan, Rocky Reach, Rock Island and Priest Rapids high dam combined, would have about the same capacity as Grand Coulee; but the surplus resulting from their combined operation would be

(Testimony of Willis T. Batchellor.)

about $4,000,000.00 per year less than the surplus
from Grand Coulee; and the production cost would
be about twenty per cent or twenty-five per cent
greater.

Cross-Examination.

I never built any irrigation project or operated
one.

In my estimate for the project (Grand Coulee) I
stated it would be necessary to divert about 3½
acre-feet to only deliver 3 acre-feet to the land. I
took the Army Engineer's report into account and
also the Bureau of Reclamation report in House
Document 7446.

Asked by plaintiff's counsel to turn to page 91 of
the Army Engineer's report of the hearing before
the Committee on Irrigation, the witness read that
the amount of water per acre to be diverted from
Grand Coulee reservoir, as shown by that report,
was 4½ feet.

I made an independent investigation of the actual
district now in existence in the Quincy area where
it is irrigated. I got my information on a very
large project from the report of the Bureau of
Reclamation. I never operated an irrigation project myself. My statement that you could deliver 3
acre-feet to the land by a diversion of 3½ acre-
feet, whereas the Army figures show a diversion of
about 5 acre-feet, was in connection with the Quincy
district. [100]

(Testimony of Willis T. Batchellor.)

The Skagit project is about 40% completed at this time. The ultimate development as planned by the department will be 1,120,000 horse-power. The present development is 75,000 horse-power. The next major unit will come on the market in 1937 with a capacity of 160,000 h.p. and the construction is about three-fourths completed.

The heaviest demand for power in the state of Washington is in two principal sections, the Puget Sound region and the area served by the Washington Water Power Company. The total production west of the mountains (Cascade) of the principal companies I have listed was for 1934 1,590,000,000 kilowatt hours, and the total in central Washington was 880,000,000 kwh or about the ratio of 35% east of the mountains and 65% west of the mountains. The 1,120,000 kw to be developed on the Skagit would be located about 105 miles north of the principal market west of the mountains. There is about $35,000,000 involved in the completion of the work now under way out of approximately $100,000,000 for the city of Seattle project. The distribution system will add $100,000,000 more. Transmission distances from Bonneville and Grand Coulee to the Puget Sound region are identical.

I do not think there was any private power plant started in the state of Washington in the last three years because there has been a temporary surplus. Due to the cessation of industrial activities, there has been a dropping off in power demand between

(Testimony of Willis T. Batchellor.)

1930 and 1933; between 1932 and 1933 there was a normal increase. In 1932 we had the bottom of the depression and in 1933-1934 there has been a normal increase in the power market in this area. None of the power companies were considering any more power plants in the years 1930, 1931, 1932 and 1933. Prior to that time they uniformly built plants very much smaller [101] than the Grand Coulee plant in preference to large developments of that size. The development at Rock Island is one of the largest private plants in the State; that is 60,000 kw or one-third of the ultimate capacity.

We would have to flood a proportionate amount of the lands in the reservoir site for any height of dam which we would build. You can not use a dam without flooding the lands in the back-water and the project would be useless without that land in the back-water. You can develop two feet of head at the damsite without extending the backwater beyond the lands we are considering. I have allowed a smaller price per acre for the lands in the reservoir than I have for the damsite. In connection with my original report I estimated the proportionate cost of the right of way for the development would be about $500,000. When I made that report and statement to Congress I was figuring on a dam at Grand Coulee somewhere between 50 and 200 feet in height. That is the figure ($500,000) that I used in all my estimates of the cost of the entire right of way of a 200-foot dam to which I referred in that report.

Plaintiff's counsel asked witness at this point to read his statement on page 113 of Senate Document 1462, Columbia Basin Reclamation Project. Reading:

"Senator McNary. Q. Will any valuable acreage be submerged by the impounding of water?

A. There will be practically none. The Columbia River flows in a canyon about a thousand feet deep at this point and for some distance further up and there are only a few little patches down the river bars that will be affected so that the areas involved are negligible."

Witness resumes his testimony: That refers to irrigated lands and that is still my opinion. At that time I thought that "valuable acreage" in Senator McNary's question meant lands that had been irrigated. My estimate [102] of $500,000 was approximately $1.00 per horse power for commercial power developed. I have included in my present estimate $5,000,000 additional for over-flow lands and damages. I mean by present estimate the one given in court today. Before I was employed in this case I estimated the cost of right of way at $500,000 based on horse power—commercial horse power.

Indian tribal lands are part of the lands to be overflowed by the dam to be built on that site. A dam however small would flood the tract marked

"12" on my map of the damsite which is Indian
tribal land. In my financial analysis I have allowed $5,000,000 additional, or $100 per acre, for
lands in the area to be flooded, other than the river
bed. I estimated the average rate per acre on the
land at the damsite at $6,000.

If you applied to the lands which are indispensable
to the project, because involved in the reservoir,
the same rate of value as I have given the land
involved in the damsite, the total cost of the right of
way would be about $300,000,000. The reservoir
lands have no value or use for any other purpose
except for use as a storage reservoir site.

Mr. Batchellor further testified on cross examination that there would be needed for the completed
reservoir other property besides land, including
property at Kettle Falls owned by the Washington
Water Power Company, the Great Northern bridge
at Marcus, the Great Northern bridge at Northport,
and it would be necessary to revise the highway
bridge crossing above Kettle Falls between the Little
Falls plant of the Washington Water Power Company and the Fish Hawk site on the Columbia River,
and that possibly the Kettle Falls branch of the
Great Northern [103] would be affected, but he was
unable to say what portion of his total estimate for
right of way was for railroad right of way, bridge
property, power site and property other than farming and grazing land.

He said that the business, as represented by power
output, of the Puget Sound Power and Light Com-

(Testimony of Willis T. Batchellor.)

pany, Washington Water Power Company, Pacific Power and Light Company, Northwestern Electric Company, and Portland General Electric Company decreased in 1933 as compared with 1932; that the business of Tacoma and the Washington Gas & Electric Company however had increased in 1933 as compared with 1932 but that such increases were completely offset by losses in the city of Seattle alone. The total kilowatt hour production on the systems in the power market area for 1932 were 380,000,000,000 and in 1933 were 370,000,000,000; that there was actually a decrease in kwh production in 1933 as compared with 1932, whereas the diagram introduced by the witness on direct examination shows an increase in 1933 over 1932.

That the Geological Survey statement, which is one of the documents provided for in the stipulation, shows with reference to power production in the state of Washington for the year 1932 a total of 2,487,000,000 kwh; for the year 1933 2,439,000.000 kwh, which is a slight decrease compared with 1932.

Witness testified that he had based his prediction on future growth on the assumption that the growth during good years preceding 1933 is to continue uninterruptedly after 1934 without any recurrence of conditions which have existed in the past five years; that in his curve he has allowed for depressions similar to the 1921 depression but has not allowed for any depression resulting in the [104] falling off of business or demand such as in the years 1931, 1932 and 1933.

(Testimony of Willis T. Batchellor.)

The witness stated that the only irrigation project that he had studied in Washington which had been refinanced by the State was the Manson project at Chelan; that he did not know what percentage of the par value of the bonds of the district the bondholders received when the project was refinanced. Upon being handed the 7th biennial report of the Department of Conservation and Development of the state of Washington, the witness read from the report that the State had refinanced nineteen districts during the biennial, paying an average price of 36.8 cents on the dollar for the district bonds.

He said that at the time he made his official report on the Grand Coulee project several years ago, in which he estimated the cost of the entire right of way as $500,000, he knew of the suitability of the Grand Coulee damsite lands for the construction of a dam to some extent but nothing like the extent to which it has developed since the Army report and studies made since; that he knew the granite outcropping to which he had previously referred extended across the river at that point and that he knew about the diamond drill borings at the time he made his report and that the lands at that point were adaptable for the construction of such a dam as he proposed and that the lands were adapted for the dumping of waste material just as they are now.

"Q. What was there about the information available at the time you made your report that

(Testimony of Willis T. Batchellor.)

would have prevented the construction of just
such a dam as you are now figuring on?

"A. My information was incomplete and I
was merely asked in my assignment to study
the feasibility of the dam. [105]

"Q. Answer the question.

"A. There was none and there is nothing
now."

He stated he had appeared before a Senate Committee in Congress asking for a survey of this project, claiming that there had been no survey before
worth anything on the part of the Government.
The witness was asked why he did not tell the Senate
Committee that the dam would flood the valuable
lands concerning which he has testified in this case,
and he answered that he considers the value of the
lands in the reservoir site as nominal; that the committee in his opinion were only asking about the
lands to be flooded and were not trying to get at
the value of all of the lands used for this project
including the damsite lands.

He stated that in his estimates of cost he has
allowed three-fourths of one mill for transmission
cost; that in his estimate he is assuming that the
primary power will be sold at 2½ mills per kwh
and the secondary power at 1 mill per kwh at the
plant. That in his plan the pump lift necessary to
get the water up from the Columbia River into the
Grand Coulee would be about 420 feet initially and

(Testimony of Willis T. Batchellor.)
that would be reduced as the height of the dam was raised so that in 1947 the lift would be about 290 feet, and that he contemplated purchasing power from a private power company who would put in a dam.

Mr. Batchellor stated that in arriving at the figure of $97.60 per acre for the development of lands in the Quincy district, he included 40,000 acres more than was estimated in the Army Engineers' report for that division of the project, it being land which he considered tributary to the Quincy district. It would take about ten years to complete settlement of 410,000 acres. The first 50,000 [106] acres would be available by 1940 when the power plant was ready to operate. It would be 1940 before the first unit is ready. He did not remember allowing for interest during the construction of that irrigation project. He said he allowed for contingencies in his main estimate. The interest during construction is a part of the $150,000 allowed for contingencies.

Mr. Batchellor continued: My estimate on the West Main Canal is $23,827,000. The Army Engineers' estimate for the same canal is $30,400,000, my estimate being about $7,000,000 less than the Army Engineers' estimate. The reason for this difference is that the Army Engineers figured it might be 50 years before this project was built and allowed for fluctuation of construction prices on that account. My estimate is based upon awarding the contract and having it done during the next four years. My West Main Canal contemplates irrigating 30,000 acres more near the upper end of the canal than contemplated in the Army Engineers' estimate for the main canal. In the event you wish for comparative purposes to include in this unit only the 370,000 acres, it would change this estimate from $98 to about $107 per acre. The power cost on the basis of pumping from the river to deliver 3.4 acre-feet on the land is about $2.50 per acre, based on a rate of 1 mill for power. If my plans miscarried in securing a power company contract to build the plant and sell the power at that price, I would not start the project. The lowest rate I know of being charged for electric power for irrigation pumping in this state is about one-half cent per kwh on relatively small installations. The average construction cost required by the government on such successful projects as the Boise project is about $2.50 per acre per year I [107] think. It is possible that it has been reduced to $1.50 per acre per year. It is true of settlers on projects where the charge has been as low as $1.50 per acre that the settlers have been aggrieved and petitioning Congress for a moratorium on the ground that they could not pay $1.50.

Re-Cross Examination

The fact that refinanced irrigation projects have continued in operation would not be of any particular benefit to the people who invested their

(Testimony of Willis T. Batchellor.)

money in constructing those projects and lost from two-thirds to three-fourths of their investment. I do not think that the fact that the investors in those districts lost their money would discourage the further construction of private projects in the State.

————

H. P. THOMAS,

being duly sworn as a witness on behalf of defendants, testified:

That he is a graduate of Wittenberg College, Springfield, Ohio, with the degree of Bachelor of Science in Engineering, in 1910. Later he was employed as engineer by the Puget Sound Power & Light Company and the Weyerhauser Timber Company. He designed the power plant for the city of Everett, Washington. From 1923 to 1932 he was employed in the Department of Public Utilities for the city of Tacoma, Washington. For about two and a half years last past he has been chief engineer for the Inter-County River Improvement Flood Control project involving the streams in the counties in which Seattle and Tacoma are situated. He has designed dams and has had experience studying the merits and appraising the value of dam sites. He has studied the possibilities of the Grand Coulee dam site, and the market for electric power in that area, comparing Grand Coulee with other available sites on the Columbia River, and [108]

(Testimony of H. P. Thomas.)

"have in fact practically exhausted the study of all the data which is at hand on the subject."

There is no other site on the Columbia River at which there might be built a dam of two hundred feet in height or more "which could be used for the dual purpose of reclamation and power." Grand Coulee "has several inherent qualities which make it an excellent site." A granite dike crosses the river at this point, furnishing a perfect foundation and abutments for a dam; the market for the power in that area is favorable; and the proximity of the site to Grand Coulee especially adapts it for use in irrigating the Quincy district. He agreed substantially with the testimony of Mr. Batchellor as to the physical characteristics of the dam site.

Mr. Thomas also testified that he had made a study as to whether private capital would be interested in acquiring and developing Grand Coulee; that the principal considerations which would determine that question are: whether the site is naturally adapted to the construction of a dam, and the development of power; whether there is a market for the power which can be generated at that point; and whether the power could be generated and sold at a profit. That he had made an exhaustive study of the market conditions and that he had found that from 1907 to 1933 there has been a very definite trend upward in the use of electricity.

At this point Mr. Thomas identified and explained Defendants' Exhibit 19, being a chart showing

(Testimony of H. P. Thomas.)

graphically the growth of the power market; that there is a normal rate of increase in the power market of nine per cent (9%) compounded annually. That he had given full consideration to the depression through which we are passing, and [109]

"in fact, I have approached this subject from the angle of one who was advising private capital. I have endeavored to be entirely conservative in my opinion in the matter, and in my prediction. I wouldn't be at all surprised, and it is my anticipation that the production of electricity will reach the curve as is predicted by the Army Engineers. * * * However, in the interest of conservatism and viewing the situation as an engineer who is informing a client who is willing to invest considerable funds, I have placed the curve at the position which I feel can be predicted with a certainty will happen. * * * This prediction is based entirely on the history of the past and shows a normal rate of increase without any unusual happenings. * * * I am satisfied there will be some development here which will contribute in a material way to make this curve reach materially above where it is shown there."

By the year 1941 all the installed electrical capacity and all uncomplete capacity will be absorbed in the state of Washington; at that time it will be necessary to have ready for production more operat-

(Testimony of H. P. Thomas.)

ing capacity in this State. With that in mind, private operation would put Grand Coulee into operation in 1941.

The growth in the power market will absorb the Grand Coulee power, not only that developed by the low dam, but all that can be generated by the ultimate development of the high dam.

It would be practicable and profitable for private capital to acquire Grand Coulee and develop it to full capacity. The first unit, with a dam two hundred feet high, would cost about $74,000,000.00.

"We would be able to sell from the plant.* * * about 300,000 kilowatt years of primary power * * * also about 100,000 kilowatt years of secondary power."

The operation of the project would produce a gross revenue of $7,466,000.00.

"As a matter of fact I think there will be a market for considerable more primary power than that. I have tried to make a very conservative estimate." [110]

After deducting all operating expenses, including cost of operation, maintenance, management, depreciation, reserves, and other necessary expenses from the gross revenue, there will remain net earnings in the amount of $5,226,000 annually from which there must be paid the carrying charges on the capital, leaving a net balance of $4,434,000.00 per annum.

(Testimony of H. P. Thomas.)

There would be no dividends the first year, but the second year would show $750,000.00 available for dividends, and there would be an increase from then on until by the 6th year "we can set aside $5,342,800.00 for dividend purposes."

Mr. Thomas testified that the method of computation employed by him "is the method that has been used right along by the Army Engineers in the study of this plant."

The development of the Grand Coulee project, using the high dam, would involve an investment of approximately $200,000,000.00. After allowing interest on the investment at six per cent and taxes at one and one-half per cent, and depreciation at the same rate, using the method of accounting employed by the Army Engineers, the plant will show a total surplus reaching on the twelfth year of $5,223,097.00, and over a period of twenty years after it is started an accumulated surplus of $61,552,884.00.

> "That to my mind shows that Grand Coulee is feasible from the viewpoint of private capital."

Mr. Thomas testified that in December, 1933, the fair market value of Defendants' lands was:

The Raths tract	$ 351,000.00
The Seaton tract	$1,088,000.00
The Julius C. Johnson and Continental Land Company tracts	$1,536,000.00

(Testimony of H. P. Thomas.)

Mr. Thomas further testified that the inherent advantages of Defendants' lands as a dam site are such that in 1933 private capital would certainly be justified in acquiring the dam site at his estimate of market value.

A selling price of two and one-half mills per kilowatt at the Grand Coulee plant would justify any distributor of electric power, such as the Washington Water Power Company, in building transmission lines to Grand Coulee to obtain the power. That rate would produce the profits testified to, and at the same time would be sufficiently attractive to bring distributing lines to the plant. A wholesale price of two and one-half mills at the plant would enable Grand Coulee to sell electric power any place in the State in competition not only with existing plants but with any future plants that are now planned.

The figures and conclusions testified to do not assume that the company owning and operating Grand Coulee will derive any profit from the retail distribution of electricity, nor from irrigation.

Mr. Thomas testified that in the generation of electric power at Grand Coulee the waters of the Columbia River must be diverted from the river out onto and over Defendants' uplands involved in this action. The water is then returned to the river below the dam. The dam will raise the water in the river and cause it to spread out over Defendants' uplands on either side of the present channel. The

(Testimony of H. P. Thomas.)
water is taken over Defendants' uplands and carried down through the penstocks onto the turbines, which also are situated on Defendants' uplands. [112]

"Q. Then, as I understand you, there is actual diversion of the water of the river out over the uplands?

"A. Yes, indeed.

"Q. And it is a fact that all the waters which in fact generate power must be diverted out over the uplands and put through the process of going through the wheels and back into the river through the tail race?

"A. That's true."

In 1914 Mr. Thomas accompanied a crew of Government engineers and cruisers making a survey of the Colville Indian reservation, preparatory to opening the reservation to entry; the land along the river bed which would be flooded by the Grand Coulee dam is

"practically all waste land * * * nothing growing on it * * * mostly rock."

Cross Examination.

We have had a serious depression and financial conditions in the last four or five years have been such that private financing of large construction enterprises is impossible. I know of no large financial arrangement for construction of hydro-electric plants.

Witness testified concerning his prediction of power market and read from unpublished plates

(Testimony of H. P. Thomas.)

prepared by the Army Engineers and also from the Army Engineer's report.

"Judge WEBSTER: I may say the point I have in mind is this: Some of this witness' testimony has been directed toward showing discrepancies in the testimony given by the witness Dibble, based on his studies made for the purposes of this case and certain figures he either prepared or collaborated in preparing that appear in the Army report. Now, we must know whether we are talking about the same thing or not to know whether there is any discrepancy. If this witness has based his computation upon a plate or other data which is not a part of the Army Engineers' report, clearly it is not permissible to charge discrepancies on the part of Dibble with that information, because his testimony is founded on the Army report. What this witness has ascertained for the purpose of his figures as showing discrepancies—if this document he referred to is not part of the Army [113] report, then, obviously, you can't predicate an opinion on discrepancies in Dibble's testimony upon that document.

"Mr. LEWIS: We are very glad to have that suggestion, your Honor. I will say that this is a point that was not called to my attention and if we can save time, I will undertake to go thru with Mr. Thomas some of this introductory matter and call it to the Court's

(Testimony of H. P. Thomas.)

attention later. If we do find that Mr. Thomas' computations are based upon something entirely unfair to Mr. Dibble, we will very gladly make the correction."

The witness then proceeds to testify further:

What I have indicated on my diagram as the prediction as to the average kw for 1950 is approximately 40% higher than the prediction for that year on page 45 of the official report of the Army Engineers. And the same comparison for 1955 shows my figures 59½% in excess of the Army Engineers'. I do not remember whether my diagram predicted a continuous increase at the rate of 9½% compounded annually. The company which built the plant will have to have transmission lines to carry their power to the distribution points. I did not include these transmission lines in the cost of this project. I do not recollect at what rate power has been contracted for sale at the Bonneville Dam. A part of my estimated returns of the Columbia Basin project is to be derived from the government project so far as the irrigation end of it is concerned if the irrigation project should be developed by the Government rather than by private capital. There is no other market for such a block of secondary power other than the proposed irrigation project that I know of. I have never financed a hydro-electric development. As to sales of secondary power, I assume that one mill per kwh of energy at the pumping station would be received for pow-

(Testimony of H. P. Thomas.)

er. I have never developed a hydro-electric power site. The proposed Grand Coulee project will be financed [114] by private capital by the sale of bonds. I have not offered any for sale. I have not been looking for anybody to buy them. I have not tried to sell any. I did not assume that any such securities could be sold between 1930 and 1933. I did not assume that I would finance it at this time. I know of no sales which would indicate that I might have sold large blocks of power securities in 1933-1934. I have used the rate of 5% for the first issue of bonds, 4% for the first issue of securities and 5% for the junior securities in my computation. I computed 6% as the average rate for the entire capital required. The feasibility from the standpoint of financing the project will depend in a degree upon the rate of interest it would have to pay.

Re-Cross Examination.

I have not considered the continued construction of additional navigation dams along the Columbia River following the completion of the Bonneville Dam, but it is possible in the distant future another dam for purposes similar to Bonneville may be constructed at The Dalles or elsewhere. I know there has been some agitation for development at Uma-tilla Rapids. After a plant is producing, another plant would not come into market without some consideration of the existing plants. I am familiar with the area that will be flooded both by a low dam and a high dam. My initial dam would flood

(Testimony of H. P. Thomas.)

flood at least 600 tracts in private ownerships. You could not make any beneficial use of the proposed dam without the flooding of lands in the reservoir site. The land in the reservoir site must be flooded after the water is raised behind the dam. I consider the lands in the damsite have an inherent value due to their natural proper- [115] ties and natural elements. Any desirability that the lands above the dam site have for use as reservoir lands depends entirely upon the inherent value of the dam site itself, and any value the dam site may have depends upon the use of the reservoir lands. It would be impossible to operate a dam without the reservoir lands.

Re-Cross Examination.

The Army Engineers consider the curve begins tapering off about 1950-1951. It is possible that there is some slight drop in increase a few years prior to that time.

"Q. Isn't there a prediction that this taperin off is to begin immediately—reducing from 9½ gradually to 4½ and finally to no further increase at all?

"A. I think you are possibly right in that, Mr. Stoutemyer—that 9½% continues only a few years.

"Q. Does it continue any years at all before it begins tapering off?

"A. I couldn't answer that right now.

(Testimony of H. P. Thomas.)

"Q. Then this Army Engineers' predicted market on the tapered basis would begin to diverge from your line almost immediately, wouldn't it, instead of waiting until 1951?

"A. It would."

WILLIAM P. CREAGER,

having been duly sworn as a witness on behalf of defendants, testified:

That he is a consulting hydraulic engineer residing in Buffalo, New York; that he was graduated from Rensselaer Polytechnic Institute in the year 1901 with the degree of Civil Engineer; that he has been employed as engineer by the Provincial Government of the Philippine Islands in river improvement work; by the New York State Barge Canal as designer in the field of dams and locks; [116] by the J. G. White Engineering Corporation of New York City, starting in the capacity of designer and ending as chief engineer of hydraulic structures. During his connection with the J. G. White Corporation he had experience on dams and hydraulic projects in every field of work, including investigations, preliminary field surveys, costs and valuation, field engineering and construction. He has been connected with the Beauharnois Development in Canada, Connecticut River Power Company, Muscle Shoals steam plant water supply for the United States Government, and Arco Nitrate plants at Alabama.

(Testimony of William P. Creager.)

From 1922 until 1930 he was Vice-President, Chief Engineer and Director of the Power Corporation of New York and the North New York Utilities, in charge of engineering and construction. In such capacity he had actual charge of construction and was in direct contact with financial interests. From 1930 to the present time he had been consulting engineer for a number of Public Service corporations, evaluating power sites and projects, and inspecting reports relating to hydro-electric power development, and the construction of dams. He is a member of the Board of Consulting Engineers on the Los Angeles Flood Control District on the San Gabriel dam, which, when completed, will be the largest earth and rock filled dam in the world. As consulting engineer he has served, among other companies, the New York Power & Light Company, North New York Utilities, Black River Irrigating District, Hudson River Irrigation District, Malone Light & Power Company, the Soviet Government of Russia, the Cities Service Company, Niagara-Hudson Power Company. He has studied and reported on Niagara-Hudson Power Company's holdings on the St. Lawrence River which will call for an expenditure of $120,000,-000.00, [117] and an installation of about 1,500,000 horse power. That was a "private development."
He is author of a number of books, among them being: "Engineering for Masonry Structures", "Hydro-Electric Handbook", the section on "Water Power" for "Pender's Handbook for Electrical

(Testimony of William P. Creager.)

Engineers'', the section on ''Dams'' in the engineering book entitled ''Concrete & Masonry Structures'', the section on ''Hydraulics'' for the coming new edition of ''Kent's Mechanical Engineers Handbook''. His book on ''Dams'' has been translated into the French and Russian languages.

He has seen and examined the Grand Coulee dam site, he heard all the evidence since the beginning of the trial, and has read the essential parts of the Report of the Army Engineers made on the Grand Coulee project. His testimony was based upon his personal experience as an engineer, his study of the Army Engineers' reports, and the investigation and reports made by Mr. Batchellor and Mr. Thomas. He has had experience in passing upon the investigations, studies and reports of other engineers, and has been accustomed to basing his conclusions and recommendations upon such studies and reports to the companies which he has served. Mr. Creager testified that ''it is both feasible and practical'' for private capital to develop the Grand Coulee project, and gave as his reasons the following:

''For a distance of a hundred miles below the dam site and a distance of seventy miles above the dam site there is no other possibility—no other possible opportunity of building a dam to any practical height. This dam site is admirably adapted for the purposes intended. I have visited, studied, and reported on hundreds of dam sites and I never yet have seen

(Testimony of William P. Creager.)

a dam site better than this, and perhaps I have
never seen any as good. A dam site at that
place in comparison with other places on the
river furnishes an enormous amount of [118]
storage which improves the water power and
navigation conditions all down the river. With
regard to the water power improvement due to
storage there is an increase in volume and necessarily would be an increase in capacity those
plants would be able to have, and the benefit
to those plants would accrue to the builders of
the Grand Coulee dam, although that has not
been taken into consideration by the witnesses.
This dam adapts itself very readily to the generation of power in steps. It's true a large
initial investment will have to be made, but
after that, according to the records it will be
built in steps, one after the other as the power
demand increases. It will provide lake navigation which, although not apparently taken
into consideration by the witnesses should have
—should provide means in the future to ready
access to the site from the Canadian boundary.
The very magnitude of this dam and power
house is sufficient to stifle competition; there
are comparatively few hazards at that site compared with other possible sites for development
on the river."

Mr. Creager testified that it was his opinion that
there was a demand and a market for dam site purposes for Defendants' uplands involved in this litiga-

(Testimony of William P. Creager.)

tion in 1933, or within a reasonable time thereafter, and as his reasons for such opinion Mr.
Creager gave the following:

"My conclusions were arrived at after a consideration of all the factors which I have just
enumerated in regard to the physical characteristics of the site and the opportunity of improving the river, and other things, and also a
consideration of the records of the case indicate a site could be built by private capital,
or any one else, generate power and sell that
power at the plant which would run into millions of dollars each year. The records also
indicate that that site is the best site for the
construction of a dam and power house for the
generation of electrical energy, and that the difference between generating electricity at that
site and any other comparable site or any other
feasible site or possible site on the river would
amount to millions of dollars each year. I have
taken those things into consideration and in my
opinion private capital would certainly be interested in purchasing that site as of that date.

* * *

My experience is that private companies are
always on the lookout for such sites where
profitable."

Mr. Creager stated that the sums of money disclosed in the evidence in connection with the development of Grand Coulee "would neither be pro-

(Testimony of William P. Creager.)

[119] hibitive nor beyond the reach of private capital."

Mr. Creager then testified that he had formed an opinion as to the fair market value of Defendants' lands, and gave the following values:

Rath tract .... $ 420,000.00
Seaton tract .... $ 960,000.00
Julius C. Johnson and
Continental Land Com-
pany tract $1,410,000.00

Mr. Creager testified that he had designed twenty-six hydro-electric power developments, and had personally constructed fifteen of them. That he had designed thirty-five dams and had made over two hundred reports to financial interests on dams and hydro-electric power development. That he had done work for such projects in thirty-five different states and in a number of foreign countries, and that in his opinion it would be practicable and in conformity with sound engineering principles to build a low dam and later add to it as proposed in the plan suggested by Mr. Batchellor and Mr. Thomas.

Cross-Examination.

I do not approve of the Reclamation Bureau's plan for raising the dam but I did not see any detail plans for that construction—all I have seen is what has been in the reports. I do not know that any detail plans were ever made by the Recla-mation Bureau for raising the dam. It is my rec-

(Testimony of William P. Creager.)

ollection in connection with the plan I have endorsed
that it would take three or four years between the
initial construction and the enlargement.

Witness was then asked by plaintiff's attorney to
make a sketch showing in a general way the extent
of the spillway section of the low dam that he recommends and to superimpose on it the section of
the high dam which he endorses. The witness
stated that what he was about to [120] demonstrate
would not be what he would say is a final design
but would be an outline of a design which would have
to be filled out by experiments and further calcula-
tions (whereupon witness makes a freehand sketch).
Now that is a suggested design which I feel perfectly confident would prove out all right.

Both Mr. Batchellor and Mr. Thomas have included in their estimates of the dam an amount of
money which I consider adequate to take care of
any reasonable experiment which would have to be
made in regard to this method of constructing the
dam. In a general way, what I have shown here is
a design of a dam I would endorse. The abutment
section would be a little different from that. The
lower cofferdam would be down in here off the sheet,
probably about 160 to 200 feet away. The concrete
heats during the time it is setting or hardening. I
have never built any concrete in that vicinity but
I have in the northern part of New York—if that
is as high a latitude as this. As it heats, concrete
expands, and as it cools down it contracts. After
the low dam has been completed and water has

(Testimony of William P. Creager.)

poured over the spillway for a year or so, the low dam would have cooled off, which would occur before I started the proposed enlargement. And the shrinkage would have taken place in the low dam before I began construction of the enlargement.

When I construct the high dam on the low dam, the new portion of the dam will be hot and when it cools off it will contract and the steps which I endorse will tend to prevent movement. If shrinkage takes place in the new concrete and movement cannot take place along the steps, the new concrete will be subject to tension. I do not think that cracks will develop as the result of [121] such tension, if there is properly cooled construction. I do not think it would either crack or sheer the steps to which I refer. I have never had anything to do with the construction of mass concrete anywhere near the size of this dam, my highest dam being only about 120 feet high. I do not know the amount of concrete in the Grand Coulee high dam except I was told it was close to 10,000,000 yards and I have never built a dam that had as much as 500,000 yards to it. I have never built a dam that had as much as 5% of the quantity of concrete as this one. If such shrinkage as occurs results in cracks, that might be detrimental to the safety of the dam. I believe that you should make a dam that you thoroughly believe to be safe. It should be built with the safest kind of reasonable construction. I am endorsing the plan by Mr. Batchellor and Mr. Thomas. I did not include in my endorsement their

(Testimony of William P. Creager.)

proposed irrigation project'. I am not an irrigation engineer. I am basing my estimate of the value of the damsite tracts on the evidence presented in court by these gentlemen (Mr. Batchellor and Mr. Thomas). I am assuming that that testimony is correct. If there are errors in their testimony as to the construction of the proposed dam and enlargement thereof, and the power plant, and the predicted power curve, and the sale of power for irrigation, and all the rest of the scheme, my testimony would also be subject to error.

The St. Lawrence project which I referred to is close to Malone—Bernhardt Island (St. Lawrence River). The population within a radius of 300 miles of that location is perhaps 10,000,000 to 15,000,000. I would assume that [122] it would be more than ten times as much as the population within 300 miles of Grand Coulee. The developments to which I refer as being somewhat near in size to this one are located in a territory where there is a very much larger population than is involved here.

In regard to my computations as to the values of the lands of the damsite, I had previously determined according to my judgment that the value of the entire site as of December, 1933 was $3,000,000. Starting out with that allocation in accordance with my judgment, I allocated to each parcel of this property which would be needed, certain amounts of this $3,000,000 in proportion to the adaptability of those

(Testimony of William P. Creager.)

different parcels of property to the construction of the damsite.

I do not know of any large sales of damsite property at that location or anywhere else in that vicinity at that time or any time near that date. There was some purchase of property by the Niagara-Hudson Corporation for the St. Lawrence development during that period. Just exactly what dates I don't know. That is adjacent to a thickly populated country. I do not know of any such sales anywhere in the Northwest. No very large projects were constructed to my knowledge during the period of the depression. There were no hydro-electric developments started in the Northwest during the period between 1930 and 1934. There was no need for them at that time. During that time nobody would have financed such construction. Financing construction requiring $70,000,000 would be found very improbable. It would be foolish to construct a development when there is no necessity for power at that particular date, December, 1933. My

(Testimony of William P. Creager.)

recollection is that the court records indicate about 600 owners in the reservoir [123] site whose property would have to be secured before the reservoir could be used. I don't know what kind of procedure you would have to go through to get the Indian lands which would be indispensable for that project, or the withdrawn lands that were withdrawn under the Reclamation act, or the state lands in the bed of the stream and the uplands. I do not know the total of that. I am not basing my testimony on my knowledge but on the court records. If private capital did not finance this proposition, it would have to finance some other on the river, but if they could not get those necessary rights of way they certainly would not throw away $3,000,000 buying land at the dam site.

Re-Direct Examination.

"Q. Just a few moments ago you distinguished between financing the development of a power project at the Grand Coulee, and purchasing the site which is involved in this law suit. Will you please explain a little to us why you made that distinction?

"A. My distinction is based on the knowledge that private companies are always on the lookout for dam sites to keep up with the market. Unless our economical structure is going to fall down flat the companies which are existing today to take care of the market and provide manufacturing power have just got to keep developing and keep supplying that market.

(Testimony of William P. Creager.)

and in order to do that they have got to look
ahead and make plans and arrange for these
dam sites. They have got to locate them and
buy them. They make investigations to determine what is best—which, in their opinion
would be the most economical and most suitable for the purpose. Now everything in court
has indicated in the circumstances surrounding
Grand Coulee that the Grand Coulee dam site
would result in a development which is better
than any other possible site on the river. Now,
private capital would be perfectly willing to go
in there to keep the project from getting into
adverse hands, to prepare for future market
supply, and to go in there and tie up that property, purchase it, even if it didn't intend to
build right at that time; even though there
were no market at that time, but knowing that
market must build up later and must develop,
and, therefore, buy that property to insure
themselves when that time comes they will have
it available for construction."

Referring to the market values testified to by
him, [124] Mr. Creager said:

"That price which I have given is, in my
opinion, one sufficiently attractive to move it
at the time of December, 1933, in full consideration of the conditions that existed at that
time. In normal times it would have been very
much greater."

(Testimony of William P. Creager.)

Re-Cross Examination.

I understand this dam site has been known for a great many years, at least 10 or 15 years. It was filed upon in 1922 by Colonel Cooper but the filing was denied, which I understand was because of the desire of the United States government to hold it for themselves. I don't know why the filer did not purchase the dam site at that time.

I doubt very much if private capital would ever have built it in 1922. It is possible it might have acquired it in 1922. Why they did not, I don't know. The power market was growing much faster in 1929 than in 1933. Nineteen twenty nine was about the peak of growth. I do not know why private capital did not purchase it then except that the previous effort to purchase it was denied on the ground that the Government wanted it. I really have not sufficient knowledge to answer the question as to why that property was not purchased in 1929 except that in my business I keep in touch with these things and I have gathered from different sources that the Government was withholding permission from private capital to build that dam from the time an attempt was made to file on it in 1921 or 1922 by Mr. Cooper.

I am not familiar with the negotiations with private capital for power sites along that river. I am familiar with the conditions on the St. Lawrence. I am not familiar with the conditions on the Columbia other than what is written in the court records

(Testimony of William P. Creager.)

and what I have seen in my [125] visits to the site (Grand Coulee).

I visited the power development at Bonneville but have visited no other part of the Columbia River besides this particular location. I base my conclusion that this is a better site than anything else on the Columbia River on the court records.

———

MARVIN CHASE,

being duly sworn as a witness on behalf of Defendants, testified:

That he resides at Wenatchee, Washington; he had lived in the state of Washington forty-three years; for eight years he was State Hydraulic Engineer for the state of Washington, from 1918 to 1925 inclusive, and he was Chairman of the Columbia Basin Survey Commission, which Commission was created by the Legislature of the state of Washington in 1919 for the purpose of inspecting the lands in eastern Washington known as the "Columbia Basin" or the "Big Bend", containing about 1,700,-000 acres.

Mr. Chase testified that he has been connected with reclamation and irrigation for many years in the Republic of Mexico, in the States of California, Oregon, Montana, Idaho and Washington; that such connection has been mostly as an engineer in laying out and building irrigation projects. That during many years his work as consulting engineer took

(Testimony of Marvin Chase.)

him into different states, and as a member of the
Washington Water Commission he helped to draft
and pass the Washington Water Code, and became
the first State Hydraulic Engineer. He has been a
member of the American Society of Civil Engineers
for about thirty years.

He made a careful study of all the Quincy District with particular reference to its availability for
reclamation and irrigation, and, in his opinion, said
district is [126] the "best and most reliable of any
irrigation project that we have." It is well adapted
for reclamation, and private capital would probably become interested.

As State Engineer, Mr. Chase became acquainted
with the Grand Coulee dam site and Defendants'
lands involved in this case. He knows of no other
place on the Columbia River between the mouth of
the Snake and the mouth of the Spokane River
which is adapted for a dam site such as is contemplated here. He has made a study of the financial
set-up and report made by Mr. Thomas as received
in evidence at the trial. From such study, and from
his acquaintance with the dam site in question, it
was his opinion that, in December, 1933, the fair
market value of Defendants' several tracts of land
was:

The Rath tract	$ 375,000.00
The Seaton tract	$1,025,000.00
Julius C. Johnson and Continental Land Company tracts	$1,450,000.00

(Testimony of Marvin Chase.)

Mr. Chase testified that during his eight years as State Hydraulic Engineer, it was his duty to pass upon all things having to do with the water resources of the state of Washington. That as receiver of the Priest Rapids power project, and as consulting engineer for the Puget Sound Light & Power Company, he had further experience in determining the value of power sites. As a member of the Columbia Basin Commission he had gained first hand information regarding the Grand Coulee site. It was upon such knowledge and experience so gained, and upon his business and engineering judgment, that he based his opinion of the market value of Defendants' lands, having in mind what had been paid for other dam sites of which he had personal knowledge. [127]

Cross Examination.

To the best of my ability to answer, there are probably 10,000 acres extending along the Okanogan, Yakima, Wenatchee and Columbia rivers which are the total of all private projects constructed in the State in the last ten years. But I do not know what is the total of all. I think it would take me some time to enumerate or study and get all of that because I have not had it in mind. I cannot answer the question as to where the largest single privately constructed project is in the state of Washington that was constructed in the last ten years. The great majority of the land on the Brewster Flat has been abandoned—gone back to the desert—

(Testimony of Marvin Chase.)

because of the lack of water supply. I do not know
why it was allowed to revert if it is feasible to pump
at such an elevation.

Plaintiff's attorney then read from the paragraph at the top of page 9 in the Seventh Biennial
Report of the Department of Conservation and Development as follows:

"It will be noted the State has refinanced 19
districts during the biennium, paying an average of 36.8 on the dollar for the district bonds."

The witness stated that of these refinanced districts he was familiar with the West Okanogan,
sometimes called Oroville-Tonasket project, Icicle,
Chelan or Manson project, but could not tell what
the refinancing was. That he knows they were refinanced but does not know what was paid for the
bonds.

My plan concerning the development of the Quincy Flats would contemplate that it would be developed for general farming. By "general farming" I
mean raising [128] hay and grain and gardening
and growing all diversified crops that are best grown
in that locality and climate. I don't recall any general farming project where the products are of the
kind I have mentioned that is being successfully
farmed with a pumping lift of over 400 feet.
I consider myself an irrigation engineer with considerable experience along the road with power. I
have gone over the figures of the proposed power
plant. In the first place, I was responsible for the

(Testimony of Marvin Chase.)

figures that were made in the Columbia Basin Survey Commission report and I also was familiar with the figures that have been made by the State in every instance. Under the law I was made adviser to the Supervisor so that the money spent on the dam site, both by the Commission and under appropriation in 1921, I had a great deal to do with and I have now been consulted and have made a study of the figures of Batchellor and Thomas. I am basing my figures on their set-up. If the figures set up by Mr. Batchellor and Mr. Thomas are all wrong, then I am all wrong on that.

Plaintiff's attorney then handed the witness the report to the Federal Power Commission on the Uses of the Upper Columbia River, signed by Board of Engineers of which M. A. Chase is one, this being one of the documents included in the stipulation. Witness reads from page 56, paragraph 7 of the report:

"Mr. W. T. Batchellor, an electrical engineer, was employed to make this estimate of electrical development and transmission, and pumping plant at the Grand Coulee site. He was not authorized by any official of the State to do any other work whatsoever, and was not competent either by training or experience to undertake the study of canals, water distribution, or any other portion of the irrigation project. We have at all times emphatically protested against his statements except on matters covered by his official employment being given

(Testimony of Marvin Chase.)

    greater weight than merely personal opinions not based on qualified judgment.''

Witness testified that he based his judgment on his [129] own investigations and checking of the reports in question. He could not explain how it is that in Mr. Batchellor's estimates of the proposed irrigation project, appearing as Defendants' Exhibit No. "7", the estimate for the North dam has been given as $205,000, while the Army Engineers' estimate for the same dam is $1,085,000. He could not state how it is that in the Army Engineers' estimate of the canal the cost is given as $4,474,330 while in Mr. Batchellor's estimate the cost of the canal has been cut down to $1,180,000.

I have never studied the Army Engineers' report and I know nothing of what their figures are. I have studied the reports of Batchellor and Thomas but have not studied their figures in connection with the Army Engineers' report. It is my recollection that Mr. Batchellor's estimated figure of $9760 per acre for the irrigation project to which he refers, includes interest during the construction or during the settlement period.

On being questioned as to whether it included interest during the settlement period, witness answered, "I can not tell you—I do not know."

Re-Cross Examination.

In answering the question as to how he arrived at the particular figures he gave and why he placed differences in value per acre on one tract as com-

(Testimony of Marvin Chase.)

pared with another, witness stated that it was the best of his judgment based on good business ability.

In making my estimates of value I assumed a total estimated value of $3,055,000 for the entire dam site. I did not allow anything for that part of the dam site owned by the State in the channel of the stream. I couldn't build a dam [130] at that site without having the lands owned by the State in the channel of the stream, and yet I did not allocate any part of the value to those lands in the channel of the stream which are indispensable to the construction of a dam. I think private money could have been secured for a development project of future construction at less than 6% interest in 1933. I cannot give any examples where private money was furnished for the construction of an irrigation project in 1933. Assuming private money would cost at least 6% and that in addition to the 6% on the construction cost of the project and the cost of operation and maintenance, you add the cost of power for pumping, the total annual cost per acre of the power project would be between $9.00 and $10.00. I cannot believe a district could pay 6%. I think it is a wrong assumption to assume a district or anyone else would pay 6%. It would not be feasible to pay 6%.

R. H. THOMSON,

being duly sworn as a witness on behalf of Defendants, testified:

That he has lived at Seattle, Washington, for fifty-four years; he was graduated as an engineer from

(Testimony of R. H. Thomson.)

Hanover College. In 1881 he entered the employ of the engineering firm of Eastman, Morris & Whitworth, Seattle; in 1887 he made a survey and appraisal of the Snoqualmie Falls, one of the outstanding power sites in the state of Washington. In 1892 he became City Engineer of Seattle, holding the office for nineteen years. During that period he studied and reported on many dam sites, and hydro-electric projects. From 1912 to 1915 he was employed by the Government of British Columbia. He studied and reported on the power sites of the Washington Power Company; also on a series [131] of dam sites in southeastern Alaska. His main duty in many of his studies and reports was to estimate the value of the sites.

Mr. Thomson then testified that he has known of the Grand Coulee dam site for some fourteen or fifteen years by reason of the published reports, including the reports of the Washington Commission in 1919 and the report made by General Goethals. That in February, 1934, he began a personal study and examination of the Grand Coulee dam site. That in co-operation with Mr. Thomas and Mr. Duffy, he had conducted an extensive study of the power market tributary to Grand Coulee, and that as a result of such studies he is of the opinion that there will be a stable rate of increase in the power consumption in the territory tributary to Grand Coulee, at the rate of nine per cent (9%) per year, and that he concurs in the estimate testified to by Mr. Thomas.

(Testimony of R. H. Thomson.)

Mr. Thomson testified that he has made such a study of Grand Coulee as he would make if he were responsible for advising a private investor, and that it is his conclusion that by the year 1940 the entire installed capacity of all power plants now in existence, or in contemplation, in the State of Washington, will be consumed. That he made a study to determine whether the market for power in the State of Washington can be supplied economically and profitably from Grand Coulee. That he took into consideration all the plants in existence around the State, adding the additions possible to be made to them, and that he concluded that the Grand Coulee site was well adapted to supply economically the increasing demand for electric power; that he had considered whether private capital would buy defendants' lands here in question in December, 1933, and that, in his judgment, said lands "would be a [132] very attractive purchase," and that he would recommend the development of the Grand Coulee project by private capital, building it in steps "just as the market demanded the power."

"Q. Do you believe that in the development of Grand Coulee you could make every step pay if the development were carried on by private capital?

"A. Yes."

Mr. Thomson testified that construction and operation of the "high dam" by private capital would pay much greater profits than the "low dam". Dur-

(Testimony of R. H. Thomson.)

ing the first four or five years of "low dam" operation, the project would about break even; by the end
of ten years it would show a net profit of $5,956,-
000.00 annually, after deducting all customary and
proper charges. An investment returning a net
profit of $5,000,000.00 per year after the tenth year,
running a period of fifty years, where there is no
demand for replacing the investment "would be
seized rapidly by the investment public". Private
capital would have acquired the Grand Coulee dam
site in December, 1933, or within a reasonable time
thereafter.

Mr. Thomson testified that he had determined
what was the fair market value of Defendants lands
in December, 1933, and that in his study of that
question he had taken into consideration prices paid
for other dam sites in the State of Washington; that
he had made allowance for difference in physical
and other characteristics between Grand Coulee and
the other sites of which he knew the prices paid.
Among other sites in the State of Washington which
he took into consideration were Snoqualmie Falls,
Cedar Falls, Sunset Falls, Baker River, Bowl &
Pitcher, Kettle Falls and Priest Rapids. The fair
market value of the several tracts was: [133]

Rath tract ....$ 250,000.00

Seaton tract ....$ 800,000.00

Continental Land Com-
pany and Julius C.
Johnson tracts $1,250,000.00

(Testimony of R. H. Thomson.)

He took into consideration the general economic and business conditions of the country which greatly tended to reduce the fair market value. Market price is arrived at by bargaining; there is no set price for dam sites. "There is always a demand for dam sites in the State of Washington."

Cross Examination.

In arriving at my statement of value which I have given on the various tracts, I used my own method based on my own judgment and experience. I estimated what the dam site ought to be worth in normal times, then took up each tract to determine at how much it would sell.

The law granting the right of way to the Government is no difficulty. The fact that the Government has the right of way does not stop me. Giving the United States right of way does not constitute deeding the land.

I have been consulting engineer on a number of irrigation projects but I have never been an operator or promoter. I do not know of any large private reclamation projects that were constructed by private capital during the last ten years nor at any other time. I know of the Sunnyside project, which is a fairly large project constructed by private capital in this state. This was constructed nearly 30 years ago. I paid no attention to the promotion of irrigation districts. My business is engineering and I neither promoted sales nor operated.

(Testimony of R. H. Thomson.)

The first power plant we proposed at Grand Coulee is for 358,000 kw capacity. The capacity of the completed plant, so far as I could determine, using the high dam up [134] to 1285, would give us firm power of 900,000 kw. We proposed using generating units of about 105,000 kw each, so for that height it would require 18 units of 105,000 kw. Nine of them would give us the 50% demand. I do not remember how many units are shown in my final setup. The one on which Mr. Thomas and I collaborated, we discussed the type of water wheel with several makers but the makers did not give us any final figures. I don't remember what speed I figured for the low dam or the high dam. I remember for the low dam we figured we would have a static head of practically 193.5 feet and with the high dam I think about 356 feet or 357 feet static head. I do not recall what space would be required between the center lines of adjacent water wheels—they would be set well apart. I don't remember what sized crane we contemplated but we figured it would cost us $80,000. I don't remember the weight of the heaviest piece of equipment to be handled during construction of the power plant. It would be a great many tons. I do not remember what would be the size of the power plant, the length and width. We have a plan somewhere; Mr. Thomas and I collaborated in the preparation of a plan. I don't remember the size. I don't remember the rating of the generators we proposed as to speed voltage. In making up the estimate as to the generating unit, we

(Testimony of R. H. Thomson.)

assembled together all the costs necessary to buy the unit in the East and pay the freight here and transport it to the dam and assemble it, including all costs and insurance. I could not tell you what figures we estimated for each unit. The type of transformers is the type recommended by the Westinghouse Electric people—what the special name is I couldn't tell you. We figured on lifting the voltage to 110,000 volts, but the generation [135] is a much less figure—I would have to see the book to say. Our understanding is the transformer would have to be erected above and back of the power-house—that is if the power-house is down on the slope, a transformer would be carried up and back. The type of transmission line that would be suitable and economical for delivery of power from Grand Coulee to Puget Sound would depend entirely on the quantity. I don't figure on delivering our power outside the switch-yard in our plant but to sell it there wholesale and every company in the state doing business with us would have to take and distribute it. The cost of transmission is a factor in the delivery of power to Puget Sound. Somebody would have to provide that transmission capacity. I don't know how many lines would be required to take the whole output to Puget Sound. I don't expect to sell the whole output over there. The power would have to be taken away from the Coulee in order to be put to use. I don't remember what investment would be required in the transmission.

(Testimony of R. H. Thomson.)

Re-Direct Examination.

The development and operation of Grand Coulee by private capital would be a financial success with electricity selling at two and one-quarter (2¼) mills per kilowatt. The success of the operation at Grand Coulee is not dependent upon selling the electricity at two and one-half (2½) mills. The estimate testified to as to the fair market value of Defendants' lands would be the same regardless of whether electricity sold for two and one-half or two and one-quarter mills. The successful operation of the Grand Coulee project, from the point of view of the fair market value of Defendants' lands, is not dependent upon the successful operation of the [136] irrigation project in the Quincy District or the Columbia Basin. The computation and testimony given is based upon the development of Grand Coulee purely as a power plant, and is not dependent on any reclamation or irrigation project.

HARVEY K. MEYER,

sworn as a witness on behalf of the Defendants, testified:

That he lives at Nespelem, Washington; that he is Superintendent of the Colville and Spokane Indian Reservations. That there are 3938 Indians on the two reservations combined, 3131 on the Colville Reservation and 807 on the Spokane Reservation as of April 1st, 1935. The Colville Reservation contains

(Testimony of Harvey K. Meyer.)
approximately 1,100,000 acres of lands, and the
Spokane Reservation approximately 140,000 acres.
Defendants' Exhibit 33, an official map of the Colville Indian Reservation, and Defendants' Exhibit
34, a map of the Spokane Indian Reservation, and
Defendants' Exhibit 35, a map showing both Reservations, were received in evidence. The red lines
along the Columbia River on Defendants' Exhibit
35 show the lands that will be flooded.

Cross Examination.

The Indian lands along the river are not considered very valuable.

Re-Direct Examination.

Mr. Meyer has been connected with the Indian
Office in the state of Washington since May 1st,
1926. During that period of time the Government
and the Department of Indian Affairs have had
applications for permits to flood or otherwise to use
lands in the Colville and Spokane Indian Reservations. Some of the applications were by the Big
Bend Transit Company and the area to be flooded
was from the Old Fort [137] Military Site, a distance of eighteen miles. That application was
granted, the land was appraised and the Big Bend
Transit Company paid for that land. It now has a
permit to construct a dam there and to overflow the
Indian lands. Frequent applications are filed for
building power lines or taking water for irrigation,
or for building highways over Indian lands. That
is true on both Reservations. It is the uniform

(Testimony of Harvey K. Meyer.)

policy of the United States Government and the Department of Indian Affairs to give very favorable consideration to such applications. Mr. Meyer has never known of any such application being denied or refused. When such applications are granted or permits given, the money received for such permit affecting allotted land is turned over to the individual Indian owner, but for tribal lands the money is paid to the United States for the benefit of the tribe.

The Indians of the Colville and Spokane Reservations have voted themselves out from under the Wheeler-Howard Act, so that Act is not applicable to the Indians of these two Reservations.

Government's verified complaint, Rules & Regulations Governing the Administration of the Federal Power Act, and Specification #570, being Sketches and Specifications of Grand Coulee Dam as a power plant; particularly paragraph 18 on page 17, paragraph 19 on page 18, and drawings numbered 8 and 9 in the Supplement, were received in evidence, as Defendants' Exhibits 39, 40, 42a, 42b, 42c and 43.

"Mr. LEWIS: Am I right in my understanding that the Constitution and the Statutes of the State of Washington will be taken judicial notice of by the Court?

"Judge WEBSTER: It may be a violent assumption, but that is the law."

DEFENDANTS REST. [138]

Rebuttal.

BARRY DIBBLE,

being recalled by the plaintiff on rebuttal, testified:

Referring to the statements made by Mr. Thomas and Mr. Batchellor in regard to alleged discrepancies in my testimony and referring particularly to Mr. Thomas' statement that

> "The Army Engineers' report assumes for the state of Washington a 9% average annual increase compounded annually and for the total area 9½%",

I would say that the report of the Army Engineers on page 866, par. 1033 states:

> "There has been selected for the rate of increase a portion of a sine curve, such that the rate of increase of production is 9.5% in 1930, decreases to 4.75% in 1960 and finally reaches zero in 1990."

That is the basis on which the study in the Seattle district office was made originally and the basis on which it appears in the report. The Seattle report was prepared by the District Engineer of the U. S. Army in Seattle and was submitted to the Division Engineer in Portland. The Division Engineer, to whom the District Engineer is subordinate, passed upon the estimates and used them as a basis for his final conclusions. These estimates appear on pages 44-45 of volume 1 of the Army Engineers' report and are summarized in table H on page 45 which gives in figures a basis for the estimate.

(Testimony of Barry Dibble.)

Plate 2 appears on page 46, and on this plate there is shown according to the title "Growth of Generation as Recorded by the U. S. Geological Survey, Historical Trend and Estimated Future Growth in the Power Market Area for Columbia River Power." The historical trends are shown for several different regions, including the states of Oregon and Washington, market area for Columbia River [139] power for the Pacific states and for the United States. Then the estimated future growth is shown for the Market Area for Columbia River power. The text states that the "graph of generation in the market area for Columbia River power has been extended from 1930 to 1960 in conformity with the estimates of Table H". Paragraph 135 on page 47 includes the statement:

"These estimates appear to give reasonable and consistent results satisfactory for the purpose of this report. Should growth continue as it has in the past, the estimates will be exceeded. Should the industry fail to continue its progress or should it be detrimentally affected by some new discovery, it may fall considerably short of the estimate."

When this report was completed about August 1, 1931, the office of the Division Engineer in Portland was discontinued and the District Engineers were transferred to the jurisdiction of the Division Engineer's office in San Francisco. The report was reviewed by the then Division Engineer Colonel Robins and he acted upon it as shown on page 1403

(Testimony of Barry Dibble.)
of volume II of the report and he stated in a memorandum to the Chief of the Army Engineers, referring to the rates of increase estimated in the report:

> "These data indicate that the estimated rate
> of power growth as used in the Columbia River
> report are over-optimistic. Using the more
> conservative prediction proposed on the diagram, it is estimated that beginning in 1940,
> about 25 years would be required to absorb the
> primary power output of the Grand Coulee
> high dam project, assuming that this power
> would be taken to the extent of excluding all
> other power development in the market area,
> which is not probable."

Acting upon the instructions from the Division Engineer, the office in Seattle revised their estimates and prepared a new estimate on the basis of paragraph 5, page 1404. This paragraph 5 states that there are two power diagrams showing the financial conditions for [140] the Grand Coulee power plant based on these assumptions: that the power market supplied from this plant will increase at a uniform rate from zero to the prime power of the site (907,-000kw) in the period of 25 years or at a rate of 36,280 (average) kw per year; that the energy sold will be paid for at a rate of $2\frac{1}{4}$ mills per kw. hr; that the cost of operation, maintenance and depreciation will be $\frac{1}{4}$ of a mill per. kw. hr. for both the energy sold and the energy used in pumping irriga-

(Testimony of Barry Dibble.)
tion water; that the load factor for commercial
power will be 55%.

The rate of growth which the Division Engineer
found to be over-optimistic was the rate of growth
I used in arriving at my conclusions. If, instead of
using the assumed rate of increase which I have
used and which was described by the Division Engineer as over-optimistic, I had used the rate of increase that was finally adopted by the Army Engineers, after instructions from the Division Engineer,
the change resulting would have been that the actual growth of the load would have been smaller than
that which I assumed and the deficit would have
been considerably increased.

Plate 125 that was submitted by the defendants
is almost identical with Plate 2 shown on page 46
of volume I of the Army Engineers' report. The
titles are slightly different. Plate 2, page 46 volume
I shows a curve which is a projection of the growth
of the Market Area for Columbia River power which
had a purported trend of 9½% instead of 9%. There
is no prediction made by the Army Engineers on
any other basis than a tapering curve, except with
this modification of the Seattle report in the letter
to which I have referred. These are on a basis of
uniform annual increase, and would also taper [141]
on a percent basis. The District Engineer of Seattle
made the report on the Columbia River above the
mouth of the Snake River and the District Engineer
of Portland made the report on the Columbia River

(Testimony of **Barry Dibble**.)

below the mouth of Snake River. The Division Engineer in Portland then prepared a summary of the two reports which begins on page 16 of volume I and was concluded, without the appendices, on page 84 of the report. The references which were made on cross-examination of Mr. Thomas to volume I are contained in the Division Engineer's report summarizing the reports of the two District Engineers. The two District Engineers were on an equality. The Division Engineer in Portland had charge of the Portland and Seattle districts. The Division Engineer in Portland accepted the figures of the District Engineers but before the report was finally transmitted to Washington the office of the Division Engineer in Portland was abolished and jurisdiction transferred to San Francisco, and the Division Engineer in San Francisco instructed the revision of the estimates and regarded the proposition as over-optimistic. The statement by Mr. Batchellor that my estimate of the average rate of increase in market demand for power assumes about one-half of what was assumed formerly and that the one-half would be somewhere in the neighborhood of four or five per cent, is not correct. The assumption for rate of increase is the same year by year as I made them and as the Army Engineers made them, except I took into account the effect of the depression and used the year 1934 as a base year instead of 1930, as had been done in the case of the Army Engineers' report. I think I did actually state that the effect of the depression was the main [142] reason for the

(Testimony of Barry Dibble.)

change in basis which I used. I had the actual figures for 1934 and used them as a basis for future predictions. There is of course a difference between the number of kilowatt hours each year that I used as a basis for the power market, but there is no difference between my figures and the Army Engineers' figures in the percentages which I applied from year to year. I felt that the depression had been so severe and the long period in which electrical production has made no growth has caused an offset in the line of development and that the industry cannot be expected to recover and get back on the curve it was following prior to 1930. The rate set up in the revised Army report under the instructions from the Division Engineer was $2\frac{1}{4}$ mills. The Bureau of Reclamation also estimated a rate of $2\frac{1}{4}$ mills.

I have made computations to determine whether Mr. Batchellor is correct in his theory that if the tables of the Army report were calculated on a basis of private development with 6% money instead of a basis of public development on 4% money they would still show the dam and power plant to be profitable for private development. I have those computations available.

(Witness produces sheet containing computations which was marked Plaintiff's Identification "O" and was admitted in evidence and became PLAINTIFF'S EXHIBIT "O")

Witness resumes: The difference between this sheet marked Plaintiff's Exhibit "O" and table 115

(Testimony of Barry Dibble.)

on pages 740-741 of the Army Engineers' report is that Exhibit "O" was computed on the assumption that the development of the low dam at Grand Coulee would be made by private enterprise with 6% money. The assumptions which the Army set up for private enterprise and 6% money are shown in the final column of Table 112 on page 736, Volume II of the Army [143] report. Following through, I have used the same step development that was used in Table 115 (pages 740-741) putting in the generating units in the power-house, giving the same capacity, using the same incomes and outputs, and the same rate, 2½ mills per kw. hr. for the revenues from the sale of power—the initial cost is modified because of the difference in the rate of interest during construction. My table shows that there will be a deficit each year, that is the revenues are insufficient to cover the interest, depreciation, taxes, operation and maintenance and therefore leave a deficit every year throughout the length of the table and the deficit is increasing at the end of the table so it would continue to increase indefinitely. At the end of the 41 years, which the table covers, the accumulated deficit amounts to over $83,000,000. This would not indicate the low dam at the Grand Coulee site to be a profitable enterprise and attractive to private capital as testified to by witnesses for defendants.

Mr. Thomson's estimate, as shown by the figures in Defendants' Exhibit 26, on which he based his conclusion that the low dam at Grand Coulee would

(Testimony of Barry Dibble.)

be profitable for private capital with interest at 6%, includes $73,900,000 for the low dam and power plant while the Army estimate for the same is $105,000,000 or more. The interest and taxes on that difference of investment would make a very large difference in the annual charges and would wipe out the surplus which Mr. Thomson estimates and leave a considerable deficit instead, and make the plan impracticable under Mr. Thomson's set-up.

(Plaintiff offered in evidence Identification "Q", entitled "Grand Coulee High Dam 6% Money" and it was admitted and it became PLAINTIFF'S EXHIBIT "Q".) [144]

Witness resumed: This Exhibit "Q" contains the results of a computation I made to see if Mr. Batchellor was correct in testifying that the Grand Coulee high dam would be profitable for private development on the Army basis. This sheet has been computed using the Army basis for private development and 6% money as shown on Table 118, page 749 of the Army report. The table is in the same form as Table 121 at pages 752-753 of the Army report except it has been necessary to modify it in order to show the differences in the computations necessitated by the Engineers' basis. I have used in this computation the same installation of units, dam capacity and kilowatts, the same output, the same revenue as was used in Army Engineers' Table 121, the cost being modified to suit the changed basis. My table shows that there would be deficits

(Testimony of Barry Dibble.)

as a result of 6% money under the Army plan for the high dam beginning with over $10,000,000 a year for the first eleven years. During that time an accumulated deficit of over $72,000,000 would be built up and it would take about 20 years more for this deficit to be wiped out by the surpluses which begin to accumulate after the eleventh year—in other words, assuming that the plant starts opera-tion in 1941, it would be 1972 before the accumulated deficit would be wiped out. After that there would be a surplus each year and at the end of 41 years there would be a total surplus of about $57,000,000. I do not think that would indicate the venture to be a profitable enterprise attractive to private capital.

The financial statement to which I just referred does not include amortization as required by the Federal Power Commission. If amortization expense were included, the amortization and the fees of the Federal Power Commis- [145] sion taken together would amount to more than the surplus that would occur. This would increase the deficit and if those items were included there would never be a surplus.

I have made a computation to determine whether Mr. Batchellor was correct in testifying that the Grand Coulee dam would be profitable for private development with 6% money, on the basis of the Bureau of Reclamation report dated January 7, 1932.

(Testimony of Barry Dibble.)

(Witness' computation was marked as Plaintiff's Identification "S" and later admitted as PLAINTIFF'S EXHIBIT "S".)

This table is in the form of the table which is found on page 142 of the report of the Bureau of Reclamation published in the hearings on H.R. 7446, Table 15. This table as it appears in the Reclamation report has been modified to show the effect of taking interest at 6% instead of 4% and making other necessary changes—taxes have been inserted and retirement of investment has been eliminated; costs of operation and maintenance have been left the same. The estimated revenue has been made the same as in Table 15. Table 15 shows revenue from sale of power by pumping at the rate of $1.00 per acre of land in cultivation on the Columbia Basin project and I have included that revenue as set up by the Bureau of Reclamation. The table follows as nearly as can be the table prepared by the Reclamation Bureau except for the change of rate of interest and other matters involved in private development. As a result of 6% money under the Bureau of Reclamation plan, my table shows the plant would start with an initial deficit of $12,000,-000 the first year of operation and that this deficit would gradually decrease for 15 years, when it would become something over $9,000,000. By that time the accumulated deficit would be $166,000,000. [146] from then on the deficit begins to accumulate

(Testimony of Barry Dibble.)

with increasing rapidity and the table is carried out for a period of 60 years, which is estimated to be necessary for bringing in all of the Columbia Basin Irrigation project, and by the end of the 60 years, on account of the compound effect of the deficit the computation shows a very enormous total of $2,100,000,000 as an accumulated deficit. This certainly would not indicate that a dam and power plant at Grand Coulee with private capital at 6% interest under the Bureau of Reclamation plan would be a profitable enterprise and attractive to private capital.

Referring to the testimony of Mr. Thomas, I have prepared a table showing figures actually used by me in estimating the rate of growth and the average kw hour output, estimated for each year.

(Witness' computation was marked "Plaintiff's Identification "T" and later admitted and marked PLAINTIFF'S EXHIBIT "T".)

Witness resumed: Identification "T" is the sheet showing the computations to which I just referred. In the first column is shown the calendar years. In the middle of the sheet is a column marked "Annual Increase Percent" showing the percentage of increase from year to year that I have assumed in making up my prediction of growth of load. In the second column beyond the one just referred to, headed "Base, 1934", the figures are the average kw estimated by me for the power market area as the annual output of each year to which they refer,

(Testimony of Barry Dibble.)

beginning with 1934. In the second column beyond that one, marked with an arrow, is the growth that was estimated to be available for Grand Coulee power development after 1940. This figure is computed from the preceding column and was taken as half of the total growth after 1940 as shown in the column just preceding. This is the load which we have [147] assumed in this study would be available for the Grand Coulee plant. These are the figures I used in preparing my testimony. The rate of load increase conforms to the prediction which has been referred to by the superior officers of the Army as too optimistic.

I have assumed Mr. Batchellor's set-up of a plan of step construction and have made up a table using the plan but applying it to a more conservative prediction of rate of power market growth than Mr. Batchellor used.

(Witness' computation marked Plaintiff's Identification "U" was admitted and became PLAINTIFF'S EXHIBIT "U".)

I worked out this data by preparing a table to show the effect of the development such as proposed by Mr. Batchellor, raising the dam in steps. We have used in this case, instead of the growth which Mr. Batchellor assumed at 10% compounded annually, a growth corresponding to that which we have used in our own study. We have also used the rate which assumed 2¼ mills per kw hour instead of 2½ mills per kw hr. When worked out this way, the

(Testimony of Barry Dibble.)

result of the Batchellor plan shows a deficit each year but two. Those two years are 1958-1959—after that the deficit occurs again. I might say in connection with the preparation of the table that because of slower growth of the power market, we have delayed installation of machinery and raising the dam to correspond with the load, rather than taking the same rate for construction work as taken by Mr. Batchellor. However, we have used his costs as applied to this lower rate of construction and have otherwise attempted to conform to his plan. The rate of growth estimated in this computation is the same percentage of growth from year to year as recommended in the original Army report which [148] was regarded as too optimistic, but uses 1934 as a starting point rather than 1930. The total accumulated deficit under Mr. Batchellor's plan of development, if I applied that rate of growth to the power market, would be an accumulated deficit of $39,482,000 at the end of 25 years. The deficit would continue to increase following that. I think that this would show the plan described by Mr. Batchellor would not be a profitable and attractive one to private capital. I do not endorse Mr. Batchellor's plan of step construction as being sound or practicable. I do not endorse his estimated costs as being adequate. I am certain that it would not be possible in December, 1933, or at any reasonable time within a period of 5 years after that date to finance the construction of the dam and power plant at Grand Coulee through private enterprise if the

(Testimony of Barry Dibble.)
project didn't promise a return in excess of 6% of
the entire investment.

PLAINTIFF'S EXHIBIT V, a certified
copy of the order of the Federal Power Commission, dated August 20, 1932, granting a
power permit to the Columbia Basin Commission for the Grand Coulee project; and Exhibit
W, the permit to the Columbia Basin Commission to construct the Grand Coulee project were
offered in evidence.

They were objected to as incompetent, irrelevant
and immaterial, and not rebuttal.

Discussion here followed.

"Judge Webster: I am not clear about it.
I wish I had a more definite view about it, but
I am inclined to think it is safer to admit it
than to exclude it, and I will allow the Permit
to be introduced. V and W will be admitted."

To which ruling Defendants except.
Discussion and Recess. [149]

"Judge Webster: There is one thought that
has come to my mind during this recess with
respect to these permits. Mr. Lewis has just
made an objection to the introduction of the
permit, and I understand that objection is
joined in by all of the defendants. * * *

"This is a delicate situation, and I will sustain the objection to both. Let the order admit-

ting Exhibits V and W be set aside, and Exhibits V and W will be rejected."

To which ruling Plaintiff excepts.

"Judge Webster: The outstanding authority upon the question of the rights of the owners of shore lands along a navigable stream when the Government, in the exercise of its power to regulate commerce with foreign countries and among the several states, and with the Indian tribes, decides to carry on the development for the purpose of navigation—the law of the State of Washington is clear upon the point that the owner of the beds of navigable streams in this state is vested in the State. It is also well settled that the character of riparian rights is a matter of local law; that is to say, the law of the State of Washington determines for the State of Washington the character of the rights which are enjoyed by owners of property riparian to navigable waters, and as I have said before, the beds of navigable streams are vested in the State.

"Now, the case of the United States v. Chandler-Dunbar Water Power Company, reported in Volume 229, United States Supreme Court Reports, page 53, is perhaps the leading and outstanding pronouncement by the Supreme Court of the United States upon the question under review. It has been followed, and in so far as my investigation of the authorities goes, in every instance upheld."

Here the Court read at length from the opinion of Mr. Justice Lurton in the Chandler-Dunbar case, and also from the opinion of Lewis Blue Point Oyster Cultivation Company v. Briggs, 229 U. S. 82.

Following the reading from the opinion in the Chandler-Dunbar and Briggs cases, there was further discussion.

"Judge Webster: Assuming a motion will be made pursuant to the ruling that I made yesterday, to strike from consideration of the jury all of the evidence relating to the adaptability of this property for a dam site—if such a motion is made it will be granted, consequently the question of availability and adaptability of this land as a dam site has no place in the consideration of the jury because I am disposing of that as a matter of law."

"Mr. Stoutemyer: In view of the court's ruling we wish to move at this time to strike from the record all testimony in regard to the market value of the lands in question for dam site purposes." [150]

"Judge Webster: And that motion will be granted."

"Mr. Lewis: Allow us an exception, if the Court please."

"Judge Webster: Let the record show each of the Defendants excepts to the ruling of the court, and each exception is allowed."

"Judge Webster: I am not at all unmindful of the importance of the ruling the court has made, nor of the far reaching consequences of it to the litigants in this case. I have given as careful and painstaking consideration to it as I am capable of giving. I have reached a definite and positive conclusion in my own mind concerning it and in that state of mind my duty is very plain, that is to rule exactly as my conclusion is, and that is what I have done. If any litigant is aggrieved by it the law provides ample remedy by which the error may be corrected.

"Bring in the jury, Mr. Bailiff."

Whereupon the jury is returned to the Court Room.

"Judge Webster: Gentlemen of the Jury: During your absence from the Court Room certain proceedings have been taken before the Court relating to a number of important aspects of this case. The most important one is a motion interposed by the Government to strike from the record and from the consideration of the jury all testimony and evidence in this case relating to the adaptability and availability of the properties involved in these cases for use as a dam site. That motion has been granted.

"I think out of respectful consideration for the jury, which is an arm of the Court, it is proper for me to briefly tell you the considerations which lead me to that conclusion.

"In the State of Washington the beds of navigable streams are not vested absolutely or qualifiedly in the owners of the shore lands along such navigable streams. The bed of navigable streams in the State of Washington is vested in the State of Washington. The decisions of the Supreme Court of the United States are at one upon this proposition, that the Congress of the United States has absolute control over the navigable streams within the borders of the country. It has that power in virtue of the provision of the Constitution of the United States which confers exclusively upon Congress the power to regulate commerce with foreign nations and among the several states and with Indian tribes. Navigable streams are great water highways, agencies and instrumentalities of commerce, and the dominant power of Congress to control the waters of such streams is clearly settled and determined by repeated decisions of the Supreme Court of the United States. The decisions of the Supreme Court of the United States are to the effect that riparian owners of shore lands along the banks of a navigable stream do not have as [151] against the United States, any interest in or title to the waters which flow in the stream when the United States undertakes to develop it or to improve those water highways for the purpose of advancing and improving navigation. That the land owner so owning these adjoining shore lands is not entitled to have any allowance made to him based upon any title to the bed of the stream or any allowance made to him for any right that he has because of the water running in the navigable stream or its potential water power.

"I am reading to you a succinct paragraph from one of the leading cases decided by the Supreme Court of the United States which to my mind fits this case like a glove, and is absolutely conclusive of the question presented:

" 'Having decided that the Chandler-Dunbar Company as riparian owners have no such vested property rights in the water power inherent in the falls and rapids of the river, and no right to place in the river the works essential to any practical use of the flow of the river, the Government cannot be justly required to pay for an element of value which did not inhere in these parcels of upland.' 'The Government had dominion over the water power of the rapids and falls, and cannot be required to pay any hypothetical additional value to a riparian owner who had no right to appropriate the current to his own commercial use. These additional values represent, therefore, no actual loss, and there would be no justice in paying for a loss suffered by no one in fact. The requirement of the 5th Amendment is satisfied when the owner is paid for what is taken from him. The question is—what has the owner lost, and not what has the taker gained.'

"These owners, in my judgment, are not entitled to have that adaptabiliy of this site taken into account for the reason they have neither title to the bed of the stream nor any right to the waters which flow in it as against the Government exercising dominant power to improve the stream for navigation purposes, and that they are not entitled to that because it has not been taken from them, and it hasn't been taken from them for the simple reason that they never owned it in the first place."

Further Rebuttal was then had on the issue of the value of certain of Defendants' lands for agricultural, grazing and orchard purposes, which is not material on this appeal.

"Mr. Lewis: Defendants respectfully move the court for leave and permission to introduce evidence to prove that all the lands, the values of which were testified to by said witnesses Batchellor, Thomas, Duffy, Creager, Chase and Thomson lay [152] above the ordinary high water level of the Columbia River.

"Judge Webster: I think there will be no contention to the contrary, will there?

"Mr. Lewis: I don't think there will be, your Honor.

"Mr. Stoutemyer: I really wasn't listening to what counsel was saying in the last few minutes.

"Judge Webster: We seem to have considerable difficulty.

"Mr. Lewis: May I finish my motion, if the Court please? In support of said motion Defendants respectfully represent and state to the Court that if permitted by the Court to do so the witnesses Batchellor, Thomas, Duffy, Chase, Creager and Thomson will testify each respectively, that the values testified to by him in the trial of this action applied only to lands belonging to the respective Defendants lying above the ordinary high water mark of said river; that each of said witnesses will testify that he knows what is the ordinary high water mark of the Columbia River, and that he has not included any value for any land whatsoever lying below the said ordinary high water mark of the river.

"Judge Webster: What does counsel have to say about that?

"Mr. Stoutemyer: We wouldn't want to concede that the witnesses testified to anything they didn't testify to.

"Judge Webster: But if there is any contention as to the value of this land—that all of the acreage involved here may be taken into consideration as above the high water mark of the river.

"Mr. Stoutemyer: There has been no contention on that.

"Judge Webster: With that part of the record clear, there will be no necessity to re-open the case."

Defendants then offered in evidence paragraph 1670, 1678, 1690, 1692, 1990 and 1999 of H. R. 103, Volume II, to which there was an objection on the ground that they come too late, which objection was sustained and exceptions allowed.

Said paragraphs are quoted as follows:

"Sec. 1670. The Columbia is a river with steep slopes, high velocities, and numerous rapids flowing [153] through a tortuous channel from 2,000 to 3,000 feet below the level of the surrounding country, much of which is semi-arid and comparatively unproductive without irrigation. The volume of water carried by the river justifies a serious consideration of its practical use for navigation, but investigation of conditions in the Columbia above the Snake shows that the cost of improvements necessary to give a satisfactory width and depth to the channel is much greater than any possible river commerce would warrant."

"Sec. 1678. The cost of this work is estimated at $165,000,000. Interest on this amount at 4 percent would be $6,600,000 annually, which would, of course, be prohibitive if any appreciable proportion of the cost were charged against navigation."

"Sec. 1690. It appears, therefore, that navigation is of no present importance and that future consideration will have to depend upon conditions as they develop."

"Sec. 1692. It is concluded that—

1. Expenditures necessary to permit through traffic by canalization on Columbia River above the Snake are not justified by any reasonable expectation of shipments by water in or out of the territory.

2. Navigation from Portland to points below Wenatchee could be made possible by the construction of locks in all dams below Wenatchee when the river is fully developed, for power.

3. The construction of any dams for the development of power would make local traffic in the pool above it possible. No special expenditure will be necessary to facilitate the development of the local commerce with the exception of the improvement of the channels at the upper end of the pool to accommodate traffic during low stages of the river.

4. Traffic on the river in and out of the territory above the Snake would represent no saving to producers, shippers, or consumers unless such traffic exceeded 250,000 tons annually.

5. The possibility of future traffic on the river above the Snake may justify Federal par-

ticipation in the construction of locks when and if such are needed."

"Sec. 1990. A high dam is proposed in the Columbia opposite the head of Grand Coulee for the generation of power for the general market and for use in connection with the irrigation of the Columbia Basin irrigation project. This dam will hold water at elevation 1,287.6 and would back the water to the international boundary. A location for locks is shown on the plans although none are contemplated for inclusion in the comprehensive plan."

"Sec. 1999. No provision is made for the control of floods on the Columbia above the Snake as none is required."

EVIDENCE CLOSED. [154]

———

Defendants then submitted to the Court eleven written requests for instructions to the jury, all of which were refused by the Court. The requests sufficient to present the questions material on this appeal and to the refusal of which exceptions were duly taken and allowed, were:

"Instruction No. IX.

"It is not necessary for defendants in order to establish a market value for the lands in question as of December, 1933, or within a reasonable time thereafter, to prove that at said time there were actual sales of lands of similar character. If you find from the evidence that said lands were inherently adapted for dam site or other purposes you are entitled to consider such adaptability in determining what, if any, market value said lands possessed at said time.''

"Instruction No. X.

"If you find from all the evidence that any of the tracts of land involved in this action, or any portion of any such tract, was especially suited or adapted for use as a dam site, in December, 1933, and that, at that time, or within a reasonable time after December, 1933, any such tract or parcel of land could have been sold for such use to any purchaser other than the United States Government, then you are instructed that you should return a verdict in favor of the owner of any such tract or parcel of land for the amount of money which you find from all the evidence, such tract or parcel of land could be sold for, in December 1933 or within a reasonable time thereafter, considering its adaptability for use as a dam site as well as all other uses for which the tract or parcel was adapted.''

INSTRUCTIONS TO THE JURY

"Judge Webster: Gentlemen of the Jury:

"We have now reached the point in these consolidated cases where it becomes the duty of the Court to explain to you the issues in the cases which you are called upon to determine by your verdict, and to instruct you as to the applicable rules and principles of law by which you must be guided in your deliberations. It is your duty to accept these instructions as correct, and so far as the law of the case is concerned be guided by them. The law provides an ample and adequate remedy whereby any mistakes in the instructions may be corrected, but it is not the province of the jury to undertake to correct mistakes of law which the Court may make, and for the purposes of your deliberations the instructions which I will give you must be accepted as the law of the case. [155]

"Under the 5th Amendment to the Constitution of the United States it is provided that private property will not be taken for public use except upon the payment of just compensation. You will note that the thing that the private owner is entitled to when his property is taken for public uses is 'just compensation'. The Government of the United States possesses what is known in law as the 'power of eminent domain', which means that in the exercise of its legitimate powers it has the right to take private property whenever such property is necessary for public use and convenience. In the exercise of that power the Government institutes an action which is commonly referred to as 'condemnation proceedings', whereby it acquired title to the property of the individual upon condition that it pay just compensation to the owners for the property of which they are deprived. And the owner of the property is entitled to have the value of that which is taken from him fixed by the judgment of a jury of his peers.

"In this particular case the Government in the exercise of its legitimate powers of eminent domain is seeking to take for legitimate public purposes lands, which are owned in five separate and distinct proprietorships, which for convenience I will refer to as the Seaton lands, the Rath Estate lands, the Continental Company lands, and the Julius Johnson lands and the lands of Eva D. Burdin.

"As I have said, the Constitution of the United States provides that separate property will not be taken for public use without just compensation to the owner. The property involved in the cases at bar has been taken in eminent domain proceedings by the United States of America for public use, and the right of the Government to so take it is in no way involved in your deliberations. The owners of the property involved are entitled to just compensation for this taking, and 'just compensation' includes all elements of value that inhere in the property. It does not exceed, however, the full, fair, cash market value of the property at the time of its taking, fairly and conscientiously arrived at. And the controlling time in this case is December 27, 1933, that being the date when the properties in question were appropriated by the Government.

"The sum required to be paid the owner does not depend upon the use to which he has devoted his land, but is to be arrived at by just consideration of all the uses for which it is reasonably and practically suitable and adaptable. The highest and most profitable use for which the property is reasonably and practicably adapted is the criterion by which its market value must be measured, not necessarily to the full measure of that value, but to the fullest content that such adaptability and availability reflects itself in and increases the market value of the land at the time it is taken. Private property, under the law of the United States, cannot be appropriated to a public use until the full and exact equivalent for it is paid to the owner. [156]

"In determining the value of the lands which in this case have been taken for public use the same considerations are to be regarded by you as in the sale of property between private persons. The inquiry in the case must be—What is the property worth in the market, viewed not merely at the time appropriated, but with reference to any use to which it was reasonably and practically adapted within the reasonably near future.

"In determining the fair market value of lands taken the just compensation to the owner is a sum of money which, considering all the circumstances, disclosed by the evidence, could have been obtained for the lands by an informed seller offering them in the open market for cash, that is, the amount that in all reasonable possibilities would have been arrived at by fair negotiations between an informed owner, willing but not compelled to sell, and an informed purchaser willing but not compelled to buy. In arriving at that value you will take into account all the considerations that may fairly be brought forward and reasonably be given substantial weight by well informed men engaged in such bargaining.

"So many and varied are the circumstances to be taken into account in determining the value of the

property condemned for public use it is impossible
to formulate an exact rule to govern its appraisal in
all cases. Exceptional circumstances will modify the
most carefully guarded rule, but the general rule
is that just compensation to the owner is to be
determined by reference to the use for which the
property is reasonably and practically suitable and
adaptable, having regard to the existing business or
wants of the community, or such as may reasonably
be expected in the reasonably near future. The market value of land taken for public use includes its
value for any use to which it may reasonably and
practically be put, and all of the uses for which
it is reasonably and practically adapted, and not
merely the condition in which it is found at the
time of the taking, and to which it was applied by
the owner at that time. Lands, by reason of their
location, surroundings, natural advantages or inherent characteristics, may be peculiarly adapted
to some particular use, and all of the circumstances
which make up this adaptability are to be taken into
consideration in determining the fair market value
of the land and just compensation to the owner
thereof.

"Property taken for public use is not to be determined worthless merely because the owner has allowed it to go to waste or hasn't seen proper to use
it to its best advantage. It is not to be regarded as
valueless because the owner does not put it to any
use, and is not to be regarded of less value because
the owner has not been able to put it to the highest

and most profitable use, but the capability and possibility of its reasonable availability for a particular use which is of such a [157] character as to reflect itself in the market value of the property at the time it was taken is the factor to be taken into consideration in determining the fair market value of the property and the just compensation to the owner.

"As I have said the market value of the property is the price which it would bring when it was offered for sale for cash by an informed person who desires to but is not obliged to sell it, and is bought by an informed purchaser who is desirous of buying but under no necessity of purchasing—in determining the value all of the capabilities of the property, and all the uses to which it may be applied, or to which it is reasonably adapted, may be considered, having regard to the existing business or wants of the community or such as may reasonably be expected in the reasonably near future, and not merely the condition it is in at the time it was taken, nor to the use to which the owner has applied it at that time. It is not the value to the owner that you are to consider, nor can the damages be enhanced by the unwillingness of the owner to sell—it is the full, fair, cash value of the property as of December 27, 1933.

"The necessities of the Government of acquiring the property must not be taken into consideration, nor must any unwillingness to sell the property by the owner be taken into consideration by you in your deliberations. The owners of the property are en-

titled to receive as compensation for the taking by
the Government the value of the property for the
use for which it is most valuable, and by this is
meant the market value for that use, not its value to
the owner for such or any other particular use, but
that price which a reasonably prudent and careful
man having knowledge as to valuations in the
locality in question, and who is desirous but not
under any necessity of purchasing would be willing
to pay for the property having such uses in view or,
if he were the owner thereof, would be willing to accept as the purchase price of it, he being under no
necessity to sell it. And while determining the fair,
cash value of the property you will properly consider its capability and availability for the different uses to which it is reasonably and practically
applied, you will, nevertheless, bear in mind that you
are to ascertain and determine the full, fair, cash
market value of the property as it existed on December 27, 1933. In determining the fair, cash
market value of the property sought to be condemned you will not permit yourselves to be in any
way influenced by the character of the petitioner as
the Government of the United States, and neither
shall you permit yourselves to be influenced in any
way by the character of the defendants, or any unwillingness on their part to part with their property.
You will, in determining the fair cash market value
of the property which is to be paid by the Government to the defendants as compensation for the
taking thereof, proceed in precisely the same amount

of fairness as to all parties that you would exercise if you were sitting on a board of arbitration to determine the value of such property between owners who were willing to sell and a private purchaser who was willing to purchase where such parties had agreed [158] upon a sale at a fair, cash market value and had submitted to them the question of determining what that fair, cash market value was. Market value does not mean what a person would be willing to pay for the premises, having no necessities for buying them, but there is the added condition that it must also be such a sum as the person who was under no obligation to sell was willing to take. These two elements, taken together, go to make up market value; either one alone does not do so, and in arriving at the market value you must arrive at such a sum as would reasonably be agreed upon between a willing seller, who was under no necessity to sell, and a willing buyer who was under no necessity to purchase. The necessity of either one to sell or buy must not be taken into consideration.

"At this point I instruct you that in determining the value of this land you must not take into consideration any added value that may be given to it because of the use for which the Government is taking it.

"On the other hand, you must not deprive the owner of the value that the land actually possessed as of December 27, 1933, because of any threatening injury that might come to it because of the proposed use which the Government is to make of the property when taken.

"The purpose of assessing damages in a condemnation proceeding such as this is to award to the owner full, fair, complete and adequate compensation for the property taken. The condemning party shall not be permitted to appropriate land for less than its fair, cash market value. On the other hand, the law does not contemplate that the owners of property shall recover excessive damages, based upon any visionary or fantastic theories of value, or to remote contingencies which may never arise, or, if so, at some time so remote and uncertain as to reflect no present element of market value in the property.

"In connection with this I instruct you that the doctrine of riparian rights obtains in the State of Washington. This doctrine is that the owner of lands which are riparian to a stream, that is, whose lands primarily touch or contact such stream, may use the waters of such stream for domestic purposes of the owner, for the watering of live stock of the owner, or for the irrigation to the full extent of the soil of such owner as are riparian to the stream irrespective of the legal subdivisions the land may contain, provided the legal subdivisions are all contiguous, that is to say, in an uninterrupted body.

"Gentlemen of the Jury, I have said to you that the Judge is the sole arbiter of the law of this case, but the jury is the sole arbiter of the facts in the case. Whilst the jury has no right to entrench upon the field of law in the trial of a law suit, the Court has no right to entrench upon the jury in the determination of the facts. You are the sole and exclusive judges of what are the facts in this case, and of the weight [159] and credit to be given to the testimony of each witness who has testified before you. In discharging that task you are at liberty to take into consideration the conduct, appearance and demeanor of each witness while testifying before you; the intelligence, or lack of intelligence displayed by the witness; the apparent candor and frankness, or want of this quality, if any such appear, in giving his testimony; the opportunity or lack of opportunity on the part of any witness of knowing or being informed concerning the matters about which he testified; the interest or lack of interest on the part of each witness in the outcome of this trial; in short, all the facts and circumstances attending the witness as they were disclosed to you from the witness stand, and in the light of all these considerations give to the testimony of each witness that fair and reasonable weight which in your practical judgments as men of common sense it impresses you as reasonably and justly entitled to receive at your hands, and no more.

"Where witnesses qualify as experts in a particular field of knowledge or learning, and are called to the witness stand and allowed to express opinions, rather than testify to facts, those opinions are for the aid and the assistance of the jury, and not for the purpose of invading its functions. The responsibility of decision rests upon the jury, and it is your duty to evaluate and appraise the testimony of the witnesses who express opinions precisely as you are called upon to evaluate the testimony of witnesses who testify to facts, and it is for you in the light of all the circumstances as disclosed during the progress of this case to place that weight and give that credit to the testimony of each witness which you conscientiously believe in the exercise of sound judgment and good sense it is entitled to have at your hands, and no more.

"You will understand that in the field of ascertaining the fair, cash market value of pieces of property as of a particular time the law has no accurate mathematical standard by which that amount can be ascertained. In that field the rules of law must be defined and much must be left to the sound judgment and good common sense of a conscientious jury, and, in their deliberations there is no room for sympathy, or sentiment, or prejudice or passion. Your deliberations must be guided as your oath obliges you to be guided, to decide the case without regard to personalities; guided so far as the law of the case is concerned by the instructions of the Court, and, so far as the facts of the case are concerned, by the testimony of the witnesses.

*　　*　　*　　*　　*　　*　　*

"It will require the concurrence of the entire jury in order to return a verdict. When you retire to your jury-room to deliberate you will select one of your number as foreman who will sign your verdicts for you when they have been agreed upon, and who will represent you as your spokesman in the further conduct [160] of this case in Court.

"There have been prepared for your convenience 5 separate forms of verdict, one in favor of each separate ownership of the property involved, and in arriving at the fair market values of the property you must apply the evidence to each tract of land separately just as though that ownership was the only question before you. Take the evidence as it relates to each parcel of land and fix the value upon it just as though that parcel was the one piece that was before you, and pursue that method until you have valued all of the lands involved.

"When in the course of my instructions I said to you that it was your function to ascertain the reasonable and practical adaptability of the property in question you, of course, will understand that I did not intend to include its value or claimed value as a dam site. That question is withdrawn from the consideration of the jury and the adaptability and availability of the property in question which you will consider will be those adaptabilities or uses disassociated from any claimed use for a dam site."

"Mr. McKevitt: The Court having submitted the issues to the jury, and the jury having not yet retired to deliberate upon its verdict, the Defendants now except:

"I. To that portion of the Court's instructions eliminating from the consideration of the jury

the element of dam site valuation, for the reason
and upon the ground that the law applicable to the
case required the submission of such issue to the
Jury.

*   *   *   ..   *   .,   *   *

"V. Defendants except to the refusal of the
Court to give Instruction No. 9 for the reason that
said instruction included the element of valuation
for dam site purposes, and said instruction is a correct statement of the law applicable to the case.

"VI. Defendants except to the refusal of the
Court to give Instruction No. 10, which instruction
included the element of dam site valuation, for the
reason that said instruction is a correct statement
of the law applicable to the case.

"May the record show, your Honor, that the exceptions just made are made on behalf of each and
all of the Defendants."

"Judge Webster: Yes, it may be understood that
each of the Defendants join in the exceptions that
have been taken, and each defendant is allowed an
exception. [161]

"Mr. Stoutemyer: We would like to withdraw
the two exhibits we offered and which were rejected
—V and W."

WHEREUPON the bailiffs were sworn to take
charge of the jury during its deliberations.

"Judge Webster: Gentlemen of the Jury: This
case is now finally submitted to you. You may retire
to the juryroom and consider of your verdict.

After deliberation a verdict was returned, on which the following judgment was entered:

[Title of Case]   No. L-4760

Judgment

Filed Sept. 25, 1935

"This cause having come on for trial on the 15th day of July, 1935, and stipulation having been made in open court between counsel for the plaintiff and counsel for the defendants herein that the United States of America has the right to condemn the property described in the complaint herein for the purposes alleged in the complaint, and the issues arising upon the complaint of the plaintiff and the answers on file herein, other than those disposed of by the said stipulation, having been duly tried before the court and a jury, and the said jury having returned their verdict herein, in and by the terms of which the said jury made the following award to the several defendants herein, to-wit:

"For the tract commonly refered to as the Continental Land Company tract, more particularly described as Tract No. 1 in the complaint on file herein, and hereinafter more fully set out, the sum of.............. $1260.63

"For the tract commonly referred to as the Johnson tract, more particularly described as Tract No. 2 in the complaint on file herein, and hereinafter more fully set out, the sum of .... $ 623.75

"For the tract commonly referred to
as the Seaton tract, more particularly described as Tract No. 3 in the
complaint on file herein, and hereinafter more fully set out, the
sum of $8491.87

"For the tract commonly referred to
as the Rath tract, more particularly
described as Tracts No. 4, No. 5,
and No. 6 in the complaint on file
herein, and hereinafter more fully
set out, the sum of...............................$2506.67

"And it appearing during the trial of the said
above entitled cause that counsel for the plaintiff
herein offered to accept a judgment in the above
entitled cause wherein it shall be expressly provided
that there is excepted from the property condemned
such mineral rights, if any, as the inter- [162]
venors D. L. Underwood et al may have in that part
of the Seaton tract within the boundaries of the
so-called Sand Hill placer claim.

"And it appearing to the Court from the records
and files in the above entitled action that under date
of December 27, 1933, a declaration of taking under
the provisions of the Act of Congress of February
26, 1931 (46 St. 1421, 1422), signed by the authority
empowered by law to acquire the lands described in
the complaint, to-wit, the Secretary of the Interior,
was filed in the above entitled cause of action and
that with the said declaration of taking there was
deposited into the registry of the court, to the use
and benefit of the persons thereto entitled on the

said 27th day of December, 1933, the sum of $11,-267.92 as the estimated just compensation for the said premises described in the said complaint and in the said declaration of taking, to-wit:

"Continental Land Company Tract (Tract No. 1)—

Lots One (1), Two (2), Three (3) and Southwest quarter of Northwest quarter (SW¼ NW¼), Section 1, Township 28 North, Range 30 East, Willamette Meridian, in Grant County, Washington, containing 169.25 acres, more or less.

"Johnson tract (Tract No. 2)—

Lots Four (4) and Five (5), also Northwest quarter of Southwest quarter (NW¼ SW¼) and Southwest quarter of Southwest quarter (SW¼ SW¼) Section 1, Township 28 North, Range 30 East, Willamette Meridian, in Grant County, Washington, containing 164.50 acres, more or less.

"Seaton tract (Tract No. 3)—

Lots one (1) and Two (2), Section 31, Township 29 North, Range 31 East; Lots Five (5), Six (6), Seven (7), Section 36, Township 29 North, Range 30 East; Lots Six (6), Seven (7), Eight (8), Nine (9), Section 1, Township 28 North, Range 30 East, Willamette Meridian, in Okanogan County, Washington, containing 315.30 acres, more or less.

"Raths tract—

(Tract No. 4) Lots Two (2), Three (3), and Four (4), Section 5, Township 28 North, Range 31 East, Willamette Meridian, in Okanogan County, Washington, containing 111.37 acres, more or less.

(Tract No. 5) Lot Three (3), Section 31, Township 29 North, Range 31 East, Willamette Meridian, in Okanogan County, Washington, containing 39.89 acres, more or less. (Tract No. 6) Lot Four (4), Section 31, Township 29 North, Range 31 East, Willamette Meridian, in Okanogan County, Washington, containing 39.97 acres, more or less.

and thereupon title in fee simple absolute vested in the United States of America and the same was deemed to be condemned and taken for the use of the United States of America and at the same time the right of just compensation vested in the persons entitled thereto, to-wit, the defendants herein. [163]

"And it appearing to the Court that under the provisions of the said Act of February 26, 1931 (46 Stat. 1421, 1422) the said defendants became entitled to interest at the rate of 6% per annum on the amount finally awarded as the value of the property, from the date of taking until the date of payment except that interest shall not be allowed on so much thereof as shall have been paid into court, and it appearing to the Court that the excess of the said award over the amount so paid into court is the sum of $1615.00 on which sum the defendants are entitled to interest at the rate of 6% per annum from said date of taking, to-wit, December 27, 1933, until the balance of the said award is paid into court for the defendants, the said interest to be paid into court and to be thereafter distributed to the several defendants on a pro rata basis as the court may direct.

"Now, Therefore, IT IS HEREBY ORDERED, ADJUDGED AND DECREED that the award of the said jury to the defendants, together with interest at the rate of 6% per annum on the sum of $1615.00 from the said 27th day of December, 1933, the date of taking, until the balance of the said award is paid into court herein, is the just and reasonable compensation to be allowed to the said defendants, and that the defendants shall have judgment against the United States of America for the said sum of Twelve thousand eight hundred eighty-two dollars and ninety-two cents ($12,882.92) plus interest on the said sum of Sixteen hundred fifteen dollars ($1615.00) at the rate of six per cent (6%) per annum from the said date of taking, December 27, 1933, until the balance of the said award is paid into court for the defendants, the said interest payment to be prorated to the said defendants as the court may direct and the said award when paid into court to be distributed to the defendants as ordered by the court as their interests shall appear.

"AND IT IS FURTHER ORDERED, ADJUDGED AND DECREED that the above described property is condemned and that fee simple title thereto has vested in the United States of America, expressly excepting therefrom, however, such mineral rights, if any, as the intervenors D. L. Underwood, et al, may have in that part of the Seaton tract within the boundaries of the so-called Sand Hill placer claim, the rights of the said intervenors (if any rights they have) to remain entirely unaffected by this suit, entirely unaffected by this judgment, and entirely unaffected by any order, decree or declaration of taking filed in this action.

    "DONE this 23rd day of September, 1935.

             (Signed) J. STANLEY WEBSTER,

                             Judge.''

    Defendants' motion for a new trial was regularly and seasonably made and duly filed, and the same having been heard by the Court, Hon. J. Stanley Webster presiding, was on September 2nd, 1935 in all respects denied, in open Court. [164]

    The following orders were signed by the Court for the purpose of keeping open the judgment term for settling the Bill of Exceptions and the perfection of the appeal:

    [Title of Court and Cause.]

             No. L-4760

             Order Extending Time Within Which to File Bill of Exceptions. Filed Aug. 9, 1935.

    "Upon reading the application of the above named defendants for an order extending the time within which to serve and file the bill of exceptions in connection with the above matter in order that an appeal may be taken to the Circuit Court of Appeals from which it appears that it is proper that an extension of time be granted,

"NOW, THEREFORE, IT IS HEREBY ORDERED that said defendants shall have an extension of time for a period of thirty (30) days from and after August 12, 1935, within which to prepare, serve and file a bill of exceptions in the above entitled action.

"DATED this 9th day of August, 1935.
                    J. STANLEY WEBSTER
                              District Judge"

[Title of Court and Cause.]

No. L-4760
Stipulation
Filed Aug. 29, 1935

"IT IS HEREBY STIPULATED AND AGREED, by and between the parties to the above entitled action, that the present term of the above entitled Court shall be extended for the purposes hereinafter mentioned, as follows:

I

"That the said defendants shall have up to and including October 10, 1935, within which time to serve and file their bills of exceptions for the purpose of appeal and that the above named plaintiff shall have thirty (30) days after the serving and filing of the bills of exceptions on behalf of the defendants within which time to serve and file proposed amendments to such bills of exceptions so filed. [165]

II

"That the Court shall thereafter settle the same.

III

"That the defendants shall have up to and including November 1, 1935, within which to serve and file their notices of appeal and the grounds on which the same shall be based.

IV

"That the present term of said Court shall also be extended for a sufficient time necessary for the determination of the issues presented by the serving and filing of the several motions for new trial interposed by the defendants, and for such other acts as may be necessary on the part of the defendants in order to perfect the appeal to the Circuit Court of Appeals for the Ninth Circuit.

"DATED this 23rd day of August, 1935.

J. M. SIMPSON
United States District Attorney
B. E. STOUTEMYER
Attorneys for Plaintiff.
PARKER W. KIMBALL
F. J. McKEVITT
E. H. CHAVELLE
I. K. LEWIS
SHUMATE & CLARKE
E. K. BROWN
Attorneys for Defendants."

[Title of Court and Cause.]

No. L-4760

Order Extending Time for:
Filing Proposed Bill of Exceptions, Filing Amendments
thereto, and Filing Notices of
Appeal.

Filed Aug. 29, 1935.

"It being stipulated in writing by the parties
appearing in said cause through their respective
attorneys for an [166] order continuing the
time for filing the bill of exceptions in the above
entitled cause over the present term, and it appearing
to the Court that under the rules of this
Court the time within which the defendants
have to file a bill of exceptions and the time
within which proposed amendments to such bill
of exceptions shall be made and within which
the said bill of exceptions shall be settled and
notices of appeal shall be given will extend
over the present term of Court,

"NOW, THEREFORE, IT IS HEREBY
ORDERED that the matter of filing and settlement
of the bill of exceptions in the above
entitled cause, and the time for serving and
filing a notice of appeal is continued over the
present term and, pursuant to the stipulation
entered into, the defendants shall have up to
and including October 10, 1935, within which
time to serve and file their bill of exceptions,
the plaintiff shall have thirty (30) days after

the serving and filing of the bill of exceptions within which time to serve and file proposed amendments to the same, and the defendants shall have up to and including November 1, 1935, within which time to serve and file their notices of appeal and the grounds on which . the same shall be based.

"That for all such purposes the present term is hereby extended.

"DATED this 29th day of August, 1935.

J. STANLEY WEBSTER,
District Judge."

[Title of Court and Cause.]

No. L-4760

Order Extending Time for Filing Proposed Bills of Exceptions, and Notice of Appeal.

Filed Oct. 19, 1935.

"This matter came on this 19th day of October, 1935, on the application of the above named defendants for an order extending the time within which to file bills of exceptions and notice of appeal, and, it appearing to the Court that it is proper that the defendants be given additional time within which to file such bills of exceptions and notice of appeal,

"IT IS THEREFORE ORDERED that said defendants shall [167] have up to and including December 2, 1935, within which time to serve and file their bills of exceptions and notice of appeal, and that the term of Court during which said cases were tried is extended for all such purposes.

"DATED this 19th day of October, 1935.

J. STANLEY WEBSTER

District Judge."

[Title of Court and Cause.]

No. L-4760

Order Extending Term for Settling Bill of Exceptions. Filed Nov. 29, 1935.

"It appearing to the Court that bills of exceptions, assignments of errors and notice of appeal have been filed in the above matter, and notice of appeal and petition for order allowing appeal have been filed in said matter in accordance with the order of the Court made in connection therewith,

"NOW, THEREFORE, IT IS HEREBY ORDERED that the term of Court during which said cases were tried is extended for 30 days for the purpose of settling the bill of exceptions or filing and approval of bond ordered in connection with said appeal.

"DATED this 29th day of November, 1935.

J. STANLEY WEBSTER,

District Judge."

[Title of Court and Cause.]

No. L-4760

Order Extending Term for Settling Bill of Exceptions. Filed Dec. 26, 1935.

"It appearing to the Court that the plaintiff in the above entitled matter has filed objections to the proposed bill of exceptions and a motion to amend the same, and it further appearing to the Court that the term during which said case was tried was extended until December 29, 1935, for the purpose of settling the bill of exceptions, and that said matter cannot be disposed of during said time, [168]

"NOW, THEREFORE, IT IS HEREBY ORDERED that the term of Court during which such case was tried is extended for a period of thirty days from and after December 29, 1935, for the purpose of hearing the objections to the proposed bill of exceptions, and for the purpose of settling said proposed bill of exceptions.

"DATED this 26th day of December, 1935.

J. STANLEY WEBSTER,
District Judge."

[Title of Court and Cause.]

No. L-4760

Order Extending Time for Settling Bill of Exceptions.

Filed Jan. 25, 1936

"It appearing to the Court that the plaintiff in the above entitled matter has filed objections to the proposed bill of exceptions, and is also preparing amendments to propose to the same, and it further appearing to the Court that the term during which said case was tried has been extended until January 29, 1936, for the purpose of settling the bill of exceptions and that said matter can not be disposed of during said time,

"NOW, THEREFORE, IT IS HEREBY ORDERED that the term of Court during which such case was tried is extended for a period of thirty (30) days from and after January 29, 1936, for the purpose of filing proposed amendments to the bill of exceptions and for the purpose of settling said bill of exceptions.

"Dated this 25th day of January, 1936.

J. STANLEY WEBSTER
District Judge."

[Title of Court and Cause.]

No. L-4760
Order Enlarging Time Within
Which to File Transcript of
Record and Docket Case.
Filed Jan. 25, 1936.

"It appearing to the Court that the proposed amendments to the bill of exceptions are being offered by the plaintiff herein and that it will be impossible to have the bill of exceptions settled and the preparation of the transcript of [169] the record made on or before January 29, 1936, being the time within which the same shall be settled and the record filed.

"NOW, THEREFORE, IT IS HEREBY ORDERED that the time within which to complete and file such transcript of record and docket the case in the Circuit Court of Appeals be and the same is hereby further enlarged up to and including February 28, 1936.

"Dated this 25th day of January, 1936.

J. STANLEY WEBSTER,
District Judge."

[Title of Court and Cause.]

No. L-4760
Order Extending Time for
Settling Bill of Exceptions.
Filed February 25, 1936.

"It appearing to the Court that the plaintiff in the above entitled matter has filed objections to the proposed bill of exceptions, and is also preparing amendments to propose to the same, and it further appearing to the Court that the term during which said case was tried has been extended until February 28, 1936, for the purpose of settling the bill of exceptions and that said matter can not be disposed of during said time,

"NOW, THEREFORE, IT IS HEREBY ORDERED that the term of Court during which such case was tried is extended for a period of thirty days from and after February 28, 1936, for the purpose of filing proposed amendments to the bill of exceptions and for the purpose of settling said bill of exceptions.

"Dated this 25th day of February, 1936.

J. STANLEY WEBSTER
District Judge." [170]

[Title of Court and Cause.]

No. L-4760
Order Enlarging Time Within Which to File Transcript of Record and Docket Case.
Filed Feb. 25, 1936.

"It appearing to the Court that the proposed amendments to the bill of exceptions are being offered by the plaintiff herein, and that it will be impossible to have the bill of exceptions settled and the preparation of the transcript of the record made on or before February 28, 1936, being the time within which the same shall be settled and the record filed,

"NOW, THEREFORE, IT IS HEREBY ORDERED that the time within which to complete and file such transcript of record and docket the case in the Circuit Court of Appeals be and the same is hereby further enlarged up to and including March 28, 1936.

J. STANLEY WEBSTER
District Judge."

[Title of Court and Cause.]

No. L-4760
Order extending time for settling Bill of Exceptions.
Filed March 23, 1936.

"It appearing to the Court that the plaintiff in the above entitled matter has filed objections to the proposed bill of exceptions and is also preparing amendments to propose to the same, and it further appearing to the Court that the term during which said case was tried has been extended until March 28, 1936, for the purpose of settling the bill of exceptions, and that said matter can not be disposed of during said time,

"NOW, THEREFORE, IT IS HEREBY ORDERED that the term of Court during which such case was tried is extended for a period of thirty days from and after March 28, 1936, for the purpose of filing proposed amendments to the bill of exceptions and for the purpose of settling said bill of exceptions. "Dated this 23rd day of March, 1936.'

J. STANLEY WEBSTER

District Judge." [171]

[Title of Court and Cause.]

No. L-4760

Order Enlarging Time Within Which to File Transcript of Record and Docket Case.

Filed March 23, 1936.

"It appearing to the Court that the proposed amendments to the bill of exceptions are being offered by the plaintiff herein, and that it will be impossible to have the bill of exceptions settled and the preparation of the transcript of record made on or before March 28, 1936, being the time within which the same shall be settled and the record filed,

"NOW, THEREFORE, IT IS HEREBY ORDERED that the time within which to complete and file such transcript of record and docket case in the Circuit Court of Appeals be and the same is hereby further enlarged up to and including April 28, 1936.

J. STANLEY WEBSTER

District Judge."

NOW, THEREFORE, in furtherance of justice and that right may be done, the defendants present and propose the foregoing as the corrected Bill of

Exceptions in this case, and pray that the same may be cited, signed, and certified by the Judge, as provided by law, and filed as a Bill of Exceptions.

> PARKER W. KIMBALL
> P. J. McKEVITT
> I. K. LEWIS
> EDWARD H. CHAVELLE
> CHARLES ATEN
> By PARKER W. KIMBALL
> Attorneys for Defendants

Copy of the foregoing is hereby admitted this 23rd day of March, 1936.

> J. M. SIMPSON
> United States Attorney

[Endorsed]: Filed Mar. 25, 1936. [172]

[Title of Court and Cause.]

ORDER SETTLING BILL OF EXCEPTIONS.

On the 23rd day of March, 1936, the above cause came on for hearing on the application of the defendants to settle the bill of exceptions in said cause. Defendants appeared by their counsel Parker W. Kimball and F. J. McKevitt, and the plaintiff appeared by B. E. Stoutemyer as attorney for the United States Reclamation Bureau, and J. M. Simpson, United States District Attorney;

And it appearing to the Court that the proposed bill of exceptions was duly served on attorneys for the plaintiff within the time provided by law, and that amendments suggested thereto by the plaintiff which were proper to be allowed have been allowed, and that the time for settling said bill of exceptions has been continued and has not expired, and the term has been extended for the purpose of allowing said bill of exceptions;

And it further appearing to the Court that said bill of exceptions contains all of the material facts occurring in the trial of said cause which bear on the claimed errors of law committed in the trial of [173] said action and all the proceedings necessary for the review of the same on appeal;

And it further appearing to the Court that the parties to said action have stipulated that the original exhibits and the exhibits offered in said action and rejected shall be forwarded to the Clerk of the Circuit Court of Appeals; and, in accordance with such stipulation, the Clerk is hereby directed to forward such original exhibits to the Clerk of the Circuit Court of Appeals for the Ninth Circuit at San Francisco, California.

NOW, THEREFORE, ON MOTION OF PARKER W. KIMBALL, one of the attorneys for defendants, IT IS ORDERED that said proposed bill of exceptions, with the amendments allowed by this Court, be and the same is hereby settled as a true bill of exceptions in said cause, and the same is hereby certified by the undersigned Judge of this court who presided at the trial of said cause that it conforms to the truth, that it is in proper form, and that it is a full, true and correct bill of exceptions; and the clerk of this Court is hereby ordered to file the same as a record in said cause and transmit the same to the United States Circuit Court of Appeals for the Ninth Circuit at San Francisco, California.

Dated this 25th day of March, 1936.

J. STANLEY WEBSTER,
District Judge.

O. K.

J. M. Simpson
U. S. Atty.
PARKER W. KIMBALL
for Defts.

[Endorsed]: Filed Mar. 25, 1936. [174]

[Title of Court and Cause.]

PRAECIPE FOR TRANSCRIPT OF RECORD.

TO: A. A. LaFRAMBOISE, CLERK OF THE ABOVE ENTITLED COURT:

You will please prepare transcript of record in this cause to be filed in the office of the Clerk of the United States Circuit Court of Appeals for the Ninth Judicial Circuit, under the appeal heretofore prosecuted and allowed in said Court, which record shall be transmitted in typed form to the Clerk of the Circuit Court of Appeals for the Ninth Circuit, and included in said transcript the following files, proceedings and papers on file, to-wit:

(1) Summons, complaint and order of possession.

(2) Answer of defendants Continental Land Company, Julius C. Johnson and wife, Emma Raths, et al.

(2½) Verdicts

(3) Judgment

(4) Amended petition for new trial.

(4½) Excerpt from Minutes showing denial of Petition for New Trial.

(5) Petition for order allowing appeal. [175]

(6) Order allowing appeal.

(7) Bond on appeal.

(8) Citation on appeal.

(9) Assignments of errors.

(10) Bill of exceptions.

(11) Stipulation for transmission of original exhibits.

(12) Order settling bill of exceptions.

(13) Praecipe.

Dated at Spokane, Washington, this 26th day of March, 1936.

I. K. LEWIS
F. J. McKEVITT
EDWARD H. CHAVELLE
PARKER W. KIMBALL
By PARKER W. KIMBALL
Attorneys for Defendants.

Copy Received this — day of March, A. D. 1936.

....

United States Attorney

[Endorsed]:Filed Mar. 26, 1936 [176]

[Title of Court and Cause.]

CERTIFICATE OF CLERK OF U. S. DISTRICT COURT TO TRANSCRIPT OF RECORD

United States of America,
Eastern District of Washington.—ss.

I, A. A. LaFRAMBOISE, Clerk of the District Court of the United States for the Eastern District of Washington, do hereby certify the foregoing typewritten pages numbered 1 to 176 inclusive, to be a full, true and correct copy of so much of the record, papers and proceedings in the above entitled cause as are necessary to the hearing of the appeal therein in the United States Circuit Court of Appeals as called for by the praecipe of counsel, as the same remains on file and of record in the office of the Clerk of said District Court, and that the same constitutes the record on appeal of the defendants from the final judgment of the District Court of the United States for the Eastern District of Washington, to the United States Circuit Court of Appeals for the Ninth Judicial Circuit, at San Francisco, California.

I further certify that I have attached hereto and herewith transmit the original citation issued in said Court and cause.

I further certify that in accordance with the stipulation of counsel and the order of this Court, I transmit under separate cover the original exhibits in this cause.

I further certify that the fees of the Clerk of this court for preparing and certifying the foregoing typewritten record amounts to $25.00 and that the same has been paid in full by Parker W. Kimball of Attorneys for Defendants and Appellants.

IN WITNESS WHEREOF, I have hereunto set my hand and affixed the seal of said District Court this 27th day of March, A. D. 1936.

[Seal]   A. A. LaFRAMBOISE
                Clerk of said District Court.

[Endorsed] No. 8162. United States Circuit Court of Appeals for the Ninth Circuit. Continental Land Company, a corporation, Julius C. Johnson, Mable Johnson, Samuel J. Seaton, Mary A. Seaton, Emma Raths, Martha Raths Baldwin, Warren Baldwin, Henry Raths, George Raths, Albert Raths, Arthur Raths, Alma Raths Clark, Fred Clark, Mary Raths Marnhart, Clarence Marnhart, Minnie Raths, Fred Raths, and Manita Raths, Appellants, vs. United States of America, Appellee. Transcript of Record upon Appeal from the District Court of the United States for the Eastern District of Washington, Northern Division.

Filed March 30, 1936.

PAUL P. O'BRIEN,
Clerk of the United States Circuit Court of Appeals for the Ninth Circuit.

United States

ircuit Court of Appea

For the Ninth Circuit ✓

CONTI NTAL LAND COMPANY, a corpora-
tion, JULIUS C. JOHNSON, MABLE JOHN
SON, SAMUEL J. SEATON, MARY A. SEA
TON, EMMA RATHS, MARTHA RATHS
BALDWIN, WARREN BALDWIN, HENRY
RATHS, GEORGE RATHS, ALBERT
RATHS, ARTHUR RATHS, ALMA RATHS
CLARK, FRED CLARK, MARY RATHS
MARNHART, CLARENCE MARNHART,
MINNIE RATHS, FRED RATHS and MA-
NITA RATHS,

Appellants,

vs.

UNITED STATES OF AMERICA,

App

Appellants' Brief

Upon Appeal from the District Court of the United
ates for the Eastern District of Washington,
Northern Division.

FILED

PAUL P. O'BRIEN,

INDEX

INDEX TO CITATIONS

STATUTES:

MISCELLANEOUS:

United States

Circuit Court of Appeals

For the Ninth Circuit

CONTINENTAL LAND COMPANY, a corporation, JULIUS C. JOHNSON, MABLE JOHNSON, SAMUEL J. SEATON, MARY A. SEATON, EMMA RATHS, MARTHA RATHS BALDWIN, WARREN BALDWIN, HENRY RATHS, GEORGE RATHS, ALBERT RATHS, ARTHUR RATHS, ALMA RATHS CLARK, FRED CLARK, MARY RATHS MARNHART, CLARENCE MARNHART, MINNIE RATHS, FRED RATHS and MANITA RATHS,

Appellants,

vs.

UNITED STATES OF AMERICA,

Appellee.

Appellants' Brief

Upon Appeal from the District Court of the United States for the Eastern District of Washington, Northern Division.

STATEMENT OF THE CASE

This appeal arises out of condemnation proceedings brought by the United States to acquire Appellants' land as a site for the Grand Coulee dam on the Columbia River in the State of Washington. The action was begun in the United States District Court, for the Eastern District of Washington, Northern Division, and the trial was had before Hon. J. Stanley Webster, and a jury.

At the trial, the Government assumed the burden of going forward, and introduced evidence tending to prove the value of the land in question for grazing and agricultural purposes, and also introduced evidence tending to support its contention that the adaptability of said land for use as a damsite could not be considered in estimating its market value. Government's testimony tended to prove that the cost of the Grand Coulee project and the financial losses, which the Government claimed will result from its operation, eliminate from consideration any possibility of development by private capital, thus leaving the Government as the only possible taker of the land for use as a damsite.

Thereafter, Defendants-Appellants introduced evidence that their land was especially adapted for use as a damsite, and rebutted the Government's evidence that the cost of the project, and the alleged losses from operation would eliminate the possibility of development by private capital. They then introduced evidence of the market value of their land for all available uses, including use for a damsite.

At the end of the trial, the Court, on his own motion, struck from the record all of Appellants' evidence which tended to prove special adaptability for use as a damsite, and market value with such adaptability and use taken into account, and instructed the jury not to take such use and adaptability into consideration in determining the fair market value of the land.

STATEMENT OF FACTS

The Government brought condemnation proceedings to acquire Defendants' lands pursuant to Act of Congress, June 17, 1902 (32 Stat. 388) entitled, **"An Act Appropriating the Receipts from the Sale and Disposal of Public Lands in certain States and Territories** (including the State of Washington) **to the Construction of Irrigation Works for the Reclamation of Arid Lands,"** and Act of June 16, 1933 (48 Stat. 195) entitled, **"An Act to Encourage National Industrial Recovery, to Foster Fair Competition, and to Provide for the Construction of Certain Useful Public Works, and for other purposes"** (Record page 5).

There is no evidence that Congress ever authorized the taking of Defendants' lands; nor that Congress ever legislated for the improvement of navigation in the Columbia River.

The development appears to have been undertaken by the Federal Emergency Administrator, as a Public Works Project (R. p. 5). The Government has undertaken to construct a dam across the Columbia River at Grand Coulee in the State of Washington. The dam is being built on Defendants' lands, which **constitute the only damsite on the Columbia River which is practicable for the purpose** (R. p. 103, 104). Defendants' lands are situated in Grant and Okanogan Counties in the State of Washington (R. p. 9-12). It is estimated that the storage of water to be made available behind the Grand Coulee dam will about double the amount of firm power which can be developed on power sites between Grand Coulee and the mouth of the Columbia River, and that the increased amount of firm power so made possible by reason of the storage behind the Grand Coulee dam is an important factor in the feasibility of each of the said lower power sites as a self-liquidating project (R. p. 7-8).

As its first witness Petitioner called **MR. F. A. BANKS,** construction engineer for the Government on the Grand Coulee dam (R. 54) who testified, that the United States Army Engineers had made a thorough study and investigation of the Columbia River from a point about 200 miles below Grand Coulee to a distance of about 125 miles above or northerly of Grand Coulee, and that said exploration disclosed that **the Grand Coulee damsite on Defendants' lands is the most feasible one for all purposes (R. p. 62).** That the Grand Coulee damsite was particularly adaptable for irrigation because of the fact that the Grand Coulee itself, which is situated near the point where the dam is being built on Defendants' lands, invites the pumping of water out of the river and storing it in the Coulee for irrigation purposes at a relatively low lift (R. p. 63). Grand Coulee, located near Defendants' lands is one of the largest examples of erosion that there is existing today. It was caused by glacial action causing the Columbia River to erode a new channel leaving the old channel as a natural storage reservoir (R. p. 63). Grand Coulee extends southerly from the present damsite for a distance of about 50 miles. A dam is to be constructed at each end of the Coulee some 25 miles apart, so that the Grand Coulee, or the old river bed, will be used as a storage and irrigation reservoir. The average depth of the water in Grand Coulee will be about 35 feet, and the average width of the reservoir will be about a mile, or more, so that there will be in the Grand Coulee a lake some 25 miles long, averaging a mile or more in width, and with an average depth of 35 feet (R. p. 64).

The physical structure of the river bed adjoining Defendants' lands is a granite formation, and furnishes a good foundation entirely suitable for any dam. The banks of the river likewise have a particularly suitable granite formation. The location of the pump which will pump the water into Grand Coulee is on Defendant Julius Johnson's property (R. p. 65). The top of the dam when completed will be about 4,200 feet in length, and **about 1,800 or 1,900 feet of the dam on each side of the river will rest upon Defendants' uplands** involved in this proceeding (R. p. 65). The high dam to be constructed on Defendants' lands will raise the water of the Columbia River about 355 feet above the ordinary low water mark of the river (R. p. 64). The water will thus be raised to elevation 1,289 feet sea level datum. The elevation at the International Boundary is considerably above that (R. p. 66).

MR. BANKS also testified, on behalf of the Government, that this large development at Grand Coulee would not be desirable for private enterprise because it requires too large an investment, and the carrying charges would be too great during the development period. **That the site had no value to anybody except the Government** (R. 67).

MR. BARRY DIBBLE, consulting engineer for the Government (R. p. 79) testified, that he had been employed on the report of the Army Engineers on Grand

Coulee as consultant on the power market feature of the report (R. p. 81). That it would not be feasibly for private capital to develop the Grand Coulee project (R. p. 84). That the development of Grand Coulee by private capital would show a deficit, or loss, in the year 1941 of $11,000,000.00. That the loss or deficit would gradually increase until in 1947 it would show an annual loss of $11,500,000.00, and that by the year 1958 the project, if developed by private capital, would show an accumulated deficit or loss of $115,000,000.00. That thereafter the deficit would continue to grow until by the year 1960 it would show a deficit of $215,000,000.00 in addition to the original investment of $197,000,000.00 (R. p. 85-86).

MR. F. A. DARLAND, a hydraulic engineer called as a witness by the Government, testified that the development of Grand Coulee by private capital would not be advisable, and that it would earn a perpetual deficit. That his figures as to those deficits are the same as Mr. Dibble's (R. p. 94).

The foregoing facts were testified to by Government's witnesses on Petitioner's case in chief. After Petitioner had introduced evidence of value based upon use of Appellants' lands for agriculture and allied purposes, which evidence is not here material, it rested its case, and Defendants then introduced the following evidence:

MR. WILLIS T. BATCHELLOR, a hydraulic engineer of long and extensive experience, who was thoroughly acquainted with the Grand Coulee site, and with most of the power projects in the Pacific Northwest, and has made an exhaustive study of the water power and irrigation possibilities at Grand Coulee and throughout the extent of the Columbia River (R. p. 95-96), testified that the inherent adaptability and peculiar fitness of Defendants' lands for use as a damsite lie in the fact that there is a granite dike which has been cut by the Columbia River to a depth of 600 feet. In other possible sites on the river this condition does not exist (R. p. 101). In the entire stretch of the Columbia River from the International Boundary to the mouth of the Snake River there is no place where there is a fall or head sufficient to generate any commercial power. The dam built on Defendants' lands creates a fall or head of 350 feet, which is a little more than twice the head at Niagara Falls. The dam also creates a storage reservoir to store water upstream which regulates the stream flow. **Every foot of the fall or head is produced by the dam. The site on which the dam is built, therefore, becomes of primary importance, and is indispensible to the development of water power.** The reservoir created behind the dam will increase the uniform flow of the Columbia River from 18,800 c. f. s. to 41,500 c. f. s., an increase of approximately two and one-half times (R. p. 102).

There is a granite formation on Defendants' lands which extends across the river bed, and also extends upward to about 600 feet above the river on either side. "It is very prominent, and you just couldn't miss it." **There is no other place on the entire river that has such characteristics.** That formation is important in building a dam, because it is necessary to have a solid foundation and a water-tight reservoir (R. p. 103).

Defendants' lands were recommended as a damsite in a report which Mr. Batchellor made following a study of the project in 1921 and 1922 (R. p. 103). **It would not be practical to construct a dam anywhere on the Columbia River which would serve the dual purpose of power and irrigation except on Defendants lands. There are prominent granite projections on Defendants' lands on both sides of the river. It would not be possible to move the location of the dam more than a few hundred feet from its present location. It would be physically impossible to construct a dam on the Columbia River without using Defendants' lands which are being taken in this proceeding "no matter how much money you wanted to spend"** (R. p. 104).

In determining whether private capital would undertake such a development as is contemplated for Grand Coulee, the controlling considerations are: Whether the physical characteristics are favorable for the construction of a dam and the generation of power, whether there is a market for the power to be generated, and whether power can be produced at a profit (R. p. 104-105).

In the development of water power three elements are important: 1, the volume of water; 2, the fall or head of water; 3, uniformity of flow resulting from storage. The most important element is the fall or head. The flow and storage are of about equal importance (R. p. 100). There is no fall or head on the Columbia River, for a distance of 110 miles upstream from Grand Coulee, and a distance of 75 miles downstream, from which any water power can be developed. The average slope or fall in the Columbia River over that entire distance of 185 miles is about 2 feet to the mile, which is insufficient to create any water power. **The entire head or fall at Grand Coulee is created and furnished by the dam, which cannot be built without using Defendants' lands. There is no other site on the Columbia River within this area of 185 miles upon which it would be possible to build a dam.** Uniformity of flow and storage are likewise created by the Grand Coulee dam built on Defendants' lands (R. p. 100-101).

Mr. Batchellor also testified that he has made an exhaustive study of the power market in the territory tributary to Grand Coulee and of the practicability of developing the project by private capital, and of operating the same at a profit; that **private capital is always ready for a proposition of that kind which will show a profit** (R. p. 105). That according to the natural and reasonably expected growth of the power market, there will be a demand, by the year 1941, for the block of power from the initial unit at Grand Coulee, and that **without the development of power at Grand Coulee there will be an actual shortage of power necessary to supply the area. That if Grand Coulee is not developed this block of power will have to be supplied from some other site** (R. p. 106). By the year 1949 the Grand Coulee project, developed by private capital, would be built to its full capacity, and the market will absorb the entire output. Power plants, when built and operated by private capital, are built to suit the market requirements, by increasing the capacity output as the market demand increases (R. p. 106). The development and operation of Grand Coulee by private capital **would**

show a surplus in the year 1952 of $15,000,000.00 annually, and that by the year 1985, the end of the license period, the Grand Coulee project would have accumulated an amortization fund of $231,000,000.00, the amount of the total investment, and in addition will develop a surplus or profit of $13,000,000.00 annually. That because of the prospects of great profits from the development of power at Grand Coulee, **private capital would be in the market to purchase the Grand Coulee damsite in the year 1933,** the time when Defendants' lands were taken in these proceedings (R. p. 107).

Mr. Batchellor testified that the market value of Defendants' lands in view of their inherent adaptability for use as a damsite in December, 1933, and taking all uses and considerations into account, was $4,500,000.00.

MR. H. P. THOMAS, a hydraulic engineer of 25 years experience, who was thoroughly familiar with the power projects in the Pacific Northwest, and who had made a study of the water power possibilities of Grand Coulee on the Columbia River, testified that he agreed substantially with the testimony of Mr. Willis T. Batchellor as to the physical characteristics which make **Defendants' lands peculiarly adapted for use as a damsite** (R. p. 121).

Mr. Thomas further testified, that by the year 1941 the output of all installed and uncompleted power projects in the Pacific Northwest would be absorbed (R. p. 122), and that it would be necessary for private capital to put Grand Coulee, or some other power project, into production by that time (R. p. 123). That the development and operation of the Grand Coulee project

for power would produce a net annual profit of \$4,-
434,000.00. That the cost of a dam at Grand Coulee, together with the first power unit would be \$74,000,-
000.00. **That there would be \$750,000 available for divi-
dends the second year, and by the 6th year \$5,342,800.00
would be available for dividends** (R. p. 123-124).

Mr. Thomas further testified that, by using the
method of accounting employed by the Army Engineers,
the Grand Coulee power project, built and operated by
private capital, would show a **surplus on the 12th year
of its operation of \$5,223,097.00, and over a period of 20
years after it is started it will show an accumulated surplus of \$61,552,884.00, after allowing interest on invest-
ment at 6%, taxes at 1½% and depreciation at 1½%.**
That accordingly **the development and operation of
Grand Coulee is feasible from the viewpoint of private
capital** (R. p. 124).

Mr. Thomas also testified that the inherent advantages of Defendants' lands for use as a damsite are such
that **in 1933 private capital would have been in the market to purchase them as a damsite** (R. p. 125).

Mr. Thomas also tesified that in generating electric
power at Grand Coulee the waters of the Columbia
River must be diverted from the river out on to and over
Defendants' uplands, and that the water is then returned
to the river, undiminished, below the dam. That the
dam raises the water in the river and causes it to spread
out over Defendants' lands on either side of the natural
channel, and is taken over Defendants' uplands and carried down through the penstocks on to the turbines, all

of which are situated on Defendants' uplands. That there is actual diversion of water out of the river channel over Defendants' uplands (R. p. 125-126). Mr. Thomas testified that the market value of Defendants' lands in view of their inherent adaptability for use as a damsite together with all other uses in December, 1933, was $2,975,000.00 (R. p. 124).

MR. R. H. THOMSON, a distinguished hydraulic engineer, with 50 years of experience in the Pacific Northwest (R. p. 150), testified that he had examined and appraised most of the power sites in the Pacific Northwest, and that he had known of the Grand Coulee site for 15 years. That he had made a study of the Grand Coulee project and prepared a report thereon, as though he were advising a private client (R. p. 152). That by the year 1940 the entire installed capacity of all existing plants, and those in contemplation, in the area tributary to Grand Coulee will be absorbed by the power market. That additional electric power will then be necessary, and that Grand Coulee is well adapted to supply the additional power necessary (R. p. 152). That there was a market for Defendants' lands for use as a damsite by private capital, and that **every step in the development of the Grand Coulee project by private capital would pay** (R. p. 152). **That after 10 years of operation by private capital, the Grand Coulee power project would show an annual net profit of $5,956,000.00** (R. p. 153). **That private capital was in the market for and would have acquired Defendants' lands for use as a damsite in the year 1933, or soon thereafter, for their fair market value of $2,300,000.00** (R. p. 154).

MR. MARVIN CHASE, who had served as **State Hydraulic Engineer for the State of Washington** for a period of eight years, and **Chairman of the Columbia Basin Survey Commission** (R. p. 144) testified, that he was acquainted with the water power resources in the State of Washington, including the power sites on the Columbia River, and that **there is no place on the Columbia River between the mouth of the Snake River and the mouth of the Spokane River which is suitable for a damsite, except Defendants' lands** (R. p. 145). That he has had experience in appraising the value of power sites and power projects, that he has been Receiver of the Priest Rapids power project and consulting engineer of the Puget Sound Light & Power Company, and has had experience in operating power plants. That he is acquainted with, and **has personal knowledge of the prices paid for other damsites in the area tributary to Grand Coulee** (R. p. 146). **That in his opinion the fair market value of Defendants' lands in December, 1933, was $2,850,000.00** (R. p. 145).

MR. WILLIAM P. CREAGER, of Buffalo, New York, who has enjoyed an extensive experience and who has had a distinguished career as a hydraulic and electrical engineer, and has served as engineer in various capacities for the Provincial Government of the Phillipine Islands, the New York State Barge Canal, the Connecticut River Power Company, Muscle Shoals Steam Plant Water Supply for the United States Government, Director of the Power Corporation of New York, the North New York Utilities, as a member of the Board of Consulting Engineers on the Los Angeles Flood Control District on the San Gabriel Dam, the New

York Light & Power Company, the Hudson River Irrigation District, and the Soviet Government of Russia, and who is author of a number of books on hydraulic and electrical engineering, some of which have been translated into the French and Russian languages (R. p. 131-133), testified that he has seen and examined the Grand Coulee damsite, and that **he has probably never seen a damsite as good as that furnished by Defendants' lands at Grand Coulee (R. p. 134). That it was entirely feasible and practicable for private capital to acquire Defendants' lands for use as a damsite in 1933,** and to develop the same as the market required, as testified to by Mr. Batchellor and Mr. Thomas. That **there was a market for Defendants' lands for use as a damsite in December, 1933; that private companies are always on the lookout for such sites.** That there are comparatively few hazards in the development of the Grand Coulee project by private capital, and that **the magnitude of this dam and power project stifles competition** (R. p. 134-135). That the cost of acquiring the damsite and developing the Grand Coulee project would not be beyond the reach of private capital (R. p. 135-136). That if private capital did not acquire and finance the Grand Coulee project it would have to finance some other power project on the Columbia River in order to supply the increase in the power market (R. p. 141).

That application was made for a permit to develop the Grand Coulee damsite by Colonel Hugh L. Cooper of New York City, in the year 1922. That the Government has withheld permission for private capital to develop the Grand Coulee project on the ground that the Government wanted it (R. p. 143).

Mr. Creager testified that the fair market value of
Defendants' lands, considering their inherent adaptability for use as a damsite, together with all other uses,
in December, 1933, was $2,790,000.00, (R. p. 136) even
under the business and financial conditions existing in
December, 1933; that the market price to which he testified was sufficiently attractive to move the property
on the market at that time. That, in normal times, the
market price would have been very much greater (R. p.
142). Mr. Creager also testified that he had made over
200 reports to financial interests on dams and hydro-
electric development, and that it was entirely practicable
to build a dam, and a power plant in steps or units, as
proposed by Mr. Bachellor and Mr. Thomas (R. p. 136).

After the foregoing evidence was all received and
Defendants had rested their case, the Trial Court invited a motion by Petitioner to strike all of said evidence, which motion was then made and granted; an exception was duly allowed to all Defendants (R. p. 175).

THE QUESTION ON APPEAL

The question on this appeal is, Whether, on the
facts contained in the record, the Court erred in striking Appellants' evidence, and instructing the jury not
to consider the adaptability of the land for use as a damsite, in determining its market value.

ASSIGNMENTS OF ERROR

I.

That the United States District Court for the Eastern District of Washington, Northern Division, erred in granting Plaintiff's motion to "strike from the record all testimony in regard to the market value of the lands in question for dam site purposes."

II.

That the Court erred in refusing to grant Defendants' request No. 9 for instructions to the jury, which request was as follows:

"It is not necessary for defendants in order to establish a market value for the lands in question as of December, 1933, or within a reasonable time thereafter, to prove that at said time there were actual sales of lands of similar character. If you find from the evidence that said lands were inherently adapted for dam site or other purposes you are entitled to consider such adaptability in determining what, if any, market value said lands possessed at said time."

III.

That the Court erred in refusing to grant Defendants' request No. 10 for instructions to the jury, which request was as follows:

"If you find from all the evidence that any of the tracts of land involved in this action, or any portion of any such tract, was especially suited or adapted for use as a dam site, in December, 1933, and that, at that time, or within a reasonable time after December, 1933, any such tract or parcel of land could have been sold for such use to any purchaser other than the United States Government, then you are instructed that you should return a verdict in favor of the owner of any such tract or parcel of land for the amount of money which you find from all the evidence, such tract or parcel of land could be sold for, in December, 1933, or within a reasonable time thereafter, considering its adaptability for use as a dam site as well as all other uses for which the tract or parcel was adapted."

IV.

The Court erred in instructing the jury, as follows:

"When in the course of my instructions I said to you that it was your function to ascertain the reasonable and practical adaptability of the property in question you, of course, will understand that I did not intend to include its value or claimed value as a dam site. That question is withdrawn from the consideration of the jury and the adaptability and availability of the property in question which you will consider will be those adaptabilities or uses disassociated from any claimed use for a dam site."

V.

The Court erred in denying Defendants' motion for a new trial.

VI.

The Court erred in entering judgment in favor of Defendants and against Plaintiff, the United States of America, "for the said sum of $12,882.92 plus interest on the said sum of $1,615.00 at the rate of 6% per an-

num from said date of taking, December 27, 1933, until
the balance of the said award is paid into Court for the
Defendants," for the reason that said judgment deprived
Defendants of their legal right to recover the fair market value of their lands for all uses for which said lands
are reasonably adapted, including their use and adaptability as a dam site; and deprived Defendants of their
right to just compensation for their said lands guaranteed by the Constitution of the United States of America and the Constitution of the State of Washington.

BRIEF OF THE ARGUMENT

SPECIAL ADAPTABILITY CONCEDED

Appellants' lands are conceded to be specially and
inherently adapted for use as a damsite and constitute
all land necessary for a dam site (R. p. 103-104).

THE GENERAL RULE

Inherent adaptability of property for a special use
must be taken into consideration in determining market value (R. p. 58-61).

> **Mississippi & Rum River Boom Co. v.**
> **Patterson,**
> 98 U. S. 403.

> **Weiser Valley Land & Water Company v.**
> **Ryan,**
> 190 Fed. 417 (9th Cir.).

> **McCandless v. U. S. (C. C. A. 9th),**
> 74 F. (2d) 596.

McCandless v. U. S.,
56 Sup. Ct. 764,
80 L. Ed. 797.

REASONS STATED BY TRIAL COURT FOR NOT
APPLYING THE GENERAL RULE (R. p. 179).

THE REASONS STATED DO NOT JUSTIFY THE
COURT'S RULINGS AND INSTRUCTIONS, BE-
CAUSE:

I. That Appellants did not own or have a license to use the river bed does not exclude evidence
of special adaptability from consideration in estimating market value.

Mississippi & Rum River Boom Co. v.
Patterson, Supra,

Weiser Valley Land & Water Company v.
Ryan, Supra,

Ford Hydro-Electric Company v. Neely,
13 F. (2d) 361,
(C. C. A. 7th Cir.).

Monongahela Navigation Company v. U. S.,
148 U. S. 312.

Olson v. United States,
292 U. S. 246.

McCandless v. U. S.,
80 L. Ed. 797.

Union Electric Light & Power Company v.
      Snyder Estate Company (C. C. A.
      8th),
  65 Fed. (2d) 297.

Cincinnati v. L. & N. R. R. Co.,
  223 U. S. 390.

San Diego Land & Town Company v. Neale,
  78 Cal. 63,
  20 Pac. 372.

Re: Arbitration between Lucas & Chesterfield
      Gas & Water Board,
  1 L. R. K. B. D. (1909) 16.

II. That Appellants did not own or have a right to use the flow of the river does not exclude evidence of special adaptability from consideration in estimating market value.

Olson v. U. S., Supra,

Boom Company v. Patterson, Supra,

State, ex rel Ham, Yearsley & Ryrie v. Superior
      Court, Northern Pacific Railway
      Company, et al,
  70 Wash. 442,
  126 Pac. 945.

Ham, Yearsley & Ryrie v. Northern Pacific
      Railway Company,
  107 Wash. 378,
  181 Pac. 898.

Ham, Yearsley & Ryrie v. Northern Pacific
Railway Company,
110 Wash. 467,
188 Pac. 527.

U. S. v. Chandler-Dunbar Company,
229 U. S. 52.

McCandless v. U. S.,
74 Fed. (2d) 596 (9th Cir.).

McCandless v. U. S.,
56 Sup. Ct. 764,
80 L. Ed. 797.

L. R. Junction Ry. v. Woodruff,
49 Ark. 381,
5 S. W. 792.

III.   That the Columbia River is navigable and
that Petitioner claims to take Appellants' lands in
aid of navigation do not exclude evidence of special
adaptability from consideration in estimating market value.

U. S. v. Chandler-Dunbar Company, Supra,

Olson v. U. S., Supra,

Ham, Yearsley & Ryrie v. N. P. Ry. Co., Supra,

Remington's Revised Statutes of Washington,
§7416.

Federal Water Power Act,
16 U. S. C. A. p. 217, §791-823,
41 Stat. at Large 1063.

Boston Chamber of Commerce v. Boston,
217 U. S. 189.

Kerr v. South Park Commissioners,
117 U. S. 379.

Shoemaker v. United States,
147 U. S. 282.

Mississippi & Rum River Boom Company v.
Patterson, Supra.

BUT THE IMPROVEMENT OF NAVIGATION IS
NOT IN THE CASE (R. p. 5).

National Industrial Recovery Act,
48 Stat. 195,

U. S. v. Arizona,
295 U. S. 174.

Monongahela Navigation Company v. U. S.,
148 U. S. 312.

Clark's Ferry Bridge Co. v. Public Service
Commission of Pennsylvania,
291 U. S. 227.

Ford Hydro-Electric Company v. Neely,
13 F. (2d) 361 (7th Cir.).

Defendants' Exhibits 42a, 42b, 42c and 43
(R. P. 159).

H. R. No. 103, Report of Chief of Engineers
and Secretary of War to the 73rd
Congress (R. p. 181-183).

Wisconsin v. Illinois,
278 U. S. 367.

ARGUMENT

The question presented for review is clear and simple. Did the trial court err in striking Appellants' evidence, in denying Appellants' requested instructions, and in his instructions to the jury, as specified in the Assignments of Error? All of the Assignments of Error involve and squarely present the one controlling question in the case, namely, **Was it proper to eliminate from consideration, in determining the fair market value of Appellants' lands, the inherent adaptability of said lands for use as a damsite?**

It will not be necessary to discuss the several Assignments of Error separately; the Court's rulings on the main question, and the reasons assigned for such rulings, will afford the most convenient basis for analysis and discussion.

Appellants' lands are conceded to be especially and inherently adapted for use as a damsite. The four tracts of land involved in this proceeding constitute the entire damsite, except the bed of the River (R. p. 103-104).

This is the only possible damsite on the entire Columbia
River which can serve the dual purpose of generating
power and impounding water in the Grand Coulee for
use in irrigation (R. p. 121). Obviously, this inherent
adaptability for special uses would, under the general
rule, be taken into consideration by the jury, along with
all other evidence, in estimating market value.

THE GENERAL RULE

**It Is the General Rule in Condemnation Proceedings,
That the Inherent Adaptability of Property for a
Special Use Must Be Taken Into Consideration in
Determining Market Value, Insofar As Such Adapt-
ability Appears to Have Affected Market Value.**

An extended discussion of this general rule is un-
necessary; it is elemental, and it was recognized by the
Trial Court (R. p. 58-61). The statement of the rule
most frequently quoted is found in:

**Mississippi & Rum River Boom Company v.
Patterson,
98 U. S. 403, 407.**

"In determining the value of land appropriated for public purposes, the same considerations
are to be regarded as in a sale of property between
private parties. The inquiry in such cases must
be, what is the property worth in the market,
viewed not merely with reference to the uses to
which it is at the time applied, but with reference
to the uses to which it is plainly adapted; that is to

say, what it is worth from its adaptability for valuable uses."

The same rule has been stated and applied by this Court in

> **Weiser Valley Land & Water Company v.
> Ryan,**
> **190 Fed. 417, 423 (9th Circ.).**

"All of the uses to which the property is available, the most advantageous as well as the less advantageous, should be taken into view, and the general estimate of the market value should be deduced; not what any one person would give for it for his particular use, but what could probably be obtained for it if a sale was desirable and a purchaser sought, applying the ordinary business methods of finding a purchaser and disposing of the property."

The rule was again applied by this Court in the recent case of

> **McCandless v. United States,**
> **(C. C. A. 9th Cir.)**
> **74 Fed. (2d) 596.**

See also **McCandless v. United States,**

> **56 S. Ct. 764,**
> **80 L. Ed. 797,**
> ....U. S............
> **Decided May 18, 1936.**

"The rule is well settled that, in condemnation cases, the most profitable use to which the land can probably be put in the reasonably near future, may be **shown and considered** as bearing upon the market value; * * * "

In its attempt to eliminate this inherent adaptability from consideration the Government, at the outset, undertook to prove that no one except the Government could develop the Grand Coulee project; because, as it claimed, the amount of capital required was too great, and because the project could not be operated at a profit; that the cost of the development would be approximately $175,000,000, and its operation, by private capital, would result in a continuous and perennial loss of more than $9,000,000 per year, showing an accumulated total deficit in 1960 of $215,000,000.

To refute the Government's evidence, and solely for the purpose of proving that there was a market for their damsite, Appellants introduced evidence tending to prove that the amount of capital required for the project was not more than private enterprise could furnish (R. p. 135-136), and that to supply the expanding market for power, less capital will be required and more profits will be produced at Grand Coulee than at any other power site available for development in that area (R. p. 105-107); that power can be developed and sold at Grand Coulee cheaper than from any other source, and that the market for power, and the revenue from its sale, are such as to attract private capital to the development of the Grand Coulee project. Their evidence proved that private capital was in the market for this damsite, and that this development and operation will produce an annual net profit of more than $5,000,-

000.00. There was competent evidence of market value ranging from $2,300,000.00 to $4,500,000 for the land in question, in view of its special adaptability for use as a damsite, as well as other uses (R. p. 100, 101, 106, 107, 109, 121-126, 134-136, 145, 146, 152-154).

On this state of the record, the evidence being conflicting, it was clearly for the jury to determine, in view of all the evidence, what was the fair market value of Appellants' lands for any and all uses for which they are inherently adapted, insofar as such adaptability and other facts and circumstances, disclosed by the evidence, were shown actually to have affected market value.

The Trial Court recognized the general measure of compensation payable on the "taking" of this class of property, and admitted all evidence offered on either side of the question. Indeed, it would be difficult to improve on the statement of the general rule which was made by the Court at the very outset of the trial (R. p. 58-61). But at the end of the trial, the Court departed from the general rule and struck out all of Defendants' evidence of special adaptability. The reasons for this ruling were stated by the Court.

REASONS STATED BY THE TRIAL COURT FOR NOT FOLLOWING THE GENERAL RULE, AND FOR STRIKING APPELLANTS' EVIDENCE OF SPECIAL ADAPTABILITY.

The reasons for the Court's ruling, and instructions to the jury were stated by him as follows:

"These landowners, in my judgment, are not
entitled to have that adaptability of this site taken
into account for the reason that they have neither
title to the bed of the stream nor any right to the
waters which flow in it as against the Government
exercising dominant power to improve the stream
for navigation purposes, and that they are not entitled to that because it has not been taken from
them, and it hasn't been taken from them for the
simple reason that they never owned it in the first
place" (R. p. 179).

These are the only reasons suggested; they are
three in number:

First, Appellants did not own the river bed upon
which a part of the dam must rest; **secondly,** Appellants
had no proprietary or vested right to use the flow of the
river; and **thirdly,** the Government claimed to take and
use Appellants' lands in aid of navigation, and accordingly, could not be required to pay its value for use as a
damsite.

The accuracy of the Court's ruling and instructions, here assigned as error, may best be determined by
examination of the reasons which he assigned therefor. It will be convenient to examine them in the order
mentioned:

I.

THE FACT THAT APPELLANTS DID NOT OWN
THE RIVER BED OR HAVE A LICENSE TO USE IT,
DOES NOT DESTROY SPECIAL USE VALUE AS A

MATTER OF LAW, OR EXCLUDE IT FROM CON-
SIDERATION IN ESTIMATING MARKET VALUE.

It will be conceded, as it must be under the authorities, that the United States, as condemnor of Appellants'
lands, stands exactly in the same position as regards
the proper measure of "just compensation" as would
any other condemnor. The constitutional guarantee
that "just compensation" must be paid for private property taken for public use applies to all takers, and to
all property.

> Mississippi & Rum River Boom Company v.
> Patterson,
> 98 U. S. 403, 407,
> 25 L. Ed. 206.

> Weiser Valley Land & Water Company v.
> Ryan,
> (C. C. A. 9th Cir.)
> 190 Fed. 417, 423.

> Ford Hydro-Electric Company v. Neely,
> 13 Fed. (2nd) 361.
> (C. C. A. 7th Cir.)
> (Certiorari denied, 273 U. S. 723).

> Monongahela Navigation Company v. U. S.,
> 148 U. S. 312,
> 13 S. Ct. 622,
> 37 L. Ed. 463.

Olson v. United States,
    292 U. S. 246,
    54 S. Ct. 704,
    78 L. Ed. 1236.

McCandless v. U. S.,
    80 L. Ed. 797 (May 18, 1936).

The taking of property by eminent domain is an exercise of sovereignty, regardless of who may exercise the power. Whether the power be exercised directly by the sovereign, or by some delegatee of the power, the obligation to pay "just compensation" remains the same.

Union Electric Light & Power Company v.
    Snyder Estate Company,
    (C. C. A., 8th Cir.),
    65 Fed. (2d) 297, 304.

Cincinnati v. L. & N. R. R. Company,
    223 U. S. 390, 404,
    32 S. Ct. 267,
    56 L. Ed. 481.

Let us suppose, then, that a corporation, which for convenience let us call the Occident Power Company, were organized to develop the same Grand Coulee project which is now being developed by the Government. Let us suppose also that it had obtained the necessary permit and license to occupy the river bed, and to build a dam across the Columbia River (as it might lawfully do according to the laws of Washington and the Federal Water Power Act) and, in furtherance of its project, it were condemning Appellants' lands for use as a damsite. Surely it could not be argued seriously, that the fact that the Occident Company had obtained the license to occupy the river bed and build the dam gives it the right to appropriate Appellants' lands, with their inherent adaptability for use as a damsite, by merely paying their value for grazing purposes! The license to use the bed of the river and to build the dam gives the holder of such license no magic or superior right or power not possessed by the owners of the uplands, which are equally necessary and valuable to the completed project. Obviously, it is largely a matter of accident or enterprise wehther the right to use the river bed and to build the dam is acquired and held by the Occident Company or by the Orient Company, or by the United States, or by the Columbia Basin Commission, which actually held a permit to construct and make this very improvement at Grand Coulee (R. p. 173).

Under the **Water Code of the State of Washington, Remington's Revised Statutes of Washington §7416,** and the

Federal Water Power Act,
(16 U. S. C. A. p. 217, §§791-823,
41 Stats, at Large 1063)

Appellants themselves, or any other person, or group of persons, might well have obtained a permit to make this improvement. Such licenses have been granted to other semi-private companies to construct dams and improvements on the Columbia River. As stated, a permit was actually issued to the Columbia Basin Commission to make the improvement now carried on by the Government.

It is a matter of common knowledge that higher values have always been paid for damsites regardless of who holds the license to build the dam. The owner of the license to occupy the river bed and to build the dam, is no more entitled to claim that the upland, on which a part of the dam must rest, is valueless as a dam site, because no dam can be built without using his license, than is the owner of the upland to claim that the license to build the dam is valueless, because no dam can be built without using his upland. Ownership of all property necessary to the completed project has never been required to entitle inherent adaptability for special use to be taken into consideration in determining market value. It is in the acquisition of additional property necessary to complete the project that the question of value based upon adaptabiliy for special use most frequently arises. Such value is not to be eliminated from consideration merely because additional property is necessary to complete the project.

Olson v. U. S. (Supra),

McCandless v. U. S. (Supra),

**San Diego Land & Town Company v. Neale
78 Cal. 63,
20 Pac. 372, 376.**

"But it is argued that the value 'as a reservoir site' should not have been taken, because there was no practicable site for a dam upon the defendants' property, the only use of which for reservoir purposes being in connection with the land of the plaintiff. * * * While it is true that the defendants' property had no value for reservoir purposes except in connection with the land of the plaintiff, it is equally true that the plaintiff's property had comparatively little value for such purposes except in connection with the land of the defendants; * * * And, this being the case, we can see no more reason for saying that the plaintiff can take the defendants' portion, without regard to its value for reservoir purposes, than for saying that the defendants, (if they had happened to commence proceedings first) could take the plaintiff's portion upon the same basis. **The question of value is distinct from the question of ownership."**

The condemnor's license or authority to make the improvement can not destroy value inherent in the property of another, if such property is necessary to the project.

In Re: **Arbitration Between Lucas and Chesterfield Gas & Water Board,**
1 L. R. K. B. D. (1909) 16, 21-22.

Condemnation of land for a storage reservoir. Counsel for the Water Board argued:

"The circumstances of the case are such as to prevent any special adaptability of the claimant's land for the purpose of the construction of a reservoir forming an element in the value of the land

---

* FOOT NOTE—(Bold face type in this brief is supplied by Counsel unless otherwise stated.)

upon an assessment of compensation . . . there is no reasonable possibility of the owner of the land being able to avail himself of its suitability for the purpose . . . Under the circumstances no one could be a competitor with the Water Board for the acquisition of this land for the purposes of a reservoir; the Board is the only possible purchaser for that purpose."

Buckley, L. J., in reading the judgment of the Court said (pp. 35-37):

"The frank cynicism of the argument which the appellants have had the courage to address to the court has occasioned me surprise. I hope I do not go too far when I say that the argument can only be seriously advanced by a speaker who studiously shuts his eyes to the immorality of its substructure . . . They contend that where one of the three is in fact desirous of using the land for that special purpose, and has in fact obtained from the legislature compulsory powers to enable him to do so, he can deprive the other two of the special value arising from the adaptability, and that upon the ground that the special purpose cannot be effectuated without his consent. **They say that they went to the legislature and obtained compulsory powers for a special public purpose, and that in fixing the fair value to be paid for the exercise of their compulsory powers they are entitled to say that the special purpose cannot be carried out, because they do not assent to the land being used for that purpose. * * ***

"The facts here are that not only is there a reasonable possibility of the site coming into the market, but that the site is wanted for the particular purpose, and is being acquired under compulsory powers for that purpose. **The land is so situated in proximity to the reservoirs already existing that within a reasonable time it will be reasonably certain that it will be required for this special purpose, with the result that it has acquired an enhanced value. That was a matter for the umpire to take into consideration.** To effectuate that purpose the Board must necessarily concur so far as they are owners of part of the site. **In this state of things there is nothing to exclude the element of adaptability.** * * *"

The fact that Appellants did not own the river and that their land could not be used as a damsite except in combination with the state-owned river bed does not justify striking Appellants' evidence of special use value, or excluding special use from consideration in determining market value.

McCandless v. U. S. (Supra),

Olson v. U. S. (Supra).

"The fact that the most profitable use of a parcel can be made only in combination with other lands does not necessarily exclude that use from consideration if the possibility of combination is reasonably sufficient to affect market value. Nor does the fact that it may be or is being acquired by eminent domain negative consideration of availability for use in the public service. **New York v. Sage, 239 U. S. 57, 61.** It is common knowledge that public service corporations and others having that power frequently are actual or potential competitors not only for tracts held in single ownership but also for rights of way, locations, sites, and other areas requiring the union of numerous parcels held by different owners. And, to the extent that probable demand by prospective purchasers or condemnors affects market value, it is to be taken into account. **Boom Company v. Patterson, ubi supra.**"

That there was "probable demand by prospective purchasers" was abundantly proved by Defendants. (R. p. 107, 125, 152, 154, 134-136, 141, 142). Application for permit to develop Grand Coulee was filed by Col. Hugh L. Cooper, New York, (R. p. 143) A power permit was issued to the Columbia Basin Commission to construct the Grand Coulee Dam. (R. p. 173) The dam could not possibly be built without taking appellants uplands. (R. p. 104, 125, 126, 145,) Private capital is always on the lookout for such dam sites. (R. p. 135)

It must be evident that the fact that Appellants did not own the river bed cannot justify the trial court's ruling and instructions, here assigned as error.

II.

THE FACT THAT APPELLANTS DID NOT OWN OR HAVE A RIGHT TO USE THE FLOW OF THE RIVER DOES NOT EXCLUDE EVIDENCE OF

SPECIAL USE VALUE FROM CONSIDERATION IN DETERMINING MARKET VALUE.

What has been said under Sub-division I hereof regarding the fact that Defendants did not own the river bed applies with equal force to their nonownership of the flow of the river. The principle is identical in respect to each.

In order to require that special use value be taken into consideration in determining the market price of property taken for public purposes, it is not necessary that such property possess all the qualities necessary to the completed project. It is enough that a tract of such property possesses, **inherently**, any one or more of the necessary qualities, provided that it is probable that, within a reasonable time, there will be a demand for such tract for said use, and that there be available a practicable and legal method whereby such tract may be united with other properties possessing the other remaining qualities necessary to the execution of the project.

Olson v. U. S. (Supra),

Boom Co. v. Patterson (Supra).

"The contention on the part of the plaintiff in error is, that such adaptability should not be considered, assuming that this adaptability could never be made available for other persons, by reason of its **supposed exclusive privileges;** in other words, that **by the grant of exclusive privileges to the company the owner is deprived of the value which the**

lands by their adaptability for boom purposes previously possessed, and, therefore, should not now receive anything from the company on account of such adaptability upon a condemnation of the lands. **We do not think that the owner by the charter of the company lost this element of value in his property."**

The Supreme Court of the State of Washington and the Supreme Court of the United States have both held squarely that the owner of upland riparian to navigable water has a legal right to prove and to recover the fair market value of his upland, considering all its adaptability for valuable uses; and he has that right even though he does not have a property right in the navigable water, nor any right to use or occupy the submerged land under it.

State ex rel Ham, Yearsley & Ryrie v.
    Superior Court, Northern Pacific
    Railway Company, et al,
      70 Wash. 442,
      126 Pac. 945.

Ham, Yearsley & Ryrie v. Northern Pacific
    Railway Company, et al,
      107 Wash. 378,
      181 Pac. 898.

Ham, Yearsley & Ryrie v. Northern Pacific
    Railway Company, et al
      110 Wash. 467,
      188 Pac. 527.

In the first of these cases the question was whether Ham, Yearsley & Ryrie or the Northern Pacific Railway Company had the right to appropriate the water of Moses Lake, and to acquire by condemnation the dam site at its outlet. Moses Lake was navigable, and the title to the bed of the lake, and to the shore land below high water mark was in the State of Washington. The same is true of the water and bed of the Columbia River in Appellants' case. The Northern Pacific Railway owned riparian upland suitable for a damsite, on the shore and at the outlet of the lake. Ham, Yearsley & Ryrie (an irrigation company) sought and claimed the right to appropriate the water and to build a dam for irrigation purposes. The Northern Pacific sought to build its own dam, for irrigating its own land, and resisted the action brought for condemnation by Ham, Yearsley & Ryrie. The Supreme Court of Washington held that Ham, Yearsley & Ryrie had made its application first, and so had the prior right to appropriate the water, and therefore, had the right to acquire the damsite by condemnation, and that **the Northern Pacific Railway had no right in the water of the lake.**

The next action was to condemn the land necessary for the damsite. The question, as in Appellants' case, was whether the adaptability of the land for use as a damsite could be considered in determining market value. The Court held that **the Northern Pacific had no right to use the water of the lake, and that it had no right to condemn land for use as a damsite, nor to build the dam.** It, therefore, necessarily followed that **the Northern Pacific could make no possible use of its damsite.** Nevertheless, the Court allowed it to prove, and required Ham, Yearsley & Ryrie to pay, the fair market value of the land considering its inherent adaptability for use as a damsite.

The Court said:

"The value of this land should be ascertained for all purposes for which it is shown to be available, either agricultural, grazing, townsite, manufacturing, * * * or **for the purpose of a damsite,** and its value for the last named purpose should be arrived at by the same test as would be applied in ascertaining its value for the first named purpose, namely: what advantages does it possess in itself as a damsite. If an adequate dam can be constructed here four hundred feet long and twelve feet wide at a cost of $35,000.00, what is the value of the site as compared with what it would have been if the dam must necessarily have been eight hundred feet long and cost $70,000.00, or but one hundred feet long and cost $10,00.00."

(110 Wash. 467 at 473, 474, 188 P. 527.)

The Northern Pacific Railway did not have any property right in the water of the lake; it did not have any right to use the water; it did not own or have any right to use the bed of the lake; it did not own all the land and property necessary to the completed project, and its land was riparian to navigable water, Moses Lake being navigable. In these respects, the Northern Pacific and its damsite were in the same position legally and factually as are Appellant and their damsite. **But the Supreme Court of Washington permitted the Northern Pacific to prove and required the condemnor to pay the**

value of the land for all purposes, including its use for a damsite.

**United States v. Chandler-Dunbar Company,
229 U. S. 52.**

Prior to the action to acquire the Chandler-Dunbar Company property, an Act of Congress had decreed that all of the submerged land, and all of the water of the river which flowed over it, as well as the riparian uplands were necessary for the improvement of navigation. The Supreme Court held that **the Chandler-Dunbar Company, therefore, had no right to use or occupy the submerged land in the bed of the river, and that it had no property right in the flow of the river, and no right to use it.**

The Government appropriated the Chandler-Dunbar Company's riparian uplands which were adapted for special use as a site for locks and a canal. **Since Chandler-Dunbar Co. had no property in, and no right to use, the bed and flow of the river, it was; relatively, in the same position as are Appellants in this action.** Yet, contrary to the ruling and instructions of the Trial Court in the instant case, **the Supreme Court held that the Chandler-Dunbar Company had a right to prove and to collect the fair market value of its uplands, in view of their inherent adaptability for lock and canal purposes.** The Supreme Court said:

(p. 74) "Coming now to the award for the **upland** taken:

"The Court below awarded to the Chandler-Dunbar Company on this account—

"a. For the narrow strip of **upland** bordering on the river, having an area of something more than 8 acres * * * $60,450. * * *

"The value of the **upland** strip fixed at $60,450 was arrived at in this manner—

"a. For its value, including railroad side-tracks, buildings and cable terminal, including also its use 'wholly disconnected with power development or public improvement, that is to say, for all general purposes, like residences, or hotels, factory sites, disconnected with water power, etc., $20,000.'

"b. For use as a factory site in connection with the development of 6,500 horse power, either as a single site or for several factories to use the surplus of 6,500 horse power not now used in the city, an additional value of $20,000.

"c. **For use for canal and lock purposes, an additional value of $25,000.** * * *

"The United States excepted to the additional value allowed in consequence of the **availability** of these parcels **in connection with the water power supposed to be the property of the Chandler-Dunbar Company,** and supposed to have been taken by the Government in this case. It **also excepted** to so much of the awards as constituted an additional value by reason of **availability for lock and canal purposes.**

"These exceptions so far as they complain of the additional value to be attached to these parcels for use as factory sites in connection with the development of horse power by the Chandler-Dunbar Company, must be sustained. These 'additional' values were based upon the erroneous hypothesis that that company had a private property interest in the water power of the river, not possibly needed now or in the future for purposes of navigation, but that that excess or surplus water was capable, by some extension of their works already in the river, of producing 6,500 horse power.

"(P. 76) the exception taken to the inclusion as an element of value of the **availability of these parcels of land for lock and canal purposes must be overruled.** That this land had a prospective value for the purpose of constructing a canal and lock parallel with those in use had passed beyond the region of the purely conjectural or speculative. That one or more additional parallel canals and locks would be needed to meet the increasing demands of lake traffic was an immediate probability. **This land was the only land available for the purpose.** It included all the land between the canals in use and the bank of the river. Although it is not proper to estimate land condemned for public purposes by the public necessities or its worth to the public for such purpose, **it is proper to consider the fact that the property is so situated that it will probably be desired and available for such a purpose. Lewis on Eminent Domain, Sec. 707; Boom Co. v. Patterson, 98 U. S. 403, 408; Shoemaker v. United States, 147 U. S. 282; Young v. Harrison, 17 Georgia 30; Alloway v. Nashville, 88 Tennessee, 510; Sargent v. Merrimac, 196 Mass. 171.**"

It would appear that the inherent adaptability of
Appellants' upland for use as **a damsite** is equivalent to
the inherent adaptability of the Chandler-Dunbar **upland** for use "for **lock and canal** purposes." It is equally
true in both cases that "This land was the only land
available for the purpose.

Furthermore, the owner of the Chandler-Dunbar
upland had no right or license to use the water or the
bed of the river, or to build a lock and canal. But that
fact did not deprive the owner of the fair market value
of the land, in view of its inherent adaptability for lock
and canal purpose. By the same principle and reasoning,
it necessarily follows that the fact that Appellants did
not have a license to build a dam across the Columbia
River, or to use the water, should not deprive them of
the fair market value of their land, in view of its inherent adaptability for use as a dam site.

Consideration of the Trial Court's ruling and
instructions in connection with the portion of the
opinion in the Chandler-Dunbar case which he read in
his remarks to the jury (R. p. 178-9) suggests that possibly the Court did not distinguish between the two
questions in the Chandler-Dunbar case. First, **what
property was in fact taken?**; secondly, **what is the
measure of compensation for the property actually
taken?**

As regards the submerged land in the river bed and
the flow of the water in the stream, the Supreme Court,
in the Chandler-Dunbar Case, held that the riparian
owner had no property right in them, and, **accordingly,**

that there was nothing for which compensation could be paid. But the riparian uplands were held to be entirely different. Property right in them must be conceded. That property may not be taken without just compensation. The question is, what is the **measure** of that compensation? In the Chandler-Dunbar case, the Supreme Court held that adaptability for special use must be considered as one of the elements.

Appellants make no claim for compensation on account of the flow of the stream. Their claim is only for the loss of their upland. Reason and authority dictate that their loss must be measured by the uses which their property is adapted to serve. Obviously, what was said in the Chandler-Dunbar case in holding that the riparian owner **has no private property in the submerged land or in the flow of the stream** can not be used to measure the value of riparian **upland in which Appellants' private property right is conceded.** It is respectfully submitted that the Trial Court did that very thing in striking Appellants' evidence and instructing the jury to disregard it.

McCandless v. U. S.,
74 Fed. (2d) 596 (9th Cir.).

Condemnation of land for naval depot. It was claimed the land was adapted to production of sugar cane. But to make it so adapted it was necessary to acquire and transport water in large quantities for irrigation. **The owner, McCandless, did not own, or have any definite arrangement to acquire or use the necessary water, or the right of way over which to bring the water to his land.** He was, in legal contemplation, in the same position as Appellants in the instant case, as regards other property necessary to complete the project for which the land was adapted.

The trial court in the McCandles case, as in the instant case, excluded evidence of special adaptability and instructed the jury to disregard it, except to the extent that the water might be developed on the land itself. This Court held that such exclusion and instruction were error, and that the owner was entitled to show that a watter supply was available, although at that time he did not own it or have any right to use it; and held that he was entitled to prove and collect the market value of his land in view of its adaptability for valuable use, in combination with other property, although he did not own or have a license to use that other property. This Court said:

> "The court limited the landowner in his showing of available water for irrigation purposes to the land itself and to the 289 acre tract on the Haleakala River immediately adjoining the land, a portion of which fact was being condemned. * * * **Limited to the land itself for sources of water it was clear from the evidence that the land could not be made available for sugar cane purposes,** since for this purpose twenty-five to thirty million gallons of water per day would be required.

> "An offer of proof was made upon the part of the landowners and denied * * *

> "Among instructions to the jury to which exception was taken was the following:

'12· In estimating the compensation to be paid to the owners of the land which the government here seeks to condemn, I instruct you that you must entirely disregard any possibility of bringing water to the land in question from any other land, excepting the land which the government here seeks to condemn and the 284 acre tract.'

"The major question upon the appeal is whether the court erred in denying the offers of proof and giving the instruction quoted."

"It appears from the evidence that in order to supply the land in question with a sufficient water supply for the cultivation of sugar cane the **water would have to be conducted not only across public lands of the Territory but also across other land held in private ownership.** It may be assumed that such a right of way may be acquired over private lands by condemnation if necessary by means of a corporation organized for such a purpose. **48 USCA §562; Rev. Laws Hawaii 1925, §§828, 829.**

* * *

"The denial of the offers of proof and the giving of the instruction above referred to were errors."

This court was of the opinion, however, that the Trial Court's error was not prejudicial, but the Supreme Court held otherwise, and granted a new trial. **McCand-**

less v. U. S. 80 L. Ed. 797, 799, 801. The Supreme Court said:

"These offers, and evidence of a similar character sought to be elicited from witnesses, were rejected by the trial court upon the ground that the possibility of bringing water from outside sources was too remote and speculative.

At the conclusion of the evidence the court gave the following instruction to the jury: (Here the Court quotes the instruction, (Supra) and continued,

"The rule is well settled that, in condemnation cases, the most profitable use to which the land can probably be put in the reasonably near future may be shown and considered as bearing upon the market value; and the fact that such use can be made only in connection with other lands does not necessarily exclude it from consideration if the possibility of such connection is reasonably sufficient to affect market value. **Olson v. United States, 292 U. S. 246, 255, 256, 78 L. Ed. 1236, 1244, 1245, 54 S. Ct. 704.**

"That the greater part of the land here sought to be condemned was adapted to the successful growth of sugar cane if provided with sufficient water for irrigation is not controverted. Proof that a supply of water was available and might be brought to the land at an expense consistent with its profitable use was, therefore, relevant and material. And this the evidence offered tended to establish. The ruling of the trial court rejecting the offers, and its instruction to the jury to disregard the possibility of bringing water from other lands other than the land sought to be condemned and the 284 acre tract adjoining, were erroneous. This is well pointed out by the court below, and we see no occasion to enlarge upon its opinion.

* *

"In an eminent-domain proceeding, the vital issue—and generally the only issue—is that of just compensation. The proof here offered necessarily related to the value of the land when used for a purpose to which it probably could be put within the rule laid down by the **Olson case, 292 U. S. 246, 78 L. Ed. 1236, 54 S. Ct. 704, supra.** To exclude from the consideration of the jury evidence of this elementary character could not be otherwise than prejudicial."

A new trial was granted.

L. R. Junction Ry. v. Woodruff,
49 Ark. 381,
5 S. W. 792.

This was an action to condemn a point of rocks suitable for a bridge site. In allowing the inherent adaptability for special use to be considered in estimating its market value, the Supreme Court of Arkansas said (p. 387):

"This is a sort of promontory that makes out into the river, and seems to have been somewhat inviting as a bridge site. The only issue in the court below was as to the value of the property. * * *"

The Court then quoted from Appellants' brief in said action, as follows:

"We contend that, having a **special right** under the law of Arkansas **to construct the road** which we have constructed, **and of erecting said** bridge, **and the defendant not having shown any such, or similar right,** that the defendants can not have any damages based upon a use to which they could not have put the property, but only for being deprived of the right to devote the property to such uses as the law allows them to devote to it. * * *

"**If Woodruff did not have the right to bridge the Arkansas, he has not been deprived of anything but his land.**"

Compare the statement of trial court in the instant case:

"These owners * * * are not entitled to have that adaptability of this site taken into account for the reason they have neither title to the bed of the stream nor any right to the waters which flow in it * * * and they are not entitled to that because it has not been taken from them * * *" (R. p. 179)

To this argument of counsel, the Supreme Court of Arkansas said:

"This is asking us to put fetters on the market value, if it is not a proposition to discard it as a criterion of damage altogether.

"It can hardly be doubted that if Woodruff
had gone upon the market to sell this property he
would not have concealed the fact that it possessed
superior advantages as a bridge site. Now, if he
would not have concealed it from a purchaser, **it
would be unfair to him for the court to conceal it
from the jury.** On the other hand, if one had been
about to purchase this property, he would hardly
have been so obtuse as to overlook an element of
value so obvious as its eligibility for a bridge site.
* * * If it were announced that a point of rocks
on the Mississippi River, at Hopefield, opposite
Memphis, was offered for sale upon the market, **it is
easy to predict that there would be no lack of bidders,** and that the price offered would be very much
above what the property would be 'worth as a piece
of land.' **In their anxiety to secure property so valuable, bidders would hardly delay until they had
obtained authority to build a bridge.** (P. 393)

"It seems to us that counsel for appellant **mag-
nifies the difficulty and overrates** the importance
of obtaining and owning a bridge franchise. Whatever may be the case elsewhere, so far as Arkansas
is concerned, perhaps the **easiest and cheapest part
of building a bridge,** or a railroad, is obtaining the
charter. **The most difficult things to obtain** are the
money with which to build and a rock upon which
to land." (P. 395)

The record proves beyond doubt that private enterprise was ready and able to supply the money, and
**Appellants' land supplied the "rock" upon which to
build the dam.** The Washington Water Code, the Fed-

eral Water Power Act and the Rules of the Federal Power Commission furnished the "legal and practical possibility" of obtaining the "franchise" or license to build the dam.

Every material fact, and every legal principle which permitted and required consideration of evidence of the adaptability of the Chandler-Dunbar land "for lock and canal purposes"; and the adaptability of the Northern Pacific land for use as a dam site, and the adaptability of the McCandless land for growing sugar cane, and the adaptability of the Woodruff rock for a bridge site is present in Appellants' case, and with equal force and reason, requires that Appellants be granted a new trial.

III.

THE FACT THAT THE COLUMBIA RIVER IS NAVIGABLE AND THAT PETITIONER CLAIMS TO TAKE APPELLANTS' LAND IN AID OF NAVIGATION DOES NOT DESTROY MARKET VALUE ARISING OUT OF INHERENT ADAPTABILITY FOR A SPECIAL USE, OR EXCLUDE EVIDENCE OF SUCH USE AND ADAPTABILITY FROM CONSIDERATION IN MEASURING "JUST COMPENSATION."

The stress placed by the trial court on the fact that the Columbia River is navigable, and on the assertion that Appellants' lands are taken in aid of navigation (R. p. 176-179) indicates that the Court was of the opinion that the navigability of the river and the purpose for which the lands are taken might modify the measure of compensation which must be paid.

It is respectfully submitted that the navigability of the Columbia River, and the purpose for which Appellants' lands are taken have no bearing whatsoever on the measure of compensation which must be paid. It is the usefulness and consequent value of Appellants' upland that must be paid for. Navigability is a quality of the river, not of the upland; its navigability is quite immaterial to the question of upland values. These values cannot be affected by the qualities or characteristics of the river nor by the use to be made of the land by the taker; provided only that it be legally practicable to obtain the right to use the water and the bed of the river to complete the project.

U. S. v. Chandler-Dunbar, (Supra).

McCandless v. U. S. (Supra).

**Ham, Yearsley & Ryrie v. Northern
Pacific (Supra).**

Olson v. United States (Supra).

In the **Chandler-Dunbar** case, the fact that the land was taken for the improvement of navigation did not destroy or eliminate from consideration its inherent adaptability for lock and canal purpose although **the lock and canal could serve no possible use except navigation. Neither did the fact that the land was riparian to navigable water, nor that the Government had already, by act of Congress determined that the land was necessary for the improvement of navigation, defeat the right to prove adaptability for special and valuable use.** In like manner, the conclusion is unescapable that, the fact

that the Columbia River is navigable, and that navigation might be improved by building a dam on Appellants' land, cannot eliminate inherent adaptability as a
dam site, from consideration in estimating the fair
market value of the upland.

The test specified in the **Olson** case is that it appear
that there is a "legal and practical possibility" that the
owner "or some other person or persons, other than the
expropriating authority could have acquired the right
to flow the land necessary for the lawful raising of the
lake." (i. e., the lawful execution of the project involving the special use). The same test was applied in the
McCandless case and the **Northern Pacific** cases
(supra).

The Washington Water Code **(Remington's Revised Stats. of Washington §7416)** as well as the Federal
Water Power Act furnish a "legal and practical possibility" for any public, or semi-public, entity to acquire
the right to use the water and the bed of the river to develop the Grand Coulee project. The State and Federal
laws not only furnish legal and practical means for acquiring such rights, but plainly indicate a public policy
to encourage and invite the development of such natural
resources by private capital.

The **WASHINGTON WATER CODE** provides:

"There is hereby granted to persons, firms and
corporations organized among other things for irrigation and power purposes **the right to construct
and maintain dams and works incident thereto
over, upon and across the beds of the rivers of the**

State of Washington in connection with such power and irrigation purposes, and there is hereby granted to such persons, etc., an easement over, upon and across the beds of such rivers for such purposes."

There is a proviso that navigation shall not be interfered with.

The **FEDERAL WATER POWER ACT** provides:

"Sec. 4. That the Commission is hereby authorized and empowered—

(a) To make investigations and to collect and record data concerning the utilization of the water resources of any region to be developed. * * *

(c) To make public from time to time the information secured hereunder, and to provide for the publication of its reports and investigations in such form and manner as may be best adapted for public information and use. The commission, on or before the first Monday in December of each year, shall submit to Congress for the fiscal year preceding a classified report showing the permits and licenses issued under this Act, and in each case the parties thereto, the terms prescribed and the moneys received, if any, on account thereof.

(d) To issue licenses to citizens of the United States, or to any association of such citizens, or to any corporation organized under the laws of the United States or in any State thereof, or to any State or municipality for the purpose of constructing, operating, and maintaining dams, water conduits, reservoirs, power houses, transmission lines, or any other project works necessary or convenient for the development and improvement of navigation and for the development, transmission, and utilization of power across, along, from or in any of the navigable waters of the United States, or upon any part of the public lands and reservations of the United States (including the Territories), or for the purpose of utilizing the surplus water or water power from any Government dam, except as herein provided: * * *"

Comformable with the State and Federal Acts, the natural water power sites in the State of Washington have been developed by private capital for many years. Dams and power developments have been permitted and developed. One dam and power development of large proportions has already been completed on the Columbia River at Rock Island, and a permit had already been issued to the Columbia Basin Commission to develop the Grand Coulee project, before these proceedings were instituted by the Federal Government. (R. p. 173)

The Washington Code expressly grants the right to use the water and the bed of the river. The Federal Government has no jurisdiction to veto such grant, except in aid of navigation; and such veto will not be presumed, but can result only by act of congress; a fact which does not exist in this case. The Federal Water Power Act and the rules of the Power Commission clearly indicate a policy to conform to the Washington Water Code, in encouraging the development of power and irrigation, excepting only where navigation may be impaired thereby.

Every desirable or possible improvement to navigation could be secured through development of Grand Coulee by private capital under Government supervision, in exactly the same way as it is now accomplished, if at all. The type of dam, as well as its operation, and the use of the water would be identical, whether the improvement were made by private capital or by the Government. There can be no question on the evidence and the law, that **there was a "legal and practical possibility" that others than the Federal Government could acquire the right to use the bed and the flow of the river, conformable with the requirements of navigation. The navigability of the river, therefore, is no reason for striking Defendants' evidence of special adaptability, or excluding it from consideration.**

Appellants introduced abundant evidence to satisfy the rule of "legal and practical possibility" stated and applied in the **Olson** and **McCandless** cases. They were, therefore, legally entitled to have the special adaptability of their lands for use as a damsite shown and considered as an element of market value.

The fact that Appellants' lands were taken in aid of navigation, if such were the fact, would likewise be immaterial. "Just compensation" is the measure of what the owner has lost, no what the taker has gained. The use made by the taker may not be considered.

> **Boston Chamber of Commerce v. Boston,**
> 217 U. S. 189,
> 30 S. Ct. 459,
> 54 L. Ed. 725.

Kerr v. South Park Commissioners,
117 U. S. 379,
6 S. Ct. 801,
29 L. Ed. 924.

Schoemaker v. United States,
147 U. S. 282, 304,
13 S. Ct. 361,
37 L. Ed. 170.

Mississippi & Rum River Boom Company v.
Patterson,
98 U. S. 403,
25 L. Ed. 206.

United States v. Chandler-Dunbar Company
229 U. S. 53,
33 S. Ct. 667,
57 L. Ed. 1063.

OLSON v. United States,
292 U. S. 246,
54 S. Ct. 704,
78 L. Ed. 1236.

On reason, as well as on authority, the fact, if it were a fact, that the Government seeks to aid navigation, and has a right to use the **bed of stream** in doing so, cannot confer on the Government the right to take Appellants' **uplands** without paying their fair market value. What is fair market value is not determined by the use which the Government intends to make of the land, nor by its paramount right to occupy the river bed. **Neither**

the navigability of the river, nor the Government's alleged purpose to improve navigation, contributes, or adds to, the inherent adaptability of Appellants' upland for use as a damsite. The geographic location, and the physical characteristics of these uplands are inherent and existed long before the Government came into being, or had any power to improve navigation. **This special adaptability for valuable use as a damsite inheres in these uplands, and, therefore, must be considered in determining market value.**

BUT, THE IMPROVEMENT OF NAVIGATION IS NOT IN THE CASE.

Even if the improvement of navigation could modify the General Rule permitting proof and consideration of special adaptability, the Government is not in position to claim modification in this case, because:

(a) The taking of Appellants' lands was not declared by Congress to be necessary in aid of navigation. In the Chandler-Dunbar case, upon which the trial court based his ruling, Congress had declared by formal enactment that the submerged lands, and all of the water of the river, as well as the uplands, were necessary for the improvement of navigation, and the Chandler-Dunbar Company and all the world were excluded therefrom. But in the instant case no one was excluded from using the bed and flow of the river. **On the contrary, a permit had been issued to the Columbia Basin Commission to use the river, and to make the very improvement now being made by the Government.** The evidence shows no action whatsoever by Congress in the matter. Congress has absolute authority and jurisdiction to determine what is necessary in aid of navigation. But until congress acts the authority over the water and bed of the river is vested in the State of Washington.

U. S. Chandler-Dunbar Company (Supra).

But Appellants' lands were taken under the claimed authority of the National Industrial Recovery Act (48. Stat. 195) R. p. 5) There was no act by Congress designed or intended to improve navigation, or in any way appropriating Appellants' lands for that purpose of navigation. The distinction between taking Appellants' uplands, as an F. E. R. A. project, and the formal taking of the Chandler-Dunbar uplands by Act of Congress in aid of navigation, is clear and controlling. Obviously, what was said in the Chandler-Dunbar case about taking water power and submerged lands in aid of navigation can have no application in the instant case.

In fact, it is probable that Petitioner had no legal right whatsoever to take Appellants' lands in this proceeding. Congress had taken no action in the matter, and the record does not show the performance of any acts, or the exercise of any lawful authority, which could amount to authority in law for this taking, or the making of the Grand Coulee improvement by the Federal Government.

U. S. v. Arizona,
295 U. S. 174,
55 S. Ct. 666,
79 L. Ed. 1371.

It is Appellants' contention that the only authority which the Government has to take their uplands in this proceeding is the stipulation entered into in open court "that the Government has a right to condemn the property described in the complaint in this case, and that the only issue for trial is the value of the property" (R. p. 42). There is no suggestion in the stipulation that improvement of navigation is contemplated, or if contemplated, that "the value of the property" is to be reduced or destroyed thereby . The stipulation clearly contemplates that the general rule for determining "the value of the property" shall govern. As already shown, the general rule is that evidence of special adaptability for use as a damsite may be introduced and must be considered, and that whether the taker uses the property in aid of navigation or for some other public purpose is wholly immaterial.

> Monongahela Navigation Company v. U. S.,
>   148 U. S. 312,
>   13 S. Ct. 622,
>   37 L. Ed. 463.

> Clark's Ferry Bridge Co. v. Public Service
>   Commission of Pennsylvania,
>   291 U. S. 227,
>   54 S. Ct. 427,
>   78 L. Ed. 767.

> Ford Hydro-Electric Company v. Neely,
>   13 F. (2d) 361 (7th Cir.).

Since Congress has taken no action to appropriate Appellants' lands in aid of navigation, and since the record is barren of anything which could possibly be construed as an authorized and lawful appropriation for that purpose, **there is no foundation in law for the claim that Appellants' uplands are taken for the purpose of improving navigation.**

(b) Furthermore, there is no foundation in fact for any such claim. As already stated, the record does not show that Petitioner, or anyone else, had in mind any intention to improve navigation. The burden was on Petitioner to prove that the land was taken to improve navigation before it could claim any privilege or advantage on that account. But, in this case, not only does the record fail to show any purpose to improve navigation, it proves exactly the contrary.

Petitioner's testimony is largely concerned with the development of and the market for hydro-electric power, and with reclamation and irrigation, and with the losses which may be expected from each.

The Government's plans and specifications for the Grand Coulee dam, Defendant's Exhibits 42a, 42b, 42c, and 43 (R. p. 159) show no locks, canals, or other devices necessary to promote navigation around the dam.

Furthermore, the report transmitted to the 73rd Congress by the Chief of Engineers, and the Secretary of War in 1932 and printed as H. R. No. 103, which Defendants offered in evidence, but which was, in view of the court's previous rulings, erroneously excluded, shows clearly that Appellants' lands were not taken for the purposes of navigation.

Vol. II, H. R. No. 103 (R. p. 181-183):

"Sec. 1670. The Columbia is a river with steep slopes, high velocities, and numerous rapids flowing through a tortuous channel from 2,000 to 3,000 feet below the level of the surrounding country, much of which is semi-arid and comparatively unproductive without irrigation. The volume of water carried by the river justifies a serious consideration of its practical use for navigation, **but investigation of conditions in the Columbia above the Snake shows that the cost of improvements necessary to give a satisfactory width and depth to the channel is much greater than any possible river commerce would warrant.**"

"Sec. 1678. The cost of this work is estimated at $165,000,000. Interest on this amount at 4 per cent would be $6,600,000 annually, **which would, of course, be prohibitive if any appreciable proportion of the cost were charged against navigation.**"

"Sec. 1690. It appears, therefore, that **navigation is of no present importance** and that future consideration will have to depend upon conditions as they develop."

"Sec. 1692. It is concluded that—

1. **Expenditures necessary to permit through traffic by canalization** on Columbia River above the Snake **are not justified** by any reasonable ex-

pectation of shipments by water in or out of the territory.

2. **Navigation from Portland to points below Wenatchee could be made possible by the construction of locks** in all dams below Wenatchee **when the river is fully developed, for power.**

3. The construction of any dams for the development of power would make local traffic in the pool above it possible. No special expenditure will be necessary to facilitate the development of the local commerce with the exception of the improvement of the channels at the upper end of the pool to accommodate traffic during law stages of the river.

4. Traffic on the river in and out of the territory above the Snake would represent no saving to producers, shippers, or consumers unless such traffic exceeded 250,000 tons annually.

5. **The possibility of future traffic on the river above the Snake may justify Federal participation in the construction of locks when and if such are needed."**

"Sec. 1990. **The high dam is proposed in the Columbia opposite the head of Grand Coulee for the generation of power for the general market and for use in connection with the irrigation of the Columbia Basin irrigation project.** This dam will hold water at elevation 1,287.6 and would back the water to the international boundary. **A location for locks is shown on the plan although none are contemplated for inclusion in the comprehensive plan."**

"Sec. 1999. No provision is made for the control of floods on the Columbia above the Snake as none is required."

Clearly, there is in the record no foundation in fact or in law for the claim that Appellants' uplands were taken in aid of navigation. They are taken as an F. E. R. A. project to supply water for irrigation and to develop hydro-elecric power. Accordingly, whatever rights Congress might have to take private property in aid of navigation in the Columbia River, such rights have not been exercised. Appellants' lands are not being taken for that purpose. It follows that considerations of navigation have no part whatever in the measure of just compensation to be paid in this proceeding.

Wisconsin v. Illinois,
278 U. S. 367, 415,
49 S. Ct. 163,
73 L. Ed. 426.

"This Court has said that while Congress in the exercise of its power may adopt any means having some positive relation to the control of navigation and not otherwise inconsistent with the Constitution, **United States v. Chandler-Dunbar Company, 229 U. S. 53, 62,** it may not arbitrarily destroy or impair the rights of riparian owners by legislation which has no real or substantial relation to the control of navigation or appropriateness to that end. **United States v. River Rouge Improvement Co., 269 U. S. 411, 419; Port of Seattle v. Oregon & Washington R. R., 255 U. S. 56, 63.**"

SUMMARY AND CONCLUSION

I.

We Believe That Is Is Fair to State That the Following Facts Are Established Either By Admission or By Competent Evidence.

1. That Appellants' lands, which are taken in these proceedings, are uplands, situated above ordinary high water mark.

2. That Appellants' uplands possess inherent adaptability for use as a damsite.

3. That they are the only lands in existence which are suitable and available for a damsite useful for the development of hydro-electric Power, and for irrigation, by using Grand Coulee as a storage reservoir.

4. That these uses can be accomplished only by building a dam across the Columbia River at Grand Coulee, and that no such dam can be built without using Appellants lands.

5. That, at the time of taking, there was a market for Appellants' lands for use as a damsite, by others than the Government, and that there was a "legal and practical possibility" of their being acquired and used for that purpose.

6. That, the market value of these lands was greatly increased because of their adaptability for a damsite, and that their market value can not be determined except by considering such adaptability.

II.

The Following Legal Conclusions Appear Justified and Unescapable:

1.   The decisions of this Court, and of the Supreme Court of the United States, and of the Supreme Court of Washington, hold that facts such as are recorded in this case give property owners the right to prove and to collect compensation measured by the adaptability of their lands for all valuable uses, including use as a damsite.

2.   The reasons stated by the Trial Court do not justify his ruling and instructions and do not require or justify a departure from the general measure of just compensation in such cases.

3.   The Trial Court erred in striking Appellants' evidence and excluding it from the jury's consideration, in estimating market value.

4.   The rulings and instructions assigned as errors, were prejudicial, and deprived Appellants of a fair trial.

5.   The verdicts and the judgments entered thereon are contrary to law and the evidence.

6.   This Court should correct the errors, and grant Appellants a new trial of their cause, together with their costs and disbursements on this appeal.

Respectfully submitted,

I. K. LEWIS,

Duluth, Minnesota.

MR. PARKER W. KIMBALL,
Spokane, Washington.

MR. F. J. McKEVITT,
Spokane, Washington.

MR. EDWARD H. CHAVELLE,
Seattle, Washington.

MR. CHARLES ATEN,
Wilbur, Washington,
Attorneys for Appellants.

MR. BRADLEY W. YOUNG,
Spokane, Washington.

MR. W. E. SOUTHARD,
Ephreta, Washington.

MR. JOHN M. PRINS,
Minneapolis, Minnesota.

Of Counsel.

In the
United States Circuit Court
of Appeals
FOR THE NINTH CIRCUIT ♂

No. 8162

CONTINENTAL LAND COMPANY, a corporation,
JULIUS C. JOHNSON, MABLE JOHNSON,
SAMUEL J. SEATON, MARY A. SEATON, EM-
MA RATHS, MARTHA RATHS BALDWIN,
WARREN BALDWIN, HENRY RATHS,
GEORGE RATHS, ALBERT RATHS, ARTHUR
HENRY RATHS, GEORGE RATHS, ARTHUR
RATHS, ALMA RATHS CLARK, FRED CLARK,
MARY RATHS MARNHART, CLARENCE MARN-
HART, MINNIE RATHS, FRED RATHS and
MANITA RATHS,   *Appellants,*

vs.

UNITED STATES OF AMERICA,

Appellee.

APPELLEE'S BRIEF

*Upon Appeal from the District Court of the United
States for the Eastern District of Washington,
Northern Division*

J. M. SIMPSON,
United States Attorney,
Spokane, Washington;

B. E. STOUTEMYER,
District Counsel, Bureau of
Reclamation,
Portland, Oregon,
Attorneys for Appellee.

In the

United States Circuit Court

of Appeals

FOR THE NINTH CIRCUIT

No. 8162

CONTINENTAL LAND COMPANY, a corporation,
JULIUS C. JOHNSON, MABLE JOHNSON,
SAMUEL J. SEATON, MARY A. SEATON, EM-
MA RATHS, MARTHA RATHS BALDWIN,
WARREN BALDWIN, HENRY RATHS,
GEORGE RATHS, ALBERT RATHS, ARTHUR
HENRY RATHS, GEORGE RATHS, ARTHUR
RATHS, ALMA RATHS CLARK, FRED CLARK,
MARY RATHS MARNHART, CLARENCE MARN-
HART, MINNIE RATHS, FRED RATHS and
MANITA RATHS,   *Appellants,*

vs.

UNITED STATES OF AMERICA,

Appellee.

APPELLEE'S BRIEF

---

*Upon Appeal from the District Court of the United
States for the Eastern District of Washington,
Northern Division*

J. M. SIMPSON,
United States Attorney,
Spokane, Washington;

B. E. STOUTEMYER,
District Counsel, Bureau of
Reclamation,
Portland, Oregon,
Attorneys for Appellee.

SUBJECT INDEX

TABLE OF CASES CITED

II

TABLE OF STATUTES CITED

In the
United States Circuit Court
of Appeals
FOR THE NINTH CIRCUIT

No. 8162

CONTINENTAL LAND COMPANY, a corporation,
JULIUS C. JOHNSON, MABLE JOHNSON,
SAMUEL J. SEATON, MARY A. SEATON, EM-
MA RATHS, MARTHA RATHS BALDWIN,
WARREN BALDWIN, HENRY RATHS,
GEORGE RATHS, ALBERT RATHS, ARTHUR
HENRY RATHS, GEORGE RATHS, ARTHUR
RATHS, ALMA RATHS CLARK, FRED CLARK,
MARY RATHS MARNHART, CLARENCE MARN-
HART, MINNIE RATHS, FRED RATHS and
MANITA RATHS,   *Appellants,*

vs.

UNITED STATES OF AMERICA,
                                        Appellee.

APPELLEE'S BRIEF

---

*Upon Appeal from the District Court of the United
States for the Eastern District of Washington,
Northern Division*

STATEMENT OF FACTS

The question and the only question involved in
this appeal is the question whether Judge Webster
was in error in instructing the jury in language
quoted from the opinion of the Supreme Court in
the Chandler-Dunbar case as follows:

"In the State of Washington the beds of
navigable streams are not vested absolutely or
qualifiedly in the owners of the shore lands
along such navigable streams. The bed of
navigable streams in the State of Washington
is vested in the State of Washington. The decisions of the Supreme Court of the United
States are at one upon this proposition, that the
Congress of the United States has absolute
control over the navigable streams within the
borders of the country. It has that power in
virtue of the provision of the Constitution of
the United States which confers exclusively
upon Congress the power to regulate commerce
with foreign nations and among the several
states and with Indian tribes. Navigable
streams are great water highways, agencies and
instrumentalities of commerce, and the dominant power of Congress to control the waters
of such streams is clearly settled and determined by repeated decisions of the Supreme
Court of the United States. The decisions of
the Supreme Court of the United States are
to the effect that riparian owners of shore lands
along the banks of a navigable stream do not
have as against the United States, any interest
in or title to the waters which flow in the stream
when the United States undertakes to develop
it or to improve those water highways for the
purpose of advancing and improving navigation. That the land owner so owning these adjoining shore lands is not entitled to have any
allowance made to him based upon any title to
the bed of the stream or any allowance made to
him for any right that he has because of the
water running in the navigable stream or its
potential water power.

"I am reading to you a succinct paragraph

from one of the leading cases decided by the Supreme Court of the United States which to my mind fits this case like a glove, and is absolutely conclusive of the question presented:

" 'Having decided that the Chandler-Dunbar Company as riparian owners have no such vested property rights in the water power inherent in the falls and rapids of the river, and no right to place in the river the works essential to any practical use of the flow of the river, the Government cannot be justly required to pay for an element of value which did not inhere in these parcels of upland.' 'The Government had dominion over the water power of the rapids and falls, and cannot be required to pay any hypothetical additional value to a riparian owner who had no right to appropriate the current to his own commercial use. These additional values represent, therefore, no actual loss, and there would be no justice in paying for a loss suffered by no one in fact. The requirement of the 5th Amendment is satisfied when the owner is paid for what is taken from him. The question is—what has the owner lost, and not what has the taker gained.'

"These owners in my judgment, are not entitled to have that adaptability of this site taken into account for the reason they have neither title to the bed of the stream nor any right to the waters which flow in it as against the Government exercising dominant power to improve the stream for navigation purposes, and that they are not entitled to that because it has not been taken from them, and it hasn't been taken from them for the simple reason that they never owned it in the first place." (Tr. pp. 177-179.)

It appears from appellants' assignments of error
(Tr. pp. 30, 31, 32) that the only instruction given
by the trial judge to which the appellants offer any
objection is the one referred to in appellants' fourth
assignment of error (Tr. p. 31) as follows:

> "The Court erred in instructing the jury, as
> follows:
>
> " 'When in the course of my instructions I
> said to you that it was your function to ascer-
> tain the reasonable and practical adaptability
> of the property in question you, of course, will
> understand that I did not intend to include its
> value or claimed value as a dam site. That
> question is withdrawn from the consideration
> of the jury and the adaptability and availability
> of the property in question which you will con-
> sider will be those adaptabilities or uses disas-
> sociated from any claimed use for a dam site.' "

The other assignments of error simply reiterate
in various forms appellants' objections to the principle most concisely announced by the trial judge
in the above quoted statement to the jury and the
principle announced by the Supreme Court in the
quoted paragraph.

All of the defendants' witnesses who offered testimony as to the value of the lands involved in this
case (Willis T. Batchellor, William P. Creager, H.
P. Thomas and R. H. Thompson) are engineers
whose expert knowledge and qualification to offer

opinion testimony are limited to engineering questions and did not include any experience as dealers in land or any experience as owners of similar land or any knowledge whatever of market values of land in the section where this land is located (Tr. pp. 95, 96, 120, 131, 132, 133, 150, 151). These engineers, who knew nothing of land values in the section in question, who made no pretense of any experience as dealers in land or even as owners of land in that section, and whose qualification to offer opinion testimony was confined to engineering questions, submitted to the jury their opinion that the 1100 acres of desert land involved in this case was worth from $3,000,000 to $5,000,000 *"if"* or *"provided"*. This is all *"if"* testimony and the *if* is the most important part of it, for the proviso is—

If the defendants or the hypothetical possible buyer could do those things which the law forbids, then in the opinion of the defendants' witnesses the lands would be valuable for dam site purposes, that is

(a) If the defendants could seize and convert to their own use the government's paramount right, title and control of the beds and waters of navigable streams without let or hindrance and regardless of the purpose of the federal government to devote such property to a project for the improvement of navigation;

(b) If in addition to the above requirement the defendants could seize and convert to their own use the state's title to the bed of the navigable stream, which the state statute (Sec. 7412, Remington's Rev. Stat.; Sec. 3380, Pierce's Code) provides shall be granted only to the United States government;

(c) If in addition to the above requirements the defendants could, without the consent of the government, seize, flood and convert to their own use the thousands of acres of government Indian reservation land, both allotted land and tribal land which will be flooded by the reservoir (see stipulation, Tr. pp. 43, 44, 46, also pp. 56, 57);

(d) If the defendants could seize, flood and convert to their own use the public lands of the United States which have been withdrawn from all forms of entry under the first form of withdrawal authorized by the Reclamation Act of June 17, 1902, 32 Stat. 388 (see stipulation, Tr. pp. 43, 44);

(e) If the defendants could seize and convert to their own use the public lands which have been withdrawn for power site purposes;

(f) If the defendants could secure the license which the Federal Power Commission has refused to grant (Tr. p. 143);

(g) If, in addition to all the above requirements concerning state and federal property, the defendants could seize and convert to their own use the essential prior water appropriation which has been secured by the Columbia Basin Commission (see stipulation, Tr. pp. 43, 44);

(h) And if in addition to all of the above requirements the defendants could in any reasonable probability bring into one ownership the more than six hundred (600) separately owned tracts of private land held by more than 900 different owners (see Tr. pp. 43, 44, 56, 130) without resorting to condemnation;

If all these legal questions are answered in the affirmative, then assuming that the market for power will reverse its trend of the last 3 years and will increase continuously and uninterruptedly during all future years at a rate of increase of 9%, 9½% or 10% per year *compounded annually* (Tr. pp. 115, 128, 129, 130, 151, 171) and assuming further that private capital in the enormous amounts required for this enterprise could be secured and that the capital required by this new and highly speculative enterprise could be secured at a low rate of interest, the defendants' witnesses expressed the opinion that the 1100 acres of desert land involved in this case have a value of $3,000,000 to $5,000,000 for dam site purposes, but it is freely admitted that unless all the legal questions which we have listed as a, b, c, d, e, f, g, and h are answered in the affirmative, that is unless the defendants could secure all of the rights and property required for the dam including the all important section across the river channel, and also all the rights and property required for the back water or reservoir above the dam, no dam or power project could be constructed and therefore defendants' lands would be worthless for dam site purposes.

For instance, Mr. William P. Creager, the most eminent of the defendants' engineers, testified on cross examination (Tr. pp. 140, 141 and 143):

"I do not know of any large sales of dam-site property at that location or anywhere else in that vicinity at that time or any time near that date. There was some purchase of property by the Niagara-Hudson Corporation for the St. Lawrence development during that period. Just exactly what dates I don't know. That is adjacent to a thickly populated country. I do not know of any such sales anywhere in the Northwest. No very large projects were constructed to my knowledge during the period of the depression. There were no hydro-electric developments started in the Northwest during the period between 1930 and 1934. There was no need for them at that time. During that time nobody would have financed such construction. Financing construction requiring $70,-000,000 would be found very improbable. It would be foolish to construct a development when there is no necessity for power at that particular date, December, 1933. My recollection is that the court records indicate about 600 owners in the reservoir site whose property would have to be secured before the reservoir could be used. I don't know what kind of procedure you would have to go through to get the Indian lands which would be indispensable for that project, or the withdrawn lands that were withdrawn under the Reclamation act, or the state lands in the bed of the stream and the uplands. I do not know the total of that. I am not basing my testimony on my knowledge but on the court records. If private capital did not finance this proposition, it would have to finance some other on the river, *but if they could not get those necessary rights of way they certainly would not throw away $3,000,000 buying land at the dam site.*"

"I understand this dam site has been known for a great many years, at least 10 or 15 years. It was filed upon in 1922 by Colonel Cooper but the filing was denied, which I understand was because of the desire of the United States government to hold it for themselves. I don't know why the filer did not purchase the dam site at that time.

"I doubt very much if private capital would ever have built it in 1922. It is possible it might have acquired it in 1922. Why they did not, I don't know. The power market was growing much faster in 1929 than in 1933. Nineteen twenty-nine was about the peak of growth. *I do not know why private capital did not purchase it then except that the previous effort to purchase it was denied on the ground that the Government wanted it.* I really have not sufficient knowledge to answer the question as to why that property was not purchased in 1929 except that in my business I keep in touch with these things and I have gathered from different sources that *the Government was withholding permission from private capital to build that dam from the time an attempt was made to file on it in 1921 or 1922 by Mr. Cooper.*"

Mr. Batchellor, the defendants' first witness, concedes (Tr. pp. 112, 113, 114):

> "You can not use a dam without flooding the lands in the back-water and the project would be useless without that land in the back-water."

> "Indian tribal lands are part of the lands to be overflowed by the dam to be built on that site. A dam however small would flood the tract marked '12' on my map of the damsite which is Indian tribal land."

> "If you applied to the lands which are indispensable to the project, because involved in the reservoir, the same rate of value as I have given the land involved in the damsite, the total cost of the right of way would be about $300,-000,000."

H. P. Thomas, another witness for defendants, testified on cross examination (Tr. pp. 126, 129, 130):

> "We have had a serious depression and financial conditions in the last four or five years have been such that private financing of large construction enterprises is impossible. I know of no large financial arrangement for construction of hydro-electric plants."

> "The proposed Grand Coulee project will be financed by private capital by the sale of bonds. I have not offered any for sale. I have not been looking for anybody to buy them. I have not tried to sell any. I did not assume that any such securities could be sold between 1930 and 1933. I did not assume that I would finance it at this time. I know of no sales which would indicate that I might have sold large blocks of power securities in 1933-1934. I have used the rate

of 5% for the first issue of bonds, 4% for
the first issue of securities and 5% for the junior securities in my computation. I computed
6% as the average rate for the entire capital
required.''

"I am familiar with the area that will be
flooded both by a low dam and a high dam. My
initial dam would flood at least 600 tracts in
private ownerships. You could not make any
beneficial use of the proposed dam without the
flooding of lands in the reservoir site. The land
in the reservoir site must be flooded after the
water is raised behind the dam. I consider the
lands in the damsite have an inherent value due
to their natural properties and natural elements. Any desirability that the lands above
the dam site have for use as reservoir lands
depends entirely upon the inherent value of the
damsite itself, and any value the dam site may
have depends upon the use of the reservoir
lands. It would be impossible to operate a dam
without the reservoir lands.''

Marvin Chase, another engineer who testified for
defendants, stated on cross examination (Tr. p.
150):

"In making my estimates of value I *assumed*
a total estimated value of $3,055,000 for the en-
tire dam site. I did not allow anything for
that part of the dam site owned by the State in
the channel of the stream. I couldn't build a
dam at that site without having the lands owned
by the State in the channel of the stream, and
yet I did not allocate any part of the value to
those lands in the channel of the stream which
are indispensable to the construction of a dam.
I think private money could have been secured

for a development project of future construction at less than 6% interest in 1933. I cannot give any examples where private money was furnished for the construction of an irrigation project in 1933. Assuming private money would cost at least 6% and that in addition to the 6% on the construction cost of the project and the cost of operation and maintenance, you add the cost of power for pumping, the total annual cost per acre of the power project would be between $9.00 and $10.00. I cannot believe a district could pay 6%. I think it is a wrong assumption to assume a district or anyone else would pay 6%. It would not be feasible to pay 6%."

Alone among defendants' witnesses, Mr. R. H. Thompson (with characteristic contempt for all law and all legal and property rights of the government and the state) declares (Tr. p. 154):

"The law granting the right of way to the Government is no difficulty. The fact that the Government has the right of way does not stop me."

Evidently prospective buyers (if there ever were any prospective buyers) did not share Mr. Thompson's contempt for the law and for the property rights of the government and the state, and most assuredly they did not subscribe to his legal opinion that "the law granting the right of way to the government is no difficulty" and "the fact that the government has the right of way does not stop me", for Mr. William P. Creager, another witness for the defendants testified (Tr. pp. 141, 143):

"But if they could not get those necessary rights of way they certainly would not throw away $3,000,000 buying land at the dam site."

"I do not know why private capital did not purchase it then except that the previous effort to purchase it was denied on the ground that the Government wanted it. I really have not sufficient knowledge to answer the question as to why that property was not purchased in 1929 except that in my business I keep in touch with these things and I have gathered from different sources that the Government was withholding permission from private capital to build that dam from the time an attempt was made to file on it in 1921 or 1922 by Mr. Cooper."

In sharp contrast to the entire lack of qualification on the part of the defendants' witnesses (who have no expert knowledge except as engineers) to give opinion testimony as to the market value of land in the vicinity of the Grand Coulee dam site, we find the plaintiff's witnesses abundantly and unquestionably qualified to give such testimony as appears in the record as follows:

"My name is W. R. Prowell. I live in Wenatchee, Washington, and have lived there for 44 years. Practically during all the period since 1891 I have bought and developed and sold real estate in the Columbia River Valley and territory adjacent thereto. These lands which I have been selling and buying include grazing and dry-farming lands in the vicinity of the Columbia River. I am familiar with the lands described in the complaint in this case and have been dealing in other lands of that character. I examined the lands involved in this case on

September 18 or October 18, 1933, and I have observed them on occasions since that date." (Tr. pp. 67, 68.)

"My name is Thomas F. Roddy and I live in Wenatchee. I have lived there something over 25 years. I have been in the orchard business and in the real-estate business buying and selling and owning and operating various kinds of land on the Columbia River and its tributaries. For the past ten years I have been exclusively in the real estate business and own land bordering on the Columbia River at the present time. I have had experience in appraising land for others than the Government. Between December 18 and 27, 1933 I examined and was over all the lands involved in this suit." (Tr. pp. 70, 71.)

"My full name is W. R. Cooley and I live in Spokane. I have lived there for 35 years. The last 25 years I have been in the general real estate business which has included handling of land all through eastern Washington. I have done appraisal work on many occasions for the government and for clients of my own. I have owned lands myself, mainly farming and grazing lands and irrigated tracts. I have owned lands in Okanogan, Lincoln and Grant counties and I own some in Grant county now. I first saw the lands in this suit in 1930 and on several occasions I went over these lands in 1933." (Tr. p. 75.)

Without exception all the qualified witnesses testified that this land did not in fact have any value for dam site purposes, the testimony on this question being as follows:

W. R. Prowell:

"The Seaton lands are most suitable for grazing, portions being used for dry-farming. * * * The Raths lands are the same—most suitable for grazing—but a portion of them were tilled and in crops and stubble at the different times I viewed them." (Tr. p. 68.)

"Leaving out of consideration the Government project, there was no value to the lands involved in this case for damsite purposes. There is no market for damsites in that territory." (Tr. p. 70.)

Thos. F. Roddy:

"There is no market value for the land for damsite purposes."

"The discussion about tthe Grand Coulee project during recent years has been a discussion with reference to the attempt to get the government interested in building that project and there never has been any private enterprise ever contemplated, to my knowledge, in all of this time." (Tr. p. 74.)

W. R. Cooley:

"None of the lands involved in this suit had any market value in December, 1933 for damsite or reservoir purposes. There was no market demand for a damsite of such size as this at this location that I know of." (Tr. p. 78.)

G. H. Sellar:

"None of the lands to which I have referred had any market value for a damsite or reservoir purposes in December, 1933." (Tr. p. 79.)

The Columbia River is the second largest stream in the United States, larger than the St. Lawrence and surpassed in volume of flow only by the Mississippi. It carries more water than the combined flow of all the other streams of the Pacific slope. It is unique among all the streams of the West in that it is the only stream which has broken through the mountain barrier of the Cascade and Sierra Nevada mountains and created a navigable channel from the interior to the Pacific Ocean. It has been used extensively for navigation purposes ever since the date of the earliest settlement of the white man, and even prior to that time was used by the Indians as a highway for such trade and travel as was carried on among the Indian tribes.

The court will take judicial knowledge of the fact that the Columbia is a navigable stream in fact as well as in law.

> *Arizona v. California,* 283 U. S., 423; 75 L. ed., 1154.

It carries about ten times as much water as the Colorado river, of which the supreme court said:

> "We know judicially from the evidence of history, that a large part of the Colorado river south of Black Canyon was formerly navigable, and that the main obstacles to navigation have been the accumulations of silt coming from the upper reaches of the river system, and the irregularity in the flow due to periods of low

water. Commercial disuse resulting from
changed geographical conditions and a congressional failure to deal with them does not amount
to an abandonment of a navigable river or prohibit future exertion of Federal control."

Arizona v. Calif., 283 U. S., 423, 454; 75
L. ed., 1154, 1164-1165.

It is alleged in the complaint (Tr. pp. 5, 6, 7, 8)
and expressly admitted in the answer (Tr. p. 16):

"VI.

"That pursuant to the acts of Congress of
June 17, 1902 (32 Stat. 388) and of June 16,
1933 (48 Stat. 195), the Secretary of the Interior of the United States of America as such
officer and as Federal Emergency Administrator of Public Works has caused surveys and
investigations to be made of the Columbia Basin
project on the Columbia River, a federal project
having for its purposes:

"Regulation of the flow of said stream by
storage reservoirs; and

"Coordinated development and use of said
stream for the various purposes for which it is
adapted, including navigation, hydro-electric power, flood control and irrigation, including irrigation of public lands of the
United States,

all in respect to the waters of the Columbia
River and contemplating the construction of
dams for storage of the waters thereof and
means for the diversion thereof and the utilization of the power generated by such storage and
diversion, all in pursuance of the Constitution
and laws of the United States; that such sur-

veys and investigations have been particularly directed to the immediate plans of construction of a dam across said Columbia River at or near the head of the Grand Coulee, which dam constitutes the first unit and an integral part of a larger Grand Coulee dam which will form a part of the complete Columbia Basin project and serve as the diversion dam therefor and also as the principal storage reservoir on said stream to regulate the flow of said stream for flood control and to serve the purposes of navigation and power development at all points on such stream below said Grand Coulee dam.

"VII.

"That under appropriations made for that purpose by Congress, the Corps of Engineers, United States Army have conducted exhaustive investigations of the Columbia River for the purpose of determining the best use of said stream and its tributaries for the various purposes to which it is adapted and has adopted a comprehensive and coordinated plan for the development and use of said stream for navigation, flood control and irrigation and for the development of electrical energy to pay the cost of the proposed construction and for irrigation, pumping and industrial and domestic use.

"VIII.

"That the said comprehensive plan for the coordinated development of the Columbia River for navigation, flood control, power, and irrigation includes the construction of a series of dams at various points on the Columbia River, the uppermost of which is the Grand Coulee Dam.

"IX.

"That the said Grand Coulee Dam is the key structure in the said comprehensive plan for the coordinated development of said stream, in that the said Grand Coulee Dam will provide the necessary storage capacity to store the peaks of the Columbia River floods and by storing the floods and releasing the stored water during the low water season will improve the flow of said stream for navigation, power development, and irrigation and will reduce the flood dangers on the lower part of the stream.

"X.

"That it is estimated that the storage to be made available behind the said Grand Coulee Dam will about double the amount of firm power which can be developed at each of the proposed dam sites between the Grand Coulee and the mouth of the Snake River and will increase by about 50% the amount of firm power that can be developed at each of the several dam sites below the mouth of the Snake and that the said increased amount of firm power made possible at each of said lower dams by reason of the storage behind the Grand Coulee Dam is an important factor in the feasibility of each of said lower dams as a self-liquidating project.

"XI.

"That in pursuance of the provisions of the said act of June 16, 1933 (48 Stat. 195) the Emergency Public Works Board and the Emergency Public Works Administrator under the authorization of the President of the United States has allocated for the construction of said first unit dam and appurtenant structures from the Emergency Public Works Fund, available by reason of said last mentioned act, a sum of money estimated as sufficient to construct said dam and acquire the necessary rights of way therefor; and in pursuance of said last mentioned act, and the allocation made thereunder, the said Secretary and Emergency Public Works Administrator has authorized the construction of said dam and the reservoir to be formed thereby and the acquisition of the necessary rights of way therefor."

The answer alleges:

"Defendants * * * 'admit paragraphs 1, 2, 3, 4, 5, 6, 7, 8, 9, 10, 11, 12, 13, 14, 15 and 16 to be true'."

The testimony of F. A. Banks, engineer in charge of the Grand Coulee project, includes the following:

"The proposed dam which is under construction at this time will serve the purposes of a diversion dam for the Columbia Basin project, improvement of navigation by creating a lake 150 miles long running from the dam to the Canadian boundary and, by regulation of the low flow of the river and increasing it, will improve navigation all the way from the dam site to the coast." (Tr. p. 55.)

This testimony has not been questioned by defendants and is not in any way disputed.

Mr. Banks also furnished the following undisputed testimony (Tr. pp. 56, 57):

"That foundation, including construction of 200 feet below the high water line of the river, is necessary before any head can be secured for power development purposes. The cost of putting in the foundation up to the point before any head is secured for power development purposes is about $60,000,000.

"There are over 600 separate tracts of private land in different ownerships which will be flooded by the low dam. There are about 900 different owners of the various tracts of private lands which will be flooded by the low dam. The number of separate ownerships of private land which will be flooded by the high dam is about twice as many as flooded by the low dam.

"The nearest tribal lands of the Colville Indian Reservation are located just a little over half a mile above the dam, as shown on the photograph Plaintiffs' Exhibit B. The Indian reservation extends along that side of the river for over 100 miles, about 120 miles above the dam. It would not be possible to construct any dam at that site without flooding both the allotted lands and the tribal lands of the Colville Indian Reservation. Another Indian reservation which will be flooded by the back waters from the dam is the Spokane Indian Reservation.

"A map showing the location of the Indian reservation lands and the reservoir site was admitted in evidence as Plaintiff's Exhibit C.

"Mr. Banks (continuing): This map, Plaintiff's Exhibit C, was prepared under my direction and shows the flow line for the dam called the Grand Coulee high dam and in single cross-hatching are shown the Indan lands and in double cross-hatching are shown the lands that are public lands withdrawn under the first form from all forms of entry. The double cross-hatched lands have been withdrawn for power

site purposes and they were so withdrawn prior
to the time these suits were filed.''

At the time this case was tried funds for this
construction had been allotted by order of the
President out of the funds appropriated by Congress under the provisions of the Public Works section of the National Industrial Recovery Act of
June 16, 1933. (48 Stat. 195.)

The Rivers and Harbors Act of August 30, 1935
(49 Stat. 1039), which was then pending before
Congress and which became a law shortly thereafter, contains the following provision:

"That for the purpose of controlling floods,
improving navigation, regulating the flow of the
streams of the United States, providing for
storage and for the delivery of the stored waters
thereof, for the reclamation of public lands and
Indian reservations, and other beneficial uses,
and for the generation of electric energy as a
means of financially aiding and assisting such
undertakings, the projects known as 'Parker
Dam' on the Colorado River and 'Grand Coulee Dam' on the Columbia River, are hereby
authorized and adopted, and all contracts and
agreements which have been executed in connection therewith are hereby validated and ratified, and the President, acting through such
agents as he may designate, is hereby authorized
to construct, operate, and maintain dams, structures, canals, and incidental works necessary to
such projects, and in connection therewith to
make and enter into any and all necessary contracts including contracts amendatory of or

supplemental to those hereby validated and ratified.''

Preferring to expedite the trial rather than to await the final enactment of the pending act of Congress, the parties to this action (at the beginning of the trial of this case) all agreed upon the following stipulation (Tr. p. 42):

"Mr. Stoutemyer: The plaintiff and all the defendants have agreed that the government has a right to condemn the property described in the complaint in this case and that the only issue for trial is the value of the property.

"To this stipulation the attorneys for defendants assented and the court then ordered:

"JUDGE WEBSTER: Let the record so show.''

by which stipulation the parties narrowed the issues of this case to the single question of the value of the property sought to be condemned.

The parties also signed, filed and introduced in evidence a written stipulation (Tr. pp. 42, 43, 44, 45, 46, 47) which contains the following provisions:

"IT IS FURTHER STIPULATED AND AGREED that the backwater from the Grand Coulee Dam now under construction (the low dam) will flood about eighteen thousand acres of privately owned land divided into six hundred tracts in different ownerships, also some public lands of the United States and lands of t he Colville and Spokane Indian Reservations including both tribal and allotted lands. That prior to the date of the filing of the complaint in the above entitled cause of action, the Columbia Basin Commission filed upon and secured a permit to appropriate under the state law 100,-000 second-feet of the water of the Columbia River for use in connection with the Columbia Basin project, and stands ready to assign such water filings to the United States for the purposes of the said project. That the lands which will be flooded by the backwaters from the said dam also include state lands of the State of Washington, both uplands and riparian lands, and lands in the bed of the stream. That under date of January 4, 1934 the Secretary of the Interior filed with the State Commissioner of Public Lands of the State of Washington the notice copy of which is hereto attached as Exhibit A and the list of lands attached hereto, which shows the various tracts of state lands to be used in whole or in part for the purposes of the said project. That the Colville Indian Reservation borders the Columbia River for a number of miles immediately above the said Grand Coulee damsite and that any power dam constructed at such site would necessarily flood some of such Indian reservation lands, including both allotted and tribal Indian lands."

ARGUMENT AND AUTHORITIES

Respondent's Position

The question whether Judge Webster was or was not in error in instructing the jury in the language of the Supreme Court quoted from the Chandler-Dunbar case, as set out on pages 2 and 3 of this brief (Tr. pp. 177, 178, 179) naturally divides itself into three parts or three questions on which our position is as follows:

First—Judge Webster's decision was correct and in harmony with the decisions of the Supreme Court on the grounds on which he placed it and should be confirmed on those grounds; that is on account of the government's paramount right, title and control over the beds and waters of navigable streams for the purpose of the improvement of navigation and the state's ownership of the same subject to the government's paramount right therein, the defendants did not own any dam site but only the worthless right to build down to but not beyond the high-water line of the river, without any right or title to, and without any ability to secure the all important section across the river channel and without any right to flood the government and state property in the reservoir site which is indispensable to any effective use of the dam.

United States v. Chandler-Dunbar Co., 229 U. S., 53; 57 L. ed., 1063;

Lewis Blue Point Oyster Co. v. Briggs, 229
U. S., 82;

Ashwander v. Tenn. Valley Authority, 80
L. ed., adv. sheets, 427;

Article 17, Sec. 1, of Constitution of State
of Washington;

Sec. 7412, Remington's Revised Stat. of
Washington, Annotated;

Arizona v. California, 80 L. ed., Advance
sheets, 877-882.

But that if this court should not agree with the
trial judge on the grounds on which the trial judge
placed his decision, the decision was nevertheless
correct and should be sustained on other grounds,
as follows:

Second—That the decision sustaining the plaintiff's motion to strike out defendants' testimony as
to claimed value for dam site purposes and instructing the jury to disregard such testimony was correct and should be sustained because all the qualified testimony was that this land did not in fact
have any additional value on account of alleged
adaptability for dam site purposes (see testimony
referred to on pages 13 and 14 of this brief) and
that the only testimony offered by defendants as to
their claimed land values was the testimony of engineers who were experts only on engineering questions but had no qualifications whatever to offer
opinion evidence as to the market value of land in

that section of Eastern Washington in which the Grand Coulee dam site is located (Tr. pp. 95, 96, 120, 131, 132, 133).

Third—Because it has been shown that the lowest dam which would be considered either for government or private construction would flood more than 600 separately owned tracts of private land held by more than 900 different owners and that the number of ownerships flooded by the high dam would be twice that many (Tr. pp. 43, 44, 56, 130) as well as thousands of acres of reserved government lands included in Indian Reservation, Power site withdrawals, and 1st form Reclamation withdrawals which are not open to appropriation by defendants (Tr. pp. 56, 57, 43, 44) and also thousands of acres of state lands, both river bottom and uplands which have been dedicated by the state statute to the use of the federal reclamation project (Sec. 7412, Rem. Rev. Stat. of Wash.) and are reserved from any other disposition or use. These facts, considered in connection with the rule established by repeated decisions of the Supreme Court that where the lands required for a dam or reservoir project are in divided ownership no owner of any one or any number of such tracts less than the whole is entitled to any part or share of the value of the whole for dam or reservoir purposes unless there is a reasonable probability that all of the different ownerships could be brought into one ownership without resorting to eminent domain,

> *McGovern v. New York,* 229 U. S., 371-372;
> 57 L. ed., 1232;
>
> *New York v. Sage,* 239 U. S., 57, 60-62;
> 60 L. ed., 143, 146;
>
> *Boston Chamber of Commerce v. Boston,*
> 217 U. S., 189, 195; 54 L. ed., 725, 727;
>
> *Chandler-Dunbar Water Power Co. v.*
> *United States,* 229 U. S., 53; 57 L. ed.,
> 1063;
>
> *Olson v. United States,* 292 U. S., 246; 78
> L. ed., 1236;
>
> *C. B. & Q. RR. Co. v. Chicago,* 166 U. S.,
> 226; 41 L. ed., 979;
>
> *United States v. Seufert Bros. Co.,* 78 F.
> (2d), 520, 523;

necessarily lead to the conclusion that on account of the divided and widely scattered ownership of the lands (government, state and private) which are indispensable to any beneficial use of the dam site and reservoir site, the defendants are not entitled to any allowance of dam site value and would not be even if the Columbia River was not a navigable stream and if the project was not being constructed for the purpose of improving navigation.

Leaving out of consideration (as the Supreme Court requires) the possibility of resort to condemnation to combine into one ownership the widely

scattered ownerships in the reservoir site, there isn't
one chance in ten thousand that 600 separately
owned tracts of private land held by more than
900 different owners could be voluntarily combined
into one ownership without any one of the 900 owners holding out, and when you add to the difficulty
of combining the more than 600 tracts of privately
owned land held by more than 900 different owners
without resorting to condemnation, the still more
difficult task of acquiring without the consent of the
government the thousands of acres of government
reserved lands held in three different kinds of reservations (Indian reservations, Power site withdrawals and 1st form Reclamation Act withdrawals) and
the thousands of acres of state lands, both submerged lands and uplands which the state statute
(Sec. 7412, Rem. Rev. Stat.) requires should be reserved for and devoted to the purposes of the federal reclamation project and not transferred for
any other purpose, the chance that the defendants
or any prospective buyer from the defendants could
acquire without condemnation and combine into
one ownership all of the lands (state, federal and
private) which would be required for the completed
dam and reservoir, is not only extremely improbable
but absolutely impossible and therefore not an element which can be considered as contributing value
to the lands involved in this action.

We will discuss in the order named above, the

three grounds on which we contend that the decision of the trial court should be sustained.

First Ground for Sustaining the Decision of the Trial Court

Discussion of Paramount Right, Title and Control of Federal Government Over the Beds and Waters of Navigable Streams.

We think it will be agreed that on this question the leading case and the one most directly in point is the case of United States v. Chandler-Dunbar Water Power Company, supra. It has been followed repeatedly and in every instance upheld by the later decisions of the Supreme Court. After a statement of the case, Mr. Justice Lurton said:

"From the foregoing it will be seen that the controlling questions are, first, whether the Chandler-Dunbar Company has any private property in the water power capacity of the rapids and falls of the St. Marys river which has been 'taken' and for which compensation must be made under the 5th Amendment to the Constitution; and, second, if so, what is the extent of its water power right and how shall the compensation be measured?

"That compensation must be made for the upland taken is not disputable. The measure of compensation may in a degree turn upon the relation of that species of property to the alleged water power rights claimed by the Chandler-Dunbar Company. We therefore pass for the present the errors assigned which concern the awards made for such upland.

"The technical title to the beds of the navigable rivers of the United States is either in the states in which the rivers are situated, or in the owners of the land bordering upon such rivers. Whether in one or the other is a question of local law. * * *

"Upon the admission of the State of Michigan into the Union the bed of the St. Marys river passed to the state, and under the law of that state the conveyance of a tract of land upon a navigable river carries the title to the middle thread. * * *

"The technical title of the Chandler-Dunbar Company, therefore, includes the bed of the river opposite its upland on the bank to the middle thread of the stream, being the boundary line at that point between the United States and the Dominion of Canada. Over this bed flows about two-thirds of the volume of water constituting the falls and rapids of the St. Marys river. By reason of that fact, and the ownership of the shore, the company's claim is, that it is owner of the river and of the inherent power in the falls and rapids, subject only to the public right of navigation."

U. S. v. Chandler-Dunbar Co., supra.

It will be readily seen that in the case above referred to the Chandler-Dunbar Water Power Company was in a far stronger position than are any of the defendants in the instant case, for under the Michigan law the Chandler-Dunbar Company as the owner of the riparian lands also owned the bed and shore of the navigable stream subject only to the paramount right of control vested in the federal government for the purposes of navigation, while the defendants in the instant case have no right, title or interest of any sort, nature or kind below the "ordinary high water line" of the Columbia River.

Article XVII, Section 1 of the Constitution of the State of Washington provides:

"The state of Washington asserts its ownership to the beds and shores of all navigable waters in the state up to and including the line of ordinary high tide in waters where the tide ebbs and flows, and up to and including the line of ordinary high water within the banks of all navigable rivers and lakes: Provided, that this section shall not be construed so as to debar any person from asserting his claim to vested rights in the courts of the state."

And Section 7412, Remington's Revised Statutes of Washington (Sec. 3380, Pierce's Code) provides:

"When the notice provided for in section 7410 shall be given to the commissioner of public lands the proper officers of the United States may file with the said commissioner a list of lands (including in the term 'lands' as here used, the beds and shores of any lake, river, stream, or other waters) owned by the state, over or upon which the United States may require rights of way for canals, ditches or laterals or sites for reservoirs and structures therefor or appurtenant thereto, or such additional rights of way and quantity of land as may be required for the operation and maintenance of

the completed works for the irrigation project
contemplated in such notice, and the filing of
such list shall constitute a reservation from the
sale or other disposal by the state of such lands
so described, which reservation shall, upon the
completion of such works and upon the United
States by its proper officers filing with the commissioner of public lands of the state a description of such lands by metes and bounds or other
definite description, ripen into a grant from the
state to the United States. The state, in the disposal of lands granted from the United States
to the state, shall reserve for the United States
rights of way for ditches, canals, laterals, telephone and transmission lines which may be required by the United States for the construction, operation and maintenance of irrigation
works."

In this connection see also the notice (Exhibit A)
attached to stipulation (Tr. pp. 46, 47, 48).

Some other respects in which the defendants in
the Chandler-Dunbar case were in an infinitely
stronger position than are the defendants in the
instant case included the following.

The development of the power "inherent in the
falls and rapids of the river" in that case

"(a) did not require the flooding of thousands
of acres of Indian Reservation lands, which can
not be secured without the consent of the Government;.

"(b) did not require the flooding of public
lands withdrawn from all forms of entry under
the 1st form of withdrawal authorized by the

Reclamation Act of June 17, 1902 (32 Stat. 388);

"(c) did not require the flooding of public lands withdrawn as power sites;

(d) did not require the bringing together into one ownership (without resort to condemnation) of over 600 separate ownerships of private land held by over 900 different owners; and

"(e) did not require the acquisition of a 100,-000 second-feet prior water appropriation under state laws, which in the instant case is indispensable to the project and held by adverse parties (the Columbia Basin Commission) and referred to in the stipulation as follows: (Tr. pp. 43, 44):

"That prior to the date of the filing of the complaint in the above entitled cause of action the Columbia Basin Commission filed upon and secured a permit to appropriate under the state law 100,000 second-feet of the water of the Columbia River for use in connection with the Columbia Basin project and stands ready to assign such water filings to the United States for the purposes of the said project."

In the instant case the defendants, in addition to the insurmountable obstacles presented by the government's paramount right, title and control over the bed and waters of the navigable stream, and the state's subordinate title thereto, would also have to overcome the additional obstacles (also unsurmountable) which we have listed above as (a), (b), (c), (d) and (e) before the defendants could realize any of the profits of the proposed private power development on which they base their claim to dam site values.

Although the Chandler-Dunbar Company actually owned the bed of the navigable streams involved in that case, subject only to the government's right of control and use for improvement of navigation, and the only obstacle which stood between the company and the realization of prospective power profits sought to be capitalized as a part of the value of defendants' property was the government's right to control and use the bed of the navigable stream for the improvement of navigation, the Supreme Court decided against the defendant on the following grounds:

> "While not denying that this right of navigation is the dominating right, yet the claim is that the United States, in the exercise of the power to regulate commerce, may not exclude the rights of riparian owners to construct in the river and upon their own submerged lands such appliances as are necessary to control and use the current for commercial purposes, provided only that such structures do not impede or hinder navigation, and that the flow of the stream is not so diminished as to leave less than every possible requirement of navigation, present and future. This claim of a proprietary right in the bed of the river and in the flow of the stream over that bed, to the extent that such flow is in excess of the wants of navigation, constitutes the ground upon which the company asserts that a necessary effect of the Act of March 3ʼ 1909, and of the judgment

of condemnation in the Court below, is a taking from it of a property right of interest of great value, for which, under the 5th Amendment, compensation must be made.

"This is the view which was entertained by Circuit Judge Dennison in the court below and is supported by most careful findings of fact and law and an elaborate and able opinion. The question is therefore one which, from every standpoint, deserves careful consideration.

"This title of the owner of fast land upon the shore of a navigable river to the bed of the river is, at best, a qualified one. It is a title which inheres in the ownership of the shore; and, unless reserved or excluded by implication, passed with it as a shadow follows a substance, although capable of distinct ownership. It is subordinate to the public right of navigation, and however helpful in protecting the owner against the act of third parties, is of no avail against the exercise of the great and absolute power of Congress over the improvement of navigable rivers. That power of use and control comes from the power to regulate commerce between the states and with foreign nations. It includes navigation and subjects every navigable river to the control of Congress. All means having some possible relation to the end in view which are not forbidden by some other provision of the Constitution, are admissible. If, in the judgment of Congress, the use of the bottom of the river is proper for the purpose of placing therein structures in aid of navigation, it is not thereby taking private property for a public use, for the owner's title was in its very nature subject to that use in the interest of navigation. If its judgment be that structures placed in the river and upon such submerged land are an obstruction or hindrance to the proper use of the river for purposes of navigation, it may require their removal and forbid the use of the bed of the river by the owner in any way, which, in its judgment, is injurious to the dominant right of navigation. So, also, it may permit the construction and maintenance of tunnels under or bridges over the river, and may require the removal of every such structure placed there with or without its license, the element of contract out of the way, which it shall require to be removed or altered as an obstruction to navigation. * * *

"Thus, in Scranton v. Wheeler, 179 U. S. 141, 163, 45 L. ed. 126, 137 * * this court said:

" 'The primary use of the waters and the lands under them is for the purposes of navigation, and the erection of piers in them to improve navigation for the public is entirely consistent with such use, and infringes no right of the riparian owner. Whatever the nature of the interest of a riparian owner in the submerged lands in front of his upland bounding on a public navigable water, his title is not as full and complete as his title to fast land which has no direct connection with the navigation of such waters. It is a qualified title, a bare technical title, not at his absolute disposal, as is his upland, but to be held at all times as subordinate to such use of the submerged lands and of the waters flowing over them as may be consistent with or demanded by the public right of navigation.'

"So unfettered is this control of Congress over navigable streams of the country that its judgment as to whether a construction in or over such a river is or is not an obstacle and a hindrance to navigation is conclusive. Such judgment and determination is the exercise of legislative power in respect of a subject wholly within its control. * * *

"It is a little difficult to understand the basis or the claim that in appropriating the upland bordering upon this stretch of water, the government not only takes the land, but also the great water power which potentially exists in the river. The broad claim that the water power of the stream is appurtenant to the bank owned by it, and not dependent upon ownership of the soil over which the river flows, has been advanced. But whether this private right to the use of the flow of the water and flow of the stream be based upon the qualified title which the company had to the bed of the river over which it flows, is of no prime importance. In neither event can there be said to arise any ownership of the river. Ownership of a private stream wholly upon the lands of an individual is conceivable; but that the running water in a great navigable stream is capable of private ownership is inconceivable.

"Whatever substantial private property rights exist in the flow of the stream must come from some right which that company has to construct and maintain such works in the river, such as dams, walls, dykes, etc., essential to the utilization of the power of the stream for commercial purposes. We may put out of view altogether the class of cases which deal with the right of riparian owners upon non-navigable stream to the use and enjoyment of the stream and its water." * * *

"To utilize the rapids and fall of the river which flows by the upland of the Chandler-Dunbar Company, it has been and will be necessary to construct and maintain in the river the structures necessary to control and direct the flow so that it may be used for commercial purposes.

* * *

"Upon what principle can it be said that, in requiring the removal of the development works which were in the river upon sufferance, Congress has taken private property for public use without compensation? In deciding that a necessity existed for absolute control of the river at the rapids, Congress has, of course, excluded, until it changes the law, every such construction as a hindrance to its plans and purposes for the betterment of navigation. The qualified t itle to the bed of the river affords no ground for any claim of a right to construct and maintain therein any structure which Congress has, by the act of 1909, decided in effect to be an obstruction to navigation, and a hindrance to its plans for improvement. That title is absolutely subordinate to the right of navigation, and no right of private property would have been invaded if such submerged lands were occupied by structures in aid of navigation, or kept free from such obstructions in the interest of navigation. * * *

"Having decided that the Chandler-Dunbar Company, as riparian owners, had no such vested property right in the water power inherent in the falls and rapids of the river, and no right to place in the river the works essential to any practical use of the flow of the river, the government cannot be justly required to pay for an element of value which did not inhere in these parcels as upland. The government had dominion over the water power of the rapids and falls, and cannot be required to pay any hypothetical additional value to a riparian owner who had no right to appropriate the current to his own commercial use. These additional values represent, therefore, no actual loss, and there would be no justice in paying for a loss suffered by no one in fact. 'The requirement of the 5th Amendment is satisfied when the owner is paid for what is taken from him. The question is what has the owner lost, and not what has the taker gained.'"

> *United States v. Chandler-Dunbar Co., supra.*

At the close of counsel's argument on this question in the trial court, Judge Webster analyzed the Chandler-Dunbar case and answered defendants' argument in a manner so clear and concise that we find it impossible to improve on the language used by the trial judge and therefore will simply quote Judge Webster's oral statement to counsel as our reply to appellants argument so far as the Chandler-Dunbar Company case is concerned. Judge Webster said:

> "Now in the syllabi of that case the writer states the principle announced in this paragraph of this opinion, it seems to me with perfect accuracy in this language:

> " 'An owner of upland bordering upon a navigable river which is taken under condemnation by the government for the purpose of improving navigation is entitled to compensation for the fair value of the property but not to any additional value based upon private interest in the potential water power of the river.'

> "The pronouncements of general principles often may be tested by subjecting them to practical application. Supposing in this case I

should undertake to follow the argument of
counsel and say to the 'jury, 'In the state of
Washington the beds of navigable streams are
vested in the State; that none of these abutting
owners have any title to the bed of the stream',
and I should also say to them 'that as riparian
owners along the shore of a navigable river
such as the Columbia River, the Government
has the right as against them to make any improvements in the river which it sees fit to
make, which in its judgment is in aid of navigation, and that these owners have no title to
the flow of the waters in the stream, nor any
title to the bed of the stream, but, in determining the value of this dam site, Gentlemen of
the Jury, you must take into account that the
ownership of the stream is not in the defendants, and the ownership of the water is not in
the defendants, but you must give it a special
value as a dam site, leaving out of consideration the Columbia River.' How can there be a
practical application of a refinement so nice?
How can it be said that the owner of the land
is confined to the special uses and adaptabilities
for which his property is valuable, and that if
it has a special adaptability for use as a dam
site 'you have a right to take its use for that
purpose into consideration, and if its special
adaptability for that purpose enhances its fair
market value you may give that additional
value to the owner, but in that consideration
you must leave out of mind that the Government isn't taking from you either the bed of
the stream or the waters which flow in it.

"The theory of these cases, to my mind, is
plain, logical and sound. The owner is not entitled to recover for the simple reason that he
has not been deprived of anything which he
owns, and the Government is compelled to pay

the owner for what it takes. The Government already owned the bed of the stream, so if these abutting owners didn't own it, or if the Government already had a right, in the exercise of its power to improve and develop navigation, to use that water and convert it to its own use, it didn't deprive these abutting land owners, because neither of them ever owned it, either in whole or in part, in the first place, so far as the Government of the United States, in the exercise of its power to control navigation is concerned.

"My conclusion, therefore is,—

"MR. LEWIS: Begging the Court's pardon for interrupting the Court's pronouncement but I wonder if the Court would permit me to ask leave to be heard briefly?

"JUDGE WEBSTER: No, the arguments are over—there comes a time when we have to finish. There was one suggestion made in the argument which, I think, deserves comment. Before going to that I wish to make this thing very plain—and I do not want to be misunderstood upon any assumption or any interpretation of what I have said, that I am holding that the availability of a particular piece of property for a particular use may not be shown in a condemnation case even though the property is being condemned for that every use. The Chandler-Dunbar case deals with that, and the overwhelming weight of authorities holds just as I have ruled in every stage of this case. The fact that property has a special adaptability as a dam site is to be taken into account in deciding its value, even though taken for the purpose of a dam site, but the point I rest my ruling upon is that it must be a taking of something which the owner possesses, and if the lands here in question are to be appraised upon their inherent value as lecided in the Chandler-Dunbar case, then it necessarily follows that you cannot take it into account as a dam site without taking into consideration the flow of the river, and you must and cannot escape transferring to the uplands the inherent qualities that are vested in the lands which it does not possess. Now, it is the value which inheres in the property taken and is the thing to be valued.

"Harking back to this again—

"'Having decided that the Chandler-Dunbar Company as riparian owners, have no such vested property right in the water power inherent in the falls and rapids of the river, and no right to place in the river the works essential to any practical use of the flow of the river, the government cannot be justly required to pay for an element of value which did not inhere in these parcels of upland.'

"Well, if they haven't any riparian rights nor rights which have been taken from them, there is nothing else you can value them upon except their inherent value as upland. If you undertake to take into consideration the flow of this stream and the waters that are used, and by that reason say that this dam has an especially attractive value, you are transferring, and cannot escape transferring the inherent quality of the riparian rights to the inherent quality of the upland, and the uplands are all these property owners own in this controversy as against the government.

"Now the portion of the case upon which counsel touched this morning as sustaining his contention: it will be noted here in the statement of the case that there were some small parcels of land, a narrow strip of upland bordering on the river, having an area of something more than eight acres, excluding the small parcels described in the pleadings and judgment as claims 95 and 96—now

" 'The exception taken to the inclusion as an element of value of the availability of these parcels of land for lock and canal purposes must be overruled. That this land had a prospective value for the purpose of constructing a canal and lock parallel with those in use had passed beyond the region of the purely conjectural or speculative. That one or more additional parallel canals and locks would be needed to meet the increasing demands of lake traffic was an immediate probability. This land was the only land available for the purpose. It included all the lands between the canals in use and the bank of the river, although it is not proper to estimate land condemned for public purposes by the public necessities or its worth to the public for such purpose, it is proper to consider the fact that the property is so situated that it will probably be desired and available for such a purpose.'

"Now all the court undertook to decide on that question was you may show the special availability of a piece of property and show its availability for that particular thing or purpose for which it is being condemned. There is no question in this instance of riparian ownership of the flow of the stream or the power which it would develop. This is a question of structures on land which in no way interferes with the development of or improvement of navigation by the Government in the exercise of its paramount right to develop and improve navigation."

If the appellants could show that the uplands
owned by them (which is the only property they
own) have a special value for canal right of way
purposes independent of the government project
for which they are being condemned and could be
used for such purpose without trespassing on the
property of the United States and the State of
Washington in the river bottom lands and shore
lands of the navigable stream and without interfering with the flow of the navigable stream over which
the government has complete and paramount right
of control and without flooding the reserved state
and federal lands in the reservoir site, they would
have the right to show that; but in the instant case
it is not claimed and cannot be claimed that the
appellants' lands have any value (other than the
amount awarded by the jury) for any purpose
which could be carried out without occupying, using
and converting to appellants' use the government
and state property and rights in the bed and shores
of the Columbia River, the water flowing therein,
and the reserved state and federal lands in the
reservoir site above the proposed dam.

What appellants are trying to do is to mulct the
government for from $3,000,000 to $5,000,000 for
1100 acres of desert land on account of alleged dam
site values arrived at by capitalizing the alleged
profits which it is assumed would be derived from
building a power dam several hundred feet high on

the river bottom lands and shore lands belonging to
the United States and the State of Washington,
impounding and interfering with the flow of the
navigable stream, and flooding many thousands of
acres of reserved state and federal lands in the reservoir site as well as private lands held by over 900
different owners, and that is just what the Supreme
Court has decided can not be done.

The next case which came before the Supreme
Court of the United States dealing with this question was at the same term and decided at the same
time and in that case also the opinion was written
by Justice Lurton. I refer to the case of *Lewis
Blue Point Oyster Co. v. Briggs,* 229 U. S., 82, 57
L. ed., 1083, in which the court said:

> "That case and the later one cited fail to
> recognize the qualified nature of the title which
> a private owner may have in the lands lying
> under navigable waters. If the public right of
> navigation is the dominant right, and if, as
> must be the case, the title of the owner of the
> bed of navigable waters holds subject absolutely
> to the public right of navigation, this dominant
> right must include the right to use the bed of
> the water for every purpose which is in aid of
> navigation. This right to control, improve, and
> regulate the navigation of such water is one of
> the greatest of the powers delegated to the
> United States by the power to regulate com-
> merce. Whatever power the several states had
> before the Union was formed, over the nav-
> igable waters within their several jurisdictions,

had been delegated to the Congress, in which, therefore, is centered all of the governmental power over the subject, restricted only by such limitations as are found in other clauses of the Constitution.

"By necessary implication from the dominant right of navigation, title to such submerged lands is acquired and held subject to the power of Congress to deepen the water over such lands, or to use them for any structure which the interest of navigation, in its judgment, may require. The plaintiff in error has, therefore, no such private property right which, when taken, or incidentally destroyed by the dredging of a deep water channel across it, entitles him to demand compensation as a condition."

Lewis Blue Point Oyster Co. v. Briggs, supra.

The last word from the Supreme Court on this important subject is found in the very recent case of *Ashwander v. Tennessee Valley Authority*, 80 L. ed. advance sheets, 427, in which the court said:

"The Act of 1916 also had in view 'improvements to navigation.' Commerce includes navigation. 'All America understands, and has uniformly understood,' said Chief Justice Marshall in Gibbons v. Ogden, 9 Wheat. 1, 190, 6 L. ed. 23, 68, 'the word "commerce" to comprehend navigation.' The power to regulate interstate commerce embraces the power to keep the navigable rivers of the United States free from obstructions to navigation and to remove such obstructions when they exist. 'For these purposes', said the Court in Gilman v. Philadelphia, 3 Wall. 713, 725, 18 L. ed. 96, 99, 'Congress possesses all the powers which existed in the States before the adoption of the national Constitution, and which have always existed in the Parliament in England.' See also Philadelphia Co. v. Stimson, 223 U. S. 605, 634, 56 L. ed. 570, 582, 32 S. Ct. 340.

"The Tennessee River is a navigable stream, although there are obstructions at various points because of shoals, reefs and rapids. * * *

"While, in its present condition, the Tennessee River is not adequately improved for commercial navigation, and traffic is small, we are not at liberty to conclude either that the river is not susceptible of development as an important waterway, or that Congress has not undertaken that development, or that the construction of the Wilson Dam was not an appropriate means to accomplish a legitimate end.

"The Wilson Dam and its power plant must be taken to have been constructed in the exercise of the constitutional functions of the Federal Government.

"*Fourth. The constitutional authority to dispose of electric energy generated at the Wilson Dam.* The government acquired full title to the dam site, with all riparian rights. The power of falling water was an inevitable incident of the construction of the dam. That water power came into the exclusive control of the Federal Government. The mechanical energy was convertible into electric energy, and the water power, the right to convert it into electric energy, and the electric energy thus produced, constitute property belonging to the United States. See Green Bay & M. Canal Co. v. Patten Paper Co., 172 U. S. 58, 80, 43 L. ed. 364, 373, 19 S. Ct. 97; United States v. Chandler-Dunbar Water Power Co., 229 U. S. 53, 72, 73,

57 L. ed. 1063, 1079, 33 S. Ct. 667; Utah Power
& L. Co. v. Pfost, 286 U. S. 165, 179, 76 L. ed.
1038, 1045, 52 S. Ct. 548. * * *

"In United States v. Chandler-Dunbar Water
Power Co., 229 U. S. 53, 57 L. ed. 1063, 33 S.
Ct. 667, the United States had condemned land
in Michigan, lying between the St. Marys River
and the ship canal strip of the Government, in
order to improve navigation. The riparian owner, under revocable permits from the Secretary
of War, had placed in the rapids 'the necessary dams, dykes and forebays for the purpose
of controlling the current and using its power
for commercial purposes.' Id., p. 68. The Act
of March 3, 1909, authorizing the improvement,
had revoked the permit. We said that the Government 'had dominion over the water power
of the rapids and falls' and could not be required to pay 'any hypothetical additional
value to a riparian owner who had no right
to appropriate the current to his own commercial use.' Id., p. 76. The Act of 1909, also
authorized the Secretary of War to lease 'any
excess of water power which results from the
conservation of the flow of the river, and the
works which the Government may construct.'
'If the primary purpose is legitimate,' said the
Court, 'we can see no sound objection to leas-
ing any excess of power over the needs of the
Government. The practice is not unusual in
respect to similar public works constructed by
state governments.' Id., p. 73. Reference was
made to the case of Kaukauna Water Power
Co. v. Green Bay & M. Canal Co., 142 U. S.
254, 35 L. ed. 1004, 12 S. Ct. 173, supra, where
the Court had observed in relation to a Wisconsin statute of 1848, which had reserved to the
State the water power created by the dam over
the Fox River:— 'As there is no need of the

surplus running to waste, there was nothing objectionable in permitting the State to let out the use of it to private parties, and thus reimburse itself for the expenses of the improvement.' "

> *Ashwander v. Tennessee Valley Authority, supra.*

In the still more recent case of *Arizona v. California,* 80 L. ed. advance sheets, 877, 882, the Supreme Court said:

"But we have no occasion to consider the arguments urged upon us in support of the adoption, in this case, of a different rule from that of appropriation, as applied locally, for we are of the opinion that in the circumstances disclosed by the bill of complaint there can be no adjudication of rights in the unappropriated water of the Colorado River without the presence, as a party, of the United States, which, without its consent, is not subject to suit even by a state. Kansas v. United States, 204 U. S. 331, 343, 51 L. ed. 510, 514, 27 S. Ct. 388.

"The Colorado River is a navigable stream of the United States. The privilege of the states through which it flows and their inhabitants to appropriate and use the water is subject to the paramount power of the United States to control it for the purpose of improving navigation. Arizona v. California, 283 U. S. 423, 75 L. ed. 1154, 51 S. Ct. 522, supra."

> *Arizona v. California, supra.*

Second Ground for Sustaining the Decision of the Trial Court

The second reason why the decision of the trial court should be sustained, namely—

That the decision sustaining the plaintiff's motion to strike out defendants' testimony as to claimed value for dam site purposes and instructing the jury to disregard such testimony was correct and should be sustained because all the qualified testimony was that this land did not in fact have any additional value on account of alleged adaptability for dam site purposes (see testimony referred to on pages 11 to 14 of this brief) and that the only testimony offered by defendants as to their claimed land values was the testimony of engineers who were experts only on engineering questions but had no qualifications whatever to offer opinion evidence as to the market value of land in that section of Eastern Washington in which the Grand Coulee Dam site is located (Tr. pp. 95, 96, 120, 131, 132, 133)— is a question of fact as shown by the record. That the record sustains our contention on this point can be readily verified by checking the pages of the transcript above referred to and those quoted on pages 11 to 14 of this brief.

Without exception all of defendants' witnesses who offered testimony on this question were engineers qualified only on technical engineering ques-

tions. None of them except Marvin Chase ever
lived in Eastern Washington or anywhere within
200 miles of the land in question. None of them
ever had any experience as dealers in land or ever
bought or sold land or even owned land in the
section in question or (so far as the record shows)
anywhere else. As engineers they were competent
to express an opinion as to what type of dam could
be built at the Grand Coulee dam site, for that was
an engineering question, but they didn't and
couldn't have any expert knowledge as to the market value of land in that locality. What they did,
when asked to express an opinion on that question,
and the only thing they could do, was just what
Mr .Marvin Chase said he did:

> "In making my estimates of value I *assumed*
> a total estimated value of $3,055,000 for the en-
> tire dam site." (Tr. p. 150.)

*Third Ground for Sustaining the Decision of the
Trial Court*

The third reason why the decision of the trial
court should be sustained, namely,

Because it has been shown that the lowest dam
which would be considered either for government
or private construction would flood more than 600
separately owned tracts of private land held by
more than 900 different owners and that the number of ownerships flooded by the high dam would

be twice that many. (Tr. pp. 43, 44, 56, 130) as well
as thousands of acres of reserved government lands
included in Indian reservation, Power site withdrawals, and 1st form. Reclamation withdrawals
which are not open to appropriation by defendants
(Tr. pp. 56, 57, 43, 44) and also thousands of acres
of state lands, both river bottom and uplands which
have been dedicated by the state statute to the use
of the federal reclamation project (Sec. 7412, Rem.
Rev. Stat. of Wash.) and are reserved from any
other disposition or use, and would also require the
use of the prior water appropriation held by the
Columbia Basin Commission. These facts, considered in connection with the rule established by repeated decisions of the Supreme Court that where
the lands required for a dam or reservoir project
are in divided ownership no owner of any one or
any number of such tracts less than the whole is
entitled to any part or share of the value of the
whole for dam or reservoir purposes unless there
is a reasonable probability that all of the different
ownerships could be brought into one ownership
without resorting to eminent domain necessarily
lead to the conclusion that on account of the divided and widely scattered ownership of the lands
(government, state and private) which are indispensable to any beneficial use of the dam site and
reservoir site, the defendants are not entitled to
any allowance of dam site value and would not be
even if the Columbia River was not a navigable

stream and if the project was not being constructed for the purpose of improving navigation—is supported by a long line of decisions, beginning with the case of *Boston Chamber of Commerce v. Boston,* 217 U. S., 189, 195; 54 L. ed. 725, 727.

In the case of *McGovern v. New York, supra,* the rule is stated by the Supreme Court as follows:

"* * * The enhanced value of the land as part of the Ashokan reservoir depends on the whole land necessary being devoted to that use. *There are said to have been hundreds of titles to different parcels of that land.* If the parcels were not brought together by a taking under eminent domain, the chance of their being united by agreement or purchase in such a way as to be available well might be regarded as too remote and speculative to have any legitimate effect upon the valuation. See Chicago, B. & Q. R. Co. v. Chicago, 166 U. S. 226, 249, 41 L. ed. 979, 989, 17 Sup. Ct. Rep. 581. The plaintiff in error was entitled to be paid only for what was taken from him as the titles stood, and could not add to the value by the hypothetical possibility of a change unless that possibility was considerable enough to be a practical consideration and actually to influence prices. Boston Chamber of Commerce v. Boston, 217 U. S. 189, 195, 54 L. ed. 725, 727, 30 Sup. Ct. Rep. 459. *In estimating that probability, the power of effecting the change by eminent domain must be left out.* The principle is illustrated in an extreme form by the disallowance of the strategic value for improvements of the island in St. Mary's river in United States v. Chandler-Dunbar Water Power Co.

(229 U. S. 53, ante, 1063, 33 Sup. Ct. Rep. 667)
decided last month.'' (Italics supplied.)

229 U. S., 363, 372; 27 L. ed., 1228, 1232.

In the case of *New York v. Sage, supra,* the same
rule is stated as follows:

> "* * * *The city is not to be made to pay
> for any part of what it has added to the land by
> thus uniting it with other lots, if that union
> would not have been practicable or have been
> attempted except by the intervention of emi-
> nent domain.* * * * (Italics supplied.)

239 U. S., 57, 61; 60 L. ed., 143, 146.

It will be noticed that the stream involved in the
cases of McGovern v. New York and New York v.
Sage, was not a navigable stream and the project
was not a project for improvement of navigation.
The stream was a non-navigable stream and the
project was a reservoir to provide a municipal
water supply for the City of New York. Yet on
account of divided ownership alone and because the
lands required for the reservoir were divided
among several hundred different owners it was decided that the defendants were not entitled to any
additional value on account of the adaptability of
the land for use as a reservoir site. The divided
ownership and large number of owners made it
extremely improbable that all these diverse ownerships could be brought into one ownership without
resorting to condemnation and therefore it was held,
following the rule which was first announced in the

case of Boston Chamber of Commerce. v. Boston, supra, that no additional value should be allowed on account of the alleged adaptability of the land for use as a reservoir site, for none of the tracts in question is adopted for use as a reservoir unless it can be united with all the other tracts in the reservoir site.

As might be expected from the statement in McGovern v. New York that, "The principle is illustrated in an extreme form by the disallowance of the strategic value for improvements of the island in St. Mary's river in United States v. Chandler-Dunbar Water Power Co.", this question is one of the questions which was passed upon by the Supreme Court in the Chandler-Dunbar case in which case the following paragraph covers this point:

"* * * In respect to the allowance of $15,000 as its 'strategic value', the court below in its opinion said:

"'Owing to its location, this property had, and always has had, a strategic value with reference to any general scheme of water development in the river, and because it must be included as a tail race site, if not otherwise, in any completely efficient plan of development by any owner, private or public. * * *'

"This allowance has no solid basis upon which it may stand. That the property may have to the public a greater value than its fair market value affords no just criterion for estimating what the owner should recieve. *It is not proper to attribute to it any part of the value which might result from a consideration of its value as a necessary part of a comprehensive system of river improvement which should include the river and the upland* upon the shore adjacent. *The ownership is not the same.* The principle applied in Boston Chamber of Commerce v. Boston, 217 U. S. 189, 54 L. ed. 725, 30 Sup. Ct. Rep. 459, is applicable."

> *U. S. v. Chandler-Dunbar Co.,* 229 U. S., 53, 79; 57 L. ed., 1063, 1082.

There is no difference in principle between the Boston case and the instant one.

Here the division of the fee is in area. In that case the division was in several estates in the same fee. In the Boston case a road way was being condemned affecting the fee as dominated by an easement for private way. There was no injury to the fee, since it was already encumbered by the dominant estate—the private way. There was no injury to the dominant estate since the super-position of the public way upon the private one obviously resulted in no damage to the latter.

By collusion of the owners of the several estates, judgment was sought in a lump sum for the entire estate. The question, the contention of the plaintiff in error, and the answer of the Supreme Court are stated thus—

(A) "* * * The only question to be considered is whether, when a man's land is taken, he is entitled, by the 14th Amendment, to recover more than the value of it as it stood at the time. * * *

(B) "The petitioners contended that they had a right, as matter of law, under the Constitution, after the taking was complete and all rights were fixed, to obtain the connivance or concurrence of the dominant owner, and by means of that to enlarge a recovery that otherwise would be limited to a relatively small sum. It might be perfectly clear that the dominant owner never would have released short of a purchase of the dominant estate, in other words, that the servitude must have been maintained in the interest of lands not before the court,—but still, according to the contention, by a simple joinder of parties after the taking, the city could be made to pay for a loss of theoretical creation, suffered by no one in fact.

(C) "The statement of the contention seems to us to be enough. It is true that the mere mode of occupation does not necessarily limit the right of an owner's recovery. Mississippi & R. River Boom Co. v. Patterson, 98 U. S. 403, 408, 25 L. ed. 206, 208; Louisville & N. R. Co. v. Barber Asphalt Pav. Co., 197 U. S. 430, 435, 49 L. ed. 819, 822, 25 Sup. Ct. Rep. 466. But the Constitution does not require a disregard of the mode of ownership,—of the state of title. It does not require a parcel of land to be valued as an unencumbered whole when it is not held as an unencumbered whole. It merely requires that an owner of property taken should be paid for what is taken from him. It deals with persons, not with tracts of land. And the question is, What has the owner lost? not, What has the taker gained?"

Boston Chamber of Commerce v. Boston,
217 U. S., 189-195; 54 L. ed., 725, 727.

Can there be any question that it would be infinitely more difficult to bring into one ownership (without resort to condemnation) all the 600 different ownerships of private land owned by over 900 different owners, involved in the instant case, and the thousands of acres of reserved government and state land, than it would to have brought together the two ownerships involved in the Boston case?

The last word on this question is found in the recent decision of the Supreme Court in the Lake of the Woods or Olson case, *Olson v. United States,* 292 U. S., 246-262; 78 L. ed., 1236, in which the Court said:

"Respondent, having obtained leave to establish foundation for objection to petitioners' offers to prove, introduced evidence of the following facts:

"The main shoreline of the Lake of the Woods, including the affected reaches of the Rainy river, exceeds 1035 miles of which more than 110 are in Minnesota. * * * Below sealevel datum 1064, established by the treaty, there are about 850 parcels owned by more than 775 individuals. If mortgagees and other claimants are counted, the number to be dealt with is not less than 1225 persons. * * * The United States owns a considerable part—about onefifth—of the shore line in Minnesota. Small areas are held under homestead entries. The

State of Minnesota owns a small piece subject
to contracts of sale. * * * On the Canadian
side about 40 Indian reservations include 8,600
acres below the established level along about
250 miles of shoreline. These lands may be
disposed of only with the assent of a majority
of the male members of the band of the full
age of 21 years at a meeting summoned for
that purpose according to the rules of the band,
and subject to the approval of governmental
authority. * * * The fact that the most
profitable use of a parcel can be made only in
combination with other lands does not necessarily exclude that use from consideration *if
the possibility of combination is reasonably sufficient to affect the market value.* * * * But
the value to be ascertained does not include,
and the owner is not entitled to compensation
for, any element resulting subsequently to or
because of the taking. Considerations that may
not reasonably be held to affect market value
are excluded. *Value to the taker of a piece of
land combined with other parcels for public use
is not the measure of or a guide to the compensation to which the owner is entitled.* New York
v. Sage, 259 U. S. 57, 60 L. ed. 143, 36 S. Ct.
25, ubi supra; United States v. Chandler-Dunbar Water Power Co., 229 U. S. 53, 76, 80, 57
L. ed. 1063, 1080, 1082, 33 S. Ct. 667; Shoemaker v. United States, 147 U. S. 282, 305, 37
L. ed. 170, 187, 13 S. Ct. 361; Kerr v. South
Park, 117 U. S. 379, 386, 21 L. ed. 924, 927, 6
S. Ct. 801; Union Electric Light & P. Co. v.
Snyder Estate Co. (C. C. A. 8th, 65 F. (2d)
297, 304.) The use of shorelands for reservoir
purposes prior to the taking shows merely the
physical possibility of so controlling the level
of the lake. But physical adaptability alone
cannot be deemed to affect market value. There

must be a reasonable possibility that the owner could use his tract together with the other shorelands for reservoir purposes or that another could acquire all lands or easements necessary for that use. * * * *Elements affecting value that depend upon events or combinations of occurrences which, while within the realm of possibility, are not fairly shown to be reasonably probable, should be excluded from consideration for that would be to allow mere speculation and conjecture to become a guide for the ascertainment of value—a thing to be condemned in business transactions as well as in judicial ascertainment of truth.* Cf. Minnesota Rate Cases (Simpson v. Shepard) supra (230 U. S. 452, 57 L. ed. 1563, 33 S. Ct. 729, 48 L. R. A. (N. S.) 1151, Ann. Cas. 1916A, 18); Smith v. Illinois Bell Teleph. Co., 282 U. S. 133, 152, 75 L. ed. 255, 265, 51 S. Ct. 65; Los Angeles Gas & E. Corp. v. Railroad Commission, 289 U. S. 287, 319, 77 L. ed. 1180, 1199, 53 S. Ct. 637. * * *

"The situation in respect of lands bordering the Lake of the Woods is essentially different. The fact that the raising of the lake would take or damage shorelands could not affect their market value. There could be no rational basis for any demand that would affect value to the owner for reservoir purposes, unless, as a legal and practical possibility, he or some other person or persons—other than the expropriating authority—could have acquired the right to flow the lands necessary for the lawful raising of the lake. The lands upon which the flowage easement is condemned are located in two counties. Neither could authorize expropriation in the other. Petitioners did not cite or offer evidence of any instance of acquisitions, without reliance upon the power of eminent domain, that are at all comparable with those under consideration. When regard is had to the number of parcels, private owners, Indian tribes and sovereign proprietors to be dealt with, it is clear that there is no foundation for opinion evidence to the effect that it was practicable for private parties to acquire the flowage easements in question.

"* * *

"As just compensation includes no increment resulting from the taking, petitioners were not entitled to elements of value arising from the prospect that the Government would acquire the flowage easements. Under the circumstances, intention to acquire was the equivalent of the formal designation of the property to be taken. Prices actually paid, and estimates or opinions based, upon the assumption that value to owners includes any such elements are not entitled to weight and should not be taken into account. On the fact shown, it conclusively appears that there was no element of value belonging to petitioners that legitimately could be attributed to use and adaptability of their lands for reservoir purposes. The evidence covered by petitioners' offers was inadmissible. The court rightly excluded reservoir uses from consideration." (Italics supplied.)

Olson v. United States, 292 U. S., 246-262; 78 L. ed., 1236, 1242-1248.

Let us test appellants claim by the rule laid down by the Supreme Court in the Olson case, namely,

"Elements affecting value that depend upon events or combinations of occurrences which, while within the realm of possibility, *are not fairly shown to be reasonably probable,* should be excluded from consideration for that would be to allow mere speculation and conjecture to become a guide for the ascertainment of value —a thing to be condemned in business transactions as well as in judicial ascertainment of truth.''

and ask the question, *''Is it reasonably probable,* that (without resorting to eminent domain) appellants could have brought into one ownership all of the more than 600 different ownerships of private land in the dam and reservoir site held by more than 900 different owners, and in addition thereto could have acquired all the reserved public lands of the United States, included in Indian Reservations, power site withdrawals and 1st form withdrawals under the Reclamation Act of June 17, 1902, 32 St. 388, and in addition to that could also have acquired the government's paramount right of control over the bed and water of the navigable stream, and the prior water appropriation made by the Columbia Basin Commission, and the state title to the bed and shores of the stream and the state-owned uplands in the reservoir site, all of which state property is required by state statute to be reserved and devoted only to the government reclamation project?''

Will this Court or any one else answer that question in the affirmative?

The question in so far as it relates to the occupation of the reserved public land of the United States is concerned has been very definitely answered by the Supreme Court in the case of *Utah Power and Light Co. v. United States,* 243 U. S., 402; 61 L. ed., 792.

REPLY TO APPELLANTS' BRIEF

Appellants have given as their statement of facts a part of the testimony of their own witnesses on direct examination but conveniently forgot to state what the same witnesses said on cross-examination. We think the Court will agree with us that the effect of what defendants' witnesses said on direct examination was utterly destroyed by what the same witnesses said on cross-examination and in some instances more than destroyed. (See testimony quoted on pages 8 to 12 of this brief.)

The first case cited by the appellants is that of *Mississippi and Rum River Boom Co. v. Patterson,* 98 U. S., 403, 25 L. ed., 206, which is typical of all the other cases cited by appellants except the Olson case and the Chandler-Dunbar case, in both of which the decision was squarely against the defendants in those cases and squarely against the contention of the appellants in the instant case.

In the Olson case (Olson v. United States, supra) which involved conditions very similar to those involved in the case at bar, the Supreme Court distinguished the case of Mississippi & R. R. Boom Co. v. Patterson by saying,

> "The boom company could not exclude others from handling logs floated in the river. The owner and others had the right to use the island

lands to construct a boom for their own purposes or for general use.''

Olson v. United States, supra.

But the United States can exclude others from building the Grand Coulee dam in the bed and across the channel of the navigable stream, and most assuredly the United States can prevent others from flooding the reserved public lands of the United States included in Indian Reservations, Power site withdrawals, and Reclamation withdrawals,

Utah Power & Light Co. v. United States, 243 U. S., 402; 61 L. ed., 792;

and also the state lands granted to the United States by state law for Reclamation purposes.

That the United States can exclude others from building the Grand Coulee Dam in the bed and across the channel of this navigable stream is expressly provided by statute in that part of 16 U. S. C. A., par. 800, which reads:

"Whenever in the judgment of the commission, the development of any project should be undertaken by the United States itself, the commission shall not approve any application for such project by any citizen, association, corporation, state or municipality.''

That this particular project has been so reserved for government construction ever since 1922 has

been shown by appellants' own witnesses (Tr. 143),
Mr. Creager testifying:

> "It was filed upon in 1922 by Colonel Cooper
> but the filing was denied, which I understand
> was because of the desire of the United States
> government to hold it for themselves."

> "I do not know why private capital did not
> purchase it then except that the previous effort
> to purchase it was denied on the ground that
> the government wanted it."

> "The Government was withholding permis-
> sion from private capital to build that dam
> from the time an attempt was made to file on
> it in 1921 or 1922 by Mr. Cooper."

This distinction makes the Boom Company case
and every other authority cited by appellants (except the Chandler-Dunbar case and the Olson case)
inapplicable and worthless as applied to the facts
of the case at bar and, as we have pointed out, the
Chandler-Dunbar case and the Olson case are
squarely against the appellants' contention.

The same distinction applies to the cases which
involve the condemnation of land for park purposes,
for such enterprises did not require the construction of a dam or other obstruction in and across the
bed of a navigable stream, and public parks might
be developed by a state, a municipality or by the
federal government and private parks might be
developed by any one. None of those cases involved
the flooding of the reserved public lands included in

Indian Reservations, Power site withdrawals, and Reclamation withdrawals. Neither did such enterprises require the acquisition of the state title to state lands dedicated and reserved by state law for the exclusive use of the federal reclamation project.

The Olson case (Olson v. United States, supra.) did involve conditions similar to the ones encountered in the instant case and in that case the district court held, for reasons which apply with equal force to the instant case, that the defendants were not entitled to any additional award whatever for the claimed reservoir values but only for agricultural values and in the case of the Olson tract for fishing values, and the decision of the district court was affirmed in every particular by the Supreme Court.

In the Olson case the court stated several conditions which were fatal to the claims of the defendants in that case and are equally fatal to the claims of the defendants in the instant case. The first is, "The fact that the most profitable use of a parcel can be made only in combination with other lands does not *necessarily* exclude that use from consideration, if the *possibility of combination is reasonably sufficient* to affect the market value," and in the same case the conclusion of the court as to such possibility is stated as follows:

> "When regard is had to the number of parcels, private owners, Indian tribes, and sov-

ereign proprietors to be dealt with, it is clear that there is no foundation for opinion evidence to the effect that it was practicable for private parties to acquire the flowage easements in question.''

Olson v. United States, supra.

The Olson case is on all fours with the instant case and is conclusive against appellants' claim. This is made even more certain in another paragraph in the same decision, where the Supreme Court, after discussing the Boom Company case and saying, "The boom company could not exclude others from handling logs floating in the river. The owners and others had the right to use the island lands to construct a boom for their own purposes or for general use," went on to say:

"The situation in respect of lands bordering the Lake of the Woods is essentially different. The fact that the raising of the lake would take or damage shorelands could not affect their market value. There could be no rational basis for any demand that would affect value to the owner for reservoir purpses unless, *as a legal and practical possibility,* he or some other persons—*other than the expropriating authority*—could have acquired the right to flow the lands necessary for the lawful raising of the lake."

Olson v. United States, supra.

So here again we find the Supreme Court announcing the same rule stated by the Circuit Court

of Appeals for the First Circuit in the case of
United States v. Boston C. C. & N. Y. Canal Co.,
271 Fed., 893, that is,

> "We are of the opinion that, in ascertaining
> the market value of property taken in a con-
> demnation proceeding the utility or availability
> of the property for the special purpose of the
> taker can not be shown if the taker is the only
> party who can use the property for that pur-
> pose."
>
> *United States v. B. C. C. & N. Y. Canal Co.,*
> 271 Fed., 893.

Here again the Olson case is on all fours with the
instant case and is conclusive against appellants'
claim.

The above quoted paragraph from the case of
United States v. Boston C. C. & N. Y. Canal Company gives, we think, a very clear and concise statement of one of the controlling distinctions between
the class of cases on which appellants rely and the
class of cases to which the Olson case, the Chandler-
Dunbar case and the case at bar belong.

On pages 42 and 48 of appellants' brief is quoted
that part of the Chandler-Dunbar case which deals
with the value allowed on account of the availability
of a certain tract of upland for canal and lock purposes. Here we have the same distinction which
has been pointed out in the Olson case and United
States v. Boston C. C. & N. Y. C. Co., supra, for

a canal could be built on the uplands belonging to the Chandler-Dunbar Company by any corporation or individual who might desire to engage in such enterprise and such enterprise would not require the construction of any dam or other structure in and across the channel of the navigable stream to control the flow of the navigable stream. Neither did it require the bringing together into one ownership of hundreds of separately owned tracts of private lands or any public lands included in Indian Reservations, power site withdrawals and Reclamation withdrawals. That paragraph of the Chandler-Dunbar case dealing with the value of defendant's uplands for canal purposes involves nothing more than was involved in the Boom Company case. But when the Supreme Court came to the consideration of the claim of the Chandler-Dunbar Company for claimed values for a purpose which would require a dam or other structure in the bed of the stream to control the flow of the navigable stream the court emphatically rejected the claim, pointing out among other things:

> "Whatever substantial private property rights exist in the flow of the stream must come from some right which that company has to construct such works in the river, such as dams, walls, dykes, etc., essential to the utilization of the power of the stream for commercial purposes."

> "To utilize the rapids and fall of the river which flows by the upland of the Chandler-Dun-

bar Company, it has been and will be necessary to construct and maintain in the river the structures necessary to control and direct the flow so that it may be used for commercial purposes.''

"Having decided that the Chandler-Dunbar Company, as riparian owners, had no such vested property right in the water power inherent in the falls and rapids of the river, *and no right to place in the river the works essential to any practical use of the flow of the river,* the government cannot be justly required to pay for an element of value which did not inhere in these parcels as upland."

U. S. v. Chandler-Dunbar W. P. Co., supra.

And when the court came to consider the claim of the Chandler-Dunbar Company for claimed values for a purpose which would require the uniting into one ownership of parcels of land then held in separate ownerships the court rejected that claim also, saying:

"It is not proper to attribute to it any part of the value which might result from a consideration of its value as a necessary part of a comprehensive system of river improvement which should include the river and the upland upon the shore adjacent. *The ownership is not the same.* The principle applied in Boston Chamber of Commerce v. Boston, 217 U. S. 189, 54 L. ed. 725, 30 Sup. Ct. Rep. 459, is applicable."

U. S. v. Chandler-Dunbar W. P. Co., supra.

So the Chandler-Dunbar case furnishes in itself

a perfect illustration of the distinction between the three classes of cases to which we have referred

Section 7416 of Remington's Revised Statutes, referred to on pages 54 and 55 of appellants' brief, has no application to the state lands involved in this case because the defendants have not acquired any rights under such statute by actual construction or otherwise and whatever right the state could grant has passed to the United States under Section 7412 of Remington's Revised Statutes, quoted on page 32 of this brief. Furthermore, if the defendants had acquired all the rights that the state could grant, they would have no greater right in the bed of the navigable stream than had the Chandler-Dunbar Company, and that was no right at all.

On page 55 of appellants' brief, appellants refer to the Federal Water Power Act as if it were a charter of right to the defendants, but the effect of the act in question is just the opposite of what appellants claim for under the provisions of the section thereof which appears as 16 U. S. C. A., 800; quoted on page 2a of this brief, the Federal Power Commission is expressly authorized and directed to deny the application of "any citizen, association, corporation, State or municipality" "whenever in the judgment of the commission, the development of any project should be undertaken by the United States itself." That it was so determined that this is a project which should be constructed by the government itself and that it has been so reserved for construction by the government itself ever since 1921 or 1922 has been shown by the testimony of appellants' own witness, Mr. Creager.

On page 59 of appellants' brief, appellants assert, "But the improvement of navigation is not in the case." We think that in making that statement counsel must have forgotten the complaint and answer, for the defendants' answer reads,

"Admits paragraphs 1, 2, 3, 4, 5, 6, 7, 8, 9, 10, 11, 12, 13, 14, 15 and 16 to be true"

and the paragraphs expressly admitted to be true contain the following allegations that the Columbia Basin project, of which the Grand Coulee dam is the first unit, is

"a federal project having for its purposes:
"Regulation of the flow of said stream by storage reservoirs; and

"Co-ordinated development and use of said stream for the various purposes for which it is adapted, including *navigation,* hydro-electric power, flood control and irrigation, including irrigation of public lands of the United States,

"* * * which dam constitutes the first unit and an integral part of a large Grand Coulee dam which will form a part of the complete Columbia Basin project and serve as the diversion dam therefor and also as the principal storage reservoir on said stream to regulate

the flow of said stream for flood control and to
serve the purposes of *navigation* and power development at all points on such stream below
said Grand Coulee dam.

"* * * and has adopted a comprehensive
and co-ordinated plan for the development and
use of said stream for *navigation,* flood control
and irrigation and for the development of electrical energy to pay the cost of the proposed
construction and for irrigation, pumping and
industrial and domestic use. * * *

"That the said Grand Coulee Dam is the key
structure in the said comprehensive plan for
the co-ordinated development of said stream, in
that the said Grand Coulee Dam will provide
the nececssary storage capacity to store the
peaks of the Columbia River floods and by
storing the floods and releasing the stored water
during the low water season will improve the
flow of said stream for navigation, power development, and irrigation and will reduce the
flood dangers on the lower part of the stream."

It is true that one of the defendants, Samuel J.
Seaton, withdrew his answer and went to trial without any answer, which he is permitted to do under
the Washington statute.

But Section 297 of Remington's Revised Statutes
provides:

"Every material allegation of the complaint
not controverted by the answer, and every material allegation of new matter in the answer
not controverted by the reply, shall, for the
purpose of action, be taken as true."

and the effect of the action of the defendant Seaton
in going to trial without an answer is the same as
that of the other defendants who expressly admitted the allegations of the complaint. That the above
quoted allegations of the complaint are material allegations can not be doubted for Section 921 of
Remington's Revised Statutes provides that the petition in eminent domain must set forth among
other things, "the object for which the land is
sought to be appropriated."

The public works section of the Act of June 16,
1933 (48 Stat. 195), under which this project was
initiated provides for the construction of public
works for the purpose of improvement of navigation and the Act of August 30, 1935 (quoted on page
22 of this brief), expressly authorizes the construction of the Grand Coulee project for the purpose
of flood control and the improvement of navigation.
The last named act is peculiar in that it not only
authorizes the construction of the Grand Coulee
project for the purposes named but expressly rati-
fies the action previously taken in connection with
the said project and the contracts previously made
in connection therewith, which contracts would include, we think, the implied contracts which arise
from the taking of private property for public
use.

> United States v. Great Falls Co., 112 U. S.,
> 745; 28 L. ed., 850.

The stipulation (Tr. p. 42) in which all the parties to this action joined, that

> "The plaintiff and all the defendants have agreed that the government has a right to condemn the property described in the complaint in this case"

necessarily includes the stipulation that the project is duly authorized by law, for otherwise the government would not have the right to condemn, and as the project has been fully described in the complaint and the purposes thereof fully set out in the complaint, all of which has been expressly admitted by the answer, the appellants have certainly waived the right to question either the legal authority for the construction of the project or the purpose for which it is being built.

Furthermore the material fact so far as the valuation of appellants' land is concerned is that this project has been removed by authority of law from the class of projects which are open to exploitation by private enterprise and that occurred, as we have pointed out, over 15 years ago under the provisions of the Federal Water Power Act. The allotment of $63,000,000 of government funds for the construction of this project prior to the filing of this suit simply ratified and confirmed what had been initiated 15 years earlier by reserving the project for construction by the government itself.

After the project has been taken out of the class of projects which are open to private construction and reserved for construction by the government only, it can make no possible difference in the valuation of appellants' lands whether the government constructs the project for the purposes of navigation or the purposes of the reclamation of arid public lands or for any other public purpose in which the federal government will engage.

That the project will in fact improve navigation has been shown by competent evidence which is in no way disputed. See the following undisputed testimony (Tr. p. 55):

> "The proposed dam which is under construction at this time will serve the purposes of a diversion dam for the Columbia Basin project, improvement of navigation by creating a lake 150 miles long running from the dam to the Canadian boundary and, by regulation of the low flow of the river and increasing it, will improve navigation all the way from the dam site to the coast."

We might also say in this connection that if the project were not authorized by law the appellants would not be entitled to any judgment.

Title and possession of the property involved in this action passed to the United States by order of court which was made at the time that the complaint was filed (Tr. pp. 14, 15) to which order appellants made no objection and took no exception and which therefore is not open to question on appeal and would not be open to question on appeal even if the appellants had not expressly waived their right to raise such question by the stipulation which they made at the beginning of the trial.

Respectfully submitted,
J. M. SIMPSON,
United States Attorney,
Spokane, Washington;

B. E. STOUTEMYER,
District Counsel, Bureau of
Reclamation,
Portland, Oregon,
Attorneys for Appellee.

NO. 8162

United States

Circuit Court of Appeals

For the Ninth Circuit

CONTINENTAL LAND COMPANY, a corpora-
tion, JULIUS C. JOHNSON, MABLE JOHN-
SON, SAMUEL J. SEATON, MARY A. SEA-
TON, EMMA RATHS, MARTHA RATHS
BALDWIN, WARREN BALDWIN, HENRY
RATHS, GEORGE RATHS, ALBERT
RATHS, ARTHUR RATHS, ALMA RATHS
CLARK, FRED CLARK, MARY RATHS
MARNHART, CLARENCE MARNHART,
MINNIE RATHS, FRED RATHS and MA-
NITA RATHS,

Appellants,

vs.

UNITED STATES OF AMERICA,

Appellee.

Appellants' Reply Brief

Upon Appeal from the District Court of the United
States for the Eastern District of Washington,
Northern Division.

FILED

NOV -5 1936

INDEX

INDEX TO CITATIONS

NO. 8162

United States
Circuit Court of Appeals
For the Ninth Circuit

CONTINENTAL LAND COMPANY, a corpora-
tion, JULIUS C. JOHNSON, MABLE JOHN-
SON, SAMUEL J. SEATON, MARY A. SEA-
TON, EMMA RATHS, MARTHA RATHS
BALDWIN, WARREN BALDWIN, HENRY
RATHS, GEORGE RATHS, ALBERT
RATHS, ARTHUR RATHS, ALMA RATHS
CLARK, FRED CLARK, MARY RATHS
MARNHART, CLARENCE MARNHART,
MINNIE RATHS, FRED RATHS and MA-
NITA RATHS,

Appellants,

vs.

UNITED STATES OF AMERICA,

Appellee.

Appellants' Reply Brief

Upon Appeal from the District Court of the United
States for the Eastern District of Washington,
Northern Division.

As stated in Appellants' brief, and as conceded in
Appellee's brief (p. 25), the controlling question on this
appeal is, **whether it was error for the trial court to
strike from the record and exclude from the considera-**

tion of the jury, in determining market value, the admitted fact that Appellants' **uplands were especially adapted for use as a damsite, and that their market value was enhanced on that account.***

Appellee's brief seeks to justify the ruling of the trial court on three grounds (Aple's Br. pp. 25-59) as follows:

"First—* * * On the grounds on which he placed it * * * that is, on account of the Government's paramount right, title and control over the beds and waters of navigable streams for the purpose of the improvement of navigation.

"Second—That the decision * * * was correct * * * because all the qualified testimony was that this land did not in fact have any additional value on account of alleged adaptability for damsite purposes * * * and that the only testimony offered by defendants as to their claimed land values was the testimony of engineers who were experts only on engineering questions."

"Third—Because it has been shown that the lowest dam which would be considered * * * would flood more than 600 separately owned tracts of private land held by more than 900 different owners, as well as thousands of acres of reserved

---

* Note—(Variations in type, and underscoring, wherever they appear in this reply brief are supplied by counsel unless otherwise indicated.)

government lands included in Indian Reservation, power site withdrawals, and 1st form Reclamation withdrawals which are not open to appropriation by defendants, and also thousands of acres of state lands, both river bottom and uplands which have been dedicated by the state statute to the use of the federal reclamation project. * * * That where the lands required for a dam or reservoir project are in divided ownership no owner of any one or any number of such tracts less than the whole is entitled to any part or share of the value of the whole for dam or reservoir purposes unless there is a reasonable probability that all of the different ownerships could be brought into one ownership without resorting to eminent domain."

Appellants' reply will analyze these three grounds in the order stated in Appellee's brief, together with the cases cited therein, in so far as they appear to have some bearing on the question in this appeal.

"FIRST"—Do the grounds stated by the trial court in support of his ruling justify the court in holding, as a matter of law, that the jury in determining just compensation may not consider adaptability of Appellants' uplands for use as a damsite?

The reasons relied on by the trial court are stated and analyzed and the errors pointed out in **Appellants' brief beginning at the foot of page 27,** to which attention is again respectfully directed to avoid repetition.

It may be significant to note that learned counsel
for Appellee offer no contribution to support the
grounds stated by the trial court as justification for his
ruling. They abandon said grounds with purported quo-
tations from the Court's statement which is not contained in the Transcript of Record, and they suggest
other grounds to justify the rulings complained of:

> "But if this court should not agree with the
> trial Judge on the ground on which the trial Judge
> placed his decision, the decision was, nevertheless,
> accurate, and should be sustained on other grounds,
> as follows:" (Aples' Br. p. 26).

It will not be necessary to duplicate here the analysis and citations contained in Appellants' Brief beginning on Page 27, but since Appellee's brief contains
what purports to be a further statement by the Trial
Court and what appears to be a misconception of the
holding in the Chandler-Dunbar case, some additional
analysis of said purported statement and of the Chandler-Dunbar case may be permissible.

At the foot of page 42, Appellee's brief the trial
court is quoted as saying:

> "But the point I rest my ruling upon is that it
> must be a taking of something which the owner pos-
> sesses, and if the lands here in question are to be
> appraised upon their inherent value **as decided in
> the Chandler-Dunbar case,** then it necessarily fol-
> lows that you cannot take it into account as a dam
> site without taking into consideration the flow of

the river, and you must and cannot escape transferring to the uplands the inherent qualities that are vested in the land which it does not possess."

It is plain from the foregoing as well as from all the statement of the Trial Court to support his ruling, that the Trial Court considered the holding in the Chandler-Dunbar case to be that **land riparian to navigable water may not, as a matter of law, possess any inherent value for a special use in which navigable waters play a necessary part.**

There is, of course, no law to that effect, and there is no reason why there should be. In **Boom Company v. Patterson, 98 U. S. 403, 25 L. Ed. 206,** the boom would have been useless without the flowing navigable water in the Mississippi River. Likewise, the Chandler-Dunbar upland would have been useless for lock and canal purposes without the right to use the navigable water of the St. Mary's River. **Yet in each of those cases adaptability for the special use, as a boom site and as a lock and canal site respectively, was considered and paid for as an element of market value.**

A close analysis of what the trial court said and what the Chandler-Dunbar case held, will disclose the starting point of the Court's error.

The trial court said (Aple's Br. p. 43):

"If the lands here in question are to be appraised upon their inherent value **as decided in the Chandler-Dunbar case**, then it necessarily follows that you cannot take it into account as a dam site without taking into consideration the flow of the river * * *."

That statement by the Trial Court discloses plainly that he thought that the Chandler-Dunbar Company was claiming the right to prove that its upland was adapted for special use in the development of hydro-electric power, and that such special use must be considered in determining the market value of the upland. The Trial Court must have thought that the Chandler-Dunbar case holds that even if it were claimed and proved that the Chandler-Dunbar uplands were especially adapted for such use, that such use could not be considered in determining its market value. The Trial Court must have so understood the Chandler-Dunbar case,—otherwise he could not have made the statement which he did. The Chandler-Dunbar case does not so hold.

U. S. V. CHANDLER-DUNBAR—ANALYZED, DISTINGUISHED AND APPLIED.

1. There was no claim and no proof that the Chandler-Dunbar uplands were especially adapted for use in the development of hydro-electric power. The Trial Court's findings of fact in that case tend to show that all the hydro-electric power was developed on the company's submerged lands over which the government had unlimited power in aid of navigation, and that the strip of upland, which corresponds to appellants' uplands in the instant case, was not a necessary part of the power development. In any event there was no claim or

suggestion that the strip of upland was adapted for use in the development of power.

The following are some of the specific findings of fact made by the Trial Court in the Chandler-Dunbar case.

"III.

* * * The fall in the river, **the water power of which** is the subject of the **main contention** herein, was in the rapids fronting on the upper part of the so-called Indian reservation."

"XIII.

Two-thirds of the total flow would, under ordinary, original, natural conditions, flow over the Chandler-Dunbar Water Power Company's **submerged lands.**"

"XXXVII.

The existing structures built by or under the Chandler-Dunbar Company are in connection with a tail-race excavated upon the **below-lying public river bed,** whereby there is, at the power house, a fall of 15 feet instead of only the 9 foot fall (effective) which exists on the Chandler-Dunbar property."

"XXXVIII.

The proposed United States structures **in the bed of the stream** will deliver 7,500 c.f.s. * * *" **

** (Note—The findings of fact, conclusions of law and the opinion of the trial court may be found in the

Supreme Court records and briefs in the Chandler-Dunbar case.)

The foregoing findings of fact indicate that the strip of upland in the Chandler-Dunbar case was not necessary to the development of hydro-electric power and that it possessed no special adaptability therefor.

2. Furthermore, **the claim** which was made for compensation in the Chandler-Dunbar case **was for** the value of **the water power** claimed to have been taken. **There was no claim based upon the inherent adaptability of the land for a special use.** The claim was solely for the value of the **flow of the river and the hydro-electric power generated thereby** as a distinct and **separate unit of property.** The question of inherent adaptability **of the land** for special use, which is the question involved in our case, was not involved and was not considered in that part of the Chandler-Dunbar case relied upon by the Trial Court in the instant case.

That the claim which was being considered by the Supreme Court in the Chandler-Dunbar case was for the **value of the flowing water of the river, and the electric power capable of being generated thereby,** and that **there was no suggestion of claim involving the inherent adaptability of the strip of upland for use in the development of electric power,** is shown beyond the possibility of doubt by the findings of fact and conclusions of law of the Trial Court in that case, and by the language of the Supreme Court with reference thereto.

The Court found as further facts in the Chandler-Dunbar case:

"XIV.

* * * I fix the annual **value of the raw power** per theoretical horse-power as follows: For the first 3,000 h. p. $10.00 each; for the second 3,000 h. p. $7.50 each; for all beyond 6,000 h. p. $5.00 each."

"XV.

The proper basis for capitalization is ten per cent."

"XLII.

Such 6,500 horse-power has an **annual value of $55,000; a present value of $550,000.**"

"OPINION OF THE COURT"

"12. **Amount of compensation.**

Under the methods already stated such 6,500 horse-power has an annual value of $55,000 and this capitalized at ten per cent amounts to a present value of $550,000.00."

It is plain from the foregoing language that the Trial Court was dealing with a claim for the value of **water power as a separate and distinct unit of property,** and that the question of **inherent adaptability of the**

land for the development of power, or for use as a damsite was in no way involved. The language of the Supreme Court clearly establishes the same fact, and clearly shows that the language quoted and relied on by the
Trial Court in the instant case **had no reference whatsoever to the question of inherent adaptability of land for
a special use.** The language of the Supreme Court upon
which the Trial Court in the instant case relied, had to
do only with the question **whether any private property
had in fact been taken.** Nothing was said as to what
might be shown in determining its market value. It did
not become necessary for the Supreme Court to discuss
elements of value because it was held that the **stream
flow and water power** in a navigable river **are not private property.** Since there was no private property there
could be no question of inherent adaptability.

The Supreme Court said:

"From the foregoing it will be seen that the
controlling questions are, **first,** whether or not the
Chandler-Dunbar Company **has any private property in the water power capacity of the rapids and
falls in the St. Mary's River** which has been 'taken'
and for which compensation must be made under
the 5th Amendment to the Constitution; and, **second,** if so, what is the extent of its water power right
and **how shall the compensation be measured?**

"**That compensation must be made for the upland taken is not disputable.** The measure of compensation may in a degree turn upon the relation of
species of property to the alleged water power rights

claimed by the Chandler-Dunbar Company. **We, therefore, pass for the present the errors assigned which concern the awards made for such upland."** (P. 60)

"The company's claim is, that it is the owner of the river and of the inherent power in the falls and rapids, subject only to the public right of navigation. * * * **This claim of a proprietary right in the bed of the river and in the flow of the stream over that bed** to the extent that such flow is in excess of the wants of navigation **constitutes the ground upon which the company asserts** that a necessary effect of the act of March 3, 1909, and of the judgment in condemnation in the court below, is a taking from it of **a property right or interest of great value,** for which, under the Fifth Amendment, compensation must be made. (P. 61) * * *

(P. 68)

"The provisions of the act in respect of compensation apply only to compensation for **such** 'property described' **as shall be held private property** taken for (P. 69) public use. Unless, therefore, the **water power rights** asserted by the Chandler-Dunbar Company **are determined to be private property,** the court below was not authorized to award compensation for such rights.

* * * (P. 69)

"Ownership of a private stream wholly upon the lands of an individual is conceivable; but that **the running water** in a great navigable stream **is capable of private ownership is inconceivable.**

"The 71st finding of fact was in these words: 'All the development works ever constructed upon the Chandler-Dunbar **submerged lands** by any one, have been constructed after obtaining from the Secretary of War a permit therefor, and each such permit has been expressly revocable by right of revocation reserved on its face, to be exercised with or without cause. Each such permit was revoked before the commencement of this proceeding.'

"Upon what principle can it be said that in requiring the removal of the **development works which were in the river** upon sufferance, Congress has taken **private property** for public use without compensation?"

* * *

(P. 72)

"That title is absolutely subordinate to the right of navigation, and **no right of private property** would have been invaded if such **submerged lands** were occupied by structures in aid of navigation, or kept free from such obstructions in the interest of navigation. **Scranton v. Wheeler, supra; Hawkins Light House Case, 39 Fed. Rep. 77, 83.** * * *

"That determination operates to exclude from
the river forever the structures necessary for the
commercial use of the **water-power. That it does not
deprive the Chandler-Dunbar Company of private
property rights follows from the considerations before stated.**"

It is plain from the foregoing language that the
Supreme Court in the Chandler-Dunbar case was not
passing upon the right to prove, or to be paid for, the
**inherent adaptability of the Chandler-Dunbar upland
for special use in the development of hydro-electric
power as an element of its market value.** As regards
stream flow and hydro-electric power, the Court went
no farther than to hold that they **were not private property,** and since they were not private property they could
have no value which was recoverable in that action. That
the Court was dealing with **"raw water"** and **"stream
flow"** as a **separate unit of property,** and not as something for which the **upland might possess inherent
adaptability** is further shown by the language of the
Supreme Court dealing with the award which had been
made for these separate units of property. On that subject the Supreme Court said:

"The compensation awarded was as follows:

    A.   To the Chandler-Dunbar Company
        $652,332.00. Of this, $550,000 was the
        estimated **value of the water power.**

"The errors assigned by the United States challenge the allowance of any compensation whatso-

ever on account of any **water power right** claimed by any of the owners of the condemned upland.

"The award of $550,000 on account of the claim of the Chandler-Dunbar Company to the undeveloped **water power** of the river at the St. Mary's Rapids in excess of the supposed requirements of navigation **constitutes the principal question in the case,** and its importance is increased by the contention of that company that the assessment of damage on that account is grossly inadequate, and should have been $3,450,000.00.

A careful reading of the opinion of the Supreme Court makes it perfectly plain that the Court in that part of the Chandler-Dunbar case relied on by the Trial Court in the instant case, and quoted in Appellee's Brief, was not dealing with the market value of the upland, nor with its inherent adaptability for any special use. The claim urged by the company, and the discussion by the Court had to do only with **water power as a separate unit of property.** What was said by the Court in reference to "upland" and "riparian owners" was said in considering whether "raw water" and the "rapids and flow of the river" could be subjects of private property or objects of private ownership. **There was no claim, and accordingly no discussion, of any possible inherent adaptability of the upland for special use in the development of hydro-electric power.**

THERE IS A PORTION OF THE OPINION IN THE CHANDLER-DUNBAR CASE, HOWEVER, WHICH DEALS EXPRESSLY WITH THE CLAIM OF

INHERENT ADAPTABILITY OF THE STRIP OF UPLAND FOR SPECIAL USES.

The special uses for which the strip of upland was claimed to be inherently adapted were expressly enumerated. **The development of hydro-electric power was not one of them.** The Supreme Court enumerated them as follows:

> "Coming now to the award for the **upland** taken:

> "The Court below awarded to the Chandler-Dunbar Company on this account:

> "a. For the narrow strip of **upland** bordering on the river, having an area of something more than 8 acres * * * $60,450.00. * * *

> "The value of the **upland** strip fixed at $60,450 was arrived at in this manner—

> "a. For its value, including railroad side-tracks, buildings and cable terminal, including also its use 'wholly disconnected with power development or public improvement, that is to say, for all general purposes, like residences, or hotels, factory sites, **disconnected with water power,** etc., $20.000.'

> "b. For use as **factory site in connection with the development of 6,500 horse power,** either as a single site or for several factories to use the surplus of 6,500 horse power not now used in the city, an additional value of $20,000.

"c. **For use for canal and lock purposes, an
additional value of $25,000.** * * *

"The United States excepted to the additional
value allowed in consequence of the **availability of**
these parcels **in connection with the water power
supposed to be the property of the Chandler-Dunbar
Company,** and supposed to have been taken by the
Government in this case. It **also excepted** to so
much of the awards as constituted an additional
value by reason of **availability for lock and canal
purposes.**

The disallowance of the claimed adaptability "for
use as factory sites" in connection with the development
of 6,500 horse power illustrates one of the controlling
principles involved. The Supreme Court said:

"These exceptions, so far as they complain of
the additional value to be attached to these parcels
for use as **factory sites in connection with the development of horse-power** by the Cahdnler-Dunbar
Company, must be sustained. These additional
values were based upon the erroneous hypothesis
that that company had a **private property** interest in
the **water power of the river** * * *.

"Having decided that the Chandler-Dunbar
Company as riparian owners **had no such vested
property right in the water power inherent in the
falls and rapids of the river,** and no right to place in
the river the works essential to any practical use of
the flow of the river, the Government cannot be

justly required to pay for an element of value **which did not inhere in these parcels of upland.**"

It is plain from the foregoing language of the Supreme Court that the claimed market value of the upland based upon **"use as factory site in connection with the development of 6,500 horse power"** was excluded, not because the strip of upland was riparian to navigable water, not because the government had the paramount right to improve the river in aid of navigation, but because of the fact, as found by the Court, that the strip of land **had no inherent adaptability** for such use. There was no showing that 6,500 horse power would ever be developed with which to operate the factories, and without the development of the hydro-electric power there would be no factories. Congress had already determined, by legislative enactment, that the submerged land and the entire flow of the river were necssary for the improvement of navigation. Accordingly, there was no likelihood that the 6,500 horse-power would be available, and there being no power available clearly the tract of land could have no inherent adaptability for use as factory sites. **Special adaptability for use as a factory site was, therefore clearly, eliminated because no such special adaptability existed, not because the land was riparian to a navigable stream.**

It is respectfully submitted that the language and holding of the Chandler-Dunbar case upon which the Trial Court relied in the instant case, when properly analyzed and understood, simply holds that where **private property right does not exist, as in the** flowing **water of a stream,** there can be no market value, and no inherent adaptability, and where private property does exist **but has no inherent adaptability for a claimed special use, as for use "in connection with the development of 6,500 horse-power"** where there is no showing that the power will be available, there can be no special use value to consider as an element of market value. The result would be the same whether navigable water, or non-navigable water, or no water at all, were an element in the case. **The navigability of the water and the Government's right to control it, cannot destroy or exclude from consideration the inherent adaptability of private property for a special use, provided the private property right and the inherent adaptability for the claimed special use actually exist in fact.** Navigable water, and the Government's paramount right of control over it, may determine **whether in fact private property does exist, and if it exists whether it possesses inherent adaptability for the claimed special use,** but it cannot destroy such special use value of private property **where it is proved that both private property and inherent adaptability for a special use exist in fact.**

THE CHANDLER-DUNBAR CASE SQUARELY HOLDS THAT WHERE PRIVATE PROPERTY EXISTS IN FACT, AND IS SHOWN TO POSSESS INHERENT ADAPTABILITY FOR A SPECIAL USE, SUCH SPECIAL ADAPTABILITY MAY BE PROVED AND MUST BE CONSIDERED IN ESTIMATING MARKET VALUE.

Neither the fact that navigable water is involved, nor that the Government has actually exercised its paramount right to control it can eliminate such adaptability from consideration, nor destroy its value. **The inclusion as an element of value of the Chandler-Dunbar strip of upland for lock and canal purposes can be accounted for on no other legal or logical ground.**

In allowing value based upon inherent adaptability for a special use where both the private property right and the inherent adaptability are proved, the Supreme Court in the Chandler-Dunbar case said:

"The exception taken to the inclusion as an element of value of the availability of these parcels of land for **lock and canal purposes** must be overruled. That this land had a prospective value for the purpose of constructing a canal and lock parallel with those in use had passed beyond the region of the purely conjectural or speculative. * * *

"This land was the only land available for the purpose. It included all the land between the canals in use and the bank of the river. Although it is not proper to estimate land condemned for public purposes by the public necessities or its worth to the public for such purpose, it is proper to consider the fact that the property is so situated that it will probably be desired and available for such a purpose."

Appellants' uplands are in identically the same position, factually and legally, as regards their **inherent adaptability for use as a damsite,** as was the Chandler-Dunbar Company land, as regards its **inherent adaptability for use for lock and canal purposes.** The trial court and Appellees' brief in the instant case have failed to note the identity of legal principles and controlling facts affecting the two tracts of land. After reading the above quoted language of the Supreme Court allowing the special use value of the Chandler-Dunbar land, the trial court in the instant case said:

> "Now all the court undertook to decide on that question was you may show the special availability of a piece of property and show its availability for that particular thing, or purpose for which it is being condemned. There is no question in this instance of riparian ownership of the flow of the stream or the power which it would develop. This is a question of structures on land which in no way interferes with the development of or improvement of navigation by the Government in the exercise of its paramount right to develop and improve navigation."

The fact is that the Supreme Court not only permitted the Company to "show the special availability" of its land for lock and canal uses, but it required that "special availability" to be considered as an element of market value, and to be paid for as such.

The Court stated accurately that "there is no question * * * of riparian ownership of the flow of the stream or the power which it would develop." It is equally true that there is no such question in the instant case. **Appellants make no claim for the flow of the stream nor for the power which it would develop.** They claim only that the market value of their land is increased by its inherent adaptability for use as a dam site, just as the Chandler-Dunbar Company claimed that the market value of its land was increased by its inherent adaptability for use for lock and canal purposes. **Appellants also claim that they are entitled to have that fact considered as an element of the market value of their land, just as it was in the Chandler-Dunbar case.**

If it be conceded that the trial court also stated accurately that in the Chandler-Dunbar case "this is a question of structures on land which in no way interferes with the development or improvement of navigation by the Government in the exercise of its parament right to develop and improve navigation," the identity of the two cases as to controlling facts and legal principles still exists. The construction of a dam on Appellants' land across the Columbia River "in no way interferes with the development or improvement of navigation by the Government." In fact, **the construction of such a dam is the only means whereby the Government can develop or improve navigation.** If the Grand Coulee dam were being constructed by private capital under Government supervision as provided by the Federal Water Power Code, the same improvement of navigation would be had with no different "interference" or "structure" than will be caused by the Government dam. **The dams or structures, and their effect upon navigation, would be identical, whether constructed by the Government or by private enterprise.**

But the statement of the trial court is not entirely accurate. The construction by private capital of a fourth canal with accompanying locks on the Chandler-Dunbar land would necessarily "interfere with the development and improvement of navigation by the Government" unless the construction and operation of said canal and locks were carried on under government control. The Government would already have three canals and accompanying locks in operation. The Government had already exercised its absolute dominion over the submerged land and the water of the St. Mary's River. Indeed, **neither private capital nor the Government could build or operate another canal and locks on the Chandler-Dunbar land without using the submerged land and the navigable water of the river over which the Government had already exercised absolute dominion.** How then can it accurately be said that the use of the Chandler-Dunbar upland for the purposes for which it was inherently adaptable would "in no way interfere with the development or improvement of navigation by the Government?" **If that statement is accurate in reference to the Chandler-Dunbar upland, it is equally true** with reference to Appellants' uplands. **The two tracts of upland, in the Chandler-Dunbar and the instant cases, are in the same identical position, as regards inherent adaptability for special uses.**

In law, and in sound practical reason, **it can make no difference that Appellants' land, any more than the Chandler-Dunbar land, can be used for the purpose for which it is inherently adapted only by using the submerged land and navigable water over which the Government has dominion.** Why should that fact make any difference? The Chandler-Dunbar upland was as necessary to the construction and operation of the fourth canal at the rapids of St. Mary's River as were the submerged land and the navigable water of the river over which the Government had absolute dominion. Likewise, **Appellants' uplands are as necessary for the construction of a dam at Grand Coulee on the Columbia River and for the development of hydro-electric power and the improvement of navigation, if such will result, as are the river bed and the water of the Columbia River.** Neither property is sufficient to accomplish the desired improvement without the use of the other.

So long as it is legal and practical to combine the properties to accomplish the use and improvement for which it is inherently adapted, **such inherent adaptability may be shown to and must be considered by the jury in estimating market value.**

> **McCandless v. U. S.,**
> > **74 Fed. (2d) 596,**
> > **80 L. Ed. 797.**

> **Olson v. U. S.,**
> > **292 U. S. 246,**
> > **78 L. Ed. 1236.**

> **San Diego Land & Town Company v. Neale,**
> > **78 Cal. 63,**
> > **20 Pac. 372.**

APPELLANTS' BRIEF pages 28-58.

The Trial Court and Government counsel appear to have disregarded the distinction between **upland** situated above ordinary high water mark and **submerged** land situated below ordinary high water mark. Both Court and counsel cite and rely on

Lewis Blue Point Oyster Co. v. Briggs,
229 U. S. 82,
57 L. Ed. 1232.

It is respectfully submitted that the question in the Briggs case has no relationship or similarity whatsoever to the question presented here on appeal. The only lands involved in the Briggs case were **submerged lands** over which the **Government had absolute dominion,** and for which, in the improvement of navigation, the Government could not be required to pay compensation. In Appellants' case, however, the only land involved is **upland** over which the **Government has no dominion whatever** either to improve navigation, or otherwise, and the Government may not take such upland without payment of just compensation.

With great respect to the learned Trial Court and able Government counsel, it is suggested that reliance on such cases as the Blue Point Oyster case, which deal exclusively with **submerged lands,** and a misconception of the real holding in the Chandler-Dunbar case, are responsible for the error committed by the Trial Court, as well as for the fallacy of Counsels' argument in their attempt to justify it. The whole structure of Appellee's case in support of its First division of its brief is based on this fundamental error.

It is respectfully submitted that the only part of the opinion in the Chandler-Dunbar case which is in point, on the question presented on this appeal, is that

part which awards compensation for the narrow strip of upland in view of its inherent adaptability for use for lock and canal purposes; and that the Chandler-Dunbar case, properly understood, is controlling authority supporting Appellants' demand for a new trial of their cause.

With due respect, it is suggested that misconception of the Chandler-Dunbar case is responsible for the confusion expressed by the Trial Court as to what instruction should be given to the jury in the event that Appellants' theory of the law were adopted (Ap-le's Br. ft. p. 40-41).

There should be no difficulty in submitting the case to the jury on Appellants' theory of the law, and under proper instruction. Appellants' 10th requested instruction, **Assignment of Error Number III,** (Appellants' Br. p. 16-17) would serve as the foundation for such instruction. The jury should be instructed that Defendants claimed that their lands possessed a higher market value because of their claimed inherent adaptability for use as a dam site; that if the jury found as a fact that such special adaptability inherred in Defendants' lands, and that their fair market value had been affected thereby, (a definition of fair market value should be given), that the jury should award such an amount as they found the fair market value of said lands actually to be in view of all uses for which said lands are reasonably adapted. The jury should also be told that the deterent facts and circumstances as well as the favorable facts and circumstances should be taken into consideration in determining fair market value. That some of such deterent circumstances were that many separate tracts of land must be unified by the exercise of eminent domain, that permits must be obtained to use the river bed and to construct the dam, that fees and expenses would necessarily be involved in accomplishing these results, that the dam must be constructed and operated conformable with Federal regulations for the promotion and improvement of navigation. These, and all other facts and circumstances, favorable as well as unfavorable, which could properly affect market value should be considered by the jury insofar as the jury found that market value had been affected thereby. These general principles, supplemented and modified by the controlling principles of law stated by the Supreme Court of the United States in **Olson v. U. S.**, would serve as instructions to the jury which would conform with the law, and would be fair to all parties concerned.

Instructions to the jury submitting somewhat similar issues may be found in

> **Sargent v. Merrimac,**
> **197 Mass. 171,**
> **81 N. E. 970, 972,**
> **11 L. R. A. (N. S.) 996.**

Approved by the Supreme Court of the United States in

> **McGovern v. New York,**
> **229 U. S. 363.**

Shoemaker v. United States,
147 U. S. 282.

U. S. v. Chandler-Dunbar Water Power Company,
229 U. S. 52, 78.

"SECOND—That the decision * * * was correct * * * because all the qualified testimony was that this land did not in fact have any additional value on account of alleged adaptability for dam site purposes * * *."

The brevity with which Appellee's "second" point is treated confirms our conviction that it could not have been urged seriously. The fact that it is urged at all indicates the difficulty under which able and experienced counsel have labored in their attempt to justify the ruling complained of. Concisely stated, Appellee's "Second" point is that the trial court was justified in excluding from the consideration of the jury all evidence of special use value because it is claimed that Appellee's witnesses were better qualified than were Appellants'. Even if the claimed superiority existed, the question of market value would still be for the jury. On Appellee's own statement, (Appellee's Br. p. 52), the testimony of Marvin Chase, for many years hydraulic engineer for the State of Washington, and Chairman of the Columbia Basin Survey Commission, was in itself sufficient to take the question of use value to the jury. The relative qualification of witnesses goes only to the weight and not to the admissibility of their testimony.

Ford Hydro-Electric Company v. Neely,
13 Fed (2d) 361,
(Certiorari denied 273 U. S. 723).

"The objection made to the question asked, and now urged to the testimony given by both witnesses, goes to the competency of the evidence sought and brought out; that is, to the competency of evidence as to the peculiar fitness of the land for particular purposes as an element in estimating its value. That this is proper evidence to be considered by the jury in determining the market value of the land has been often decided. * * * The evidence objected to threw light upon the availability of the land for water power purposes and the value of such element, as bearing upon what might be paid for it by one desiring to purchase it, and thus bore upon its market value. By objecting to this evidence, plaintiff in error sought to exclude it altogether. As remarked by the trial court, **the objection went rather to the weight to be given the evidence than to its competency. The availability of the land for the development of water power, and the value of it for such purposes, was a proper element to be considered by the jury in fixing its market value.** * * *"

But Appellee's "second" point is not well taken for the further reason that it begs the very question at issue. The question is whether Appellee should pay for a **dam site** as claimed by Appellants, or for **"1100 acres of desert land"** as claimed by Appellee (Aple's Br. foot p. 45). If a dam site was taken from Appellants than Appellee's witnesses were not qualified to estimate its value. If only desert land was taken there would be no question on this appeal. **Whether a dam site or merely desert land was taken is a question which can be determined only on full consideration of the evidence which was stricken from the record and excluded from consideration, as well as on all the evidence, and circumstances in the case.** Obviously, that question cannot be determined by comparing the qualification of the respective witnesses.

"THIRD"—Briefly stated Appellee's third and last point is that Appellants are not entitled to have the inherent adaptability of their upland for use as a dam site shown to the jury, nor to have the jury consider such adaptability in estimating fair market value, because:

(a) Appellants do not own all the land required for the dam site, in that the river bed must also be used.

(b) Many hundreds of acres of both private and public lands, including Indian lands, must be acquired for use as a storage reservoir.

(c) The right to use the navigable water of the Columbia River must be acquired in order to make the Grand Coulee development practicable.

(d) Appellee has acquired the right to use the said land and the river bed,—therefore, neither Appellants nor anyone else could acquire such right without which no one would build the dam.

(e) Appellee has declined to permit private capital to develop the Grand Coulee project, and has taken steps to make that development a Government PWA project, thereby excluding any possibility that Appellants or anyone else might use Appellants' lands as a dam site.

(f) The unification in one ownership of all land necessary to complete the Grand Coulee project can be accomplished only by the exercise of eminent domain. Therefore, special adaptability of Appellants' land may not, as a matter of law, be shown to or considered by the jury.

These six propositions urged by Appellee in support of the Trial Court's ruling, are so inter-related that convenience and brevity will be served by considering them together.

It is now much too late in the development of the law of eminent domain for these propositions, which Appellee urges, to receive serious consideration. **No Court of last resort** so far as disclosed by Appellee's Brief, or by our search of the authorities has ever held with Appellee on these propositions.

It is a basic and necessary element in all enterprise and in all improvement, that the value of any unit of

property, as well as the value of any human effort or
contribution is measured not by what it is worth **standing alone,** but by what it is worth in view of its inherent
adaptability for service **in combination with other property,** with other rights and obligations, and with other
human effort. Accordingly, the courts, with good reason and unanimity, have held that market value which
exists in fact, in view of all available uses must be paid,
and that the propositions advanced in Appellee's Brief
do not justify excluding evidence of inherent adaptability as an element of market value.

The cases so holding are legion, but due to their
unanimity and to the general treatment of the subject
found in Appellant's Brief, pages 27-58, only a few of
the leading and more recent cases will be referred to
here:

(a) **That Appellants do not own all the property necessary to the completed project does not
justify the trial court's ruling.**

McCandless v. U. S.,
74 Fed. (2d) 596.

"Limited to the land itself for sources of
water it was clear from the evidence that the
land could not be made available for sugar cane
purposes. * * *

"I instruct you that you must entirely disregard any possibility of bringing water to the
land in question from **any other land,** excepting

the land which the Government here seeks to condemn and the 284 acre tract. * * *

"The major question upon the appeal is whether the court erred in denying the offers of proof and giving the instruction quoted. * * *

"The denial of the offers of proof and the giving of the instruction above referred to were errors."

Olson v. U. S.,
    292 U. S. 246,
    78 L. Ed. 1236.

"The fact that the most profitable use of a parcel can be made **only in combination with other** land, does not necessarily exclude that use from consideration if the possibility of combination is reasonably sufficient to affect market value."

(b)   That the right to use public land and Indian land must be acquired before private capital can develop the project, and that such right had not been acquired, does not justify the trial court's ruling.

See Appellants' Brief, pages 28-52.

McCandless v. U. S., supra.

"It appears from the evidence that in order to supply the land in question with sufficient water supply for the cultivation of sugar cane the **water would have to be conducted not only across public lands of the Territory,** but also across other land held in private ownership."

Ever since 1926 the Department of Indian Affairs has had frequent applications for building power lines and using water for irrigation and for public highways over Indian lands. It is the uniform policy of the U. S. Government and the Department of Indian Affairs to give very favorable consideration to such applications. **Mr. Harvey K. Meyer, Superintendent of the Colville & Spokane Indian Reservations,** which are the two reservations involvved in this proceeding, testified that he had never known of any such application being denied or refused (Transcript of Record 158-159).

(c) **That the right to use the navigable waters of the Columbia River must be acquired in order to operate the project does not justify the trial court's ruling.**

See Appellants Brief pages 36-59.

Ham, Yearsley & Ryrie vs. N. P. Ry. Co., et al.,
107 Wash. 37.
181 Pac. 898.

For other citations and analysis and discussion of the Ham, Yearsley & Ryrie case see Appellants' Brief pages 38-40.

U. S. v. Chandler-Dunbar Company, supra.

For analysis and discussion see Appellants' Brief pages 41-45.

(d & e)   That Appellee has decided to conduct the Grand Coulee improvement as a PWA project and has acquired the necessary permits from the State of Washington, and, accordingly, has excluded Appellants and all the world from possibility of using Appellants' land for that purpose, does not justify the trial court's ruling.

There is no competent evidence to prove when Appellee decided to conduct the Grand Coulee improvement as a government project. Appellee states:

"This particular project has been so reserved for Government construction ever since 1922,"

(Aple' Br. 2A).

There follows a statement of Mr. Creager made on cross-examination on an entirely different point. Clearly, Mr. Creager was not a competent witness to prove the policy of the Government with reference to this subject. What Mr. Creager said necessarily could be nothing more than a conclusion based purely on hearsay. It was not the best evidence. Government policy cannot be proved by that class of evidence.

But neither the fact nor the time of the Government's determination to make this improvement is material to accomplish the result claimed by Appellee. The

Government is in no different position, as regards its obligation to pay just compensation for Appellants' upland, than a private corporation would be, after it had acquired permits from the State of Washington and from the Federal Government to make this same improvement. The power of eminent domain as well as state and Federal permits are sovereign in character. Whether such rights are exercised by the sovereign itself or by its grantee makes no difference. **If this development were being conducted by private capital, under Government authority and supervision, exactly the same steps and procedure would be followed as the Government has taken in the acquisition of the rights and property which it now possesses, and exactly the same results to navigation, regulation of stream flow, and the development of power would be accomplished.**

If a private or semi-public corporation had acquired the right to make this development, Appellants and all the world would be excluded from that right as effectively and completely as they have been by Government action. A development of this character is necessarily exclusive and monopolistic, but that fact does not affect the measure of just compensation.

> **Remington's Revised Statutes of Washington, Chapt. 4, Use of State Waters.**
> **Sec. 7408—Eminent Domain by U. S.**
>
> "The United States is hereby granted the right to exercise the power of eminent domain to acquire the right to the use of any water * * * and such power of eminent domain shall be exercised

under and by the **same procedure as now is or may be hereafter provided by the law of this State** for the exercise of the right of eminent domain by **ordinary railroad corporations** * * *."

Sec. 7411—Appropriations—Title to Beds and Shores.

This section provides for appropriation of the **"unappropriated waters"** of the State, and then expressly provides:

"Such appropriation by or on behalf of the United States shall inure to the United States, and its successors in interest, **in the same manner and to the same extent as though said appropriation had been made by a private person, corporation or association.**"

Chapt. I, Water Code, Sec. 7351.

This section specifies the procedure for the "appropriation for a beneficial use," and then expressly provides that:

"As between the appropriations, **the first in time shall be the first in right.**"

From the foregoing facts and provisions of the Washington Statute it follows that the power site withdrawal, water appropriation, reservation of public lands and similar measures upon which Appellee appears to rely, are nothing more or less than the usual and necessary steps in the process of taking and acquiring the rights and property necessary to complete the public improvement. Substantially the same steps would be taken if the improvement were being made by private capital. Of course exclusive rights acquired by the taker in the process of the taking can not operate to exclude elements of inherent value, or in any way to affect the rights of the parties.

In **McCandless v. U. S., Supra,** nothing could be more exclusive than the right being acquired by the Government to build a "naval ammunition depot" on Mr.McCandless' land. It does not appear when the Government decided to make that improvement. The Court did not appear to consider the question to be material, but when the Government decided to develop an ammunition depot on Mr. McCandless' land there was no more possibility of his ever growing sugar cane than that Appellants' land shall be used for dam site purposes by any one other than the Government.

There was an offer of proof in the McCandless case which this court held should have been admitted:

"That Mr. McCandless had every reason to expect that within a short time, **if it had not been for the intervention of this suit,** this water would have been developed * * * and that he had been assured that the policy of the **Land Commissioner and of the Land Board** of the Territory **would be in favor of granting a license** or a fee simple right-of-way * * *, that is **as far as concerns the right-of-way over government land only.**"

Likewise, in the Chandler-Dunbar case, Congress, by Legislative Act had excluded the Chandler-Dunbar

Company, and all the world, from the water and the submerged lands in the river. No right or power is more conclusive than the power of Congress in aid of navigation. Congress had enacted that the Chandler-Dunbar land was necessary for that purpose. Thereafter, there was no possibility that the Chandler-Dunbar Company, or anyone else, except the Government, could ever use that strip of upland for lock and canal purposes. The Court in that case found as a fact:

"Finding of Fact VII.

A fourth lock was then, and now is, in indefinite contemplation."

"Finding of Fact VIII.

In March, 1909, Congress by Act approved March 3, 1909, enacted that the United States would take not merely the land **presently necessary for the third lock,** but all the privately owned property between the northerly existing canal strip and the international boundary line."

In both the McCandless and Chandler-Dunbar cases the landowners had been completely and perpetually excluded by the Federal Government from any possibility of using their land for its claimed adaptability. **In both cases the land, for which special use value was paid by the Government, never could have been used for the purposes for which it was inherently adapted without first obtaining a Government permit, and the right to use Government property,** the public lands in the McCandless case, and the navigable water and submerged

land in the Chandler-Dunbar case. Yet, in both cases the
Supreme Court of the United States ordered evidence of
the inherent adaptability of the land for a special use to
be received in evidence, and to be considered, as an element of market value.

(f) That the unification of properties necessary to complete the development can be accomplished only by the exercise of eminent domain does
not justify the ruling of the trial court.

There is no law and no reason excluding inherent
adaptability from consideration merely because the
necessary properties are unified by eminent domain. If
there were, all that anyone would ever need to do to
escape paying special use value, would be to begin condemnation proceedings. No one can seriously contend
that the measure of just compensation depends on the
procedure by which the property is acquired, or that a
higher value should be paid if the property is acquired
by private negotiation than would have to be paid if it
were acquired by the exercise of eminent domain. There
is no case, properly understood, which so holds. The
Statutes of the State of Washington expressly give the
right of condemnation in such a case. Why should the
exercise of that power destroy values naturally inherent in the property.

Remington's Revised Statutes of Washington.
Sec. 7354—Eminent Domain for beneficial use of water.

"The beneficial use of water is hereby declared
to be a public use, and any person may exercise the

right of eminent domain to acquire any such property or right now or hereafter existing, when found necessary for the storage of water for or the application of water to any beneficial use. * * *"

"Sec. 11572—Right of eminent domain.

The right of eminent domain for the purpose of appropriating real estate is hereby extended to all corporations * * * for the purpose of conveying water by flumes, pipe-lines, channels or any other means for the utilization of water power * * *."

Olson v. U. S., Supra.

"Nor does the fact that it may be or is being acquired by eminent domain negative consideration of availability for use in the public service."

This Court in the McCandless case said:

"It appears from the evidence that, * * * the water would have to be conducted not only across public lands of the Territory but also across other land in private ownership. It may be assumed that such a right of way may be acquired over private land by condemnation; if necessary, by means of a corporation organized for such a purpose."

The fact that the right-of-way over which water might be conducted to the McCandless property could be acquired only by condemnation did not deter this court from permitting consideration to be given to the inherent adaptability of the McCandless land for growing sugar cane. The following are a few illustrative cases holding to the same effect:

U. S. v. Chandler-Dunbar Company, Supra.

Weiser Valley Land & Water Company v. Ryan,
190 Fed. 417, 423.

Ford Hydro-Electric Company v. Neely,
13 Fed. (2d) 361.

Writ denied, 273, U. S. 723.

Emmons v. Utilities Power Company,
141 Atl. 65,
82 N. H. 181.

Niagara Lockport & Ontario Power Co. v.
Horton,
247 N. Y. Supp. 761.

City of Stockton v. Vote,
76 Cal. App. 369,
244 Pac. 609.

Obstacles such as are enumerated in Appellee's brief are merely deterent factors to be considered by the jury along with all other facts, favorable and unfavorable, that naturally and properly would affect market value. Such obstacles merely bear **on the issues of fact.** They cannot operate to exclude inherent adaptability from the record, and from the consideration of the jury **as a matter of law,** provided such adaptability may "reasonably be held to affect market value;" and that there be a "**legal and practical possibility** that he, or some other person other than the expropriating authority could have acquired the right to flow the land necessary for the lawful raising of the lake," that is, for the development of the project.

Olson v. U. S., Supra.

OLSON V. UNITED STATES—ANALYZED, DISTINGUISHED AND APPLIED.

Appellee cites the holding in the Olson case as authority supporting the ruling of the Trial Court, seemingly overlooking the distinction between the facts in the Olson case and the record now before the Court. That distinction is very clear and controlling. Inherent adaptability was excluded from consideration in the Olson case, not because of multiplicity of ownerships, nor because public lands and Indian lands were involved; not because the Lake of the Woods was a navigable body of water, nor because numerous properties were being acquired and unified by eminent domain, but use value was excluded because, in the Olson case, **the lands necessary to the development of the Lake of the Woods Storage Reservoir were situated in two countries,** in the United States and Canada. **Neither country had any legal right to condemn land in the other, and** the residents of one country could not acquire the right of eminent domain in the other country. **There was no law or practicable means whereby the landowners, or any other person or entity, could lawfully acquire and unify the lands** necessary to make the Lake of the Woods reservoir. **The only way** in which the project could possibly be accomplished in a lawful manner **was by the two Governments entering into an international treaty.** The legal effect of that situation was that **the Government was the only possible taker which could use Appellants' lands for reservoir purposes.**

The controlling fact that lands, absolutely necessary to the creation of the storage reservoir were located in **two countries** (erroneously stated in Aples' Br. P. 61, as "two counties") **with no legal means of unification** puts the decision in the Olson case on a set of facts, and consequently on a legal principle, in no way involved in the instant case. That the decision in the Olson case was placed on its own peculiar facts is recognized and clearly stated by the Supreme Court:

> **"The situation** in respect of lands bordering the Lake of the Woods **is essentially different. * * ***
> There could be no rational basis for any demand that would affect market value to the owner for reservoir purposes, unless as a legal and practical possibility, he, or some other person or persons, other than the expropriating authority, could have acquired the right to flood the lands necessary for the lawful raising of the lake. **The lands upon which the flowage easement is condemned are located in two countries. Neither could authorize expropriation in the other."**

The court then referred to the practical impossibility of uniting the large number of tracts, variously owned, without the right to exercise the power of eminent domain, and, as stated, there was no law authorizing the exercise of that power. Lands located in both countries were necessary to develop the project. **The necessary and inevitable result was that, as to the owner of the shore lands, there was no "legal or practical possibility that he, or some other person or persons other than the expropriating authority could have acquired**

the right to flood the lands necessary for the lawful raising of the lake."

Referring to the Canadian lands necessary to the
completed reservoir, the Supreme Court said:

"Additional reservoir capacity **could not lawfully be created without them, and they could not
be purchased or condemned.** There was no justi-
fiable basis for competition for the flowage rights
from private owners."

The controlling distinction that **there was no "legal
or practical possibility" for acquiring the lands necessary to complete the improvement** puts the holding in
the **Olson case** in a class by itself. It is not an authority on the facts in Appellants' case where the **"legal and
practical possibility" clearly exists** (Appellants' Brief
pages 54-57).

Appellants' uplands are admitted to be inherently
adapted for use as a dam site. It would be physically and
financially impossible to make the Grand Coulee improvement without them. There was abundant evidence
that profits of many millions of dollars annually would
result from the development; that private capital could
and would have acquired Appellants' lands and undertaken the improvement if the Government had not occupied the field; that their market value is substantially
increased by their inherent adaptability for use as a
dam site; that "private companies are always on the
lookout for such sites." (Appellants Brief pp. 6-15).

Since Appellants' land constitute the only dam site available for the Grand Coulee improvement, the price paid for other lands, not suitable for use as a damsite, is of no assistance as a measure of the market value of Appellants' lands. Dam sites, in this area, were not currently bought and sold. Under these circumstances expert opinion was the proper proof of market value.

Olson v. U. S., Supra.

"Flowage easements upon these lands **were not currently bought or sold to such an extent as to establish prevailing prices,** at or as of the time of the expropriation. As that measure (U. S. v. New River Collieries Company, 262 U. S. 341, 344, 67 L. Ed. 1014, 1017) is lacking, **the market value must be estimated** * * *. In making that estimate there should be taken into account all considerations that fairly might be brought forward and **reasonably be** given substantial weight in such bargaining. Brooks-Scanlon Corporation v. U. S., 265 U. S. 106, 124, 68 L. Ed. 934, 941."

All lands involved in the Grand Coulee development are in the State of Washington. The laws of the United States and of the State of Washington, and the policy of the Government with reference to Indian lands and public lands, the rules and regulations of the Federal Power Commission, controlling developments in navigable waters, are ample to provide **"legal and practical possibility"** for the use of Appellants' lands as a dam site; and it is a matter of common knowledge that, **under these laws and rules and regulations, permits, uniformly** and frequently, have been granted to private and semi-public corporations to build and operate similar dams and structures on the Columbia River and in other navigable waters of the United States.

Every principle and every requirement laid down in the **Chandler-Dunbar case,** in the **Olson case,** and in the **McCandless case,** as prerequisite to requiring evidence of inherent adaptability to be received and considered as an element of value, have been met and satisfied in the record now submitted to this court for review. It is, therefore, urged with great earnestness and confidence that Appellants be granted a new trial.

I. K. LEWIS,
Duluth, Minnesota.
MR. PARKER W. KIMBALL,
Spokane, Washington.
MR. F. J. McKEVITT,
Spokane, Washington.
MR. EDWARD H. CHAVELLE,
Seattle, Washington.
MR. CHARLES ATEN,
Wilbur, Washington.
Attorneys for Appellants.

MR. BRADLEY W. YOUNG,
Spokane, Washington.
MR. W. E. SOUTHARD,
Ephreta, Washington.
MR. JOHN M. PRINS,
Minneapolis, Minn.
Of Counsel.

NO. 8162

United States
Circuit Court of Appeals
For the Ninth Circuit

CONTINENTAL LAND COMPANY, a corpora-
tion, JULIUS C. JOHNSON, MABLE JOHN-
SON, SAMUEL J. SEATON, MARY A. SEA-
TON, EMMA RATHS, MARTHA RATHS
BALDWIN, WARREN BALDWIN, HENRY
RATHS, GEORGE RATHS, ALBERT
RATHS, ARTHUR RATHS, ALMA RATHS
CLARK, FRED CLARK, MARY RATHS
MARNHART, CLARENCE MARNHART,
MINNIE RATHS, FRED RATHS and MA-
NITA RATHS.

Appellants,

vs.

UNITED STATES OF AMERICA,

Appellee.

Appellants' Petition for Reargument

Upon Appeal from the District Court of the United
States for the Eastern District of Washington,
Northern Division.

INDEX

Cases

NO. 8162

United States
Circuit Court of Appeals
For the Ninth Circuit

CONTINENTAL LAND COMPANY, a corporation, JULIUS C. JOHNSON, MABLE JOHNSON, SAMUEL J. SEATON, MARY A. SEATON, EMMA RATHS, MARTHA RATHS BALDWIN, WARREN BALDWIN, HENRY RATHS, GEORGE RATHS, ALBERT RATHS, ARTHUR RATHS, ALMA RATHS CLARK, FRED CLARK, MARY RATHS MARNHART, CLARENCE MARNHART, MINNIE RATHS, FRED RATHS and MANITA RATHS.

Appellants,

vs.

UNITED STATES OF AMERICA,

Appellee.

Appellants' Petition for Reargument

Upon Appeal from the District Court of the United States for the Eastern District of Washington, Northern Division.

Subsequent to the filing of the Court's opinion in the above entitled action on February 15, 1937, and within the extended time allowed therefor by the Court,

April 17, 1937, Appellants respectfully petition the
Court for the privilege of rearguing their said cause on
appeal, and as grounds for such reargument respectfully specify the following:

The Court's opinion appears to be founded on two
main reasons:

I.

**The reason specified by the Trial Court in sup-
port of his order striking from the record all evidence of the special adaptability of Appellants' uplands for use as a damsite.**

II.

**A new reason, not relied on by the Trial Court,
and not discussed in the briefs or on the oral argument, namely: that, as a matter of law, it is held that
there was no market for Appellants' uplands for
use as a damsite.**

APPELLANTS BASE THEIR REQUEST FOR A
REARGUMENT OF THE FIRST OF SAID MAIN
REASONS, ON THE FOLLOWING GROUNDS:

*(Note)

1. **The Court's opinion appears to be founded, in
part, on the assumption that Appellants' claim is for a
value arising out of "the development of electric**

---

*Note—Modifications in type are supplied by counsel,
wherever it appears in this brief, unless otherwise
indicated.

power"; and the Court finds that "the development of electric power in this case, it may be said, is purely incidental". (Mid. p. 11, Op.)

Appellants respectfully submit that the opinion misconceives the foundation of Appellants' claim. Appellants make no claim on account of the "development of electric power". The generation of electric power "is purely incidental" as stated in the opinion. Electric Power was referred to in Appellants' evidence only to show the foundation for the market for Appellants' damsite by private capital. It is the inherent adaptability for a damsite that Appellants claim as an element of value and not the adaptability for the "development of electric power". Though the development of electric power is incidental the adaptability of the land for a damsite is direct and primary. It makes no difference what the dam shall be used for, whether for power, pleasure, navigation, reclamation, or any other purposes. It is the fact that the land is inherently adapted for use as a damsite that is controlling. That fact gives the land increased value on the market, according to the evidence in the record. Therefore, such inherent adaptabiliy should be considered in determining market value.

> U. S. v. Chandler-Dunbar Water Power Company,
> 229 U. S. 52.

> Olson v. United States,
> 292 U. S. 246,
> 78 L. Ed. 1236.

McCandless v. United States,
74 Fed. (2d) 596
298 U. S. 342.
80 L. Ed. 797.

The Government is taking **a damsite** from Appellants, in this proceeding. It is not taking **"the development of electric power"**. Therefore it is **a damsite** that should be appraised and paid for.

2. **The Court's opinion and decision rests, in part, on the assumption of law that the "appellants have, as against the dominant right of navigation, no private property right in uplands 'adaptable to special use' in connection with the flooding of such uplands by the construction of a dam for navigation purposes above the reasonable market value to which the land is adaptable."** (ft. P. 11, Op.)

With great deference and respect, Appellants feel that the Court undoubtedly has failed to distinguish between the Government's right to appropriate **submerged land** in aid of navigation, and its rights in **uplands** taken for the same purpose. **Submerged lands,** in aid of navigation, may be taken by the Government without payment of compensation. The Government has no such right in **uplands** taken for that purpose.

The fact that upland is taken in aid of navigation and that the owner of the upland has no property or right in the navigable water, does not deprive the owner of the value of his upland arising out of its inherent adaptability for a special use.

U. S. v. Chandler-Dunbar Water Power Co.,
Supra,

Olson v. United States, Supra.

Please see Appellants' Reply Brief, P. 6-26.

3. Appellants respectfully submit that the opinion
is contrary to the holding in the Chandler-Dunbar case,
and appears not to have given due consideration to the
distinction between value arising out of water power
and value arising out of the special adaptability of the
upland for lock and canal purposes.

The first claimed value, **for water power,** was dis-
allowed by the Supreme Court in its discussion of the
main point in the case. The latter value, that is the value
of the uplands based on their **special adaptability for
lock and canal purposes,** was allowed. This latter value,
it is respectfully submitted, is identical with the value
claimed by Appellants arising out of the admitted
adaptability of their uplands for use as a damsite. (See
discussion of the Chandler-Dunbar case in Appellants'
Appellants' Brief, pgs. 41-45.) (Reply Br. P. 6-26)

THE SECOND OF SAID MAIN REASONS IS STATED BY THE COURT IN ITS OPINION:

"There is not left the shadow of a doubt that
there was no reasonable probability of utilizing this
land by private capital." (P. 13, Op.)

The Trial Court did not urge the above conclusion
in support of his ruling and judgment, being of the

opinion, no doubt, that there was abundant evidence to make that a question of fact for the jury. In that, we respectfully submit the Trial Court was right; and this Court, in forming a contrary opinion, overlooked material portions of the record.

The evidence on the question of **marketability** was not emphasized either in the briefs or on the oral arguments, for the reason that the point did not appear in the case. The Trial Court in support of his ruling relied exclusively on the navigability of the Columbia River, and the fact that the Apellants had acquired no right to use either the water or the bed of the river. The briefs and the oral arguments were directed, by both parties to the appeal, to the propositions relied on by the Trial Court.

Since the question of marketability is brought into the case for the first time in the opinion of this Court, and since there has been no necessity or opportunity to discuss either the facts or the law bearing on that question, Appellants respectfully ask for a reargument in order that a full discussion may be had. As a basis for their petition Appellants briefly point out the following:

A.—THE FACTS IN THE RECORD.

The record proves, by competent evidence, that Appellants' damsite was marketable.

MR. R. H. THOMSON, hydraulic engineer of recognized standing and ability, practising his profession in the State of Washington since 1881, testified that he was familiar with all of the principal dam sites in the State of Washington, and most of the principal dam sites in the Pacific northwest, and hat he was familiar with the prices that had been paid f r many of them.

Mr. Thomson testified that there will be a stable rate of increase in the power consumption in the territory tributary to Grand Coulee at the rate of 9% per year (R. P. 151). That he had made such a study of Grand Coulee as he would make if he were responsible for advising a private investor, and that by the year 1940 the entire installed capacity of all power plants now in existence, or in contemplation, in the State of Washington, will be consumed. That he had taken into consideration all power plants in existence, and all additions possible to be made, and that the Grand Coulee damsite was well adapted to supply economically the increased demand for power.

Mr. Thomson testified that he recommended the development of Grand Coulee by private capital, and that the development of Grand Coulee by private capital would pay satisfactorily. (R. P. 152).

Mr. Thomson further testified that the development of Appellants' damsite by private capital would show a **net profit of $5,756,00.00 annually after deducting all customary and proper charges.** That the investment "would be seized rapidly by the investment public", and that private capital would have acquired the Grand Coulee damsite in December, 1933, or within a reasonable time thereafter, except for the fact that the Government had acquired it. He stated that **"there is always a**

demand for damsites in the State of Washington". (R. P. 153-154)

MR. MARVIN CHASE, a resident of the State of Washington for 43 years, **hydraulic engineer for** the **State of Washington** for 7 years, and **Chairman of the Columbia Basin Survey Commission**, testified that as State Hydraulic Engineer it was his duty to pass upon the water resources of the State of Washington, and that **as Receiver of the Priest Rapids Power Project**, and as **engineer for the Puget Sound Light & Power Company**, he had experience in determining the value of power sites. That as a member of the Columbia Basin Commission he **had first-hand information regarding Appellants' damsite**. Mr. Chase testified that based upon his experience and his knowledge gained officially in the State of Washington, and **from first-hand information as to what had been paid for other damsites** in the State of Washington, it was has judgment that **Appellants' damsite had a market value of $2,850,000.00**. (R. P. 145-146)

MR. H. P. THOMAS, a graduate engineer, with experience in the employ of the Puget Sound Power & Light Company and the Weyerhauser Timber Company, and in the Department of Public Utilities for the city of Tacoma, testified that he had made a thorough study of the market for electric power in the area tributary to Grand Coulee; that he was acquainted with Appellants' damsite, and with other available sites on the Columbia River. He testified that Grand Coulee "has several inherent qualities which make it an excellent site, and that he had made a study to determine whether private capital would be in the market to acquire Appellants' damsite. That there has been a normal rate of increase in the power market tributary to Grand Coulee of 9% compounded annually. That by 1941 all the installed electrical capacity and all uncompleted capacity in the State of Washington will be absorbed, and that in view of that fact private capital would put Grand Coulee into operation by 1941 (R. P. 120-123).

Mr. Thomas testified that it would be practicable for private capital to acquire Appellants' damsite and to develop it to its full capacity. That after deducting all operating expenses, including cost of operation, maintenance, management, depreciation, reserves, and other necessary expenses, there will remain a net balance of earnings of **$4,434,000 annually, and** that **over a period of 20 years after the plant is started the investment will show an accumulated surplus of $61,562,844.00** (R. P. 123-124).

MR. WILLIAM P. CREAGER, consulting engineer residing in Buffalo, New York, who had served many of the principal power companies of the country and some foreign countries, and who had served the U. S. Government in connection with its Muscle Shoals plant (R. P. 131-132) **testified, that he was in direct contact with financial interests** (R. P. 132). That he had examined Appellants' Grand Coulee damsite, and that he had **studied the Army Engineers' reports thereon. Mr. Creager testified that there was a market for Appellants' damsite,** and that "it is both feasible and practical" for private capital to acquire and develop Appellants' property. That he had studied and reported on hundreds of damsites, and **"I never yet have seen a damsite better than this, and perhaps I have never seen any as good."** Further, the "very magnitude of this dam and power house is sufficient to stifle competition; **there are comparatively few hazards at that site compared with other possible sites on the river"** (R. P. 133-134).

Mr. Creager testified that there was a **demand and a market for Appellants' damsite by private capital** (R. P. 134-135). That Appellants' damsite is the best site on the river for the construction of a dam and power house, and that the difference between the profits derived from electricity generated at Appellants' damsite and profits available from any other comparable site **or any other possible site on the river,** would amount to millions of dollars each year. **That private capital would certainly be interested in purchasing Appellants' damsite as of that date** (R. P. 135).

Mr. Creager testified that the cost of developing Appellants' damsite **"would neither be prohibitive nor beyond the reach of private capital"** (R. P. 135-136). Further, that if private capital did not finance Appellants' Grand Coulee damsite it would have to finance some other site on the river. That private companies are always on the lookout for damsites to keep up with the market, and that **"The Grand Coulee damsite would result in a development which is better than any other possible site on the river."** (R. P. 141-142)

Mr. Creager further testified that the **market price** which he had testified to was **"sufficiently attractive to**

move it at the time of December, 1933, in full consideration of the conditions that existed at that time. In normal times it would have been very much greater." (R. P. 142)

MR. WILLIS T. BATCHELLER, a graduate in electrical engineering from the University of Washington, with a master's degree in electrical engineering, testified, that he had been employed by the Puget Sound Power & Light Company, and that he had had experience in determining the suitability, and appraising the market value of damsites. That he had been employed by the State of Washington to make engineering studies and to report to the Director of Conservation on the development of the Grand Coulee project. That he had made such study and report in 1921 and 1922.

Mr. Batcheller testified that there is no other site **on the Columbia River where a dam can be built at any cost** which will serve the purposes accomplished by Appellants' damsite. That Appellants' lands are most suitable for a damsite. The reasons given by Mr. Batcheller will be found on pages 100 to 104 of the printed record. **It would be physically impossible to construct a dam without using Appellants' damsite "no matter how much money you wanted to spend"** (R. P. 104).

Mr. Batcheller testified that there is and will be a market for all electric power which can be generated on Appellants' damsite. **That there was a demand and market for Appellants' damsite by private capital,** and that private capital "is always ready for a proposition of that kind which will show a profit,"_ * * * (R. P. 105).

Mr. Batcheller's chart (Defendants' Exhibit 13) received in evidence, shows graphically the estimated growth of the power market in the area tributary to Grand Coulee, and he testified that other power sites beside Grand Coulee must be developed, because the entire electrical output of Grand Coulee, together with the capacity of all other developed sites, will not be sufficient to supply the estimated market. That by the year 1950 it will be necessary to have a billion kilowatt hours from other plants, and that without the Grand Coulee power there will be an actual shortage of power in this area. That if Grand Coulee is not developed that block of power will have to be supplied from some other site. (R. P. 105-106).

Mr. Batcheller testified that after paying all expenses and creating an amortization fund, out of which by the end of the license period, the total investment will have been returned to the investors, the Grand Coulee project in addition to all that, will develop a surplus of $13,000,000.00 annually. That except for the fact that the Government had decided to acquire Appellants' damsite, and to develop the Grand Coulee project, private capital would be in the market to purchase Appellants' damsite in the year 1933 (R. P. 107).

Mr. Batcheller testified "there is no other single site on the Columbia River or elsewhere where a similar block of power could be developed at any price." That there are several other sites on the Columbia River where similar blocks of power may be developed, but that the production cost would be about 20% or 25% greater than the production cost at Appellants' damsite, and the surplus resulting from their combined operation would be about $4,000,000.00 per year less than the surplus from Grand Coulee (R. P. 109-110).

Appellants believe that the Court could not have had in mind the foregoing testimony in the record when, in referring to the question of marketability, the Court said:

"The speculative theorizing of expert witnesses as to private capital's seeking this suite for development is of no value."

If this Court had been advised of the foundational facts on which the opinions of the Engineers were based, it is believed that their testimony would not have impressed the Court as mere "speculative theorizing of expert witnesses". The Trial Court had these foundational facts in mind. It was for that reason, no doubt, that he did not base his ruling and judgment on the hypothesis that there was no market for the damsite.

As a foundation for the opinion of the engineers on both sides of the case it was stipulated (R. P. 42-45) that certain engineering data and reports might be used and relied on as being in evidence. A large number of such documents and reports were used as a part of the foundation for the testimony of experts on both sides. These documents were used freely by both parties to the litigation in connection with the direct testimony and on cross examination. In this petition for reargument only a brief reference to such documents will be made. A more complete citation of these foundational facts may be presented to the Court on a reargument.

A report by the U. S. Army Engineers on the Columbia River and minor tributaries to the 73rd Congress, First Session, "House Document No. 103, Volumes 1 and 2, 1934", was made a part of the record by said stipulation; likewise the printed report of the hearings before the Committee on Irrigation and Reclamation of the House of Representatives, 72nd Congress, First Session, on the "Bill H. R. 7448", June, 1932, was stipulated into the record (R. P. 51). The following brief statements from said documents will suffice to indicate some of the foundational facts upon which expert testimony was based, and which apparently satisfied the Trial Court that there was sufficient evidence in the record to make the question of whether there was a market for Appellants' damsite a question of fact for the jury:

THE MARKET FOR POWER JUSTIFIED THE DEVELOPMENT OF APPELLANTS' DAMSITE.
H. D. 103, Page 482-483, Vol. I:

"During 1920 to 1930 power requirements in this territory increased at an average rate of 9.5 per cent per year, compounded annually. For this report, a gradually decreasing rate of increase has been assumed beginning with 8 per cent in 1930 and decreasing to 4 per cent in 1960. Practically all of the power of the major hydroelectric developments on which construction has been started by the variout power companies and municipalities will have been absorbed by 1940, which is the earliest date that power from the Columbia River development could be made available. The additional generating capacity required during the 15 year period 1940 to 1955 would amount to about 3,000,000 kilowatts, whereas the proposed installation at the Columbia River Dam is 1,500,000 kilowatts or only one-half of the expected increase. With proper co-operation on the part of the various power companies and municipalities the proposed Columbia River development should be absorbed in this 15 year period."

H. D. 103, Page 521, Vol. I:

"**Absorption of Columbia River Power**—The installed generator capacity in the territory in which the power from the proposed Columbia River development would have to be absorbed now amounts to a little over 1,000,000 kilowatts, and if the load continues to increase in the next decade as it has in the past, but at a gradually reduced rate of increase as suggested above, the installed capacity will have to be doubled by 1940 in order to supply the demand. **Practically all of the major hydroelectric developments** on which construction has been started by the various power companies and municipalities will **have been absorbed by 1940, which is the earliest date that power from the Columbia River development could be made available.**

Assuming that the power load continues to increase after 1940 in accordance with curves B on drawing No. 222-D-6, there would be required a total of 5,000,000 kilowatts of generating capacity by 1955. The additional generating capacity that would have to be provided during the 15 year period 1940 to 1955 would amount to about 3,000,000 kilowatts, whereas the proposed installation at the Columbia River power plant is 1,500,000 kilowatts. In other words, the proposed installation of 1,500,000 kilowatts would take care of approximately half of the expected increase in power requirements during the 15 year absorption period. **The other half of** the **expected increase would have to be supplied by other hydro or steam development."**

MAJOR BUTLER—HEARINGS ON BILL H. R. 7446, page 18

"Studies show that the sale of the power at 2 mills per kilowatt hour net, or about 2.1 mills gross, would **repay all construction costs of the dam and power plant, plus interest, in 30 years,** and that at the end of 40 years **the accumulated net annual revenue,** after full repayment of costs, including interest, **would amount to $140,000,000.** This would total $168,070,000 with interest at 4 per cent compounded annually. This power could be absorbed into the normal power market tributary to said dam within 15 years after its completion."

On such a showing of market for electricity, the volume of power which can be developed on Appellants' damsite, and by the financial returns on the investment, as estimated by the Army Engineers, it is respectfully submitted that it may not properly be held as a matter of law that there was no market for the damsite.

THAT THE IMPROVEMENT OF NAVIGATION IS INSIGNIFICANT AND THAT THE DEVELOPMENT OF POWER IS PARAMOUNT IS SHOWN BY:

H. D. 103, Vol. 1, pages 6-7:

"5. Above the Snake River conditions are not

favorable to the development of any considerable amount of commerce, but the interests of navigation should be safeguarded by reserving to the United States the right to construct or to require the construction of locks in power dams built in this section.

* * *

"9. In the nontidal section **the development of power is of paramount importance.** It will have no adverse effect on navigation in the tidal section; it can and should be made to aid navigation in the nontidal section. Irrigation development will need the economic support of power developed for the general power market."

H. D. 103, Vol. 1, page 20:

"24. * * * Class (c) streams are the streams upon which **'the apparent benefits to navigation** that could be derived from power developments **would be insignificant.'**

"25. * * * Above the mouth of the Snake the stream may rather, at the present time, be classified as a class (c) stream."

H. D. 103, Vol. 1, page 82-83:

(e) "Commerce on the river between the head of tidewater and the mouth of the Snake is not assured to an amount sufficient to justify the expenditure of more than $5,000,000 of Federal funds as a navigation contribution on a power development (other than for locks) if such power development is **at an expense other than Federal,** nor to justify charging more than $5,000,000 of the cost of a power development to navigation (other than for locks) **if such power development is made with Federal funds contributed or loaned."**

* * :

(f) "In the section of the Columbia **above the mouth of the Snake no steps should be taken in the interest of navigation in connection with power development** except to reserve to the United States the right to install locks or similar works or require them to be installed when navigation requires them, leaving to the future the question of the time such works should be installed and the allocation of costs.

* *

(g) **"The Columbia in its nontidal section is primarily a power stream and other uses should, in general, be subordinate to power development,** provided always that development above the head of tidewater should not adversely affect the rights of navigation in the tidal section.

* * *

"The conclusion that **power development is paramount** in the nontidal section is reached with full appreciation of the just claims of navigation, and is not inconsistent with due regard therefor. Dams for navigation alone would not be justified. No works for navigation alone, other than dams, would on this steep river, adversely affect power development. Power development through creation of reservoirs by means of dams can be made to serve navigation. Power considerations should, in the main, control the location and height of the dams. At the appropriate time due provision should be made for passing navigation through or past the power dams, as stated in (e) and (f) above, and power pool levels and regulation of flow should always be so controlled that navigation will not be unduly and adversely affected."

* * *

(j) "There are numerous sites for power development on the Columbia. Three of these are of special interest for the reasons given below:

* * *

2. At the head of Grand Coulee in the State of Washington. A dam at this point might be constructed for power alone, or for power and irrigation of the large area of land in Washington known as the Columbia Basin irrigation project. A dam at this isolated point would serve only a local river traffic, which may not occur."

On the foregoing findings of the Army Engineers it is apparent that the improvement of navigation is not the impelling motive for the taking of appellants damsite. **The record proves, and everyone knows that it is being taken for the development of hydro-electric power. That purpose, and the profits to be made, are the foundation for the market which existed for Appellants' damsite. Clearly it may not be held as a matter of law that there was no market.**

THAT THERE WAS A MARKET FOR APPEL-
LANTS' DAMSITE AND THAT THE DAMSITE
COULD BE DEVELOPED BY PRIVATE CAPITAL
AT A SATISFACTORY PROFIT, IS SHOWN BY:

H. D. 103, Vol. 1, page 37:

"It was 1902 before the generation and consumption of electricity had gained sufficient importance to be reported upon as a separate industry
by the Bureau of the Census. Since that time it has
made a steady and rapid growth, reaching out into
all departments of human activities until it is now
one of the most important industries of the United
States, with an annual revenue from the sale of
electric service estimated to have been $2,155,000,-
000 in 1930. In the State of Washington the 1930
revenue was about $31,000,000; in Oregon, $17,-
000,000."

H. D. 103, Vol. 1, pages 50, 51, 52:

"The principal Columbia River sites are within
reasonable transmission distance of all the more
important load centers of Oregon, Washington,
northern Idaho and Western Montana. It is logical
to consider the utilities occupying this region as
forming a single market to be supplied by radiating
transmission lines. Such an arrangement makes it
possible to draw on a single source for all or a large
part of the growth of the power sales until the
capacity of that particular power site has been fully
utilized. **A long step in this direction has already
been made by interconnection of the systems of
independent and related power companies.**

"The business of all these utilities is growing rapidly. Frequent increase in generating capacity and other facilities for securing electric power is required to meet the needs of the consumers. **Construction programs are constantly under way.**

"**Puget Sound Power & Light Company is now constructing under Federal** license a dam and power plant at **Rock Island near Wenatchee,** Washington. This is the first dam to be built on the Columbia River. Two 15,000 kilowatt units are to be in service by January 1, 1932. **The entire capacity of 150,000 kilowatts to 200,000 kilowatts is expected to be needed by 1937.**

"**Washington Water Power Company has applied for a Federal license to develop Kettle Falls on the Columbia** 41 miles south of the international boundry. Plans propose an ultimate capacity of 230,000 kilowatts. The original program contemplated completion prior to 1940. The application has been held pending the completion of this report.

"**Portland General Electric Co.** is beginning the development of storage on Clackamas River, a tributary of Willamette River, which will increase the firm output of its power plants on that stream. This company has tentative plans for the construction of power plants at other sites on the Clackamas as they are needed to meet its requirements.

"Inland Power & Light Company is constructing under Federal license a storage dam and power plant at Ariel on Lewis River about 30 miles from Portland, Oregon. One 45,000 kilowatt unit will be ready for service in the autumn of 1931. This power site is planned for the installation of three additional units of the same size. The power will be supplied to Northwestern Electric Co. and Pacific Power & Light Company at Portland, Vancouver, Condit, and elsewhere. Preliminary plans of the company contemplate the progressive development of a number of power and storage sites on Lewis River with a possible ultimate capacity of 1,200,000 kilowatts.

"Montana Power Co. is constructing under Federal license a 100,000 kilowatt power plant on Flathead River 4 miles below the outlet of Flathead Lake in Montana. This plant is to be completed in 1933 or 1934."

H. D. 103, Vol. 1, pages 67-68:

"The margin of economic feasibility of the development of one of these large sites is increased if there be concentrated upon it a large part of the growth of the power market of the Northwest until its total potential output is absorbed. Several years will be required for preliminary work and construction at any of these sites. It has been assumed that 1940 is about as early as first-power production will begin. By that time most of the present construction programs of the several utilities will be completed and their power plants loaded. It should not

be impossible to find a plan under which these pub-
lic-service organizations could pool their interests
to the extent of drawing upon a single large development for the supply of a major part of the prospective growth of their business over a term of
years, especially if such plan would result in lower
cost to them and would help the expansion of business in the whole region. There is enough of an
analogy between the separation of the electrical
business into generation, transmission, and distribution and the customary division of merchandising
into manufacturing, transportation, and retailing
to establish the possibility of mass production of
power and its disposal in wholesale quantities to
large distributing organizations.

"The above discussion has concerned the cost
of power. There is a considerable margin between
the estimated cost of production at Grand Coulee or
The Dalles and the competitive cost of steam power
in favor of hydroelectric power. This margin represents the limit of possible profit. It is illustrated in
table Z, which shows in parallel columns the cost
of energy delivered at the principal load centers.
It is neither necessary or desirable that the initial
selling price of the hydroelectric energy be kept
down to absolute cost provided it is kept within
reasonable limits. Should the selling price be fixed
somewhat about the estimated cost, one or all of
the several things can be accomplished. Among
them are: First, the undertaking can be made a
financial success even though sales are less than
estimated; second, reserves can be built up to be

used in advancing additional development; third, applying particularly where public credit has been used, the investment can be retired or amortized in less than the 40 years estimated."

H. D. 103, Vol. 1, pages 83-84:

"(1)   Prime power from either The Dalles or Grand Coulee sites can be delivered in large quantities at the load centers in the Pacific Northwest **at one half or two thirds the cost at which steam power can be produced in large modern generating stations** where the price of fuel oil is $1 per barrel."

H. D. 103, Vol. 1, p. 535:

"Based on the above assumptions, **the revenue** would be sufficient to **repay the cost** of the Columbia River Dam and power plant **with interest at 4 per cent per annum within 50 years,** in addition to providing for the operation, maintenance, and depreciation of the dam and power plant, and **also provide a surplus of approximately $144,000,000** which would be available for repayment of the cost of the irrigation development and other purposes."

Statement of Major John S. Butler, Corps of Engineers, hearings on Bill H. R. 7446, page 18:

"Studies show that the sale of the power at 2 mills per kilowatt hour net, or about 2.1 mills gross, would **repay all construction costs of the dam and power plant, plus interest, in 30 years,** and that at the end of 40 years the accumulated net annual revenue, after full repayment of costs, including interest, **would amount to $140,000,000.** This would total $168,070,000 with interest at 4 per cent compounded annually. **This power could be absorbed into the normal power market tributary to said dam within 15 years after its completion.**"

(Page 34, same report):

"**The Grand Coulee power is, beyond question, the cheapest large block of power in the United States.**"

Surely it can not be held as a matter of law that a damsite which will develop such a block of cheap power, and repay "all construction costs of the dam and power plant, plus interest, in 30 years", and, in addition thereto, provide an "accumulated net annual revenue" which "would amount to $140,000,000.00", at the end of 40 years, would have no takers on the open market.

THAT IT WAS NOT THE ORIGINAL INTENT THAT THE GRAND COULEE SITE SHOULD BE DEVELOPED BY THE GOVERNMENT, AND THAT IT WAS CONTEMPLATED THAT DEVELOPMENT MIGHT BE CARRIED ON BY PRIVATE CAPITAL, IS SHOWN BY:

H. R. 103, Volume 1, pages 4, 5.

Recommendation of the Chief of Engineers to the Secretary of War.

Conclusions:

"19· I recommend as follows:

    (d)   The power developments on the Columbia

River shall be made **on application of** local governmental authority or **private interests** under restriction of **the Federal Water Power Act** with the prescription of reserved demands of power at cost of production, in such amount as may be made and determined in the interest of irrigation by the Secretary of the Interior.

* *

(f) That no **license be issued for the purpose of constructing dams or for power development** on the Columbia River which is not in accordance with the general plan for combined development for navigation, and power as recommended by the Board, - - - "

H. D. 103, Vol. 1, pages 6-7:

"5. Above the Snake River conditions are not favorable to the development of any considerable amount of commerce, but **the interests of navigation should be safeguarded by reserving to the United States** the right to construct or to require the construction of locks in power dams built in this section.

H. D. 103, Vol. 1, pages 8-9:

"He (the Division Engineer) recommends that this plan be adopted by the United States as its guide **in controlling and supervising development of** the **Columbia River** above tidewater, navigation being considered chargeable with the cost of locks through dams below the mouth of Snake River and subject to contribution of not over $5,000,000 toward the cost of these dams; and that the plan for the tidal section of the river remain as at present.

＊   ＊

"Based upon the information now available, **the Board** concurs in general in the views of the division engineer as to the best general plan for a comprehensive development of this river except as to the number of dams which should be constructed between the mouth of Snake River and tidewater."

H. D. 103, Vol. 1, page 11:

"Suggestions have also been made to the effect that in order to secure for the people the maximum possibilities of cheap power, it might be desirable for the United States to construct transmission lines to the chief centers of population or industry. The Board is not prepared to recommend development on such basis. **It does not understand that the action of Congress in the Boulder Canyon case was intended to be considered as a precedent in the establishment of a policy for the development of water power by the Federal Government on its navigable rivers. On the contrary, it believes that the policy set forth in the Federal Water Power Act is the adopted policy for such development.** This view is supported by the action taken in the case of the Tennessee River where there is also a large amount of potential power. The Report thereon (H. Doc. No. 328, 71st Cong. 2nd Sess.) was under the same provision of law as in this case. It submitted a comprehensive project for the development of the river and **recommended in substance that the power be developed under the provisions of the Federal Water Power Act by private interests, States, or municipalities.** This project was adopted by Congress in the River and Harbor Act of 1930. **There does not appear to be any insuperable difficulty in the development of the Columbia River power on the same basis** at any time when it can be demonstrated beyond question that the value of the power is such as to justify its development **on a purely business basis.**

*   *   *

H. D. 103, Vol. 1, page 85:

"249:,It is recommended that the above stated plan be adopted by the United States as its guide **in controlling and supervising development of the Columbia River above tidewater,** navigation being considered chargeable with the cost of locks through dams below the mouth of Snake River and subject to contribution of not over $5,000,000 toward the cost of those dams;   *   *   *"

*   *

See also Exhibits V and W (R. P. 173)

All Exhibits were transmitted to the Circuit Court of Appeals by Stipulation (R. P. 40).

H. D. 103, Vol. 2, Page 1066
    "Recommendations.

"2036. It is, therefore, recommended:

First. That the comprehensive plan as given and summarized in Chapter IV be adopted as covering the attitude of the United States toward future work on the Columbia above the Snake.

Second. That when **applications for preliminary permits or licenses for power dams on the Columbia are referred to the War Department by the Federal Power Commission, as required by Sec. 4 (d) of the Federal Water Power Act,** no dams be approved the plans of which do not contain provision for the construction of navigation locks when future cnditions may require.

Third. That no **construction of power dams at Kettle Falls or Grand Coulee on the Columbia** nor at the Narrows or Fish Hawk sites on the Spokane **be permitted** until provision has been made for irrigation on the Columbia Basin irrigation project area or until it is certain that that area is not to be irrigated.

Eighth. **That the Federal Government participate** in the execution of the comprehensive plan **to the extent of supervising the work** to see that the general principles of the plan are adhered to and the fullest utilization obtained; that it **participate in** the **construction of navigation locks** through the power dams when prospecive traffic justifies such work.

Ninth. **That the Federal Government do** not **contribute to the cost of these power developments as an aid to navigation,** as the benefit to navigation would not be sufficient to justify such participation."

From the foregoing, it is perfectly clear that it was the original intention that Appellants' damsite should be developed by private capital, under Government supervision, pursuant to the terms of the Federal Water Power Act. As stated in the Report of the Army Engineers, "There does not appear to be any insuperable difficulty in the development of the Columbia River power on the same basis", that is **"that the power be developed under the provisions of the Federal Water Power Act, by private interests".**

Mr. F. A. Banks, the Government's Engineer in charge of the Construction of the Grand Coulee dam, and a government witness, concurs in the Army Engineer's Reports. At the Annual Meeting of the National Reclamation Association held at Salt Lake City, Utah, November 16, 1936, Mr. Banks delivered a public address, which has been published and given wide circulation of which the Court may take judicial notice. Mr. Banks, among other things, said:

"An important factor in the feasibility of this project as a whole is the market that may be available for the power that is to be produced at the Grand Coulee Dam. The market area in which this power may be absorbed includes the area within a radius of 300 miles of the dam and includes all of the State of Washington, the northern part of Oregon, and the northern part of Idaho and the western part of Montana.

"If we may judge the future by the past, there is every reason to believe that the rate of increase in power production for the ten year period prior to 1930, amounting to 9.5 per cent compounded annually will continue after 1934. But if we assume that the rate of increase starts off at but 8 per cent compounded annually and decreases uniformly to 4 per cent during the next 30 years, and if we assume further that Grand Coulee will absorb only one-half of the increase after its completion leaving the other half to Bonneville and other new and additional developments, **all of the Grand Coulee commercial market will be absorbed by the market in 15 years.** And if the commercial power can be sold at $2\frac{1}{4}$ mills at Grand Coulee, equivalent to 3 mills on the Coast, the cost of the Grand Coulee dam and Power Plant with interest at 4 per cent can be liquidated in 50 years **with a surplus of \$144,-500,00** available for the partial liquidation of the irrigation investment or other purposes and after the 50th year **the annual surplus would amount to \$15,000,000.**"

The fundational facts which were included in the record by stipulation, some of which are cited above, were not called to this Court's attention in the briefs or on the oral arguments, because no question was raised in the Trial Court as to the market for Appellants' damsite. The said foundational facts were freshly in the mind of the Trial Court, and, accordingly, the trial court did not question the existence of a market for the damsite, but justified his ruling and judgment on the exclusive proposition that the Columbia River is a navigable stream and that Appellants had no rights in it as against the Government's paramount right to improve navigation. That was the only proposition relied on by the Trial Court, and, accordingly, that was the only proposition presented to this Court on appeal. It is, therefore, not surprising that this Court should not be advised of these foundational facts which abundantly prove that there was a market by private capital for Appellants' damsite.

Before this Court shall conclude as a matter of law that there was no evidence which would justify a holding that there was a market for Appellants' damsite, Appellants feel justifiably confident, in view of the foregoing facts which have not heretofore been called to the Court's attention, that the Court will desire to be fully advised of all facts affecting the market for the damsite before reaching a conclusion on that question. For that reason Appellants respectfully and confidently request a reargument of their cause, in order that they may be of assistance to the Court in that matter.

B—THE LAW APPLICABLE TO THE RECORD FACTS

Appellants respectfully submit that the law does not require evidence that others were in the market bidding against the Government for the purchase of the damsite.

No evidence of actual competition for the purchase of the property is required in order that inherent adaptability for a special use may be taken into consideration in determining market value. It is enough that facts appear which reasonably tend to support the opinion of experts that there was a market for the land for the particular use claimed.

> "Flowage easements on these lands were not currently bought or sold to such an extent as to establish prevailing prices, at or as of the time of the expropriation. **As that measure is lacking** the **market value must be estimated.**"

Olson v. U. S., supra

That is, market value may be determined from the testimony of expert witnesses.

As stated in the opinion of this Court, "McCandless v. U. S. case, 298 U. S. 342, decided May 18, 1936, points the way." In that statement Appellants concur. It is to be observed, however, that in the McCandless case there was no evidence that others desired to buy the land, and "there was no offer of proof that this land was sought by private capital." It did appear, however, that the "owner's land was adaptable for growing sugar cane if supplied with water for irrigation" (P. 13 Op.)

Similarly, Appellants' land was adaptable for the building of a dam, and the dam so built by the investment of private capital would prove extremely profitable. It was legally and economically feasible for private capital to make such development. **There was a** "legal and practical possibility" that Appellants' damsite could be developed by private capital. No additional legislation was required. It is apparent from the report of the Army Engineers, quoted above, that most of the hydroelectric developments in the Pacific Northwest have been made by private capital under Federal Permits, pursuant to the terms of the Federal Water Power Act. And this is true of development in the Columbia River at Rock Island. Everything which the Government has done, and is doing, at Grand Coulee, could be done equally well by private capital by the exercise of rights already provided by law. That is sufficient to conserve to the owners the value for special use which inheres in their uplands. (Olson v. U. S.) Exactly the same means could be lawfully employed by private capital as are being enployed by the Government in making this development.

The diversity of ownerships, the fact of Indian lands, competing power plants, and other matters of similar character referred to in the opinion (P. 13) cannot operate, as a matter of law, to eliminate inherent adaptability for use as a damsite from consideration. The facts mentioned in the opinion should be considered along with all other facts, favorable and unfavorable, including the fact of adaptability for use as a damsite; and the market value should be determined from a fair and full consideration of all the facts. The deterent factors enumerated in the Court's opinion would prove no greater obstacle to the development by private capital than to the development by the Government. The Federal Water Power Code and the Constitution and laws of the State of Washington provide legal means whereby private capital could overcome these obstacles, exactly as the Government is now overcoming them. The "legal and practical possibility" were supplied and were already at hand. They were expressly referred to in the Army Engineers' Reports. They are sufficient to require consideration of the adaptability for use as a damsite.

Olson v. U. S., supra

U. S. v. Chandler-Dunbar, supra

It is respectfully submitted that "judicial knowledge of the Congressional attitude with relation to such permission, and the requirements for the granting of such benefits; * * *" (P. 13 Op.) may not operate to eliminate from consideration the inherent adaptability for use as a damsite. Congress, by withholding permission to build a dam by private capital, and by deciding that the Government should build it, to the exclusion of everyone else, does not eliminate inherent adaptability for a damsite from consideration, in estimating the market value of the property so taken.

The inherent adaptability of Appellants' land as a damsite was not created or conferred by the Government. Just so, its inherent adaptability for a valuable use cannot be destroyed or eliminated from consideration by Government action, or by its withholding of a permit. The quality which makes Appellants' upland peculiarly adapted for use as a damsite inheres naturally in it, and when the Government takes it, it is only right and fair that it should pay whatever of value such naturally inherent quality possesses and contributes to the market price.

It is well settled that the law requires that such payment be made, and the fact that the Government has seen fit to exclude private capital from the development and has decided to take and develop the property itself as a public project, does not relieve the Government from paying the fair market value, with inherent adaptability for a special use taken into consideration.

For a further discussion of this point Appellants respectfully refer to pages 37-39 of Appellants' Reply Brief.

Appellants have deemed it appropriate to present the foregoing outline, without complete detail, in support of their petition for a re-argument. On a re-argument, if permitted, a full presentation of both the facts and the law may be made.

Since the marketability of Appellants' damsite has never been brought into the case until the Court's opinion was written, and since, accordingly, no discussion of that question has been had by either side, it is respectfully urged that a re-argument be granted in order that the parties may have a full opportunity to be heard, in the hope that they may be of assistance to the

Court in doing justice between the parties.

Respectfully submitted,

I. K. LEWIS,

Duluth, Minnesota.

MR. PARKER W. KIMBALL,

Spokane, Washington.

MR. F. J. McKEVITT,

Spokane, Washington.

MR. EDWARD H. CHAVELLE,

Seattle, Washington.

MR. CHARLES ATEN,

Wilbur, Washington.

Attorneys for Appellants.

MR. BRADLEY W. YOUNG,

Spokane, Washington.

MR. W. E. SOUTHARD,

Ephreta, Washington.

MR. JOHN M. PRINS,

Minneapolis, Minnesota.

Of Counsel.

CERTIFICATE

STATE OF MINNESOTA,)
               ·   ) SS.
COUNTY OF ST. LOUIS.)

    I. K. LEWIS, being duly sworn, certifies that he is one of the attorneys and counsel for Appellants in the foregoing appeal. That in his opinion Appellants' petition for a rehearing is meritorious and well founded, and that it is not interposed for delay. That this certificate is made in conformity with Rule 29 of the Rules of the United States Circuit Court of Appeals for the 9th Circuit.

....

                      I. K. LEWIS

Subscribed and sworn to before me

this 5th day of April, 1937.

....

    Margaret J. Palmer

Notary Public, St. Louis County, Minn.

My commission expires July 18, 1943.

      (Notarial Seal)

CERTIFICATE

STATE OF MINNESOTA)
) ss
COUNTY OF ST. LOUIS)

        I. K. Lewis, being first duly s
that he is one of the attorneys and counsel
in the foregoing appeal. That in his opinio
petition for rehearing is meritorious and we
and that it is not interposed for delay. Th
is made in conformity with Rule 29 of the Ru
United States Circuit Court of Appeals for t

Subscribed and sworn to before me
this 5th day of April, 1937.

Margaret J. Palmer

Margaret J. Palmer
Notary Public, St. Louis County, Minn.
My commission expires July 18, 1943
         (Notarial seal)

United States

Circuit Court of Appeals

For the Ninth Circuit. 6

NEUSTADTER, JOSEPHINE D.
NEUSTADTER, FLORENCE N. STETT-
HEIMER, JAMES D. HART and ELLEN K.
ART,

Appellants,

vs.

UNITED STATES OF AMERICA,

Appellee.

Transcript of Record

---

on Appeal from the District Court of the United
States for the Northern District of California,
Southern Division.

PARKER PRINTING COMPANY, 545 SANSOME STREET, SAN FRANCISCO

No. 8176

United States
Circuit Court of Appeals
For the Ninth Circuit.

NEWTON H. NEUSTADTER, JOSEPHINE D.
NEUSTADTER, FLORENCE N. STETT-
HEIMER, JAMES D. HART and ELLEN K.
HART,

Appellants,

vs.

UNITED STATES OF AMERICA,

Appellee.

Transcript of Record

Upon Appeal from the District Court of the United
States for the Northern District of California,
Southern Division.

INDEX

NAMES AND ADDRESSES OF ATTORNEYS.

ADOLPHUS E. GRAUPNER, Esq.,
  1120 Balbour Bldg., San Francisco, California.
                    Attorneys for Appellants

H. H. McPIKE, U. S. Attorney,
ESTHER B. PHILLIPS, Assistant U. S. Attorney,
  P. O. Bldg., San Francisco, California
                    Attorneys for Appellee

In the District Court of the United States for the
  Northern District of California Southern Division.

In Equity—No. 3639L.

UNITED STATES OF AMERICA,
                              Complainant,

vs.

NEWTON H. NEUSTADTER, JOSEPHINE D.
  NEUSTADTER, FLORENCE N. STETT-
  HEIMER, JAMES D. HART, ELLEN K.
  HART,
                              Defendants.

BILL OF COMPLAINT.

To the Honorable Judges of the District Court of
the United States for the Northern District of California, Southern Division.

The complainant, the United States of America,
by its attorney, H. H. McPike, United States Attorney for the Northern District of California, com-
plains of the defendants and respectfully shows to
the Court:

I.

That at all times hereinafter mentioned, the complainant was, and now is, a corporation sovereign and body politic.

II.

That the defendants, Newton H. Neustadter, Josephine D. Neustadter, Florence N. Stettheimer, James D. Hart, and Ellen K. Hart, are citizens of the United States and of the State of California, and are inhabitants of, and reside in the Northern Judicial District of California, Southern Division thereof, and within the jurisdiction of this Court. [1*]

III.

That this is a suit in equity of a civil nature arising under the laws of Congress providing for internal revenue and the collection thereof.

IV.

That David Neustadter, hereinafter referred to as the decedent, died testate in the City and County of San Francisco, State of California, on February 13, 1923, being at the time of his death a resident of the said City, County and State, leaving estate therein, and leaving him surviving as his sole next of kin and heirs at law, and who under the terms of the last will and testament of said decedent are his sole and only legatees and devisees, the following named persons, to-wit:

---

*Page numbering appearing at the foot of page of original certified Transcript of Record.

Josephine D. Neustadter, surviving widow of said decedent. Newton H. Neustadter, surviving son of said decedent. Florence N. Stettheimer, surviving daughter of said decedent. Ellen K. Hart, surviving granddaughter of said decedent. David D. Hart, surviving grandson of said decedent.

V.

That the last will and testament of David Neustadter, deceased, was filed in the office of the Clerk of the Superior Court in and for the City and County of San Francisco, State of California, on February 21, 1923; that thereafter said will was duly and regularly admitted to probate by said Superior Court; that Newton H. Neustadter, Walter W. Stettheimer and Julian Hart were duly appointed executors under said will on March 8, 1923 by the Superior Court in and for the City and County of San Francisco; that thereafter the executors entered upon their duties and proceeded to administer the estate under the provisions of the said will; that the decedent provided in his will that his widow, Josephine D. Neustadter, should receive one-half of his estate; and further provided that the balance of said estate was to be divided into eight equal parts, and that of the said eight parts three parts were bequeathed and devised [2] to Newton H. Neustadter, three parts to Florence N.

Stettheimer, one part to Ellen K. Hart, and one
part to James D. Hart.

VI.

That on November 23, 1923, the executors of said
estate filed an inventory of the property and assets
of said estate showing a value thereof of $601,-
630.77; that the executors of said estate proceeded
to distribute the same in accordance with the provisions of the will of the decedent; and that the
above-named defendants, as heirs at law of David
Neustadter, deceased, have each received as distributees of said estate money and property in
excess of $30,000.00.

VII.

Complainant further states that pursuant to the
provisions of an Act of Congress approved November 23, 1921, entitled "An Act to reduce and equalize
taxation, to provide revenue, and for other purposes", Newton H. Neustadter, executor of the
estate of David Neustadter, deceased, on December
31, 1923, filed with the Collector of Internal Revenue
for the First District of California a return for
Federal estate taxes for the estate of David
Neustadter, deceased; that said return disclosed a
total gross estate having a value of $601,630.77,
and a net estate subject to estate tax in the sum of
$204,847.50, and an estate tax in the sum of $4,145.43
which was paid.

VIII.

That said return was incorrect, misleading and
false in that the gross estate was reported to be

$601,630.77, and the net estate was reported to be $204,847.50, whereas, in truth and in fact it should have shown a gross estate of $603,888.88 and a net estate in the sum of $506,844.18, subject to estate tax.

IX.

That subsequent to the filing of said return the Commissioner of Internal Revenue, upon additional information and facts submitted to [3] him, directed a review and audit to be made of said decedent's estate tax return, and as a result thereof the gross estate, deductions, net estate and estate tax as theretofore reported by the executor of said estate were corrected and determined to be as follows:

Gross estate	$603,888.88
Deductions	98,044.70
Net estate	$505,844.18
Tax determined herein	16,850.65
Tax paid on return $4,035.77	
Balance of return tax paid 109.66	
Additional tax paid 692.23	
Total paid	4,337.66
Deficiency tax	$ 12,012.99

X.

That thereafter the Commissioner of Internal Revenue, within the time provided by law and pursuant to Section 318 of the Revenue Act of 1926, on September 21, 1926, mailed a sixty-day letter to Newton H. Neustadter and the other executors of the estate of David Neustadter proposing the assessment against said estate of the deficiency in estate tax in the sum of $12,012.99, and advised the estate of its right to appeal to the United States Board of Tax Appeals from the proposed deficiency; that thereafter and on November 2, 1926, an appeal was duly taken from said proposal so made by the Commissioner of Internal Revenue to the United States Board of Tax Appeals; that said appeal was docketed as No. 20988; that such proceedings were thereafter had before the United States Board of Tax Appeals; that thereafter on March 14, 1929, an order was entered by the United States Board of Tax Appeals as follows, omitting formal parts: [4]

"DECISION

"Pursuant to the Board's findings of fact and opinion, promulgated March 13, 1929, it is

"ORDERED and DECIDED: That there is a deficiency of $12,012.99 in estate tax.

Enter: Entered March 14, 1929.
(Signed) JOHN B. MILLIKEN,
Member,
United States Board of Tax Appeals."

XI.

That said decision so made and entered by the United States Board of Tax Appeals has never been modified, set aside or reversed and has now become and is the final order and decision of said Board of Tax Appeals, no appeal having been taken within the period provided by law.

XII.

That thereafter and in accordance with the decision of the United States Board of Tax Appeals so made and entered in said appeal, as hereinbefore set out, the Commissioner of Internal Revenue, on September 27, 1929, duly and regularly assessed the deficiency in estate tax in the sum of $12,012.99 so determined by said Board; that although notice and demand for the payment of said tax was duly made by the Collector of Internal Revenue on October 18, 1929, no part of said tax or interest has been paid; that there is now due and outstanding an additional estate tax in the sum of $12,012.99, together with interest thereon at the rate of 1 per centum a month from October 18, 1929.

XIII.

That prior to the assessment of the estate tax as hereinbefore set out, and on February 25, 1924, Newton H. Neustadter, Walter W. Stettheimer and Julian Hart, executors of the last will and testament of David Neustadter, deceased, filed their first and final account of their administration of the estate of said decedent, and their report as executors of the last will [5] and testament of said decedent, and their petition praying for a settlement of said first and final account, and their petition praying for a final distribution of said estate; that said report was duly approved by Honorable Thomas F. Graham of the aforesaid Superior Court in and for the City and County of San Francisco; that although final distribution has been made of the entire estate of David Neustadter, deceased, the executors have not been finally discharged; that the executors, as such, are not made parties defendant in this suit for the reason that they hold no property or assets of said estate at the present time.

XIV.

That the defendants, Newton H. Neustadter, Josephine D. Neustadter, Florence N. Stettheimer, James D. Hart, and Ellen K. Hart, have each received as distributees of said estate money or property in excess of the amount of the tax and interest involved in this suit.

XV.

That by reason of the settlement and distribution of all the property, money and assets of said estate to the next of kin and heirs at law of the decedent, the defendants named herein, the estate is left without any property or assets of any kind with which to pay said estate tax due and owing the United States as hereinbefore specifically set out; that the defendants received as distributees of said estate the aforesaid money, property and assets of said estate charged with a trust in favor of the United States to the extent of the tax and interest as heretofore set forth.

XVI.

That the complainant has no clear, adequate or complete remedy at law against the defendants herein, and therefore brings this suit. [6]

XVII.

That the Commissioner of Internal Revenue authorizes and sanctions these proceedings.

WHEREFORE, in consideration of the facts herein stated, complainant being without a clear, adequate and complete remedy at law comes before this Court and prays:

1. That this Honorable Court order, adjudge and decree that the aforesaid assets of said estate so distributed to the defendants constitute a trust fund for the payment of the additional estate tax due and owing by the said estate to the United States and that the said defendants shall account to this Court for the aforesaid trust property and that the fund aforesaid be applied to the payment of the additional estate tax and interest due and owing to the complainant.

2. That this Honorable Court order, adjudge and decree that the defendants be accountable to the complainant for the aforesaid tax to the extent of the amount distributed to or received by them and each of them from the assets of the said estate and that each of the said defendants be ordered to pay to the complainant to the extent of the amount distributed to and received by them from the assets of the said estate the amount herein shown to be due

to the complainant for additional estate tax, together with interest at the rate of 1 per centum a month from October 18, 1929.

3. That the complainant have such other, and further and general relief as is just and equitable as well as a decree for costs.

And may it please the Court to grant unto the complainant a writ of subpoena to the United States of America issued out of and under the seal of this Honorable Court directed to the above-named defendants and commanding them on a day certain and under certain penalties therein expressed personally to appear before this Honorable Court then and there to answer all and singularly the premises, answer under oath being ex- **[7]** pressly waived, and to stand to and perform and abide by such orders, directions and decrees as may be made against them in the premises, and complainant will ever pray, etc.

H. H. McPIKE,

United States Attorney,

Northern District of California,

Southern Division.

By ESTHER B. PHILLIPS,

Ass't U. S. Attorney. **[8]**

State and Northern District of California,
City and County of San Francisco.—ss:

ESTHER B. PHILLIPS, being first duly sworn, deposes and says:

I hold the office of Assistant United States Attorney for the Northern District of California, and am charged with the responsibility of prosecuting this case. I verify this complaint on behalf of the United States in my official capacity. I have read the foregoing complaint and know its contents. It is true of my own knowledge save as to matters therein alleged on information and belief, and as to those matters I believe it to be true.

ESTHER B. PHILLIPS.

Subscribed and sworn to me before me this 3rd day of October, 1933.

[Seal]   J. A. SCHAERTZER,
Deputy Clerk, U. S. District Court,
Northern District of Calfornia.

[Endorsed]:   Filed Oct. 3, 1933.   [9]

———

[Title of Court and Cause.]

ORDER GRANTING LEAVE TO FILE
AMENDED ANSWER.

Upon stipulation of the parties to the above-entitled suit that the defendants thereto may file an amended answer to the Bill of Complaint therein,

IT IS HEREBY ORDERED that the said defendants may and are hereby granted leave to file an amended answer to said Bill of Complaint in lieu of the Answer now on file.

Dated January 5th, 1935.

> HAROLD LOUDERBACK,
>> Judge of the District Court of the United States for the Northern District of California, Southern Division.

[Endorsed]: Filed Jan. 5th, 1935. [10]

[Title of Court and Cause.]

AMENDED ANSWER TO BILL OF COMPLAINT.

Come now the above named defendants, by their attorneys Herbert L. Rothschild, Esq., and Adolphus E. Graupner, Esq., and, under order of court duly made and entered, file this their amended answer to the Bill of Complaint in the above entitled suit, and allege, admit and deny as follows: [11]

I.

Allege that this court is without jurisdiction in equity in the above entitled proceeding because a plain, adequate and complete remedy may be had at law by complainant herein, because complainant has abandoned various other proceedings at law which offered an adequate and complete remedy at law, and because proceedings in equity against the parties named as defendants are barred by the statute of limitations. In making this answer defendants do so with reserve and without waiver of their challenge of the jurisdiction of this court to hear and/or determine any other issue than those above-mentioned.

II.

Admit the allegation contained in paragraph I of the Bill of Complaint herein.

III.

Admit the allegations contained in paragraph II of the Bill of Complaint herein.

IV.

Deny all the allegations contained in paragraph III of the Bill of Complaint herein, and specifically deny that this suit is authorized by the laws of Congress or any act of the Congress of the United States.

V.

Admit the allegations contained in paragraph IV of the Bill of Complaint herein.

VI.

Admit the allegations contained in paragraph V of the Bill of Complaint herein.

VII.

Admit the allegations contained in paragraph VI of the Bill of Complaint herein, and in addition thereto allege that the decree of distribution therefor was made and ordered by [12] the Superior Court of the State of California on the 25th day of February, 1924.

VIII.

Admit the allegations contained in paragraph VII of the Bill of Complaint herein.

IX.

Deny the allegations contained in paragraph VIII of the complaint and particularly the specific statement contained therein "that said return was incorrect, misleading and false".

X.

Deny the allegations contained in paragraph IX of the Bill of Complaint therein and, in lieu thereof allege the following:

That on or about September 21, 1926, nearly three years after the estate tax return was filed and approximately a year after the final assessment of estate tax was made by the Commissioner of Internal Revenue and paid in full by the estate of David Neustadter, deceased, said Commissioner proposed to assess only against the alleged executors of said estate a deficiency in estate tax in the amount of $12,012.99. That said proposed deficiency was asserted in a purported notice of deficiency under section 318 of the Revenue Act of 1926 and in the pertinent part thereof said Commissioner stated:

> "In view of the decision of the United States Supreme Court in the case of United States v. Robbins, 269 U. S. 315, rendered January 4, 1926, and an opinion of the Attorney General of the United States issued June 24, 1926, (Treasury Decision 3891), the Bureau now

holds that the entire value of the community property should have been included in the gross estate of this decedent and the tax has been redetermined on that basis."

"The following tabulations shows the unpaid deficiency:

"Gross Estate $603,888.88
Deductions 98,044.70

Net Estate $505,844.18
    Carried forward $505,844.18

[13]

            Brought forward $505,844.18
Tax determined herein 16,850.85
Tax paid on return.............$4,035.77
Balance of returned
    tax paid 109.66
Additional tax paid 692.23

Total paid 4,837.66

Deficiency tax ....$12,012.99"

XI.

Deny the allegations contained in paragraph X of the Bill of Complaint and in lieu thereof allege as follows:

That on or about September 21, 1926, and purportedly under the authority of section 318 of the Revenue Act of 1926, the Commissioner of Internal Revenue mailed a purported notice of deficiency addressed to "Newton H. Neustadter et al, Execu-

tors, Estate of David Neustadter'', advising them
of a proposed deficiency in estate tax of $12,012.99.
(A copy of said letter Marked as Exhibit A is
hereunto attached and made a part of this amended
answer.)

That thereafter and on November 2, 1926, the
parties named in said notice as executors of the
estate, on their own behalf, filed a petition with
the United States Board of Tax Appeals, No. 20988
(a copy of which is hereunto attached and marked
"Exhibit B"), wherein the parties appeared and
pleaded, as restricted by said notice of deficiency,
only on behalf of themselves and not on behalf of
said estate against the tax liability sought to be
imposed upon them by the above-mentioned deficiency letter addressed to them solely as the executors
of a distributed and barren estate. That thereafter
the proceedings came before the Board of Tax
Appeals for hearing and on March 14, 1929, long
after the estate of said decedent had been distributed, the said Board rendered a decision (15
B. T. A. 839. 851) in which it held that it had no
jurisdiction to determine any liability against the
executors personally and then held that: "All we
determine is that the executors in their representative [14] capacities are liable for the deficiency
determined by respondent." That on the same date
said Board made and entered a final order in said
proceeding in which it was "Ordered and Decided:
That there is a deficiency of $12,012.99 in estate
tax", but which did not determine that the estate

was liable therefor. That said decision and order were without the jurisdiction of said Board and were invalid and void.

XII.

Deny the allegations contained in paragraph XI of the Bill of Complaint in so far as the allegation that said order "is the final order and decision of said Board of Tax Appeals" and allege that the reason that no appeal was taken was because the decision of the Board of Tax Appeals was beyond the jurisdiction of the Board and void.

XIII.

Deny the allegations contained in paragraph XII of the Bill of Complaint but in lieu thereof allege that thereafter the Commissioner of Internal Revenue caused to be made a pretended and unauthorized assessment in the amount of $12,012.99 against the said estate of David Neustadter and on November 20, 1929, the Collector of Internal Revenue for the Northern District of California caused a form of notice and demand for payment to be made upon one of the asserted executors under said pretended and unauthorized assessment; also, that, on the service of said form of notice and demand the representative of the Collector was informed that the estate of David Neustadter had been distributed long before and was without assets; and, also, that said Collector made no further attempt toward collection of said alleged deficiency and neither filed or recorded any notice of lien on the former property of the estate. Defendants further allege that said pretended assessment was addressed to a non-existent person and one which had not been a person addressed in [15] the above mentioned purported deficiency letter and had not been made a party to the above mentioned proceedings before said United States Board of Tax Appeals.

XIV.

Admit the allegations as set forth in paragraph XIII of the Bill of Complaint.

XV.

Admit the allegations contained in paragraph XIV of the Bill of Complaint.

XVI.

Answering paragraph XV of the Bill of Complaint filed herein, defendants admit that the entire estate of David Neustadter, deceased, was distributed to the defendants herein as legatees under the last will and testament of said decedent, and allege that said distribution was made under order of the court in which said estate was probated and only after the final determination by the Commissioner of Internal Revenue of the proper and complete estate tax due, the legal assessment of said tax in February 1926, the payment of said tax on March 15, 1926, and the receipt from the Bureau of Internal Revenue showing payment in full of said final and legally assessed tax.

Defendants deny that said estate was, at the time

the Bill of Complaint was filed herein, charged with any trust in favor of the United States for any amount whatever, and that there was any estate, or property and assets of any estate, charged with a trust under which defendants herein were liable to complainant for any tax or interest. Allege that the only trust or lien imposed on the property of said estate was that imposed under section 409 of the Revenue Act of 1921 and that, as to such lien, no attempt was ever made by Complainant to enforce the same and that such lien was barred by the statute of limitations on February 13, 1933, before this suit was commenced. [16]

XVII.

Deny the allegations contained in paragraph XVI of the Bill of Complaint and allege that defendants herein are not liable for the payment of $12,012.99 or any other amount to Complainant herein, and further allege that the Bill of Complaint herein fails to state a cause of action, and, if it does state what appears to be a cause of action, the remedy therefor is barred by the statute of limitations, and that said Bill of Complaint should be dismissed and judgment ordered for the defendants.

XVIII.

Deny the allegations contained in paragraph XVII of the Bill of Complaint.

XIX.

Allege that the decision of the United States Board of Tax Appeals upon which complainant re-

lies as the basis of the pretended assessment was
beyond the jurisdiction of said Board and void in
that there was no existent estate and the executors
were without possession of any property of the
distributed estate of David Neustadter, deceased,
which they could represent or against which said
decision of said Board might be effective and legal.
And, further and for the same reasons, that said
pretended assessment is void and insufficient to extend the statute of limitations to give this Court
jurisdiction to render any judgment, order, or decree
whatsoever against the defendants herein.

> HERBERT L. ROTHSCHILD,
> Mills Tower, San Francisco
> ADOLPHUS E. GRAUPNER,
> Balfour Bldg., San Francisco.
> Attorneys for Defendants.
> [17]

State of California,
City and County of San Francisco.—ss.

NEWTON H. NEUSTADTER being first and
duly sworn deposes and says: I am one of the defendants in the foregoing entitled action; that I
have read the foregoing Amended Answer and am
familiar with the statements therein contained, and
that the facts stated are true, except as to those
facts stated to be upon information and belief, and
as to those facts he believes that they are true.

> NEWTON H. NEUSTADTER.

Subscribed and sworn to before me this 5th day of January, 1935.

[Seal]   P. J. HARLIS,

Notary Public in and for the City and County of San Francisco, State of California. [18]

[Printer's Note: Exhibits "A" and "B" have not been set forth at this place. They may be found at p. 42 and p. 38].

[Title of Court and Cause.]

AMENDMENTS TO AMENDED ANSWER

Come now the above named defendants, by their attorney Adolphus E. Graupner, Esq., and under order of court duly made and entered, file these amendments to their Amended Answer to the Bill of Complaint in the above entitled suit. [23]

XI.

In answer to paragraph X of the Bill of Complaint defendants admit that on September 21, 1926, and under the asserted authority of section 318 of the Revenue Act of 1926, the Commissioner of Internal Revenue mailed a notice of deficiency to "Newton H. Neustadter, et al., Executors, Estate of David Neustadter, 62 First Street, San Francisco, California," proposing the determination of a deficiency in estate tax for the "Estate of David Neustadter," deceased, in the amount of $12,012.99.

(A copy of said deficiency notice marked "Exhibit A" is attached to the Amended Answer on file herein and, by reference, is hereby made a part of this amendment to said Amended Answer.)

Admit that following the receipt of said notice and on November 2, 1926, Newton H. Neustadter, Walter W. Stettheimer and Julian Hart, the former executors of said estate, filed a petition with the United States Board of Tax Appeals, docketed as No. 20988, in appeal from said notice; that thereafter hearing on said proceeding was had before said Board and thereafter and on March 13, 1929, said United States Board of Tax Appeals made its findings of fact and rendered its decision as reported in volume 15, United States Board of Tax Appeals Reports, at pages 839 to 851, both inclusive, to which reference is hereby made as a part of this answer; that thereafter and on March 14, 1929, an order was entered by the said Board in the words and figures quoted in paragraph X of the Bill of Complaint herein.

Deny the allegations contained in and as stated in paragraph X of the Bill of Complaint.

XII.

Answering paragraph XI of the Bill of Complaint herein defendants admit that the above mentioned findings of [24] fact, decision, and order have never been modified, set aside, or reversed and that no appeal therefrom was taken, but deny the allegations contained and as stated in said paragraph XI alleged.

XIV.

Answering paragraph XIII of the Bill of Complaint defendants deny the allegations thereof, but admit the following.

That prior to the assessment of the estate tax alleged to have been made in paragraph XII of the Bill of Complaint and on February 7, 1924, Newton H. Neustadter, Walter W. Stettheimer and Julian Hart, as executors of the last will and testament of David Neustadter, deceased, filed their first and final account of their administration of the estate of said decedent, and their report as executors, and their petition praying for a settlement of said first and final account, and their petition praying for a final distribution of said estate; that said first and final account, report, petition for settlement of final account, and petition for final distribution of said estate came on duly for hearing before and were allowed and approved by the Honorable Thomas F. Graham, Judge of the Superior Court of the State of California in and for the City and County of San Francisco on February 25, 1924, and the orders and decrees necessary for the allowance and approval of said report and petitions were filed with the County Clerk of the City and County of San Francisco, State of California, on March 1, 1924; that, although final distribution of the entire estate of David Neustadter, deceased, was made, the said appointed executors have not been finally discharged under section 1697 of the Code of Civil Procedure or section 1066 of the Probate Code of California

or under section 313(b) of the Revenue Act of 1926;
that said appointed executors, as such, hold no property or assets of said estate at the present time [25]
nor held any such property or assets at the time
this suit was commenced.

Following paragraph XIX of defendants'
amended answer and as a separate paragraph and
prayer, the following is added to said amended
answer.

WHEREFORE, defendants pray this Court
either to dismiss this cause for lack of jurisdiction
and equity or to render judgment in favor of defendants and grant defendants such other and further relief as it may deem proper, including a decree
for costs.

> ADOLPHUS E. GRAUPNER,
> Balfour Bldg., San Francisco.

[26]

State of California,
City and County of San Francisco.—ss.

FLORENCE N. STETTHEIMER being first and
duly sworn deposes and says:

I am one of the defendants in the foregoing suit;
that I have read the foregoing Amendments to
Amended Answer and am familiar with the statements therein contained, and that the facts stated
are true, except as to those facts stated to be upon
information and belief and as to those facts she
believes them to be true.

> FLORENCE N. STETTHEIMER.

Subscribed and sworn to before me this 18th day of October, 1935.

[Seal]   WINIFRED BELLAM
                Notary Public in and for the
                City and County of San Fran-
                cisco, State of California.

My Commission expires Dec. 31, 1938.

Receipt of a copy of the foregoing Amendments to Amended Answer this 29th day of October, 1935.

H. H. McPIKE

By ESTHER B. PHILLIPS
                Attorneys for Complainant.

[Endorsed]: Filed Nov. 20, 1935.   [27]

———

[Title of Court.]

AT A STATED TERM of the Southern Division of the United States District Court for the Northern District of California, held at the Court Room thereof, in the City and County of San Francisco, on Tuesday, the 14th day of January, in the year of our Lord one thousand nine hundred and thirty-six.

PRESENT: the Honorable Harold Louderback, District Judge.

[Title of Cause.]

This case having been heretofore tried and submitted, being now fully considered, it is Ordered that objection of attorney for defendant to portions of deposition of Commissioner of Internal

Revenue, is hereby overruled, and that a decree be entered in favor of the United States, upon findings of fact and conclusions of law, to be filed. [28]

[Title of Court and Cause.]

FINDINGS OF FACT AND CONCLUSIONS OF LAW.

The above-entitled matter having come regularly on for trial on November 20, 1935, the plaintiff appearing by its Attorney H. H. McPIKE, United States Attorney for the Northern District of California, and ESTHER B. PHILLIPS, Assistant United States Attorney for the Northern District of California, and the defendants appearing by their Attorney A. E. GRAUPNER, and evidence oral and documentary having been received, and the cause having been submitted upon argument and briefs, and the Court having considered the evidence and the argument of counsel now makes findings of fact as follows:

FINDINGS OF FACT.

I.

DAVID NEUSTADTER died testate in the City and County of San Francisco, State of California, on February 13, 1923, being at the time of his death a resident of said City and County and State, and leaving an estate therein, and surviving him as his next of kin, heirs-at-law, legatees and devisees under his will, the defendants, J O S E P H I N E D. NEUSTADTER, NEWTON H. NEUSTADTER,

FLORENCE N. STETTHEIMER, JAMES D. HART and ELLEN K. HART. Thereafter his last will and testament was admitted to probate by the Superior Court of the State of California and NEWTON H. NEUSTADTER, WALTER W. STETTHEIMER and JULIAN HART were appointed his executors. Thereafter they qualified and entered upon their duties. They have never been discharged as executors of said estate.

II.

On December 31, 1923, said Executors filed an estate tax return of the estate of DAVID NEUSTADTER with the Collector of Internal Revenue for the First Collection [29] District of California at San Francisco, California. In this return they disclosed a total gross estate of the value of $601,630.77, and a net estate subject to estate tax in the sum of $204,847.50, and an estate tax due to the United States of America in the sum of $4,145.43, which was paid at or about the time of the filing of said return. In said return the executors deducted from the gross estate the community property interest of the surviving widow, JOSEPHINE D. NEUSTADTER. Said executors acted in good faith in making said deduction.

On February 7, 1924, said executors filed their first and final account of their administration, their report as executors, their petition praying for settlement of their first and final account, and their petition praying for the final distribution of said estate with the Superior Court of the State of California in and for the City and County of San Francisco, the court having jurisdiction of the probate of said estate. On February 25, 1924, said account, report and petition were allowed and approved and a decree for the final distribution of said estate was made by said Court. Property and money in excess of $30,000 was distributed to each of the defendants from the assets of said estate. The entire estate of DAVID NEUSTADTER, deceased was distributed by said executors prior to the date of mailing a deficiency notice by the Commissioner of Internal Revenue to the above-named executors on September 21, 1926. The above-named executors have never been discharged under the provisions of section 1697 of the Code of Civil Procedure or section 1066 of the Probate Code of California or under section 313(b) of the Revenue Act of 1926.

III.

On July 30, 1924, said executors wrote the Commissioner [30] of Internal Revenue requesting an early determination of the estate tax for said Estate of DAVID NEUSTADTER, deceased. On November 10, 1925, said Commissioner advised said executors of a deficiency in tax of $692.23, which amount was paid.

IV.

Thereafter an audit of said return was made by agents of the United States Commissioner of Internal Revenue and, as a result of said audit, the

Commissioner of Internal Revenue determined that the community interest of the widow, JOSEPHINE D. NEUSTADTER, was properly to be included as a part of the estate subject to tax and, as a result thereof, found that there was a deficiency in estate tax in the principal amount of $12,012.99. On September 21, 1926, the Commissioner of Internal Revenue mailed a 60-day letter (as required by Section 316 of the 1926 Revenue Act) to said executors of the estate of DAVID NEUSTADTER, proposing an additional assessment in the amount of said deficiency in estate tax. On November 2, 1926, and within the time allowed by law, an appeal was taken from said proposed deficiency assessment to the United States Board of Tax Appeals by said executors. An answer was filed by the Commissioned to said executors' petition of appeal and thereafter proceedings were had before the United States Board of Tax Appeals, and the cause submitted. On March 14, 1929, an order was entered by the United States Board of Tax Appeals determining a deficiency in estate tax in the sum of $12,012.99, as proposed by said Commissioner of Internal Revenue. No appeal was taken from said decision of the United States Board of Tax Appeals, and said order became final, without modification. Thereafter, in accordance with said decision of the United States Board of Tax Appeals, [31] the Commissioner of Internal Revenue on September 27, 1929, assessed a deficiency in estate tax in the sum of $12,012.99 against said executors of the

estate of DAVID NEUSTADTER, deceased, and
against said estate.

The amount of the estate tax due to the United
States from the estate of DAVID NEUSTADTER
was in fact $12,012.99 (principal) in addition to
the previous accounts paid by the executors, and
the deficiency notice given by the Commissioner on
September 21, 1926 correctly computed the estate
tax due to the United States.

V.

No part of said deficiency in tax, and no part of
the interest thereon, has been paid.

VI.

This suit was authorized and sanctioned by the
United States Commissioner of Internal Revenue.

From the foregoing Findings of Fact, the Court
states these.

CONCLUSIONS OF LAW.

I.

The assets of the estate distributed to these defendants, in the manner previously found by the
Court, constituted a trust fund for the payment of
estate taxes owing to the United States of America.
The defendants being the distributees of the estate,
and each of them a distributee in an amount exceeding the amount of tax involved herein, are
accountable to this Court for the property so distributed to them from the assets of said estate, in
the amount of said tax, namely, $12,012.99, to-wit:

NEWTON H. NEUSTADTER,
JOSEPHINE D. NEUSTADTER,
FLORENCE N. STETTHEIMER,   [32]
JAMES D. HART, and
ELLEN K. HART,

together with interest thereon at 6 per centum from September 27, 1929.

Let judgment be entered accordingly against each of the above-named defendants in the sum of $12,-012.99, with interest thereon at 6 per centum per annum from September 27, 1929, together with costs as may be taxed.

HAROLD LOUDERBACK
United States District Judge.

[Endorsed]: Filed Feb. 5th, 1936.   [33]

In the Southern Division of the United States District Court for the Northern District of California.

In Equity—No. 3639-L.

UNITED STATES OF AMERICA,

Plaintiff,

vs.

NEWTON H. NEUSTADTER, JOSEPHINE D. NEUSTADTER, FLORENCE H. STETTHEIMER, JAMES D. HART and ELLEN K. HART,

Defendants.

DECREE.

The above entitled cause came regularly on for trial on November 20, 1935, the plaintiff appearing by its Attorneys H. H. McPIKE, United States Attorney for the Northern District of California, and ESTHER B. PHILLIPS, Assistant United States Attorney for the Northern District of California, and the defendants appearing by their attorney A. E. GRAUPNER, and trial was thereupon had. Evidence oral and documentary having been introduced and the cause having been submitted upon argument and briefs of counsel, and the Court having made his Findings of Fact and Conclusions of Law;

It is hereby ORDERED, ADJUDGED and DECREED, that the assets of the Estate of DAVID NEUSTADTER, which were distributed to the defendants in the manner previously found by the Court in property and money in excess of $30,000.00 to each defendant, constituted a trust fund for the payment of the taxes owing by said estate and executors of said estate to the United States, and that the defendants, the distributees thereof, are accountable to this Court for said trust property so distributed not exceeding the amount distributed to each of them from the assets of said estate; [34]

It is FURTHER ORDERED, ADJUDGED and DECREED that the plaintiff do have and recover against each of the above named defendants the amount of tax due to the United States, namely, a principal amount of $12,012.99, with interest thereon at 6% per annum from September 27, 1929, as follows:

> NEWTON H. NEUSTADTER
>> Principal amount $12,012.99, with interest thereon at 6% per annum from September 27, 1929, until paid.
>
> JOSEPHINE D. NEUSTADTER
>> Principal amount $12,012.99, with interest thereon at 6% per annum from September 27, 1929, until paid.
>
> FLORENCE H. STETTHEIMER
>> Principal amount $12,012.99, with interest thereon at 6% per annum from September 27, 1929, until paid.

JAMES D. HART

> Principal amount $12,012.99, with interest thereon at 6% per annum from September 27, 1929, until paid.

ELLEN K. HART

> Principal amount $12,012.99, with interest thereon at 6% per annum from September 27, 1929, until paid.

It is FURTHER ORDERED, ADJUDGED and DECREED that plaintiff do have and recover its costs herein as may be taxed. Costs taxed at $40.60.

HAROLD LOUDERBACK
United States District Judge.

February 18, 1936.

[Endorsed]: Receipt of copy admitted this 6th day of Feb. 1936.

ADOLPHUS E. GRAUPNER
Attorney for Defendants

[Endorsed]: Filed and entered Feb. 19, 1936.

[35]

[Title of Court and Cause.]

It is hereby stipulated and agreed by and between counsel for the above entitled parties that the time within which the above named defendants may propose, have settled, and file their Bill of Exceptions in the above-entitled suit be and the same is hereby extended to and including the 31st day of March, 1936.

> H. H. McPIKE,
> ESTHER B. PHILLIPS,
> > Attorneys for Complainant.
> ADOLPHUS E. GRAUPNER,
> > Attorney for Defendant.

Dated: March 30th, 1936.

[Endorsed]: Filed Mar. 30, 1936. [36]

[Title of Court and Cause.]

DEFENDANT'S BILL OF EXCEPTIONS

BE IT REMEMBERED that on the 20th day of November and the 7th day of December, 1935, the above-entitled cause came on for trial before the Court, sitting in equity and without a jury, the Honorable Harold Louderback, District Judge, presiding and H. H. McPike, Esq., United States Attorney, and Miss Esther B. Phillips, Assistant United States Attorney for the Northern [37] District of California, appearing for the complainant and Adolphus E. Graupner, Esq., appearing for the defendants, and on the 20th day of November, 1935, the following proceedings were had:

The defendants moved for permission to file an amendment to their amended answer and said motion was granted without objection, and, after service of said amendments, the same were filed with the clerk of the Court.

Complainant offered in evidence a certified copy of the Federal Estate Tax return for the Estate of David Neustadter, deceased, which was admitted in evidence without objection and marked

EXHIBIT 1.

Said Exhibit showed the following material facts:

That David Neustadter died testate February 13, 1923, and was a resident of San Francisco, California; that he left an estate consisting entirely of community property of a gross value of $601,-630.77, one-half of which, or $300,815.38, was returned as the gross estate of the decedent subject to Federal estate tax; that from such gross estate the sum of $95,967.88 was deducted for exemption, expenses of administration, etc., leaving a net estate for tax of $204,847.50, upon which a Federal Estate Tax in the amount of $4,145.43 was computed and paid. Said Exhibit will be transmitted to the Clerk of the Circuit Court of Appeals for the Ninth Circuit by the Clerk of the United States District Court when the record is docketed with the Clerk of said Circuit Court of Appeals for detailed reference by said Court.

Complainant offered in evidence a certified copy of a portion of the miscellaneous tax assessment certificate for January, 1924, signed by the Commissioner of Internal Revenue on March 5, 1924, which was made upon the estate tax return filed above stated and assessed estate tax against said estate in the amount [38] shown by such return. The assessment certificate offered was admitted in evidence without objection and marked

EXHIBIT 2

and, insofar as material, reads as follows:

ASSESSMENT CERTIFICATE

District First California, Estate Tax List, January, 1924

2099 Neustadter, David, Estate of 9 c/o Newton
H. Neustadter, 62 First St., San Francisco.

Old Balance—

Date—12-31-23

Debit—4,035.77

Credit—4,035.77

New Balance—

Remarks—Died, February 13, 1923. 706 Original
Tax Block 445.

Complainant offered in evidence certified copies of a petition to the United States Board of Tax Appeals in the proceeding entitled Newton H. Neustadter, et al. v. Commissioner of Internal Revenue, Docket No. 20988, the deficiency notice upon which said petition was founded, dated September 21, 1926, and constituting an exhibit to said petition, the answer to said petition and an order of said Board determining a deficiency in tax in said proceeding. Without objection the above mentioned records were admitted in evidence and marked

EXHIBIT 3

and are as follows:

[Title of Board and Cause.]

PETITION

The above-named petitioners, Newton H. Neustadter, Walter W. Stettheimer and Julian Hart, Executors of the Estate of David Neustadter, hereby petition for a redetermination of the alleged deficiency set forth by the Commissioner of Internal [39] Revenue in his notice of deficiency (MT-ET-2099-C1.-CLMcC) dated September 21, 1926, and as a basis of this proceeding allege as follows:

1. The petitioners are Executors of the Estate of David Neustadter, who died on February 13, 1923. The address of the petitioners is 62 First Street, San Francisco, California.

2. The notice of deficiency (a copy of which is attached and marked Exhibit "A") was mailed to the petitioners on September 21, 1926.

3. The taxes in controversy are Estate taxes asserted against said Estate in the sum of $12,012.99.

4. The determination of tax set forth in the said notice of deficiency is based upon the following errors:

(a) The respondent erred in reopening this case and in asserting a deficiency when he, the respondent, had on November 10, 1925, closed the case by sending to the petitioner a registered sixty days letter from which determination petitioner did not appeal. The period of time within which a deficiency could be legally asserted against petitioners has expired, in view of the application for final determination and discharge hereinafter referred to.

(b) The respondent erred in including in the gross Estate of the decedent, for Estate tax purposes, the entire value of the community property, one-half of which belonged to his wife.

5. The facts upon which petitioners rely as the basis of this proceeding are as follows:—

(a) Under dates of July 30, 1924, and September 6, 1924, petitioners made application to the Commissioner of Internal Revenue for an audit of the Estate tax return and determination of the Estate taxes due from said Estate. Pursuant to the said [40] application respondent audited the return filed for the Estate and determined a deficiency of $692.23 which petitioners were notified by respondent by registered letter dated November 10, 1925. This letter from respondent was a notice of deficiency in which petitioners were given sixty days in which to take an appeal to this Board; no petition was filed, however, and the deficiency of $692.23 was paid by petitioners.

By reason of petitioner's application as aforesaid for a determination and assessment of the total taxes due by the said Estate and respondent's determination of the tax liability evidenced by his notice of deficiency dated November 10, 1925, and the payment of the deficiency of $692.23 shown therein, petitioners assert that the said notice of deficiency of respondent, dated November 10, 1925, was a final determination and that respondent erred in reopening the case and determining the deficiency herein complained of. In any event, the Executors (petitioners herein) having filed a complete return and having made written application to respondent not later than September 6, 1924, for a determination of the amount of the Estate tax and for a discharge of petitioners from personal liability therefor, respondent was limited to one year after the receipt of such notice in which to give notice to petitioners of any additional Estate tax liability or to assert any deficiency against petitioners.

(b) At the date of his death, (February 13, 1923), the decedent, David Neustadter, was a married man living with his wife, and domiciled in the State of California. Under the laws of that State, one-half of the community property was owned, at the decedent's death, by his wife. Respondent, however, has now erroneously included in the taxable Estate the value of the entire community property, not merely one-half thereof. For reasons stated, only one-half of the value of the community [41] property should be included in the taxable Estate of the decedent, and it was error, therefore, to include in such Estate of the decedent the value of his wife's interest in the community property.

WHEREFORE, petitioners pray that this Board may hear the proceeding, and that it be held by the Board that the errors above mentioned were made by respondent and that no liability rests upon the petitioners to pay the taxes asserted in the notice of deficiency, and for such other relief as may appear equitable and proper as this cause progresses.

W. W. SPALDING
Counsel for Petitioners,
Woodward Building,
Washington, D. C.

State of California,
City and County of San Francisco—ss.

NEWTON H. NEUSTADTER, WALTER W. STETTHEIMER and JULIAN HART, being duly sworn, say that they are the duly appointed and qualified Executors of the Estate of David Neustadter, deceased, and are duly authorized to verify the foregoing petition; that they have read the said petition and are familiar with the statements contained therein, and that the facts stated are true, except as to those facts stated to be upon information and belief, and those facts they believe to be true.

NEWTON H. NEUSTADTER
WALTER W. STETTHEIMER
JULIAN HART

Subscribed and sworn to before me this 25th day of October, 1926.

[Seal]   ALICE SPENCER
Notary Public in and for the
City and County of San
Francisco, State of California. [42]

EXHIBIT A

COPY

TREASURY DEPARTMENT
Washington

Sep 21 1926

MT-ET-2099-C1.-CLMcC
District of First California
Estate of David Neustadter
Date of death—February 13, 1923
Deficiency tax $12,012.99
Newton H. Neustadter, et al., Executors,
  Estate of David Neustadter,
    62 First Street,
      San Francisco, California.

Sirs:—

Reference is made to the return on Form 706, filed in the above named estate in the audit of which the value of the wife's community interest was excluded from the gross estate of this decedent and tax was paid on that basis.

In view of the decision of the United States Supreme Court in the case of United States v. Robbins, 269 U. S. 315, rendered January 4, 1926, and an opinion of the Attorney General of the United States issued June 24, 1926 (Treasury Decision 3891), the Bureau now holds that the entire value of the community property should have been included in the gross estate of this decedent and the tax has been redetermined on that basis.

The following tabulation shows the unpaid deficiency:

Gross estate		$603,888.88
Deductions		98,044.70
Net estate		$505,844.18
Tax determined herein		16,850.65
Tax paid on return	$4,035.77	
Balance of returned tax paid	109.66	
Additional tax paid	692.23	
Total paid		4,837.66
Deficiency tax		$ 12,012.99

[43]

Pursuant to Section 318 of the Revenue Act of 1926, notice of deficiency, amounting to $12,012.99, in estate tax with respect to the estate of David Neustadter is hereby given, with a view to the assessment and collection thereof. Any portion of the amount assessed, not paid within thirty days from the date of notice and demand from the Collector, will bear interest at the rate of one per centum a month from the date of such notice and demand, unless an extension of time for payment should be granted.

Within sixty days (not counting Sunday as the sixtieth day) after the mailing of this notice you may, in accordance with the provisions of Section 308 of the Revenue Act of 1926, file a petition with the Board of Tax Appeals for a redetermination of the deficiency. The address of the Board is: United States Board of Tax Appeals, Earle Building, 13th and E Streets, N .W., Washington, D. C.

No claim in abatement of any deficiency which may be assessed in this case will be entertained.

If you acquiesce in this determination, either in whole or in part, you are requested to sign the enclosed waiver of restrictions on the assessment and collection of so much of the deficiency as results from the adjustments in which you acquiesce, and forward it to the Commissioner of Internal Revenue, Washington, D. C., marked for the attention of the Estate Tax Division, Miscellaneous Tax Unit.

Respectfully,

(Signed) C. R. NASH,

Acting Commissioner.

Enclosure

MPH

[Title of Board and Cause]

ANSWER

The Commissioner of Internal Revenue by his Attorney, A. W. Gregg, General Counsel, Bureau of Internal Revenue, in answer to the petition of the above named taxpayers, admits and denies as follows:

1. Admits the allegations set forth in the paragraph of the petition numbered 1.

2. Admits the allegations set forth in the paragraph of the petition numbered 2. **[44]**

3. Admits the allegations set forth in the paragraph of the petition numbered 3.

4. Denies that the determination of the defi-

ciency tax is based upon errors as alleged in the paragraph of the petition numbered 3.

5. (a) Admits so much of subparagraph (a) of the paragraph of the petition numbered 5 as alleges that under date of July 30, 1924, the executor of the estate requested the Commissioner of Internal Revenue to arrange at his earliest convenience for an examination of the return of the estate of David Neustadter; that under date of November 10, 1925, the Commissioner addressed a letter to the executor showing a deficiency tax of $692.23, which amount was paid by the petitioners, and denies every other allegation contained in said subparagraph (a).

(b) Admits so much of subparagraph (b) of the paragraph of the petition numbered 5 as alleges that on February 13, 1923, the decedent was married and living with his wife in the State of California, but denies every other allegation contained in said subparagraph (b).

6. Denies each and every allegation contained in the petition not hereinbefore specifically admitted or denied.

WHEREFORE, it is respectfully prayed that the determination of the Commissioner be approved.

A. W. GREGG,
General Counsel,
Bureau of Internal Revenue.

Of Counsel:

J. F. GREANEY,
Special Attorney,
Bureau of Internal Revenue.

[Title of Board and Cause.]

DECISION

Pursuant to the Board's findings of fact and opinion promulgated March 13, 1929, it is [45]

ORDERED and DECIDED: That there is a deficiency of $12,012.99 in estate tax.

[Seal]   (a) JOHN B. MILLIKEN

Member

United States Board of Tax Appeals

Entered: March 14, 1929.

The published opinion and decision of the Board of Tax Appeals in said proceeding of Neustadter v. Commissioner, appearing in Volume 15 of United States Board of Tax Appeals Reports at pages 839 to 851, both inclusive, was stipulated to be in evidence and is hereby incorporated by reference as a part of this bill as though fully transcribed herein.

Complainant offered in evidence a certified copy of a portion of a miscellaneous tax-estate-assessment certificate signed by the Commissioner of Internal Revenue on September 27, 1929, which, as far as material to this suit, is as follows:

ASSESSMENT CERTIFICATE

District, First — California, Miscellaneous — Estate, List August, 1929

Neustadter, David, Est. of. c/o Newton Neustadter, et al., Exec. 62 1st Street, San Francisco, Cal.

Old Balance—

Date—

Debit—12,012.99
Credit—
New Balance—12,012.99
Remarks—Def. Tax MT:ET-2099

The certified copy so offered in evidence was admitted in evidence and marked

EXHIBIT 4.

Whereupon, counsel for complainant advised the Court and counsel for defendant that the Government would rely upon all admissions of defendants in their amended answer and in their amendments to the amended answer to allegations of fact in the bill of complaint as being a part of proofs on behalf of complainant.

Thereupon, counsel for complainant announced that: "The Government rests." [46]

Complainant having rested its case, counsel for defendants moved the Court to dismiss the suit for want of jurisdiction and want of proof. Whereupon counsel for complainant asked leave of the Court to re-open the case to introduce further evidene on behalf of complainant. Such leave being granted by the Court, counsel for complainant then moved that the cause be continued for further hearing in order to permit the taking of depositions on behalf of complainant in Washington, D. C. Whereupon the Court granted the motion and continued hearing of the cause to December 7, 1935.

On the 7th day of December, 1935, the above entitled suit came on for further hearing before the Court and the following proceedings were had:

The deposition of Guy T. Helvering, Commissioner of Internal Revenue, identifying his signature to a letter addressed to "Honorable H. H. McPike, United States Attorney, San Francisco, California," dated September 26, 1933, was read in evidence, which letter stated the substance of the pleadings and the decision in the proceeding before the United States Board of Tax Appeals in the case entitled "Newton H. Neustadter, Walter Stettheimer and Julian Hart, Executors of the Estate of David Neustadter v. Commissioner of Internal Revenue, Docket No. 20988," and requested, sanctioned and authorized said H. H. McPike to institute suit in the name of the United States against the defendants herein for the purpose of collecting payment of the additional assessment of estate tax in the sum of $12,012.99 made by the Commissioner of Internal Revenue on September 27, 1929. Thereupon plaintiff rested.

Thereupon, counsel for defendants moved the Court to dismiss the suit upon the ground of want of jurisdiction of the Court to grant any relief to complainant and upon the further ground that, as the Court was one of limited jurisdiction, its jurisdiction could not be presumed on the facts shown and it was without equity to proceed by reason of failure of complainant to prove its jurisdiction in the following particulars:

I

(a) Complainant failed to prove and defendants deny [47] that it was without a plain, complete and adequate remedy at law at the time this suit was filed.

(b)   Complainant failed to prove any reason for its failure to avail itself of the plain, complete and adequate remedies provided by law and existing before and/or at the time of institution of this suit.

(c)   Complainant failed to prove any of the exceptions to the restrictions of section 267 of the Judicial Code to entitle it to equitable relief.

(d)   Complainant failed to prove that either the former executors or the defendants herein failed to pay the additional tax or deficiency alleged to have been assessed against the estate of David Neustadter, deceased.

(e)   For the reasons stated above, this suit does not involve a dispute or controversy properly within the jurisdiction of this Court and the intendment of section 37 of the Judicial Code.

(f)   That on the pleadings and proofs in this suit there is a want of equity and the suit should be dismissed under section 37 of the Judicial Code upon the following particulars, viz:

1—Complainant has failed to prove the liability of defendants as transferees for any tax or that there is any tax or deficiency in tax now due, outstanding and unpaid for which defendants are liable as transferees and, without such proof this court is without jurisdiction in equity.

2—Complainant is estopped from seeking to establish an equitable trust because it permitted the trust enforceable in equity and created by section 409 of the Revenue Act of 1921 to lapse without at-

tempt at enforcement before the expiration of the
ten year period of limitation and before the commencement of this suit.

Defendants further moved, in event of the denial
of [48] the foregoing motion to dismiss, that this
Court direct, order and enter judgment for defendants on the following and each of the following
grounds, viz:

1.   Complainant has failed to prove that it is
within the equitable jurisdiction of this court.

2.   Complainant has failed to prove that there is
any tax or deficiency in tax for which, under the
equitable trust doctrine relied upon, defendants or
any of them are liable as transferees.

3.   Complainant is not entitled to any equitable
relief because it has not complied with the prerequisites necessary to recognition by a court of equity,
viz:

(a)   That he who comes into equity must come
with clean hands.

(b)   That equity aids the vigilant and not those
who slumber on their rights.

4.   Complainant has failed to prove any right
of suit or to remedy in equity.

5.   Complainant's right of suit, if any it had, is
barred by limitation, and defendants are entitled
to judgment.

After the making of the foregoing motions to the
Court, arugment thereon was made by counsel for
the defendants and complainant and thereupon the
court denied the motions to dismiss and for judgment, without prejudice to complainant to renew

the same, and granted exception to the order of denial.

EXCEPTION NO. 1

Thereupon,

WALTER W. STETTHEIMER

was called and sworn as a witness on behalf of defendants and, on

Direct Examination

orally testified in substance as follows:

I was at one time an executor of the Estate of David Neustadter, deceased. The estate was distributed during the years [49] 1923 and 1924 and was, to the best of my knowledge, completely distributed prior to September 1, 1926.

On Cross Examination

by counsel for complainant, the witness testified in substance as follows:

I do not know whether the executors have ever been discharged. The estate was distributed between 1923 and 1924 but I do not recall whether it was by one decree or several. I have a dim recollection that in the decree of distribution the executors held out a certain sum to apply upon a possible additional estate tax for some time. However, it is my recollection that everything was distributed prior to September of 1926. I am not a defendant in this suit.

"Miss PHILLIPS: That is all.

"Mr. GRAUPNER: We rest.

"The COURT: Any rebuttal?"

"Miss PHILLIPS: No rebuttal, your honor. I would like at this time to have the record show a motion for judgment for the plaintiff as prayed in the complaint, upon all the issues involved."

"Mr. GRAUPNER: I would at this time like to have the record show a motion for judgment in favor of the defendants upon all of the issues involved, upon the grounds asserted in the motion to dismiss and the motion for judgment heretofore submitted to your Honor, and upon which your Honor ruled adversely; and in addition thereto upon the following grounds:"

1.   The proceedings before the Board of Tax Appeals in the proceeding of Neustadter et al. v. Commissioner, Docket No. 20,988, were beyond the jurisdiction of the said Board and were and are illegal and void.

2.   The notice of deficiency addressed to Newton H. Neustadter, Walter Stettheimer and Julian Hart, as executors of [50] the estate of David Neustadter, deceased, and mailed to them by the Commissioner of Internal Revenue on or about September 21, 1926, was insufficient, illegal and contrary to statute and could not vest said Board of Tax Appeals with any jurisdiction to receive or hear any proceeding before it which would attempt to determine and adjudge a liability binding in any way upon defendants herein for any estate tax or deficiency in estate tax which, if not paid, is due or

owing from the estate of David Neustadter, deceased.

3. Any order, judgment or decree made by said Board in said proceeding pretending to determine a liability for estate tax or deficiency in estate tax against Newton H. Neustadter, Walter Stettheimer and Julian Hart as executors or representatives of the estate of David Neustadter, deceased, is null and void and any attempt in this suit to rely upon any such order, judgment or decree is without and beyond the jurisdiction of this court and in contravention of the provisions of the Constitution of the United States.

4. If the assessment list (Exhibit 4), in the absence of present proof, may be presumed to be in any way founded upon or result from any order, judgment, or decree of said Board of Tax Appeals in said proceeding, then such pretended assessment is void, a nullity and insufficient to extend the statute of limitations or to confer any jurisdiction on this court.

5. Complainant has failed to prove any case entitling it to any relief in equity in this suit.

Thereafter the Court granted time to the parties to present briefs and, all briefs having been filed, the Court, on motion of complainant, ordered the cause submitted on January 10, 1936. On January 14, 1936, the Court ex parte made and caused to be entered its order "that a decree be entered in favor [51] of the United States, upon findings of fact and conclusions of law, to be filed."

The defendants hereby except to the order of the

Court "that a decree be entered in favor of the United States" made and entered January 14, 1936, as being contrary to law, the facts and the rules of equity.

EXCEPTION NO. 2

Thereafter and on January 22, 1936, complainant filed and presented to defendants proposed findings of fact and conclusions of law. On January 25, 1936, defendants served and filed objections and proposed amendments and additions to complainant's proposed findings of fact and conclusions of law. On January 26, 1936, complainant served and filed an amended draft of its proposed findings of fact and conclusions of law wherein it accepted certain of defendants proposed amendments and additions and rejected others. On January 28, 1936, defendants served and filed objections and proposed amendments and additions to said amended draft wherein defendants objected to and requested the Court to strike the following portions of said amended draft of findings of fact and conclusions of law, viz:

1. The last line of proposed finding I containing the words "They have never been discharged as executors of said estate", for the reason that it was contrary to law and the proofs and redundant.

2. That part of proposed finding of fact IV found in the first paragraph thereof and consisting of the parenthetical clause "(as required by Section 316 of the 1926 Revenue Act)" for the reason that it was a conclusion not supported by proof and contrary to the proofs adduced.

3. That part of proposed finding of fact IV contained [52] in the last sentence of the first paragraph thereof and consisting of the clause "in accordance with said decision of the United States Board of Tax Appeals," for the reason that it is a conclusion not supported by any proof.

4. All of proposed finding of fact V for the reason that it is a conclusion not supported by any evidence or proof.

5. All of the Conclusions of Law as being beyond the jurisdiction of the Court and not supported by the evidence.

As an addition to proposed amended finding IV, defendants requested that preceding the sentence commencing with the words "On March 14, 1929", in the first paragraph thereof, the following be inserted: "On March 13, 1929, the United States Board of Tax Appeals made findings of fact and rendered its opinion directing that judgment be entered for the Commissioner of Internal Revenue."

Said objections and proposed amendments and additions to said amended draft of proposed findings of fact and conclusions of law were, except as to such as were accepted by complainant in its amended draft, identical with those made by defendants to the first draft of proposed findings of fact and conclusions of law.

On February 1, 1936, said proposed amended findings of fact and conclusions of law, together with defendants' objections and proposed amendments and additions thereto, came before the Court for settlement and were ordered submitted subject to exception by defendants. On February 5, 1936,

said amended findings of fact and conclusions of law
as prepared by complainant and objected to by defendants were approved and signed by the judge
of the above entitled Court.

The defendants hereby except to said findings of
fact and conclusions of law upon the grounds that
they are not supported by the facts, and are contrary to law. [53]

EXCEPTION No. 3

On February 19, 1936, the above entitled Court
made and caused to be entered its decree and judgment in which it decreed and adjudged that the
assets of the Estate of David Neustadter distributed to defendants herein "constituted a trust fund
for the payment of taxes owing by said estate and
the executors of said estate to the United States"
and that defendants were accountable for said distributed property in an amount not exceeding
$30,000, distributed to each of them from the assets
of said estate. The Court further adjudged and
decreed that complainant recover from each of the
defendants the principal amount of the tax found
of $12,012.99, with interest thereon at 6% per an-
num from September 27, 1929, and that complainant have its costs.

Defendants hereby except to said decree and
judgment entered in favor of complainant on the
ground that it is contrary to the facts and the law.

EXCEPTION No. 4

The foregoing constitutes defendants' bill of exceptions to be used upon appeal from the decree

and judgment heretofore entered herein.

Dated: March 15th, 1936.

ADOLPHUS E. GRAUPNER
Attorney for Defendants [54]

STIPULATION RE BILL OF EXCEPTIONS

Settlement of the foregoing bill of exceptions having been regularly continued to the present term of court and having been presented within due time IT IS HEREBY STIPULATED AND AGREED that said bill of exceptions is a true bill of exceptions taken upon the trial of the above entitled action and the same may be presented to and settled and allowed and certified by the Judge who tried the above-entitled cause.

Dated: March 30, 1936.

H. H. McPIKE
United States Attorney.
By ESTHER B. PHILLIPS
Attorneys for Complainant.
ADOLPHUS E. GRAUPNER
Attorney for Defendants [55]

ORDER SETTLING BILL OF EXCEPTIONS

Settlement of the foregoing bill of exceptions having been regularly continued to the present term of court and said bill of exceptions having been duly and regularly prepared and served in due time and found to be correct, the same is hereby settled, certified and allowed as a true bill of exceptions of the proceedings taken on the trial of the above-entitled cause, and the same is hereby made a part of the record in the above entitled cause.

Dated: March 30th, 1936.

HAROLD LOUDERBACK
Judge of the above-entitled
Court.

[Endorsed]: Receipt of a copy of within Defendants bill of exceptions admitted this 21st day of March, 1936.

H. H. McPIKE
United States Attorney
By ESTHER B. PHILLIPS,
Ass't U. S. Attorney
Attorneys for Complainant.

[Endorsed]: Filed Mar. 30, 1936. [56]

———

[Title of Court and Cause.]

PETITION FOR AND ORDER ALLOWING APPEAL [57]

To the Honorable, the Judge of the United States District Court, in and for the Northern District of California, Southern Division:

Defendants herein, Newton H. Neustadter, Josephine D. Neustadter, Florence N. Stettheimer, James D. Hart and Ellen K. Hart, feeling themselves aggrieved by the decree and judgment entered in this cause on the 19th day of February, 1936, in favor of complainant and against defendants, in that in the record and proceedings had in

said cause and also in the rendition of said decree
and judgment against said defendants manifest
error has happened to the damage and prejudice of
said defendants, and your petitioners are desirous
of appealing from said decree and judgment to the
United States Circuit Court of Appeals for the
Ninth Circuit.

Now come the said defendants by their counsel
and petition the above-entitled court for an order
allowing an appeal from the decree and judgment
given, made and entered in the above-entitled cause
on February 19, 1936, to the Honorable, the United
States Circuit Court of Appeals for the Ninth Circuit, under and in accordance with the laws of the
United States in such cases made and provided,
and that a citation be issued as in such cases made
and provided.

WHEREFORE, defendants pray for an order
allowing said appeal and for an order fixing the
amount of bond for costs which said defendants
shall give and furnish upon said appeal, and that
upon the giving of such security, all further proceedings in this court be suspended and stayed until the determination of said appeal in said United
States Circuit Court of Appeals for the Ninth Circuit, and that a transcript of the record and proceedings with all things concerning the same, duly
authenticated, be sent to said United States Circuit Court of Appeals, and for such other order and
process as may cause such error to be [58] corrected by said United States Circuit Court of Appeals.

And your petitioners will'ever pray, etc.

Dated March 30, 1936.

ADOLPHUS E. GRAUPNER

Attorney for Defendants [59]

ORDER ALLOWING APPEAL AND FIXING AMOUNT OF COSTS BOND

Upon motion of Adolphus E. Graupner, Esq., attorney for defendants, and upon the filing of a petition for an order allowing appeal to the United States Circuit Court of Appeals for the Ninth Circuit, and the assignment of errors herein,

IT IS ORDERED that an appeal is hereby allowed to have reviewed in said United States Circuit Court of Appeals a decree and judgment heretofore entered in the above-entitled suit in favor of complainant and against defendants, which said decree and judgment were given, made and entered on the 19th day of February, 1936, and that the amount of the supersedeas bond on said appeal is hereby fixed in the sum of Twenty Fve Thousand Dollars and a cost bond in the sum of $250.00.

And that upon the filing of such bond, all proceedings on the judgment of said cause be and the same are hereby stayed, pending the prosecution of said appeal.

Dated: March 30th, 1936.

HAROLD LOUDERBACK

United States District Judge.

[Endorsed]: Receipt of a copy of the within Pe-

tition For and Order Allowing Appeal is hereby admitted this 30th day of March, 1936.

H. H. McPIKE

Attorney for Complainant.

[Endorsed]: Filed Mar. 30, 1936. [60]

[Title of Court and Cause.]

DEFENDANTS' ASSIGNMENT OF ERRORS.

[61]

Now come the defendants above named and
specify and assign the following as the errors upon
which they will rely on their appeal to the United
States Circuit Court of Appeals for the Ninth
Circuit in the above entitled suit:

1. That the United States District Court erred
in denying defendants' motion for dismissal and
motion for judgment made upon complainant resting its case in the following particulars:

(A) It erred in denying the defendants' motion to dismiss the suit for the reason that the
court was without jurisdiction in equity to grant
relief to complainant because: (1) complainant
failed to prove that it was without a plain, complete
and adequate remedy at law when the suit was filed,
(2) complainant failed to prove any reason for its
failure to avail itself of the plain, complete and
adequate remedies at law available to it before or at
the time the suit was filed, (3) complainant failed
to prove that the alleged deficiency in tax had not
been paid, (4) the suit did not involve a dispute

or controversy within the jurisdiction of the court
and the intendment of section 37 of the Judicial
Code, (5) complainant failed to establish a right
to equitable relief by adequate proof, (6) complainant is estopped from establishing an equitable
trust for the reason that it permitted the trust enforceable in equity and created by section 409 of
the Revenue Act of 1921 to lapse without attempt
at enforcement, and (7) it is barred from any
relief by limitation;

(B) Said court erred in denying defendants'
motion for judgment upon all of the grounds specified above on motion to dismiss and for the following additional reasons: (1) complainant failed to
prove that it was within the equitable jurisdiction of the District Court, (2) complainant failed
to prove any tax or deficiency in tax to be due and
unpaid, upon which [62] defendants might be held
liable as transferees, (3) complainant is not entitled to equitable relief because (a) it does not
come into court with clean hands and (b) its claim
is stale, (4) complainant failed to prove its right
to a remedy in equity, and (5) complainant's right
of suit is barred by limitation.

DEFENDANTS' EXCEPTION No. 1

2. Said court erred in making and entering its
order "that a decree be entered in favor of the
United States."

DEFENDANTS' EXCEPTION No. 2

3. Said Court erred in making findings of fact
contrary to the proofs and which failed to show

equitable jurisdiction, and, also, in stating conclusions of law contrary to the proofs and based upon inadequate and erroneous findings of fact.

DEFENDANTS' EXCEPTION No. 3

4. Said Court erred in rendering judgment against defendants because: (a) the court was without jurisdiction, (b) the judgment was contrary to the proofs, (c) all taxes legally assessed against the Estate of David Neustadter, deceased, had been fully paid, (d) there was no liability on the part of defendants, as transferees, to pay any tax claimed in this suit, and (e) the proceedings and findings upon which said judgment was founded are violative of the Fifth Amendment of the Constitution of the United States.

DEFENDANTS' EXCEPTION No. 4

WHEREFORE, defendants pray that said decree and judgment of the District Court herein in favor of complainant be vacated, set aside, corrected, or reversed and that said [63] court be directed to enter judgment in favor of defendants and for their costs of suit.

Dated: March 30, 1936.

ADOLPHUS E. GRAUPNER,
Attorney for Defendants.

[Endorsed]: Receipt of a copy of the within Defendants' Assignment of Errors is hereby admitted this 30th day of March, 1936.

H. H. McPIKE
Attorney for Complainant.

[Endorsed]: Filed Mar. 30, 1936. [64]

[Title of Court and Cause.]

STIPULATION FOR OMISSIONS FROM PRINTED RECORD IN TRANSCRIPT ON APPEAL

It is hereby stipulated and agreed by and between [65] the above named parties to this suit that there may and shall be omitted from the printed transcript of record upon appeal of the above entitled suit to the United States Circuit Court of Appeals for the Ninth Circuit the following described portions of the record to be transmitted by the Clerk of the above entitled court to the Clerk of said United States Circuit Court of Appeals, viz:

1. Exhibits A and B to defendants' amended answer, for the reason that the same appear in full in Complainant's Exhibit No. 3 in defendants' Bill of Exceptions, which will form a part of said transcript, and

2. Complainant's Exhibit No. 1, the Estate Tax Return filed in the Estate of David Neustadter, deceased, for the reason that said exhibit is to be transmitted to said United States Circuit Court of Appeals to permit reference thereto by the Honorable Judges of said Court.

March 30, 1936

                    H. H. McPIKE
                    By ESTHER B. PHILLIPS
                        Ass't U. S. Atty.
                        Attorneys for Complainant.
                    ADOLPHUS E. GRAUPNER
                        Attorney for Defendants.

[Endorsed]: Filed Mar. 30, 1936. [66]

[Title of Court and Cause.]

> The premium charged for this bond is $10.00 Dollars per annum.

WHEREAS, the above named Defendants have prosecuted an appeal to the United States Circuit Court of Appeals for the Ninth Circuit, from a judgment made and entered against them in the above entitled court on February 19, 1936, and

WHEREAS, an undertaking for costs is required in connection with said appeal.

NOW, THEREFORE, in consideration of the premises, the undersigned, FIDELITY AND DEPOSIT COMPANY OF MARYLAND, a Corporation duly organized and existing under the laws of the State of Maryland and duly authorized and licensed by the State of California to do a general surety business in the State of California, does hereby undertake and promise on the part of the Defendants, that the said Defendants will prosecute their said appeal to effect and answer all costs if they fail to make good their plea, not exceeding the sum of TWO HUNDRED FIFTY AND NO/100 ($250.00) DOLLARS, to which amount it acknowledges itself justly bound.

And further, it is expressly understood and agreed that is case of a breach of any condition of the above obligation, the Court in the above entitled matter may, upon notice to the FIDELITY AND DEPOSIT COMPANY OF MARYLAND, of not less than ten days, proceed summarily in the action or suit in which the same was given to ascertain the amount which said Surety is bound to pay on account of such breach, and render judgment therefor against it and award execution therefor.

Signed, sealed and dated this 30th day of March, A. D. 1936.

FIDELITY AND DEPOSIT COMPANY
[Seal] OF MARYLAND

By C. K. BENNETT
Attorney-in-Fact

Attest: C. A. BEVANS
Agent. [67]

State of California,
City and County of San Francisco—ss.

On this 30th day of March, A. D. 1936, before me, Charles H. Cunningham, a Notary Public in and for the City and County of San Francisco, residing therein, duly commissioned and sworn, personally appeared, C. K. Bennett, Attorney-in-Fact, and C. A. Bevans, Agent, of the Fidelity and Deposit Company of Maryland, a corporation, known to me to be the persons who executed the within instrument on behalf of the corporation therein named and acknowledged to me that such corporation executed the same, and also known to me to be the persons whose names are subscribed to the within instrument as the Attorney-in-Fact and Agent respectively of said corporation, and they, and each of them, acknowledged to me that they subscribed the name of said Fidelity and Deposit Company of Maryland thereto as principal and their own names as Attorney-in-Fact and Agent respectively.

IN WITNESS WHEREOF, I have hereunto set my hand and affixed my official seal at my office in the City and County of San Francisco the day and year first above written.

[Seal]   CHARLES H. CUNNINGHAM,
Notary Public in and for the City and County of San Francisco, State of California.

My commission expires December 26, 1938.

[Endorsed]: Approved 3/31/36
HAROLD LOUDERBACK
U. S. Dist. Judge.

[Endorsed]: Filed Mar. 31, 1936. [68]

[Title of Court and Cause.]

PRAECIPE

To the Clerk of Said Court:
Sir:

Please issue for transmission to the Clerk of the United States Circuit Court of Appeals for the Ninth Circuit at San Francisco, California, a certified copy of the record on appeal to said Circuit Court for preparation of the transcript, including therein the following papers:

Complaint.

Order granting leave to file an amended answer.

Amended Answer.

Amendments to Amended Answer.

Complainant's Exhibit No. 1 (Estate Tax Return).

Order for entry of decree in favor of Complainant.

Findings of Fact and Conclusions of Law.

Judgment or decree.

Defendants' Bill of Exceptions. [69]

Stipulation extending time to file Bill of Exceptions.

Petition for Appeal and Order allowing petition for appeal and fixing Cost Bond.

Assignments of error.

Cost Bond on Appeal.

Citation on appeal.

Stipulation for Omission from Printed Record in Transcript.

Your Certificate.

This praecipe.

Dated: March 31, 1936.

> ADOLPHUS E. GRAUPNER
> Attorney for Defendants.

[Endorsed]: Receipt of a copy of the within Praecipe is hereby admitted this 31st day of March, 1936.

> H. H. McPIKE
> U. S. Attorney
> By ESTHER B. PHILLIPS,
> Ass't U. S. Attorney
> Attorneys for Complainant.

[Endorsed]: Filed Mar. 31, 1936. [70]

[Title of Court.]

CERTIFICATE OF CLERK TO TRANSCRIPT OF RECORD ON APPEAL

I, WALTER B. MALING, Clerk of the United States District Court, for the Northern District of California, do hereby certify that the foregoing 70 pages, numbered from 1 to 70, inclusive, contain a full, true, and correct transcript of the records and proceedings in the cause entitled UNITED STATES OF AMERICA, Plaintiff, vs. NEWTON H. NEUSTADTER, et al., Defendants, In Equity No. 3639-L, as the same now remain on file and of record in my office.

I further certify that the cost of preparing and certifying the foregoing transcript of record on appeal is the sum of $11.75 and that the said amount has been paid to me by the Attorney for the appellants herein.

IN WITNESS WHEREOF, I have hereunto set my hand and affixed the seal of said District Court, this 15th day of April A. D. 1936.

[Seal]   WALTER B. MALING, Clerk.

J. P. WALSH

Deputy Clerk [71]

[Title of Court and Cause.]

CITATION ON APPEAL

United States of America—ss.

The President of the United States of America,
to the United States of America, Greeting:

YOU ARE HEREBY CITED AND ADMON-ISHED to be and appear at a United States Circuit Court of Appeals for the Ninth Circuit, to be holden at the City and County of San Francisco, in the State of California, within thirty days from the date hereof, pursuant to an order allowing an appeal, of record in the Clerk's office of the United States District Court for the Northern District of California, Southern Division, wherein Newton H. Neustadter, Josephine D. Neustadter, Florence N. Stettheimer, James D. Hart and Ellen K. Hart are appellants and you are appellee, to show cause, if any there be, why the decree or judgment rendered against the said appellants, as in the said order of appeal mentioned, should not be corrected, and why speedy justice should not be done to the parties in that behalf.

WITNESS, The Honorable HAROLD LOUD-ERBACK, United States [72] District Judge for the Northern District of California, this 31st day of March, A. D. 1936.

HAROLD LOUDERBACK
United States Dsitrict Judge.

[Endorsed]: Receipt of a copy of the within Citation On Appeal is hereby admitted this 31 day of March, 1936.

H. H. McPIKE,

U. S. Attorney.

By ESTHER B. PHILLIPS,

Asst. U. S. Attorney.

Attorney for Complainant.

[Endorsed]: Filed Mar. 31, 1936. Walter B. Maling, Clerk. By J. P. Welsh, Deputy Clerk.

———

[Endorsed]: No. 8176. United States Circuit Court of Appeals for the Ninth Circuit. Newton H. Neustadter, Josephine D. Neustadter, Florence N. Stettheimer, James D. Hart and Ellen K. Hart, Appellants, vs. United States of America, Appellee. Transcript of Record. Upon Appeal from the District Court of the United States for the Northern District of California, Southern Division.

Filed April 18, 1936.

PAUL P. O'BRIEN,

Clerk of the United States Circuit Court of Appeals for the Ninth Circuit.

No. 8176

IN THE

United States Circuit Court of Appeals

For the Ninth Circuit 7

NEWTON H. NEUSTADTER, JOSEPHINE D. NEU-
STADTER, FLORENCE N. STETTHEIMER, JAMES
D. HART and ELLEN K. HART,

Appellants,

vs.

UNITED STATES OF AMERICA,

Appellee.

BRIEF FOR APPELLANTS.

ADOLPHUS E. GRAUPNER,
Balfour Building, San Francisco,
Attorney for Appellants.

FILED

AUG 29 1936

PERNAU-WALSH PRINTING CO , SAN FRANCISCO

Table of Contents

Appendix

Table of Authorities Cited

No. 8176

IN THE

United States Circuit Court of Appeals
For the Ninth Circuit

NEWTON H. NEUSTADTER, JOSEPHINE D. NEU-
STADTER, FLORENCE N. STETTHEIMER, JAMES
D. HART and ELLEN K. HART,

Appellants,

vs.

UNITED STATES OF AMERICA,

Appellee.

BRIEF FOR APPELLANTS.

I. STATEMENT OF THE CASE.

This appeal is taken from a decree in equity adjudging
that appellants, as distributees of the estate of David
Neustadter, deceased, are accountable and liable as equitable trustees for estate taxes alleged to have been
assessed against and to be due from said estate in the
amount of $12,012.99, with interest at 6% per annum
from September 27, 1929. Appellee relies upon a purported assessment against said estate as the sole basis of
its right to relief. Appellants contend that no liability
of appellants was proven, that the assessment relied on
was illegal and void, that appellee's claim is barred by
limitation, that appellee is not entitled to relief in equity,
that appellee's procedure to assert a liability is not due
process, and that the District Court lacked jurisdiction.

2

II. THE FACTS.

(For convenience, all material dates are set forth in calendar form following this statement. Where this statement conflicts with the findings, such conflict is shown in footnotes.)

David Neustadter, a resident of San Francisco, died testate February 13; 1923, leaving as his devisees the five appellants herein. Newton H. Neustadter, Walter W. Stettheimer and Julian Hart were duly appointed and qualified as the executors of the estate of said decedent. (R. p. 26.)

Said executors filed a federal estate tax return on December 31, 1923, and paid the federal estate tax therein computed in the amount of $4145.23. (R. p. 27.)

On February 7, 1924, said executors filed the first and final account of their administration, their report, petition for settlement of said account, and petition for final distribution with the Superior Court of the State of California, in and for the City and County of San Francisco, which court had jurisdiction of the probate of said estate. On February 25, 1924, said account, report, and petitions were allowed and approved and a decree for the final distribution of said estate was made and ordered entered by said court. (R. p. 27.)

On July 30, 1924, the executors wrote the Commissioner of Internal Revenue requesting an early final determination of the estate tax for said estate. On November 10, 1925, said Commissioner mailed to said executors a notice of deficiency in estate tax of $692.23, which amount was assessed and paid. (R. p. 28.)

The entire estate of David Neustadter, deceased was completely distributed by said executors under the above mentioned decree of final distribution prior to September 1, 1926 (R. p. 51) and the executors thereby were discharged as representatives of said estate.[1]

On September 21, 1926, *after said estate had been completely distributed,* said Commissioner mailed a second deficiency notice, addressed to "Newton H. Neustadter et al., executors", proposing an additional deficiency in estate tax against said estate in the amount of $12,012.99, "pursuant to Section 318 of the Revenue Act of 1926". (R. p. 42.)[2]

The parties named as executors appealed from said notice of deficiency to the United States Board of Tax Appeals on November 2, 1929. Said Board, after hearing on the proceeding, promulgated its decision directing judgment in favor of said Commissioner on March 13, 1929 (15 B. T. A. 839) and on March 14, 1926, made an order determining a deficiency in estate tax in the amount of $12,012.99. (R. p. 46.) Said decision of said Board is stipulated in evidence (R. p. 46) and is reprinted in the appendix, pages i-xxiv thereof.

On September 27, 1929, said Commissioner signed an assessment certificate asserting a deficiency in estate tax of $12,012.99 against "David Neustadter, Est. of" which does not disclose that it was signed "in accordance with said decision" of said Board of Tax Appeals or any part

---

1. The court below, over the objection of appellants (R. p. 54) and contrary to the evidence (R. p. 51), found that said executors had never been discharged. (R. p. 27.)

2. The court below, adversely to objections and proposed amendment of appellants and contrary to Exhibit 3-A (R. p. 43) found as a fact that such deficiency notice was "as required by Section 316 of the 1926 Revenue Act." (Finding IV, R. p. 29.)

of any revenue act. (R. p. 46.)[3] It is upon such assessment that appellee relies to sustain its right to maintain the suit here on appeal. The suit was filed more than ten years after the death of David Neustadter and more than seven years after the final distribution of his estate.

III. CALENDAR OF MATERIAL DATES.

February 13, 1923, David Neustadter died. Ten year lien on property of estate became imposed by Section 409 of the Revenue Act of 1921.

March 8, 1923, will probated; executors appointed and qualified.

December 31, 1923, estate tax return filed and tax paid.

February 7, 1924, petition for final distribution, etc. filed.

February 13, 1924, due date of tax (returned and paid as above).

February 25, 1924, decree of final distribution of estate made.

March 4, 1924, assessment of estate tax, as returned, certified.

July 30, 1924, executors wrote Commissioner requesting early final determination of estate tax.

November 10, 1925, amended notice of deficiency of $692.23 in estate tax mailed to executors; no appeal taken.

---

3. Without proof or any evidence in support thereof, and adversely to appellants' specific objection and proposed amendment, the court below found that said certificate of assessment was made ''in accordance with'' the above mentioned decision of said Board. (Finding IV, Tr. p. 29.)

March 13, 1926, assessment of $692.23 deficiency in estate tax made.

March 15, 1926, deficiency of $692.23 paid.

September 1, 1926, entire estate distributed before this date.

September 21, 1926, deficiency notice for $12,012.99 mailed to "Newton H. Neustadter et al.", as executors.

November 2, 1926, petition on appeal from deficiency notice filed with Board of Tax Appeals, Docket No. 20,988.

December 4, 1928, proceedings heard before Board of Tax Appeals.

March 13, 1929, decision of said Board promulgated.

March 14, 1929, final order of Board determining deficiency entered.

September 27, 1929, certificate of assessment of deficiency of $12,012.99 illegally signed by Commissioner.

November 10, 1929, collector demanded payment of deficiency from one of former executors.

March 13, 1932, expiration of six year period from last legal assessment under which appellants might be sued on liability as transferees. (See March 13, 1926.)

February 13, 1933, lien and equitable trust created by Section 409 of Revenue Act of 1921 expired by limitation.

October 6, 1933, bill of complaint in this suit filed.

February 19, 1936, decree for appellee entered in District Court.

IV. CONFLICTS BETWEEN PLEADINGS, PROOFS AND FINDINGS.

Appellee alleged in its complaint that: (1) the suit was one in equity (Par. III, R. p. 2); (2) the assessment of September 27, 1929, was made "in accordance with the decision" of the Board of Tax Appeals (Par. XII, R. p. 7); (3) no part of said tax had been paid and all thereof was due and outstanding (Par. XII, R. p. 7); (4) the appointed executors have not been finally discharged (Par. XIII, R. p. 8; (5) the property and assets of the estate distributed to appellants was "charged with a trust in favor of the United States" (Par. XV, R. p. 8); and (6) appellee had "no clear, adequate or complete remedy at law" against appellants.

All such allegations were denied by appellants and *no* proof to substantiate any of them was offered by appellee.

The District Court *did not find* that the proceeding was one in equity, or that appellee had no clear, adequate, or complete remedy at law", or that the court had any jurisdiction of the cause.

Contrary to or without proof, the court found that: (1) the assessment of September 27, 1929, was made in accordance with a decision of the Board of Tax Appeals (R. p. 29); (2) the deficiency notice, upon which the decision of the Board and the assessment were supposedly founded, was "as required by Section 316 of the 1926 Revenue Act" (R. p. 29); (3) the executors have never been discharged (R. p. 27); the property distributed from the estate was charged with a trust in favor of appellee (R. p. 30); and (5) no part of the tax had been paid. (R. p. 30.)

V. ASSIGNMENT OF ERRORS.

The errors assigned are detailed on pages 61 to 63 inclusive of the record. All are relied upon and because of their extent are here summarized as follows:

1. Appellee failed in its proofs and is not entitled to relief;

2. Appellee is barred from relief by limitation;

3. Appellee is estopped from equitable relief;

4. The District Court lacked jurisdiction of the cause; and

5. The proceedings upon which appellee relies violate the Fifth Amendment to the Federal Constitution.

6. The trial court erred in denying appellants' motion to dismiss and their motion for judgment in their favor on each and every of the above-mentioned grounds.

VI. ARGUMENT.

1. APPELLEE FAILED TO PROVE A RIGHT TO RELIEF.

The full burden of proof rested on appellee and it failed to sustain that burden. A complainant in equity must establish by evidence *every averment* of its bill essential to entitle it to relief. *There is no presumption to favor equitable relief.*

> *Smith v. McCullough,* 270 U. S. 456, 459; 46 S. Ct. 338, 339;
>
> *Norton v. Larney,* 266 U. S. 511, 516; 45 S. Ct. 145, 147.

8

Where the government sues for the collection of a tax, the burden rests upon it to prove the liability of the person sued.

> *Little Miami etc. Co. v. U. S.*, 108 U. S. 277, 281, 2 S. Ct. 627, 629;
>
> *U. S. v. Boston & Montana etc. Co.*, 1 Fed. (2d) 31, 32.

Although appellee is the sovereign, it has no greater standing before the court or any greater privilege to relief than if it were the lowliest citizen or subject.

> *U. S. v. Stinson*, 197 U. S. 200, 205, 25 S. Ct. 426, 427;
>
> *U. S. v. Midway Northern Oil Co.*, 232 Fed. 619, 331;
>
> *Walker v. U. S.*, 139 Fed. 409, 413-415, affd. 148 Fed. 1022.

(a) Appellee failed to prove that a tax liability existed or was due from anyone.

Appellee alleged (R. p. 7, Par. XII) that "no part of said tax or interest has been paid; that there is now due and outstanding an additional estate tax in the sum of $12,012.99, together with interest thereon". That allegation was denied in appellants' amended answer. (R. p. 17, Par. XIII.) In the court below, appellee argued that its failure of proof was saved by what it termed "admissions" in said paragraph XIII of said amended answer. Conceding the widest and wildest interpretation of appellants' pleading in that paragraph, there is no admission of non-payment or of a tax being due which could cure appellee's failure to prove an unpaid legal deficiency in tax. The allegation that the "Collector made no further attempt toward collection'' *is not* an admission that the alleged deficiency was not paid.

Whether a judgment or lack of a remedy at law is a prerequisite to a suit such as this, the fundamental essential to equitable relief, viz.: *the existence of an unsatisfied debt, must be proven.* This rule in equity is thus succinctly stated:

> "In this case the bill alleges that executions were issued upon the judgments of the claimants and were returned 'unsatisfied', but *the allegation was not admitted,* and *no proof on the subject was produced* at the hearing. The case therefore stands as a suit in equity commenced for the satisfaction of judgments before any attempt had been made for their collection at law, by the issue of execution thereon. *That the suit cannot be maintained under these circumstances is clear,* both upon principle and authority.
>
> "*The decree appealed from must, therefore, be reversed and the court below directed to enter a decree for the defendant, dismissing the suit.*" (Italics supplied.)
>
> *Jones v. Green,* 68 U. S. 330, 332, 17 L. Ed. 553, 555.

The doctrine that "in all cases where a court of equity interferes to aid the enforcement of a remedy at law *there must be an acknowledged debt proven*", is one firmly established in equity by both federal and state courts and has been consistently followed.

> *Cates v. Allen,* 149 U. S. 451, 37 L. Ed. 804, 808;
>
> *Scott v. Neely,* 140 U. S. 106, 113, 35 L. Ed. 358, 361.

It naturally follows that a debt must exist and its non-payment established (as it was not in this case) before transferees of an alleged creditor may be held liable in equity. A paraphrase of the above quoted language from *Jones v. Green,* seems conclusive argument of appellants' position:

> "In this case the bill alleges that 'no part of said tax or interest has been paid; that there is now due and outstanding an additional estate tax in the sum of $12,019.99, together with interest thereon', but *the allegation was not admitted and no proof on the subject* was produced at the hearing. The case therefore stands as a suit in equity commenced to enforce an alleged equitable lien or trust for the satisfaction of an alleged liability for a tax without any showing that such liability exists. *That the suit cannot be maintained under these* circumstances is clear, both upon principle and authority.
>
> "The decree appealed from must, therefore, be reversed and *the court below directed to enter a decree for appellants herein, dismissing the suit."*

(b) Appellee failed to prove any legal assessment against the estate of David Neustadter, deceased, or appellants, which would entitle it to relief in equity.

This is fatal to appellee's cause for the reason that, without a valid assessment, its right of recovery is barred by limitation and the suit should be ordered dismissed. As failure of proof of a legal and binding assessment affects other issues, it will be more fully discussed hereinafter.

(c) Appellee has failed to prove that it has any right whatever to equitable relief.

1. It failed to prove that its proceeding was one properly in equity;

2. It failed to plead or prove any excuse or reason for its delay in seeking equitable relief or its failure to resort to available legal remedies;

3. It failed to prove that it was without a plain, speedy and adequate remedy at law;

4. It failed to prove that its cause was within the equitable jurisdiction of the court;

5. It failed to prove any lien on the distributed property to exist at the time the suit was filed, under which it might seek to establish an equitable trust.

Due to its failure of proof in the above specified particulars, appellee was not entitled to any relief in the court below and the decree therein should be reversed with order for dismissal of appellants. The merits of appellants' foregoing specifications will be argued hereinafter.

----

2. RECOVERY IS BARRED BY LIMITATION.

The defense of the statute of limitations is not technical, but substantial and meritorious, and appellants are entitled to judgment on their plea thereof.

> *United States v. Oregon Lumber Co.*, 260 U. S. 290, 43 S. Ct. 100.

Also, statutes of limitation may not be extended by implication and should be construed liberally in favor of the taxpayer.

> *United States v. John Barth Co.*, 279 U. S. 370, 377, 49 S. Ct. 366, 367.

Argument on plea of the bar of limitation must of necessity be somewhat confused, because of the inconsistencies between appellee's pleadings, proofs and findings. The case was tried and submitted on the theory that appellants were liable as a result of proceedings had before the Board of Tax Appeals under a deficiency notice mailed to the former executors under assumed authority of Section 318(a) of the Revenue Act of 1926. (R. p. 42.) After entry of the order for a decree (R. p. 25), appellee shifted its position by preparing a finding which stated that the proceedings before the Board of Tax Appeals upon which it relied were had on a deficiency notice "as required by section 316 of the 1926 Revenue Act". (R. p. 29.) Such finding was protested by appellants when proposed and, also, when presented to the trial judge (R. p. 54), but, nevertheless, was not amended by appellee and was signed by the judge. Such finding completely negatives the effect of the decision of the Board of Tax Appeals in evidence (App. p. i) and changes the entire theory of the case as tried and argued below. The result of this situation is the necessity for appellants to present varied and extended argument.

Appellee's suit was brought upon the theory that an assessment extended the time for its filing to within the period when the bill was filed. The theory fails to afford a remedy because the alleged assessment was illegal and void.

If Section 316 controlled, as the court found, then Sections 310 and 311 of the 1926 Act bar relief by limitation; if Section 318(a) applied, then Section 1109 bars recovery; in either case, Section 409 is a bar to transferee liability.

(a) **Under Section 316 of the Revenue Act of 1926, appellee is barred from relief.**

Finding IV (R. p. 29) states that the deficiency notice, resulting in proceedings had before the Board of Tax Appeals, was mailed "as required by Section 316 of the 1926 Revenue Act". Under that section, the decision of the Board and the assessment which appellee contends was made "in accordance with said decision" could not extend the statute of limitations to permit this suit. Said Board has jurisdiction only in so far as the deficiency notice is authorized by a specific section of a Revenue Act and *then only over the persons named in said notice.*

> *Melczer v. Commissioner,* 23 B. T. A. 124, 127 (appeal dismissed by this court, 63 Fed. (2d) 1010);
>
> *Liebermann's Committee* (C. C. A. 2), 54 Fed. (2d) 527, 530.

Under the above stated finding of fact this court can do naught else than reverse the lower court and order dismissal. This because Section 316 (App. p. xxvii) authorizes deficiency notices to only two classes of persons, viz.: (1) transferees of property of estates of decedents and (2) fiduciaries who are liable under R. S. Section 3467, *infra.* As the deficiency notice in evidence (R. p. 42), under which proceedings were brought before the Board of Tax Appeals, was addressed *only* to the *functus officio* executors, it is obvious that a decision and consequent assessment under a deficiency notice "required by Section 316" could apply *only to the personal fiduciary liability* of the former executors.

R. S. Section 3467 contains such restrictive language that any assessment on liability for taxes imposed in reliance thereon could not affect the property of the estate or its distributees.

> "R. S. sec. 3467. Every executor * * * who pays any debt due by the * * * estate from whom or for which he acts, before he satisfies and pays the debts due to the United States from such * * * estate, shall become answerable *in his own person and estate* for the debts so due to the United States." * * * (Italics supplied.)

Any assessment made as a consequence of proceedings had before the Board under a deficiency notice "as required by section 316" and as addressed to the former executors would be ineffective as against the persons and property of appellants and could in no way suspend the running of the statute of limitations to their detriment. Appellants, not being named in said deficiency notice, were not and could not become parties or privies to the proceedings against the *functus officio* executors in their fiduciary capacities.

Sections 310, 311 and 316(b) (see App. pp. xxv, xxvii) provide the statute of limitations applicable to transferees of estates. Section 310(a) of the 1926 Act provides:

> "Except as provided in section 311, the amount of the estate taxes imposed by this title shall be assessed within three years after the return was filed, and no proceeding in court *without assessment* for the collection of such taxes *shall be begun after the expiration of three years after the return was filed.*" (Italics supplied.)

The executors of the estate of David Neustadter filed estate tax return December 31, 1923, and the three year period of limitation for assessment against the estate expired December 31, 1926. The additional period of one year under Section 316(b)(1) of the 1926 Act (App. p. xxvii) for assessment of liability of appellants as transferees expired December 31, 1927.

If the assessment in evidence (R. p. 46) was "in accordance with said decision" of the Board of Tax Appeals and based on proceedings had on a deficiency notice "as required by Section 316 of the 1926 Revenue Act" (R. p. 29), there then would be no suspension of the above mentioned period of limitation applicable to appellants. This because, under the finding, there could be no proceeding against the estate or its distributees to create such a suspension.

Section 316(c) of the 1926 Act provides the specific limitation as to the scope of an assessment, also that for suspension of the running of the statute of limitations, as affecting transferees and fiduciaries, viz.:

> "(c) The running of the period of limitation upon the assessment of the liability of a transferee *or* fiduciary shall, after the mailing of the notice under subdivision (a) of section 308 to the transferee or fiduciary, be suspended for the period during which the Commissioner is prohibited from making the assessment with respect to the liability of the transferee *or* fiduciary." (Italics supplied.)

The word "or", used as above, clearly distinguishes an assessment against a "fiduciary" from one against a "transferee". No deficiency notice under any section of the 1926 Act was mailed to appellants as transferees, nor was any assessment made with respect to their liability. Consequently, under the finding, there could be no suspension of the period of limitation applicable to either appellants or the estate. Therefore, the period of "six years after the assessment of the tax" for bringing "a proceeding in court" for collection, as permitted by Section 311(b) (App. p. xxv), was never available to appellee.

Appellee, under the findings and decree, had only the three year period provided in Section 310(a), *supra*, to bring the suit here on appeal. Not having proceeded within that period, it is barred from relief.

The finding that the deficiency notice in evidence was mailed to the former executors of the estate of David Neustadter "as required by Section 316 of the 1926 Revenue Act" was drafted by appellee's counsel and signed by the trial judge over appellants' objections. (R. p. 54.) This fact should make the finding binding on appellee, estop it from denying the bar of limitation, and justify this court in ordering a decree in favor of appellants.

> *Jones v. U. S.,* ....Fed. Sup........, 4 C. C. H. Tax Service (1936) 9371.

(b) Appellee is barred from relief by Section 1109 of the Revenue Act of 1926.

Until findings were prepared by appellee, appellants had no inkling that it was relying upon Section 316 as the basis of the assessment, from the date of which it claimed a period of six years within which this suit might be instituted. Consequently, in pleading the statute of limitations (R. p. 19) and presenting their defense in the court below, appellants relied upon the bar provided by Section 1109 of the Act of 1926 (App. p. xxviii), which is the applicable section under Section 318(a) of that Act. (App. p. xxviii.)

If this court disregards the finding upon which the decree under appeal is based, it must then consider the bar of limitation presented to but ignored by the District Court. Appellants contend that this suit was barred by limitation under Section 1109(a) of the 1926 Act and the assessment relied upon by appellee to extend the bar was insufficient, illegal, null and void.

Section 318(a) of the Revenue Act of 1926, under which the deficiency notice in evidence appears to have been given (R. p. 42), applies *only* to additional taxes to be imposed against estates under revenue acts prior to that of 1926. That section specifically provides that "the period of limitation prescribed in section 1109" of the 1926 Act "shall be applied in lieu of the period prescribed" in Section 310(a). This precludes the application of Section 311, which would be applicable under Section 316.

(1) The assessment certificate and the proofs fail to disclose that the assessment relied upon by appellee was made in accordance with any section of any revenue act which would suspend the operation of the statute of limitations.

Appellee contends and the District Court found that the assessed deficiency in estate tax (Ex. 4 R. 46) was made "in accordance with said decision" of the Board of Tax Appeals. (R. p. 29.) There is *no proof* to support this contention and finding. Contrary to Bureau practice, the assessment certificate does not disclose any section of the revenue act under which it might be authorized. Therefore, this court may not assume or presume that the assessment was made under a section which would suspend the operation of the statute of limitations or that it was made "in accordance with" a decision of the Board. When the certificate is so uncertain that appellee may elect between Sections 318 and 316 as the authority for the assessment and the trial court may find the assessment to have been made under a different section than that upon which the Board of Tax Appeals based its decision, the authority for the assessment, without proof thereof, is too vague and indefinite to warrant presumption or conclusion.

If the assessment in evidence was *not* proven to be based on a valid decision of the Board of Tax Appeals and, also, *not* to be founded on a specific section of the Revenue Act of 1926 which would suspend the operation of the statute of limitations, it could *not* operate to remove the bar of limitation pleaded by appellants.

Section 318(a) (App. p. xxviii) restricts the authority of the Commissioner to assess for additional estate taxes arising under any Revenue Act prior to that of 1926, by requiring the mailing of a deficiency notice *"to the person liable for such tax"*. The tax for the estate of David Neustadter was imposed under the 1921 Act. When it was sought to impose the additional tax and the deficiency notice was addressed to "Newton H. Neustadter, et al., Executors" (R. p. 42), the persons addressed were not "liable for such tax", excepting in a fiduciary capacity. The estate had been distributed under decree of final distribution before the deficiency notice was mailed (R. p. 28), the one-time executors were *functus officio,* they were not "liable for such tax" as executors, for they no longer represented the estate, its property, or its distributees. All privity between the one-time executors and appellants had ceased.

> *Lindley v. U. S.* (C. C. A. 9), 59 Fed. (2d) 336, 338, and additional authorities hereinafter cited.

The courts may not stretch the meaning of the statute to hold that an illegal assessment erroneously made or that any assessment made against any person will operate to suspend the bar of limitations against all persons, as appellee contends.

Therefore, under Section 1109(a)(1) of the 1926 Act (App. p. xxviii) there could be no proceeding in court for the collection of the tax alleged to be due "after the expiration of five years after such tax became due". The tax on the estate of David Neustadter became due under Section 406 of the Revenue Act of 1921 on February 13, 1924, and the five years to bring suit expired February 13, 1929,—more than four years before this suit was brought.

(2) An assessment made against a person not the owner of the property chargeable with the tax is null and void.

The District Court found: "The entire estate of David Neustadter, deceased, was distributed by said executors prior to the date of mailing a deficiency notice by the Commissioner of Internal Revenue to the above-named executors on September 21, 1926." (R. p. 28.) This finding is supported by the evidence. (R. p. 51.) Such finding is one which is determinative of the fact that *the persons named as executors had ceased to have any right of title or possession to or representation of* the one-time assets of the estate and could no longer be considered in privity with or representative of appellants or their property in the least degree.

> *Lindley v. U. S.* (C. C. A. 9), supra.

Under California law, title to the distributed property of an estate vests completely in the distributees under a degree of final distribution and the distributed estate is beyond the power of representation by its one-time executors. The status of estates and executors is controlled by the law of the state of domicile and the decree of final distribution by a competent state court is determinative of the property rights of the parties *to all federal courts.*

> *Hurlburd v. Commissioner,* ———— U. S. ————, 56 S. Ct.
> 197, 204, and other cases hereinafter cited.

The certificate of assessment in evidence (Ex. 4, R. p. 46) attempts to assess "Neustadter, David, Est." At the time the certificate was signed the Commissioner knew the estate had been distributed, because both the decree and the effect of the distribution were before the Board of Tax Appeals when it considered the proceeding of *Neustadter, et al. v. Commissioner,* 15 B. T. A. 847. (Appendix p. xvi.) Furthermore, under Section 1668 of the Code of Civil Procedure requiring posting of notice of time and place of hearing of a petition for distribution of an estate before final distribution could be decreed, the Commissioner as representative of appellee, *must* be presumed to have had notice that final distribution was pending and to be finally decreed on the day fixed in said notice: i. e., February 25, 1924.

> *Miller v. Pittman,* 180 Cal. 540, 543;
> *Goodrich v. Ferris,* 214 U. S. 71, 79, 29 S. Ct. 580,
> 582.

The estate not being the owner or holder of any property, and being defunct, and the Commissioner having
knowledge of those facts when the assessment was made,
rendered the certificate of assessment in evidence null and
void. It was not such an assessment as contemplated by
Section 1109(a)(3) (App. p. xxix) and could not serve
to extend the time to bring a proceeding in court for
collection of the alleged tax to "within six years after"
its date.

An assessment against someone not the owner of the
property chargeable with a tax is null and void.

> *Bird v. Benlisa,* 142 U. S. 664, 670, 35 L. Ed. 1151,
> 1153;
>
> *Rich v. Braxton,* 158 U. S. 375, 404, 39 L. Ed. 1022,
> 1032;
>
> *People v. Castro,* 39 Cal. 65, 69.

This doctrine has been recognized in its application to
income taxes in

> *Dreyfuss Dry Goods Co. v. Lines* (C. C. A. 5), 24
> Fed. (2d) 29, 30, 31;
>
> *United States v. S. F. Scott & Sons* (C. C. A. 1), 69
> Fed. (2d) 728, 730, 731.

These cases hold that the revenue act contemplates a legal
assessment and distraint against the property of the delin-
quent taxpayer and not the property of someone other than
the taxpayer, and an assessment against the wrong party
would be invalid. By logical analogy the same doctrine
would apply to estate taxes. An assessment against an
estate is merely an assessment against the property of an
estate while in the possession of an executor as representative.

"An estate of a decedent signifies broadly the property left from the time the owner died until settlement and distribution is completed (at which time there ceases to be an estate)."

Ballentine Law Dict., *"Estate of a Deceased Person"*;

Commissioner v. Beebe (C. C. A. 1), 67 Fed. (2d) 662, 664;

Lindley v. United States (C. C. A. 9), supra.

Hence, assessment against the estate could only be against the property in the estate and, without property in the estate, the assessment certificate in evidence is null and void and could not extend or suspend the bar of limitation. There is no assessment within the contemplation of Section 1109(a) which would permit this suit to be brought at the time the complaint was filed (see App. p. xxviii), viz.: "within six years after the assessment of the tax."

The trial court found, regarding the appointed executors of the estate of David Neustadter, "They have never been discharged as executors of said estate". (R. p. 27.) This finding is made contrary to proof and conflicts with the subsequent finding that: "The above-named executors have never been discharged under the provisions of Section 1697 of the Code of Civil Procedure or Section 1066 of the Probate Court of California or under Section 313(b) of the Revenue Act of 1926." (R. p. 28.)

The second finding is based on an allegation in appellant's amendments to their amended answer (R. p. 23) and copies a part of its language. (R. p. 28.) The court finding omits the concluding language of the allegation, viz.: "that said appointed executors, as such, hold no property

or assets of said estate at the present time nor held any
such property or assets at the time this suit was commenced." (R. p. 24.) This allegation was in answer to the
allegation in appellee's complaint: that although final
distribution has been made of the entire estate of David
Neustadter, deceased, the executors have not been finally
discharged." (R. p. 8.) Appellants' allegation went solely
to an admission of the fact that, when the suit was commenced, *the appointed executors had not been discharged
from their personal or fiduciary liability,* that, therefore,
appellee had a remedy at law against them and, consequently, had no right to relief in equity.

In the first finding mentioned the trial court ignored the
fact that executors are deprived of all representative
capacity by final distribution under decree. The same
error which it made and which this Court reversed in
Lindley v. U. S., 59 Fed. (2d) 336, 530. That decision held
that final distribution terminated the representative capacity of executors. If executors cease to represent an
estate and there is no estate remaining to be represented,
no proceeding to reach the property of the distributed
estate can be effective or in due process of law which
attempts to hold property liable through action against
persons whose representative functions have been terminated. Such proceeding could in no way toll the bar of
limitation.

(3) If the assessment in evidence was made in accordance with the decision of the Board of Tax Appeals in Neustadter v. Commissioner, it was null and void and could not suspend or remove the bar of limitation.

Appellee depends upon the decision of the Board of Tax Appeals (App. p. i) to suspend the bar of limitation and to validate an assessment (Ex. 4, R. p. 46) which, it contends, extended the time to collect the alleged estate tax by proceeding in court against appellants for six years from the date thereof. This extended time for suit was claimed under Section 1109(a)(3) of the Revenue Act of 1926. (App. p. xxix.)

If the Board of Tax Appeals was without jurisdiction over the parties to its proceeding, then *its decision and any assessment* which might have been made "in accordance with said decision" *would be null and void.* A void assessment could not suspend the bar of limitation or render Section 1109(a)(3) operative to permit this proceeding in court.

(a) *The decision of the Board of Tax Appeals is not res adjudicata as to appellants* because appellants were not parties to the proceeding before the Board and were not in privity with the parties therein.

> "The rule regarding *res adjudicata,* generally, is that in order to render a matter *res adjudicata* there must be identity of the thing sued for, identity of the cause of action and the identity of the parties in the character in which they are litigants. *Washington, etc. Steam-Packet Co. v. Sickels,* 24 How. 333, 341, 342; *Lyon v. Perin & Gaff Mfg. Co.,* 125 U. S. 678, 700; *Aspden v. Nixon,* 4 How. 467."

(Rule adopted in *Appeal of Suhr,* 4 B. T. A. 1198, 1200; Acquiescence by Commissioner, VI—1 C. B. 6.)

15 *R. C. L. p.* 841, Section 314 and cases cited.

(b) *Said decision of said Board is subject to collateral attack and impeachment in this suit.* The Board was without jurisdiction over the estate of its former executors as representatives thereof and its decision is null and void.

> *Rich v. Town of Metz,* 134 U. S. 632, 644, 645, 10
> S. Ct. 610, 614;
>
> *Hatch v. Ferguson* (C. C. A. 9), 68 Fed. 43, 45.

It is a settled rule that "the jurisdiction of any court exercising authority over a subject may be inquired into in every other court, when the proceedings in the former are relied upon and brought before the latter by a party claiming the benefit of such proceedings". As appellee claims benefit from the extrajurisdictional decision of said Board, this court may inquire into and impeach that decision.

> *Williamson v. Berry,* 8 How. 495, 540; 49 L. Ed.
> 1170, 1189;
>
> *Guaranty Trust etc. Co. v. Green Cove etc. Co.,* 139
> U. S. 137, 147, 11 S. Ct. 512, 516;
>
> 15 *R. C. L.* pp. 841-843, Section 136 and cases cited.

Courts and tribunals, such as the Board of Tax Appeals, constituted by statutory authority cannot exceed their delegated powers. If they act beyond that authority their judgments and orders are regarded as nullities. They are not voidable but void.

> *Old Wayne Life Assn. v. McDonough,* 204 U. S.
> 8, 27 S. Ct. 236;
>
> *Vallely v. Northern F. & M. Ins. Co.,* 254 U. S.
> 348, 353-354, 41 S. Ct. 116, 117;
>
> *U. S. v. Davis,* 8 Fed. (2d) 907, 909;
>
> *Hatch v. Ferguson* (C. C. A. 9), 68 Fed. 43, 45.

Nothing is presumed in favor of the judgment of a court of inferior or limited jurisdiction against collateral attack.

> *Galpin v. Page,* 18 Wall. 350, 21 L. Ed. 959;
>
> *Grigum v. Astor,* 2 How. 319, 11 L. Ed. 283;
>
> *John II Estate v. Brown,* 201 Fed. 224, 247;
>
> *In re Central Irrigation Dist.,* 117 Cal. 382, 49 Pac. 354.

(c) *The proceedings had before the Board of Tax Appeals were beyond its jurisdiction, its decision therein was void, and any assessment made thereunder was a nullity.*

The only deficiency notice which could confer jurisdiction on the Board of Tax Appeals under Section 318(a) of the Revenue Act of 1926 (App. p. xxviii) would be one mailed "to the person liable" for the tax. *The deficiency notice in evidence* (R. p. 42) *was not addressed or mailed to such a person.* It was addressed to executors who had lost all power to represent the estate.

When that deficiency notice was mailed, there were two groups of persons liable for the alleged tax, viz.: (1) the appellants herein, as distributees, and (2) the former executors, as fiduciaries. The section which would authorize a deficiency notice that could confer jurisdiction on said Board over either of said groups was Section 316 of the 1926 Act (App. p. xxvii), and no such notice is in evidence. Belated recognition of the fact that Section 316 was the applicable section probably led appellee's counsel to prepare the erroneous finding (R. p. 29) that the deficiency notice was "as required by Section 316 of the 1926 Revenue Act", contrary to the evidence.

The Board of Tax Appeals held in its decision that it was without jurisdiction to determine any liability against the former executors as fiduciaries because the deficiency notice here in evidence was not based on Section 316. The Board could not attempt to determine any liability against appellants because they were not named in the deficiency notice and could not become parties to the proceeding.

The Board erroneously assumed jurisdiction, despite knowledge of the distribution of the estate of David Neustadter, under the false conclusion that "the executors were then (and now are in office)" (App. p. xx) and "that the executors in their representative capacities" were liable for the deficiency determined "by the Commissioner in his deficiency notice". (App. p. xxiv.) This error is identical with that made by the trial court in *United States v. Lindley,* and which this Court reversed on appeal, saying:

> "Whatever may be the rule in other jurisdictions wherein the relation of the parties to an estate is different from that in California, we think, that under the California rule, where an estate is administered under the jurisdiction of the court and the executors derive their authority from their appointment by the court (11 Cal. Jur. 214, sec. 6) and *where they are obligated by a decree of distribution to turn the property over to those to whom it is distributed* by the decree of the court, and have no authority to retain that property after the decree, such a decree being enforceable against the executors by contempt proceedings if they neglect to distribute the property in accordance with the terms of the decree (12 Cal. Jur. 222, sec. 955), *the authority of the executors over the funds of the estate ceases upon distribution* (12 Cal. Jur. 199, sec. 940), and that, having disposed

of the property in accordance with the requirements of the law under which they act, *they cannot be subsequently held in their representative capacities* to repay moneys which they have collected for and on behalf of and paid to the distributees, although that collection may have been erroneously made. *The money did not belong to the executors. They had no authority to withhold it from the legatees upon the theory that the government might subsequently seek to reclaim it. Their full duty was performed when they turned it over to the distributees.* We conclude that, in so far as the judgment is against the executors of Curtis Lindley in their *representative capacities,* it is erroneous and should be reversed.'' (Italics supplied.)

Lindley v. U. S., 59 Fed. (2d) 336, 338.

See:

Nauts v. Clymer, 36 Fed. (2d) 207, 208;

Liebermann's Com. v. Commissioner, 54 Fed. (2d) 527, 530.

The Board of Tax Appeals, in attempting to assume jurisdiction to determine a deficiency liability against the estate of David Neustadter, ignored its own rulings and the law as settled by decisions of the federal courts.

"A plea to the jurisdiction of a body of limited jurisdiction, such as is the Board, may be raised at any time. *Jurisdiction cannot be granted by the parties nor can it be acquired by a failure to plead the lack thereof.*" (Italics supplied.)

French & Co. v. Commissioner, 10 B. T. A. 665, 671.

See:

Bell v. Commissioner (C. C. A. 2), 82 Fed. (2d) 499.

Though the former executors did not plead lack of jurisdiction in their petition to the Board, they could not confer jurisdiction by their appearance. When the proceeding came to trial they did challenge the Board's jurisdiction (App. p. xvi) and were overruled. The distribution of the estate of David Neustadter and the resulting release of its executors from representative capacity were beyond any jurisdiction of the Board and its *ipse dixit* that the executors were in office and could make the distributed estate liable for a tax by their appearance before the Board is grossly erroneous.

> "Federal courts *have no jurisdiction to make or control distribution,* which is a mere incident of administration proceedings from which such courts are excluded."

> 11 B. *Cal. Juris.* 740, Section 1256.

Estates, like corporations, exist only for specific purposes and then only by legislative act. If the life of an estate can be prolonged after distribution for purposes of litigation, it is necessary, as in the case of corporations, that there should be some statutory authority for the prolongation. There is no such statutory authority in California. In considering the estate of David Neustadter the Board of Tax Appeals should have treated the petition of the *functus officio* executors in the same manner as it treated the *functus officio* officer of a dissolved corporation, viz.:

> "All of the rights which it as a corporation had theretofore had were completely extinguished. It no longer had any right to do anything. Having been thus wiped out, no legal entity remained to institute this proceeding. *The attempt on the part of one of its*

former officers to institute a proceeding in its behalf has resulted in nothing since he could not by his own acts raise the dead. A petition filed for and on behalf of a wholly dissolved corporation *does not give this Board jurisdiction.*

*   *   *   *   *   *   *

"Our determination of a deficiency under such circumstances *would be a nullity,* and accordingly, *on our own motion,* we hold that we have no jurisdiction." (Italics supplied.)

> *Hirsch Distilling Co. v. Commission,* 14 B. T. A. 1073, 1078.

See:

> *Louisiana Naval Stores, Inc. v. Commissioner,* 18 B. T. A. 533, 536.

The law governing the release of property of an estate from administration and the termination of the representative capacity of executors is that of the state of the decedent's domicil and situs of probate, and federal tribunals are bound by the same rules that govern local tribunals.

> *Security Trust Co. v. Black River Nat'l Bank,* 186 U. S. 211, 227, 237, 23 S. Ct. 52, 58, 61;
>
> *Hurlburd v. Commissioner,* .... U. S. ...., 56 S. Ct. 197, 201, 202.

The decree of final distribution in the estate of David Neustadter was that of a competent local court and was controlling on the Board of Tax Appeals and is conclusive as to this court.

> *Hurlburd v. Commissioner,* .... U. S. ...., 56 S. Ct. 197, 204.

The administration of an estate in California is terminated for all purposes by entry of the decree of final distribution and the distribution of the estate. After the distribution the executors become *functus officio,* their representative capacity is ended, they can neither sue nor be sued as representatives of the estate, and any suit brought against them after decree of final distribution is one against them individually, *not as representatives.*

> *Fidelity Deposit Co. v. Lindholm* (C. C. A. 9), 66 Fed. (2d) 56, 59;
>
> *Estate of Baird,* 181 Cal. 742, 744, 186 Pac. 351;
>
> *Western Pac. Ry. Co. v. Godfrey,* 166 Cal. 346, 351, 136 Pac. 284, 285;
>
> *St. Mary's Hospital v. Perry,* 152 Cal. 338, 340, 92 Pac. 864;
>
> *Union Savings Bank v. DeLaveaga,* 150 Cal. 395, 398, 89 Pac. 84, 85;
>
> *Mackay v. San Francisco,* 128 Cal. 678, 684-685, 61 Pac. 382, 384;
>
> *More v. More,* 127 Cal. 460, 462-463, 59 Pac. 823, 824;
>
> *Johnson v. Superior Court,* 77 Cal. App. 599, 601, 247 Pac. 249, 250;
>
> *Rafferty v. Mitchell,* 4 Cal. App. (2d) 491, 494.

The failure of the executors to obtain a decree discharging them from all liability, as permitted by Section 1697 of the Code of Civil Procedure, left them subject *only* to proceedings against them on their personal liability.

> *Fidelity Deposit Co. v. Lindholm* (C. C. A. 9), supra;

Melone v. Davis, 67 Cal. 279, 282, 7 Pac. 703, 704;

Renwick v. Garland, 1 Cal. App. 237, 238, 82 Pac.
89, 90;

Southern Pac. Co. v. Swanson, 73 Cal. App. 229,
234, 238 Pac. 736, 738.

The Board of Tax Appeals lacked any jurisdiction to determine a liability against the estate of David Neustadter in the proceedings had before it. An assessment made under such a determination would be void as a charge against the one-time assets of the estate or the property of appellants as distributees. If any one was to be charged there would be need of a new assessment, and there is no new assessment in evidence in this case under which appellants would be liable. Such being the law and the facts, there is no assessment which would entitle appellee to six years extension of the bar of limitation within which to bring proceedings in court against appellants.

Hurlburd v. Commissioner, ———— U. S. ————, 56 S.
Ct. 197, 200.

Appellee seems to find some comfort in the fact that no appeal was taken from the decision of the Board upon which it relies. Had such an appeal been taken, this court would have been required to hold on its own motion that it *had no jurisdiction* because right of the executors to proceed in court as representatives had abated when the decree of final distribution became effective.

Standifer Const. Co. v. Commissioner (C. C. A.
9), 78 Fed. (2d) 285, 286;

Oklahoma Nat. Gas Co. v. Oklahoma, 273 U. S. 257,
47 S. Ct. 391.

(c) **Appellee is barred from relief by Section 409 of the Revenue Act of 1921.**

No parallel to Section 409 is to be found in the provisions relating to income or miscellaneous taxes in any of the revenue acts. The section fixes a limited term of burden of liability for estate tax.

Section 409 of the 1921 Act (also Section 315(a) of the 1926 Act) provides:

> "That unless the tax is sooner paid in full it shall be a lien for ten years upon the gross estate of the decedent."

Numerous cases hold that such lien becomes impressed on the property of an estate and the ten year period becomes effective as of the date of death of a decedent.

See:

> *Rosenberg v. McLaughlin* (C. C. A. 9), 66 Fed. (2d) 271, 272.

So, from February 13, 1923, to February 13, 1933, the property of the estate of David Neustadter was subject to a lien for any additional estate tax, even though the estate had been entirely distributed.

Such a restricted period of limitation is both fair and wise. Unlike persons or corporation, estates are expected to have but a short period of existence. The government has no cause to expect their continued existence nor the continuous preservation of assets. Under such circumstances, it is to be presumed that the fixing of a ten year period was intended to foreclose any interference with the property rights of distributees after its expiration.

During the ten year period appellee had a right to collect by distraint, or to resort to proceedings in equity to enforce the constructive trust resulting from distribution of the estate, against the property distributed to appellants. Appellee failed to exercise either of these rights within the ten year period and was thereby barred by limitation from the relief sought when this suit was commenced.

Appellee may contend that it had alternative remedies. It did, but failed to avail itself of them. Equity will not permit appellee to allow its legal and equitable remedies to expire by limitation and then countenance an attempt to adopt an illegal course in order to extend the period of limitation in the guise of seeking equity.

Appellants are entitled to a reversal of the decree of the District Court and to order of a decree in their favor.

---

3. **UNDER FUNDAMENTAL RULES OF EQUITY, APPELLEE IS NOT ENTITLED TO ANY RELIEF.**

In seeking equitable relief, appellee has offended the maxims of equity and should be denied any remedy.

He who comes into equity must come with clean hands. This maxim *expresses a doctrine independent of that of laches.* It assumes that the suitor has himself been guilty of conduct in violation of the fundamental conceptions of equity jurisprudence, and *therefore refuses him all recognition and relief* with reference to the subject matter or transaction in question.

> *Pomeroy's Equity Jurisprudence* (4th Ed), Sec. 397;
>
> *Story's Equity Jurisprudence* (14th Ed.), Sec. 98.

Appellee did not promptly or diligently proceed to collect the asserted estate tax from the persons liable therefor, either through administrative or court proceedings. It did not resort to jeopardy assessment before the estate was distributed, nor to distraint; nor did it seek equity to enforce the lien or trust created by Section 409 of the 1921 Act. It did not proceed against appellants under Section 316 of the Revenue Act of 1926, nor did it bring action at law against the former executors under R. S. 3467 (31 U. S. C. Section 192) to enforce their fiduciary liability. Moreover, appellee offered no explanation for its neglect to resort to available and timely legal and equitable remedies.

Furthermore, in offense to equity, appellee seeks to collect a tax upon a tax by praying for judgment for interest computed on a period of unexplained delay which is chargeable only to its neglect or failure to act promptly and which results to appellants' disadvantage.

Appellee sought equity more than twelve years after decedent's death, without notice or demand being made on appellants for payment. Neither reason, law, nor equity may expect a distributed estate to remain intact or not undergo disadvantageous changes during such a long period.

Equity aids the vigilant and not those who slumber on their rights.

> "A court of equity, which is never active in relief against conscience, *has always refused its aid to stale demands,* where the party has slept upon his rights and acquiesced for a great length of time. Nothing

can call this court into activity but conscience, good faith and *reasonable diligence."* (Italics supplied.)

> *Pomeroy's Equity Jurisprudence* (4th Ed.), Section 419.

Appellee did not exercise reasonable diligence, but slumbered on its rights by failing to resort to its many available remedies which it allowed to lapse. Even after attempting to recover through an illegal deficiency notice and discovery of that fact, appellee, for reasons unexplained, delayed more than four years before filing this suit. Appellee's failure to act is unconscionable and should deprive it of any standing in equity.

The established practice of courts of equity is to grant no aid to one who delays his assertion of relief for an unreasonable period, especially where, as in this suit, the delay is to the disadvantage of the party against whom relief is sought. *If the claimant fails to show in his bill or by proof an excuse for such delay, then his cause is beyond equitable jurisdiction.*

> *Hays v. Port of Seattle,* 251 U. S. 233, 239, 40 S. Ct. 125, 127;
>
> *Young v. Southern Pac. Co.,* 34 Fed. (2d) 135, 137.

Appellee failed to prove any facts which would minimize the effect of or permit it to escape from the foregoing principles of equity. Therefore, it is without right to relief and the decree of the District Court should be reversed.

(a) Appellee is estopped from equitable relief.

Appellee seeks to *restore* the trust or lien which it once had under Section 409 of the 1921 Act and which it ignored. By its omission, appellee is estopped by limitation, staleness and lack of vigilance from the relief prayed for in its bill.

On distribution of the estate of David Neustadter, appellants took the property subject to a trust to satisfy additional taxes proposed against the estate within the ten year period created by said Section 409. After distribution of the estate and during the remainder of that ten year period—until February 13, 1933—appellee had the right to proceed in equity against appellants as trustees of the resultant equitable trust, provided it proved a tax to be due and unpaid.

The right to enforce the trust resultant from Section 409 for taxes determined subsequent to distribution of an estate is a statutory substitute for the right of equitable relief herein sought by appellee, i. e. the right to pursue the distributed assets to collect additional taxes for which the estate was liable. In this case, the additional tax sought to be recovered by appellee was discovered within four years after the ten year lien attached, yet appellee did not act upon it within the remaining period of more than six years.

Appellee may not have two opportunities for relief in equity upon the same cause, particularly when it allowed its primary right to such relief to lapse.

> *Case v. New Orleans etc. R. R. Co.*, 101 U. S. 689, 25 L. Ed. 1104.

The expiration of the trust resultant from said Section 409 was the expiration of a specific statutory limitation upon equitable remedies to pursue assets which had passed to appellants as distributees.

Where the legislature creates a specific liability and restricts the period thereof, this court, after the expiration of such period, may not supplement or extend the statute by decreeing an additional period of limitation. At all times during the ten year period appellee had a statutory legal remedy as well as equitable remedy. Where both a legal and an equitable remedy existed and were permitted to expire by limitation, equity will recognize the bar of limitation and not entertain a claim for equitable relief, because the claim is stale. The court may not by analogy declare an equitable trust or lien to replace a specific lien and resultant trust provided by statute, which appellee deliberately allowed to lapse and makes no excuse for its failure to act.

> *Hall v. Law*, 102 U. S. 461, 466, 26 L. Ed. 217, 219.

It is a principle of equity that the sovereign is bound by its own acts and those of its officers and departments, within the scope of their authority, and *the courts will visit estoppel* on the sovereign where, in cases like this, it invokes judicial action.

> "The underlying principle of all the decisions is that, when the sovereign comes into court to assert a pecuniary demand against the citizen the court has authority, and is *under duty, to withhold relief to the* sovereign, except upon terms which do justice to the citizen or subject, so determined by the jurisprudence of the forum in like subject-matter between man and man. The act or omissions of its officers, if they be authorized to bind the United States or to shape its *course of conduct* as to a particular transaction, and they have acted within the purview of their authority, may in a proper case *work an estop-*

pel against the government.'' (Citing many cases.)
"The principle that the sovereign is bound by his
own acts, and *those of his lawfully authorized agents*
within the purview of their authority, *is a wholesome
one, and* requires the courts to visit an estoppel on *the
sovereign* in a proper case, *where he invokes judicial action.''* (Italics supplied.)

> *Walker v. U. S.,* 139 Fed. 409, 413-415, affirmed
> (C. C. A. 5) 148 Fed. 1022;
>
> *Ritter v. U. S.,* 28 Fed. (2d) 265, 267;
>
> *U. S. v. Midway Oil Co.,* 232 Fed. 619, 631;
>
> *Cook v. U. S.,* 91 U. S. 389, 23 L. Ed. 237.

The Commissioner had authority to enforce or not enforce the lien or trust imposed by Section 409 of the
1921 Act. His failure to enforce cannot be presumed as
laches, but properly can be presumed to be a deliberate
intention not to enforce. When the Commissioner failed
or refused to proceed under Section 409, his unexcused
action or omission to act was that of appellee and it is
bound and estopped thereby.

Where powers are vested in the Commissioner, whereby
he may or may not perform some act, his power of
omission is as great as that of commission. Such omission may not be presumed to be laches, but must be considered a deliberate intent not to act.

> "Whenever an affirmative act is necessary on be-
> half of the United States to effect or enforce a
> pecuniary right against an individual, the officer or
> department whose duty is to do that act represents
> the United States as to that matter and *it is bound
> by his action or nonaction.''* (Italics supplied.)

> *Walker v. U. S.,* 139 Fed. 409, 414;
>
> *Ritter v. U. S.,* 28 Fed. (2d) 265, 267;

U. S. v. Barker, 12 Wheat. 559, 561, 6 L. Ed. 728, 729;

U. S. v. Bank of the Metropolis, 15 Pet. 377, 10 L. Ed. 774.

"When a sovereignty submits itself to the jurisdiction of a court of equity, and prays its aid, *its claims and rights are adjudicable by every other rule and principle of equity* applicable to the claims and rights of private parties under similar circumstances." (Italics supplied.)

The Falcon, 19 Fed. (2d) 1009, 1014.

Appellee, through or by the acts or omissions of its representatives or attorneys, may waive its rights and be precluded from having them restored.

Jones v. U. S., ...Fed. Sup........, 4 C. C. H. Tax Service (1936) 9371.

Under the above declared principles, appellee is estopped from a renewal of the trust or lien which it deliberately allowed to lapse and this court should reverse the judgment appealed from and direct a decree in favor of appellants.

(b) **This suit to establish an equitable trust fails to meet the requirements of that doctrine.**

The remedy sought by appellee is in the nature of a creditor's bill to collect a debt not recovered or recoverable at law. A tax liability is considered in the nature of a debt and the government is considered as a creditor for the purpose of pursuing transferred assets of a debtor.

Dyer v. Stauffer, 19 Fed. (2d) 922; ·

Hatch v. Morosco Holding Co., 50 Fed. (2d) 138,
139;

First Nat'l Bank v. Blackwell, 51 Fed. (2d) 282,
283.

Such suits have come to be classified as suits to enforce
equitable trusts or liens in favor of creditors.

Comr's Freedman's S. & T. Co. v. Earle, 110 U. S.
710, 4 S. Ct. 226.

Ordinarily, such a suit could not be maintained until
a judgment at law had been obtained against the debtor
and execution returned unsatisfied.

Cates v. Allen, 149 U. S. 451, 458, 13 S. Ct. 883,
884.

However, this rule is relaxed where the creditor is able
to show that he has exhausted his remedies at law and
is without remedy save in equity or where the debtor
is stripped of assets and the creditor lacks a remedy at
law, but this last privilege is generally recognized *only
when the creditor has a lien* on the property of the debtor
which passed to transferees.

Case v. New Orleans etc. R. R. Co., 101 U. S. 688,
690, 25 L. Ed. 1004, 1005.

To establish an equitable trust certain essential elements must be proven. In this case it was incumbent on
appellee to prove:

(a) That a debt was due and unpaid at the time
of trial. On this element, appellee offered no proof
and there was no admission.

(b) That the executors of the estate of David
Neustadter, as representatives, transferred its assets
to appellants in fraud on the creditor appellee. There

was no attempt made to prove any fraudulent act of the executors or that they had any knowledge of an impending additional tax when they made distribution.

(c) That appellants held property subject to a lien for estate tax, as equitable trustees for the benefit of appellee, when the suit was brought. There was no attempt to prove any such lien, but the proofs offered disclosed that the ten year lien, which would have permitted recovery, had been permitted to expire.

(d) That the appellee was without a plain, adequate, or complete remedy at law when the suit was filed. No proof was offered on this essential point. On the contrary, the bill alleges (Par. XIII, R. p. 8) that "the executors have not been finally discharged" and court found, as admitted by appellants that the executors have never been discharged as to their fiduciary liability under the provisions of Section 1697 of the Code of Civil Procedure or Section 1066 of the Probate Code of California or under Section 313(b) of the Revenue Act of 1926. (R. p. 28.) This is a finding that appellee did have a plain, adequate and complete remedy at law under R. S. 3467. This finding should defeat and cause reversal of the decree.

Appellee failed to establish any right to the declaration of an equitable trust on all four of the elements required under the doctrines of equity applicable thereto. Consequently the decree under appeal should be reversed and decree ordered in favor of appellants.

(c) The District Court lacked jurisdiction to grant equitable relief to appellee.

The jurisdiction of the District Court is limited and, relief through equity being restricted by statute (Jud. Code, Sec. 267), the presumption is against its equitable jurisdiction, unless it is affirmatively and distinctly made to appear. *Lack of affirmative and distinct pleading and proof cannot be helped by presumptions or argumentative inferences.*

> *Norton v. Larney,* 266 U. S. 511, 516, 69 L. Ed. 413, 416;
>
> *Smith v. McCullough,* 270 U. S. 456, 459, 46 S. Ct. 338, 339.

Appellee's bill alleged: "That this is a suit in equity of a civil nature". (R. p. 2.) An allegation of a conclusion, denied by appellants (R. p. 13), on which no proof was offered. The burden of proving the equitable jurisdiction of the trial court rested on appellee.

> *Marra v. Doran,* 44 Fed. (2d) 829, 830;
>
> *Schoenthal v. Irving Trust Co.,* 287 U. S. 92, 94, 95, 77 L. Ed. 185, 187, 188.

The rule governing the jurisdiction of a court of equity is thus succinctly stated:

> "A court of equity will not entertain a case for relief where the complainant has an adequate legal remedy at law. The complaining party *must,* therefore, *show that he has done all that he could at law* to obtain his rights." (Italics supplied.)
>
> *Case v. New Orleans, etc. Co.,* 101 U. S. 688, 690, 25 L. Ed. 1004.

The fact that appellee is the sovereign does not relieve it from this mandate of equity.

> *U. S. v. Detroit Lumber Co.,* 200 U. S. 321, 50
>   L. Ed. 499;
>
> *U. S. v. Board, etc.,* 254 Fed. 570, 166 C. C. A.
>   128;
>
> *U. S. v. Midway etc. Co.,* 232 Fed. 619, 631.

Appellee herein failed to prove and the court failed to find this suit to be one within the jurisdiction of equity. As this court may not presume, in the absence of proof and findings, that the suit was within the equitable jurisdiction of the District Court, its decree should be reversed and dismissal ordered.

Under Section 267 of the Judicial Code (28 U. S. C., Sec. 384) no suit in equity can be sustained "in any court of the United States in any case where a plain, adequate and complete remedy may be had at law". Under this section this court has held to the effect that any remedy at law which would reimburse the claimant sufficed to bar equitable jurisdiction.

> *Thompson v. Schwaebe,* 22 Fed. (2d) 518.

Appellee pleaded (R. p. 9) that it had no remedy at law. Appellants denied this allegation. (R. p. 19, Par. XVII.) Appellee offered no proof whatever and the court made no finding to sustain the allegation. These facts alone sustain appellants' contention that the District Court was without equitable jurisdiction of the suit.

However, the findings in effect declare that appellee had a plain, adequate and complete remedy at law against the former executors as fiduciaries under R. S. Section

3467 (31 U. S. C. Sec. 192) when the bill herein was filed. When the court found (R. p. 28) that said executors had "never been discharged" from their personal liability "under the provisions of Section 1697 of the Code of Civil Procedure or Section 1066 of the Probate Code of California or under Section 313(b) of the Revenue Act of 1926", it made a finding to the effect that, when this suit was commenced, appellee had a remedy at law contemplated by Judicial Code Section 267 and authorized by R. S. 3467.

R. S. Section 3467 is a statutory adoption, made in 1799, of the common law right to recover preferences by actions of trover and money had and received and, therefore, provides a remedy at law.

> *Schoenthal v. Irving Trust Co.,* supra;
> *Baker v. Cummings,* 169 U. S. 189, 206, 42 L. Ed. 711, 718;
> *Metropolitan Nat'l Bank v. St. Louis etc. Co.,* 149 U. S. 436, 450, 37 L. Ed. 799, 804.

That legal remedy was open to appellee when this suit was filed and appellee was without right to equitable relief and the District Court was without jurisdiction.

Also, appellee failed to prove that it had exhausted all adequate administrative remedies before it resorted to court. Such proof is essential to equity jurisdiction.

Furthermore, appellee failed to prove the existence of any of the exceptions which might entitle it to equitable relief despite the prohibition of Section 267 of the Judicial Code, viz.:

(a) That a multiplicity of actions would have resulted;

(b) That a fraud was committed by the defendants which had its remedy in equity alone;

(c) That any misrepresentation or concealment of facts on the part of the appellants existed.

In no way was the jurisdiction of the trial court established. Its jurisdiction was challenged by appellants. (R. pp. 48, 49, 50, 52, 53.) The court did not inquire into its jurisdiction nor did appellee seek to prove the jurisdiction. Therefore, the decree should be reversed and dismissal ordered.

---

4. THE DECREE UNDER APPEAL VIOLATES THE FUNDAMENTAL PRINCIPLES OF LAW.

Be it understood that appellants do not challenge the constitutionality of any of the federal statutes relied upon by either of the parties. However, appellants assert that the action of appellee's administrative officers was contrary to law and violated the due process clause of the Fifth Amendment to the Constitution of the United States. The illegal actions of appellee's administrative officers cannot confer jurisdiction on a court of equity nor render appellants liable, even though appellee as sovereign seeks to avail itself of such unlawful acts.

The administrative officers and courts of the United States, when attempting to exercise jurisdiction over an estate or its executors, are administering the laws of the state of domicile of the decedent, and are bound by the same laws which govern local tribunals.

> *Security Trust Co. v. Black River Nat'l Bank,* 187
> U. S. 211, 237, 23 S. Ct. 52, 61;
>
> *Hurlburd v. Commissioner,* _____ U. S. _____, 56 S. Ct.
> 197, 294.

The decree of final distribution of the estate of David Neustadter by the Superior Court of the State of California, sitting in probate, was a decision of a court of special competence and its decision, unless it exceeded the bounds of jurisdiction, is binding on the Commissioner, the Board of Tax Appeals, and the Federal Courts.

> *Hurlburd v. Commissioner,* supra.

Under the law of California, the legal effect of a decree of final distribution is to remove the estate of the deceased from the jurisdiction of the court and to render the office of executor, which depends upon such jurisdiction, *functus officio.*

The decree of final distribution is conclusive as to the rights of the heirs, legatees, or devisees to the property of the estate, subject only to reversal or modification by appeal. (C. C. P. 1666.) There was no appeal from the final decree in the estate of David Neustadter. If the executors fail to distribute the estate as required by the final decree, the probate court continues to have jurisdiction over the executors—but *only* by means of contempt procedings to compel distribution.

> *In re Kennedy's Estate,* 129 Cal. 384, 387, 62 Pac.
> 63, 65;
>
> *St. Mary's Hospital v. Perry,* 152 Cal. 338, 340,
> 92 Pac. 864, 865.

If an *action* is brought against an executor to enforce distribution or payment of a claim *after* a final decree is made, such action is one against him individually and *not against him in his representative capacity. It is not an action against the estate.*

    Melone v. Davis, 67 Cal. 279, 281, 7 Pac. 703, 704;

    St. Mary's Hospital v. Perry, supra;

    Renwick v. Garland, 1 Cal. App. 237, 238, 82 Pac. 89, 90;

    Southern Pac. Co. v. Swanson, 73 Cal. App. 229, 234, 238 Pac. 736, 738.

Had additional property been discovered for the estate after the decree and distribution, the executors could not have administered it without new letters testamentary being granted as required by C. C. P. Section 1698.

    In re Yorba's Estate, 176 Cal. 166, 171, 167 Pac. 854, 856;

    O'Brien v. Nelson, 164 Cal. 573, 575, 129 Pac. 985.

No action founded on misfeasance in office can be maintained against an executor in his representative capacity under California law.

    Eustace v. John, 38 Cal. 2, 23;

    Sterrett v. Barker, 119 Cal. 492, 494, 51 Pac. 695, 696;

    St. Mary's Hospital v. Perry, supra.

Section 1669 of the Code of Civil Procedure did not require payment of federal taxes before final distribution could be decreed. Therefore, when the court made final decree of distribution in the estate of David Neustadter, it did not exceed its jurisdiction nor did the executors, in distributing the estate, commit any misfeasance under

the California law. If there was any misfeasance in relation to distribution, it would relate solely to failure to pay
federal estate taxes. Appellee had the legal right to proceed in court at law against the executors on their personal
and fiduciary liability under R. S. Section 3467. (31 U. S.
C. Sec. 192.) The government did not resort to this "due
process" method.

Other than the course mentioned above, the Commissioner had three alternative legal courses open to him
when he proposed to determine a deficiency against the
estate of David Neustadter, viz.:

    (1) To mail a deficiency notice to appellants as
transferees under Section 316 of the Revenue Act of
1926; or

    (2) To mail such a notice to the former executors
as fiduciaries under said Section 316; or

    (3) To mail a deficiency notice to appellants, as
the persons whose property was liable for the tax
under the lien imposed by Section 409 of the Revenue
Act of 1921, as permitted by Section 318(a) of the
1926 Act.

Appellants would have been subject to said third course
because, under the definition of "executor" in Section
300(a) of the 1926 Act (App. p. xxv) as the appointed
executors had become *functus officio* and ceased to act as
representatives, "any person in actual or constructive
possession of any property of the decedent" became an
executor for the purpose of the Act.

The Commissioner ignored the legal avenues open to
him. Instead, he adopted a course beyond authority of the

statute and law. His illegal method *could not confer juris-diction on the Board of Tax Appeals* nor could the appearance of the, former executors confer jurisdiction.

> *French & Co. v. Commissioner,* 10 B. T. A. 665, 671;
> *Hirsch Distilling Co. v. Commissioner,* supra.

The right of the *functus officio* executors to bring proceedings on behalf of the estate and to bind appellants by so doing, abated under the decree of final distribution.

> *Standifer Const. Corp. v. Commissioner* (C. C. A. 9), 78 Fed. (2d) 285;
> *Oklahoma Nat. Gas Co. v. Oklahoma,* supra.

By this suit appellee seeks to replace proper legal remedies which its responsible officers did not use. In other words it seeks to utilize an illegal administrative action, which was contrary to law and not "due process", as a ground for equitable relief.

The decision of the Board of Tax Appeals is void because beyond its jurisdiction.

In the proceedings instituted by the former executors of the estate of David Neustadter upon the deficiency notice mailed to them (R. p. 42), the Board held that the executors were "in office" (App. p. xx) and "in their representative capacities" were liable for the deficiency determined by the Commissioner. (App. p. xxiv.) Upon this decision the Board made its order that there was a deficiency in estate tax. Appellee contended that the assessment (R. p. 46) made against "Neustadter, David, Est. of" was "in accordance with said decision" and the trial court so found. (R. p. 29.) The decision of the Board, the assessment, and the decision of the District Court are all void and contrary to "due process" because they violate the established rule governing the status of executors and estates, viz.:

> "The courts of the United States, in enforcing claims against executors and administrators of a decedent's estate, are administering the laws of the state of domicile, and are bound by the same rules that govern the local tribunals."
>
> *Security Trust Co. v. Black River Nat'l Bank,* supra;
>
> *Hurlburd v. Commissioner,* supra.

At the hearing of the proceedings before the Board of Tax Appeals, the petitioners urged the lack of jurisdiction of the Board to determine any liability against them as representatives of the estate of David Neustadter or personally as fiduciaries. The Board brushed aside this fundamental challenge to its jurisdiction over the petitioners "as representatives", though admitting its want of jurisdiction over them "as fiduciaries". This action of the Board was exactly the reverse to what it held in *Hurlburd v. Commissioner* (27 B. T. A. 1123), which was affirmed by the Supreme Court, which stated:

> "In this case there was neither waiver or estoppel, but a steady insistence that the deficiency had been assessed against the estate and no one else, and that the liability of the estate had ended. *To hold that by consent,* either tacit or express, the *proceeding had been turned into one to review the validity of a different assessment,* and one never in fact made, *would be a preversion of the record."* (Italics supplied.)
>
> *Hurlburd v. Commissioner,* .... U. S. ......, 56 S. Ct. 197, 201.

The decision of the Board of Tax Appeals in *Neustadter et al. v. Commissioner* is based upon the fallacious premise that, because the executors had not been discharged from their personal liability by "a receipt or writing" issued by the Commissioner under authority of Section 313(b) of the Revenue Act of 1924, they continued "in office" as "representatives". This premise ignores the California law relating to release of executors from representative capacity. Had the executors retained funds of the estate in their hands until after the deficiency notice in evidence had been mailed to them, the proceeding by the Commissioner against them could only have been one legally against them on their personal liability. The proceeding could not be one against the estate.

> *Melone v. Davis,* supra;
>
> *St. Mary's Hospital v. Perry,* supra, and other cases cited under subheading 4;
>
> *Fidelity & Deposit Co. v. Lindholm* (C. C. A. 9), 66 Fed. (2d) 56, 59.

When appellee seeks to utilize the assessment in evidence (R. p. 46) as a foundation upon which to claim an extension of the bar of limitations under Section 1109(a)(3) of the 1926 Act, it again violates the "due process" clause under the above quoted portion of the opinion in *Hurlburd v. Commissioner.* Appellee's resort to that assessment as a foundation for this suit is, in the language of the Supreme Court, "a perversion of the record" because:

> (a) The assessment was made against an estate which the evidence shows had ceased to exist, by reason of final distribution, before the Commissioner

mailed any deficiency notice and is void under the authorities cited hereinabove in part 2(b)(2) of this argument;

(b) There is an entire failure of proof to disclose any statutory authority for the making of the assessment;

(c) The certificate of assessment does not show on its face that it was made in accordance with any valid decision of the Board of Tax Appeals or any applicable section of any revenue act;

(d) The authority for the certificate of assessment is so uncertain and vague that appellee without proof or excuse readily translated its application from Section 318(a) to Section 316 of the 1926 Act and, also, the District Court, in its findings (R. p. 29), finds its source to be Section 316 of said Act without any proof or argument being presented to in any way show that Section 316 applied to any proceeding had in relation to any tax liability of the estate of David Neustadter, its former executors, or appellants as distributees.

VII. CONCLUSION.

Apologies are offered the court for the length of this brief. Appellee's belated shift of its theory as to its right to relief and the inconsistencies between theory and fact, conclusions and evidence, proofs and findings, as well as misapplication of the law and the rules of equity, constitute our excuse.

Appellants respectfully submit that the decree of the District Court should be reversed and that this court should direct either the dismissal of this suit or entry of decree in favor of appellants.

Dated, San Francisco,
August 28, 1936.

ADOLPHUS E. GRAUPNER,
Attorney for Appellants.

(Appendices A and B Follow.)

Appendices A and B.

United States Board of Tax Appeals

Newton H. Neustadter, Walter W. Stettheimer and Julian Hart, Executors, Estate of David Neustadter, Petitioner, vs. Commissioner of Internal Revenue, Respondent.	Docket No. 20,988 Promulgated March 1

This proceeding involves the redetermination of a deficiency in estate tax in the amount of $12,012.99. The errors alleged are—(1) that respondent erred in reopening this case and in asserting a deficiency when he had on November 10, 1925, closed the case by sending to petitioner a registered sixty-day letter from which determination petitioners did not appeal, and that the period within which a deficiency could be legally asserted against petitioners had expired in view of their application for final determination and discharge; and (2) that respondent erred in including in the gross estate of decedent for estate-tax purposes the entire value of the community property, one-half of which belonged to his wife. The facts have been stipulated, and in accordance with the stipulation we make the following

Findings of Fact.

David Neustadter, a citizen and resident of the State of California died testate on February 13, 1923, and Newton

H. Neustadter, Walter W. Stettheimer and Julian Hart were, on the 8th day of March, 1923, duly appointed and qualified as executors of his estate, and have been since the date of their appointment and qualification and now are the duly qualified bonded and acting executors of the estate of David H. Neustadter, deceased.

On December 31, 1923, the said Newton H. Neustadter, Walter W. Stettheimer and Julian Hart, as executors, duly filed with the Collector of Internal Revenue for the First District of California an estate tax return for said estate of the said David Neustadter. In said return the tax shown to be due by said estate was $4,145.43, which was assessed and paid by said estate.

On July 30, 1924, one of the executors of the estate of David Neustadter, to-wit, Newton H. Neustadter, addressed a letter to the Commissioner of Internal Revenue at Washington, D. C., which letter was duly received, and which reads as follows:

July 30th, 1924.

Commissioner of Internal Revenue,
Washington, D. C.
Dear Sir:

Will you kindly arrange at your earliest convenience for an examination of the Income Tax Returns of David Neustadter, Deceased, and for an examination of the returns of the Estate of David Neustadter, Deceased; also for an examination of the Federal Tax returns of the Estate of David Neustadter, Deceased.

The reason for this request is that the executors desire to take the necessary steps for their discharge.

Respectfully yours,
(Signed) Newton H. Neustadter,
Executor, Est. of David Neustadter,
Deceased.

On August 25, 1924, C. B. Allen, Deputy Commissioner of Internal Revenue, addressed a letter to Newton H. Neustadter, Executor of the Estate of David Neustadter, in which he acknowledged the receipt of the letter of July 30, 1924. Said letter of August 25, 1924, reads:

Mr. Newton H. Neustadter,
    c/o Neustadter Brothers,
        62 First Street,
           San Francisco, California.

Sir:

Receipt is acknowledged of your letter dated July 30, 1924, requesting the early determination of the income tax liability of the Estate of David Neustadter.

If an application is filed in accordance with the provisions of Treasury Decision 3329, a copy of which is enclosed, it will be given careful consideration. A Court Certificate showing your authority to administer upon the estate of the decedent should accompany the application.

The determination of the estate tax liability will be made the subject of a separate communication from the Bureau.

In your reply please refer to IT:R:BGC:S.

        Respectfully,
           (Signed)   C. B. Allen,
               Deputy Commissioner.

Treasury Decision 3329 referred to in the above letter is as follows:

Expeditious disposition of tax cases in which an emergency has been found to exist.

Treasury Department
Office of the Commissioner of Internal Revenue
Washington, D. C.

To Collectors of Internal Revenue
and Others Concerned:

If, upon application of any taxpayer, it be shown to the satisfaction of the Commissioner (1) that the taxpayer is in the hands of a receiver and a reorganization is necessary; (2) that the taxpayer is in financial difficulties, either actual or imminent, and refinancing is necessary; or (3) that the distribution of a fund in which a large number of people may be interested is held up pending the determination of the amount of income or profits taxes which must be paid out of the fund—then the Commissioner will declare an emergency to exist with reference to such case and will direct that the matter be given priority of consideration with a view to the expeditious determination of the particular tax liability.

Application for such priority of consideration shall be in the form of a letter addressed to the Commissioner and shall be supported by statements under oath setting forth in detail the facts upon which the request for special consideration is based, and the particular reason why such person believes himself entitled to have the case expedited as provided herein.

On August 29, 1924, M. F. Snider, Acting Deputy Commissioner of Internal Revenue, addressed a letter to Newton H. Neustadter, Executor, acknowledging the receipt of said letter of July 30, 1924. Said letter of August 29, 1924, reads:

In reply to your letter of July 30th, wherein you request an early determination of the Federal Estate Tax due from the above-named estate, please be advised that this case is being assigned for audit and review, and you will be notified of the result thereof at an early date.

On October 14, 1925, the Commissioner of Internal Revenue mailed to Newton H. Neustadter, et al., Executors, Estate of David Neustadter, 62 First Street, San Francisco, California, a deficiency notice, as provided by Title III, Part I, of the Revenue Act of 1924, in which it was stated that the tax liability of the Estate of David Neustadter had been finally determined and the deficiency found to be due was $801.89. The material parts of said notice are as follows:

October 14, 1925

Newton H. Neustadter, et al., Ex.,
    Estate of David Neustadter,
       62 First St.,
          San Francisco, Calif.

Sirs:

The Bureau has examined the protest, filed by you as executors of the above-named estate, against the tentative findings as set out in its letter addressed to you under date of May 16, 1925.

No adjustment is made of funeral expenses, attorney's fees, miscellaneous administration expenses, and support of dependents, as one-half instead of the full amount of such charges are deductible under the provisions of the Federal Estate Tax Law.

Deductions	Returned	Determined
Debts of decedent	$3,666.63	$2,967.13

Debts of decedent are adjusted by allowing the additional sums of $500, being one-half the amount pledged to the Community Chest of San Francisco, and $650, being one-half the total for accountant's fees.

Pursuant to the above, the gross estate is determined to be $301,944.44, the deductions $74,022.35, and the net estate $227,922.09, the tax upon the transfer of which is $4,837.66. The tax shown by the return is $4,145.43 of which amount, $4,035.77 has been paid. Accordingly, there is a balance due on the original tax of $109.66. The deficiency tax as herein determined is $801.89.

As the entire tax shown by the return was not paid within one year and six months after the date of decedent's death, as provided by Section 406 of the Revenue Act of 1921, the unpaid balance of $109.66, together with the deficiency tax, bears interest at the rate of six per centum per annum from one year after the date of death until payment is received by the Collector.

In accordance with the provisions of Title III, Part I of the Revenue Act of 1924, you are allowed sixty days form the date of this letter within which to file an appeal to the Board of Tax Appeals, contesting in whole, or in part, the correctness of this determination.

*   *   *   *   *   *

No appeal was taken to the Board from said notice of October 14, 1925.

On November 10, 1925, C. R. Nash, Acting Commissioner of Internal Revenue, mailed to Newton H. Neustadter, et al., Executors of the Estate of David Neustadter, a second deficiency notice for the purpose of correcting an "inadvertent typographical error in the letter of Ocober 14,

1925''. In said letter of November 10, 1925, the deficiency finally proposed was changed to $692.23 instead of $801.89. The material parts of said letter read:

The Bureau has considered the request of the executors to correct an inadvertent typographical error in its adjustment letter of October 14, 1925. Accordingly, this letter is in lieu of the Bureau's prior letter dated October 14, 1925.

No adjustment is made of funeral expenses, attorneys' fees, miscellaneous administration expenses and support of dependents as one-half instead of the full amount of such charges are deductible under the provisions of the Federal estate tax law.

	Returned	Determined
Debts of decedent	$3,666.63	$2,967.13

Debts of decedent are adjusted by allowing the additional sum of $500, being one-half the amount pledged to the community chest of San Francisco, and $650, being one-half of the total for accountants' fees.

Pursuant to the above, the gross estate is determined to be $301,944.44, the deductions $74,022.35, and the net estate $227,922.09, the tax upon the transfer of which is $4,837.66. The tax shown by the return is $4,145.43, of which amount $4,035.77 has been paid. Accordingly, there is a balance due on the original tax of $109.66, and the deficiency tax as herein determined is $692.23, making the total amount due $801.89.

As the entire tax shown by the return was not paid within one year and six months after the date of decedent's death, as provided by Section 406 of the Revenue Act of 1921, the unpaid balance of $109.66, together with the deficiency tax, bears interest at the rate of six per centum per annum from one year after date of death until payment is received by the Collector.

In accordance with the provisions of Title III, Part I, of the Revenue Act of 1924, you are allowed sixty days from the date of this letter within which to file an appeal to the Board of Tax Appeals, contesting in whole or in part, the correctness of this determination.

*   *   *   *   *   *   *

No appeal was taken to the Board from said notice of November 10, 1925.

On September 21, 1926, C. R. Nash, Acting Commissioner, mailed to Newton H. Neustadter, et al., Executors, Estate of David Neustadter, 62 First St., San Francisco, California, a deficiency notice under the provisions of Section 308 of the Revenue Act of 1926, in which notice it was proposed to assess a deficiency in tax against the Estate of David Neustadter in the amount of $12,012.99. Said letter reads:

Reference is made to the return on Form 706, filed in the above-named estate in the audit of which the value of the wife's community interest was excluded from the gross estate of this decedent and tax was paid on that basis.

In view of the decision of the United States Supreme Court in the case of United States v. Robbins, 269 U. S. 315, rendered January 4, 1926, and an opinion of the Attorney General of the United States issued June 24, 1926 (Treasury Decision 3891), the Bureau now holds that the entire value of the Community property should have been included in the gross estate of this decedent and the tax has been redetermined on that basis.

The following tabulation shows the unpaid deficiency:

Gross Estate		$603,888.88
Deductions		98,044.70
Net estate		$505,844.18
Tax determined herein		16,850.65
Tax paid on return	$4,035.77	
Balance of returned tax paid	109.66	
Additional tax paid	692.23	
Total paid		4,837.66
Deficiency tax		$12,012.99

Pursuant to Section 318 of the Revenue Act of 1926, notice of deficiency, amounting to $12,012.99, in estate tax with respect to the estate of David Neustadter is hereby given, with a view to the assessment and collection thereof. Any portion of the amount assessed, not paid within thirty days from the date of notice and demand from the Collector, will bear interest at the rate of one per centum a month from the date of such notice and demand, unless an extension of time for payment should be granted.

Within sixty days (not counting Sunday as the sixtieth day) after the mailing of this notice you may, in accordance with the provisions of Section 308 of the Revenue Act of 1926, file a petition with the Board of Tax Appeals for a redetermination of the deficiency. The address of the Board is: United States Board of Tax Appeals, Earle Building, Washington, D. C., 13th and E Streets, N.W.

No claim in abatement of any deficiency which may be assessed in this case will be entertained.

If you acquiesce in this determination, either in whole or in part, you are requested to sign the enclosed waiver of restrictions on the assessment and collection of so much of the deficiency as results from the adjustments in which you acquiesce and forward it to the Commissioner of Internal Revenue, Washington, D. C., marked for the attention of the Estate Tax Division, Miscellaneous Tax Unit.

From the notice of September 21, 1926, the Executors of the Estate of David Neustadter filed a petition for appeal to the Board.

On or about the 25th day of February, 1924, the Superior Court of the State of California, in and for the City and County of San Francisco, entered its final decree settling accounts and distributing the Estate of said David Neustadter in accordance with the terms of his will. The pertinent parts of said decree read:

Newton H. Neustadter, Walter W. Stettheimer and Julian Hart, as executors of the last will and testament of David Neustadter, deceased, having filed in this Court their first and final account of their administration of the estate of said deceased, and their report as executors of the last will and testament of said deceased, and their petition praying for a settlement of said first and final account, and their petition praying for a final distribution of said estate;

And it duly appearing that due and legal notice of the hearing of said accounts, report and petition for distribution has been given in the manner and form required by law; and it duly appearing that the special notice as prescribed by Section 1380 of the Code of Civil Procedure of the State of California was duly and regularly given to all persons interested in said proceeding and in said estate, and to their said attorneys, who were entitled to or had requested notice thereof; and said matter coming on duly and regularly to be heard this day;

And it duly appearing that said account and report are in all respects true and correct and supported by proper vouchers, and that since the rendition of said account there have been no receipts in the matter of said estate;

And it further appearing that due and legal notice has been given to the creditors of and all persons having claims against said decedent and said estate, for the time required by law and the order of this Court, and that heretofore the above-entitled Court duly made and entered and filed its order, adjudging and decreeing that due and legal notice had been given to the creditors of and all persons having claims against said decedent and said estate;

And it further appearing that all state, county and municipal taxes upon the property of said estate have been duly paid, and that the inheritance tax due from said estate and from the heirs, legatees and devisees of said estate to the State of California, and the estate tax due from said estate to the United States of America, and all other taxes of every kind and character have been duly paid and discharged;

And it further appearing that all the debts of said decedent and of said estate, and all expenses of administration thereon thus far incurred have been paid, and that no claims have been presented, allowed or filed against said estate;

And it further appearing that said David Neustadter died, testate, at the City and County of San Francisco, State of California, on the 13th day of February, 1923, being at the time of his death a resident of said City, County and State, leaving estate therein, and leaving him surviving as his sole next of kin and heirs at law, and who under the terms of the last will and testament of said decedent are his sole and only legatees and devisees, the following named persons, to-wit:

Josephine D. Neustadter, surviving widow of said decedent, of adult age, and a resident of the City and County of San Francisco, State of California;

Newton H. Neustadter, surviving son of said decedent, of adult age, and a resident of the City and County of San Francisco, State of California;

Florence N. Stettheimer, surviving daughter of said decedent, of adult age, and a resident of San Mateo County, State of California;

Ellen Kathleen Hart, surviving granddaughter of said decedent, of minor age, and a resident of the City and County of San Francisco, State of California; and

James David Hart, surviving grandson of said decedent, of minor age, and a resident of the City and County of San Francisco, State of California;

And it further appearing that the estate of said decedent was the community property of said decedent and said Josephine D. Neustadter, his wife, and consists entirely of real and personal property more particularly described hereinafter;

And it further appearing that the name of said executor Julian Hart has been variously spelled in the above-entitled proceeding, both as Julian Hart and as Julien Hart, but said name applies to one and the same person, one of the executors of said last will and testament;

And it further appearing that all matters and things in said first and final account and in said report accompanying the same and in said petition for final distribution filed therewith are true and correct and supported by evidence introduced and considered;

And it further appearing that said Newton H. Neustadter and Florence N. Stettheimer, surviving children of said decedent, have received their full share and portion of said estate to which they are entitled under the last will and testament of said decedent by virtue of a certain decree of partial distribution heretofore made, entered and filed in the above entitled proceeding on or about the 17th day of November, 1923;

And it further appearing that all the balance of said estate, with the certain exceptions hereinafter distributed unto Ellen Kathleen Hart and James David Hart, should be distributed unto the surviving widow of said decedent, to-wit: Josephine D. Neustadter.

And it appearing that the decree of partial distribution made in favor of Ellen Kathleen Hart on or about the 8th day of January, 1924, and the decree of partial distribution made in favor of James David Hart on or about the 30th day of January, 1924, in the above-entitled estate, were never executed, and that the distribution in this decree of final distribution is in full of said respective decrees of partial distribution, as well as in full of distribution under this decree, and in full of all the interests and rights and title and claims of said Ellen Kathleen Hart and James David Hart, as heirs, legatees and devisees under the last will and testament of said decedent;

Now, therefore, it is hereby ordered, adjudged and decreed, that the first and final account of said executors be and the same is hereby settled, allowed and approved.

It is further ordered, adjudged and decreed, that due and legal notice of the hearing of said accounts and of said petition for distribution was given in the manner and form required by law, and to all persons entitled thereto.

It is further ordered, adjudged and decreed, that due and legal notice to the creditors of said decedent and to all persons having claims against said decedent or against said estate has been given in the manner and form required by law and by the order of this Court heretofore duly given, made and filed.

It is further ordered, adjudged and decreed, that the inheritance tax due from said estate and from the respective heirs, devisees and legatees under the last will and testament of said decedent to the State of California, and the estate tax due from said estate to the United States of America, and all other taxes of very kind and character chargeable against said estate or the persons in interest therein, have been duly paid, satisfied and discharged.

It is further ordered, adjudged and decreed, that the estate of said decedent in the hands of said executors be and the same is hereby distributed as follows:

Unto Ellen Kathleen Hart, granddaughter of said decedent, and unto James David Hart, grandson of said decedent, equally, share and share alike, the following personal property, to-wit:

(Here follows description of property)

* * * * *

And it appearing that the said executors are holding ten thousand dollars ($10,000.00) to apply to any Federal taxes which may hereafter be levied in adjusting returns for taxes to the United States Government;

Now, therefore, it is hereby ordered, that said executors hold said ten thousand dollars ($10,000.00) until they receive a full clearance and acquittance from the United States Government with respect to all Federal and United States taxes claimed or to be claimed against said estate.

It is further ordered, that, upon said executors receiving such clearance, acquittance and receipts in full from said United States Government, then said ten thousand dollars ($10,000.00) or as much thereof as may remain after any payment which may be made to said United States Government, be and the same is hereby distributed as follows: to-wit:

One-half of said money, or balance thereof, unto Josephine D. Neustadter, surviving widow of said decedent.

Three-sixteenths of said money, or balance thereof, unto Newton H. Neustadter, surviving son of said decedent.

Three sixteenths of said money, or balance thereof, unto Florence N. Stettheimer, surviving daughter of said decedent.

One-sixteenth of said money, or balance thereof, unto Ellen Kathleen Hart, surviving granddaughter of said decedent.

One-sixteenth of said money, or balance thereof, unto James David Hart, surviving grandson of said decedent.

All the rest, residue and remainder of said estate, of every kind and character, be the same real, personal or mixed and wheresoever situate, it is hereby ordered, adjudged and decreed, shall be and the same is hereby distributed unto Josephine D. Neustadter, surviving widow of said decedent.

The rest, residue and remainder of said estate distributed unto said Josephine D. Neustadter as aforesaid is all that certain property described as follows, to-wit:

(Here follows description of property)

*   *   *   *   *   *   *

It is further ordered, adjudged and decreed, that all other property belonging to said estate, or in which said estate may have any interest, right, title or claim, not now known or discovered, or not mentioned herein, and wheresoever situate, and be the same real, personal or mixed, be and the same is hereby distributed unto said Josephine D. Neustadter, surviving widow of said David Neustadter, deceased.

Done in open Court this 25th day of February, 1924.

After the Executors of said Estate of David Neustadter received the deficiency notice of November 10, 1925, they paid on behalf of the Estate of David Neustadter, deceased, the deficiency in tax of $692.23 shown to be due and the deficiency in payment of $109.66 on the original tax assessed.

Opinion.

Milliken: Petitioners do not now contend that respondent erred in including for estate tax purposes the entire value of the community property in the gross estate of David Neustadter, deceased. Neither do they now raise any question as to the amount of the deficiency. See *Estate of Isidore Rosenberg, Deceased,* 14 B. T. A. 1340, and cases therein cited. They admit that the determination of such a deficiency would be unobjectionable in a proper case. They, however, vigorously contend that since, as they assert, they have distributed the whole of the estate to the various devisees and legatees, they and each of them would have incurred a personal liability for the deficiency but for the fact that they have been, as they contend, relieved from such liability by reason of the letter of July 30, 1924 (written by Newton H. Neustadter, as executor) to respondent and the subsequent correspondence between them, and by reason of the payment by them prior to the receipt of the deficiency letter upon which this proceeding is based of the whole tax then determined against them. They assert that since said deficiency letter was addressed to them as executors, respondent has determined they are personally liable for the deficiency, and further assert that, since they have been released from all personal liability and since as they now have in their hands no assets of the estate from which payment can be made, the Board should determine that there is no deficiency as against them.

The contention that they have been released of personal liability is based upon Section 313 of the Revenue Act of 1924. That section reads:

Sec. 313 (a). The collector shall grant to the person paying the tax duplicate receipts, either of which shall be sufficient evidence of such payment, and shall entitle the executor to be credited and allowed the amount thereof by any court having jurisdiction to audit or settle his accounts.

(b). If the executor makes written application to the Commissioner for determination of the amount of the tax and discharge from personal liability therefor, the Commissioner (as soon as possible, and in any event within one year after the making of such application, or, if the application is made before the return is filed, then within one year after the return is filed,

but not after the expiration of the period prescribed
for the assessment of the tax in section 310) shall
notify the executor of the amount of the tax. The
executor, upon payment of the amount of which he
is notified, shall be discharged from personal liability for any deficiency in tax thereafter found to be due
and shall be entitled to a receipt or writing showing
such discharge.

(c). The provisions of subdivision (b) shall not
operate as a release of any part of the gross estate
from the lien for any deficiency that may thereafter be
determined to be due, unless the title to such part of
the gross estate has passed to a bona fide purchaser
for value, in which case such part shall not be subject to a lien or to any claim or demand for any such
deficiency, but the lien shall attach to the consideration
received from such purchaser by the heirs, legatees,
devisees, or distributees.

See also Section 407 of the Revenue Act of 1921.

Respondent asserts that petitioners have not complied
with the above sections and for the reason these provisions
have no application. Respondent further contends that the
question of personal liability on the part of the executors
is not involved in this proceeding. This latter contention,
we think, is the controlling issue. In this connection, it is
to be noted that the decree of the Superior Court entered
in February, 1924, recites that petitioners had in their
hands the sum of $10,000, which they were to hold until
they had received a full acquittance from the United States
Government with respect to all United States taxes
claimed or to be claimed against the estate of David
Neustadter, deceased. Petitioner contends that since it is
shown that they had paid the deficiency determined by the

letter of October 14, 1925, as redetermined by the letter of November 10, 1925, we must assume that petitioners have distributed the said amount to the persons entitled as required by the decree. Respondent does not assent to this contention. It is also pertinent to note that petitioners have not been discharged from their office and are now proceeding in this appeal in their executorial capacity and not as individuals.

Whether the issue of personal liability is before us depends on what respondent has determined in his letter of September 21, 1926, which is the basis of this proceeding. That letter is addressed to "Newton H. Neustadter, et al., Executors, Estate of David Neustadter". A careful reading of the letter of September 21, 1926, discloses that there is nothing in that letter which refers to any personal liability on the part of the executors. It asserts only a "deficiency" in estate tax. It is further most important to note that the letter was written pursuant to Section 318 of the Revenue Act of 1926, and informs petitioners of their right under Section 308 to appeal to the Board. The pertinent part of Section 318 reads:

> If after the enactment of this Act the Commissioner determines that any assessment should be made in respect of any estate or gift tax imposed by the Revenue Act of 1917, the Revenue Act of 1918, the Revenue Act of 1921, or the Revenue Act of 1924, or by any such Act as amended, the Commissioner is authorized to send by registered mail to the person liable for such tax notice of the amount proposed to be assessed, which notice shall, for the purposes of this Act be considered a notice under subdivision (a) of section 308 of this Act. * * *

As shown by the above excerpt, this section applies to both estate and gift taxes and the requirement is that the registered letter be mailed "to the person liable for such tax * * *". By Section 406 of the Revenue Act of 1921 it is provided:—"The executor shall pay the tax to the collector or deputy collector * * *". By Section 400 of the same Act it is provided:

> The term "executor" means the executor or administrator of the decedent, or, if there is no executor or administrator, any person in actual or constructive possession of any property of the decedent; * * *

Since the executors were then (and now are) in office, the plain requirement of the statute is that the deficiency letter be addressed to them. It is only where "there is no executor or administrator" that the letter may be addressed to "any person in actual or constructive possession of any property of the decedent." It is a further requirement of Section 318 of the Revenue Act of 1926 that said notice "shall for the purpose of this Act be considered a notice under subdivision (a) of section 308 of this Act." Turning to subdivision (a) of Section 308, we find that it contains the following:

> If the Commissioner determines that there is a deficiency in respect of the tax imposed by this title, the Commissioner is authorized to send notice of such deficiency to the executor by registered mail. Within 60 days after such notice is mailed (not counting Sunday as the sixtieth day), the executor may file a petition with the Board of Tax Appeals for a redetermination of the deficiency. * * *

The definition of the term "executor" in Section 300 of the Revenue Act of 1926 is the same as that in Section

400 of the Revenue Act of 1921. It thus appears that respondent could have determined a deficiency in estate tax under Section 308 against the estate of David Neustadter, deceased, in no way other than by addressing his letter to the executors than in office. If petitioners' contention be followed to its logical conclusion, it would result that it matters not that the estate was liable for the tax, whether in the hands of the executors or in the hands of the devisees or legatees, no deficiency under Section 308 could be determined in a case like this where the executors are still in office. We do not concur in such a contention.

Upon an appeal under Section 308 of the Revenue Act of 1926, the jurisdiction of the Board is limited to a redetermination of a deficiency in estate tax due from the executors in their representative capacities. However, in redetermining such a deficiency, the Board is not limited to a mere recomputation, but may determine that there is no deficiency on the ground that the deficiency is barred by the Statute of Limitations (Section 906 (e), or because it is illegal in that it violates the provisions of any of the revenue acts or for any other reason. *National Refining Co. of Ohio,* 1 B.T.A 236. We have approved the deficiency asserted by respondent against the executors in their representative capacities, and in so doing, we are of opinion that we have exhausted our jurisdiction in so far as this proceeding is concerned. In approving the deficiency we have not decided whether the additional tax shall be paid by the executors as their personal liability. This view is in accord with the decision of the United States District Court for the Eastern District of Pennsylvania in *United States v. Rodenbough,* 21 Fed. (2d) 781, where the Court said:

One other matter remains to be disposed of. The defendant argued that, under the limitation provision of section 407 of the Revenue Act of 1921 (Comp. St. §6336 ¾h), this action against the defendant is barred. The discharge from liability provided for by that statute, however, is a discharge from personal liability. This action is not against the executor personally, but against him in his representative capacity as executor of the estate. A judgment rendered in this action would not subject him directly to any personal liability. If for any reason, as a result of the judgment in this case, recourse against the executor in his personal capacity should be attempted, the question could then be raised. As the record stands at present, it is not involved.

This portion of the opinion of the District Court was affirmed by the Circuit Court of Appeals in *Rodenbough v. United States,* 25 Fed. (2d) 13.

Respondent can determine the personal liability of an executor only under Section 316 of the Revenue Act of 1926, the pertinent parts of which read:

Sec. 316(a). The amounts of the following liabilities shall, except as hereinafter in this section provided, be assessed, collected and paid in the same manner and subject to the same provisions and limitations as in the case of a deficiency in a tax imposed by this title (including the provisions in case of delinquency in payment after notice and demand, the provisions authorizing distraint and proceedings in court for collection, and the provisions prohibiting claims for suits for refunds):

(1) The liability, at law or in equity, of a transferee of property of a decedent or donor, in respect of the tax (including interest, additional amounts, and

additions to the tax provided by law) imposed by this title or by any prior estate tax Act or by any gift tax Act.

(2) The liability of a fiduciary under section 3467 of the Revised Statutes in respect of the payment of any such tax from the estate of the decedent or donor.

Any such liability may be either as to the amount of tax shown on the return or as to any deficiency in tax.

Thus we find that the Revenue Act of 1926 contains a distinctively separate provision for the redetermination of "The liability of a fiduciary under Section 3467 of the Revised Statutes * * *". Section 3467 of the Revised Statutes reads:

Every executor, administrator, or assignee, or other person, who pays any debt due by the person or estate from whom or for which he acts, before he satisfies and pays the debts due to the United States from such person or estate, shall become answerable in his own person and estate for the debts so due to the United States, or for so much thereof as may remain due and unpaid.

Three things are to be noted at this juncture:—First, petitioners are asserting their release from the personal liability created by Section 3467 of the Revised Statutes; second, that the liability under this section can be asserted by respondent only under Section 316 of the Revenue Act of 1926; and, third, that Section 316 is distinct from and exclusive of Sections 308 and 318 of the Revenue Act of 1926.

We are of opinion that we cannot under a proceeding based on a deficiency letter issued under Sections 308 and 318 determine a "liability" under Section 316. All we determine is that the executors in their representative capacities are liable for the deficiency determined by respondent. We hold that where our jurisdiction is based upon a deficiency letter written pursuant to Sections 308 and 318, and which determines only a "deficiency" in estate tax, we have no jurisdiction to decide the question of the "liability" of a fiduciary under Section 3467 of the Revised Statutes. Since respondent has proceeded under Sections 308 and 318; since he has determined only a deficiency in estate tax against the executors in their representative capacities; and since he has determined no personal liability on the part of the executors under Section 3467 of the Revised Statutes, we are of opinion that we exhaust our jurisdiction as concerns this proceeding when we approve the deficiency as determined by respondent.

Reviewed by the Board.

Judgment will be entered for respondent.

Sterhagen concurs in the result.

Appendix B

Sections of Revenue Act of 1926 cited, but not quoted, in argument:

Sec. 300. *Definitions.* "When used in this title—

"(a) The term 'executor' means the executor or administrator of the decedent, or, if there is no executor or administrator appointed, qualified, and acting within the United States, then any person in actual or constructive possession of any property of the decedent;"

*　　　*　　　*　　　*

Sec. 310. *Limitation of Time.*

"(a) Except as provided in section 311, the amount of the estate taxes imposed by this title shall be assessed within three years after the return was filed, and no proceeding in court without assessment for the collection of such taxes shall be begun after the expiration of three years after the return was filed.

"(b) The running of the statute of limitations provided in this section or in section 311 on the making of assessments and the beginning of distraint or a proceeding in court for collection, in respect of any deficiency, shall (after the mailing of a notice under subdivision (a) of section 308) be suspended for the period during which the Commissioner is prohibited from making the assessment or beginning distraint or a proceeding in court (and in any event, if a proceeding in respect of the deficiency is placed on the docket of the Board, until the decision of the Board becomes final), and for 60 days thereafter."

Sec. 311. *Enforcement of Tax.*

"(a) in the case of a false or fraudulent return with intent to evade tax or of a failure to file a return the tax may be assessed, or a proceeding in court for the collection of such tax may be begun without assessment, at any time.

"(b) Where the assessment of any tax imposed by this title or of any estate or gift tax imposed by prior act of Congress has been made (whether before or after the enactment of this act) within the statutory period of limitation properly applicable thereto, such tax may be collected by distraint or by a proceeding in court (begun before or after the enactment of this act), but only if begun (1) within six years after the assessment of the tax, or (2) prior to the expiration of any period for collection agreed upon in writing by the Commissioner and the executor."

Sec. 313. *Receipt.—Discharge of Executor.*

"(a) The collector shall grant to the person paying the tax duplicate receipts, either of which shall be sufficient evidence of such payment, and shall entitle the executor to be credited and allowed the amount thereof by any court having jurisdiction to audit or settle his accounts.

"(b) If the executor makes written application to the Commissioner for determination of the amount of the tax and discharge from personal liability therefor, the Commissioner (as soon as possible, and in any event within one year after the making of such application, or, if the application is made before the return is filed, then within one year after the return is filed, but not after the expiration of the period prescribed for the assessment of the tax in section 310) shall notify the executor of the amount of the tax. The executor, upon payment of the amount of which he is notified, shall be discharged from personal liability for any deficiency in tax thereafter found to be due and shall be entitled to a receipt or writing showing such discharge.''

Sec. 316. *Transferee Liability.*

''(a) The amounts of the following liabilities shall, except as hereinafter in this section provided, be assessed, collected, and paid in the same manner and subject to the same provisions and limitations as in the case of a deficiency in a tax imposed by this title (including the provisions in case of delinquency in payment after notice and demand, the provisions authorizing distraint and proceedings in court for collection, and the provisions prohibiting claims and suits for refunds):

(1) The liability, at law or in equity, of a transferee of property of a decedent or donor, in respect of the tax (including interest, additional amounts, and additions to the tax provided by law) imposed by this title or by any prior estate tax act or by any gift tax act.

''(2) The liability of a fiduciary under section 3467 of the Revised Statutes in respect of the payment of any such tax from the estate of the decedent or donor. Any such liability may be either as to the amount of tax shown on the return or as to any deficiency in tax.

''(b) The period of limitation for assessment of any such liability of a transferee or fiduciary shall be as follows:

''(1) Within one year after the expiration of the period of limitation for assessment against the executor or donor; or''

Sec. 318. *Deficiency Under Prior Acts.*

"(a) If after the enactment of this Act the Commissioner determines that any assessment should be made in respect of any estate or gift tax imposed by the Revenue Act of 1917, the Revenue Act of 1918, the Revenue Act of 1921, or the Revenue Act of 1924, or by any such Act as amended, the Commissioner is authorized to send by registered mail to the person liable for such tax notice of the amount proposed to be assessed, which notice shall, for the purposes of this Act, be considered a notice under subdivision (a) of section 308 of this Act. In the case of any such determination the amount which should be assessed (whether as deficiency or additional tax or as interest, penalty, or other addition to the tax) shall be computed as if this Act had not been enacted, but the amount so computed shall be assessed, collected, and paid in the same manner and subject to the same provisions and limitations (including the provisions in case of delinquency in payment after notice and demand and the provisions prohibiting claims and suits for refund) as in the case of a deficiency in the tax imposed by this title, except that in the case of an estate tax imposed by the Revenue Act of 1917, the Revenue Act of 1918, or the Revenue Act of 1921, or by any such Act as amended the period of limitation prescribed in section 1109 of this Act shall be applied in lieu of the period prescribed in subdivision (a) of section 310."

*   *

Sec. 1109. *Limitation on Assessments and Suits by the United States.*

"(a) Except as provided in sections 277, 278, 310, and 311—

"(1) Notwithstanding the provisions of section 3182 of the Revised Statutes or any other provision of law, all internal-revenue taxes shall (except as provided in paragraph (2) or (3) of this subdivision) be assessed within four years after such taxes became due, and no proceeding in court without assessment for the collection of such taxes shall be begun after the expiration of five years after such taxes became due."

*　　　*　　　*　　　*　　　*　　　*　　　*

"(3) Where the assessment of any tax imposed by this Act or by prior Act of Congress has been made (whether before or after the enactment of this Act) within the statutory period of limitation properly applicable thereto, such tax may be collected by distraint or by a proceeding in court (begun before or after the enactment of this Act), but only if begun (A) within six years after the assessment of the tax, or (B) prior to the expiration of any period for collection agreed upon in writing by the Commissioner and the taxpayer."

No. 8176

IN THE

United States Circuit Court of Appeals

For the Ninth Circuit

NEWTON H. NEUSTADTER, JOSEPHINE D. NEU-
STADTER, FLORENCE N. STETTHEIMER, JAMES
D. HART and ELLEN K. HART,

Appellants,

VS.

UNITED STATES OF AMERICA,

Appellee.

On Appeal from the District Court of the United States for the
Northern District of California, Southern Division.

BRIEF FOR APPELLEE.

H. H. McPIKE,
United States Attorney,

ESTHER B. PHILLIPS,
Assistant United States Attorney,

ROBERT H. JACKSON,
Assistant Attorney General of the United States,

J. LOUIS MONARCH,

JULIAN G. GIBBS,
Special Assistants
to the Attorney General of the United States,
Post Office Building, San Francisco,

Attorneys for Appellee.

PERNAU-WALSH PRINTING CO., SAN FRANCISCO

Subject Index

Table of Authorities Cited

Cases

Statutes   Pages

No. 8176

IN THE

United States Circuit Court of Appeals
For the Ninth Circuit

NEWTON H. NEUSTADTER, JOSEPHINE D. NEU-
STADTER, FLORENCE N. STETTHEIMER, JAMES
D. HART and ELLEN K. HART,

Appellants,

vs.

UNITED STATES OF AMERICA,

Appellee.

On Appeal from the District Court of the United States for the
Northern District of California, Southern Division.

BRIEF FOR APPELLEE.

JURISDICTION.

This is an appeal from the judgment of the District
Court of the United States for the Northern District
of California, Southern Division, involving Federal
estate taxes due on the estate of David Neustadter, deceased, in the principal amount of $12,012.99, with in-
terest thereon at 6% per annum from September 27,
1929. The judgment of the District Court was entered
on February 19, 1936. (R. 34.) Appeal was allowed
on March 30, 1936. (R. 60.) The jurisdiction of this
Court is invoked under Section 128 of the Judicial
Code as amended by the Act of February 13, 1935.

QUESTIONS PRESENTED.

1. Were the steps taken by the Commissioner of Internal Revenue for assessment and collection of the tax in controversy in accordance with law?

2. Is the appellee entitled to equitable relief?

3. Does the decree of the lower Court violate the "due process" clause of the Fifth Amendment to the Federal Constitution?

4. Did the appellee sustain the burden of proof in the lower Court?

STATUTES INVOLVED.

The statutes involved will be found in the Appendix, *infra,* pp. i-viii.

STATEMENT.

The decedent, David Neustadter, died testate in San Francisco, California, on February 13, 1923, being at the time of his death a resident of said city and state, and leaving estate therein, and surviving him as his next of kin, heirs at law, legatees and devisees under his will, the appellants named in this proceeding. (R. 26-27.) His last will and testament was admitted to probate by the Superior Court of California, and Newton H. Neustadter, Walter W. Stettheimer and Julian Hart were appointed his executors. They thereafter qualified and entered upon their duties as such, and have never been discharged as executors of said estate. (R. 27.)

The executors filed a Federal estate tax return on behalf of the estate on December 31, 1923, disclosing a total gross estate valued at $601,630.77, a net estate subject to estate tax in the sum of $204,847.50, and an estate tax due of $4145.43 which was paid at or about the time of the filing of said return. (R. 27.) In this return the executors deducted from gross estate the community property interests of the surviving widow, Josephine D. Neustadter. (R. 27.)

On February 7, 1924, the executors filed their first and final account of their administration, their report as executors, their petition praying for a settlement of their first and final account, and their petition praying for the final distribution of said estate with the probate court. (R. 27-28.)

On February 25, 1924, their account, report and petitions were allowed and approved, and a decree for the final distribution of the estate was made by the probate court. (R. 28.) Property and money in excess of $30,000 were distributed to each of the appellants in this proceeding from the assets of said estate. (R. 28.) The executors have never been discharged under the provisions of Section 1697 of the Code of Civil Procedure or Section 1066 of the Probate Code of California or under Section 313(b) of the Revenue Act of 1926. (R. 28.)

On July 30, 1924, the executors wrote the Commissioner of Internal Revenue requesting an early determination of the estate tax for said estate of the decedent. (R. 28.) On November 10, 1925, the Commissioner advised the executors of a deficiency in tax of $692.23, which was paid. (R. 28.)

On January 4, 1926, the Supreme Court rendered its decision in the case of *United States v. Robbins,* 269 U. S. 315, holding that the community property interests of a surviving widow should be included in taxable gross estate and a tax paid thereon. Pursuant thereto the Commissioner of Internal Revenue determined that the community interests of the decedent's widow, Josephine D. Neustadter, were properly to be included as a part of the estate subject to tax, and as a result thereof found that there was a deficiency in estate tax in the principal amount of $12,012.99. (R. 29, 42.)

On September 21, 1926, the Commissioner mailed to the executors of the decedent's estate a so-called sixty-day letter or notice of deficiency of $12,012.99 under Section 318 of the Revenue Act of 1926, the merits of which deficiency rested upon the decision in the above-mentioned *Robbins* case. (R. 29, 42-43.)

On November 2, 1926, and within the time allowed by law, the executors filed a petition with the United States Board of Tax Appeals to redetermine and disallow the deficiency just mentioned upon the grounds (1) that the Commissioner erred in reopening the case and asserting a further deficiency subsequent to the one covered by its prior deficiency notice of November 10, 1925, and (2) that the deficiency had been computed erroneously on the merits. (15 B. T. A. 839.) (R. 29, 38, 39.) An answer was filed by the Commissioner and thereafter proceedings were had before the Board of Tax Appeals, and the cause submitted. (R. 29.) On March 14, 1929, an order was entered by the Board determining a deficiency in estate tax in the sum of

$12,012.99 as proposed by the Commissioner. (R. 29.) No appeal was taken from said decision of the Board, and the order became final without modification. (R. 29.)

On September 27, 1929, pursuant to and in accordance with said decision of the Board, the Commissioner assessed a deficiency in estate tax in the sum of $12,012.99 against the executors of the decedent's estate and against the estate. (R. 29-30.) No part of said deficiency and interest has been paid. (R. 30.) This suit was commenced on October 3, 1933, against the appellants as transferees of the decedent's estate. (R. 1-11.)

SUMMARY OF ARGUMENT.

1. A notice of deficiency in estate tax mailed to the executors (undischarged) of a distributed estate meets the requirements of Section 318(a) of the Revenue Act of 1926, which provides that such notice be mailed to the one liable for the tax. Said notice was mailed within the four-year period provided therefor by Section 1109(a)(1) of said Act. The statute of limitations was tolled during the pendency of the estate's appeal to the United States Board of Tax Appeals from said notice of deficiency. The assessment was made within sixty days after the decision of said Board became final, which was in accordance with Section 310(b) of said Act. The assessment was therefore valid. The suit was entered on October 3, 1933, which was in accordance with Section 1109(a)(3) of said Act provid-

ing for the filing of such suit within six years from the date of the assessment. All steps for the assessment and collection of the tax in controversy were therefore validly and timely taken.

2. Appellee is entitled to equitable relief in this proceeding. The remedies open to the Government for the collection of unpaid Federal taxes of distributed estates from the distributees thereof are cumulative and not exclusive. As long as all of the statutory requirements of the course pursued are met, the remedy chosen is not subject to attack.

3. The decree of the lower Court does not violate the "due process" clause of the Fifth Amendment to the Federal Constitution because all of the steps taken looking towards assessment and collection of the tax in controversy were taken under and by virtue of the statutes heretofore cited, and there could therefore be no such thing as lack of "due process" under such circumstances.

4. The appellee fully met the burden of proof imposed upon it by law in the Court below. The only exceptions taken thereto by the appellants relate to the proof of non-payment of the tax in controversy and to its assessment against both the estate and the distributees. The answer of appellant in the Court below sufficiently admits non-payment of said tax. Assessment of the tax against the distributees was not necessary under the law as a condition precedent to maintenance of the suit herein. The evidence shows non-payment of the tax and assessment against the estate.

ARGUMENT.

I.

THE ACTION IS BASED ON SECTIONS 318(a), 1109(a)(1) AND
1109(a)(3) OF THE REVENUE ACT OF 1926, AND IS THERE-
FORE IN ACCORDANCE WITH THE LAW.

The decedent having died on February 13, 1923, his
estate was subject to the Revenue Act of 1921 for
Federal estate tax purposes. The estate tax return was
filed on December 31, 1923. The deficiency notice in
question was mailed to the executors on September 21,
1926, pursuant to the provisions of Section 318(a) of
the Revenue Act of 1926, which provides, in so far as
is material, as follows:

> Sec. 318. (a) If after the enactment of this
> Act the Commissioner determines that any assess-
> ment should be made in respect of any estate * * *
> tax imposed by the Revenue Act of * * * 1921,
> * * * or by such act as amended, the Commis-
> sioner is authorized to send by registered mail to
> the person liable for such tax notice of the amount
> proposed to be assessed, which notice shall, for the
> purposes of this Act, be considered a notice under
> subdivision (a) of section 308 of this Act. [See
> Appendix.] In the case of any such determination
> the amount which should be assessed (whether as
> deficiency or additional tax or as interest * * *
> or other addition to the tax) shall be computed
> as if this Act had not been enacted, but the
> amount so computed shall be assessed, collected,
> and paid in the same manner and subject to the
> same provisions and limitations * * * as in the
> case of a deficiency in the tax imposed by this
> title, except that in the case of an estate tax im-
> posed by the * * * Revenue Act of 1921, or by

any such Act as amended, the period of limitation prescribed in section 1109 of this Act shall be applied in lieu of the period prescribed in subdivision (a) of section 310.

Section 1109 of the Revenue Act of 1926, in so far as is material, provides as follows:

Sec. 1109. (a) Except as provided in sections 277, 278, 310, and 311——

(1) Notwithstanding the provisions of section 3182 of the Revised Statutes or any other provision of law, all internal revenue taxes shall * * * be assessed within four years after such taxes became due, and no proceeding in court without assessment for the collection of such taxes shall be begun after the expiration of five years after such taxes became due. * * *

(3) Where the assessment of any tax imposed by this Act or by prior Act of Congress has been made (whether before or after the enactment of this Act) within the statutory period of limitation properly applicable thereto, such tax may be collected by distraint or by a proceeding in court (begun before or after the enactment of this Act), but only if begun (A) within six years after the assessment of the tax, * * *.

Therefore, under Section 1109(a)(1) of the Revenue Act of 1926, *supra,* the Commissioner of Internal Revenue had four years from the date of the filing of the estate tax return on December 31, 1923, within which to take steps looking towards a valid assessment. The Commissioner took such steps when he mailed a deficiency notice to the estate on September

21, 1926. The taxpayer took an appeal from the Commissioner's determination to the United States Board of Tax Appeals. The statute of limitations was tolled during the time the matter was pending before the Board. The Board's order determining the deficiency against the estate was entered on March 14, 1929. (R. 29.) The Commissioner was further prohibited for a period of six months thereafter from making an assessment under Section 1001(a) of the Revenue Act of 1926, which provides, in so far as is material, as follows:

> Sec. 1001. (a) The decision of the Board rendered after the enactment of this Act * * * may be reviewed by a Circuit Court of Appeals * * *, as hereinafter provided, if a petition for such review is filed by either the Commissioner or the taxpayer within six months after the decision is rendered.

The Commissioner was therefore prohibited from making an assessment until after September 14, 1929.

Under Section 310(b) of the Revenue Act of 1926, the Commissioner had a further period of sixty days from September 14, 1929, within which to make a valid assessment against the estate, said section providing, in so far as is material, as follows:

> Sec. 310. * * *

> (b) The running of the statute of limitations provided in this section or in section 311 on the making of assessments and the beginning of distraint or a proceeding in court for collection, in respect of any deficiency, shall (after the mailing of a notice under subdivision (a) of section 308)

be suspended for the period during which the Commissioner is prohibited from making the assessment or beginning distraint or a proceeding in court, and for 60 days thereafter.

The assessment having been made on September 27, 1929, was made within such sixty-day period and was therefore timely.

The suit was filed on October 3, 1933, which was within the six-year period from the date of the assessment of September 27, 1929, and fulfilled the requirements of Section 1109(a)(3) of the Revenue Act of 1926, *supra,* requiring that the suit be brought within six years from the date of the assessment. There is no question, therefore, of the timeliness of the action taken with respect to assessment and collection of the tax in controversy.

One of the attacks of appellant upon the validity of the assessment against the estate is on the ground that the Commissioner's notice of deficiency was not addressed to the correct party and not to the one liable for the tax. The lower Court found as a fact that the executors had not been discharged under the provisions of Section 1697 of the Code of Civil Procedure of California or Section 1066 of the Probate Code of California or under Section 313(b) of the Revenue Act of 1926. (R. 28.) Since the executors had not been discharged, the estate and/or the executors in their representative capacity were the ones liable for the tax deficiency and the ones to whom a notice of deficiency should have been sent. It was sent to the executors of the estate. (R. 29.)

The executors were not liable under Section 3467 of the Revised Statutes and no notice should have been sent them under Section 316(a)(2) of the Revenue Act of 1926 providing for such procedure if the executors are liable under said Section 3467 of the Revised Statutes. Apropos thereto, and under authority of Section 407 of the Revenue Act of 1921, the executors gave the Commissioner notice in the year 1924 to determine and assess immediately any outstanding estate tax liability against the estate. This relieved them of any personal liability. The appellants seem to contend, however, that when the executors gave the Commissioner such notice and a relatively small deficiency was asserted as a result thereof, the decedent's estate as well as the executors were discharged from any further liability even if the Commissioner thereafter, and within the applicable period of limitation running from the date of the return, should ascertain and determine any further deficiency in the estate tax liability.

Although Section 407 of the Revenue Act of 1921 (which corresponds to a substantial extent to Section 313(b) of the Revenue Acts of 1924 and 1926) makes provision, to a limited extent, for shortening the period for determination of estate tax liability "if the executor files complete return and makes written application for such immediate determination", the material part of that section is as follows:

> The Commissioner, as soon as possible and in any event within one year after receipt of such application, shall notify the executor of the amount of the tax, and upon payment thereof the

executor shall be discharged from personal liability for any additional tax thereafter found to be due, * * *; *Provided, however,* that such discharge shall not operate to release the gross estate from the lien of any additional tax that may thereafter be found to be due while the title to such gross estate remains in the heirs, devisees, or distributees thereof; but no part of such gross estate shall be subject to such lien or to any claim or demand for any such tax if the title thereto has passed to a bona fide purchaser for value.

No question was raised by the Government, therefore, that the former executors of the decedent's estate have not been released from personal liability as fiduciaries under Section 3467 of the Revised Statutes. Furthermore, the Board of Tax Appeals in its decision pointed out that no attempt had been made to assert any liability for unpaid taxes of the decedent's estate by any summary administrative proceedings against them as fiduciaries or transferees of the decedent's estate under Section 316 of the Revenue Act of 1926 (15 B. T. A. 839, 851). (R. 46.) Since the executors were not discharged as such and since they were not liable under Section 3467 of the Revised Statutes, the notice of deficiency was properly sent under authority of Section 318(a) of the Revenue Act of 1926.

The fact that an executor has been released from personal liability as a fiduciary, however, does not release him in his representative capacity from liability of his decedent's estate for unpaid Federal taxes. *Rodenbough v. United States,* 25 F. (2d) 13, 18 (C. C. A. 3d), affirming 21 F. (2d) 781 (E. D. Pa.) as to points cited here.

So far as the original liability of the decedent's estate or of the former executors in their representative capacity for the outstanding deficiency is concerned, such liability was determined by the Commissioner and was redetermined and approved by the Board of Tax Appeals under an appeal of the executors taken subsequent to the effective date of the Revenue Act of 1926; and the executors did not avail themselves of their right under Section 1001(a) of the Revenue Act of 1926, *supra,* to obtain a review of the Board's decision by the Circuit Court of Appeals. Section 1005(a) of the Revenue Act of 1926 provides that the decision of the Board shall become final—

> (1) upon the expiration of the time allowed for filing a petition for review, if no such petition has been duly filed within such time; * * *

These statutes have been construed as holding that where, under appeal subsequent to the effective date of the 1926 Act, the Board redetermines a tax deficiency and such redetermination becomes final under the above-mentioned statute, the District Courts are without jurisdiction thereafter to inquire into the merits or amount of such tax liability. *Old Colony Trust Co. v. Commissioner,* 279 U. S. 716; *Green v. McLaughlin,* 55 F. (2d) 423 (E. D. Pa.); *Bankers Reserve Life Co. v. United States,* 44 F. (2d) 1000 (C. Cls.); *Bindley v. Heiner,* 38 F. (2d) 489 (W. D. Pa.).

Moreover, in its findings of fact and decision affirming the Commissioner's determination of March

14, 1929, the Board (15 B. T. A. 839) held that the deficiency was properly assessable upon the merits insofar as it was a liability of the decedent's estate which had been redetermined under Sections 308 and 318 of the Revenue Act of 1926, and expressly limited that determination to one of liability of the executors in their representative capacity as the representatives of the decedent's estate. The Board, in its opinion, said (p. 851):

We are of opinion that we can not under a proceeding based on a deficiency letter issued under Sections 308 and 318 determine a "liability" under section 316. All we determine is that the executors in their representative capacities are liable for the deficiency determined by repondent. We hold that where our jurisdiction is based upon a deficiency letter written pursuant to sections 308 and 318, and which determines only a "deficiency" in estate tax, we have no jurisdiction to decide the question of the "liability" of a fiduciary under section 3467 of the Revised Statutes. Since respondent has proceeded under sections 308 and 318; since he has determined only a deficiency in estate tax against the executors in their representative capacities, and since he has determined no personal liability on the part of the executors under section 3467 of the Revised Statutes, we are of opinion that we exhaust our jurisdiction as concerns this proceeding when we approve the deficiency as determined by respondent.

The assessment was therefore made against the executors in their representative capacity and consequently against the estate.

Appellants rely to a great extent upon the decision of the Supreme Court rendered December 9, 1935, *Hulburd v. Commissioner*, 296 U. S. 300, wherein the Court passed upon the liability of a legatee under the will of a deceased stockholder in a dissolved corporation, under the transferee provisions of Section 280 of the Revenue Act of 1926. In that case a corporation was dissolved in September 1919, and its assets distributed in liquidation among its stockholders. Its return for the fiscal year ended September 30, 1919, was filed in December 1919. The Commissioner assessed a deficiency against the dissolved corporation within the applicable five-year period after the return was filed on or about November 17, 1924. In the meantime, a stockholder named Charles H. Hulburd, who had received a liquidating distribution from the dissolved corporation, died on January 14, 1924. On October 27, 1926, the Commissioner mailed a notice under Section 280 of the Revenue Act of 1926 addressed to the "Estate of Charles H. Hulburd, c/o De Forest Hulburd, Chicago, Illinois," of a proposed assessment against the estate "by reason of its liability as a transferee of the property of the dissolved corporation." Prior to the issuance of that notice of transferee liability, the estate of the deceased stockholder had been settled, the assets distributed, and the executor discharged. In that proceeding the Commissioner attempted to fasten liability upon De Forest Hulburd as a distributee of the Charles H. Hulburd estate. De Forest Hulburd, in addition to being former executor of the Charles H.

Hulburd estate, was also a legatee and distributee thereof.

In the *Hulburd* case, *supra,* the Supreme Court held that the former executor of the deceased stockholder's estate was not chargeable in *that* proceeding with liability *as a transferee of a transferee* for the unpaid tax of the dissolved corporation; and that he was not subject to a *transferee assessment* in his *representative capacity* after the estate had been settled and its executors had been discharged *in conformity with local law prior to notice* from the Commissioner of the outstanding tax liability of the dissolved corporation. The Supreme Court further pointed out that when the former executor appealed to the Board of Tax Appeals and put the Commissioner upon notice of his defense against the asserted transferee liability, there was still time for the Commissioner to proceed under the transferee provisions of the Revenue Act of 1926, as amended, against that petitioner as a transferee of a transferee, but that the Commissioner had stood upon his previous transferee notice and had not availed himself of the opportunity to commence a new and further transferee proceeding.

The *Hulburd* case, therefore, is not in any way analogous or applicable to the case under consideration. There is no attempt here, as in the *Hulburd* case, to convert a proceeding against the executors in one capacity into a proceeding in a different capacity. This is a separate and distinct action from the Board proceeding and is not subject to the same infirmities which existed in the *Hulburd* case. The *Hulburd* case was a transferee proceeding under the Revenue Acts and an appeal from a Board of Tax Appeals decision, whereas the instant case originated in the District Court on a suit under the trust fund doctrine.

Another contention of appellants is that the notice of deficiency to the estate in the instant case was insufficient since the estate was distributed, and that such notice may be given to the executor only when the estate has not been distributed. The law attaches no such condition to giving notice to the executor. In this connection appellants cite and rely upon *Lindley v. United States,* 59 F. (2d) 336 (C. C. A. 9th). In that case the *executors of the estate of Curtis Lindley* paid an estate tax computed by including as part of the estate the community interest of the wife. Thereafter, their claim for refund was filed and a refund was allowed and paid to the executors in the sum of $1,669.87, which was computed by excluding the wife's community interest. The refund was paid to the executors of the estate of Curtis Lindley. Under the will, the refund was distributable to the widow and the two children. As the widow was dead when the refund was paid, the executors distributed it direct to the two children, Curtis Lindley, Jr., and Elizabeth Lindley Rood, who received one-sixth and one-third of it as heirs of their father. The widow's half of the refund went to them as the heirs of their mother.

After the decision in *United States v. Robbins,* 269 U. S. 315, the United States filed suit against the executors of the estate of Curtis Lindley in their representative capacity, and against Curtis Lindley, Jr., and Josephine Lindley Rood personally, as distributees, to recover the amount of the refund as being an erroneous payment to them of Government money by mistake of its officers. This Court held that the executors were not liable in their representative capacity because they made the payment under an order of the probate court, but that the distributees were liable to return the money in their proportionate shares.

The *Lindley* case, *supra,* therefore, is not authority for saying that suit does not lie against undischarged executors in their representative capacity *to determine the merits of a tax* merely because they have distributed the estate. Such a ruling would be in conflict with the ruling of this Court in the later case of *Rosenberg v. McLaughlin,* 66 F. (2d) 271 (C. C. A. 9th), certiorari denied 290 U. S. 696. As a matter of fact, the record in the *Lindley* case shows that the Commissioner gave notice to the executors of redetermination of tax, just as he did in the case at bar, and in the *Rosenberg* case. The suit was not to recover an additional tax, but to recover an erroneous refund of money belonging to the United States. Such an action lies, but in character it is not a recovery of tax, but recovery of money belonging to the United States. *Talcott v. United States,* 23 F. (2d) 897 (C. C. A. 9th); *Kelley v. United States,* 30 F. (2d) 193 (C. C. A. 9th); *United States v. Pusey,* 47 F. (2d) 22 (C. C. A. 9th). Therefore the Circuit Court held that the suit did not lie against the executors (who were protected by the probate court's order), but only against the distributees who had actually received the money.

In *Rosenberg v. McLaughlin, supra,* the estate had been distributed at the time the Commissioner gave notice of deficiency to the administrator. The administrator appealed to the Board of Tax Appeals, which affirmed the determination of the Commissioner. No appeal was taken from the Board's decision, and the Commissioner assessed the deficiency accordingly. The Collector then asserted the Government's estate tax lien upon real property in the hands of the distributees for the unpaid balance of the deficiency tax determined by the Board. The distributees sought to enjoin collection. One of the grounds urged by the distributees before the Circuit Court of Appeals was that the determination of the tax deficiency by the Board was not a determination as to them, and that it had never been adjudicated that they (the distributees) were liable for the tax. The right of the Collector to distrain for the deficiency as determined was sustained. It will be noted that in this case the notice of deficiency was addressed and mailed to the administrator of the estate after it had been distributed, which is the exact situation that we have in the instant *Neustadter* case.

Since the Board of Tax Appeals' record (15 B. T. A. 839) in the instant case shows that the deficiency notice was issued under Section 318 of the Revenue Act of 1926, any finding of the lower Court contrary thereto should be ignored. (R. 29.) The notice of deficiency in question also appears in the record as Exhibit A attached to the petition before the Board of Tax Appeals. (R. 42-43.)

We submit, therefore, that the steps taken by the Government for assessment and collection of the taxes in controversy were in accordance with the law and should be sustained.

II.

THE UNITED STATES MAY PURSUE ANY OF THE REMEDIES OPEN TO IT AGAINST THE DISTRIBUTEES OF AN ESTATE FOR UNPAID STATE TAXES, AND IS THEREFORE ENTITLED TO THE EQUITABLE RELIEF SOUGHT IN THIS CASE.

Appellants contend that appellee is not entitled to equitable relief in this case because (1) it "did not promptly or diligently proceed to collect the asserted estate tax from the persons liable therefor, either through administrative or court proceedings"; (2) it "did not resort to jeopardy assessment before the estate was distributed, nor to distraint"; and (3) it did not "seek equity to enforce the lien or trust created by Section 409 of the 1921 Act." (Br. 35.) Section 409 of the Revenue Act of 1921 creates a lien against an estate for unpaid Federal estate taxes for a period of ten years from the date of the filing of its return. Such a lien was created in this case until December 31, 1933, the estate tax return having been filed on December 31, 1923.

On the question of whether or not the Government was bound to exercise its lien under Section 409 of the Revenue Act of 1921, it has never been the rule that the United States is bound to use distraint proceedings through the Collector rather than to avail itself of court proceedings. In *United States v. Ayer,* 12 F. (2d) 194 (C. C. A. 1st), it was held that the United States may resort to court proceedings for collection of an estate tax without relying on an assessment and without the aid of the Collector. In *Blacklock v. United States,* 208 U. S. 75, it was held that the remedy for collection by distraint and the remedy by suit in equity for foreclosure of a lien were two remedies which could co-exist in the absence of action by Congress to make one remedy exclusive.

It has heretofore been argued that the executors were not personally liable under Section 3467 of the Revised Statutes, and that the Commissioner of Internal Revenue was correct in not attempting to hold them liable based on said Section 3467, Revised Statutes. In addition to what has been heretofore said with respect thereto, it should be noted that at the time the executors distributed the estate they had no notice of the deficiency assessment in question, and that they could have had no such notice since the deficiency tax in question is based upon the inclusion in the decedent's gross estate of the wife's community property as a result of the decision of the Supreme Court in *United States v. Robbins, supra,* of January 4, 1926, the executors having distributed the estate on or about February 25, 1924. (R. 28, 29.)

Chief Justice Marshall of the United States Supreme Court, in *United States v. Fisher,* 2 Cranch

358, held that the executor or other fiduciary was liable under Section 3467 of the Revised Statutes only if they received notice of the debt or claim prior to distributing the estate. It is obvious that a judgment against the executors in their representative capacity would have been worthless. It is likewise obvious that a judgment against the estate would have been worthless. To require the United States to secure judgments would have necessitated futile acts. The United States is not required to get a worthless judgment. *Hatch v. Morosco Holding Co.*, 50 F. (2d) 138 (C. C. A. 2d); *Baumgartner v. Commissioner*, 51 F. (2d) 472 (C. C. A. 9th).

Even if the executors were personally liable and a judgment had been entered against them, this would not relieve the distributees. *United States v. Cruikshank*, 48 F. (2d) 352 (S. D. N. Y.). In that case the United States Trust Company, the distributee of funds of the estate, was joined with executors in a suit to recover additional estate taxes. The judgment ran against the distributee to the extent of the assets in its possession. The judgment entered by the Court for the tax was made payable by the distributee-trustee out of trust assets previously distributed to it, and, in default of such payment, by the defendant-executor. This case was also cited with approval by Judge Kerrigan of this Court in *Rosenberg v. McLaughlin, supra,* and has never been overruled.

Where a liability arises in law or in equity for unpaid income taxes of a transferor taxpayer as against his transferee, it is no longer open to question that summary administrative remedies provided by statute are cumulative and not exclusive, and that the failure upon the part of the Government officials to resort to same within a shorter period of limitation applicable to such summary remedies does not preclude the Government from maintaining a civil suit in equity against transferees to enforce their liability for unpaid Federal taxes. *Phillips v. Commissioner,* 283 U. S. 589; *Leighton v. United States,* 289 U. S. 506; *Rosenberg v. McLaughlin, supra.* For all practical purposes material here, Section 280 and Section 316 of the Revenue Act of 1926 are identical and should be construed the same way by the Courts.

It is not necessary to obtain a judgment against a dissolved corporation as a condition precedent to a suit against stockholders where it is either impossible to obtain judgment against the corporation or obtaining judgment is manifestly useless and an idle formality. *United States v. Fairall,* 16 F. (2d) 328 (S. D. N. Y.); *United States v. Garfunkel,* 52 F. (2d) 727 (S. D. N. Y.). Nor does the fact that the dissolution of the corporation and transfer of its assets occurred prior to the assessment affect the Government's right to sue the stockholders as transferees. *United States v. Garfunkel, supra.* Nor is assessment against the appellants as transferees necessary as a condition precedent to the maintenance by the Government of a suit against transferees. *Leighton v. United States, supra; Rosenberg v. McLaughlin, supra.*

So long as the action taken by the Government is within the time allowed by statute for the taking thereof, and against the parties liable, any charges of inequities or laches on its part are immaterial. *Dox v. Postmaster General,* 1 Pet. 317; *Simmons v. Ogle,* 105 U. S. 271; *Stanley v. Schwalby,* 147 U. S. 508; *United States v. Drielinger,* 21 F. (2d) 211 (S. D. N. Y.); *United States v. Converse Cooperage Co.,* 42 F. (2d) 227 (N. D. Ill.).

It has been established that under the law and the authorities (1) the Government was not bound to exercise its lien under Section 409 of the Revenue Act of 1921; (2) the executors were not personally liable under Section 3467 of the Revised Statutes; (3) the remedies open to the United States against the distributees of a closed estate for the collection of its just and legally due unpaid taxes are cumulative and not exclusive; and (4) the instant suit was brought within the six-year period after assessment of the tax against the taxpayer as provided for by Section 1109 (a)(3) of the Revenue Act of 1926, and assessment was made within the four-year period after the filing of the estate tax return as provided for by Sections 318(a) and 1109(a)(1) of said Act.

We submit therefore that the United States was in the first place without any plain, adequate and complete remedy at law, and that it is entitled to the equitable relief sought for that reason alone. We further submit, however, that separate and apart from such reason, it is entitled to such relief on the basis of its choice of remedies, it having elected to pursue such remedy in this case.

III.

THE DECREE OF THE LOWER COURT DOES NOT VIOLATE THE "DUE PROCESS" CLAUSE OF THE FIFTH AMENDMENT TO THE FEDERAL CONSTITUTION.

Appellants here do not challenge the constitutionality of the Federal statutes under which the tax in question is assessed, but they do say that the acts of the administrative officer of the Government in this case were "contrary to law and violated the due process clause of the Fifth Amendment to the Constitution of the United States." At page 50 of their brief, appellants say as follows: "By this suit appellee seeks to replace proper legal remedies which its responsible officers did not use. In other words it seems to utilize an illegal administrative action, which was contrary to law and not 'due process,' as a ground for equitable relief."

Since it has been shown that all steps looking towards assessment and collection of the tax in controversy were valid and were timely taken under the statutes in such cases made and provided by Congress, as well as under the authorities cited, it follows that there is no merit to appellants' contention in this respect.

IV.

THE APPELLEE FULLY MET THE BURDEN OF PROOF IN THE LOWER COURT.

The appellants contend that the "Appellee failed to prove that a tax liability existed or was due from anyone." (Br. 8.) A certified copy of the "Assess-

ment Certificate" introduced in evidence shows that
the tax in controversy has not been paid. The space
thereon provided for and entitled "Credit" is blank.
(R. 46, 47.) Moreover, the lower Court found that
"No part of said deficiency in tax, and no part of the
interest thereon, has been paid." (R. 30.) This finding is based on the pleadings wherein it is alleged in
Par. XII of the Bill that "no part of said tax or
interest has been paid; that there is now due and
outstanding an additional estate tax in the sum of $12,-
012.99, together with interest thereon" (R. 7); and
Par. XIII of the amended answer, wherein it is stated
(R. 17):

> Deny the allegations contained in paragraph
> XII of the Bill of Complaint but in lieu thereof
> allege that thereafter the Commissioner of In-
> ternal Revenue caused to be made a pretended
> and unauthorized assessment in the amount of
> $12,012.99 against the said estate of David Neu-
> stadter and on November 20, 1929, the Collector
> of Internal Revenue for the Northern District of
> California caused a form of notice and demand
> for payment to be made upon one of the asserted
> executors under said pretended and unauthorized
> assessment; also, that, *on the service of said form
> of notice and demand the representative of the
> Collector was informed that the estate of David
> Neustadter had been distributed long before and
> was without assets; and, also, that said Collector
> made no further attempt toward collection of said
> alleged deficiency* * * *. (Italics supplied.)

Par. XII of the complaint referred to an assessment which the Commissioner made, of which the Col-

lector of Internal Revenue gave notice and made demand for payment. (R. 7.) Par. XIII of the amended answer (R. 17) specifically refers to said assessment, concerning which it is specifically *alleged* that the Collector gave notice and made demand for payment, to which the executors made reply by stating the reason for non-payment, and further *alleging* that the Collector made "no further attempt toward collection." There would be no basis for any action against the transferees if the tax had in fact been paid, and in view of the presumption of legality attaching to the acts of public officers, it must be presumed in the absence of denial that the tax has not been paid. Appellants do not assert that the tax has been paid; they merely rely on the technical ground that the failure to pay has not been proved. Their answer admits that they failed to respond to the Collector's demand and asserts that the Collector made no further attempt to collect.

The lower Court having found as a fact that "no part of said deficiency in tax, and no part of the interest thereon, has been paid" is sufficient, and there being a substantial basis therefor in the record, including the pleadings, the matter is not open to review on appeal. *McCaughn v. Real Estate Co.,* 297 U. S. 606.

Appellants further argue that the appellee failed to prove any legal assessment against the estate of the decedent in this case, or the appellants, which would entitle it to relief in equity. (Br. 10.) As heretofore asserted, assessment against the appellants as transferees is not a condition precedent to the maintenance by the Government of a suit against the transferees under the trust fund doctrine. *Leighton v. United States, supra; Rosenberg v. McLaughlin, supra.* With respect to assessment against the original taxpayer, the certified copy of the "Assessment Certificate," heretofore referred to and offered in evidence, shows not only that the tax in controversy had not been paid at the date of the trial but that it had been duly assessed against the estate. (R. 46, 47.) The lower Court having found as a matter of fact that such assessment had been made, and there being a substantial basis therefor in the evidence adduced at the trial, the matter is not open to review on appeal. *McCaughn v. Real Estate Co., supra.*

We submit that the record shows that the appellee fully met the burden of proof required of it in proving its case in the lower Court.

CONCLUSION.

In view of the foregoing facts and circumstances and authorities cited, it is submitted the judgment should be for the appellee.

Dated, San Francisco,
October 7, 1936.

Respectfully submitted,

H. H. McPike,
United States Attorney,

Esther B. Phillips,
Assistant United States Attorney,

Robert H. Jackson,
Assistant Attorney General of the United States,

J. Louis Monarch,

Julian G. Gibbs,
Special Assistants
to the Attorney General of the United States,

Attorneys for Appellee.

(Appendix Follows.)

Appendix.

Appendix

Revenue Act of 1921, c. 136, 42 Stat. 227:

Sec. 407. That where the amount of tax shown upon a return made in good faith has been fully paid, or time for payment has been extended, as provided in section 406, beyond one year and six months after the decedent's death, and an additional amount of tax is, after the expiration of such period of one year and six months, found to be due, then such additional amount shall be paid upon notice and demand by the collector, and if it remains unpaid for one month after such notice and demand there shall be added as part of the tax interests on such additional amount at the rate of 10 per centum per annum from the expiration of such period until paid, and such additional tax and interest shall, until paid, be and remain a lien upon the entire gross estate.

The collector shall grant to the person paying the tax duplicate receipts, either of which shall be sufficient evidence of such payment, and shall entitle the executor to be credited and allowed the amount thereof by any court having jurisdiction to audit or settle his accounts.

If the executor files a complete return and makes written application to the Commissioner for determination of the amount of the tax and discharge from personal liability therefor, the Commissioner, as soon as possible and in any event within one year after receipt of such application, shall notify the executor of the amount of the tax, and upon payment thereof the executor shall be discharged from personal liability for any additional tax thereafter found to be due, and shall be entitled to receive a receipt or writing showing such discharge: *Provided, however,* that such discharge shall not operate to release the gross estate from the lien of any additional tax that may thereafter be found to be due while the title to such gross estate remains in the heirs, devisees, or distributees thereof; but no part of such gross estate shall be subject to such lien or to any claim or demand for any such tax if the title thereto has passed to a bona fide purchaser for value.

Revenue Act of 1924, c. 234, 43 Stat. 253:

Sec. 313 * * *

(b) If the executor makes written application to the Commissioner for determination of the amount of the tax and discharge from personal liability therefor, the Commissioner (as soon as possible, and in any event within one year after the making of such application, or, if the application is made before the return is filed, then within one year after the return is filed, but not after the expiration of the period prescribed for the assessment of the tax in section 310) shall notify the executor of the amount of the tax. The executor, upon payment of the amount of which he is notified, shall be discharged from personal liability for any deficiency in tax thereafter found to be due and shall be entitled to a receipt or writing showing such discharge.

Revenue Act of 1926, c. 27, 44 Stat. 9:

Sec. 280. (a) The amounts of the following liabilities shall, except as hereinafter in this section provided, be assessed, collected, and paid in the same manner and subject to the same provisions and limitations as in the case of a deficiency in a tax imposed by this title (including the provisions in case of delinquency in payment after notice and demand, the provisions authorizing distraint and proceedings in court for collection, and the provisions prohibiting claims and suits for refunds): * * *

Sec. 308. (a) If the Commissioner determines that there is a deficiency in respect of the tax imposed by this title, the Commissioner is authorized to send notice of such deficiency to the executor by registered mail. Within 60 days after such notice is mailed (not counting Sunday as the sixtieth day), the executor may file a petition with the Board of Tax Appeals for a redetermination of the deficiency. Except as otherwise provided in subdivision (d) or (f) of this section or in section 312 or 1001, no assessment of a deficiency in respect of the tax imposed by this title and no distraint or proceeding in court for its collection shall be made, begun, or prosecuted until such notice has been mailed to the executor, nor until the expiration of such 60-day period, nor, if a petition has been filed with the Board, until the decision of the Board has become final. Notwithstanding the provisions of section 3224 of the Revised Statutes the making of such assessment or the beginning of such proceeding or distraint during the time such prohibition is in force may be enjoined by a proceeding in the proper court.

Sec. 310. * * *

(b) The running of the statute of limitations provided in this section or in section 311 on the making of assessments and the beginning of distraint or a proceeding in court for collection, in respect of any deficiency, shall (after the mailing of a notice under subdivision (a) of section 308) be suspended for the period during which the Commissioner is prohibited from making the assessment or beginning distraint or a proceeding in court, and for 60 days thereafter.

The provisions of Sec. 313(b) are the same as those of Sec. 313(b) of the Revenue Act of 1924, *supra.*

The provisions of Sec. 316(a) are the same as those of Sec. 280(a), *supra.*

Sec. 318. (a) If after the enactment of this Act the Commissioner determines that any assessment should be made in respect of any estate or gift tax imposed by the Revenue Act of 1917, the Revenue Act of 1918, the Revenue Act of 1921, or the Revenue Act of 1924, or by any such act as amended, the Commissioner is authorized to send by registered mail to the person liable for such tax notice of the amount proposed to be assessed, which notice shall, for the purposes of this Act, be considered a notice under subdivision (a) of section 308 of this Act. In the case of any such determination the amount which should be assessed (whether as deficiency or additional tax or as interest, penalty, or other addition to the tax) shall be computed as if this Act had not been enacted, but the amount so computed shall be assessed, collected, and paid in the same manner and subject to the same provisions and limitations (including the provisions in case of delinquency in payment after notice and demand and the provisions prohibiting claims and suits for refund) as in the case of a deficiency in the tax imposed by this title, except that in the case of an estate tax imposed by the Revenue Act of 1917, the Revenue Act of 1918, or the Revenue Act of 1921, or by any such Act as amended, the period of limitation prescribed in section 1109 of this Act shall be applied in lieu of the period prescribed in subdivision (a) of section 310.

Sec. 1001. (a) The decision of the Board rendered after the enactment of this Act (except as provided in subdivision (j) of section 283 and in subdivision (h) of section 318) may be reviewed by a Circuit Court of Appeals, or the Court of Appeals of the District of Columbia, as hereinafter provided, if a petition for such review is filed by either the Commissioner or the taxpayer within six months after the decision is rendered.

Sec. 1003. (a) The Circuit Courts of Appeals and the Court of Appeals of the District of Columbia shall have exclusive jurisdiction to review the decisions of the Board (except as provided in section 239 of the Judicial Code, as amended); and the judgment of any such court shall be final, except that it shall be subject to review by the Supreme Court of the United States upon certiorari, in the manner provided in section 240 of the Judicial Code, as amended.

Sec. 1005. (a) The decision of the Board shall become final—

(1) Upon the expiration of the time allowed for filing a petition for review, if no such petition has been duly filed within such time; * * *

Sec. 1109. (a) Except as provided in sections 277, 278, 310, and 311—

(1) Notwithstanding the provisions of section 3182 of the Revised Statutes or any other provision of law, all internal revenue taxes shall (except as provided in paragraph (2) or (3) of this subdivision) be assessed within four years after such taxes became due, and no proceeding in court without assessment for the collection of such taxes shall be begun after the expiration of five years after such taxes became due. * * *

(3)   Where the assessment of any tax imposed by this Act or by prior Act of Congress has been made (whether before or after the enactment of this Act) within the statutory period of limitation properly applicable thereto, such tax may be collected by distraint or by a proceeding in court (begun before or after the enactment of this Act), but only if begun (A) within six years after the assessment of the tax, or (B) prior to the expiration of any period for collection agreed upon in writing by the Commissioner and the taxpayer.

Revenue Act of 1921, c. 136, 42 Stat. 227:

Sec. 409.   That unless the tax is sooner paid in full, it shall be a lien for ten years upon the gross estate of the decedent, except that such part of the gross estate as is used for the payment of charges against the estate and expenses of its administration, allowed by any court having jurdisdiction thereof, shall be divested of such lien.   If the Commissioner is satisfied that the tax liability of an estate has been fully discharged or provided for, he may, under regulations prescribed by him with the approval of the Secretary, issue his certificate, releasing any or all property of such estate from the lien herein imposed.

If (a) the decedent makes a transfer of, or creates a trust with respect to, any property in contemplation of or intended to take effect in possession or enjoyment at or after his death (except in the case of a bona fide sale for fair consideration in money or money's worth) or (b) if insurance passes under a contract executed by the decedent in favor of a specific beneficiary, and if in either case the tax in respect thereto is not paid when due, then the transferee, trustee, or beneficiary shall be personally liable for such tax, and such property, to the extent of the decedent's interest therein at the time of such transfer, or to the extent of such beneficiary's interest under such contract of insurance, shall be subject to a like lien equal to the amount of such tax. Any part of such property sold by such transferee or trustee to a bona fide purchaser for a fair consideration in money or money's worth shall be divested of the lien and a like lien shall then attach to all the property of such transferee or trustee, except any part sold to a bona fide purchaser for a fair consideration in money or money's worth.

Revised Statutes:

Sec. 3467. *Liability of fiduciaries.* Every executor, administrator, or assignee, or other person, who pays, in whole or in part, any debt due by the person or estate for whom or for which he acts before he satisfies and pays the debts due to the United States from such person or estate, shall become answerable in his own person and estate to the extent of such payments for the debts so due to the United States, or for so much thereof as may remain due and unpaid. (U. S. C. Title 31, Sec. 192.)

No. 8176

IN THE

United States Circuit Court of Appeals
For the Ninth Circuit

Newton H. Neustadter, Josephine D. Neustadter, Florence N. Stettheimer, James
D. Hart and Ellen K. Hart,

Appellants,

vs.

United States of America,

Appellee.

APPELLANTS' REPLY BRIEF.

Adolphus E. Graupner,
Balfour Building, San Francisco,
Attorney for Appellants.

FILED

OCT 17 1936

PAUL P. O'BRIEN,
CLERK

Pernau-Walsh Printing Co., San Francisco

Subject Index

Table of Authorities Cited

Statutes and Rules

No. 8176

NEWTON H. NEUSTADTER, JOSEPHINE D. NEU-
STADTER, FLORENCE N. STETTHEIMER, JAMES
D. HART and ELLEN K. HART,

Appellants,

vs.

UNITED STATES OF AMERICA,

Appellee.

APPELLANTS' REPLY BRIEF.

PRELIMINARY STATEMENT.

The questions which appellee presents for consideration
(Brief p. 2) attempt to restrict the issues raised by appellants. Appellee seeks to ignore certain fatal defects in its
case and to subordinate other important points in effort
to escape from its dilemma.

Appellee does not present a statement of facts (Brief
p. 2) but a composite of facts and conclusions which are
confusing. Appellants presented a statement of the
material facts in their opening brief (pp. 2-5) and, for
that reason, will not cumber this brief by restating them.
Appellee's conclusions will be answered in argument.

REPLY ARGUMENT.

We believe that failure of proof on the part of appellee is the first issue. Appellee has sought to minimize the effect of the weakness of its proof by placing that issue in fourth and last place in its argument. In our reply, we restore the question to first place because we believe that issue alone warrants this court in ordering dismissal or entry of judgment for appellants.

I. APPELLEE FAILED TO SUSTAIN ITS BURDEN OF PROOF AND ITS CAUSE MUST FAIL.

Appellee has not denied or attempted to controvert appellants' position that "the full burden of proof rested on appellee." (Opening Brief p. 7.) It only attempts to argue that it sustained that burden. Therefore, we will respond to appellee on each item in the order in which it presents its contentions.

1. Appellee failed to prove that a tax liability existed or was due from anyone.

To controvert our assertion appellee rests upon four items which it calls proof (Appellee's Brief pp. 25-27), viz:

(a) That the "Assessment Certificate" (Ex. 4, R. 26) shows the tax has not been paid;

(b) That the trial court found that "No part of said deficiency in tax, and no part of the interest thereon has been paid";

(c) That appellants' answer contains admissions equivalent to an admission of non-payment upon which the above stated finding was based; and

(d) That appellants have referred to an "assessment" in their answers and, *ergo ad absurdum,* they have thereby admitted that the tax (?) was not paid.

(a) The Assessment Certificate is proof of nothing more than that the Commissioner attempted to assess.

Record page 46 shows that Exhibit 4 was introduced under the following circumstances:

"Complainant offered in evidence a certified copy of a portion of a miscellaneous tax-estate-assessment certificate signed by the Commissioner of Internal Revenue on September 27, 1929."

The certified copy was admitted in evidence without explanation of its purpose or attempt to enlarge its evidentiary effect. Therefore, there could be no presumption that it was offered for any other purpose than to prove that *the Commissioner* had taken steps to attempt an assessment.

Exhibit 4 was signed September 27, 1929, nearly a month before the alleged attempt to collect (R. 7) was made. The fact that the spaces on the certificate form entitled "Old Balance" and "Credit" are blank proves nothing more than that on *September 27, 1929,* there was no overdue unpaid tax and no overpayment of tax. It is appellee's position that the alleged assessment was based on the determination of a deficiency by the Board of Tax Appeals. If that be true, which we admit only for argument, then Exhibit 4 is definitely linked to the deficiency notice in evidence (Ex. A, R. 42) which definitely shows (R. 43) that there was no unpaid "Old Balance" to go to assessment. Nowhere in the record is there any indication of an overpayment of tax to be given as a "Credit" against the deficiency claimed by the Commissioner. Therefore, there was nothing to be inserted under the two headings left blank in Exhibit 4.

Exhibit 4 does not indicate from its context that the blank spaces were to be utilized in any way after its execution. There is absolutely no evidence to support any presumption by this court that Exhibit 4 was intended to be anything else than what it purports to be—"assessment certificate". There is no evidence and appellee did not seek to introduce any proof that Exhibit 4, in addition to being an "assessment certificate" was an accounting record. In view of this lack of proof and the known fact that the collection of taxes and accounting therefor is the duty of *the Collector of Internal Revenue,* this court may not presume that Exhibit 4 is evidence of nonpayment, as appellee contends.

(b) The finding that "no part of said deficiency in tax" has been paid is not proof.

Appellee seeks to utilize the challenged findings of the trial court as proof of nonpayment. The court found (R. 30):

> "No part of said deficiency in tax, and no part of the interest thereon has been paid."

To such finding appellants excepted. (R. 55, 56.) Such exception is here under attack on appeal. Being under exception and on appeal it is not such proof as may be considered by this court to sustain appellee's argument. Particularly when appellee admits (Brief p. 26) that such finding is based on the pleadings to be considered in the following subdivisions ((c) and (d)) of this part of our argument.

Appellee argues (Brief p. 27), that, because the trial court made the above quoted finding, this court may not review the truth of the finding on this appeal and cites *McCaughn v. Real Estate Co.*, 297 U. S. 606.

That case was one at law, where a jury was waived and the court rendered a general verdict. The plaintiff's exceptions there "raised no question save the one at law, whether the court's verdict was wholly without evidence to support it." The decision of that case creates no rule to govern this case.

In this case appellants specifically excepted to the findings of fact (R. 54-56), as well as the conclusions of law, as being contrary to the proofs. In equity cases the appellate court considers the whole case, *both fact and law.* Appeals in equity are trials *de novo.*

> *Boynton v. Moffat Tunnel Imp. Co.*, (C. C. A. 10)
> 57 Fed. (2d) 772, 777, with cases there cited,
> Cert. Den. 287 U. S. 620;
> *Presidio Mining Co. v. Overton*, (C. C. A. 9) 270
> Fed. 388, 390, Cert. Den. 256 U. S. 694.

(c) **There is no admission in any of appellants' pleadings that any tax was due from or not paid by them.**

Appellee contends (Brief p. 26) that its allegation that "no part of said tax or interest has been paid; that there is now due and outstanding an additional estate tax in the sum of $12,012.99, together with interest thereon", is admitted by the portion of appellants' answer quoted by appellee. Please note that appellee does not claim and the record clearly discloses that no direct effort was made to prove the allegation quoted above.

By reference to the quotation on page 26 of appellee's brief or to paragraph XIII of appellants' amended answer (R. 17), the court will see that appellants denied the above quoted allegation of appellee's complaint. Therefore, the question resolves itself into the following: After denial of appellee's allegation of nonpayment, may appellants' affirmative allegation, which made no mention of payment or nonpayment, be considered as an admission when no attempt was made to prove the allegation and appellee never admitted the truth of the allegation? We respectfully submit the answer must be "No."

Before discusing this question, we desire to call the attention of the court to the statement of appellee's counsel on resting its case. After introduction of Exhibit 4 (supra) appellee's counsel stated in substance "that the Government would rely upon all admissions of defendants in their amended answer and in their amendments to the amended answer to allegations of fact in the bill of complaint as being a part of proofs on behalf of complainant" and then stated "The Government rests." (R. 47.)

There was no admission of the truth of any of the quoted affirmative allegations contained in appellants' pleadings. Nor, was there any specific mention of what appellee's counsel considered as admissions of fact. Appellants, after denial of their motion to dismiss and their motion for judgment (R. 47-50), offered evidence on but one point, i. e., the distribution of the estate before the mailing of the deficiency notice on record. (R. 51.) Appellants then rested and no rebuttal was offered by appellee. (R. 52.) Appellants were not required to prove what appellee had failed to prove.

The position of appellee entirely ignores the Rules of Practice in Equity, particularly Section 31 thereof, which in part reads:

> "Unless the answer assert a set-off or counter-claim, no *reply shall be required* without special order of the court or judge; but *the cause shall be deemed at issue* upon the filing of the answer, and *any new or affirmative matter therein shall be deemed to be denied by the plaintiff.*" * * * (Italics ours.)

Under this rule, there being no allegation of "set-off or counterclaim," the allegations in appellants' pleadings were "deemed to be denied" by appellee when the cause went to trial. As appellee did not specifically or generally admit the truth of appellants' "new or affirmative matter" and as appellants did not attempt to prove those affirmative allegations which appellee seeks to distort into admissions, its reliance on such allegations as proof completely fails. Neither the rules of equity practice nor those of ethics will permit appellee, *after a suit has been tried and submitted,* to claim as admissions those affirmative allegations of appellants' pleadings which were "deemed to be denied" and never specifically admitted during the trial.

If the portion of the appellants' amended answer quoted by appellee (Brief p. 26) be relied upon as a confession under equity rule 30, we then call attention to the fact that nowhere do appellants admit or confess the regularity or legality of the processes upon which appellee depends. "A pretended and unauthorized assessment" does not entitle appellee to relief. "A form of notice and demand for payment" "made upon one of the asserted executors under said pretended and unauthorized assessment'' is not a confession of a legal assessment and demand. The assertion ''that said Collector made no further attempt toward the collection of said alleged deficiency'' is not a confession of non-payment of the tax liability claimed by appellee, particularly when no proofs thereon were offered by either party. If the quoted appellants' allegations (Appellee's Brief, p. 26) were to be considered as admissions or confessions properly accepted by appellee, then ''a pretended and unauthorized assessment'' must be admitted by appellee. Such an admission entitled appellee to no relief and entitled appellants to decree in their favor.

(d) Appellants' reference to an assessment in their answers is neither an admission of the validity of any assessment nor a confession that any tax was not paid.

Appellee contends that there is a ''presumption of legality attaching to the acts of public officers,'' and, therefore, ''it must be presumed in the absence of denial that the tax has not been paid.'' (Brief p. 27.) This contention is based upon what appellee classes as admissions in paragraph XIII of appellants' answer. (R. 17.)

Paragraph XII of the bill of complaint (R. 7) is the paragraph wherein appellee alleges assessment ''duly and regularly'' made and ''that no part of said tax or interest has been paid.'' The opening of paragraph XIII of appellants' amended answer denies ''the allegations contained in paragraph XII of the Bill of Complaint.'' This is a denial *in toto* of appellee's allegations, and we cannot see how it can argue, as it does, that there was an ''absence of denial.''

Appellee's specious argument to create presumptions from what it asserts to be admissions is made the more difficult to understand when the remainder of paragraph XIII, which appellee did not quote, is read (R. 18):

"Defendants further allege that said *pretended assessment* was addressed to a non-existent person and one which had not been a person addressed in the above mentioned *purported deficiency letter* and had not been made a party to the above mentioned proceeding before said United States Board of Tax Appeals." (Italics supplied.)

Reading the foregoing, particularly with reference to paragraph XII (R. 17) of appellants' amended answer, makes it apparent that appellants took the position that the whole proceeding was beyond the jurisdiction of the Board and the assessment was null and void. If appellee accepts appellants' allegations as admissions of fact, it confesses the irregularity and illegality of the decision and assessment upon which it relies. If it so confesses, it has no right to claim relief.

We submit that all of appellee's argument fails to show that there is any proof that the alleged "tax liability" was not paid. As appellee has not sought to overcome the rule presented by appellants (Brief pp. 8-10) that "there must be an acknowledged debt proven" in order to obtain relief in equity, we must assume that it recognizes that rule. The rule being recognized and the proof having failed, appellants are entitled to judgment.

2. **The failure to prove a legal assessment is fatal to appellee's plea for judgment.**

Without proof of a valid and legal assessment appellee's cause fails, because, under Section 1109 (a) (1) of the Revenue Act of 1926, appellee was barred from bringing this suit "after the expiration of five years after" the estate tax became due. The five years expired February 13, 1929, while this suit was filed October 6, 1933. (See: Brief for Appellants, pp. 11-34 for enlarged argument and authorities.)

——————

II. APPELLEE'S SUIT IS NOT SANCTIONED BY ANY APPLICABLE STATUTE.

This part of our argument is in response to part I of appellee's argument. (Brief pp. 7-20.) Again we find that appellee has shifted its position. If the findings of the trial court are as *sacro-sanct* and binding as appellee elsewhere in its brief contends, then its argument in part I of its brief is immaterial and inapplicable. This, because the trial court found that the proceedings had before the Board of Tax Appeals were under "a 60-day letter (as required by Section 316 of the 1926 Revenue Act)." If that finding is beyond the power of this court "to review on appeal" as appellee has argued (Brief pp. 26, 28), then appellee by reverting to Section 318 (a) has argued itself into a position wherein it has no case.

In hope that appellee will not again shift its position, conceding only for argument that it is privileged to play the part of Janus, we will reply to its now contentions. To sustain appellee's argument, this court must ignore the law of the State of California terminating the representative capacity of executors. Also, it must abandon the rule approved by the Supreme Court and recognized by this court: "that the courts of the United States, when exercising jurisdiction over executors and administrators of the estates of decedents within a state, are administering the laws of that state, and are bound by the same rules which govern the local tribunals."

We call attention of the court to the fact that appellee has not disputed the following determined legal principles which appellants set forth in their opening brief, viz:

(a) The decision of the Board of Tax Appeals in *Neustadter v. Commissioner* is not *res adjudicata* as to appellants.

(b) Said decision of said Board is herein subject to collateral attack.

(c) The law governing the release of property of an estate from administration and the termination of the representative capacity of executors is that of the state of the decedent's *domicil* and *situs* of probate.

(d) The administration of an estate in California is terminated for all purposes by entry of the decree of final distribution and the distribution of the estate. The representative capacity of executors ends with distribution of the estate and they can neither sue or be sued as representatives of the estate.

The foregoing settled principles of law have been presented at length in the Brief for Appellants (pp. 24-34, 46-52.) Their correctness is not disputed by appellee and we will not here present further argument thereon.

1. Appellee's suit is not in accordance with either law or equity.

Appellee's argument on pages 7 to 10 of its brief is predicated upon a theory which completely ignores the above stated principles. *If* the deficiency notice under Section 318 of the 1926 Act had been mailed to the executors of the estate of David Neustadter, deceased, before the estate had been entirely distributed it would have been effective because the executors would have retained representative capacity. Or, *if* the deficiency notice had been addressed to the appellants herein after distribution it would have been effective because Section 303 (a) of the Revenue Act includes "any person in actual or constructive possession of any property of the decedent" within the meaning of executor. As these "ifs" were not met, and because the deficiency letter was mailed to *functus officio* executors who had distributed the entire estate, appellee's contentions fail.

We do not dispute that, *if* the pretended assessment had been achieved in a legal manner as the result of a legal determination by the Commissioner of Internal Revenue and the Board of Tax Appeals, the statute of limitations would be as appellee represents.

We contend, however, that the deficiency notice was a worthless scrap of paper when addressed to *functus officio* executors; that the Board of Tax Appeals was without any jurisdiction to entertain the proceedings on the petition filed or to render any other decision than one of dismissal for want of jurisdiction; that, when the Board entered a decision, it was void for want of jurisdiction; that such decision did not warrant any assessment against anyone; that, when the Commissioner attempted to assess, his certificate of assessment was void for all purposes, and that the mistaken deficiency notice, the void decision of the Board, and the void assessment of the Commissioner could neither toll the statute of limitations nor produce such an assessment as would permit appellee to sue appellants within six years from the date of such pretended and void assessment. These contentions have been argued *in extenso* in our opening brief (pp. 11-34) and, as appellee has sought to evade rather than controvert the authorities there presented by us, we will not indulge in other citations.

Appellee seeks to have this court validate the illegal actions of its responsible servant, the Commissioner, and to ignore his mistakes. We respectfully submit that equity was never intended for such a purpose. *If illegal acts of administrative officers are to be given the same effect as legal acts, then equity and protection of the law pass into the abyss as far as citizens are concerned.*

2. The Executors were liable at law and appellee had a remedy at law when this suit was filed.

Apparently in defense against our assertion that appellee was not entitled to equitable relief because: "It failed to prove that it was without a plain, speedy and adequate remedy at law" (Brief for Appellants, pp. 11, 43-45), appellee argues that: "The executors were not liable under Section 3467 of the Revised Statutes." (Brief p. 11.) Appellee cites no authorities to sustain this statement but argues: "under authority of Section 407 of the Revenue Act of 1921, the executors gave the Commissioner notice in the year 1924 to determine and assess immediately any outstanding estate tax liability against

the estate. This relieved them of any personal liability."
This is the assertion of another inconsistent and contrary
position by the Government.

When the proceeding of *Neustadter v. Commissioner,*
was on hearing before the Board of Tax Appeals the
petitioners therein contended that they had been released
from personal liability because they had given the very
notice to which appellee refers in the above quoted portion
of its argument. There *the government contended that the*
executors had not been discharged from personal liability
and the opinion states: "Respondent asserts that petitioners have not complied with the above sections and
for that reason these provisions" (Sections 407 and 313)
"have no application." (15 B. T. A. 848, Appendix to
Brief for Appellants XVIII.)

The foregoing quotation shows that appellee had one
interpretation for one phase of its tax search and ad-
vances another for a different phase. Consistency in the
interpretation of statutes is of no moment to appellee.

Appellee's quotation from Section 407 of the Revenue
Act of 1921 (Brief pp. 11, 12) is not complete. Where it
inserts stars in the quotation, it omits the following
statutory language:

"and" (the executor) "shall be entitled to receive
a receipt or writing showing such discharge." (Italics
supplied.)

It was because the Commissioner claimed that the estate
tax return was not complete and that he *did not* issue
discharge in writing to the executors, that the Government contended before the Board of Tax Appeals on

trial of *Neustadter v. Commissioner* that the petitioners therein had not been discharged from personal liability.

As appellee must and does rely upon the invalid decision of said Board to validate the present suit, it must be bound by the position taken by it before that Board in its attempt to validate that decision. As one of its defenses there was that the executors had not been discharged from their personal liability, it came before the trial court in this suit with the burden of proving that before the filing of this suit that the executors had been discharged. Appellee failed to meet this burden at the trial, so that the trial court assumed jurisdiction without proof that appellee was without a plain, speedy and adequate remedy at law. The record of the proceedings of the Board of Tax Appeals was in evidence and showed that appellee had not considered that such remedy at law had been erased. Until it was erased appellee was not entitled to relief in equity. Appellee cannot validate the decision of the Board by here changing the position that it took before that tribunal.

We call the attention of the court to the fact that appellee does not challenge the adequacy of the right to a remedy at law under R. S. Section 3467. It only seeks to evade the applicability of that section to this suit.

III. THE PETITIONERS BEFORE THE BOARD OF TAX APPEALS IN NEUDSTADTER v. COMMISSIONER WERE NOT REPRESENTATIVES OF EITHER THE DEFUNCT ESTATE OR THE APPELLANTS HEREIN.

We have never contended that release of an executor from personal liability under Section 407 of the 1921 Act of itself operated to release him from his representative capacity. Only distribution of the estate could effect that. So appellee's citation of *Rodenbaugh v. U. S.*, 25 Fed. (2d) 13, has no application to this suit. We contend that *distribution of an estate under a decree of final distribution removes the executor from all representative capacity,* and that, when the deficiency letter herein involved was mailed, the persons named therein had been removed from their representative capacity and that they could not confer, nor could the Board of Tax Appeals assume, any jurisdiction to determine any liability whatever against them in such capacity. (See authorities cited and argument in Brief for Appellants, pp. 26-32.)

Appellee has not attempted to controvert nor to cite any authorities to dispute the principles of law advanced by appellants in behalf of their above stated position. We believe our position to be beyond legal dispute and to be one which this court must sustain. Appellee attempts to show by rather disingenuous analysis of *Hurlburd v. Commissioner*, 296 U. S. 300, 56 S. Ct. 197, and *Lindley v. U. S.*, 59 Fed. (2d) 336 (Brief pp. 15-18), that those two cases do not present a principle of law applicable to this suit because the facts differ. However, this court has but to read the two decisions to determine that both of them sustain our contention that the termination of representative capacity of executors depends on the law of the state of domicile and probate of the estate of the decedent, and that *Lindley v. U. S.* (supra) sustains our contention that under the law of California (the State within which David Neustadter was domiciled and his estate probated) the representative capacity of the executors ended when they distributed the estate.

See:

> *Fruler v. Helvering,* 291 U. S. 35, 45; 54 S. Ct. 308, 312;
>
> *Commissioner v. Blair,* 83 Fed. (2d) 655.

Appellee cites *Rosenberg v. McLaughlin,* 66 Fed. (2d) 271. Whatever may have been the similarity of facts between that suit and this, the principles of law and equity therein involved differed from those in this suit in all but one particular, viz.: that the ten-year lien created by Section 409 of the Revenue Act of 1921 took effect at the time of death. We have accepted the decision on that point in this case and it is to the detriment of the cause of appellee. In that case the legality of the decision of the Board of Tax Appeals and of the resulting assessment were not challenged, were not before this court for consideration, and were not passed upon in the decision, so that the decision is of no force in disputing our position in this case.

IV. THE DISTRICT COURT AND THIS COURT HAVE JURISDICTION TO INQUIRE INTO THE PROCEEDINGS HAD BEFORE THE BOARD OF TAX APPEALS.

The arguments of appellee are in such disarray that they are difficult to discuss in the order of their presentation and with certainty as to their intent. On page 13 of its brief, appellee cites *Old Colony Trust Company v.*

Commissioner, 279 U. S. 716; *Green v. McLaughlin,* 55 Fed. (2d) 423; *Banker's Reserve Life Co. v. U. S.,* 44 Fed. (2d) 1000, and *Bindley v. Heiner,* 38 Fed. (2d) 489. These cases apparently are cited to support a contention that because the petitioners in *Neustadter v. Commissioner* did not appeal to this court from the decision of the Board of Tax Appeals that decision is binding on everyone directly or indirectly affected thereby, whether they were parties or not parties to the proceedings.

The citation of the above named cases appears to be a deliberate attempt to mislead the court. All that such cases decide and all that Section 1001 (a) of the Revenue Act of 1926 contemplates is this: *Where the party before the Board* fails to appeal and the decision of the Board becomes final, such party may not thereafter maintain a suit or action in the District Court to in any way challenge such decision. We do not dispute such ruling. Such a condition of affairs was not before the District Court in this case nor is it brought before this court on the appeal.

As we carefully pointed out in our opening brief appellants were not parties to the proceedings before the Board and could not in any way have become parties to make the decision of the Board binding on them or to give them right to appeal to this court from the decision of the Board.

If this court were to sustain appellee's position on this point, it would thereby establish a rule that would deprive all persons who were not made parties to a proceeding before the Board of Tax Appeals of their right to a day in court. It would enable appellee, through its servants, to adopt illegal or mistaken methods of asserting tax liability and thus bind people, who were not liable and not parties, to undisputable liability by decisions of the Board which would be illegal and void. Appellee's position on this point is convincing of the truth of appellants' assertion that appellee does not come into equity with clean hands and that it seeks equity without being willing to do equity. (Brief p. 34.)

Appellee's argument in no way overcomes or controverts the arguments and authorities of appellants to the effect that the decision of the Board of Tax Appeals in controversy is not *res adjudicata* as to appellants and is subject to collateral attack and impeachment in this suit. (Brief for Appellants pp. 24-26.)

V. THE UNITED STATES MAY PURSUE ONLY THOSE REMEDIES WHICH WERE OPEN TO IT UNDER LAW OR THE RULES OF EQUITY.

Under Point II of its brief (pp. 20-24) appellee presents a confused and confusing argument which seems to rest upon the claim that the Government is not bound by any limitation, statute, rule of equity, or decision of court. As we can best disassemble the confusion of its arguments, we will discuss appellee's points under separate headings:

1. How far is the Government bound by Section 409 of the Revenue Act of 1921?

Appellants admit that while the ten-year lien created by Section 409 of the 1921 Act was in force and until February 13, 1933, appellee had the right to elect between the enforcement of that lien by distraint under a lawful assessment or by establishing the lien, without assessment, by a suit in equity to declare the owners of the property to be equitable trustees for the Government and thereupon obtain a judgment and execution thereon to collect the amount adjudged due.

However, the contention made in our opening brief (pp. 33-34, 36-40) is that *after the lapse of the ten-year period* the Government having failed to distrain or sue, *the Government is barred by limitation* from enforcement of any tax liability against the owners of the distributed property and is estopped from seeking equity to restore the trust or lien which it allowed to expire.

Appellee cites *Blacklock v. U. S.,* 208 U. S., 75, 28 S. Ct. 228 (Brief p. 21) to sustain its point. That case involves no question concerning a period of limitation. Apparently neither of the Government's optional remedies was barred by limitation and it had the right of election which we admitted above. Appellee thus completely evades the issues of limitation and estoppel which appellants assert, cites no authority to controvert appellants' position, and thereby admits the soundness of their contentions.

2. The Government was barred from bringing proceedings in this suit without assessment.

In citing *U. S. v. Ayer,* 12 Fed. (2d) 194 (Brief p. 21), appellee apparently seeks to overcome our plea of the bar of limitation by broadly stating that "the United States may resort to court proceedings for collection of an estate tax without relying on an assessment." Of course it may. We have never disputed that fact. But, it does not have until eternity to so resort.

With respect to the facts involved in this suit the United States had until February 13, 1929, to bring suit against appellants without assessment under Section 1109 (a) (1) of the Revenue Act of 1926. After that date it was barred by that same section from bringing a suit without assessment or one based on a void assessment. Appellee brought no suit within that period and the citation of *U. S. v. Ayer*, supra, is an attempt to mislead this court.

3. Revised Statutes, Section 3467, rendered the executors liable.

Appellee reverts to further consideration of Section 3467 of Revised Statutes in attempt to avert its defeat by the applicability of that section. This is its second attempt to escape from its failure to prove its lack of a remedy at law in order to come within the jurisdiction of equity.

Appellee apparently contends that, because the executors did not know that an additional deficiency in tax was to be claimed when they distributed the estate, they could not be held liable under Section 3467. (31 U. S. C. sec. 192.)

U. S. v. Fisher, 2 Cranch 358, is cited in support. That case interprets the Bankrupt Law of 4th April, 1800, and it in no way supports appellee's contention. Following this citation, appellee states (Brief pp. 22):

> "It is obvious that a judgment against the executors in their representative capacity would have been worthless. It is likewise obvious that a judgment against the estate would have been worthless."

After making these statements, appellee should confess its errors and move this court to enter decree in favor of appellants. These admissions directly support appellants' contention that the decision of the Board of Tax Appeals in *Neustadter v. Commissioner* was worthless—void—and that the assessment (the execution) based thereon was worthless and void.

Appellee cites *Hatch v. Morosco Holding Co.*, 50 Fed. (2d) 138 and *Baumgartner v. Commissioner*, 51 Fed. (2d) 472, apparently to show the generally accepted rule that, where a judgment at law would be worthless, resort to equity may be had. Appellee omits the relevant factor, that, to sustain equity jurisdiction under Section 267 of the Judicial Code, appellee was required to first prove that a judgment against the former executors under Revised Statutes, Section 3467 (31 U. S. C. sec. 192) was worthless. It did not make such proof and it is on failure of such proof that appellants assert that the trial court was without jurisdiction in equity.

Baumgartner v. Commissioner (supra) asserts principles of law which, while not relevant to the particular point under immediate discussion, sustain appellants' contention that the ten-year lien provided by Section 409 of the Revenue Act of 1921 creates an equitable trust. This court held in that case (p. 473) that such "lien may be asserted in equity" and that the distributee of the estate "held the property in trust." Therefore, when the period of lien and trust created by Section 409 expired by limitation, the Government was without right to attempt to re-create the lien or the trust by tardy resort to equity. (See Brief for Appellants, pp. 33-34, 36-40.)

Returning to reply of appellee's Point II (Brief p. 22) we will consider its citation of *United States v. Cruick-*

shank, 48 Fed. (2d) 352, in its application to the facts of this case. In that case the Government sued the executors in their individual as well as in their representative capacity, and joined the legal trustee of the estate as a party, (p. 353)—*something it did not do in this suit.* The decision opens with a definite premise of law which fully supports appellants' position in this case (p. 354):

> "*As a general proposition, it cannot be disputed that an executor who distributes an estate without payment of the estate tax becomes personally liable for the tax.*" * * * "It is sufficient to cite Section 3467 of the Revised Statutes. It is likewise clear that the tax is a lien for ten years upon the gross estate."

The foregoing is a direct support of appellants' position and adverse to appellee. The decision then proceeds to state:

> "It is also clear that the statute of limitations on collection of the tax by proceedings in court had not run when this suit was commenced."

This is contrary to the state of facts in this case. Here the *ten-year period had run when this suit was filed.*

The conclusions of the court in the above cited case are not as appellee interprets them. The legal trustee, which the court held liable, was created by the will of the decedent to carry out the provisions of the will and the estate was distributed to the trustee for that purpose. In its bill of complaint, the government did not ask for relief against the trustee beyond the value of the assets held by it, and, in granting decree, the court held that the lien was to be satisfied from the estate assets in the hands of the legal trustee and, if they were inadequate, the executor in his personal capacity would be liable for all the balance. Certainly this decision is no support to appellee. The attempt to follow the assets of the estate through equity was before the expiration of the limit of the ten-year lien, *in this case the attempt was made after the period of limitation had expired.*

U. S. v. Cruickshank (supra), merely declares the established rule that a transferee cannot be held liable beyond the value of the assets received by him, while the personal liability of the former executor is limited only by the amount of the charge against him.

The remainder of appellee's arguments under Point II are equally inapplicable, because they entirely ignore the bar of limitations. Appellants have fully discussed the operative provisions of limitation in their opening brief. Appellee has not overcome, or even controverted them— its reply is one of evasion only.

VI. THE DECREE OF THE TRIAL COURT IS IN VIOLATION OF THE FUNDAMENTAL PRINCIPLES OF LAW.

Under Point III of its argument (Brief p. 25), appellee blandly ignores the contentions of appellants (Brief pp. 46-53) and without counter citations disposes of the authorities cited by disclaiming their merit. Thus appellee's counsel seek to sweep aside decisions of the Supreme Court of the United States, of this and other Federal courts, and of the Supreme Court of the State of California. Thus it places its *ipse dixit* beyond the rule of *stare decisis.*

Appellee suavely assures us that it has "shown that all steps looking towards assessment and collection of the tax in controversy were valid and were timely taken." (Sic.) Five counsel for appellee thus readily dispose of constitutional questions.

The Federal Constitution declares that no person shall "be deprived of life, liberty, or property, without due process of law." We reiterate that what the Commissioner of Internal Revenue sought to do and appellee here seeks to do violates that prohibition.

The Supreme Court of the United States declared in *Security Trust Co. v. Black River Nat'l Bank*, 187 U. S. 211:

> "Another principle, equally well settled, is that the courts of the United States, *in enforcing claims against executors* or administrators of a decedent's estate, *are administering the laws of the state of domicil*, and are bound by the same rules that govern the local tribunals." (Italics supplied.)
>
> 23 St. Ct. 52, 58.

This was the declared rule of law in 1902, before it was reiterated on December 9, 1935 in *Hurlburd v. Commissioner*, 296 U. S. 300. Appellee's five counsel do not challenge the rule laid down above—they simply ignore it. As ordinary citizens we still have enough faith to believe the Supreme Court to be the final arbiter of the applicability of the rules of law, and hence contend:

> (a) That the Commissioner, who must be presumed to know the law, violated the foregoing rule when he addressed a deficiency notice to the former executors of the estate of David Neustadter, deceased,

when the estate had been distributed and, under California law, the former executors were relieved of all representative capacity.

> *St. Mary's Hospital v. Perry,* 152 Cal. 384, 387, 92
>   Pac. 864, 865;
>
> *Lindley v. U. S.,* (C. C. A. 9) 59 Fed. (2d) 336, 338.

(b) That the Board of Tax Appeals was without jurisdiction over either the estate or the former executors, when the appeal came before it and when its jurisdiction was challenged on the ground that it was without jurisdiction and the evidence before it included the decree of final distribution of a court of competent jurisdiction, said Board was powerless to do other than dismiss the proceeding for want of jurisdiction.

> *Herbert Brush Mfg. Co. v. Commissioner,* 22 B. T.
>   A. 646;
>
> *Standifer Construction Corp. v. Commissioner,* (C.
>   C. A. 9) 78 Fed. (2d) 285, 286.

(c) That because of the foregoing, the decision of said Board in the proceeding of *Neustadter v. Commissioner,* 15 B. T. A. 839, was void.

> *Hirsch Distilling Co. v. Commissioner,* 14 B. T. A.
>   1073, 1078.

(d) That consequently the attempt of the Commissioner to assess was a nullity and the assessment certificate (Ex. 4) in evidence is void and, moreover, that such assessment certificate could have no effect because not made against a person chargeable with any tax when it was made. (Brief for Appellants, pp. 20-23.)

(e) That any attempt by the Commissioner, appellee or the trial court to utilize such a void assessment to' toll the statute of limitations in order to hold appellants liable for an alleged tax is an attempt to deprive them of their property without due process.

(f) That, after appellants' plea of bar of the statute of limitations (R. p. 20), the trial court violated said constitutional provision on attempting to take jurisdiction to decree against appellants upon the evidence of such illegal and void acts.

Appellee did not controvert the foregoing principles which appellants presented in their opening brief, and we submit that it is not entitled to the relief which the trial court erroneously gave it.

CONCLUSION.

In concluding our argument we desire to briefly present the failings of appellee's argument.

1. Appellee has failed to deny or controvert the following principles of law and equity submitted by appellants:

(a) The burden of proof rested on appellee. (Appellants' Brief p. 9.)

(b) Under the finding that Section 316 of the Revenue Act of 1926 was the basis for the decision of the Board of Tax Appeals (*Neustadter v. Commissioner*, 15 B. T. A. 839, Appendix to Appellants' Brief p. i) appellee has not denied that it is barred from relief as contended by appellants. (Appellants'

Brief pp. 13-16.) As it has not in any way excused or explained its imposition on the trial court to find Section 316 to be the applicable section, it has waived its right to claim that it is not barred by limitation and is estopped from asserting any right under Section 318.

(c) Appellee has not disputed or controverted the rule of law that an assessment made against a person not the owner of property chargeable with a tax is null and void. (Appellants' Brief pp. 19-23.) As the only evidence of an attempt at an assessment (Ex. 4, R. 46) is a purported certificate of assessment addressed to ''Neustadter, David, Est. of'' and, as appellee admits and the court found, that estate had been distributed long before attempt to assess was made, appellee has confessed its lack of right to a remedy.

(d) Appellee has not denied or attempted to controvert the fact that the decision of said Board is not *res adjudicata* as to appellants, or that said decision is subject to the collateral attack made by appellants. (See Appellants' Brief pp. 24-25.)

(e) Appellee has neither denied or controverted the rule that the distribution of an estate under decree of final distribution terminates the ''representative capacity'' of the executors. (See Appellants' Brief pp. 27-32.)

(f) Appellee has not denied or controverted the fact that the right to file the bill of complaint in this suit expired by limitation, under Section 409 of the Revenue Act of 1921, ten years after the death of

David Neustadter or on February 13, 1933. (See Appellants' Brief p. 33.)

(g) Appellee has in no way overcome the maxims of equity invoked by appellants (Brief pp. 34-46) by excusing or explaining the conduct of its responsible officers. Therefore, it rests under the charge of having sought equity with unclean hands and having slumbered on its rights.

(h) Appellee has evaded but not avoided the doctrine of estoppel advanced by appellants (Brief pp. 36-40) and by not controverting the principles of equity invoked by appellants has admitted their applicability.

2. Appellee has no right in equity and the trial court had no jurisdiction of the cause in equity, because:

(a) Appellee failed to prove any unpaid tax liability;

(b) It failed to prove any valid assessment against the estate of David Neustadter, deceased, which would bind appellants;

(c) It failed to prove any assessment based on any decision of the Board of Tax Appeals;

(d) It failed to prove that it was without a plain, speedy and adequate remedy at law;

(e) It failed to prove that appellants held any property subject to any lien for any tax; and

(f) It failed to prove any of the exceptions which would permit it to seek equitable relief under the prohibitions of Section 267 of the Judicial Code.

It is therefore respectfully submitted that the decree of the trial court should be reversed and this court should make its order directing dismissal of appellants or the entry of a decree in favor of appellants.

Dated, San Francisco,
 October 16, 1936.

ADOLPHUS E. GRAUPNER,
Attorney for Appellants.

No. 8179 8208

In the United States
Circuit Court of Appeals
For the Ninth Circuit.

10

JOHN F. MUYRES AND GEORGE J. MUYRES,

Appellants,

vs.

UNITED STATES OF AMERICA,

Appellee.

Transcript of Record.

Upon Appeal from the District Court of the United States for the
Southern District of California, Central Division.

FILED

NOV 4 – 1936

PAUL P. O'BRIEN,
CLERK

Parker, Stone & Baird Co., Law Printers, Los Angeles.

No.

In the United States
Circuit Court of Appeals
For the Ninth Circuit.

JOHN F. MUYRES AND GEORGE J. MUYRES,

Appellants,

vs.

UNITED STATES OF AMERICA,

Appellee.

Transcript of Record.

Upon Appeal from the District Court of the United States for the Southern District of California, Central Division.

Parker, Stone & Baird Co., Law Printers, Los Angeles.

INDEX.

[Clerk's Note: When deemed likely to be of an important nature, errors or doubtful matters appearing in the original record are printed literally in italics; and, likewise, cancelled matter appearing in the original record is printed and cancelled herein accordingly. When possible, an omission from the text is indicated by printing in italics the two words between which the omission seems to occur.]

PAGE

v.

Names and Addresses of Attorneys.

For Appellant John F. Muyres:

HARRY GRAHAM BALTER, Esq.,

Van Nuys Building,

Los Angeles, California.

L. A. BLOOM, Esq.,

124 West Fourth Street,

Los Angeles, California.

For Appellant George J. Muyres:

RUSSELL GRAHAM, Esq.,

Chapman Building,

Los Angeles, California.

For Appellee:

PEIRSON M. HALL, Esq.,
United States Attorney,

JOHN J. IRWIN, Esq.,
Assistant United States Attorney,

Federal Building,

Los Angeles, California.

DISTRICT COURT OF THE UNITED STATES FOR
THE SOUTHERN DISTRICT OF CALIFORNIA
CENTRAL DIVISION

—

UNITED STATES OF)
AMERICA,)
      vs.)   No. 12,619-C-Crim.
GEORGE J. MUYRES,)

STATEMENT OF DOCKET ENTRIES
UNDER RULE IV,

SUPREME COURT OF THE UNITED STATES

1. Indictment for violation of Sections 415 and 88, Title
   18, United States Code, December 11, 1935.

2. Defendant arraigned December 16, 1935.

3. Plea to indictment, Not Guilty, entered December 16,
   1935.

4. Trial by jury March 18, 19 and 20, 1936, and March
   24, 25 and 26, 1936.

5. Verdict of Guilty, March 26, 1936, 2nd count; Not
   Guilty 1st count.

6. Defendant sentenced to a United States Penitentiary
   to be designated by the Attorney General of the
   United States or such representative as he may authorize to act, for the term and period of two years
   on the second count of the indictment, and pay a
   fine of $1,000.00 on said second count and stand
   committed to said penitentiary until payment of fine.
   Sentence for non-payment of fine to begin and run
   consecutively with the penitentiary sentence of two
   years; April 7, 1936.

7. Notice of Appeal filed April 7, 1936.
   Date, April 9, 1936.

DISTRICT COURT OF THE UNITED STATES FOR
THE SOUTHERN DISTRICT OF CALIFORNIA
NORTHERN DIVISION

UNITED STATES OF)
AMERICA,)
)
vs.) No.12,619-(S)-C-Crim.
)
JOHN F. MUYRES,)

STATEMENT OF DOCKET ENTRIES
UNDER RULE IV,

SUPREME COURT OF THE UNITED STATES

1. Indictment for violation of Sections 415 and 88, Title 18, United States Code, filed December 11, 1935.

2. Defendant arraigned December 16, 1935.

3. Plea to indictment, Not Guilty, entered December 23, 1935.

4. Trial by jury March 18, 19, 20, 24, 25, 26, 1936.

5. Verdict of Guilty, March 26, 1936.

6. Defendant sentenced to a Federal Penitentiary, to be hereafter designated by the Attorney General of the United States, or such representative as he may authorize to act, for the term and period of five (5) years on the first count and two (2) years on the second count, consecutively, (total of 7 years), and to pay a fine of $1000.00 on the second count and stand committed to said penitentiary until paid; April 7, 1936.

7. Notice of Appeal filed April 13, 1936.

Date, April 15, 1936.

4

No. 12619. S.   Filed............................

Viol: Sections 415 and 88, Title 18, United States Code.

IN THE DISTRICT COURT OF THE UNITED STATES IN AND FOR THE SOUTHERN DISTRICT OF CALIFORNIA CENTRAL DIVISION

At a stated term of said court, begun and holden at the City of Los Angeles, County of Los Angeles, within and for the Central Division of the Southern District of California on the second Monday of September in the year of our Lord one thousand nine hundred thirty-five:

The grand jurors for the United States of America, impaneled and sworn in the Central Division of the Southern District of California, and inquiring for the Southern District of California, upon their oath present:

That

EDWARD HAROLD RYMAN,

           alias Edward Raymond,
           alias Edward Roberts,
           alias Edward Harold,
           alias F. Rost,

THOMAS BURKE RYAN, alias Don Thompson,
FRANKLIN DOLPH LE SIEUR,
KARL L. WOOLSEY, alias Ham Woolsey,
JOHN F. MUYRES,
GEORGE J. MUYRES, and
JOHN MURRAY CHENEY,

hereinafter called the defendants, whose full and true names are, and the full and true name of each of whom is, other than as herein stated, to the grand jurors unknown, each late of the Central Division of the Southern District of California, heretofore, to-wit: on or about the 22nd day of October, 1935, did knowingly, wilfully, unlawfully and feloniously transport and cause to be transported in interstate commerce from the State of Arizona, to Huntington Park, County of Los Angeles, State of California, and within the jurisdiction of the United States and of this Honorable Court, certain securities, of the value of more than Five Thousand Dollars ($5,000.00), to-wit: of the value of Forty-two Thousand Five Hundred Dollars ($42,500.00), to-wit:

HOME OWNERS LOAN CORPORATION BONDS

$5000.00 denomination – Serial   V-18693-C
$1000.00 denomination – Series B, 2-3/4%-
                         Serials M-312775-E
                                  M-264197-H
                                  M-172105-E
                                  M-172107-H
$ 500.00 denomination – Serial   X-132530-L
$ 100.00 denomination – Serials T-521315-E
                                  T-283400-L

GERMAN CENTRAL BANK BONDS FOR AGRICULTURE, 6% GOLD BONDS

$1000.00 denomination – Serials M3597
                                 M-3742 or M-37042
                                 M-37044
                                 M-37045
                                 M-37043

GERMAN INTERNATIONAL LOAN BONDS

$1000.00 denomination, Serials   C-65342
                                            C-65343
                                            C-65349

AUSTRIAN GOVERNMENT INTERNATIONAL LOAN 1930, SINKING FUND BONDS

$1000.00 denomination – Serials M6013 to M6019 inc.
                                            M6030
                                            M12958
                                            M12960
                                            M12962

KANSAS CITY POWER & LIGHT CO. BONDS

$1000.00 denomination – Serials CM3041
                                            CM3042
                                            CM3043

all of said securities being then and there the property of Nellie P. Covert, and having been theretofore stolen from the said Nellie P. Covert, the said defendants and each of them then and there well knowing said securities to have been stolen.

Contrary to the form of the statute in such case made and provided and against the peace and dignity of the United States of America.

SECOND COUNT.

And the grand jurors aforesaid, upon their oath aforesaid, do further present:

That EDWARD HAROLD RYMAN, alias Edward Raymond, alias Edward Roberts, alias Edward Harold, alias F. Rost, THOMAS BURKE RYAN, alias Don Thompson, FRANKLIN DOLPH LE SIEUR, KARL L. WOOLSEY, alias Ham Woolsey, JOHN F. MUYRES, GEORGE J. MUYRES, and JOHN MURRAY CHENEY, hereinafter called the defendants, whose full and true names are, and the full and true name of each of whom is, other than as herein stated, to the grand jurors unknown, each late of the Central Division of the Southern District of California, heretofore, to-wit: prior to the dates of the commission of the overt acts hereinafter set forth, and continuously thereafter to and including the date of finding and presentation of this indictment, did knowingly, wilfully, unlawfully, corruptly and feloniously conspire, combine, confederate, arrange and agree together and with each other, and with divers other persons whoses names are to the grand jurors unknown, to commit an offense against the United States of America and the laws thereof, the offense being to knowingly, wilfully, unlawfully and feloniously transport and cause to be transported in interstate commerce from the State of Arizona to the County of Los Angeles, California, certain securities of the value of more than Five Thousand Dollars ($5000.00), to-wit: those securities described in count one of this indictment, all of said securities being then and there the property of Nellie P. Covert, and having been theretofore stolen from the said Nellie P. Covert, as the defendants well knew;

And the grand jurors aforesaid, upon their oath aforesaid, do further charge and present that at the hereinafter stated times, in pursuance of, and in furtherance of, in execution of, and for the purpose of carrying out and to effect the object, design and purposes of said conspiracy, combination, confederation and agreement aforesaid, the hereinafter named defendants did commit the following overt acts at the hereinafter stated places:

1. That on or about the 22nd day of October, 1935, defendant EDWARD HAROLD RYMAN, alias Edward Raymond, alias Edward Roberts, alias Edward Harold, alias F. Rost, at Tucson, Arizona, stole from Nellie P. Covert the securities more particularly described in count one of this indictment;

2. That on or about the 23rd day of October, 1935, defendant EDWARD HAROLD RYMAN, alias Edward Raymond, alias Edward Roberts, alias Edward Harold, alias F. Rost, at Huntington Park, County of Los Angeles, state, division and district aforesaid, and within the jurisdiction of the United States and of this Honorable Court, received from the Railway Express Agency the securities more particularly described in count one of this indictment;

3. That on or about the 25th day of October, 1935, defendants met at the U. S. Hotel in the City of Los Angeles, County of Los Angeles, state, division and district aforesaid, and within the jurisdiction of the United States and of this Honorable Court;

4. That on or about the 26th day of October, 1935, defendants met at the U. S. Hotel in the City of Los An-

geles, County of Los Angeles, state, division and district aforesaid, and within the jurisdiction of the United States and of this Honorable Court;

5. That on or about the 26th day of October, 1935, defendant GEORGE J. MUYRES cashed interest coupons cut from said securities at the Figueroa and Adams Branch of the Security First National Bank of Los Angeles, Los Angeles, County of Los Angeles, state, division and district aforesaid, and within the jurisdiction of the United States and of this Honorable Court;

6. That on or about the 26th day of October, 1935, defendants JOHN F. MUYRES, KARL L. WOOLSEY, alias Ham Woolsey, EDWARD HAROLD RYMAN, alias Edward Raymond, alias Edward Roberts, alias Edward Harold, alias F. Rost, and GEORGE J. MUYRES divided the proceeds of said coupons, at Los Angeles, County of Los Angeles, state, division and district aforesaid, and within the jurisdiction of the United States and of this Honorable Court;

7. That on or about the 28th day of October, 1935, defendant GEORGE J. MUYRES met with defendant JOHN M. CHENEY at Los Angeles, County of Los Angeles, state, division and district aforesaid, and within the jurisdiction of the United States and of this Honorable Court, and gave him a list of the aforesaid securities;

8. That on or about the 29th day of October, 1935, defendants JOHN F. MUYRES and GEORGE J. MUYRES· met defendant JOHN MURRAY CHENEY at

Los Angeles, County of Los Angeles, state, division and district aforesaid, and within the jurisdiction of the United States and of this Honorable Court, and discussed sale of said securities;

9. That on or about the 30th day of October, 1935, defendant GEORGE J. MUYRES, at Los Angeles, County of Los Angeles, state, division and district aforesaid, and within the jurisdiction of the United States and of this Honorable Court, brought some of said stolen securities to defendant JOHN MURRAY CHENEY who sold four of said securities to E. F. HUTTON & CO., for about Seven Thousand Dollars ($7000.00);

10. That on or about the 1st day of November, 1935, defendant JOHN F. MUYRES met defendant GEORGE J. MUYRES at Los Angeles, County of Los Angeles, state, division and district aforesaid, and within the jurisdiction of the United States and of this Honorable Court, and defendant GEORGE J. MUYRES sold two of said stolen securities to the Figueroa and Adams Branch of the Security First National Bank of Los Angeles, for Eleven Hundred Dollars ($1100.00), and the defendant GEORGE J. MUYRES received Seventy Dollars ($70.00) of the said sale price;

11. That on or about the 9th day of November, 1935, defendant JOHN MURRAY CHENEY returned to defendant JOHN F. MUYRES at Los Angeles, County of Los Angeles, state, division and district aforesaid, and within the jurisdiction of the United States and of this

Honorable Court, three of said stolen securities of the value of about Three Thousand Dollars ($3,000.00), which said defendant JOHN MURRAY CHENEY was unable to sell to E. F. HUTTON & CO.

12. That on or about the 9th day of November, 1935, defendants JOHN F. MUYRES, KARL L. WOOLSEY, alias Ham Woolsey, and GEORGE J. MUYRES buried some of said stolen securities mentioned in overt act No. 11 above, in a field about 9/10 of a mile north of the intersection of Beverly Boulevard and San Gabriel Boulevard in Los Angeles, County, state, division and district aforesaid, and within the jurisdiction of the United States and of this Honorable Court;

Contrary to the form of the statute in such case made and provided and against the peace and dignity of the United States of America.

PEIRSON M. HALL,
United States Attorney,
Wm Fleet Palmer
Assistant United States Attorney.

A true bill.

Jno. O. Knight
Foreman.

Bail $10,000 –

[Endorsed]: Filed Dec. 11, 1935 R. S. Zimmerman, R. S. Zimmerman, Clerk

At a stated term, to wit: The September Term, A. D. 1935, of the District Court of the United States of America, within and for the Central Division of the Southern District of California, held at the court room thereof in the City of Los Angeles, on Monday the 16th day of December in the year of our Lord one thousand nine hundred and thirty-five.

PRESENT: THE HONORABLE Albert Lee Stephens District Judge.

United States of America,	)
Plaintiff,	)
vs.	) No. 12619-S Crim.
Karl L. Woolsey, Alias Ham Woolsey, et al.,	)
Defendants.	)

This case coming before the Court for the arraignment and plea of defendants Karl L. Woolsey, alias Ham Woolsey, and John F. Muyres and Geo. J. Muyres; J. J. Irwin and Hal Hughes, Assistant U. S. Attorneys, appearing for the Government; defendant Woolsey, being present in court with his attorney, John C. Lee, Esq., states his true name to be Karl L. Woolsey, and, upon being required to plead, enters his plea of not guilty, and this case as to defendant Woolsey is hereby continued to December 23, 1935, for setting for trial; defendant John F. Muyres, being present in court with his attorneys, L. A. Bloom and Chas. Ostrom, Esqs., states his true name to be John F. Muyres, and this case as to defendant John F. Muyres is hereby continued one week for entry of plea; defendant Geo. J. Muyres, being present in court with his attorney, Russell Graham, Esq., states his true name to be Geo. J. Muyres, and, upon being required to plead, enters his plea of not guilty, and this case is hereby continued to December 23, 1935, for setting for trial; after which,

John C. Lee, Esq., moves the court for reduction of bail of defendant Woolsey, which motion is denied without prejudice; following which,

Upon motion of Attorneys Graham and Bloom, it is ordered that the bonds of defendants John F. and Geo. J. Muyres are reduced to $5.000.00 each, the bond of defendant John F. Muyres to cover his leaving the District to go to Arizona and he is allowed to leave the jurisdiction of the Court.

At a stated term, to wit: The September Term, A. D. 1935, of the District Court of the United States of America, within and for the Central Division of the Southern District of California, held at the court room thereof in the City of Los Angeles, on Monday the 23rd day of December in the year of our Lord one thousand nine hundred and thirty-five.

PRESENT: THE HONORABLE Albert Lee Stephens District Judge.

United States of America,

Plaintiff,)

vs.) No. 12619-S Crim.

Karl L. Woolsey, et al.,)

Defendants.)

This case coming before the Court for entry of plea of defendant John F. Muyres, for setting for trial as to defendants Karl L. Woolsey and George J. Muyres, and for arraignment and plea of defendant John Murray Cheney; J. J. Irwin, Assistant U. S. Attorney, appearing for the Government; defendant John F. Muyres, being present in Court with his attorneys, L. A. Bloom and Chas. Ostrom, Esqs., upon being required to plead, enters his plea of Not Guilty, and this case is hereby continued

two weeks for setting for trial as to the said defendant
John F. Muyres; defendant Karl L. Woolsey being present
in court with his attorney, John C. Lee, Esq., and defendant George J. Muyres being present in Court with his
attorney, Russell Graham, Esq., this case is hereby continued two weeks for setting for trial as to the said defendants Karl L. Woolsey and George J. Muyres; and,
defendant John Murray Cheney, being present in court
with his attorney, Fenton Garfield, Esq., states his true
name to be as given in the indictment, and this case is
hereby continued one week for entry of plea as to defendant Cheney. At the request of L. A. Bloom, Esq., a
copy of the Indictment is delivered to him.

At a stated term, to wit: The February Term, A. D. 1936, of the District Court of the United States of America, within and for the Central Division of the Southern District of California, held at the court room thereof in the City of Los Angeles on Wednesday the 18th day of March in the year of our Lord one thousand nine hundred and thirty-six.

PRESENT: THE HONORABLE Geo. Cosgrave District Judge.

United States of America,   )
)
                  Plaintiff,   )
)
        vs.   )   No. 12619-S. Crim.
)
Edward Harold Ryman, et al.,   )
)
              Defendants.   )

This case coming before the court for pronouncement of sentence upon defendants Edward Harold Ryman and Karl L. Woolsey, and for trial of defendants John F. Muyres, George J. Muyres, John Murray Cheney and Thomas Burke Ryan; J. J. Irwin, Assistant U. S. Attorney, appearing for the Government; defendant Edward Harold Ryman being present without his attorney, D. G. Taylor, Esq.; defendants Karl L. Woolsey and Thomas Burke Ryan each appearing in propria persona; defendant John F. Muyres being present with his attorneys, L. A. Bloom and Chas. Ostrom; defendant George J. Muyres being present with his attorney, Russell Graham, Esq.; defendant John Murray Cheney being present without his attorney, Fenton Garfield, Esq.; and C. W. Johnson and A. Wahlberg, official stenographic reporters, being present and alternating as such,

Good cause appearing therefor, it is by the Court ordered that the case be transferred to Judge Cosgrave's Department for further proceedings, all parties consenting thereto; and,

Upon motion of J. J. Irwin, Esq., it is by the Court ordered that this case, as to defendant John Murray Cheney, be dismissed, and that sentence of Edward Harold Ryman and Karl L. Woolsey be continued to Monday, March 23, 1936; and thereupon it is by the Court ordered that a Jury be impanelled herein for the trial of defendants John F. Muyres, George J. Muyres and Thomas Burke Ryan; whereupon,

The following twelve names are drawn from the box at the hour of 10:15 o'clock a. m.: R. H. Jenkins, George W. Yates, Dewey R. Barber, Adolph M. Kast, James Smith, Sr., Alfred Y. Soule, Ernest K. Walker, Lyndon J. Stanley, Frederick D. Parker, Harold R. Hilton, Walter W. Norton and Jacob H. Leeds.

The twelve prospective jurors, now seated in the jury box, are examined for cause by the Court and by J. J. Irwin and Russell Graham, Esqs., and Walter W. Norton is excused by the Court for cause; whereupon, it is ordered that one more name be drawn from the jury box, and the name of Chauncey H. Dekker being thereupon drawn therefrom, the said prospective juror is examined for cause by the Court and by J. J. Irwin and Russell Graham, Esqs.,

Adolph M. Kast is now excused on the defendant's peremptory challenge; whereupon, it is ordered that one more name be drawn from the jury box, and the name of Walker Smith being thereupon drawn therefrom, the said prospective juror is examined for cause by the Court and by J. J. Irwin and Russell Graham, Esqs.,

Walker Smith is excused by the court on the plaintiff's peremptory challenge; whereupon, it is ordered that one more name be drawn from the jury box, and the name of Loren W. Babcock being thereupon drawn therefrom, the said prospective juror is examined for cause by the court and by J. J. Irwin and Russell Graham, Esqs.,

R. H. Jenkins is excused by the court on the defendants' peremptory challenge; whereupon, it is ordered that one more name be drawn from the jury box, and the name of Andrew I. Conlin being thereupon drawn therefrom, the said prospective juror is examined by the Court and by J. J. Irwin and Russell Graham, Esqs., respectively,

Loren W. Babcock is excused by the court on the plaintiff's peremptory challenge; whereupon, it is ordered that one more name be drawn from the jury box, the name of Harry S. Hargrave being thereupon drawn therefrom, and the said prospective juror being thereafter examined for cause by the Court and by J. J. Irwin and Russell Graham, Esqs., respectively, is thereafter excused on the defendants' peremptory challenge; whereupon,

It is ordered that one more name be drawn from the jury box, and the name of Charles J. Foley being thereupon drawn therefrom, the said prospective juror is examined by the Court and by J. J. Irwin and Russell Graham, Esqs., respectively,

James Smith, Sr. is excused on the defendants' peremptory challenge; whereupon it is ordered that one more name be drawn from the jury box, and the name of Alfred W. Hookway being thereupon drawn therefrom, the said prospective juror is examined by the court and by J. J. Irwin and Russell Graham, Esqs., respectively,

Charles J. Foley is excused on the defendants' peremptory challenge; whereupon, it is ordered that one more name be drawn from the jury box, and the name of R. E. Berkeley being thereupon drawn therefrom, the said prospective juror is examined for cause by the court and by J. J. Irwin and Russell Graham, Esqs., respectively.

The twelve jurors now in the jury box are accepted and sworn in a body as the jury to try this cause, the names of the jurors so sworn being as follows:

THE JURY

Andrew I. Conlin	Ernest K. Walker
George W. Yates	Lyndon J. Stanley
Dewey R. Barber	Frederick D. Parker
R. E. Berkeley	Harold R. Hilton
Alfred W. Hookway	Chauncy H. Dekker
Alfred Y. Soule	Jacob H. Leeds

Now, at the hour of 11:14 o'clock a. m., the Court admonishes the jury that, during the progress of this trial, they are not to speak to anyone about this cause, or any matter or thing therewith connected; that until said cause is finally submitted to them for their deliberation under the instruction of the court, they are not to speak to each other about this cause, or any matter or thing therewith connected, or form or express any opinion concerning the merits of the trial until it is finally submitted, to them, and declares a recess to the hour of 11:24 a. m.

At the hour of 11:25 o'clock a. m., Court reconvenes, and all being present as before, Russell Graham, Esq., requests that all witnesses be excluded from the court room, except certain Government Agents, and the court having so ordered, and Government Agents Sisk, Whitson and Small having been permitted to remain,

J. J. Irwin, Esq. makes opening statement to the jury for the Government, and the defendants reserving opening statement to the jury,

At the hour of 11:55 o'clock a. m., the jury is told to remember the admonition heretofore given herein, and the Court declares a recess to the hour of 2:00 o'clock p. m., today.

At the hour of 2:00 o'clock p. m., Court reconvenes, and all being present as before,

Miss Nellie P. Covert is called and sworn, and testifies for the Government on direct examination conducted by J. J. Irwin, Esq., and said witness being thereafter cross-examined by Russell Graham, Esq., now testifies on redirect examination conducted by J. J. Irwin, Esq., and is thereafter cross-examined by Chas. Ostrom, Esq.

Harold Edward Ryman is called and sworn, and testifies for the Government on direct examination conducted by J. J. Irwin, Esq., and the following exhibits are offered and admitted in evidence:

Gov't Ex. 1: Suit Case

"   " 2: Registration card of State of Arizona, 1935, name Eddie Ryman.

"   " 3: List of figures on sheet of paper.

At the hour of 3:16 o'clock p. m., the Court declares a recess for ten minutes, and, at the hour of 3:30 o'clock p. m., Court reconvenes, and all being present as before,

Witness Harold Edward Ryman resumes the stand and testifies further on examination by J. J. Irwin, Esq., said witness being thereafter cross-examined by Chas. Ostrom, Esq., and the following exhibits are offered and admitted in evidence, to-wit:

Gov't Ex. 4: Two cards, both marked "Guenther's Murrieta Mineral Hot Springs", one for Tom Ryan and one for Ed Roberts

Gov't Ex. No. 5: Two coupons from bonds, January and July, 1935, resp. by Federal Republic of Austria No. 12,958.

" " " 6: One sheet of paper with list of figures thereon.

" " " 7: Railway Express Agency receipt No. 1861 — shipper Eddie Ryman.

John F. Muyres Ex. A: Four page typewritten statement of Harold Edward Ryman, dated Galveston, Texas, November 16, 1935.

At the hour of 4:30 o'clock p. m., the Court reminds the jury of the admonition theretofore given herein and declares a recess to the hour of 10:00 o'clock a. m., to-morrow.

22

At a stated term, to wit: The February Term, A. D. 1936, of the District Court of the United States of America, within and for the Central Division of the Southern District of California, held at the court room thereof in the City of Los Angeles on Thursday the 19th day of March in the year of our Lord one thousand nine hundred and thirty-six.

PRESENT: THE HONORABLE Geo. Cosgrave District Judge.

United States of America,

Plaintiff,

vs.

Edward Harold Ryman, et al.,

Defendants.

)
)
)
)
)
)
)
)
)
)

No. 12619-S. Crim.

This case coming before the court for further jury trial of defendants John F. Muyres, George J. Muyres and Thomas Burke Ryan; J. J. Irwin, Assistant U. S. Attorney, appearing for the Government; defendant John F. Muyres being present in court with his attorneys, Chas. Ostrom and L. A. Bloom, Esqs.; defendant George J. Muyres being present in court with his attorney, Russell Graham, Esq.; defendant Thomas Burke Ryan being present in court in propria persona; and E. D. Conklin being present and acting in his official capacity as court reporter of the testimony and proceedings; and the jury being present,

The Court orders trial herein to proceed, and, at the request of J. J. Irwin, Esq., attorney John Carlisle Lee, representing defendant Karl L. Woolsey, is ordered to remain in attendance during trial.

Harold Edward Ryman, heretofore sworn, resumes the stand and is cross-examined by Chas. Ostrom, Esq., and said witness being thereafter cross-examined by Russell Graham, Esq., now testifies on cross-examination conducted by defendant Thomas Burke Ryan; and defendant Thomas Burke Ryan having stated that he desires to obtain counsel to represent him,

At the hour of 10:38 o'clock a. m., the Court declares a recess for ten minutes, and, at the hour of 10:54 o'clock a. m., Court reconvenes, and all being present as before,

Upon motion of Russell Graham, Esq., the said attorney, John Carlisle Lee, of Arizona, is admitted to practice in this case only, and attorney John Carlisle Lee now appearing as attorney for defendant Thomas Burke Ryan, the said John Carlisle Lee, Esq., having also represented defendant Karl L. Woolsey who heretofore pleaded guilty,

Harold Edward Ryman, heretofore sworn, resumes the stand, and attorney John Carlisle Lee for Thomas Burke Ryan not having any further cross-examination of Harold Edward Ryman, the said Harold Edward Ryman now testifies on re-direct examination conducted by J. J. Irwin, Esq., and said witness being thereafter examined by the Court,

E. B. Howarth is called and sworn, and testifies for the Government on direct examination conducted by J. J. Irwin, Esq., there being no cross-examination of said witness at this time, and the following exhibit is marked for identification, to-wit:

Gov't Ex. No. 8 for Ident: One bond for $1,000.00, No. M-12960, of Austrian Government International Loan 1930, with coupons attached.

The following exhibits are now offered and admitted in evidence, to-wit:

Gov't Ex. No. 9:   Two bonds, each for $1,000.00 with coupons attached, of The Kansas Power and Light Company, Nos. CM-3041 and CM3042, respectively.

"   "   " 10:   One bond for $1,000.00 of Austrian Government International Loan 1930; No. M-12958 and coupons attached.

"   "   " 11:   Three bonds, each for $1,000.00 of Deutsche Rentenbank-Kreditanstalt Landwirtschaftliche-Zentralbank,

Nos. M-37042; M-37044 and M-37045, respectively, and coupons attached.

"   "   " 12:   One $1,000.00 bond of Home Owners' Loan Corporation, of U. S. A., No. M-172105-E with coupons attached.

Karl L. Woolsey is called, sworn and testifies for the Government on direct examination conducted by J. J. Irwin, Esq., and the following exhibit is marked for identification:

Gov't Ex. No. 13 for Ident: Eight page statement signed by Karl L. Woolsey, dated Phoenix, Arizona, December 2, 1935.

At the hour of 12:00 o'clock noon, the Jury is told to remember the admonition heretofore given herein and the Court declares a recess to the hour of 2:00 o'clock p. m., today.

At the hour of 2:00 o'clock p. m., the Court reconvenes, and all being present as before, and C. W. Johnson, official stenographic reporter, also being present and acting in his official capacity;

Karl L. Woolsey resumes the stand, and, Attorney John Carlisle Lee having made a statement, the Jury is excused, and in their absence discussion takes place relative to the propriety of John Carlisle Lee, Esq., cross-examining Karl L. Woolsey, his former client, in behalf of defendant Thomas Burke Ryan;

Defendant Karl L. Woolsey does object to his former attorney John Carlisle Lee cross-examining him as counsel for defendant Thomas Burke Ryan, and Attorney John Carlisle Lee thereupon withdraws as attorney for defendant Thomas Burke Ryan;

At the hour of 2:17 o'clock p. m., the Court declares a recess for ten minutes, and, at the hour of 2:22 o'clock p. m., Court reconvenes, and all being present as before,

Chas. Ostrom, Esq., says Thomas Burke Ryan has requested him to represent him, and Attorney Chas. Ostrom not being in a position to represent defendant Thomas Burke Ryan as his attorney, a recess is declared for five minutes to obtain other counsel for Thomas Burke Ryan, and,

At the hour of 2:40 o'clock p. m., Court reconvenes, and all being present as before, and the Court being unable to obtain counsel for Thomas Burke Ryan, and the Court having ordered the trial to proceed,

Witness Karl L. Woolsey is cross-examined by Russell Graham, Esq., and the said witness being thereafter cross-examined by defendant Thomas Burke Ryan and by Chas. Ostrom, Esq., respectively,

At the hour of 3:15 o'clock p. m., Attorney J. Geo. Ohannesian appears in Court and the Court appoints him as attorney for Thomas Burke Ryan, and said witness Karl L. Woolsey being thereafter further cross-examined by Chas. Ostrom, Esq., and thereafter testifying on re-direct examination conducted by J. J. Irwin, Esq.,

Robert Barr is called and sworn, and testifies for the Government on direct examination conducted by J. J. Irwin, Esq., said witness Barr thereafter testifying on cross-examination conducted by Chas. Ostrom, Esq., and the following exhibit is offered and admitted in evidence, to-wit:

Gov't Ex. No. 14: Registration card of Longfellow Hotel, Huntington Park, California; Eddie Ryman; and yellow sheet attached entitled "front office Cashier's Report", etc.:

Elias J. Tavor is called and sworn, and testifies for the Government on direct examination conducted by J. J. Irwin, Esq., and the following exhibits are offered and admitted in evidence, to-wit:

Gov't Ex. No. 15: Railway Express Agency Receipt, Eddie Ryman, October 22, 1935, and delivery sheet attached, consignee Eddie Ryman, Huntington Park, California, Oct. 22, 1935.

" " " 16: Two documents as follows: Registration Card, T. B. Ryan and E. Roberts, October 28, – ; and card attached, T. B. Ryan – E. Roberts.

At the hour of 3:46 o'clock p. m., the Court declares a recess for ten minutes, and after said recess, court having reconvened,

Douglas Ward is called and sworn, and thereafter testifies for the Government on direct examination conducted by J. J. Irwin, Esq., said witness Ward thereafter testifying on cross-examination conducted by J. G. Ohanneson, Esq., and the following exhibit is offered and admitted in evidence, to-wit:

Gov't Ex. No. 17:   (Not physically marked and not left with clerk) that portion of register of Rex Hotel, Page 10 thereof, 1st and 2nd entries;

Max Vogel is called and sworn, and thereafter testifies for the Government on direct examination conducted by J. J. Irwin, Esq., and there being no cross-examination at this time, the following exhibit is marked for identification, to-wit:

Gov't Ex. No. 18:   (Not physically marked and not left with clerk) That portion of United States Hotel Register under year 1935 – 10/23/ – ; John H. Bane; T. B. Bryan and J. Eberhart.

Fred Ernest Bakeberg is called and sworn, and thereafter testifies for the Government on direct examination conducted by J. J. Irwin, Esq., and said witness being thereafter cross-examined by Russell Graham and Chas. Ostrom, Esqs., respectively,

H. F. Small is called, sworn and testifies for the Government on direct examination conducted by J. J. Irwin, Esq., and the following exhibit is marked for identification, to-wit:

Gov't Ex. No. 19 for Ident: Eleven page statement in ink, signed by John F. Muyres, dated November 28, 1935.

John Murry Cheney is called, sworn and testifies for the Government on direct examination conducted by J. J. Irwin, Esq., and the following exhibits are marked for identification, to-wit:

Gov't Ex. No. 20 for Ident: (Later in evidence): One sheet with list of figures in in pencil, and small sheet attached in ink, "Home Loan 5,000", etc.;

" " " 21 for Ident: One sheet of paper with pencil notation thereon, "5,000 Home @ 99.23", etc.;

The following exhibits are thereafter offered and admitted in evidence, to-wit:

Gov't Ex. No. 22: Receipt of E. F. Hutton & Company, October 30, 1935, – "Received of John M. Cheney", etc.

" " " 23: Three documents of E. F. Hutton & Company, with John M. Cheney, re sale of securities.

" " " 24: Promissory note for $6,500.00, October 30, 1935, signed John M. Cheney.

" " " 25: Two documents of E. F. Hutton & Company, re John M. Cheney account.

At the hour of 4:55 o'clock p.m., the Court declares a recess.

At a stated term, to wit: The February Term, A. D. 1936, of the District Court of the United States of America, within and for the Central Division of the Southern District of California, held at the court room thereof in the City of Los Angeles on Friday the 20th day of March in the year of our Lord one thousand nine hundred and thirty-six.

PRESENT: THE HONORABLE Geo. Cosgrave District Judge.

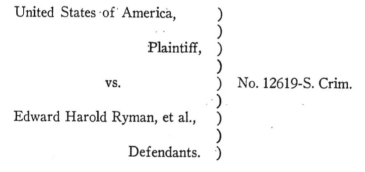

United States of America,

          Plaintiff,

         vs.   No. 12619-S. Crim.

Edward Harold Ryman, et al.,

          Defendants.

This case coming before the court for further jury trial of defendants John F. Muyres, George J. Muyres and Thomas Burke Ryan; J. J. Irwin, Assistant U. S. Attorney, appearing for the Government; defendant John F. Muyres being present in court with his attorneys, Chas. Ostrom and L. A. Bloom, Esqs.; defendant George J. Muyres being present in court with his attorney, Russell Graham, Esq.; defendant Thomas Burke Ryan being present in court with his attorney, J. Geo. Ohanneson, Esq.; and A. M. Randol being present and acting in his official capacity as court reporter; and the jury being present,

H. F. Small, heretofore sworn, is recalled to the witness stand and cross-examined by Chas. Ostrom, Esq., and,

Gov't Ex. No. 19, heretofore marked for identification, is now admitted in evidence, being an eleven-page statement, signed by John F. Muyres, dated November 28, 1935; after which

John Murray Cheney, heretofore sworn, resumes the witness stand and testifies on further examination conducted by J. J. Irwin, Esq., and said witness thereafter testifying on cross-examinations conducted by Chas. Ostrom and J. G. Ohanneson, Esqs., respectively,

Daymon Curtis Bassett is now called and sworn; following which,

Arthur E. Dusenberry is called and sworn, and said witness thereafter testifying on direct examination conducted by J. J. Irwin, Esq., on cross-examination conducted by Russell Graham, Esq., and on redirect examination conducted by J. J. Irwin, Esq.,

Daymon Curtis Bassett, heretofore sworn, is called to the witness stand, and said witness thereafter testifying on direct examination conducted by J. J. Irwin, Esq.,

At the hour of 10:52 o'clock a.m., the Court reminds the Jury of the admonition heretofore given herein and declares a recess for ten minutes; after which recess, at the hour of 11:03 o'clock a.m., Court reconvenes, and all being present as before, including the Jury,

Daymon Curtis Bassett resumes the witness stand, and said witness being thereafter further examined by J. J. Irwin, Esq., now testifies on cross-examination conducted by Russell Graham, Esq., and on re-direct examination conducted by J. J. Irwin, Esq.; following which,

Mrs. Henrietta Rosa Woolsey is called and sworn, and thereafter testifies for the Government on direct examination conducted by J. J. Irwin, Esq., and said witness thereafter testifying on cross-examination conducted by Chas. Ostrom, Esq., and on re-direct examination conducted by J. J. Irwin, Esq.,

Lish Whitson is called and sworn, and thereafter testifies for the Government on direct examination conducted by J. J. Irwin, Esq., and said witness having been thereafter cross-examined by Russell Graham, Esq., and having testified on re-direct examination conducted by J. J. Irwin, Esq., now testifies on cross-examination conducted by Chas. Ostrom, Esq.; and Government Exhibit No. 26 being thereafter offered and admitted in evidence, and Government Exhibits Nos. 27 and 28 being thereafter marked for identification, said exhibits being as shown below,

Gov't Ex. No. 26 in Evid: Fruit jar (glass), and yellow sheet, "file in agents notes", attached, and white sheet attached, with notation, "Bottle in which $7,000.00 worth of bonds were found";

" " " 27 for Ident: Statement, four pages, dated November 27, 1935, signed by George J. Muyres;

" " " 28 " " Four page typewritten
statement signed by
George J. Muyres, Los
Angeles, December 3,
1935;

Tom H. Sisk is called and sworn, and said witness thereafter testifying for the Government on direct examination
conducted by J. J. Irwin, Esq., and the following exhibit
having been offered and admitted in evidence:

Gov't Ex. No. 29: One German Government International 5½ % Loan 1930; $1,000.00
bond with coupons attached, No.
C-65344;

At the hour of 12:08 o'clock p.m., the Court declares
a recess to the hour of 2:00 o'clock p.m., today; and, at
the hour of 2:00 o'clock p.m., Court reconvenes, and all
being present as before, except that A. Wahlberg is
present and acting in his official capacity as official court
reporter,

Witness Tom H. Sisk, heretofore sworn, resumes the
stand and testifies further on direct examination conducted
by J. J. Irwin, Esq., said witness thereafter testifying on
an examination conducted by the Court, and the following listed exhibits having been offered and admitted in
evidence, to-wit:

Gov't Ex. No. 30: Small note book with red cover,
"The Beer Box";

" " " 31: Four German Government International 5½ % Loan 1930 bonds,
each for $1,000.00 with coupons
attached, Nos. C-65,345; C-65,346,

C-65,347 and C-65,348, respectively; One Austrian Government International Loan 1930, $1,000.00 bond with coupons attached, No. M-12,957; one Deutsche Rentenband Kreditanstalt Landwirtschaftliche Zentral Bank $1,000.00 Bond with coupons attached No. M-40518; 8 Home Owners Loan Corporation Bonds, with coupons attached, each for $1,000.00; One Home Owners' Loan Corporation Bond for $100.00 with coupons attached; and one Home Owners Loan Corporation Bond for $50.00 with coupons attached;

Glen A. Watkins is called and sworn, and thereafter testifies for the Government on direct examination conducted by J. J. Irwin, Esq., said witness thereafter testifying on cross-examination conducted by Russell Graham, Esq., and the following listed exhibit having been offered and admitted in evidence, to-wit:

Gov't Ex. No. 32: Cashier's Check No. 1661, Bank of America, dated November 2, 1935, $1004.06, signed L. Valprega; (not left with clerk)

Ira C. Hilgers is called and sworn, and thereafter testifies for Gov. on direct examination conducted by J. J. Irwin, Esq., and said witness having been cross-examined by Russell Graham, Esq., now testifies on re-direct examination conducted by J. J. Irwin, Esq.; after which,

Miss Nellie P. Covert is recalled to the witness stand, and thereafter testifies further on direct examination conducted by J. J. Irwin, Esq., there being no cross-examination of said witness, at this time; and Government Exhibit No. 33 having been offered and thereupon admitted in evidence, said exhibit being as shown below, to-wit:

Gov't Ex. No. 33: Letter, June 18, 1935, to Mr. S. W. Izard, from Nellie P. Covert;

Government Exhibits, Nos. 27 and 28, heretofore marked for identification, are both admitted in evidence upon motion of J. J. Irwin, Esq., and,

At the hour of 3:17 o'clock p.m., the Court declares a recess for ten minutes; after which recess, at the hour of 3:37 o'clock p.m., Court reconvenes, and all being present as before,

Tom H. Sisk, heretofore sworn, resumes the witness stand and testifies further on direct examination conducted by J. J. Irwin, Esq., and there having been offered and admitted in evidence the following listed exhibit, to-wit:

Gov't Ex. No. 34: Envelope for auto license plates, canvas cover, and piece of cellophane paper;

Morris Higbie Remsen, Jr., is called and sworn, and thereafter testifies for the Government on direct examination conducted by J. J. Irwin, Esq., said witness thereafter testifying on cross-examination conducted by Russell

Graham, Esq., and there having thereafter been offered and admitted in evidence the following listed exhibits, to-wit:

Gov't Ex. No. 35: Photostatic copy of ledger sheet of Security Bank, Figueroa & Adams Branch;

" " " 36: Photostatic copy of selling order, Security First National Bank of Los Angeles, November 1, 1935;

" " " 37: Photostatic copy of confirmation and statement of bond department of Security Bank, November 1, 1935, Total—$1103.44;

" " " 38: Photostatic copy of check for $300.00 to J. F. Muyres, dated November 9, 1935;

" " " 39: Photostatic copy of check, November 9, 1935, to Geo. Muyres $3,000.00, signed by John M. Cheney, and endorsement of Geo Myers;

" " " 40: Photostatic copy of check to Geo. Muyres for $2,000.00, dated November 12, 1935, signed by John M. Cheney;

James Thomson is called and sworn, and said witness thereafter testifying for the Government on direct examination conducted by J. J. Irwin, Esq., and testifying on cross-examination conducted by defendant's counsel,

Avery Corpestin is called out of order and sworn, said witness thereafter testifying as witness for defendant John F. Muyres on direct examination conducted by Chas. Ostrom, Esq., and there being no cross-examination, at this time,

The Government rests, subject to the introduction of further testimony, the admissibility of which will be presented to the Court; whereupon,

The Court reminds the jury of the admonition heretofore given herein and excuses the Jury until next Tuesday, March 24, 1936, 10:00 o'clock a.m.; and,

In the absence of the Jury, Russell Graham, Esq., for defendant George J. Muyres, moves for an instructed verdict of not guilty and argues in support thereof; after which,

Chas. Ostrom, Esq., for defendant John F. Muyres, moves for an instructed verdict and argues in support thereof; following which,

J. G. Ohanneson, Esq., for defendant Thomas Burke Ryan, moves for a directed verdict and argues in support thereof; and,

J. J. Irwin, Esq., having thereafter argued in opposition, and the Court having made a statement,

At the hour of 5:12 o'clock p.m., Russell Graham, Esq., argues further for his client; whereupon,

It is by the Court ordered that this case stand submitted, and, at the hour of 5:18 o'clock p.m., the Court declares a recess in this case to next Tuesday, March 24, 1936.

At a stated term, to wit: The February Term, A. D. 1936, of the District Court of the United States of America, within and for the Central Division of the Southern District of California, held at the court room thereof in the City of Los Angeles on Tuesday the 24th day of March in the year of our Lord one thousand nine hundred and thirty-six.

PRESENT: THE HONORABLE Geo. Cosgrave District Judge.

United States of America, 　　　　　　　　Plaintiff, 　　　　vs. 　　 Edward Harold Ryman, et al., 　　　　　　Defendants.	))) No. 12619-S. Crim.)))

This case coming before the court for further trial of defendants John F. Muyres, George J. Muyres and Thomas Burke Ryan; J. J. Irwin, Assistant U. S. Attorney, appearing for the Government; defendant John F. Muyres being present in court with his attorneys, Chas. Ostrom and L. A. Bloom, Esqs.; defendant George J. Muyres being present in court with his attorney, Russell Graham, Esq.; defendant Thomas Burke Ryan being present in court with his attorney J. Geo. Ohanneson, Esq.; A. Wahlberg and E. D. Conklin being present and acting alternately in 'their official capacity as court reporters of the testimony and proceedings; and the jury being absent,

The motions heretofore made by defendants to dismiss, and taken under submission, are hereby denied, and exception noted; following which,

At the hour of 10:02 o'clock a. m., the jury return into court, and all being present as before, J. Geo. Ohanneson, Esq., moves to strike certain testimony and evidence in behalf of defendant Thomas Burke Ryan, and argues in support thereof, which motion is denied, and exception noted; after which,

At the hour of 10:12 o'clock a. m., the Court declares a recess for five minutes, and, at the hour of 10:19 o'clock a. m., Court reconvenes, and all being present as before, including the jury,

Thomas M. Cushman is called as a witness for the defendants and is sworn, and thereafter testifies on direct examination conducted by J. G. Ohanneson, Esq., and said witness thereafter testifying on cross-examination conducted by J. J. Irwin and Chas. Ostrom, Esqs.,

Thomas Burke Ryan, defendant, is called and testifies on direct examination conducted by J. Geo. Ohanneson, Esq., in behalf of the defendants, and said witness being thereafter cross-examined by Chas Ostrom, Esq.,

John F. Muyres is called and sworn, and thereafter testifies for the defendants on direct examination conducted by Chas. Ostrom, Esq., and

At the hour of 11:00 o'clock a. m., the Court declares a recess for ten minutes, and, at the hour of 11:00 o'clock a. m., Court reconvenes, and all being present as before,

John F. Muyres, heretofore sworn, resumes the witness stand and is further examined by Chas. Ostrom, Esq., and,

At the hour of 12:00 o'clock noon, the Court declares a recess to the hour of 2:00 o'clock p. m., the jury having been told to remember the admonition heretofore given herein, and,

At the hour of 2:00 o'clock p. m., Court reconvenes, and all being present as before, except that D. G. Taylor, Esq., appears for defendant Thomas Burke Ryan, the said defendant's attorney, J. G. Ohanneson, Esq., being absent,

Judge Irvin Taplin is called and sworn, and thereafter testifies for the defendants on direct examination conducted by Chas. Ostrom, Esq., and there being no cross-examination of said witness at this time,

Henry M. Guenser is called, sworn, and testifies for the defendants on direct examination conducted by Chas. Ostrom, Esq., and there being no cross-examination at this time,

Ralph Reynolds is called, sworn and testifies for the defendants on direct examination conducted by Russell Graham, Esq., and thereafter the said witness, Reynolds, testifies on cross-examination conducted by J. J. Irwin, Esq.; after which,

John F. Muyres, heretofore sworn, resumes the witness stand and testifies further on direct examination conducted by Chas. Ostrom, Esq., and J. G. Ohanneson, Esq., comes into court at the hour of 2:30 o'clock p. m. and now represents defendant Thomas Burke Ryan, and there being no cross examination of said witness John F.

Muyres, the witness is examined by the Court, and thereafter testifying on cross-examination conducted by J. G. Ohanneson, Esq.,

Robert Lyle Kelly is called and sworn, and thereafter testifies for the defendants on direct examination conducted by Chas. Ostrom, Esq., and said witness being thereafter cross-examined by J. J. Irwin, Esq.,

Albert G. Brouwers is called, sworn and testifies for the defendants on direct examination conducted by Chas. Ostrom, Esq., and said witness being thereafter cross-examined by J. J. Irwin, Esq.,

Thomas Walter Fairchild is called, sworn and testifies for the defendants on direct examination conducted by Chas. Ostrom, Esq., and said witness being thereafter cross-examined by J. J. Irwin, Esq.,

John Carlisle Lee, attorney, is called, sworn and testifies in behalf of the defendants on direct examination conducted by Chas. Ostrom, Esq., and there being no cross-examination of said witness, at this time,

Walter D. Dunham is called, sworn and testifies for the defendants on direct examination conducted by Russell Graham, Esq., and said witness being thereafter cross-examined by J. J. Irwin, Esq.,

Milton L. Sutter is called, sworn and testifies for the defendants on direct examination conducted by Russell Graham, Esq., and there being no cross-examination of said witness, at this time,

Defendant George J. Muyres rests, and, at the hour of 3:04 o'clock p. m., the jury is excused until sent for, and, in the absence of the jury, Chas. Ostrom, Esq., makes offer of proof, which is denied, and exception noted, and all three defendants having rested,

Russell Graham, Esq., renews motion for defendant George J. Muyres for instructed verdict of not guilty and argues in support thereof; Chas. Ostrom, Esq., for defendant John F. Muyres joins in said motion; J. G. Ohanneson, Esq., for defendant Thomas Burke Ryan joins in said motion; and all three motions are denied, and exception noted; after which,

At the hour of 3:13 o'clock p. m., the court declares a recess for ten minutes, and, at the hour of 3:23 o'clock p. m., Court reconvenes, and all being present as before,

At the hour of 3:27 o'clock p. m., J. J. Irwin, Esq., argues to the jury in behalf of the Government, and,

At the hour of 4:30 o'clock p. m., the jury is told to remember the admonition heretofore given them herein, and the Court excuses the jury until tomorrow at the hour of 10:00 o'clock a. m., and declares a recess to the hour of 10:00 o'clock a. m., tomorrow.

At a stated term, to wit: The February Term, A. D. 1936, of the District Court of the United States of America, within and for the Central Division of the Southern District of California, held at the court room thereof in the City of Los Angeles on Wednesday the 25th day of March in the year of our Lord one thousand nine hundred and thirty-six.

PRESENT: THE HONORABLE Geo. Cosgrave District Judge.

United States of America, Plaintiff, vs. Edward Harold Ryman, et al., Defendants.	No. 12619-S. Crim.

This case coming before the court for further trial of defendants John F. Muyres, George J. Muyres and Thomas Burke Ryan; J. J. Irwin, Assistant U. S. Attorney, appearing for the Government; Chas. Ostrom and L. A. Bloom, Esqs., appearing as counsel for defendant John F. Muyres, who is present in court; defendant George J. Muyres being present in court with his attorney, Russell Graham, Esq., Thomas Burke Ryan being present in court with his attorney, J. Geo. Ohanneson, Esq.; E. D. Conklin, official stenographic reporter, being present and acting as such; and the jury being present,

J. Geo. Ohanneson, Esq., argues to the jury for defendant Thomas Burke Ryan, and, at the hour of 10:30

o'clock a. m., Chas. Ostrom, Esq., argues to the jury, and, thereafter, upon motion of Russell Graham, Esq., it is by the Court ordered that George J. Muyres have an exception noted to the ruling of the Court yesterday in over-ruling motion of said defendant for directed verdict, and,

At the hour of 10:58 o'clock a. m., the Court declares a recess for five minutes; after which recess, at the hour of 11:03 o'clock a. m., Court reconvenes, and all being present as before,

Russell Graham, Esq., argues to the jury in behalf of defendant George J. Muyres, and, at the hour of 11:45 o'clock a. m., the Court declares a recess in this case until the hour of 1:30 o'clock p. m.;

At the hour of 1:30 o'clock p. m., Court reconvenes, and all being present as before, including the jury; J. J. Irwin, Esq., argues in reply for the Government;

At the hour of 2:34 o'clock p. m., the Court instructs the jury on the law in this case; Russell Graham Esq., notes exception to the court's charge and to failure of the Court to give certain instructions requested, and the Court instructs the jury further; after which,

At the hour of 3:15 o'clock p. m., Greenlief C. Welch is sworn as Bailiff and the jury retire to deliberate upon a verdict, and the Court declares a recess until the return of the jury;

At the hour of 6:00 o'clock p. m., the Court orders that the jury be taken to dinner at the expense of the Government, and Frank Turner is sworn as additional

Bailiff to care for the jury, and the jury go to dinner at 6:35 o'clock p. m.

At the hour of 8:10 o'clock p. m., the Jury return from dinner and deliberate further upon a verdict;

At the hour of 10:36 o'clock p. m., pursuant to stipulation of all counsel in the case, it is ordered that the jury may be locked up for the night; and, in the event it reaches a verdict it is ordered to seal same and place it in the hands of the bailiff and be permitted to disband and reconvene at the hour of 10:00 o'clock in the morning, at which time the verdict will be opened and read in its presence; and, if it does not reach a verdict, it is ordered taken to breakfast at the customary time and then returned to its meeting place for further deliberations at 8:30 o'clock a. m. or 9:00 o'clock a. m., or such time as may be convenient.

At the hour of 10:50 o'clock p. m., Court reconvenes, and all counsel being present, and the jury and the defendants being present, and E. D. Conklin, court reporter, being present, the Court instructs the jury further, and, at the hour of 10:55 o'clock p. m., the Jury retire to the jury room for further deliberations, and, at this time, Court adjourns until the hour of 10:00 o'clock a. m. tomorrow.

At the hour of 11:30 o'clock p. m., the jury, after deliberating further, are locked up for the night, in charge of Frank Turner and Greenlief C. Walsh, Bailiffs.

At a stated term, to wit: The February Term, A. D. 1936, of the District Court of the United States of America, within and for the Central Division of the Southern District of California, held at the court room thereof in the City of Los Angeles on Thursday the 26th day of March in the year of our Lord one thousand nine hundred and thirty-six.

PRESENT: THE HONORABLE Geo. Cosgrave District Judge.

United States of America,
                    Plaintiff,)
          vs.   )   No. 12619-Crim.
)
Edward Harold Ryman, et al.,)
               Defendants.)

This case coming before the court for further trial of defendants John F. Muyres, George J. Muyres and Thomas Burke Ryan; J. J. Irwin, Assistant U. S. Attorney, appearing for the Government; defendant John F. Muyres being present in court with his attorney, Chas. Ostrom, Esq.; defendant George J. Muyres being present in court with his attorney, Russell Graham, Esq., defendant Thomas Burke Ryan being present in court with his attorney, J. Geo. Ohanneson, Esq.;

At the hour of 2:00 o'clock a. m., today, the Jury having presented its sealed verdict to Greenlief C. Welch, Bailiff, and the Jury having been permitted to disband, and the said Bailiff having instructed the jury to return in court today at the hour of 10:00 o'clock a. m.; at the hour of 10:04 o'clock a. m., Court reconvenes, and all being present as aforesaid, including the jury, and E. D. Conklin being present as court reporter; Bailiff Greenlief C. Welch presents sealed verdict of the Jury to the Court in the presence of the Jury, which is in the jury box, and the Verdict is read in open court by the Clerk of the Court, said verdict, which is thereupon ordered filed and entered, being as follows, to-wit:

UNITED STATES DISTRICT COURT, SOUTH-ERN DISTRICT OF CALIFORNIA, CENTRAL DIVISION. United States of America, Plaintiff, vs. Edward Harold Ryman, et al., Defendants. No. 12619-S. Crim. VERDICT OF THE JURY. We, the jury in the above entitled case, find the defendant, JOHN F. MUYRES: is guilty as charged in the first count of the Indictment; and is guilty as charged in the second count of the Indictment; the defendant, GEORGE J. MUYRES: is not guilty as charged in the first count of the Indictment; and is guilty as charged in the second count of the Indictment; and defendant, THOMAS BURKE RYAN: is guilty as charged in the first count of the Indictment; and is guilty as charged in the second count of the Indictment. Dated: Los Angeles, California, March 26th, 1936, 1:00 A. M. H. R. HILTON, Foreman of the Jury.

The jury is thereafter excused until notified; following which,

Each of the three defendants on trial notes an exception to the verdict of the jury; whereupon,

J. J. Irwin, Esq., having moved that the time for sentence of said three defendants be fixed at this time, it is by the court ordered that sentence be fixed for March 30, 1936, at 2:00 o'clock p. m.; and J. J. Irwin, Esq., having moved the court to exonerate the bond of defendant John F. Muyres in the sum of $2500.00 and commit said defendant to the custody of the United States Marshal pending the giving of new bond, and Chas. Ostrom, Esq., having argued in opposition thereto, it is by the court ordered that the bond of John F. Muyres in the sum of $2500.00 be exonerated and that he be remanded to the custody of the U. S. Marshal pending his furnishing of a new bond which is fixed in the sum of $5000.00, until sentence, and it is further ordered that defendants George J. Muyres and Thomas Burke Ryan be permitted to go on their present bonds until time of sentence.

At a stated term, to wit: The February Term, A. D. 1936, of the District Court of the United States of America, within and for the Central Division of the Southern District of California, held at the court room thereof in the City of Los Angeles on Tuesday the 7th day of April in the year of our Lord one thousand nine hundred and thirty-six.

PRESENT: THE HONORABLE Geo. Cosgrave District Judge.

United States of America,)
                Plaintiff,)
          vs.) No. 12619-S. (C) Crim.
)
Edward Harold Ryman, et al.,)
           Defendants.)

This cause coming before the court at this time for pronouncement of sentence upon defendants Edward Harold Ryman; Karl L. Woolsey; John F. Muyres, and Thomas Burke Ryan, on the first and second counts of the Indictment; and for hearing on motion, filed March 30, 1936, of George J. Muyres for a new trial and for pronouncement of sentence upon said defendant on the second count, only, of the Indictment; Jack Irwin, Assistant United States Attorney, appearing as counsel for the Government; defendant, Edward Harold Ryman, being present in court with his attorney, D. G. Taylor, Esq.; defendant, Karl L. Woolsey, being present in court in propria persona; defendant John F. Muyres, being pres-

ent in court with his attorneys, Chas. Ostrom, Esq., and
L. A. Bloom, Esq.; defendant, George J. Muyres, being
present in court with his attorney, Russell Graham, Esq.,
and defendant, Thomas Burke Ryan, being present in
court with his attorney, J. Geo. Ohannesian, Esq., and
A. M. Randol being present in court in his official capacity
as court reporter of the testimony and the proceedings;
the said Russell Graham, Esq., argues to the court in
support of the motion of George J. Muyres for a new
trial, and Jack Irwin, Esq., having argued in opposition
thereto, and the Court having made a statement, it is by
the Court ordered that said motion for a new trial be,
and the same is hereby, denied, and an exception noted;
and Attorney Chas. Ostrom, Esq., having thereupon made
a statement to the court relative to application for probation for John F. Muyres, and J. Geo. Ohannesian, Esq.,
having made a statement for leniency for defendant
Thomas Burke Ryan; Russell Graham, Esq., thereupon
makes a statement to the court and asks for probation
for defendant George J. Muyres; and Attorney Jas. D.
Randles, representing Nellie P. Covert, claimant of certain bonds, having made a statement to the court, and
Attorney Jack Irwin, Esq., having made a further statement, it is by the court ordered that the applications of
said defendants for probation be, and the same are hereby, denied; and thereupon the court pronounces sentence
upon defendants John F. Muyres, Edward Harold Ryman
and Thomas Burke Ryan for the crime of which they
now stand convicted, namely, violation of Sections 415

and 88 of Title 18 of the United States Code, and upon
defendant George J. Muyres for violation of Section 88
of Title 18 of the United States Code; and it is the judgment of the Court that said defendant, George J. Muyres,
be imprisoned in a United States Penitentiary to be designated by the Attorney General, or by such representative whom he may designate to act, for the term and
period of two years on the second count of the Indictment; and, in addition thereto, pay unto the United States
of America a fine in the sum of one thousand dollars on
the said second count, and stand committed until said
fine shall have been paid, the said sentence for non-payment of fine to commence to run at the expiration of
said two years' sentence; that defendant John F. Muyres
be imprisoned in a United States Penitentiary to be designated by the Attorney General, or by such representative
whom he may designate to act, for the term and period
of five years on the first count of the Indictment, and for
the term and period of two years on the second count of
the Indictment, the said sentence of two years on the
second count to begin at the expiration of the five years'
sentence on the first count, making a total of seven years;
and, in addition thereto, pay unto the United States of
America a fine in the sum of one thousand dollars on the
second count, and stand committed until said fine is paid,
the sentence for non-payment of fine to commence to run
after the expiration of said seven years' sentence;
* * * and the court having ordered that all defendants, as aforesaid, with the exception of Karl L. Woolsey,

be remanded to the custody of the United States Marshal forthwith; and Russell Graham, Esq., having informed the court that it is the intention of defendant George J. Muyres to appeal, and Attorney Chas. Ostrom, Esq., having served verbal notice of appeal as to defendant John F. Muyres, it is by the Court ordered that the bond of George J. Muyres for his release, etc., pending decision on appeal, be fixed in the sum of $3500.00, and that his former bond be exonerated; and an exception to the adverse rulings of the court having been noted for defendant George J. Muyres at the request of Russell Graham, Esq., and an exception to the adverse rulings of the court having been noted for defendant John F. Muyres at the request of Chas. Ostrom, Esq., it is by the court ordered that Attorney Chas. Ostrom, Esq., be, and he is hereby, permitted to withdraw as attorney from this case; * * *.

[TITLE OF COURT AND CAUSE.]

ENGROSSED BILL OF EXCEPTIONS.

BE IT REMEMBERED that on the 11th day of December, 1935, the Grand Jurors of the United States, for the Southern District of California, Central Division, returned into the above entitled Court an indictment accusing Edward Harold Ryman, alias Edward Raymond, alias Edward Roberts, alias Edward Harold, alias F. Rost, Thomas Burke Ryan, alias Don Thompson, Franklin Dolph Le Sieur, Karl L. Woolsey, alias Ham Woolsey, John F. Muyres, George J. Muyres and John Murray Cheney, of the offense of transporting in interstate commerce certain securities described in said indictment, which securities had theretofore been stolen as the said defendants then and there well knew and also of the offense of conspiring so to transport said securities.

Thereafter, to wit, on the 23rd day of December, 1935, the said defendants duly and regularly entered their pleas of not guilty with the exception of Edward Harold Ryman who entered a plea of guilty as charged in the indictment, also with the exception of Franklin Dolph Le Sieur who was not present.

Thereafter, to wit, on the 10th day of March, 1936, the defendant, Karl L. Woolsey withdrew his plea of not guilty theretofore entered and entered a plea of guilty as charged in the indictment.

This cause came on duly and regularly for trial in the above entitled Court before the Honorable George Cosgrave, Judge Presiding, on March 17th, 1936, at which time Thomas Burke Ryan acting as his own counsel,

(Testimony of Nellie P. Covert)

John F. Muyres through his attorneys, Chas. W. Ostrom
and L. A. Bloom, George J. Muyres, through his attorney
Russell Graham and John Murray Cheney, through his
counsel Fenton Garfield, and John J. Irwin, Assistant
United States Attorney for the United States of America,
announced themselves ready for trial. On motion of
John J. Irwin, Assistant United States Attorney, the cause
was dismissed as to defendant John Murray Cheney,
whereupon a jury was duly impaneled and sworn after the
Court had explained the nature of the charges contained
in the indictment to the jury impaneled.

Mr. John J. Irwin, Assistant United States Attorney
then made an opening statement in behalf of the plaintiff,
after which the following evidence was presented on behalf
of the plaintiff:

NELLIE P. COVERT

called as a witness on behalf of the Government, having
been first duly sworn, testified as follows:

(DIRECT EXAMINATION)

By Mr. Irwin:

My name is Nellie P. Covert. I live in Tucson, Arizona.
It has been my home for thirty years. I had some
banker's note cases in my house and they were locked. I
had some bonds. Some of them were foreign bonds and
some of them Home Owners Corporation Bonds. One
of the officers came and told me my bonds were stolen.
Then I looked in the boxes and they were gone. There
were a lot of letters that I had stored away and the big
envelopes were filled with those letters, and I thought

(Testimony of Nellie P. Covert)

they were my bonds; and I never missed them until he said they were gone.

(Whereupon, it was stipulated by all parties that the bonds which the witness had referred to, included the bonds described in the indictment; that the witness owned them and last saw them in the box which she had described.)

(CROSS EXAMINATION)

BY MR. GRAHAM:

I couldn't say right offhand when I did look in the boxes last. I received a letter from Stern Brothers & Company, Kansas City, Missouri, from whom I bought some bonds. I received the bonds with the letter and placed the letter and bonds in my box. No one had access to my boxes except me until the party, whoever it was, came in and searched the house and found the boxes that I had hidden in my closet. Before the officers had told me that my bonds had been stolen, I looked in my boxes for a mortgage and there was something peculiar about the appearance of the boxes. That was maybe a month or two before they notified me. The envelopes did not look as big as they should and I wondered at the time had I taken some out of my box, but there was no suspicion aroused and I thought maybe I had taken some out and forgotten about it. It may not have been as long as a month before the officer came in. The officer came to my house on November 10th. The last time before

56

that when I looked in my boxes must have been June or July. I sent a bond to Stern Brothers & Company to collect for me and that must have been about June. There were things that I noticed in my house that I couldn't understand. For one thing, I noticed the red entry lamp, the shade was bent and it was sitting near the window. The window itself was locked, but I noticed the screen, the hook was loose, and I couldn't understand that. I also noticed that some of those letters were gone from the box in which I filed them. I don't think the bonds were taken as early as May, 1935. They were taken later on in the year.

(REDIRECT EXAMINATION)
BY MR. IRWIN:

I haven't received any of my bonds back.

(CROSS EXAMINATION)
BY MR. OSTROM:

The first time that I noticed anything about my box was when I went to look for my mortgage. One of my Kansas City Power & Light bonds was called. I was ill at the time and I might have waited several months. They sent me another notice to send in the bond; that it wouldn't draw any interest from the time that they notified me. It must have been several months after that because I was feeling too bad to attend to anything very much.

(Testimony of Harold Edward Ryman)

HAROLD EDWARD RYMAN

called as a witness on behalf of plaintiff, having been first duly sworn, testified as follows:

(DIRECT EXAMINATION)

BY MR. IRWIN:

My name is Edward Harold Ryman. I am one of the defendants in this case and I have previously entered my plea of guilty. In December of 1935 I was residing in Phoenix, Arizona. I know Miss Covert, the witness who just came down from the stand. I know where she resided at that time. I stayed in one of her big houses at Park and Second Street, that she owned. I first saw her securities two or three months or maybe four months previous to the time that I took them. Miss Covert had gone away to Phoenix and had been gone about three or four days, and I went over to feed the dogs, the dogs had been hungry, and I went around to the side of the house and opened the window and got into the house to see if there was anything to feed the dogs. I didn't find anything. I looked around, and kind of rummaged through the house, and I went to the back closet and I saw a tin box in back, and I looked around and found some keys to the box, and when I opened that there were thousands of dollars worth of bonds in the box. I didn't do anything about them then. I returned the box in the position in which I found it and then left the house. Three or four months after that when I was in Phoenix, I talked to another person about what I had seen. Later I took the bonds. Three or four months after I had first seen the bonds, I talked to the defendant Ryan about

58

them. (Whereupon, the witness identified the defendant
Thomas Burke Ryan as the man to whom he talked.)
I was in the Avalon Club in Phoenix at the time. He
had come out there quite a bit. He had been taking care
of some slot machines, pin machines and marble machines.
We were reading the newspaper there and I told him I
knew where there were a lot of bonds. We got interested
and we talked. I can't recall the conversation, but, nevertheless, the outcome was that I told him I knew where
I could get all these bonds, and he asked me if they were
hot. I told him no, of course they weren't. They weren't
then. That is the way it started. It went on for two
or three weeks, or maybe a month, and nothing was done
about it. And one day he told me that he knew somebody
that could sell them. He said it would have to be done in
Los Angeles. That they would have to be sold in Los
Angeles, California. I told him when everything was all
right and ready, that I would go and get them. I don't
remember exactly what was said but it went on and about
a week later he said they were ready to sell them over on
the Coast and he said to go and get them, and I did.

"Q Then did you get the word from him, or hear
from him, pursuant to that conversation?

"A From Mr. Ryan?

"Q Yes. Did you hear from him again then?

"MR. GRAHAM: I presume it is understood that
this conversation is not being offered against the defendant
George J. Muyres?

"MR. IRWIN: Not at this time."

About three or four weeks after my first conversation
with him, he told me to go ahead. This was about a

(Testimony of Harold Edward Ryman)

week after he told me they would have to be handled in Los Angeles. He met me at the Avalon Club and told me to go and get them. I was to come by and meet him in Phoenix at the Avalon Club after I got the bonds. After I left Tucson with the bonds I came back to Phoenix. This was about a week later. Then I went to the Avalon Club to find him and he wasn't there. He had been down some place getting a glass of beer, or something, and I couldn't find him. So I left a note telling him I was going to Los Angeles. About a week or perhaps a little longer intervened between the time he told me to go ahead and get them, and the date that I did get them and come up to Phoenix and left this note for him. The reason it took so long was because I had to drive to Tucson where Miss Covert lives and because she stayed at home for a while. I just stayed around and one day she left and went to Phoenix. After leaving this note for Ryan, I took the bonds in a suitcase and shipped them to Huntington Park, California. Then I drove right over here. Sometime before we left and when I was talking to him in the Avalon Club, we had agreed that he was to meet me in the Post Office, in this building, at the General Delivery Window. I don't remember the date but it was before he told me to go ahead and get them. He was to meet me at noon or 5 o'clock, either time. We were to wait every day until we met each other around that time. The suitcase which is now handed to me is mine in which I shipped the bonds from Tucson to Huntington Park. I shipped it by express and obtained it at Huntington Park. (Whereupon, the suitcase was introduced in evidence as Plaintiff's Exhibit No. 1.) When I

(Testimony of Harold Edward Ryman)

arrived at Huntington Park, I think I went to the hotel
first and then to the express office for the suitcase. The
date upon which I left the note for Ryan and came on to
Los Angeles was October 22nd. The card which is
handed to me bearing the name of Eddie Ryman was
issued to me by the State of Arizona, Motor Vehicle
Department. It bears the statement on the back "Entered
California, October 22, 1935, Blythe #2". A man whom
I knew in Tucson but who had no connection with this
transaction came with me to California. We left that
day and drove all that day and night. The first night
we stopped at Redlands, California. (The registration
card referred to was received in evidence and marked
Plaintiff's Exhibit No. 2.) If I remember right I got
the bonds from Nellie Covert's house some time in the
morning around 10 o'clock and I got in Phoenix that
afternoon around 5 o'clock and left after a few minutes.
That was the same day I drove into California. Before
I left, I shipped the bonds from Phoenix to Huntington
Park, After I had been unable to find Ryan. I was staying at the house of the man who came with me from
Tucson. He left me at Redlands. Then I went to a
hotel and stayed the rest of the night by myself. I stayed
at the Longfellow Hotel in Huntington Park. I did not
bring all of the bonds which I stole to Los Angeles. A
part of them I hid in Arizona the same day that I stole
them. I think it was the next day after my arrival in
Los Angeles that I first saw Ryan. All I know about
the face value of the bonds that I stole then was that I
read in the indictment that it was $42,000.00 worth. I
don't know the actual value. The German bonds weren't

(Testimony of Harold Edward Ryman)

worth very much at the time, I know. I buried eight or nine or ten of them in Arizona. I took two or three of each kind. There were Home Loan, Australian Government, two different kinds of German bonds, Agriculture and International and there was also some Kansas City Power bonds. I met Ryan at the Post Office pursuant to our appointment. We went to the U. S. Hotel. I had previously left a note for Ryan in Phoenix and when I got over here I wrote him a postcard on the 23rd of October. I came down to the Post Office on the morning of the 23rd and he wasn't down there, and so I wrote him a postcard, but I saw him that same night at 5 o'clock, I think it was, but I'm not sure. He was registered at the U. S. Hotel. I think, but I am not sure, that he was staying there under the name of Ryan. I think his room was on the third floor, way in the back on the east side. I think we went up to his room. We had a conversation about the bonds and he wanted a sample of each one to show these other people who were going to sell them. I gave him samples, as I remember, that same afternoon. I had to go back to Huntington Park and get them. I first met John F. Muyres in a room in the U. S. Hotel. I can't be positive of the date but I think it was a couple of days after I gave Ryan the samples, either the next day or the day after. I can't remember which. It may have been I saw him that same day that I gave Ryan the bonds and went upstairs. Anyway, I went upstairs to see what they were doing, or he was doing. This fellow was supposed to be up there. I didn't know him at that time, whoever he was, and I went upstairs to see what they were doing. They were

(Testimony of Harold Edward Ryman)

locked in their room and Mr. Muyres and Mr. Woolsey
was in the room at the time. (Whereupon, the witness
identified the defendant, John F. Muyres.) I know Ham
Woolsey. He was there. If I remember right, I walked
in the room and Mr. Woolsey was laying on the bed there
and I said, "Hello, Ham," like that, because I had seen
him before, as he is a bartender at the Avalon Club, and
I had seen him before. I knew him, knew who he was,
but he didn't know me. I did not go up to the room
pursuant to Ryan's request but went on my own account.
I had a conversation with John F. Muyres in the room
there but I just kind of forget what he said. At the time I
walked in the room, I remember distinctly Mr. Muyres
was copying down a list. I think you have it there—of
the bonds. I made up a list of all the bonds that I had
and he was copying the list of them which I had given
to Ryan. The list which is handed to me is the list of
which I was speaking. It is in my writing. It is the
one which Muyres was copying when I walked into the
room. (The list referred to was received in evidence and
marked Plaintiff's Exhibit No. 3. It is a list of the
serial numbers and the denominations of the bonds which
the witness testified that he stole from Mrs. Nellie P.
Covert and shipped to California.) I think that list was
later given back to me by Ryan. I put it in my grip.
The list which I had copied contained the numbers of
all the bonds which I had shipped over there. As I recall, at the time, the reason that the list was given to
him, the reason I wrote the list out, was there seemed to
be some doubt in their minds if the bonds had been
stolen, and the idea was that I wrote the list out so

(Testimony of Harold Edward Ryman)

they could check up and see if they were reported stolen or not. I mean, reported stolen. I think the time I first approached Ryan back in Arizona during the discussion of these bonds, I told him they were Government bonds and naturally they were negotiable. I looked at that, of course. I had given this list to Ryan before I got up in the room and John F. Muyres was making a copy of that list. I do not recall that he spoke about the list at that time. I can't recall what was said. I was arrested November 8th and made a written statement which I signed after my arrest. It was read to me before I signed it. I think my recollection as to the events which had occurred from October 22nd to November 1st, was clearer the date I made the statement than today. It has been so long ago, four and a half months ago and I forget lots of details. I don't recall whether I saw any bonds with anyone else other than Ryan that day in the room. There were a lot of things said by those three present about the samples which I had given Ryan, but I can't recall offhand what they were. We finally left the room together and split as we got down to the street. We were supposed to meet the next day back in the hotel. All four of us. When we split up Muyres and Woolsey went together and I think I went back to the hotel, my hotel in Huntington Park, and I don't know where Ryan went. We met there again the next day. Mr. Muyres told us something about the other fellow had the bonds and was doing something with them but I don't quite remember what was said. It was just put off, postponed. We separated again at that time. We met again the next day. We met down in the U. S. Hotel either three or

(Testimony of Harold Edward Ryman)

four times, I don't recall how many times, but we went there every few days, every day for a series of days, four or five days. Nothing happened at any of these times. I gave them the samples of the bonds and Uncle Muyres came back and told me somebody was doing something about the bonds. The day before that I had given the bonds to Ryan and within a matter of a few minutes after giving the bonds to Ryan I walked over there and met Uncle Muyres and Woolsey in that room and Muyres was copying the list. And the next day Uncle Muyres told me somebody was doing something about the bonds and we met there the following day again, that happened two or three times and it was postponed on account of Saturday and Sunday. On Saturday Uncle Muyres told us we could cash the coupons, that we could sell the coupons on the bonds. I went and clipped the coupons off and gave them to Uncle Muyres. I and Uncle Muyres then went down to a street, in the Southern part of the city, where there was a sort of a park in the middle, a lot of grass and that is all I know about it. He left me there and went on down South. He was gone about a half-hour or forty-five minutes or maybe an hour. He came back with just enough money as I recall so that each got a share of $68.00 and some odd cents. Then we went back to the Hotel and the four of us met. As a matter of fact, we did not meet in the Hotel, we met in the parking lot where he had his car behind the Hotel. This was Saturday and it was agreed that we would all go to Murietta Hot Springs for Sunday. Ryan and I drove my car on Saturday night and Uncle Muyres, Woolsey and a girl came along later on that evening. We stayed there over the week-end. I came back to town Monday morning

(Testimony of Harold Edward Ryman)

early. We didn't go back to the Hotel, we went out on Whittier Boulevard and stayed at the Tabor Hotel in the 4600 block. That is I and Ryan. I left my place in Huntington Park. When we left Murietta Hot Springs we were to meet Uncle Muyres and Woolsey at 4801 Whittier. The Tabor Hotel was two or three blocks from there. I met Uncle Muyres at the service station. Nothing was said about the bonds then and we were supposed to meet again that afternoon at the service station. Uncle Muyres said the deal was going through. Then it was just postponed, somebody was doing something about the bonds and that is all I understand about it. That went along for two or three days or more and it began to get tiresome. We didn't know whether he would sell or what had happened. Up to the time when we returned from Murietta Hot Springs I had not turned over any of the bonds to anybody other than the samples which I described. When we came back on Monday and it went along for two or three days afterwards, then Uncle Muyres said that it was all set and that he wanted the rest of the bonds so I went out and got them all except I should say about $16,000.00 worth of Home Loans. I got all the Power Bonds and all the Australian Government, and all the German Bonds and one $5,000.00 Home Loan Bond, and gave them to him in his car on a little side street. That is the last I ever saw of them. That was the gross amount of them. Later on he did return a few of them, two or three of them. I saw him again that evening about five o'clock. He said that they were doing something with them; a fellow had them but that the sale hadn't gone through yet. I left Los Angeles about the first or

(Testimony of Harold Edward Ryman)

second of November and about three days before then I asked Uncle Muyres why he didn't bring the money in for the bonds and he said that the deal was going through. Pretty soon it got so we wanted to leave and he didn't bring the money in. I asked him where they were and he said this fellow had them and was trying to put through a deal. I told him that if he didn't put it through by tomorrow that we were going to leave and we wanted them back. He said that they had shipped them to New York so it was agreed that when the money was sent back for them it would be sent to me and Ryan, but before we left, I think it was the last day, I gave him first a $100.00 bond which he took out somewhere and sold and brought back the money. Then I gave him a $1000.00 bond and he was gone about an hour or an hour and a half and he came back with the money. That was about the day I left. The $500.00 bonds I gave them were all Home Loan Bonds. Before I left he came back and said they couldn't sell only a part of them and if I remember he gave me a couple of Austrian, onr or two of the German and I forget how many he gave me. He didn't give me back the $5,000.00 Home Owners Loan Bond. I didn't get any money from Uncle Muyres from the first large amount of bonds which I turned over to him. I didn't get any of the samples back which I turned over to Ryan and which Uncle Muyres reported he was working on. After I left we went to Houston, Texas. We did not take the suitcase, Government's Exhibit No. 1, to Texas but we shipped it to Texas. I had clothes and shirts and my coat and the remaining $16,000.00 of Home Loan Bonds in that suitcase. I was arrested in

(Testimony of Harold Edward Ryman)

Texas. That list which is Government's Exhibit 3, I concealed in a part of the suitcase and a list was there when I was arrested. I recognized Special Agent Sisk who is sitting here. He found that list and he knew what it was. As I recall it is the same list which I gave to Ryan and which I saw Muyres copy. With regard to the $500.00 bond which Uncle Muyres cashed for me the day before I left he said that the fellow who cashed it was to receive 30%. He brought back the remainder and that was the money that was split up between myself, Mr. Ryan, Mr. Woolsey and himself. With regard to the $1,000.00 bond which Uncle Muyres sold the day before I left there was 30% taken off for whoever was supposed to have cashed it and then it was to have been split four ways between I and himself and Woolsey and Mr. Ryan.

EXCEPTION NO. ONE

Whereupon the following took place:

"Q. Was that general agreement entered into at the outset, as to the split of all bonds?

MR. GRAHAM: Pardon me. I object to that as calling for a conclusion of the witness.

THE COURT: Objection sustained.

MR. IRWIN: All right. We will go around the long way.

Q. Did you have any conversation when you first got together after you had come to Los Angeles with the

(Testimony of Harold Edward Ryman)

bonds with anybody about what would be done with the proceeds of the sale of any bonds that might be sold?

A. It was supposed to have been divided equally among us, and after it was evenly divided, 20% of each one was to go to me.

MR. GRAHAM (Interrupting): Just a minute. That is the same thing. I have no objection to stating any conversation that he had with them.

MR. IRWIN: If you will just wait a minute, I prefer to examine my witness myself.

Q. When you say "us", who do you mean by "us"?

A. I and Mr. Muyres—as a matter of fact, it was agreed by all four of us that were present at that time.

THE COURT: When you say "was agreed", just what do you mean?

THE WITNESS: Well, it was between I and Mr. Ryan—it was agreed between I and Mr. Ryan.

THE COURT (Interrupting): Tell us just what was said.

MR. GRAHAM: If the Court please, I have another objection to this conversation: On the ground that it is immaterial, and that it could have no tendency to prove or disprove transportation of bonds in interstate commerce, a transportation which had already taken place; it could have no tendency to prove or disprove a conspiracy to transport bonds, the transportation having been completed, so the conspiracy, if any, was therefore completed.

THE COURT: What do you think about that, Mr. Irwin?

MR. IRWIN: The answer to that is this, your Honor: One of the elements that must be proved is the knowledge that they were knowingly transported, and

(Testimony of Harold Edward Ryman)

knowing that the same were stolen. The materiality of
showing the split, since it has been shown here the Home
Owners Loan bonds were negotiable bonds, if we show
that, and the witness has testified that 30 per cent went
to the man who cashed a thousand dollar bond and a five
hundred dollar bond, with 70 per cent coming back to the
four of them, Uncle Muyres, this man, and the other
two, why, it is material to show the knowledge of the
group in cashing that bond. If a bond is on the up-and-
up, you don't discount it 30 per cent, a bond of the United
States Government which is negotiable.

MR. GRAHAM: The answer to that, your Honor, is
that he is trying to prove knowledge after the crime was
complete instead of before.

MR. IRWIN: Which is entirely

THE COURT (Interrupting): Of course, all the
surrounding facts and circumstances could be shown.

The objection is overruled. I think the evidence itself
is admissible.

I think, though, the witness should give a more—
show the time and place of this conversation, and that
should be definitely fixed. We cannot leave it in saying
that it was understood, et cetera.

Strike out all of the statement of this witness as to
what was understood, with reference to the distribution
of these bonds.

Now, put this witness down to the time, place and
persons present in the regular and customary way.

MR. IRWIN: Very well, your Honor.

(Testimony of Harold Edward Ryman)

MR. GRAHAM: And may the record show it is going in over my objection, and on the grounds stated?

THE COURT: Yes.

MR. GRAHAM: And an exception noted?

THE COURT: Yes."

DIRECT EXAMINATION

CONTINUED:

Before I came to Los Angeles the only one I had discussed this deal with was Ryan. Before leaving Arizona, Ryan and I had a discussion as to what would be done with these bonds after I reached Los Angeles. I don't know how to say just what that discussion was except by saying they were all to be sold. He knew somebody else that knew somebody else that would sell them. While we were in Arizona it was not decided between Ryan and myself as to what would be done with the money that might be obtained when the bonds were sold. When I came to Los Angeles and met Ryan and gave him the samples there was nothing said between us as to what would be done with the proceeds from any of the bonds that might be sold. And later on when I met Ryan together with Uncle Muyres and Woolsey in Ryan's room where I saw Uncle Muyres copying the list which I had given Ryan and there was nothing said by anyone in the presence of the other three concerning the proceeds from any bonds that might be sold. On that same Saturday after the coupons were cashed by Uncle Muyres when I had ridden out a ways with him and he had returned with some money, there was a conversation held in Ryan's

(Testimony of Harold Edward Ryman)

room in the U. S. Hotel where Uncle Muyres, myself, Ryan and Woolsey were present. We were discussing the matter of dividing the money up. I told them what I had done in getting them and taking them over here. That I should be entitled to more for my share. Therefore I should receive 20% of each individual share. In other words, I was to take 20% of each one of their parts. It was all agreed. Muyres, Woolsey and Ryan consented. Of these coupons which I had given to Uncle Muyres and which he had cashed he brought back the face value minus 30%. We all agreed when Uncle Muyres told us that 30% had to be deducted. There was nothing that could be done about it. We all had to take it. He came back with the money and you couldn't say anything about it as long as it was stolen. The split which I proposed was of the remaining money. After the remaining money was split four ways I was to receive from each of the three, namely, Uncle Muyres, Woolsey and Ryan 20% of their fourth. Because of the extra work which I had done, and the chances I had taken in stealing the bonds. That was the split for any other sales that might be made. This was all agreed upon at that time. We went to Murietta Hot Springs on the afternoon of the same Saturday when the first proceeds from the coupons of the bonds were divided among us. (There were then offered in evidence as Plaintiff's Exhibit No. 4 two postcards sent from Murietta Hot Springs and which the witness identified.)

I did not remain at the Tabor Hotel after I returned from Murietta Hot Springs. I moved to a little hotel at 4192 Whittier Boulevard. The Rex, as I recall. We

(Testimony of Harold Edward Ryman)
stayed there about three or four or five days. That is
until we left.

When I was arrested in Texas I had on a jacket and I
had concealed in the lining a coupon. It was one of the
coupons that was clipped off the bonds that was given to
Uncle Muyres and when he brought back the money there
was some discussion why it could not have been sold and
it was left among the rest of the money given me. I put
that in my jacket. I did not see Uncle Muyres between
the time I left Los Angeles and the time of my arrest.
I left on the first or second of November.

(There was then offered in evidence as Plaintiff's Exhibit No. 5 two coupons which the witness had heretofore
identified as being those found in the lining of his jacket
at the time of his arrest.)

I never met nephew Muyres. I wasn't invited to meet
Uncle Muyers that day at the U. S. Hotel, I just walked in.

(There was then offered in evidence as Plaintiff's Exhibit No. 6 a piece of paper identified by the witness as
being a list of some securities given to him by Uncle
Muyres at the Tabor Hotel about four or five days before
the witness left and which list the witness testified was a
list of the bonds which the witness did not get back from
Uncle Muyres and were retained by somebody and were
made up of a $4,000.00 German bond and $2,000.00 Austrian, $2,000.00 Home Owners Loan and $2,000.00 of the
Kansas Power equalling $13.00.00.)

(Testimony of Harold Edward Ryman)

This note book which has the reverse cover off and
which has the initials T. B. Tom Ryan, Avalon Club,
Phoenix, is my book and the handwriting is mine. I put
that name and address there before I left Phoenix for
Los Angeles. I have seen this Railway Express receipt
which I am shown and which you sign when you get your
merchandise. I signed this when I got my bag which I
have previously identified as the one I received in Houston,
Texas. The date November 2nd, 1935 which appears
on this receipt is the day that I shipped the bag with the
bonds in it to Houston. (Thereupon this document was
received as Plaintiff's Exhibit No. 7. But only for the
purpose of indicating the date of departure of the witness
from Los Angeles to Houston, Texas, and for no other
purpose.)

(CROSS EXAMINATION)

BY MR. OSTROM:

In the summer of 1935 I was living in Phoenix, part
of the time I was in Tucson. I knew Miss Covert in
Tucson before I went to Phoenix. I have a house trailer
that I live in. I had the house trailer on part of her
property, taking care of a big house which she owned.
I can't tell you exactly when I left Tucson for Phoenix
but it was sometime around August or September. It
was after I had seen these bonds. I told you on direct
examination that the occasion for entering her house was
to feed the dog. But I don't recall seeing anything about
that in the statement that I made in Houston, Texas.

(Testimony of Harold Edward Ryman)

(Whereupon there was offered as Defendant's Exhibit No. A on behalf of the defendant, John Muyres only, the statement made to government officers by the witness at Galveston, Texas, dated November 16th, 1935) Whereupon this statement was read to the jury as follows:

"I, Harold Edward Ryman, age 28, make the following voluntary statement to Special Agent T. H. Sisk, Federal Bureau of Investigation, U. S. Department of Justice. No threats, promises or inducements of any kind have been made to me in connection with this statement; I am fully aware of my rights and that I need make no statement unless I so desire, and also realize that anything I say herein can be used for prosecutive purposes.

"I am acquainted with a woman named Miss Nellie P. Covert, who lives at 1242 North Park Street, Tucson, Arizona. I have known her about eight months, and have done odd jobs for her. I have a trailer wagon which I kept on her property from about March to the end of April, 1935. I knew this woman had a lot of property and from my knowledge of her I believed she had money or gold concealed around the house. Some time in July, 1935, while she was away I entered the house through a window and looked around, and found a lock box in a closet on the floor. I found the key in a steel cabinet, opened the box and observed a large number of bonds therein. I did not take any of them at this time.

"On or about October 8, 1935, I told Thomas B. Ryan, who worked around the Avalon Club, Phoenix, of what I had seen at Miss Covert's house. Ryan said he thought he had connections through which he could handle them. He did not at this time state the identity of his connec-

(Testimony of Harold Edward Ryman)

tions. I told Ryan I could get the bonds any time he gave the word. He indicated I should wait a few days until he saw his friend about the matter. I say Ryan nearly every day at the club. I never did know where he lived. And we had many conversations about the bonds. On or about October 15th, Ryan told me to go get the bonds as his friend was in Los Angeles waiting to handle them. I watched Miss Covert's house every day or so from then on but did not have an opportunity to get the bonds as she stayed at home all the time.

"On October 22, 1935, about 10:00 a. m., I went to her home and noticed she was away. I entered the house through a side window which was not locked. I found the lock box in the closet as previously described and took all the bonds therefrom. They were in envelopes and I substituted paper in *cash* envelope. I am not positive but it is my recollection there was $42,000 worth. I do not know how many individual bonds there were. The list tucked in my suitcase lining contains the serial numbers of all of them except these which I buried as hereinafter described.

"Immediately after obtaining the bonds I drove out St. Mary's Road, Tucson, past the front of St. Mary's Hospital, turned right at the first gravel road, approximately two blocks from the hospital, and continued along this gravel road, which eventually leads to the mountains, and which runs east and west for about one-fourth of a mile, till I came to a dry wash or creek bed, which can be located through a dip in the road. The wash is about 20 feet wide and is at right angles to the road. I walked to the right in a northerly direction, and paced off 200

(Testimony of Harold Edward Ryman)

steps, until I came to a small island or mound, about 10 by 30 feet, which was right in the center of the wash bed. I then made a small ring or circle of rocks on the bank, to the southeast, the circle being about one yard in diameter, and readily perceivable from the bed of the dry wash. About nine feet away in a southeasterly direction I buried 11 or 12 bonds in a steel box wrapped in canvas, in a hole about one foot deep. The hole is about two feet from the base of a sage brush bush, and may have a stone over it as a marker but I am not sure as to this. The buried bonds are of mixed varieties and none of the coupons have been clipped from them, i. e. by me."

The first page is signed in pen and ink, "Harold Eddie Ryman."

"After burying the bonds in question I placed the balance of them in the car in back of the rumble seat, and drove to Phoenix where I spent two hours looking for Tommie Ryan, but couldn't find him. I left a note for him at the desk in the Avalon Club stating that I was leaving for Los Angeles and to meet me there in front of the main post office at either noon or between 5:00 and 6:00 p. m. as soon as possible. Ryan and I had previously arranged to go there when I got the bonds.

"I left Phoenix about 5:00 p. m., October 22nd, in my Ford coupe, bearing Arizona license D6 D8 with a friend of mine named Russell E. Baird, whom I had picked up at Tucson after burying some of the bonds. Baird knew nothing about the bonds being in the car and is entirely innocent. Baird resided at 2500 Oracle Road, Tucson, and has an orange juice business there. He wanted to

(Testimony of Harold Edward Ryman)

accompany me west to visit his wife who resides at 144 Fourth Street, Redlands, California. I drove to California via Blythe and arrived in the state on the night of the same date, October 22nd. I drove straight through to Redlands where I left Baird off at his wife's, and I haven't see him since.

"I registered at a hotel in Redlands but do not recall the name of it. I remember it was one block off Main Street and about four blocks from Baird's house, and is a two or three story red brick building. I registered as Eddie Ryman or Roberts, and the room rent was 50 cents. I stayed there one night only. The next morning, the 23rd, I drove alone to Huntington Park, California, and registered that evening at the Longfellow Hotel as Eddie Ryman or Eddie Roberts.

"I stayed there about three days until October 26th. In the meanwhile, every day, I was driving into Los Angeles, and met Ryan on October 24th, about noon, in front of the post-office. He told me he had arrived the night before and registered at the U. S. Hotel across the street near the post-office. He was registered as either T. B. Bryan or Ryan. As soon as I saw him I told him about getting the bonds, and he said right away that he wanted samples of each kind for his friend to look at. Ryan requested that I meet him the next day at his room which I did, on October 25th.

"In the room I was introduced to Jack Muyers and Ham Woolsey, neither of whom I had ever known before, although I recalled having seen Ham Woolsey bartending at the Avalon Club in Phoenix. Ryan made the remark in front of all of us that Jack knew the man who was

(Testimony of Harold Edward Ryman)

going to handle the bonds. As I recall, Jack Muyers asked me how many I had and I told him about $30,000 worth. Muyers said he could handle all of them. I described what kind of bonds they were, mentioning the fact they weren't registered, etc. He said he wanted samples of each kind I gave him, either three or four bonds. I believe they were as follows: one, HOLC, $100; one-Kansas City Light & Power, $1,000; and one-Austrian, $1000. I might have given him one German bond but am not sure. Muyers was to show the bonds to his prospective purchaser or friend and let us know the next day if they could be handled.

"The next morning, Saturday, the 26th, the four of us again met in Ryan's room at the U. S. Hotel, at which time Muyers said nothing could be done until Monday, but that the bonds that I had left. We had the coupons already on the samples I had given him the previous day. It was agreed among the four of us that the proceeds from cashing the coupons would be split four ways, also that Muyers' friend would receive 30 per cent of the amount realized for his trouble in cashing them. I do not recall exactly how many coupons were due on the bonds. However, I remember that they had accumulated for several months back."

That is also signed in pen and ink, "Harold Eddie Ryman."

"We all went out to the hotel together. Ryan and Woolsey went shopping, and Muyers and I got in his car and drove to an exclusive residential district where he let me out on the street corner, close to Figueroa, and some other street which had a grass parkway down the middle.

(Testimony of Harold Edward Ryman)

It took us about 20 minutes to drive there from the U. S. Hotel, and we drove in a southwest direction. Muyers said he was going to see his friend and cash the coupons. He was gone about one-half hour and came back with the money in an envelope of the First Security National Bank of Los Angeles, but I do not recall what branch it was. If I recall correctly, Muyers had obtained $344 and some odd cents from cashing the coupons. This amount was the balance left over after his friend took out 30 per cent. Muyers gave me about $137 as my share. He also gave me $68 to give to Ryan as his share, which I did not give him as he was drunk. Muyers stated he would give Woolsey his $68 share and kept the additional $68 as his own share. Muyers drove back to the U. S. Hotel where we met Woolsey and Ryan.

"Inasmuch as nothing more could be done until Monday, Muyers suggested we all spend the week end at a resort known as Murrieta's Hot Springs, which he indicated he owned an interest in. Ryan and I drove there in my car, leaving Los Angeles and checking out of our respective hotels about 2:00 p. m., Saturday, the 26th. The resort is about 75 miles southwest of Los Angeles in the mountains. I registered as Eddie Roberts and Ryan as T. B. Ryan. Woolsey, Muyers and the latter's sweetheart, one Katie Condo, arrived late that night in Muyer's car. We all stayed there for the week end and returned to Los Angeles early Monday morning, October 28th. Upon arrival Ryan and I registered at the Tabor Hotel about noon. Ryan did the registering and I do not know what names he gave.

80

"Muyers had told us he owned the Jackson Service Station, 4801 Whittier Boulevard, Los Angeles, and to communicate with him there. On the way into the city from the mountains we stopped at this gas station and met Muyers and Woolsey at the restaurant which is operated in conjunction with the station. During a conversation Muyers said he was going down town to see his friend who had the bonds. Thereafter, we saw Muyers and Woolsey every day but he never did produce the cash derived from selling the bonds, claiming that his friend had not yet been able to dispose of them. About October 29th he asked me to give him all the bonds I had left as his friend could handle them right away. I gave him $21,100 worth of the bonds distributed as follows: One, $5,000 HOLC; one- $100 HOLC; two- Kansas Power & Light, at $1,000 apiece; four- Austrian Government, at $1,000 apiece; ten- German Government, at $1,000 apiece. In addition, Muyers still had the samples which I had previously given him. No one was present when I gave him the additional bonds as I turned them over to him on the street near the Tabor Hotel. The others knew about it afterwards as I told them, and Woolsey must have known of it as he was living with Muyers in a small bungalow at about 3414 Topez Street, Los Angeles. It is a brownish maroon frame house on the side of a steep hill.

"Muyers was to give me the money derived from sale of the bonds the next day, October 30th, but he came around to the Tabor Hotel room and stated the deal was delayed. Woolsey and Ryan were present at the time. On the 31st it was the same thing again.

(Testimony of Harold Edward Ryman)

"The night of October 31st, Ryan and I demanded some action on the bonds during a conversation with Muyers and Woolsey in the hotel room. Muyers had an excuse that his friend couldn't make contact with some other person who had gone out of town.

"The next morning, November 1st, Ryan and I checked out of the Tabor into the Rex Hotel, 4194 Whittier Boulevard, where we had room No. 25. Ryan suggested we use some other name, as when I Registered I used"—

That is signed also in pen and ink, "Harold Eddie Ryman."

"the name of Eddie Roberts and registered Ryan as Don Thompson.

"During the morning of November 1st I told Muyers in the presence of Woolsey and Ryan that I wanted the bonds back or else the money that same day. He said he'd get them back, and he and Woolsey came around to the hotel again later in the day at which time Muyers said that his friend couldn't get them back as he'd sent them to New York. I told him I, at least, wanted the samples back and he then left stating he would get all he could. He returned in about an hour with $8,000 worth, a total of eight individual bonds, six German and two Austrian. He handed me a piece of a lunch menu, on the back of which in his handwriting are two lists of bonds. The list to the left are what he still has, (plus the samples), and the list to the right are what he returned to me, except the $100 HOLC which he kept, and through which a line is drawn. The smaller figures at the bottom of the paper are my handwriting. Special Agent T. H. Sisk has

82

shown me the paper in question which was among either
mine or Ryan's effect, and I have initialed same while
making this statement. During this same conversation
Muyers wanted me to give him all the HOLCs, stating
that he could cash them right away. I refused to do so
until he gave me the money for the other bonds, but did
give him one $500 HOLC. He said he'd have service
station man cash it, and would give him 20 per cent for
his trouble.

"He came back in an hour and a half with about $400
cash, of which I got $160 and Ryan and Woolsey and
Muyres got $80 apiece. Muyres then said to give him a
$1000 HOLC and he'd do the same thing, which I did.
He came back again with the proceeds; as I remember it
was $700. He claiming a different man cashed this bond
and demanded 30 per cent commission. I got $280 and
each of the others $140. Muyres again suggested I give
him all the HOLCs, but I refused to do so. He said he
expected to obtain the money from the bonds shipped to
New York in about a week. Ryan and I had decided to
leave and told him to hold our shares. Ryan said he'd
pick his share up at Phoenix from Woolsey or else that
Woolsey could send it to him at Houston, Texas, where
we intended going. Both Muyres and Woolsey said they
would return to Phoenix that same day, November 1st.
This was the last I saw of them and I do not know whether
they returned or not. I told Muyres I would write him
my address as he could communicate with me. I was to
communicate with him care the Twin Barrels beer place,
19th and Madison Streets, Phoenix, which Muyres said
he owned.

(Testimony of Harold Edward Ryman)

"Ryan and I left Los Angeles, November 2nd, in my Ford car. Before leaving I placed the remaining bonds in my suitcase and expressed them collect, 'will call', to Houston, Texas.

"Enroute to Houston, we stopped over-night at Van Horn in an auto camp; also at the Dixie Hotel, San Antonio. We arrived in Houston, November 6th, and registered at the Austin Hotel. Ryan said he could dispose of the bonds in Houston, where he knew lots of people, which is the reason we came there.

"On November 7th, I concealed $14,150 of the bonds under a vacant house in Houston alongside of where my car was parked. I kept two bonds out, one $1000 HOLC and one $1,000 German International, both of which I gave to Ryan as samples. He said he was going to show them to someone, and on November 7th introduced me to a man named 'Les' Le Sieur, at a used car lot across the street from Raymond Pearson Motor Company. Nothing was said about bonds. I looked at a Cadillac car he had for sale and for which he wanted $495. Ryan was not trying to buy the car as he didn't have enough money.

"I omitted to mention that when I left Phoenix on October 22nd, I did not take the bonds with me but shipped them via Railway Express before leaving to Huntington Park, 'will call,' collect, under the name of Eddie Ryman.

"This statement consists of four typewritten pages, each of which bears my signature, and is true to the best of my knowledge and memory. I will plead guilty to violation of the National Stolen Property Act, and will testify for the Government if requested to do so."

Signed in writing, "Harry Eddie Ryman."

84

(Testimony of Harold Edward Ryman)

And on the back, in handwriting:

"Witnesses:

"A. C. Martindale, City Detective, City of Houston;

"T. J. Eubanks, City Detective, City of Houston;

"T. H. Sisk, Special Agent, Federal Bureau of Investigation, U. S. Department of Justice, San Antonio, Texas."

The first time I entered Miss Covert's house I looked around the house and found the bonds. I can't exactly give the reason, I am not a burglar. I just happened to be in the house. I knew she had lots of property and was worth money. I just took it for granted from what other people told me, and I had never been in the house before, but, as I told you, this time the dogs were hungry, and I went in the house to look around and found the bonds. I knew they were there but I didn't take them. The reason was that I did not know where to dispose of them and they were no good to me. Then I moved to Phoenix. I had met Mr. Ryan occasionally and happened to meet him accidentally in the beer parlor in Phoenix. Then about a week after I talked to Ryan the last time, I went over to Tucson with the intention of stealing the bonds and I spent about a week in Tucson. I waited until Miss Covert was out of the house. I got in through the window and I went to the box where the bonds were kept. I opened the box and took out the bonds. Then I carried the bonds and put them in the car and I drove to St. Mary's hospital and I buried some of the bonds, because I didn't know what these fellows that I had made the agreement with might cheat me out of them, and I would have some left for me, anyway, if they did. Although there was

(Testimony of Harold Edward Ryman)

only other fellow that I had any agreement with I took it for granted that there would be other people because he told me there were other people whom he had contacted. But the only person I talked to about stealing the bonds and disposing of them before I left Arizona was Ryan. And after I hid the bonds I went back to Phoenix, which was a four hour drive from Tucson, to look for Ryan in the Avalon Club. He wasn't there so I left the note to meet me in Los Angeles either at 12 o'clock noon or between 5 and 6 o'clock. It was agreed that if he wasn't there I was to go right through and leave a note for him. I left Phoenix on October 22nd, I don't remember what day of the week it was, but it probably was Tuesday. The next day I contacted Ryan. I arrived in Redlands on the 23rd about 2 o'clock in the A. M., and I came to Huntington Park on the 23rd. I did not contact Ryan until Thursday the 24th. I met him inside the Post Office about noon. But I am not positive it may have been five or six o'clock. He told me he was at the U. S. Hotel. When I met him down stairs in the Post Office I first told him I had the bond with me. He told me he wanted a sample of them. I told him I would have to get them. The bonds were in my room at the Huntington Park Hotel. I left and went alone to the hotel. The hotel was called the Longfellow. Ryan asked for one sample of each bond but I didn't have one of each, I brought one HOLC and I only brought back three or four. That was on Thursday the 24th. I was supposed to meet him back in the hotel in the lobby as soon as I could get back. I saw John F. Muyres on either Thursday the 24th or Friday the 25th, I don't remember which. It was the next day after I met Mr. Ryan in the Post Office. Until then

(Testimony of Harold Edward Ryman)

I had never seen Mr. Muyres or known him in any way.
When I walked into the hotel room Woolsey was lying on
the bed and I just looked at him and said, "Hello, Ham";
that is the fellow I had seen at the beer parlor in Phoenix
but I hadn't known him. He was a bartender that I had
seen off and on. Then Mr. Woolsey introduced me to
Mr. Muyres. We remained in the room about a half hour
or an hour. Mr. Muyres was copying some figures and .
somebody asked, "Are you done with the figures?"
Pretty soon he handed them to me and I think Muyres
asked me if I had all the bonds with me here and I said
yes. I don't remember just what was said about the copying of the list but Muyres wanted a list of the bonds and
I gave them a list of the numbers so he could check to
see if they had been reported stolen. That was the object
of the list. No one said it, it was just a recognized fact
that this is what they were for. I don't remember
whether Ryan asked me to get the list. I think he did.
You see it all happened so unexpected, I wasn't even to
go up to the room, I just broke in there and it all happened so unconcerned, so quick without forethought, it
wasn't arranged. I just broke in this room and it was all
unexpected. As I remember it, it seems to me that
Muyres asked me where I got them, it is all very vague
in my mind. I don't think I told him. I don't remember if I did. There was nothing said whether they were
stolen or not.

I remember taking an automobile ride wtih Mr. Muyres
the week following the week of October – ending Saturday, October, the 26th.

(Testimony of Harold Edward Ryman)

Q. Do you remember Mr. Muyres saying to you "Are those bonds stolen"?

A. Do I remember that?

Q. Yes.

A. I think I do.

Q. And you admitted to him then that they were stolen?

A. Yes.

Q. And that is the first time you ever told Mr. Muyres that those bonds were stolen?

A. That is the first time I had ever seen him; yes.

Q. No, no, I mean − I am talking about an automobile ride about the following Wednesday?

A. No, we never went for a ride on Wednesday. It was Saturday, the first automobile ride I had with Mr. Muyres. That was when we went to this street out there to Figueroa to cash the coupons. That was the first ride I ever had with him. I do not recall a ride with him the following week. I know for sure that I took one ride, that was the day we cashed the coupons, October 28th or 29th, I mean the 26th, the day we went to Murietta Hot Springs. I now recall that subsequent to our return from Murietta Hot Springs, either Wednesday or Thursday, I remember taking an automobile ride with Mr. Muyres to his home on Topaz, out there in a little house along the hill. That was the time that I was living at this hotel on Whittier Boulevard. I cannot recall whether it was practically said at that time by Mr. Muyres, "Are those bonds stolen?", and I said "yes".

Before I went to Los Angeles, Ryan told me I was to receive around $20,000.00. This conversation took place

(Testimony of Harold Edward Ryman)

at the Avalon Cafe in Phoenix. I don't remember the
exact date but it was about a week before I came here.
I know a man in Phoenix by the name of Bushford. I
met him in Tucson. I don't remember whether I told Mr.
Muyres that one of my friends had $50,000.00 worth of
bonds that I could get from Tucson and asked him if
he could dispose of them for me and I don't recall whether
I told Bushford that some of these bonds were Home
Owners Loan Bonds. I didn't tell Bushford that the
holder of these bonds would discount them 40% or more
and I didn't tell Bushford that these bonds were part of
the loot of the Dillinger-Hamilton gang. I didn't tell
Bushford on May 16th, 1935, that some of these bonds
were German Government bonds and Austrian Government Bonds. I forget when it was but when Bushford
was in Phoenix I did talk to him about the bonds, and
asked if he knew of any way to sell them. At that time
I didn't have the bonds. I knew about the bonds. I don't
remember any exact dates but I did speak to Bushford
about the bonds. I saw him once on the street and once
at his house. I don't remember the dates at all. I knew
Bushford for a considerable time before I knew Ryan
and I discussed with Bushford the disposal of these bonds
that I have testified about. I told him that I knew where
there were some bonds and I remember Bushford saying
he didn't want to have anything to do with them. I left
the house and that was all there was to it. I didn't tell
Bushford I had $50,000.00 worth of these bonds. I
didn't have them. But I did tell Bushford that I knew
someone who did have $50,000.00 worth of bonds. But
I am not positive as to what I said. I don't recall
whether or not I told him that these bonds, referring

(Testimony of Harold Edward Ryman)

to the Home Owners Loan Bonds, the Austrian bonds, the German bonds, *the German bonds,* the Kansas City Power & Light Bonds had been stolen or whether or not I told him the names, denominations or the total amount. I don't remember whether I told him these bonds could be stolen or were stolen. Bushford had some dress shops in town, then he went broke and is now selling Indian Jewelry and stuff of that sort. At least that is what he told me. I don't know why he told me, he would not have anything to do with the disposal of the bonds, because he was in business. He may have given me a lecture and told me that I should not *to* ahead and steal bonds but I don't remember if he did. No, I don't recall telling him I would give him $1,000.00 if he could find a buyer for these bonds. Referring again to Government's Exhibit No. 3, the list of the numbers of the bonds, I can't recall clearly remember what Mr. Muyres told me. I do remember very clearly that when I came into the room he was sitting on the window sill copying these numbers off. I never knew or talked to John F. Muyres until I met him in the hotel room in Los Angeles.

CROSS EXAMINATION BY MR. GRAHAM

This list of bonds, Government's Exhibit #3 is in my handwriting. I copied these numbers from the bonds themselves sometime within the first three days after I arrived in Los Angeles. I gave the list to Ryan. I don't recall what the conversation was when I gave the list to Ryan. But I gave him that list when I gave him the bonds. Ryan did not ask me for a list of the bonds with their serial numbers and did not tell me that he would have nothing to do with these *g*onds until he had such a

(Testimony of Harold Edward Ryman)

list to see if they had been stolen. Mr. Muyres did not say that, because at that time I had not seen Mr. Muyres and he didn't say that after I saw him. But it is a fact that I gave this list of bonds to Ryan so that he could check them to see if they were stolen. When I used the name Muyres it was with reference to the Uncle, John F. Muyres, and not to the nephew. I have never had any conversation with the nephew.

CROSS EXAMINATION BY MR. RYAN

I first met you in Phoenix at the Avalon Club. You were operating automatic merchandise machines and marble tables. We were then discusing the machines and talking generally. I told you that I was interested in buying machines and also an automobile and also that I needed some money for an operation for my father. My father is blind, but I don't recall that I wanted to buy a car because I had a car already. After some conversations we discussed the matter of bonds and I told you I knew where there were a lot of bonds and I think I asked you whether you knew where you could sell some bonds. I told you, first, that I would have to take them from somebody' else's house. I didn't tell you I had them. If they had belonged to me I would have taken them to a bank. If they had belonged to me I would not have gone to you to have you sell them for me. After discussing the bonds you told me you would look around to see if you knew anybody who had a little extra money to invest in bonds. After you told me you had a buyer for the bonds you asked me to produce the bonds. I told you that I needed a tire or two for my car and that I would have to get various things for it and there would be various expense

(Testimony of Harold Edward Ryman)

to go for them. It would take three or four days to get them and I wanted to be sure that you had a buyer for them and you explained to me that there wasn't any question in your mine that if the bonds were not counterfeit, were not hot, that you had a sale for them. I was gone for the bonds approximately a week. The next time you heard from me was when I left a note for you at the Avalon Club.

(At this point, at the suggestion of Mr. Graham, the defendant, Ryan, requested that he be permitted to retain counsel to continue the cross-examination and Mr. John Carlisle Lee, a member of the Bar of the State of Arizona, and entitled to practice in the United States District Court for Arizona was permitted to practice in this Court for the purpose of this one case only and to represent the defendant Ryan for the balance of the trial.)

MR. IRWIN: May it please the Court, in compliance with our law, the records in this court and in this case show Mr. Lee entered an appearance for Mr. Woolsey at the time he entered a plea of not guilty, which plea had been withdrawn after Mr. Lee stepped out of the case. I believe that under the law he should be given his consent that Mr. Lee represent him in the case.

THE COURT: It is the right of the defendant to choose any reputable person to appear as his counsel, and the Court will not investigate any previous arrangements. I don't think that would be fair. If there is anything in the nature of the regularity, that can, at a proper time, be brought before the Court, Mr. Irwin.

(Testimony of Harold Edward Ryman)

MR. LEE: , It seems that my client has acquitted himself *himself* in the cross examination, and I need ask no further question at this time.

RE-DIRECT EXAMINATION BY MR. IRWIN

The purpose of giving the list was not to see whether the bonds had been stolen but whether they had been reported stolen. I lived in Arizona about three years before the events took place concerning Nellie Covert. I went there on account of my health, I am tubercular. I did not know John Dillinger. I just happened to be there at the time when they were caught. Before coming to Tucson I lived in Seattle. I worked in canneries in Alaska for two years. At the time when I had the first conversation with Ryan concerning my knowledge of the availability of the bonds I said there was an awful lot of them, I imagine I said around $25,000.00 to $50,000.00, I don't recall the exact amount. At that time I had see*m* them but I didn't know how much was there at all. It was two or three days before I left Los Angeles that I requested Mr. Muyres to either produce the money or return the bonds that I had given him. I made numerous requests for them and was given very evasive answers. My recollection is not very clear about what was said by Mr. Muyres and myself when I had the automobile ride with him around the 31st of October.

Referring to Government's Exhibit 3, which I identified as a list which I prepared of the bonds and gave to Mr. Ryan there is a faint pencil notation "October 22nd" that is in my handwriting. I put that on there the same time I wrote the list that was the date I had stolen the bonds and so as to know the day they were stolen if the list was

(Testimony of E. B. Howarth)

checked. Then they could check from that day back. They would not be reported stolen before that day.

QUESTION BY THE COURT:

I am sure that I told Ryan before I stole the bonds that I was going to steal them.

E. B. HOWARTH

called as a witness on behalf of the Government, having been first duly sworn, testified as follows:

DIRECT EXAMINATION

BY MR. IRWIN:

My name is E. B. Howarth. I reside in Los Angeles. I am in charge of the claim department, local branch of the American Surety Company. I am here in response to a subpoena duces tecum. I have produced the documents requested of me in that subpoena.

The witness then handed to Mr. Irwin a $1,000.00 Austrian Government International Loan Number 12960 bond which was ordered marked Government's Exhibit No. 8 for identification.

Whereupon, there was offered in evidence as Government's Exhibit No. 9, two $1,000.00 Kansas City Power & Light Company bonds, Serial Numbers CM-3041 and 3042 which were described in the indictment and which it had theretofore been stipulated were among those bonds which were the property of Nellie P. Covert.

There was thereupon offered in evidence as Government's Exhibit No. 10, one $1,000.00 Austrian Government Bond Number M-12958 which was one of the bonds

(Testimony of Karl L. Woolsey)

described in the indictment and which it had theretofore been stipulated was among those bonds which were the property of Nellie P. Covert.

There was thereupon offered in evidence as Government's Exhibit No. 11, three $1,000.00 German Government bonds, Serial numbers M-37045, 37044 and 37042 which were the bonds described in the indictment and which it had theretofore been stipulated were among those bonds which were the property of Nellie P. Covert.

There was thereupon offered in evidence as Government's Exhibit No. 12, one $1,000.00 Home Owners Loan Corporation bond, Serial Number M-172105-E which was one of the bonds described in the indictment and which it had theretofore been stipulated was among those bonds which were the property of Nellie P. Covert.

KARL L. WOOLSEY

called as a witness on behalf of the Government, having been first duly sworn, testified as follows:

DIRECT EXAMINATION

BY MR. IRWIN:

My name is Karl L. Woolsey. I reside in Phoenix, Arizona. I am one of the defendants indicted in this case and have heretofore entered a plea of guilty to both counts of the indictment. I am married. I reside at 1105 South First Avenue, Phoenix, Arizona. My wife now lives there. I know the defendants John F. Muyres, Ryan and Ryman. In the summer and fall of 1935, I was employed at 28 South Central Avenue, at the Avalon Cafe in Phoenix, in the capacity of bar-tender. I have known Jack Muyres for approximately four years. I met Ryan,

(Testimony of Karl L. Woolsey)

to the best of my recollection, the early part of last September, 1935. I have known him from September until now. He was working in the capacity of a slot machine mechanic for the same man I was working for at the time I met him. I had a conversation with Ryan after I met him in September concerning bonds and securities. (Whereupon, Mr. Graham, attorney for defendant George Muyres requested that this testimony be considered not binding against the defendant George Muyres unless it be proved to the satisfaction of the jury that at the time the conversation took place, the defendant George Muyres was a party to the conspiracy, which request the Court granted). Ryan approached me and said he noticed I had quite a few personal friends there, leading business men of the city and he told me he had a bunch of "hot" bonds and asked me if I thought I could dispose of them. I told him I would let him know a little later, that I would look into the thing. I asked him from what source they came and he said that he and his partner had won them through gambling and I asked him where and he said "back in the east". I said what part of the east" and he said "Kansas City", so I said "I'll see what I can do". Besides Jimmy Hicks, a friend of mine had been connected with Arizona Bank Examiners, I talked to Jack Muyres. Owing to the fact that I had a lot of business dealings with Muyres and we had been in business together, he dawned on me as a prospect who might know of some place to place a bond. I knew he had big connections in Los Angeles so I went to him and told him that Ryan had approached me with a bunch of bonds that he called "hot" bonds and that at the time Ryan ap-

(Testimony of Karl L. Woolsey)

proached me, he thought there was in the neighborhood of $74,000.00. I asked Muyres if he knew where we could dispose of them. His remark to me was "hell yes, get me some of the bonds". I later went back and asked Ryan for some of the bonds. He said he would have to send his partner after them. He was supposed to have gone after them and Muyres and his mother-in-law in the meantime made a trip to California on some kind of business and he said he would look into it while he was over here. He had in mind seeing some firend of his here about it. When he returned back, he told me that friend that he had intended to see was up in Canada on a big game hunt and he didn't get to see him. He told me later that he contacted his nephew at 4801 Whittier Boulevard and they talked it over.

MR. GRAHAM: Just a minute; just a minute, your Honor. May we have the same instructions in regard to this conversation as we have in regard to the others?

THE COURT: Yes, yes.

BY MR. IRWIN:

Q. Go ahead. What did he tell you then? Had you finished when counsel interrupted?

A. He said he had some contact with his nephew there; that him and his lady friend had met him at 4801 Whittier Boulevard, and they talked it over, and would get—and if I would get in the bonds, why, he could—he was sure he could find a sale for them.

Q. Who could get the bonds?

A. If I could get the bonds from Ryan, why, then, he would dispose of the bonds.

(Testimony of Karl L. Woolsey)

Q. Where?

A. He could bring them to California to sell.

Q. All right.

MR. GRAHAM: Just a minute. I move to strike out all of the testimony of this witness on the ground that his testimony affirmatively shows that up to that time there had been no conspiracy entered into to transport any stolen bonds.

THE COURT: Up to what time?

MR. GRAHAM: Up to the time of the conversation. Because, your Honor—

THE COURT (Interrupting): Motion denied.

MR. GRAHAM: His testimony shows that in the first place—

THE COURT (Interrupting): Just a moment, please. I withdraw my ruling. Mr. Graham desires to argue this question. Go ahead, Mr. Graham.

MR. GRAHAM: His testimony is to the effect that Ryan approached him and said that he had some bonds. It is true he called them "hot" bonds.

THE COURT: That was in Phoenix?

MR. GRAHAM: Yes, and Ryan approached him and said he had some "hot" bonds; but he didn't say, "stolen" bonds; and when pressed by this witness as to where they had come from, he said they had been won in a gambling game; and at that time there was no agreement to transport the bonds—even no suggestion to transport the bonds in interstate commerce. Consequently, the conspiracy alleged in the indictment had not been entered into, and no act done prior to the formation of the conspiracy is permissible to the conspiracy.

(Testimony of Karl L. Woolsey)

THE COURT: Do I understand from this witness that he spoke to Mr. John Muyres in Phoenix?

MR. GRAHAM: Yes.

THE COURT: Was Mr. Muyres in Phoenix?

Mr. Irwin: This is Uncle Muyres.

THE COURT: He lived in Phoenix?

MR. GRAHAM: There is no suggestion of transporting these bonds.

THE COURT: It depends on what interpretation the jury might give to it. Your argument does not appeal to me.

Overruled. Now, not another thing. Let us have the question. Let us have the evidence in this case.

WHEREupon, the Court repeated its instructions with respect to the applicability of this testimony to the defendant George Muyres). That Jack Muyres's nephew and his lady friend had met him there and that if I would get him the bonds, why he was sure he could find a sale for them. He would bring them to California to sell. I went back and told Ryan that I would like to have the bonds. He said his partner was away for them so Muyres got in his car and returned to California and Ryan and Ryman were to come and meet him there so, he was over here for a period of three or four days time. It seems though Ryman hadn't made the connection; he intended to; and Ryman was waiting around, waiting for him to inform him when he was coming to California. The morning of October 22nd, Ryan came in and asked me to loan him $10.00 so that he could come to California. He said this man had left with the bonds for California

(Testimony of Karl L. Woolsey)

and asked me where Muyres was. I said "over there
waiting for you" in California. Before Muyres left, I
had talked to Muyres that he could be reached in Los
Angeles at 4801 Whittier Boulevard at Jack's Filling
Station by which I understood that he meant it was his
station. When Ryan asked me who could sell the bonds,
I told him one of his best customers. He said "who";
I said, I'll just let you guess; he said "Jack Muyres?" I
said: "Yes". So he evidently went out and had a talk with
Muyres because he said "Muyres is ready to talk to me".
Before Ryan left for Los Angeles, I was going to give
him Muyres' address there but Ryan pulled out a card and
apparently had it in his pocket himself. When Ryan asked
me for $10.00 I only had $7.00 in my pocket. I gave it
to him and he got on the bus. On the evening of the
same day which was October 22nd, I went out to Muyres'
place and told his cook to tell Muyres that in the event
he returned from California, he was to come to my house
to see me at once. About 7 or 7:30 that evening, Muyres
came to my door and asked me what I wanted. I said
Ryan was in to see me that morning. He said Ryman
was in California with the bonds and to come over there
immediately. I referred to Ryman as Ryan's partner. I
didn't know Ryman by name at that time. Muyres then
said he would go back that night if he wasn't so tired.
He said that if I would get up and put on my clothes
and go with him and keep him awake, he would drive
over tonight. We had a conversation for quite a while
and I decided to put on my clothes. I looked up my boss
and made arrangements for me to come to California
with Muyres and I was to be back there the next day

(Testimony of Karl L. Woolsey)

or so, so I got in the car and came over with him. We came to Los Angeles and went to his mother-in-law's house. I believe it is some place on Anhurst Street. We got in there around 4 o'clock in the morning and we went to bed. We got up about 7 o'clock and went to Jack's Service Station at 4801 Whittier Boulevard and while we were sitting having our breakfast, there was a telephone call. He was asked out to the station to answer the call. He came back and told me "that is Ryan". "He just told me he is at the U. S. Hotel and wanted to see me right away". We came down and met him at the U. S. Hotel. Muyres said "Well, have you got some of the bonds?" He said no, but he said he was to meet his partner at 11 o'clock here in front of the post office. That he would have everything for him then. He came out and was gone awhile. Then he came back and he had three bonds wrapped in a newspaper. We looked them over and Muyres said "Well, if you will get me the numbers of these bonds, I will go out and check up on them right away and some samples, so I can see whether they are bogus bonds or not". By bogus I mean counterfeit. Ryan left and pretty soon he returned and then Ryman came in. There was no introduction but when Ryman came in he said "hello Ham" meaning speaking to me. I didn't know who the man was. After he told me, I remembered him. Then Muyres said to Ryan, let's get down to business. Then they were away together. I saw Muyres again that evening. He said that Ryman had turned a bunch of the bonds over to them and he had taken them down and turned them over to his nephew. But he said they had to make some kind of arrangement before the bonding house would accept them. They had to take some-

(Testimony of Karl L. Woolsey)

body and make them a member of the Southern California
Athletic Club and also have to deposit $100.00 in the bank
so that the man would have a place of residence and so
that the man who bought the bonds would have somebody
to refer back to in the event the bonds were illegal. At
that time, he told me that he had turned them over to a
man named George Muyres but I later found out it was
his nephew. There was a little difficulty among these boys
being short of money and being in a hurry to get some
money together while we were waiting for the sale of
these bonds; some of us suggested the coupons be clipped
on the bonds and sold for cash to tide us over until the
sale was made. One of the things said back in Arizona
was that Ryan told me "we'll get away from the fact that
they were won by gambling. The bonds were 'hot' enough
but they will never be missed until the first of the year
owing to the fact that they have all of these coupons on
them and the party wouldn't go to them until the first of
the year and we can sell them and clean up and all go
before the bonds were missed". Now getting back to the
day when the boys were short of money, the coupons were
clipped and sold and the same statement I just made there,
Ryman made here in the hotel in the presence of all four
of us here in Los Angeles. Ryman clipped the coupons
and turned them over to John Muyres. George Muyres
had signed them all and put them in the bank. I did not
see the coupons clipped. I don't know whether they were
clipping them in the room. I saw these coupons that
morning. To the best of my recollection, I received
$68.00 for my cut of the coupons later that day. There
were no pennies or nickels to be counted. Then I kicked
back 20% to Ryman which was agreed with all of us was

(Testimony of Karl L. Woolsey)

to be given back to him. The split was with Jack Muyres, Tom Ryan, Eddie Ryman and myself. I do not know whether or not the money which was brought back and divided among us four ways was the entire amount which had been received from the sale of the coupons. I just had to take their word as to what they handed me. The principal negotiators among the four were Ryman and Muyres. They did all the trading and everything. After we received this money for the coupons, we had a few days to wait around here for the returns. Muyres told me the bonds had been shipped to New York City for sale. One $5,000.00 Home Owners Loan bond and I think three or four other thousand dollar bonds. He said while we were waiting on the return of these bonds, we all might as well have a little pleasure trip. The four of us agreed to go down to Murrieta Hot Springs. I don't remember whether this was the night of the same day when I received the $68.00 I referred to as my part of the *of the* coupons before I went down to Murrieta Hot Springs. When we came back, Muyres went to negotiate some more. He told me he was putting a thousand dollar bond first with one friend and then another to sell. Besides George Muyres, Muyres told me that he had talked with his attorney one day when they were out to lunch. He mentioned Bloom's name and said he had asked Bloom what his idea was in disposing of the bonds and that Bloom had informed him he never messed with anything like that but that his idea was in handling anything like that to go to some foreign country like China or Russia and sell them. He said he wouldn't mind taking a vacation on something like that himself. Besides the $68.00 referred

(Testimony of Karl L. Woolsey)

to, I received some other money. As I have said, there
was a thousand and five thousand dollars put out around
town for sale among friends of his and he came back with
some money, I don't know how much. Muyres and I were
at the Rex Hotel then on Whittier Boulevard. That
was where Ryan and Ryman were living at that time. I
don't know how much money we received there but some
bonds were sold and Uncle Muyres and Ryman ran Ryan
and me out of the room while they checked up on it.
This must be about a week after we came back from the
springs. Muyres said that he wanted to check with Ryman alone. It seemed that he and Ryman were getting
along well. I had intended to return immediately to
Phoenix. I was to be back for Saturday service on the
bar and I stayed over almost ten days. Muyres asked me
each day to remain and I think he said we'll have the thing
finished up tomorrow. I wired my boss twice and told
him I was detained on business and couldn't make it.
After Uncle Muyres came back from Los Angeles on his
very first trip following my conversation with him about
the bonds when he told me had made arrangements with
George Muyres, he returned to Los Angeles again and I
communicated to Ryan what he had said. Then some little
time elapsed before Ryan told me his partner had gotten
the bonds and gone to Los Angeles. I sent Muyres a wire
in Los Angeles telling him that the boys had been delayed
but he came back to Phoenix anyway. Now getting back
to the time when I left Ryman and Uncle Muyres in the
hotel room, Ryan and I came back and waited for a
while and finally they called us up into the room. Neither
one of us questioned the figures. I just got whatever

104

they gave me because they were doing the business. They divided it and to the best of my recollection, they gave me $489.83. Then I gave back to Ryman 20% of what was given me. Now getting back to the wire which I sent Uncle Muyres while he was in Los Angeles and before the time that Ryan borrowed the money from me and left for Los Angeles, I sent this wire to Uncle Muyres in Los Angeles about two days before Ryan left. I sent it Western Union. I signed it Ham. I addressed it to Jack Muyres, 4801 Whittier Boulevard. Jack Muyres or J. F. Muyres. It must have been a straight wire because I sent it in the morning. Now getting back to the split of the money at the Rex Hotel, Muyres wanted to know how each man would get his money. The boys were fixing to leave town so Ryan told me to get his money and to send it to him to the Denver Hotel in Dallas, Texas. This was the same day when I left and went back to Phoenix. Ryan and Ryman said they were leaving the same day that I left. I told Ryan I would send him the money there and we all broke up. Muyres and I made arrangements to return to Phoenix. The others made arrangements to go where they were going. It wasn't positive where they were going just to Texas. Muyres and I drove back to Phoenix. On the way there somebody threw a rock at our car and smashed the radiator. Muyres told me I still had a credit of $24.00 coming and that would pay for the repair of the radiator. We returned to Phoenix and I went back to my job. A few days later, Muyres returned back to Los Angeles to see what had happened to the bonds. Before we all broke up, Muyres told me that in the neighborhood of $10,000.00 had been

(Testimony of Karl L. Woolsey)

shipped for sale, and to keep the boys from getting away with all the bonds before we realized, the rest of them were in a safe in the Couthern California Automobile Club; that they would be sold just as soon as the return came back from the others; by that I mean to keep Ryman and Ryan from leaving town with the bonds. As I understood it, Ryman turned $19,000.00 worth of bonds over to Muyres' possession and $10,000.00 of these were shipped to New York so Uncle Muyres told me. I remember when we made our split, all of us took money except Muyres and he had taken two $1,000.00 bonds for his cut. When we went back, he had taken them back to Arizona with him. That was the last time I saw those bonds. After we returned to Phoenix, Muyres was to return back to Los Angeles for there was a part of the $19,000.00 worth of bonds that were supposed to be gone to New York in the safe of the Southern California Automobile Club, so he told me. When he got back, he told me he was scared to death. He had bought a Houston paper. He said Ryman and Ryan had been taken into custody and they had got what bonds they had with them and they had implicated Muyres and me. I believe the four of us was all that the paper said was implicated. He said that he had buried the bonds that were in the safe of the Automobile Club out in some suburb here in Los Angeles. Uncle Muyres told me that he had kept these bonds at the Automobile Club with (George) Muyres for safe keeping. In the event he got a sale on the other ones, he said "all right" he would give them to the broker and have them put through.

This document consisting of eight pages of longhand on the letterhead of the Federal Bureau of Investigation,

(Testimony of Karl L. Woolsey)
United States Department of Justice, is in the handwriting of Rutzen, one of the Agents. I initialed each page and I signed the document on the last page with my signature "Karl L. Woolsey". I suppose the date of December 2nd, 1935, which appears on the document as the date that I signed it is correct because it was after I was in custody. To the best of my recollection, the statement was correct when I signed it.

Whereupon, the document theretofore identified by the witness was marked Plaintiff's Exhibit No. 13 for identification.

After Uncle Muyres and I were arrested, we had some conversation in jail in Phoenix. We tried to make up a story that would sound truthful. We discussed what we would say about where the bonds came from and we had decided that we were to say that the bonds were presented to us as bonds won through gambling and that Ryan had said that he and his partner had won them in Kansas City. This wasn't a true statement. I later withdrew that plea in this case. I never met George Muyres, that is, Nephew Muyres until I saw him in Court. I never had any dealings with him. All of these matters which I relate were told to me by Uncle Muyres.

CROSS EXAMINATION

BY MR. LEE:

"MR. LEE: Q I do not believe, Mr. Woolsey that you were in the courtroom this morning when I was engaged as counsel for Mr. Ryan, were you?

"THE WITNESS: No.

(Testimony of Karl L. Woolsey)

"MR. LEE: Q It is a fact that I have heretofore represented you in this matter in some capacity, have I not?

"THE WITNESS: Per my wife's say yes, and not of my own accord.

"MR. LEE: Q Your wife engaged me to represent you?

"THE WITNESS: Yes.

"MR. LEE: Q And I did consult with you pursuant to that engagement?

"THE WITNESS: Yes sir.

"MR. LEE: Q Now, then, you have the privilege of claiming immunity for anything that was said between you and I, if you wish to do so, and I will ask you if you now waive that privilege?"

At this point, a lengthy discussion took place between Mr. Irwin, Mr. Lee, Mr. Graham, Mr. Ostrom and the Court respecting the propriety of Mr. Lee cross-examining Mr. Woolsey on matters which Mr. Woolsey may have confided to Mr. Lee while Mr. Lee had acted as counsel for Mr. Woolsey and before Mr. Lee became attorney of record for Mr. Ryan, a co-defendant. The witness finally objected to such an examination as to such matters and thereupon, and as all counsel agreed that in view of Mr. Woolsey's objection, such cross examination would be improper. Mr. Lee made no further cross-examination and withdrew as attorney of record for the defendant Ryan.

(Testimony of Karl L. Woolsey)

CROSS EXAMINATION

BY MR. GRAHAM:

Mr. Ryan is the man who spoke to me first about these bonds. He told me that he had some hot bonds that he and his partner had won at gambling. He said they come from out east. "We'll say Kansas City". This was early in September, 1935. Ryan was working in Phoenix for the same man I was working for. Whether he lived there in Phoenix, I don't know. I saw him almost every day in the bar where I worked. I worked for Jack Muyres in arranging his entertainment programs which he held twice a week at his place of business called the Twin Barrel*l*s. I also worked at the Avalon Club. I worked at both places at the same time. About a week or ten days after Ryan talked to me about these bonds, I first talked to Uncle Muyres about them. Before I talked to Muyres about the bonds, I have had frequent conversations with Ryan about them after the first time he mentioned them. The first time I talked to Muyres about them, I approached him and said "Mr. Muyres, I have been approached by a man who says he has a bunch of hot bonds and wanted to know if I could handle it and knowing you like I do and knowing you have a business contact, what do you think about it?" He said "hell yes, we can sell them". In that conversation when I said "hot bonds", I believe I also said "bonds that had been won on a gambling game by these men who have them". After this conversation, Muyres and I talked frequently about the bonds. Shortly after this conversation, Muyres and his mother-in-law went to Los Angeles. I don't know how long he was gone. It was probably two or three

(Testimony of Karl L. Woolsey)

days. When he returned, he said he had made a contact in Los Angeles and that he was positive he could dispose of them and for me to get in touch with Ryman and have him give him some bonds. Muyres made another trip to Los Angeles before the bonds were ever brought there. I can't tell you the date when I had this conversation with Muyres in which he told me he thought he could sell the bonds in Los Angeles. After this conversation, I told Ryan that the bonds could be sold. Ryan said he would send his partner after the bonds immediately. This conversation took place in Phoenix. Ryan told me his partner had to go east and get them. He never told me what town he had to go to but he said it would take some time to go and come. This conversation with Ryan was as near as I can remember about a week after Muyres told me he could sell the bonds. This conversation with Muyres after he returned from Los Angeles was the first time to my recollection that there was anything ever said about where the bonds could be sold. We talked so much about the sale of the bonds it would be impossible for me to state how soon before October 22nd which was the date when Ryan went to California, I had this conversation with Jack Muyres when he told me he could sell the bonds in Los Angeles. My object in getting these bonds sold was to make some money out of it. I realized that the only way I was to make some money out of it was by having the bonds sold. When I first learned that it was possible to sell these bonds, that made no impression on me, because it was a known fact with us all at the time according to Muyres that he would absolutely sell the bonds and I was more or less just quiet in the case all the way through. I relayed Ryan's message to Muyres.

(Testimony of Karl L. Woolsey)

Until Ryan and Muyres got together everybody understood it. It is not true that the first time I heard any conversation about these bonds between Jack Muyres and Ryan was over in the U. S. Hotel in Los Angeles. We talked so frequently both here and in Arizona about the bonds that I can't recall just where my first hearing them conversing over that particular matter was. I saw Ryan and Jack Muyres conversing together many times in Muyres' place of business in Arizona. I can't recall whether Ryan and Jack Muyres ever talked about these bonds in Arizona, because we negotiated over the deal so much but I don't say that they didn't have such conversations in Arizona. I never had any conversation with George Muyres. I never saw the gentleman.

CROSS EXAMINATION

BY MR. RYAN:

You worked at the Avalon Club in Phoenix on the repairing and operation of the slot machines. I saw you there very regularly. The only place I saw you repairing a machine was at Muyres because I don't ever go out. I have received calls for you at that place. You borrowed $7.00 from me when you left. When you left Phoenix, there was no agreement between you and me that we were to meet over here in Los Angeles. In fact, it was a surprise for me to meet you here and when I walked in the first thing you did was to shake hands and you asked me what my business was over here. It wasn't understood by me that it would take fifteen days to get these bonds. You told me it would take a matter of a few days. I am not being given immunity by the Government for testifying.

(Testimony of Karl L. Woolsey)

CROSS EXAMINATION

BY MR. OSTROM:

I worked in the Avalon Cafe in Phoenix as bar-tender. My regular hours were from 6 o'clock in the morning to 4 o'clock in the afternoon and then on holidays and busy nights I would double-back once in a while to help out in the rushes. The Avalon Cafe is a big and busy place and a busy man like I am doesn't see everybody in and out of the place. To the best of my recollection the first time that Ryan approached me relative to any bonds was in the early part of September. A few days after I had the first conversation with Ryan, I got in touch with Jack Muyres. Ryan approached me when I was behind the bar on duty and no one else heard the conversation that he approached me on but I presume there were other people in the building. Ryan approached me and said he had some hot bonds that he and his friend had won in a gambling game. He named the destination Kansas City and asked if I knew anyone who could dispose of the bonds and I said I would see if I could locate somebody. I am sure he used the word "hot". As I stated before, Ryan and I talked frequently of the bonds and it would be impossible for me to answer how many times and how often and when and what hour we talked about the bonds.

(At this point, the Court appointed J. George O'Hanneson to act as counsel for the defendant Ryan for the remainder of the trial, which appointment Mr. O'Hanneson accepted.)

I do not know Thomas M. Kushman to whom you have just directed my attention. To the best of my knowledge,

I have never seen him before. This gentleman was not present when the conversation between Ryan and me took place the first time. Muyres and I left Phoenix on the night of October 22nd between 8 and 9 o'clock, somewhere around there and arrived here in Los Angeles to the best of my knowledge, between 4 and 5 in the morning of October 23rd. The only dates that I remember through this whole case are those two dates and the fact I remember those is because my boss called October 22nd to my attention and told me that without failure, I was to be back to help him out on Halloween night which is the 31st of October. I don't know what day of the week it was we came here. Jack Muyres did not ask me repeatedly to go back to Phoenix. He insisted that I stay here and keep Ryan straight. The first time I saw Ryman was in the U. S. Hotel. He came in the room where Ryan was, where Jack Muyres was and where I was. He stayed for only a few minutes conflab there. We all got up and walked out of the room to go and in the corridor, Ryman asked me if Ryan was a man and I said "I suppose so". He approached him and said "Let's get down to business". I remember that before Ryman came in, Muyres suggested that Ryan get him the number of all the bonds so he could check on them and he wanted some samples to check to see if they were counterfeits. Ryman went out and got what he called a full list and Muyres copied them all off. Muyres wanted them so that he could check to see if they were counterfeit and he told us he was going to check to see if he had learned whether the bonds had got "hot" yet or not. Up to this time, these bonds were not referred to as "stolen", not to my recollection, but they were at all times referred to as "hot" bonds. We all spoke of them as "bogus" and "hot" bonds. I have worked for Jack Muyres and I know his number of the service station on Whittier Boulevard for at least two or three years. Muyres and I both gave it to Ryan because when I told Ryan that Muyres was over here and said that he left word for me to give him his address, I pulled out my card and he pulled out his card, and said these were both the same addresses so there was no addresses exchanged. To the best of my knowledge, before we left Phoenix, in my conversations with Ryan, the agreement on the slip was that they were to give Ryman 20% of what they grossed and then later there was another arrangement made. Ryan said that Ryman would get 20% and whoever helped to sell them we would split.

"Q   Did he mention Ryman's name?

"A   No. His partner's name. I didn't know Ryman at that time by name."

The first conversation was sometime early in September. To the best of my knowledge, I had one conversation with Ryan about the division of the proceeds before I left Phoenix. Muyres and I talked about that same proposition that Ryan made there before we came over here. That was when we first started talking about the deal in Phoenix. It would be almost impossible to answer how many conversations I had with Jack Muyres relative to the division of the proceeds prior to my leaving Phoenix because he and I talked so much about the case all the time that we were driving over here and different times that I would meet him in town that I couldn't tell you just how many times that one article or question was brought up. Before we left Phoenix, I

(Testimony of Robert Barr)

couldn't answer how many times we talked about the division of the proceeds and I wouldn't say a dozen times. To the best of my recollection more than once. After we left Phoenix and came over here, there was, to my recollection, nothing said after Muyres and Ryman talked about the division.

REDIRECT EXAMINATION
BY MR. IRWIN:

It is true as I stated that my reason for dealing in the bonds was to make money and it is also true that in order to make the money the bonds would have to be brought to Los Angeles owing to the fact that Jack Muyres had connections there and he so told me. A moment ago I said that while in Phoenix, Ryman told me that his partner would get 20% of the money. I didn't mean Ryman, I meant Ryan was the man I dealt with all of the time at Phoenix. I had never met Ryman there.

ROBERT BARR

called as a witness on behalf of the plaintiff testified as follows:

DIRECT EXAMINATION
BY MR. IRWIN:

My name is Robert Barr. I live at the Longfellow Hotel in Huntington Park. I am the manager and I was so engaged in October of last year. I have brought with me the registration card of the guests of the hotel as of October 23rd. On this card is the signature of Eddie Ryman registered as of the 23rd day of October, 1935. I think he stayed for three days and he paid for two nights.

(Testimony of Robert Barr)

"Q Can you state from an examination of that ledger sheet as to what day that payment was entered?

EXCEPTION NO. 2.

"MR. GRAHAM: That is objected to as entirely irrelevant and immaterial for this reason: Ryman had apparently registered in that hotel. The offense charged in each count of this indictment had been fully completed, and the man whom it concerned is not on trial. Neither of those documents, nor any of this testimony, could have the slightest tendency to show that any of the defendants who are on trial either aided or abetted Ryman in transporting these bonds to Los Angeles County, or that they conspired with him to do so.

"THE COURT: Overruled. I think that the mere—

"MR. GRAHAM: (Interrupting) Exception.

"THE COURT: (Continuing)—testimony to the effect that he was at this hotel on this day, whatever it is, would itself be admissible, in corroboration of the other testimony.

"THE COURT: Overruled.

"MR. GRAHAM: Exception."

EXCEPTION NO. 3.

THE WITNESS CONTINUING: The payment was apparently made on October 23rd, 1935.

"MR. IRWIN: I offer the card and ledger sheet as Government's Exhibit next in order in corroboration of the testimony of the witness Ryman as to the time he arrived in Los Angeles.

"MR. GRAHAM: To which I make the objection, the same objection, as the last objection made.

(Testimony of Elias J. Tabor)

"THE COURT: Overruled.

"MR. GRAHAM: Exception."

Thereupon, the registration card and ledger sheet referred to by the witness were received in evidence and marked Government's Exhibit No. 14.

CROSS EXAMINATION

BY MR. GRAHAM:

He paid on the 23rd for the 23rd and 24th, and on the 25th he paid for one more day.

Whereupon,

ELIAS J. TABOR

was called as a witness on behalf of the plaintiff and having been first duly sworn, testified as follows:

(Before the testimony of Mr. Tabor commenced, it was stipulated between counsel for the government and counsel for the defendants that a railway express agency "uniform express receipt" showing the destination office to be Huntington Park, California, and the consignee to be Eddie Ryman and showing the date of shipment to be October 22nd, 1935, and the name of the forwarding office to be Phoenix, Arizona, and the declared value being $40.00 and the description of the article being one roped old valise, could be introduced as Government's Exhibit No. 15, whereupon the said railway receipt was received in evidence and marked Government's No. 15. At the bottom of said exhibit appeared the signature of Eddie Ryman. It was further stipulated that the smaller receipt is what it purports to be.)

(Testimony of Elias J. Tabor)

Whereupon, the direct examination of Mr. Tabor continued:

I am the owner of the Tabor Hotel which is located at 4522 Whittier Boulevard.

EXCEPTION NO. 4.

Whereupon, it was stipulated by counsel for the defendants that there was registered at the hotel a person giving his name as T. B. Ryan and another person giving his name as E. Roberts and it was stipulated that one of these names is that of the defendant Ryan, excepting that an objection was made by counsel for the defendant George Muyres on the ground that this testimony was entirely immaterial as to him. The objection being overruled, an exception was noted.

These parties were registered in Room 21.

Whereupon, there was received in evidence as Government's Exhibit No. 16 as one exhibit, two cards, one being a registration card and the other a smaller card, both identified by the witness and which cards indicate the dates when the guests arrived, what rooms they occupied, how much was charged and when they checked out of the hotel.

CROSS EXAMINATION

BY MR. GRAHAM:

These two men checked out on November 1st, 1935.

118

(Testimony of Douglas Ward)

DOUGLAS WARD

called as a witness on behalf of the plaintiff, having been first duly sworn, testified as follows:

I reside at the Rex Hotel, 4194 Whittier Boulevard and I have brought with me the registration book for that hotel for the month of October, 1935. On page 10 thereof, the second entry is that of Eddie Roberts and Don Thompson which are the names of two people registered at the hotel. The column entitled "In" and the figures thereafter is the date upon which they checked in and the column entitled "Out" is the date when they checked out. The column having the "Room" and "25" is the number of the room assigned to them. Whereupon, there was offered and received in evidence as Government's Exhibit No. 17, that portion of the register book of the Rex Hotel identified by the witness being page 10 thereof and showing as the first entry: "Room 8, Deloris and Ronna Reed, 10/31/35, In; Out, 11/14/35"; second entry: "Room 12, Eddie Roberts and Don Thompson, Out, 11/3/35"; the next entry: "Room 25, Mr. and Mrs. Fred Masero, 11/1/35 In; Out, 11/13/35".

CROSS EXAMINATION
BY MR. O'HANNESON:

My name is Ward. I was present when the parties whose names appear in this register Exhibit No. 17, were present. I do not now recognize any of these parties. I don't recognize anybody in the courtroom as being either of these two men who registered on that day. Mr. Irwin thereupon requested that the record show that Ryman is not in the courtroom.

(Testimony of Max Vogel)

Whereupon,

MAX VOGEL

was called as a witness in behalf of the plaintiff and having been first duly sworn, testified as follows:

I own the U. S. Hotel over here across the street and I owned it in October of last year. I have with me the register for the month of October.

Whereupon, it was stipulated by his counsel that the defendant Ryan was registered at the hotel.

Whereupon, there was offered in evidence as Government's Exhibit No. 18, the register of the U. S. Hotel for the month of October, identified by the witness and particularly that portion of the register which counsel has stipulated indicated the defendant Ryan was registered at that hotel.

I believe that he was there on the week-end about two or three days; around October 24th, 1935. The defendant Ryan had some callers there. He had a couple of gentlemen come up there maybe once or twice a day in his room but I don't know what they would be doing in his room. They stayed there a half hour and left again. They always changed suits before they came down. This occurred at least twice. This is what directed my attention to them. I do not recognize any of these parties in the courtroom except Ryan. The reason I recall the fact that Ryan had visitors is because I have a sign that any visitors or guests have to call at the office first so these gentlemen came and asked for Ryan. I never saw these gentlemen with Ryan. They went up alone and came down alone.

FRED ERNEST BAKEBERG

called as a witness in behalf of the plaintiff, having been first duly sworn, testified as follows:

I reside at 4801 Whittier Boulevard. I have lived there about eight or nine years. I have known Jack Muyres since 1918. I was in business with him at 4801 Whittier Boulevard for about four years. These relationships terminated about four years ago. Since that time, he has been living in Phoenix, Arizona. Since he moved to Phoenix, I have seen him in Los Angeles from time to time. When he came to Los Angeles, he came to my address at 4801 Whittier Boulevard. I received messages for him when they came. During the summer and fall of last year, Jack Muyres made some trips to Los Angeles and called at my station at 4801 Whittier Boulevard and made some 'phone calls from my place of business. On some of these trips, he was accompanied by a person whom I do not know. He did not introduce me to him. On this one trip that I am talking about, I do not remember whether he and the stranger arrived in the morning or in the afternoon. I know the defendant Jack Muyres' nephew, George Muyres. As a general rule, the defendant Jack Muyres communicated with his nephew when he came in from Phoenix to Los Angeles. When he came to Los Angeles, he would call his nephew by 'phone from my station. I have definitely fixed in my mind the date sometime in October of last year when Uncle Myres appeared at my station with a stranger whom I did not know and was later joined by two other strangers. At about the same time, the nephew George Muyres appeared at the

(Testimony of Fred Earnest Bakeberg)

station accompanied by a girl. My best recollection is that George Muyres and his girl were out to the station to see his Uncle before the time when I saw Uncle Muyres together with these strange men.

CROSS EXAMINATION

BY MR. GRAHAM:

I had no conversation between these people. I did not hear the telephone conversations that took place between the Uncle and his nephew. I did not see the number he dialed. I know that Jack Muyres communicated with his nephew on these occasions because he would have his nephew call back if he wasn't there. On several times the nephew called there for his Uncle and he would come out sometimes. This went on for a period of four years but I only saw him out there at the station once around last fall. That was the time when he was out there with the girl. At that time I saw him conversing with his Uncle. The girl was present.

CROSS EXAMINATION

BY MR. OSTROM:

I do not remember seeing Jack Muyres at the station with strangers other than the occasion I mentioned in October, 1935. He formerly owned this gas station. During the four years that I speak of I was a partner with Jack Muyres and four years ago, he sold the business to me and he went to Phoenix.

(Testimony of H. F. Small)

H. F. SMALL

being called as a witness in behalf of the plaintiff, having been first duly sworn, testified as follows:

DIRECT EXAMINATION

BY MR. IRWIN:

I reside in Phoenix, Arizona. I am a special agent in the Federal Bureau of Investigation, United States Department of Justice. I was so engaged during the summer and fall of last year. I was stationed at Phoenix, Arizona during November of last year. I am here pursuant to a subpoena. I know the defendant John Muyres. I met him on the 27th of November, 1935 at Phoenix. At that time, special agent Arthur C. Rutzen and I proceeded to his establishment, the Twin Barrels at Phoenix and took him into custody on the information received from Los Angeles. At that time, he was fully advised as to his constitutional rights. I informed him that any statement he made would be held against him in a court of law. Any statement that he would make would have to be given voluntarily. There would be no coercion, no duress, no inducement to make him make any statement and that if he made a statement, he would make it of his own free will. At the time I placed him under arrest, I took him to our headquarters at 318 Security Building. (The jury was instructed that this evidence was admissible only against the defendant John F. Muyres.) He made a statement at the time that he feared he would be taken

(Testimony of H. F. Small)

into custody and that he was not surprised when special agent Rutzen and I took him into custody at the Twin Barrels establishment and that he was involved in the stolen bond deal. The following day after I placed him in custody, I again saw Muyres and I had a conversation with him. At that time, special agent Rutzen was also there. At that time, he executed a written statement.

(At this time, a written statement in longhand, dated November 28th, 1935, at Phoenix, purported to be signed by John F. Muyres was offered as Government's Exhibit No. 19 for identification.)

This statement is in my handwriting. The initials appearing in the upper lefthand corner of each page, 1 to 11 inclusive, are the initials of Mr. John Muyres. That statement was taken at the County Jail and Muyres sat there and explained the entire situation to me and as he explained it, I wrote it down in longhand and then after the statement was all written out, he read it and signed it and initialed each one of these pages. He read it in my presence. The signature "signed, John F. Muyres, Phoenix, Arizona, November 28, 1935" was signed by John F. Muyres the defendant in this case on the date which it bears. The term "Witnesses, H. F. Small" is my signature. The term "Arthur C. Rutzen" is the signature of Arthur C. Rutzen who signed it at the time in the presence of myself and Mr. Muyres.

At this point, the cross-examination of this witness by counsel for John F. Muyres was postponed until a later time.

JOHN M. CHENEY

called as a witness on behalf of the plaintiff, having been
first duly sworn, testified as follows:

DIRECT EXAMINATION

BY MR. IRWIN:

I am the Mr. Cheney who was originally indicted in
this case and against whom the indictment was dismissed
at the opening of this trial yesterday morning. I reside
at 846 W. 85th Street. I am married. In the month of
October, 1935, I was employed at the University of
Southern California as a men's equipment clerk in the
department of physical education in the gymnasium. I
have been there four and one-half years. I know the defendant George Muyres. I met him through an acquaintance at the Automobile Club about five years ago. I was
introduced to him by some relative of mine. I have seen
George Muyres approximately twice a week during these
five years. He came to the university and played squash.
That is where I saw him twice a week. Except at the
university, I have never seen George Muyres more than
two or three times prior to October, 1935. I was not married during the month of October, 1935. I have had a
conversation with George Muyres regarding bonds. George
Muyres called me on the 'phone approximately the 23rd
of October. He asked me if I knew anyone that knew
anything about bonds. I have never been engaged in the
bond business myself. Prior to this 'phone call from him,
I had never told him I knew anything about bonds. He
asked me if I knew anyone that knew anything about
bonds. I said yes, having in mind a friend of mine named

(Testimony of John M. Cheney)

Bassett. I didn't tell him that at that time. I arranged to have him meet Bassett that same afternoon when George Muyres came over to play squash pursuant to George's request. This was T. C. Bassett a friend of mine. He is a graduate student at the University. I thought of him because he has an account with E. F. Hutton & Company and his major in his work at the university is banking and finance. I knew he knew something about stocks and bonds. He is still a student. In my presence, George Muyres said to me and Bassett that he would have some bonds for sale. He had nothing with him at that time except that George Muyres had a list of the bonds that he had for sale. 1 don't recall whether he gave me that list then or within the next few days. I don't know whether he gave the list to Bassett. I don't even recall whether he had the list with him that day or not. As I recall, he didn't have it that day. He asked Bassett and myself if he could sell the bonds. Bassett told him he had an account at E. F. Hutton & Company and asked him to find out what bonds were for sale. On the first day that I introduced George Muyres to Bassett I don't believe any agreement was reached nor did we arrive at any course of action. Bassett said he would look into it. We met again the next time George came to the school, not by appointment, he just came in. As I recall, the next time he came in, he came in with a list of bonds. Bassett was there too. George Muyres said "here are the bonds I would have for sale." He gave the list to Bassett. Bassett said he would take the list and check on the negotiability of the bonds to see if they could be sold. On the first day that Muyres and Bassett and I met, nothing was said about these bonds being negotiable or non-

126

negotiable or about the nature of the bonds. Subsequently when George Muyres produced the list he said nothing about the nature of them. Anyway, Bassett was going to check to see if they were negotiable and we separated at that. About three days afterward, the defendant John Muyres and the nephew George Muyres came together to the gymnasium. George came first and the uncle came later. Bassett was there. Uncle Muyres stated he would have a $5,000 bond and could we sell it. Bassett said yes. Uncle Muyres then said "I'll bring the bond to you tomorrow." Later, George Muyres delivered the bond to me. There were also some other bonds which he delivered the following day after the uncle and the nephew were there together. They were delivered to me. I was to take them to E. F. Hutton & Company and offer them for sale. It wasn't stated previously that I was to take them to E. F. Hutton & Company but I did take them there and opened an account in my name. I would say that at the second meeting that George and I had it was discussed that I was to go down and open the account. That is the day that George Muyres brought the list.. George offered to pay me a commission for selling the bonds and I agreed to do so. Bassett suggested that he offer me the regular salesmen's commission of 5% on the face value of the bonds. That was agreeable with me. When they showed up with the bonds, George turned this group of bonds over to me. I left the bonds in the locker after he gave them to me. I then called Bassett and told him I had the bonds. George delivered the bonds to me personally alone the day following that the uncle and nephew had come to see me. The next morning, I called Bassett and told him I had the bonds. I then went to the bank and clipped

(Testimony of John M. Cheney)

some coupons off several of the bonds and sent them in for collection. I went to the Security-First National Bank at University and Jefferson Streets. I did this at the suggestion of Bassett. He stated that was the proper way to send the coupons in for collection. I had never sent any in before. I reopened an account at the bank which had been closed for about a year. The value of the coupons I clipped was $140.00. It was credited to my account later. Then Bassett and I went to E. F. Hutton & Company. George Muyres didn't go with us. Bassett showed me how to open an account under my name. I presented these bonds as mine and opened an account and offered them for sale. I got a receipt for them. I then told George Muyres what I had done. The face value of the bonds that George Muyres turned over to me was approximately $8,000. I took them down to E. F. Hutton & Company the same day. I didn't keep them over night. I told George Muyres that they had accepted the bonds and that they went to New York to be sold. As a matter of fact they had refused to accept three $1,000 bonds. I believe German Central Bank Bonds. I took these back to my office and I told George Muyres they didn't accept them because there were coupons missing on them. He said he'll try to locate the coupons. I kept the bonds at that time. I made a copy of the list of bonds that George Muyres had given to Bassett and I also made a copy of the bonds which George had turned over to me. I made a separate list of the numbers of these bonds amounting to about $8,000.00, which list included the three bonds which Hutton & Company had refused. The two papers referred to were now marked as Government's Exhibit No. 20 for identification.

(Testimony of John M. Cheney)

The witness continuing:

The larger piece of paper is a copy of the list which I copied from the list George gave me which is the list of bonds George gave to Bassett. The small piece of paper represents a list of the bonds George gave me and which I took down to E. F. Hutton & Company. On this piece of paper are listed the three bonds which Hutton & Company refused to take. They are the last three on the list and it is all in my handwriting. I made this smaller list before I took them to E. F. Hutton & Company, the same day the bonds were given to me as evidence I had all the bonds including the ones they refused.

At this time, the lists referred to and heretofore received as Government's Exhibit No. 20 for identification was now offered and received as Government's Exhibit No. 20.

The witness continuing:

This sheet of paper which you show me represents the bonds that Hutton & Company accepted for sale and these prices are the prices that the bonds sold at. These notations were made by me. They were made as soon as Hutton & Company notified me the bonds were sold. The list referred to was received and marked as Government's Exhibit No. 21 for identification. The paper which you show me on the letterhead of E. F. Hutton & Company listing certain bonds received from John M. Chaney is the receipt that I obtained from Hutton & Company on the day that I took the bonds down to them and these are the bonds that George gave to me and which they had accepted for sale. This receipt referred to was now re-

(Testimony of John M. Cheney)

ceived in evidence and marked Government's Exhibit No. 22. Referring to Government's Exhibit No. 20, which includes in part the bonds which George Muyres turned over to me, the figures 5, 6, 7, 8, 9, 10, 11 that indicates the total number of bonds which he turned over to me. $11,000 and $8,000 in bonds were the amounts E. F. Hutton & Company accepted and $3,000 that they did not take. I later received word from Hutton & Company that they did sell these bonds. The notice of sale under the letterhead of E. F. Hutton & Company, dated October 31, 1935, was received by me on the following day as far as I can recollect and the notice was received before I received the money and I communicated the fact that the bonds had been sold to George Muyres. Another receipt dated November 7, 1935, and having the name John M. Cheney, German Government Bonds, Share $1,000, is also a receipt which I received. This other receipt, E. F. Hutton & Company; John M. Cheney; November 1, 1935, "shares" $2,000 Austrian Government Bonds, I received notification of this sale approximately the day ·following the date appearing on the receipt. The news of all of these sales I communicated to the nephew George Muyres.

·The three receipts referred to were at this time offered in evidence as Government's Exhibit No. 23.

The note which you hand me signed by John M. Cheney in the amount of $6500, dated October 30, 1935, to the order of George Muyres, that is my note and my signature, which note I gave to George Muyres. I made it at the suggestion of Mr. Bassett for the protection of Mr. Muyres if anything would happen to me with all these bonds.

(Testimony of H. F. Small)

This note referred to was now received in evidence and marked Government's Exhibit No. 24.

These two statements which you show me in account with E. F. Hutton & Company, first one dated October 30 and the second one October 31, I received and they reflect the account which I had with them for the bonds which I turned over to them. I did not turn over any other bonds to E. F. Hutton & Company other than the $8,000 that I have testified to and George Muyres did not turn over any more to me for sale other than this amount. (These two statements referred to were now received in evidence and marked Government's Exhibit No. 25.)

H. F. SMALL

recalled as a witness on behalf of the plaintiff, having been previously sworn testified as follows:

CROSS-EXAMINATION

By MR. OSTRUM

Mr. John F. Muyres was arrested November 27th, about five P. M. We first took him to the Federal Bureau's office in the Security Title Building in Phoenix. We had arrested him at his place of business at Eighteenth and Madison Streets in Phoenix. It was a place known as the "Twin Barrels," a refreshment stand. It was quite a large place. The statement which has been marked GOVERNMENT EXHIBIT #19 for identification is all facts given on the day of November 28th. At that time there were present Mr. Muyres, Mr. Rutzen and myself. We took Mr. Muyres from the jail to our office. At the time the statement was taken I did not say, "you come clean Jack or else I will close your place of business

(Testimony of H. F. Small)

up," or anything to that effect. I simply told him to give us the true facts of the case and I warned him as to his constitutional rights as set out in the fore part of the statement. We started to take this statement about one o'clock in the afternoon. We talked with Mr. Muyres for quite a while. I do not recall the exact length of time; it was considerable time however. We first got what we considered the facts and then wrote it out in long hand. I got the entire story and then as I proceeded with the writing I would refresh Mr. Muyres' memory as to each and every paragraph. I actually finished writing this statement in long hand after six o'clock in the evening but I do not recall the exact hour. It was sometime in the early evening. We stayed right on the job until we had finished. I feel confident I never made a statement such as "you better come clean John, it will be better for you, or Jack." (Whereupon Plaintiff's Exhibit # 19 for identification was received in evidence as PLAINTIFF'S EXHIBIT #19). Plaintiff's Exhibit No. 19 is as follows:

"November 18, 1935

"Phoenix, Arizona

"I, John F. Muyres make this free and voluntary statement to Special Agents A. C. Rutzen and H. F. Small on this date, November 28, 1935. I make this statement freely and voluntarily. There has been no force or duress of any kind exercised to have been given this statement. This statement is the absolute truth and I fully realize it can be used against me in a court of law.

"I have known Karl or Ham Woolsey for several years here in Phoenix. He has worked for me at different occa-

132

sions at my business establishment, the Twin Barrel Thirst Station located at 19th Avenue and Madison, on the corner.

"I have known Tommy Ryan about two months. He was working for a company installing nickel derrick machines in drink and lunch stands, and he installed one in my place, at which time I met him.

"About the middle of October, 1935, Ham Woolsey met me and told me that he knew a fellow who had a bunch of bonds and that he had asked Ham if he knew where they could be sold or disposed of. Ham asked me if I knew anybody this fellow could turn the bonds to. I told him I did not know anyone right at the time, but that I might know somebody in Los Angeles, California, who might know someone. I asked Ham at this time why the party or parties owning these bonds did not dispose of them, and Ham told me that these men were gamblers and they had got the bonds through gambling and that if they attempted to dispose of them, someone might be suspicious, that they were hot and thus destroy the deal.

"A few days after meeting Ham I drove to Los Angeles, Calif., with my mother-in-law, Mrs. Martha Litch, in my car, which is a 1933 Plymouth grey coupe. We stopped in Los Angeles at my mother-in-law's home which is located at 3418 Amethyst St. On this occasion I and she went simply for the trip, and also to get some repairs on my frigidaire at my place of business. I at no time made any mention of bonds on this trip. We stayed there about a week and returned together on October 23, 1935; on the same night I returned I met Ham Woolsey, that is on my return to Phoenix and Ham told me that two

(Testimony of H. F. Small)

men, Eddie Ryman and Tom Ryan were in Los Angeles with the bonds, and that we should go to Los Angeles immediately, as Ryman and Ryan would be there when we got there. Ham had told Ryan that if they wanted to contact us in Los Angeles they could do so by calling Jack's Service Station in Los Angeles, located at 4801 Whittier Boulevard. Ryan had for some unknown reason told Ham that the bonds were in the East, or gotten in the east.

"Ham and I drove directly to Los Angeles, where we stayed at 3418 Amethyst St. or my mother-in-law's home, she not being there at the time but in Phoenix. We stayed at this place until about 9 A. M. and then went over to Jack's Service Station, where we were informed by a fellow named Bakeberg, an attendant at the station, that a party called for us and that this party would call again. About ten o'clock Ryan called me and told me and Ham to come down to the United States Hotel.

"Ham and I went down to the hotel and met Ryan, and Ryan told us that the fellow with the bonds was in town. Ryan had one $100 HOLC bond, one $1,000 Kansas Power & Light Company bond, and two $1,000 German bonds, the exact description of these two bonds I cannot recall. Ryan turned these four bonds over to me, and I went out to see a fellow whom I thought might be able to tell me where to go with the bonds. I could not find this fellow; he is not living in Los Angeles. I had left Ham with Ryan at the United States Hotel, when I went out to find the above mentioned party. Later in the day I drove out to Jack's Service Station, and at this place I called my nephew George Muyres on the phone and asked him to come over to the filling station. George

134

came over to this station and we discussed a car trade that I was trying to put through. I wanted to trade a lot down on 4105 Canto Drive in Los Angeles for a Chrysler Sedan. I thought George could help me with this deal, as he sold car insurance at the Southern California Auto Club, where he was employed, and he thus knew about all the car dealers in the city. Upon the completion of this conversation, I called George out of the car, he having his girl with him at the time, and asked him whether he knew anyone who could handle bonds. I did not tell him anything about these bonds. George told me he did not know anyone who handled bonds.

"The next day while I was at the Service Station, George called me and told me he had a very good friend who was in the bond business, but whom George states he did not know previous to this time that he was a bond broker. George told me that this broker wanted to see the bonds, and that I should bring the bonds over to him at the Auto Club. I drove over to the Auto Club and gave George the four bonds I had received from Ryan on the preceeding day.

"Later in the day George told me that the broker wanted the number on the rest of bonds that I had, or got hold of; he also said the four bonds that I had turned over to him would have to be checked to ascertain whether they were good; that this would take a few days.

"On Saturday morning, the 26th of October, I got the number off the rest of the bonds, the exact number of bonds I don't recall, and took them over to George at the Auto Club. At this time George returned to me the four bonds I had given him previously.

(Testimony of H. F. Small)

"I might mention here that the time I got the numbers off the bonds from Ryan in his room at the United States Hotel, that this was the first time I met Eddie Ryman, at which time Ham introduced us and told me that this was the fellow who had the rest of the bonds.

"It being Saturday, we went, that is Ham, Katie Cando and I, in my car, and Ryan and Ryman in their car to Murietta Hot Springs, California, and spent the week end. I want to state here that Katie Cando knew nothing about our bond negotiations, in any respect. I had met her in July, 1935, while she was employed at a restaurant at 4805 Whittier Voulevard, and at which time I had taken her to night clubs. She did not know any of the rest of the men in the party.

"Upon return from the Springs on Monday morning, October 28, 1935, Ryman and Ryan registered at some hotel at the 4100 block on Whittier Boulevard. Where Ryman stayed previous to the time I met him, I don't know.

"On the 28th I called George, my nephew, to ascertain whether the numbers I had given him previously were all right, and he told me he did not know as yet that it would take a couple of more days.

"On this same date, Ryman and I went to the Auto Club I putting Ryman out of the car before I got there, and I turned over to George one $5,000 HOLC bond, one $100 HOLC bond, two $1,000 Kansas Power & Light Company bonds, two $1,000 Austrian Government bonds, and ten $1,000 German bonds of which description I cannot remember. The amount of these bonds totaled $19,100. I also had several HOLC coupons and several other types of coupons. Relative to the HOLC coupons George gave me between $450 and $500 for these coupons on the 28th. The coupons which were not HOLC type George kept with the bonds.

"At the time I turned these bonds over to George, he told me that the broker had told him that he did not want the bonds until they got a report on them as to whether they were all right; however, told George to keep the bonds and coupons.

"That night which was the 28th, I met George at the club about 5 o'clock and asked him about the outcome of the bonds, whether they were good. At this same time, George turned over to me between $450 and $500 that he had realized from the broker on the sale of the HOLC coupons. I turned this amount to Ryman at the hotel.

"A couple of days later as I recall, I went again to George to find out whether he had realized anything off of the bonds. George asked me whether the bonds had been stolen, as well as the coupons; that the broker had mentioned that there were so many of the bonds that might have been stolen. I told him I did not know whether they had been stolen, but I would find out from Ryman or Ryan. At this time George turned over to me $700 for the sale of one of the HOLC bonds, which was valued at $1000. I went to Ryman and turned this $700 over to him, at the same time I asked Ryman whether the bonds were stolen and he said they were and that he had stolen them from an old woman in Tucson, Arizona; that he had entered her house and stole them.

"I might mention here that the time George gave me the $700 for the HOLC bond, I turned another HOLC bond $1000 value to him.

(Testimony of H. F. Small)

"After I found out these bonds were stolen, I tried to find George and tell him the bonds were stolen, but I could not locate him until the morning of October 31, 1935, at which time I told him the bonds had been stolen and that he should get them back as soon as possible and meet me tonight in front of Maier's Brewery on *Alicia* Street.

"George met me that night about 7 o'clock and turned over to me a package containing the bonds, all the coupons, except the HOLC coupons, were returned to me. George told me that at this time he could not return all the bonds, as the broker had sent some of them to New York.

"I kept the bonds that night and turned them over on Saturday morning, November the 2nd, 1935, to Ryman at the hotel where he and Ryan were stopping, and I told them I was through.

"I had made arrangements with George at the outstart that he was to get 10 per cent for the sale of each bond, for the amount he got from the broker. I don't know how much the broker got.

"Ham Woolsey, Ryan, Ryman and I were to split equally four ways for the sale of these bonds, or the proceeds derived from George, through the broker, and in addition, Ryman was to get in addition 20 per cent of each one of our shares. This did not include the Broker or George.

"Therefore, roughly speaking, Woolsey got about $370, Ryan $370, Ryman got $370, plus 20 per cent of our cuts, and in addition all of my cut, except $45. This $45 was all the cut I got and I got that off the sale HOLC coupons, which George has gotten between $450 and $500.

138

(Testimony of H. F. Small)

"I want to truthfully state at this time I did not know the broker or his location, or anything about the party, George was disposing these bonds with.

"After the men had taken their cut that is, Ryan, Ryman, Ham and I, on the second of November, 1935, Ryman turned over to me one $1,000 HOLC bond and one $1,000 Austrian bond, which was my cut. Upon leaving the hotel this was the last time I saw Ryan and Ryman, as Ham and I returned to Phoenix on this date. Before leaving, however, I took these two bonds and went out to my mother-in-law's house, 3418 Amethyst Street, and I hid the two bonds in my bedroom, down-stairs, on the north side of the house, in a closet under a paper on the shelf in this closet.

"I had told George on the night he returned the bonds to me in front of the brewery to be sure and get the rest of the bonds back; that I would be back in Los Angeles, about November 8th, 1935, to get them back.

"I returned to Los Angeles November 8th. I went out and saw George and he turned over to me three $1,000 German bonds and two $1,000 Kansas Power & Light Company bonds. I made this trip to Los Angeles alone and returned alone. I did not see Ryan or Ryman while I was there.

"George told me that the broker did not feel good about the bond deal and at the same time George told me that I met this broker on my first trip to Los Angeles, or the time I went with my mother-in-law, at an Athletic Club, which address I do not recall, at which place a squash game was being played. However, at this time I did not know this man was a broker, nor neither did George, and I am unable to recall his name.

(Testimony of H. F. Small)

"Upon leaving Los Angeles, California, on November 12, 1935, I took the bonds, the two I had left in the closet and the five I had gotten from George, the three German and two Kansas Power & Light Company bonds, which I had secreted under the house in the middle of the house, since it is on a high foundation, and put all seven of them in a fruit jar. I did not want to leave the bonds at the house because I was afraid a search might be made out there and I did not want to implicate my mother-in-law in this case as she knew nothing about it.

"I took the fruit or glass jar containing the bonds and drove alone, telling no one where I was going to hide them. I started out on Featherley Street in Los Angeles until I came to Beverley Boulevard. I drove east approximately ten ot twelves miles. Beverley Boulevard ia a cement road and although there are many branches leading off this road, I continued on this road, which is the main traveled road and which I think is Beverley Boulevard, the distance which I am not sure until I crossed a bridge which is about 150 feet long and traveled until I came to either the second or third intersection after crossing the bridge at this intersection.

"I think there is at present a gas station on the northeast corner, another gas station on the southwest corner, on the southeast corner there is another structure, which stands back a short ways from this corner, with many lights aroung it. At this place I turned to the left and traveled north on this intersection about a mile and a half. I do not know the name of the road I traveled north on, or the intersection, but it is concrete, but I do remember crossing a very small bridge which runs over a stream about 6 to 10 feet wide, about 1,000 feet north of this

(Testimony of H. F. Small)

bridge on the same road, I came to a place where there was a telephone line running east to west across the road. Right at this point there is a number of telephone poles and I stopped the car and walked toward the left in a westerly direction as far as the fourth telephone pole. There is a fence line that runs right on the telephone line, some of the telephone poles being used as fence posts, since the wire is tacked to them. At the fourth telephone pole and about 10 feet in a southwesterly direction I dug a hole about two feet deep, right near a clump of brush and buried the bonds, covering them over with dirt and placing on top of the dirt a stick of wood about five or six feet long and about four inches in diameter.

"There are some shacks about a block or 300 feet south of the telephone line, which can be recognized from the road, and these shacks are about a block on the same side of the road that the bonds are buried,

"I want to state that this statement is the absolute truth and I have mentioned the names of all parties that I know that have been involved in this case.

"It is my intention to plead guilty for what I have done in this case and throw myself on the mercy of the Court, so I can get this matter dispensed with as soon as possible, and get it over with as quickly as permissible. I sign this statement and initial the ten preceding pages of handwritten material, which I have read.

Signed   "John F. Muyres,
               "19th Ave. & Madison,
               "Phoenix, Arizona,
               "Nov. 28th, 1935.

(Testimony of John Murray Cheney)

"Witnesses:

"H. F. Small,
"Special Agent, Fed. Bur. Investigation,
"U. S. Dep't of Justice,
#318 Security Bldg.,
"Phoenix, Ariz.

Arthur C. Rutzen (Special Agent),
"Federal Bureau of Investigation, U. S. Department of Justice, Phoenix, Arizona."

JOHN MURRAY CHENEY

recalled as a witness on behalf of the Government, having been previously sworn, resumed the stand and testified as follows:

DIRECT EXAMINATION:

BY MR. IRWIN.

I deposited the money that was obtained by E. F. Hutton & Company and credited to my account from the sale of these bonds, in a bank. This account had been closed for a year and I reopened it. The amount deposited was $5500.00. After I had deposited this money in the bank, George asked me to get him $5000.00 in cash. I told him I couldn't get it in cash, as I had deposited it in the bank. He said to give him a $5000.00 check, and then he changed his mind and said to give him a $2000.00 check and a $3000.00 check, which I did. I did not tell him why I couldn't give it to him in cash. The total amount I received from E. F. Hutton & Company was a cashier's check for $5500.00, which I deposited in the bank. There was no other money credited to my account at E. F. Hut-

(Testimony of John Murray Cheney)

ton & Company. I know that Government's Exhibit 23 shows sales for my account and a credit to my account of $5014.07 under date of October 31, 1935, and on November 1, 1935, and sale and a credit to my account of $1806.07, and on November 7, 1935, a sale and a credit to my account of $318.74, making a total of approximately $7200.00 or $7150.00. The balance over and above the $5500.00 which I received is still in Hutton & Company, credited to my account. As I was notified of each sale of a portion of these bonds I communicated that fact to Mr. Muyres. Since my arrest and prior to the dismissal of the indictment, I had a conversation with George Muyres concerning the balance which is credited to my account. That conversation took place in the early part of January in Judge Stephens' Court room. No one else was present. George Muyres said, "That money in the account at Hutton's is yours. Why don't you take it?" I had not taken it. I said I didn't want it.

CROSS EXAMINATION:

BY MR. OSTROM.

I saw John F. Muyres with George J. Muyres the day before George gave me the bonds; that is, on October 29th. And Mr. Bassett was present with George Muyres, John Muyres and myself. The conversation lasted about two minutes. As near as I can recall, John F. Muyres said, "Here is a $5000.00 bond. Can you dispose of this $5000.00 bond for me?" That is about all.

CROSS EXAMINATION

BY MR. O'HANNESON:

I never at any time discussed the bonds or the character of the bonds with Mr. Ryan.

(Testimony of Daymond Curtis Bassett—Arthur E. Dusenberry)

DAYMOND CURTIS BASSETT

recalled as a witness in behalf of the Government, having been first duly sworn, testified as follows:

My full name is Daymond Curtis Bassett.

Whereupon, Mr. Bassett was temporarily excused from the witness stand.

ARTHUR E. DUSENBERRY

called as a witness on behalf of the Government, having been first duly sworn, testified as follows:

DIRECT EXAMINATION

BY MR. IRWIN:

I am employed at the Security First National Bank and was so employed during the Fall of last year. I know George Muyres, one of the defendants, and knew him at that time. Last Fall, I had a conversation with him at the Figueroa and Adams branch of the Security First National Bank. I made no notes on the matter and no one else was present. He wanted to know if we could sell certain bonds, or any bonds. I said, "Yes." He showed me some bonds. Nothing was said about the ownership or origin of those bonds. At the first conversation nothing was said with reference to the ownership of the bonds. I didn't question that at all. But later on it was explained to me those bonds were given to him by his uncle who was receiving them from an estate. I had possibly two or three conversations with Mr. Muyres. It was at the latter conversation that this statement was made by George Muyres · as to the source of the bonds. The other Manager at the

(Testimony of Arthur E. Dusenberry)

bank handled the sale of the bonds about that time. Sometime after the first conversation I cashed some coupons. These conversations took place over a course of about thirty days. I have no recollection of the date, but could look it up. I will have the other officer from our bank bring the records, showing the time when these transactions were handled. I saw that the bonds which Mr. Muyres exhibited were foreign government bonds and I didn't pay any attention as to what kind. I handed them back to him. The bonds from which the coupons were clipped were government bonds. I don't recall right now whether they were HOLC or treasury bonds.

Whereupon it was stipulated between counsel that the bonds from which the coupons were clipped were HOLC bonds.

CROSS EXAMINATION

BY MR. GRAHAM:

Mr. George Muyres had an account in the Figueroa and Adams branch of the Security First National Bank for a good many years and is well known to the officers and employees in that branch. I have known him for a good many years. At one of the later conversations he stated that he got these bonds from his uncle. As I remember he said that his uncle received them from an estate. I do not recall the exact words that he used. My best recollection is that he said these bonds came from an estate to his uncle and his uncle had given them to him.

(Testimony of Daymond Curtis Bassett)

DAYMOND CURTIS BASSETT

recalled as a witness on behalf of the Government, having been previously sworn, testified as follows:

DIRECT EXAMINATION

BY MR. IRWIN:

I reside at 301 South Witmer Street, Los Angeles. In the Fall of last year I resided at 3781-3/4 Menlo Avenue. I know the defendant George F. Muyres. At the time I met him I went over to the Gymnasium one day and Mr. Cheney asked me if I knew anything about stocks and bonds and I told him that I had taken a few "coasters" concerning them and tried once in awhile—I told him that I knew something about it, and he told me that he had a friend that wanted to sell some, and I asked him the fellow's name and occupation, and he told me that Mr. Muryes had been with the Auto Club of Southern California for a good many years and he told me he would like me to meet him. A couple of days after that Mr. George Muryes came over and explained that he had some bonds to sell. That was something like the latter part of October, I don't remember the exact date. Mr. Muryes told me he had some bonds there and intimated that they came from some foreign country and part of them were— came from some North Central State and as a result of some mortgage deal up there. He said he would bring a few over in a day or two and let me look them over. Cheney told me the reason for Mr. Muryes not selling them was because he had some domestic troubles. Mr. Muryes said that. Then in two or three days he brought over some bonds. As well as I recall one was a Home

146

(Testimony of Daymond Curtis Bassett)

Loan bond, some German bonds, a Kansas power and another German bond. He brought over these bonds and I took down the numbers and the title of them and the maturity date and the interest and things, and intended to check the values of them and during this time Mr. Muryes said he had already checked the negotiability and found it was all right and there was no claim against them. Mr. Muryes exhibited to me a letter from some foreign country and supposed to be from some relative of his. I don't know what language it was written in, but I think it was in German. I do not know German. This was when Mr. Muryes was talking about the source of these bonds. I don't know what the letter said. I merely took Mr. Muryes' word that the letter was in German. After I took down these numbers Mr. Muryes said that he had already done that and checked them, and I went downtown to a brokerage company and talked with some friends. I waited around and investigated and decided not to handle the bonds.

EXCEPTION NO. 5

MR. GRAHAM: (Interrupting)

Just a moment. I move to strike out the testimony that he decided not to handle these bonds.

THE COURT: He said he decided not to handle them. No, I think that is part of the narrative of the witness and it is necessarily an explanation of his action. Mr. Muryes suggested a certain course of action to him and he decided not to follow it. I don't think you have any objection.

(Testimony of Daymond Curtis Bassett)

MR. GRAHAM:

I have no objection to telling what he told Mr. Muyres, but what he had in his own mind is certainly not binding upon Mr. Muryes.

THE COURT:

Well, for instance, if he said he decided not to go any further in it, that is the usual form and the general course of testimony of a witness. There would be no objection. The objection is overruled.

MR. GRAHAM:

An exception.

I didn't sell any of the bonds or do anything with them. At the time the samples were exhibited to me and I took down the numbers I simply saw them in my hands and gave them back. I didn't take them away or take them down to check them up for a few days. I had under consideration the question of whether or not I would handle these bonds. Mr. Muryes said, what was the usual rate of commission for handling such a transaction and I told him I never heard of any before and he said, "How would 5% suit you?" And I told him. He said that would probably net him about $1200.00 or something like that for him on the whole thing. I have a brokerage account of my own. I have dealt in stocks and bonds for sometime. The commission paid by the brokerage houses for the sale of bonds is $1.25 a thousand. After this date that I took down the numbers and was making this investigation I had taken quite a time to investigate and Mr. Muryes seemed to be quite anxious for me to sell them. He asked me whether I intended to handle them and I told him I had not definitely decided. He said, "I would like you to handle them as soon as possible, because I need some money."

(Testimony of Daymond Curtis Bassett)

CROSS EXAMINATION

BY MR. GRAHAM:

I stated that Mr. Cheney told me that Mr. Muyres didn't want to sell these bonds on account of some domestic trouble and later Mr. Muyres said there was some domestic trouble. Simply intimated he had separated from his wife. I don't remember the exact words. It just came up as a casual remark on his part. It wasn't very definite whether Mr. Cheney referred to the domestic trouble of George Muyres or of John F. Muyres, but I thought he was referring to George Muyres. I was dealing with George. He approached me on the subject and I assumed that conversation was referring to him. He said his uncle got them from some estate or something and figured it was his share of them. It seemed like I learned someway in the conversation that his uncle's name was Muyres. He said both the nephew and the uncle had the same name and I assumed it referred to the nephew. Nobody definitely told me they were referring to the nephew. I just gathered that from the conversation there. I went down to Hutton & Company with Mr. Cheney and showed him the Cashier's desk. That is about all. I was acquainted there. I had had an account down there for a few years. He was not acquainted there and I told him the cashier would take care of the opening of the account for him. Mr. Cheney asked me to go down with him. I told him to present it to the cashier. That was after I had decided not to handle the bonds myself. I have seen Mr. Cheney quite awhile around U. S. C. and we were friends.

RE-DIRECT EXAMINATION

BY MR. IRWIN:

I just met George J. Muyres over there. I don't know him very well.

(Testimony of Mrs. Henrietta Woolsey)

MRS. HENRIETTA WOOLSEY

called as a witness on behalf of the Government, having been first duly sworn, testified as follows:

DIRECT EXAMINATION

BY MR. IRWIN:

I am the wife of Mr. Ham Woolsey. I reside in Phoenix, Arizona. Mr. Woolsey has previously pleaded guilty in this case. I recall the time he was arrested, and after that I engaged counsel for him. In January of this year I received a communication from my husband with regard to keeping counsel I had retained. I then went to the office of that attorney. I told him what my husband had to say. That attorney was John Lee, who is in the Court Room. I know John F. Muyres. I saw him at my home since my husband was arrested. He first came to my home after he got his bond and returned to Phoenix. He came there alone. It was before Christmas. He was there in January, before the 31st, alone. He also came there in connection with the case in the month of February. At all times when he called it was in connection with the case. I was living with my mother. He was there around the 6th of February, because I was in bed then. He was alone that time and he talked to me in connection with the case. He came to my house in the month of March. On one of these visits John F. Muyres was accompanied by Mr. Lee, the attorney I had engaged for my husband. As far as I knew, Mr. Lee was then representing my husband. They were down there on the 7th of March of this year. I had just had my baby and they came down on Friday, the 6th, and mother would not let them see me and both came the next day to see me. I

(Testimony of Mrs. Henrietta Woolsey)

have been in bed. This is just two weeks today since I had my baby, since I have been up. On the 7th they talked to me about my husband, about what he was going to do and what his attitude was in this case.

EXCEPTION NO. 6

BY MR. IRWIN:

Q. I will ask you what was said by Mr. Lee or yourself or Mr. Muyres when Mr. Muyres was present on this occasion, the 7th of March, concerning the coming trial of this case?

MR. O'HANNESON:

This is only against Mr. Muyres.

MR. IRWIN:

John F. Muyres.

MR. OSTROM:

To which we object, if your Honor please, as being incompetent, irrelevant and immaterial and not tending to prove or disprove any of the points involved in this case.

THE COURT:

I cannot say, as it might be a statement against interest and if so it would be admissible.

MR. IRWIN:

It is so offered.

THE COURT:

Overruled.

MR. OSTROM:

Exception, your Honor.

(Testimony of Mrs. Henrietta Woolsey)

Mr. Lee asked whether I wanted him to come over and defend my husband against his wishes or not, and he said that I did have the right, if I wanted to, and my husband had wrote and said he didn't want him, and I asked him what he would do since my husband had pleaded guilty, and he said that there was only one thing he could do and that was to make a plea to the court to have him withdraw that plea on the allegation that my husband, being up in the jail like he has been, didn't know what he was talking about and didn't know what he had done. He wanted—I told him that I would not do anything until I talked to my sister, and after I talked to my sister I told him that I didn't want him to come over there, because my husband had said he didn't want him to and I didn't want to go against his wishes. So he told me if I wanted to come over by Tuesday, he would arrange transportation for me. When he left, after I told him that I didn't want him to go to defend my husband, why he said, "If you change your mind by Tuesday, you can let me know and I will see that you get transportation." I told him that I—I asked him if he was coming over anyhow, and he said yes, he thought he was, and if I wanted to come, he would see that I got transportation over. I didn't know my husband was going to change his plea. I didn't know it then, because that was before the 10th. He made his plea on the 10th. I knew it on the 10th. I knew it then, because he made his plea on the 10th and this was after the 10th of March. That was after they came for that conversation. He had already changed his plea to guilty, and Mr. Muyres came down and that conversation was had at my house. At the time when Mr. Lee and Mr. Muyres were down there talking to me I told them I didn't have any money

(Testimony of Mrs. Henrietta Woolsey)

at all. They said there was some money over here and that if they could keep the money, the lawyers' fees would be paid out of that. They didn't say that that money would come right off from the bonds. They said that the money was tied up over here in the bank and they were not allowed to use it.

CROSS EXAMINATION

BY MR. OSTROM:

Mr. Lee and Mr. Muyres came there on the 6th, but I didn't see them. I was in bed and mother wouldn't let them in. One came first and then the other. On the 7th they came and I saw them both in the presence of each other. My mother was in and out of the room. This conversation took approximately half an hour or so. Mr. Lee told me on that occasion that Mr. Woolsey had never communicated to him the facts that would warrant a plea of guilty. Around the 7th of that month my husband had told Mr. Lee he didn't want him. I don't remember Mr. Lee making the statement to me that Mr. Woolsey had told him the facts of the case. Mr. Lee said to me in substance that from what information he, Mr. Lee, had obtained from my husband, that he, Mr. Lee, did not feel that my husband should have entered a plea of guilty. Mr. Lee on that same occasion said to me that he, Mr. Lee, did not believe that my husband was in a state of mind where he knew what he was doing when he entered his plea of guilty. Mr. Lee also told me that from what he had learned from Mr. Woolsey when he was representing my husband, that he did not believe my husband was guilty, or words to that effect.

(Testimony of Lish Whitson)

RE-DIRECT EXAMINATION
BY MR. IRWIN:

These conversations were had on the 7th before leaving to come over here, and the day of sentence was set for March 10th. They came back when I had this conversation in that connection. When they called on March 7th I had been in bed two days.

LISH WHITSON

called as a witness on behalf of the Government, after being first duly sworn, testified as follows:

DIRECT EXAMINATION
BY MR. IRWIN:

I reside in Los Angeles. I am a Special Agent of the Federal Bureau of Investigation, United States Department of Justice, and was so employed from September, last year, on. I was assigned to this office. I engaged in an investigation of this case.

I first saw the fruit jar which was just handed me, in a field nine-tenths of a mile north of the intersection of San Gabriel Boulevard and Beverly Boulevard, where it was dug up by Special Agent A. P. Lecke, Special Agent L. V. Boardman and myself, upon telegraphic instructions received from the Phoenix office. Those instructions contained the direction that led me to that spot. They were set out in the statement given by Uncle Muyres to Special Agent Small. When we dug up the jar, it contained $7000.00 worth of bonds. I made a record of those bonds. The writing, which I now hand to Mr. Irwin, was removed from that jar at that time. The bonds which were in the jar have already been introduced in evidence. This

(Testimony of Lish Whitson)

paper is the list I made of the bonds at that time—the kind and serial number. The paper in the jar was placed there by me for identification of the jar but was not in the jar at the time. It is a description of what this jar is (whereupon the jar, the descriptive paper and the list of the serial numbers of the bonds were admitted in evidence as against John F. Muyres only, as Government's Exhibit No. 26) I know the defendant George J. Muyres. I first met him in Commissioner Head's office on December 2nd, when he was present with Mr. Walter Keene, his attorney. I met them both. (Whereupon a document consisting of four pages was marked Government's Exhibit 27 for identification.) I have seen Government's Exhibit 27 for identification before.

At the time I first met George J. Muyres I had a conversation with him concerning this statement, which is Exhibit No. 27 for identification, in the office of the Federal Bureau of Investigation in this building. There were present George Muyres, Walter Keene, Special Agent Boardman and myself. We asked George Muyres if he had signed this particular statement and he said that he did. We went over all the points in the statement, and after refreshing his memory upon certain matters that were not exactly clear in here, he consented to sign a supplementary statement. He said it was the statement he signed in Denver. (Whereupon the supplemental statement was marked Government's Exhibit 28 for identification.)

(Whereupon Mr. Graham, attorney for defendant George F. Muyres, stated that he had no objection to the introduction of Exhibit No. 28 for identification, but waived the foundation for it.)

(Testimony of Lish Whitson)

CROSS EXAMINATION

BY MR. GRAHAM:

Mr. George Muyers and Walter Keene, who was acting as his attorney in an advisory capacity, came to my office voluntarily and told me that they wished to make a supplementary statement. They said that since Mr. Muyres had returned from Denver, that he had been thinking it over and was trying to recall everything that had happened and that he had refreshed his recollection on some points on which his recollection was not clear at the time he gave the statement at Denver and it was as a result of that statement and of his coming there with Mr. Keene that No. 28 for identification was taken.

RE-DIRECT EXAMINATION

BY MR. IRWIN:

Mr. Muyres was then on bond. He was not in custody at the time he read over number 27 for identification, the one dated in Denver, and he said he had made it. Where-upon it was stipulated that there was no duress, threats or promises made.

CROSS EXAMINATION

BY MR. OSTROM:

I found Government's Exhibit No. 26 at the place that was described to me in a communication from officer Small in Phoenix. I went there the same day I received the instructions, which was Thanksgiving day, November 28th, the day of Mr. John Muyres' statement. We went there near the middle of the day.

(Testimony of Tom H. Sisk)

TOM H. SISK

called as a witness on behalf of the Government, having
been first duly sworn, testified as follows:

DIRECT EXAMINATION

By Mr. Irwin:

I am a special agent with the Federal Bureau of Investigation, United States Department of Justice, and my
residence is Houston, Texas. I am one of the investi-
gators working on this case. I know the defendants Ryman and Ryan. I was present when they were apprehended on November 8, 1935. I was in Houston for
several days thereafter. Whereupon it was stipulated that
certain Houston papers of general circulation carried an
account of their arrest, on the 9th and 10th of November,
and that they were to be held for investigation in connection with stolen bonds and securities.

WITNESS:

That is substantially correct. The newspapers carried
news as to alleged stolen bonds and that these two parties and one other man had been arrested and were being held for investigation. This was prominently displayed in Houston papers.

I had a conversation with defendant Ryan after he was
arrested. Before this another agent, Mr. McInnerney of
my office had, in my presence warned him as to his constitutional rights.

(Testimony of Tom H. Sisk)

VOIR DIRE EXAMINATION

By Mr. O'Hanneson:

No written statement was taken from Mr. Ryan; the first time we discussed the case with him was in the presence of Special Agent McInnerney and Special Police detectives of the City of Houston. I had a previous conversation with him but we did not go into the case. Before the first conversation we had advised Mr. Ryan of his constitutional rights and we did not feel it was necessary to do so again.

DIRECT EXAMINATION (Cont)

By Mr. Irwin:

This conversation, at which he was advised of his constitutional rights was at Police Headquarters in Houston, Texas on the night of November 8, 1935. The parties present were Detective Tom Eubanks and A. C. Martindale, Special Agent McInnerney and myself. Agent McInnerney told Ryan that he did not have to talk to us unless he so desired and that any statement that he did make could be used against him for prosecution purposes. After agent McInnerney completed what he was saying to him about his rights Ryan said "yes, I know my rights", and then we went into the discussion. This was not the first conversation I had with Ryan but was the first one about the case, I had a previous conversation a few days before when he was arrested and was asked his name and a few things like that. We did not discuss the bonds at all with him at that time.

At the conversation at the Police Station which we were speaking of, we asked Ryan where he came from and gen-

(Testimony of Tom H. Sisk)

eral facts of this nature. We asked him what he knew
about HOLC bonds that we had recovered; we asked him
about the German bonds we had recovered. The $1,000
German Bond #C56344 has my initials on it. I first
saw this bond on the night of November 8, 1935 in a
dresser drawer in a room of the Austin Hotel, Houston,
Texas, the night Mr. Ryan and Eddie Ryman were registered at that room. We asked Ryan if he knew a man
by the name of Ryman. Ryman was registered there under the name of Roberts, or at least was known there under the name of Eddie Roberts and we asked if Mr. *Ryan*
was his room mate, and he said he knew a Mr. Roberts
there; we asked him if Eddie Roberts was not Eddie Ryman, so Mr. Ryan said that Robert's true name was probably Ryman. However, he did say the suitcases which
contained articles bearing the name of Ryman were the
belongings of Eddie Roberts and not himself. I saw
Ryan four or five days. I found out that some of the
effects in the room which Ryan said belonged to Roberts
belonged to Ryman; for instance some of the things were
in the dresser drawer; the middle dresser drawer in which
we found the bond had a number of shirts and socks and
underwear and we asked Ryan if they were his things
and he said no; then later after Ryman was arrested we
asked him if they were his things and he said no, so about
three days later I believe it was, we took all of their clothes
and mixed them up and put them on a table at the Police
Station and told them to segregate them and put in suit
cases the things which belonged to each of them, and when
they picked out their own clothes the ones Ryan put in
his suit case had this bond in. I do not think we told

(Testimony of Tom H. Sisk)

them what the charge against them was when we told them to pick out the clothes. Whereupon the bond which had been identified by the witness was received in evidence as GOVERNMENT EXHIBIT #29.

WITNESS;

I first saw Mr. Ryan the evening of November 8, 1935 at approximately 4;35 o'clock and he was in a used car lot conversing with another man who worked at the lot. We had had this used car lot under *survelience* and were watching whatever activity might take place there. About five minutes to six that same evening Ryan left the lot and walked up the street to a nearby grill and went in there and had a couple of drinks at the bar. At about 6:45, or about the neighborhood of that time, Detective Eubanks and I arrested him. The initials in the corner of the note book which was just handed me are my initials. I found this note book in the pocket of defendant Ryan, and the pencil notations in the inside of the book were all there at the time I took the note book from Mr. Ryan. It was in a bill fold in the pocket of his clothes. Whereupon it was stipulated that the note book belonged to defendant Ryan and the note book was then offered as GOVERNMENT EXHIBIT #30. The first page of Exhibit #30 contains the notation "Jack Muyres, 4801 Whittier Blvd., Jack's Ser. Stat."; the next page—"F. E. Bakeberg, Whittier Blvd., Angelus 9838, Phone"; the next page "Jack Muyres 4801 Whittier Boulevard, record Jack's Ser. Station" on the third following page on the right hand side "Don Thompson, 4194, Room 25". Reversing the book there is the name Ham Woolsey in pencil and crossed out in pencil.

(Testimony of Tom H. Sisk)

The five $1,000 Government International Bonds and one Australian International bond which have just been handed me we found under a vacant house in the 1400 block on Dallas Ave., Houston, Texas. We had located a Ford Automobile with an Arizona license plate on it in the rear of this house. It was the defendant Ryan's automobile. We searched around there and on the morning of November 9th, about 6;30 or 7;00 o'clock we found this bond under the house with those others that you have there. Ryman and Ryan occupied the same room but they were not both registered. As I recall it Mr. Ryan was registered under the name of T. B. Ryan. The nine $1,000 HOLC bonds and the 1-$100 and 1-$50 corporation bonds which have just been handed me I have seen before but not under the same circumstances. These were with those under the house. This bond we got elsewhere. That is a $1000 bond, #M172104D.

I had a conversation with Mr. Ryan after the bond was found. He said he knew nothing about them. The bond that I found on him that I identified this morning was a German bond. It has the date 11-8 on it, whereas those others have the date 11-9 on.

BY THE COURT:

I talked with a certain colored gentleman on the premises and thereafter I burrowed around under the house and found these bonds, after a search. Whereupon those bonds referred to were received in evidence as GOVERNMENT EXHIBIT #31.

(Testimony of Glen A. Watkins)

GLEN A. WATKINS

called as a witness on behalf of the government, having
been first duly sworn, testified as follows:

DIRECT EXAMINATION

by Mr. Irwin.

I reside in Los Angeles, and am Assistant Vice President of the Bank of America. On November of last year
I was engaged at the International Office of that bank at
220 North Main. I recognize the defendant George J.
Muyres. On the morning of November 2nd, Mr. Thompson, who was then connected with the Maier Brewing
Company, called me on the phone and asked me whether
we had facilities to purchase Home Owners Loan Bonds.
I told him "Yes". About 11.30 that morning he called
at the Branch Office and offered me this bond. I took
him back to the Collection Department of the Bank. I
don't recall whether he introduced me to Mr. Muyres at
that time or during the time the transaction was being
had there he came with Mr. Muyres. While the cashier's
check and order of sale was being made out, I believe
Mr. Thompson introduced me to Mr. Muyres. During the
course of the conversation Mr. Muyres stated he had a
relative who had died in Holland and that he expected
to receive a portion of the estate. I asked him the assets
of the estate, and he said there were some German bonds,
some War Savings stamps, and I believe he said some
Home Owners Loan Bonds. I asked him if we could
be of any assistance in having the bonds shipped over
here we would be glad to do so. About that time the
transaction was completed and the check was issued to

(Testimony of Glen A. Watkins)

Mr. Thompson. Mr. Thompson endorsed the check. I O. K'd his endorsement and he turned the check over to Mr. Muyres. They went over to the window and cashed the check. After returning from cashing the check Mr. Muyres entered into a conversation with Mr. Thompson and myself, during which time I asked him about a bank account for our branch. He told me at that time that he could not open an account, as he and his wife were estranged and he was afraid that if he opened an account there might be an attachment or something levied against it. That was about the total conversation. When I asked him about opening the account, the money had been already turned over to Mr. Muyres. At the time they came in I was under the impression that the bond belonged to Mr. Thompson, but later in talking with Mr. Muyres, I was certain the bond belonged to Mr. Muyres.

(Whereupon it was stipulated between counsel that George Muyres received the money on the check and the check was introduced in evidence as Government's Exhibit "No. 32". Government's Exhibit "No. 32" is a cashier's check No. 16-61, International Office, Bank of America, National Trust and Savings Association, No. 2,188,281, dated November 2, 1935, in favor of James Thompson in the sum of $1004.06, and is endorsed "James Thompson" and initialed O. Kay G. A. W. It was paid November 2, 1935.)

THE WITNESS:

Before the bond was cashed I had checked the value and found that it was worth about $98 or $99. Then there was some accrued interest. There had been very little

(Testimony of Ira C. Hilgers)

fluctuation in the value of that bond for several weeks preceding that date.

CROSS-EXAMINATION

BY MR. GRAHAM:

The way this transaction was handled was that Mr. Thompson came into the bank with Mr. Muyres. Mr. Thompson was acquainted with me and Mr. Muyres was not, so Mr. Thompson presented the bond. I check up on the value of it, had a check made out for the value of it, gave the check which is Government's Exhibit "No. 32" to Mr. Thompson, who endorsed it, gave it to Mr. Muyres, who took the check over to the window and got it cashed.

IRA C. HILGERS

called as a witness in behalf of the Government, having been first duly sworn, testified as follows:

DIRECT EXAMINATION

BY MR. IRWIN:

I reside at 528 11th Street, Santa Monica. I am a broker. We are members of the Los Angeles Stock Exchange and deal in bonds. That was my occupation in October and November of last year. I know the defendant George J. Muyres who is in the court room. I had a brief conversation with him on the telephone and later met him in my office. I called him on the telephone and solicited his business. I was told by a friend of mine that Mr. Muyres had inherited some money and might be a good prospect. He needed some guidance. This acquaintance contacted me. I told Mr. Muyres that I had

164

been in business for a number of years and could recommend our firm. This was about October 23 or 24. I told Mr. Muyres that Mr. Robinson had given me his name and had outlined to me briefly that Mr. Muyres was possibly in need of some help in view of the fact that he had no experience in securities before, and that we would solicit his business and he could use as reference for our firm two men in the Automobile Association with which he was connected. He said that the amount in the estate was not as much as Mr. Robinson had indicated. Robinson had indicated it was about $160,000. He was the mutual friend who suggested that I call Mr. Muyres. Mr. Muyres said he thought it was approximately $48,000 or $49,000. Mr. Muyres came into the office five or six days or a week later alone. I introduced myself and he sat down at my desk and brought from his pocket four specimen bonds and asked me the proximate market on these bonds at that time, which I checked as closely as possible without doing any wiring. Mr. Muyres asked me if the bonds could be checked as to whether there would be anything the matter with the bonds, as to their title, and I said we could check that very easily if he cared to have me do so, and if so I would do so right then by either checking with the banks or with any New York brokerage firm. He said that he was afraid there may be something the matter with the title to the bonds because of his uncle's past reputation. The uncle had previously come into the conversation during the phone conversation. At that time he said that these bonds were coming to him through his uncle who had brought them back from an estate that had been settled

(Testimony of Ira C. Hilgers)

of his grandparents in Holland, and this was his share of the estate, and he was also going to help his uncle in the selling of his bonds. Mr. Muyres had nothing with him except the samples of the bonds to indicate the type of bonds which he wanted to sell. He had no list and nothing was said about a list. I said that if there was any question about the title to the bonds we naturally would not want to be connected with the transaction and we would like to check it right then and there. He said he preferred not to have us check it then because he did not want to cause his uncle any undue trouble. I said, well that was his choice and I would not check the numbers of the bonds that he had if he didn't want me to. I told him I could check them very easily if he cared to have us do so, but he refused that suggestion.

CROSS-EXAMINATION

BY MR. GRAHAM:

At the time Mr. George Muyres was in my office he told me that he had become a little bit suspicious about the title of those bonds and wanted to check them and be sure there was nothing wrong with the title before he sold any of them. He also said that unless he could find out there was nothing wrong with the title he would have nothing to do with the sale of them himself. I told him that I could check the title to these very easily through any bank or through any New York brokerage house, and in that connection I specifically mentioned Hutton and Company. I believe I also told him that all of the banks and all of the large New York brokerage houses had lists of stolen bonds so that any of those big brokerage houses could check them. I told Mr. Muyres that I thought between

(Testimony of Ira C. Hilgers)

the banks and Hutton and Company we could check them very easily. I did not tell Mr. Muyres that the serial numbers of the bonds could be checked specifically through Hutton and Company, but I did say that all the New York Brokerage houses including Hutton and Company, which I mentioned by name, had lists of bonds which were reported as stolen.

RE-DIRECT EXAMINATION

BY MR. IRWIN:

With regard to my offer to check these bonds, I advised Mr. Muyres that if I had the list I could check them very easily in a very short time. I don't think I went into the details with him as to whether I could tell whether or not there was anything wrong with them, or whether there was anything of record wrong with them, or whether they were reported as stolen, but I told him as far as we could determine we could check them. I do not have a record of all negotiable bonds, all government bonds that are in circulation if there has been no report on them. On those bonds, whatever may have been their condition, if there was no report on them available I could not check them, nor could anyone else. I told Mr. Muyres what means were available to me to check those bonds at the time I offered to do so. The most feasible way of checking this in a hurry I told him would be for us to go to the bank which generally had lists of stolen bonds or to a New York wire house like Hutton and Company. I said that could be done. If they were not reported stolen I would not be able to check them.

(Testimony of Nellie P. Covert)

RE-CROSS-EXAMINATION

BY MR. GRAHAM:

What I mean to say is, if they were not stolen they would not be on a list of stolen bonds.

NELLIE P. COVERT

Recalled as a witness in behalf of the Government, having been previously sworn, testified as follows:

DIRECT EXAMINATION

By Mr. Erwin:

I remember the testimony we had here the day before yesterday about the date when I sent that Kansas City Light & Power Bond back to be redeemed. I sent that to that broker Company, Stern and Company. The letter which you have just handed me is in long hand in my writing, dated June 18, 1935. I enclosed the bond with this letter on the date it bears. (Whereupon, the letter referred to was received in evidence as Government "Exhibit Number 3". This letter is as follows:

"1242 N. Park Ave.,
Tucson, Arizona,
June 18, 1935.

"Mr. S. W. Izard,
P. O. Box 3088.
"Dear Sir:

Enclosed find Bond # C. M. 3043 for $1,000.00. You say you can handle this money. In what? A good investment?

"Your other letter was misplaced. Forgot name and address.

"Yours respectfully,
N. P. Covert.")

(Testimony of Nellie P. Covert)

Whereupon, it was stipulated between counsel that in the middle of Adams Boulevard running west from Figueroa, in the City of Los Angeles, is a parkway of about fifteen feet in width, in which is planted grass, shrubbery and trees, and the Automobile Club of Southern California is on the Southwest corner of the intersection of Figueroa and Adams.

At this point Government's Exhibits Nos. 27 and 28 for identification were received in evidence, as Government's "Exhibits Numbers 27 and 28, respectively.

Government's "Exhibit #27 is as follows:

"Denver, Colorado,
November 27, 1935.

I, George J. Muyers, make this statement to Special Agent in Charge E. P. Guinane, and Special Agents L. M. Chipman and L. G. Healey, whom I have been advised are Special Agents of the Federal Bureau of Investigation, U. S. Department of Justice, and have been advised that I do not have to make a statement, but desire to state the following in order to tell everything that I know concerning this matter.

I am thirty-five years of age, and reside at 712 South Wilton Place, Los Angeles, California, and have a wife, Alice, and two children Alice Jean and Jack Muyres.

I have been asked whether I know Edward H. Rhyman, Thomas Burke Ryan, Franklin Dolph Le Sieur, Ham Woolsey, Jack Muyres and John Cheney, and state that I do not know them, and have never met any of these men, with the exception of Jack Muyres, who is my uncle,

(Testimony of Nellie P. Covert)

and John Cheney, who is employed at the University of California gymnasium, Los Angeles, California. I have known John Cheney for about 5 or 6 years.

About October 12th or 15th Jack Muyres saw me at the Automobile Club of Southern California, at the automobile Club building, and told me that he had some bonds, and that he would like me to find out what he could sell them for, and I asked him where they came from and he said they were all right, and would let me know in a day or two, and in a day or two he called me and told me to come out to the gas station on Whittier Boulevard, which is called "Jack's Station", and there he had a couple of samples of these bonds. I don't know how many. He gave me an envelope, but I didn't pay much attention to them. (in ink:) I gave them back to Jack Muyres.

I did not hear anything further from Jack about these bonds until about October 12th or 15th, at which time Jack came up to my office in the automobile Club Bldg., and said, "Here's these bonds you were asking about," and he asked me if I was going to give them to Cheney, and he gave me five or six bonds, which I believe were in one thousand dollar denominations, which were brown and green in color, and which I believe were German or Austrian bonds. At this time the understanding was that he (in ink: Cheney) was to sell these bonds and give the money to Jack Muyres, and he said he would make it right with me.

I took these bonds to Mr. Hilgers of the Montjoy, Hilgers, (and some other partner) Bond Brokers, located in the 500 or 600 block of South Spring Street in Los Angeles—and I asked Mr. Hilgers to find out for me all

170

he could about these bonds, particularly where they came from, and if they came from an estate of my grandfather, whose name is Frank Muyres, had written to Holland concerning the estate about January or February, 1936, and when Jack Muyres gave me these bonds, I asked Jack where he got these bonds, but he told me not to worry, that they were okeh, and I thought he had obtained these bonds from the estate of my grandparents, as Jack had recently returned from a trip to Holland about June or July of 1935.

Mr. Hilgers took the numbers and descriptions of these bonds, and said he would look into them, and I returned the bonds to Jack Muyres. A few days later Mr. Hilgers called me and told me that the bonds were all right, and he wanted me to let him dispose of the bonds and invest in other securities, and I told him that I would have to let him know, because I was not sure about these bonds, that I was expecting to get more bonds from Jack Muyres or money in settlement of the estate.

I never held these bonds a secret from anybody. I sat in an office with a dozen fellows and everybody saw them, and they all kidded me, and laughed, and the employees of the Automobile Club thought it was a big joke. They knew about the estate before and knew that I expected money. And I still didn't know what to do about it. I went across the street to see Mr. Evans at the First National Bank, and told him the proposition, that is I told Mr. Evans, the manager of the bank, about them. I told him what I thought and he said, you can clear up the mortgage you have on your place, which I borrowed on the place to bury my Dad and Mother, and take care of

(Testimony of Nellie P. Covert)

other bills. He said to wait until we see if this thing is all right, and that was all the conversation, because he handled the other things for me—he took care of my real estate, and took care of the mortgage.

I went over to the University of Southern California gym and played "Squash", and they kidded me about being a "Big Bond Holder," and I said, "Don't get premature on this, because I don't know anything about it, and I want to find out more about these bonds, and they said Jack Cheney (in ink) knew a fellow who knew about ~~is in the bond business, and let him see them~~ (crossed out in ink) I said I haven't got time yet, but I will get time later on. I saw Cheney after I saw Hilger, and he kept asking me about them, and in about two or three days I brought him over. Cheney said (in ink:) <u>this party he knew could get some data on bonds,</u> if you let me have these bonds, ~~I can get more dope on them,~~ and I hesitated, but finally I gave them to Jack Cheney, and never heard anything more about them. And the next time I heard about them was about two *week* later when Cheney gave me this money—one check for $2000 and one check for $3000, and they were Cheney's personal checks. And Cheney said these bonds had been sold, but I didn't pay much attention to what they sold for, and I said I am supposed to give this money to my uncle, but I didn't be-

(In ink:) Securing 1st Natl.

cause they went through so quick. I went to the ∧ ~~First~~ National Bank and saw Mr Evans, and I told Mr. Evans that I thought something was funny about this. He Mr. Evans, said to let it lay here. Mr. Evans said, I don't think your uncle would do anything like that, and I said I

(Testimony of Nellie P. Covert)

would do that, and I did. I then deposited both checks in the Security First National Bank. I deposited both checks to a checking account, and switched $3500 to the savings account—this took place about Nevember 18th, 1935.

I talked to a Walter Keen, Attorney, and I explained the situation to him, and told him that I had the money in my possession and did not want to get in a jam, and asked him what I had better do, and he said you are going to Denver this weekend and to wait until you come back, and in the meantime I will find out what could happen if something is wrong with these bonds. At first he suggested for me to go to the United States Attorney in Los Angeles and explain the situation to him, and in that way if there was anything wrong he would know and if there wasn't, I would be clear— and I explained to him that this uncle of mine might get terribly angry about that procedure and would figure that I thought *we* was crooked, and make it uncomfortable for me, and I hesitated about it and didn't do anything, figuring that when I got back to Los Angeles, Cheney would either have some money or more information about this, thinking the bond company would find out more information about these bonds, that is if they were "Hot Bonds", and they would tell him, and he in turn would tell me, and I could straighten it out that way.

As above related, the only bonds which I received in this transaction, or any other transaction, from Jack Muyres were the five or six bonds which he gave me as above described, the proceeds of which amounted to $5000, and which I deposited in my bank as above related. I had never had any other bond transactions with my uncle,

(Testimony of Nellie P. Covert)

Jack Muyres, or any other business transaction whatsoever. I had this trip to Denver, Colorado, planned with my Dad the first part of this year, and he became ill the latter part of March and passed away in April, and so naturally the trip was postponed—the reason of the trip was to see my mother's mother, Mrs. Catherine Rohrs, 2370 South Broadway, whom I understood was having a tough time of it, who was being bothered and annoyed quite badly by her son, my uncle, John Rohrs, who lives at 2374 or 2376 South Broadway, having taken a week of my vacation in the summer with my two children to the Catalina Islands, thereby saving a week for this trip which week I would have to take before the first of the year or lose it, and not wanting to come to Colorado too late in the year, I decided this would be the time to do it or not at all.

The above statement consisting of four pages has been partially dictated by Mr. Guinane and partially by myself, and the same is true. I am not sure as to dates and addresses, but have given them as closely as I recall.

(Signed)   Geo. J. Muyres.

(Signed)   E. P. Guinane.

(Signed)   L. M. Chipman,

Witneses: E. P. Guinane Special Agent in Charge, Federal Bureau of Investigation, U. S. Department of Justice, 722 Midland Savings Bldg., Denver, Colorado. L. M. Chipman, Special Agent, Federal Bureau of Investigation, U. S. Department of Justice, 722 Midland Savings Bldg., Denver Colorado.

(Testimony of Nellie P. Covert)

Government's "Exhibit Number 28" is as follows:

Los Angeles, California,
December 3, 1935.

I, GEORGE J. MUYRES, make this statement to Special Agents L. V. Boardman and Lish Whitson, who, I have been advised, are Special Agents of the Federal Bureau of Investigation, U. S. Department of Justice, of my own free will, without threat or coercion, and in the nature of a supplemental statement to that previously given by me to Special Agents of the Denver, Colorado, Bureau Office on November 27, 1935.

With respect to Paragraph 4 of the statement signed by me on November 27, 1935, I wish to make these additional remarks. I recall that on October 14 or 15, 1935, my uncle, Jack Muyres, of Phoenix, Arizona, phoned me at my office, the Automobile Club of Southern California Building, Los Angeles, California, and asked me to come out to Jack's service station and during the ensuing conversation he mentioned that he had some bonds which he would like to have me dispose of for him. I did not commit myself one way or the other in regard to such disposition of the bonds mentioned. He had no bonds with him at this time as far as I know. I established this date as being October 14 or 15 from a conversation with Miss Denise Berry.

On or about the 23rd or 24th of October, 1935, my uncle Jack Muyres phoned me at the Automobile Club and asked me to come out to Maier's Brewery, 440 Aliso. I went down there the evening of that day and he gave me an envelope which contained four to six bonds. I did

(Testimony of Nellie P. Covert)

not examine the bonds at that time. The brewery was closed at the time I met my uncle there, and he handed me the bonds in front of the brewery. At this time he did not give me any list of bonds, either of those in the envelope handed to me or of any other bonds, and at no time did I ever receive from my uncle or have in my possession, or see, any list of bonds which my uncle was alleged to have or which were sold or disposed of in any way for my uncle by me or by anyone else. In addition, Special Agents Boardman and Whitson showed to me a plain sheet of paper upon which appeared a list of approximately thirty-one bonds. I wish to state that the handwriting which appears on this sheet of paper is not my handwriting; sthat this list of bonds was not made in my presence; that this list of bonds was not handed by me to John Cheney in whose possession this list was found; that I have never, to the best of my knowledge, seen this list of bonds, or any list of bonds, until the present list was shown me by Special Agents Boardman and Whitson as noted above.

With respect to my contact with Mr. Hilgers of Montjoy, Hurry & Hilgers, I wish to state that to the best of my recollection, I contacted Mr. Hilgers on or about October 24 or 25, 1935, the day following the receipt of the bonds from my uncle. I was referred to Mr. Hilgers by a Mr. Robinson of N. D. Dunham & Company, Ford Dealers, at the corner of Washington and Los Angeles, California. At the time I spoke to Mr. Hilgers he told me that it would take some time to check the validity of these bonds.

(Testimony of Nellie P. Covert)

On or about the 25th of October, 1935, my uncle Jack Muyres came into the courtyard of the Automobile Club Building and told me that he needed some ready money, and asked me if I could cash some interest coupons from his bonds for him. I went over to the Figueroa & Adams Branch of the Security-First National Bank of Los Angeles, with quite a handful of interest coupons, and cashed them for my uncle. On the back of each coupon the bank employee wrote the name "Muyres". I explained to him that these interest coupons were not mine but my uncle's. Inasmuch as some of these coupons required an affidavit of ownerwhip, I did not cash all of these coupons but returned approximately eight to twelve of these coupons to my uncle Jack Muyres. The amount received on these coupons to my present recollection was about $347. which amount I turned over to Jack Muyres.

On or about the day I cashed the interest coupons for my uncle, I returned to him the bonds I had taken down to Montjoy, Hurry & Hilgers. I remember this because I was planning a trip into the mountains over the 26th and 27th of October, 1935. I am sure I did not have these bonds with me while I was up in the mountains, and also that I did not have them with me at home.

John Cheney, at the University of Soutyern California gymnasium, told me that he had a friend named Bassett who, because of his knowledge of bonds, would be able to give me some information concerning my uncle's bonds. I had seen Bassett around the gymnasium several times but did not know his name and did not know his business until being so told by Cheney. On October 28 or 29, my uncle Jack Muyres, came into the Automobile Club Offices

(Testimony of Nellie P. Covert)

and I told him that I had someone that I could take the bonds to. He thereupon gave me an envelope containing four to six bonds which I presumed were the same bonds which I had had before. I took these bonds to the University of Southern California gymnasium and handed them to John Cheney. At the time I gave these bonds to Cheney we made no arrangements regarding the disposition of any proceeds from their possible sale. Later in the afternoon, when Bassett was present, he stated that the customary compensation for disposing of bonds was five per cent, whereupon I said I supposed the commission would be satisfactory if that was the procedure. I did not agree to any other compensation to be paid to Cheney or Bassett in the event these bonds were sold in a larger or smaller sum. With respect to any remuneration I was to receive for the disposition of these bonds, no arrangements had been made between my uncle and myself other than the fact that my uncle had stated that he would take care of me. At this time, on the suggestion of Bassett, Cheney gave me a receipt, the form of which I can not definitely remember and the *some* of which I can not remember; however, I do remember that it was supposed to represent the approximate value of the bonds which Cheney had received from me, which approximate value was given by Bassett who was supposed to know the value of the bonds. I do not now have this receipt in my possession, and I have no idea what became of it. It may be possible that when Cheney gave me two checks which represented the proceeds from a subsequent sale of these bonds that I might have given this receipt back to him, but I do not remember definitely. I have looked

(Testimony of Nellie P. Covert)

through my personal effects and am unable to find this receipt.

On November 1, 1935, my uncle Jack Muyres came to the Automobile Club offices and requested me to cash two bonds for him. One was what I believed to be a *V*Federal Home Loan bond in the amount of $100.00, but which I am now advised were Home Owners Loan Corporation bonds in the amounts mentioned above, I took these two bonds over to the Figueroa & Adams Branch of the Security First National Bank and showed them to Mr. A. E. Dusenberry. Mr. Dusenberry said the bonds were "O. K.", so I cashed both bonds and took the money back to my uncle Jack Muyres. Of this amount I paid to the bank $70.00 as part payment of a real estate loan which I owed to the bank. I had told my uncle previous to our going to the bank that I was borrowing this amount from him, and afterwards explained that I had paid the bank this sum of $70.00. At this time my uncle asked me what had been done with the other bonds which he had given me at the first part of the week, and I told him that they were up in a fellow's office. So far as I know my uncle never did meet or know John Cheney.

On November 2, 1935, my uncle Jack Muyres came around to the automobile club offices with another $1,000.00 bond which was of the same type as the bonds disposed of at the Security-First National Bank the preceding day. I drove down to Maier's Brewery at 330 Aliso Street and told James Thomson. I did not go down to the brewery specifically for the purpose of seeing Thomson. about this bond, but I had other business there. I told Thomson that my uncle wanted this bond cashed

(Testimony of Nellie P. Covert)

immediately, and he told me that he could get it cashed for me right up the street at the bank. He and I went over to the International Branch of the Bank of America where Thomson took the bond and cashed it for me. The bond was paid by the bank by a check to Thomson which he cashed, and then he gave the money to me. Thomson refused to accept any remuneration for assisting me in cashing this bond. I took the money from the sale of this bond back to my uncle Jack Muyres who later came to the auth mobile club office and got the money. I received no compensation at this time for my assistance in getting the bond cashed.

On the day of the U. S. C. Stanford Football game, which was on November 9, 1935, John Cheney gave me two checks, one for $2,000.00 and the other for $3,000.00, which he told me were proceeds from the sale of the bonds which I had left with him. Cheney told me that the bonds had sold for around $7,000.00 and that he had a remaining credit of approximately $2,000.00 with the E. F. Hutton & Company at which place he was supposed to have disposed of the bonds. No arrangements were made at that time for any disposition of this credit balance which he said remained at the Hutton Company.

After receiving these checks from Cheney, I wrote out a $300.00 check for my uncle which was in the nature of a loan. My uncle had phoned me that morning and wanted $300.00 "right away". I told him I could write a check but could not promise him it would be good until the following Tuesday, which would be the day after Armistice Day. I did not tell him I had received any check from Cheney as I did not know at that time whether or not the

180

checks were good or that they would clear the bank, which information I expected to know by the next Tuesday. I wrote out this check for $300.00 and placed it in an envelope on my desk with my uncle's name on the envelope. My uncle came into the office sometime during that day and picked up the $300.00 check in my absence. I saw him in a few days later when he came into the club, but I did not mention, nor did he the check for $300.00 at that time. He asked me what I knew about the bonds and I told him I did not know of any news regarding them. I have not seen him since that time; however, around the 14th or 15th of November, 1935, my uncle phoned the office during my absence and requested me to call him at Jack's service station on Whittier Boulevard. I neglected to return this call.

I wish to state *tha* aside from the $5,000.00 in my bank account and the $70.00 loan from my uncle Jack Muyres, which I received about November 1, 1935, I received no other moneys from the proceeds of the sale of the bonds which my uncle had.

At the time I made the statement in Denver I gave all the information I recalled at that time, and I did not attempt to withhold any information whatsoever. Since returning to Los Angeles from Denver, and after refreshing my memory, I have recalled the above.

I have read the foregoing statement consisting of four pages, and I wish to state that the same is true to the best of my knowledge and belief.

GEORGE J. MUYRES

(Testimony of Tom H. Sisk)

WITNESSES:

....

L. V. Boardman, Special Agent, Federal Bureau of Investigation, U. S. Department of Justice, Los Angeles, California.

....

Lish Whitson, Special Agent, Federal Bureau of Investigation, U. S. Department of Justice, Los Angeles, California.

TOM H. SISK

Recalled as a witness on behalf of the Government, having been previously sworn, further testified as follows:

DIRECT EXAMINATION

BY MR. IRWIN:

I have seen the document enclosed in an envelope which has just been handed me. The bonds concerning which I have previously testified were enclosed in this envelope when found. This piece of canvass which has just been handed me was wrapped around the envelope. (The envelope and the piece of canvass which the witness testified had been wrapped around the bonds found under the house in Texas were then admitted as Government's Exhibit "No. 34". On the envelope is the wording "Merchandise, Fourth Class Mail, Post Master: This parcel may be opened for postal inspection, if necessary. Return postage guaranteed. Department of Motor Vehicles, Division of Registration, Sacramento, California." It also con-

(Testimony of Morris Higbie Remsen, Jr.)

tains a statement concerning the automobile license plates contained on the registration certificate which was also contained. On the envelope is also a stamp of the numbers "2 V 9330".)

BY THE WITNESS:

I found that a license of that number was on a car which was sold November 4, 1935, by the W. D. Dunham Company, Los Angeles, to a man named Chambers, of Oakland. I understand that Dunham Company are automobile dealers.

(Whereupon it was stipulated that there was a W. D. Dunham Company in Los Angeles, which had a Ford agency.

MORRIS HIGBIE REMSEN, JR.

called as a witness on behalf of the Government, having been first duly sworn, testified as follows:

DIRECT EXAMINATION:

BY MR. IRWIN:

I live at 710 Adelaine Avenue, South Pasadena. Am eployed at the Security First National Bank, Figueroa and Adams Branch, Los Angeles and was so employed during the months of October and November of last year. I know the defendant George J Muyres, and have known him about eight months. He had a bank account with our institution in October and November of 1935. I have a photostatic copy of the ledger.

(Testimony of Morris Higbie Remsen, Jr.)

(Whereupon the photosatic copy of the statement of the account of George J. Muyres was introduced as Government's Exhibit "No. 35".) Government's Exhibit "No. 35" shows the balances and the amounts withdrawn as follows:

MR. IRWIN: October 9th, $14.30; October 11th, $4.30; October 14th, deposited $143.96, balance $118.26; October 15th, $73.26; October 16th, $61.26; October 17th, $47.76; deposited $60 on October 17th, balance $107.76; October 18th, $102.76; October 18th, $67.76; October 22nd, $64.46; October 22nd, $44.46; October 23rd, $24.46, October 23rd, $9.46; deposited $143.96; balance $152.42; October 31st, $122.08; November 1st, $107.08; November 1st, $87.08; November 5th, $47.08; November 6th, $32.08; deposited $28.52, balance $60.60 on November 7th; November 7th, $45.60; November 9th, deposited $3,000, balance $3,045.60; November 12th, $3,037.87; November 12th, deposited $2,000, balance $4,772.60; November 13th, $4,462.60; November 14th, deposited $141.96, balance $4,566.47; November 15th, $4,553.47; November 15th $4,503.47, November 18th, $4,477.69."

On November 18th he withdrew $3500 which, according to the stipulation between counsel and myself, we are agreed that that was deposited in a savings account in the name of George J. Muyres in the same bank, in the same branch. I took an order from Mr. Muyres to sell two Home Owners Loan bonds for him on November 1, 1935.

(Testimony of Morris Higbie Remsen, Jr.)

(A photostatic copy of that selling order was entered in evidence as Government's Exhibit No. 36. One bond had a face value of $100.00 and the other of $1000.00.)

BY THE WITNESS:

As I recall it, he explained to me that these bonds came from an estate. An uncle had died in Holland, and another uncle in this country was acting as Executor of the estate—that these bonds came from the Executor.

(Whereupon it was stipulated between counsel that photostatic copies which this witness produced were correct photostatic copies of what they purported to be.

(Whereupon the photostatic copy of a selling order of the Bond Department of the Security First National Bank was introduced in evidence as Government's Exhibit "No. 37"). This exhibit showed that that bank had sold a $1000.00 and a $100.00 Home Owners Loan Bond on November 1, 1935, for the sum of $1103.44. Pursuant to that stipulation a check dated November 9, 1935, drawn to J. F. Muyres on the Security First National Bank, Figueroa and Adams Branch, and signed by George J. Muyres for $300.00, bearing endorsement of J. F. Muyres, and a cancellation payment stamp was introduced in evidence as Government's Exhibit "No. 38" and a photostatic copy of a check dated November 9, 1935, on the University and Jefferson Branch to George F. Muyres in the sum of $3000.00 signed by J. M. Cheney was introduced in evidence as Governments Exhibit "No. 39". A photostatic copy of a check on the University and Jefferson Branch of the same bank, dated November 12, 1935, to George

(Testimony of Morris Higbie Remsen, Jr.)

Muyres in the sum of $2000.00 signed by John M. Cheney was introduced in evidence as Government's Exhibit No. 40.

CROSS-EXAMINATION

BY MR. GRAHAM:

I had known George Muyres about eight months. I knew he was employed at the Automobile Club which is right across street from our bank. I don't know for certain whether he deposited his pay checks in that bank twice a month or not. I don't think I have seen his pay checks.

(Whereupon it was stipulated that the item of deposit dated October 14, 1935 in the amount of $143.96 and the item of the same amount of October 30, and the item on November 14 of $141.96 were George J. Muyres pay checks from the Automobile Club.)

I know that Mr. Muyres had some small real estate holdings here from which he had a small income and which he deposited in the bank. He had a mortgage with our bank. He said he got these bonds from an uncle who had died in Holland, and that his other uncle from whom he got these bonds was the Executor of that estate. I am positive he said uncle, not grandmother. We were not accepting these bonds as an estate letter. I thought it was personal bonds. If I was selling securities for an Executor, securities which belonged to the estate, I would demand certified copies of Letters Testamentary and certified copies of the court's order authorizing the sale, that is if we were handling it for the Executor. I did not ask for any of those certified copies.

(Testimony of James Thompson)

JAMES THOMPSON

called as a witness on behalf of the Government, having
been first duly sworn, testified as follows:

DIRECT EXAMINATION

BY MR. IRWIN:

I reside at 400 South Rossmore. I know Glen Watkins,
connected with the Bank of America. He was connected
with that bank in November of last year. I know the defendant George J. Muyres and had a conversation with
him in November of last year concerning the handling of
some bonds. George called me on a Saturday morning,
which was November 2, and asked me if I could sell a
bond for him. I called Mr. Watkins of the Bank of
America and asked him if he could sell a bond and he said
"Yes". So when Mr. Muyres came down to the Brewery
we went down to the office and Mr. Muyres told me on the
way down that this bond belonged to his uncle, and he was
not exactly sure about it, and I said "All right". We will
take it to Mr. Watkins. We will tell Mr. Watkins the
story of where it came from." I took the bond from
him when we entered the bank and gave it to Mr. Watkins. He took it back to the Foreign Department in the
rear of the bank; found out it was O. K.; made out a
check for it. I endorsed the check and Mr. Watkins
O. K'd. it and Mr. Muyres cashed it and got the money.
Mr. Muyres mentioned the fact that there were some
bonds and War Savings Stamps and some other things
connected with his grandmother's estate in Holland; that
they would be coming over here, and Mr. Watkins told
me that if he could be of any assistance to him in selling

(Testimony of Averoy Corpestin)

them that he would be glad to do it. I don't recall anything was said about Mr. Muyres opening a bank account. Mr. Muyres left us and went across to cash the draft. I am partially hard of hearing, and he may have said something. There was a further conversation, but I didn't hear it.

CROSS EXAMINATION

BY MR. GRAHAM:

Mr. Muyres went across the room to cash the draft. I have known him since 1932 and knew his father quite well. I came in contact with him every day while working at the Brewery. No, I never heard George Muyres and his father discuss the estate of this grandmother in Holland until October of 1935.

AVEROY CORPESTIN

called out of order, as a witness on behalf of defendant John F. Muyres, having been first duly sworn testified as follows:

DIRECT EXAMINATION

By Mr. Ostrom:

I reside in Pheonix, Arizona. My brother and I have a Lumber Company in Phoenix. I know the defendant, John F. Muyres and have known him about four years. I know his reputation for truth, honesty and veracity in the community in which he lives. It is very good.

Whereupon the plaintiff rested its case.

(Testimony of Thomas Cushman)

EXCEPTION NO. 7.

Whereupon the following motion was made by Mr. Graham:

If the Court please, at this time, on behalf of the defendant George J. Muyres, I move the Court to direct the Jury to find the defendant George J. Muyres not guilty upon the ground that the evidence in the case is insufficient to warrant a conviction of this defendant on either count of the indictment.

(After argument by counsel for plaintiff and the defendant George J. Muyres, the Court denied the foregoing motion to which ruling the said defendant excepted.)

THOMAS CUSHMAN

called as a witness on behalf of defendant Ryan, having been first duly sworn testified as follows:

DIRECT EXAMINATION

By O'Hanneson:

I reside at the San Carlos Hotel Garage for the time being. In the month of December 1935 I resided at the Apache Hotel. About the 24th or 25th of September 1935 I was in the Avalon Buffet in Phoenix, Arizona. At that time I saw the defendant Woolsey who was a bar tender in the Avalon Buffet. I heard the conversation between him and defendant Ryan. Mr. Ryan, as I know him now, mentioned that he knew where he could get, or where there were, some bonds won in gambling and asked Mr. Woolsey to help him dispose of them. There was nothing said by the defendant at that time as to the bonds being "hot" bonds.

(Testimony of Thomas Cushman)

CROSS EXAMINATION

By Mr. Irwin:

I reside for the time being at the San Carlos Hotel in Phoenix. I have been there for the past month; I am a mechanic. Prior to living at the San Carlos I lived at the Apache Hotel since September 22, 1935, until the first of February. I have lived in Phoenix since the 18th of September. Before living at the Apache I was at the Arizona Hotel from the 18th to 22nd of November; before that I was in San Francisco for a month and eight days. I came there from Boston, Mass. That was my home. I left there in August 1, 1935. My address in Boston was 60 Southgate Park, West Newton. I arrived in Phoenix from San Francisco on September 18th, 1935 and I heard the conversation that I was talking about in the latter part of the week. I conducted a filling station for myself in Boston. I was in San Francisco on pleasure, no business. I was a transient. I came to San Francisco by bus, train and boat. I went from San Francisco to Arizona by bus. While I was in Phoenix I was doing nothing up until the middle of February this year. I am now employed by myself in a garage. From September 1935 to February 1936 I was not doing anything. I first communicated the substance of the conversation which I claim I heard last week to be exact the 18th of this month, to Mr. John Lee, who is here in Court and temporarily was representing Mr. Ryan and who formerly represented

(Testimony of Thomas Cushman)

Mr. Woolsey who has pleaded guilty in this case. It came to my attention that Mr. Lee was looking for a party that happened to be in the Avalon Cafe on September 1935; an elevator boy in the Security Building mentioned that fact to me. I do not know his name. After that was brought to my attention I called Mr. Lee up and came over here with him. No one has advanced me any money for coming here to testify in this case. I have been in my own business for the first time since I came here since the middle of February. I do not know these people that had the conversation and did not know who they were. I was in the Avalon Buffet once or twice since. I was unemployed from September 18th to the middle of February. At the time I heard the conversation I was standing at the east end of the bar, Mr. Ryan was standing at my elbow and cater cornered with his back to me. Woolsey was behind the bar. I had never known either of these gentlemen and had never talked to them. Ryan asked Woolsey if he knew where he could dispose of bonds which had been won in gambling. The first of the week before last it was first brought to my attention by some of the boys at the garage that this prosecution was pending in this case. I fix the approximate date of this conversation by the fact that it was the first week I was there. I heard many other conversations during the first week I was there. I do not know that there is any other one that stuck in my mind particularly. I have been in other bars since and have heard conversations there. I expect to go back east some time in May. I do not think I have ever seen Mr. Woolsey before. I do not think I have ever seen him since that time.

(Testimony of Thomas Cushman)

DIRECT EXAMINATION

By Mr. Ostrom:

I used to be in the cage and on the street for Stone & Webster of Boston, Mass. I have handled many bonds and that is what made the conversation stick in my mind. I was employed by Stone & Webster, Inc. that is a large bond house in Boston. I worked for them for more than a year in the cage and on the Street.

RE-CROSS EXAMINATION

By Mr. Irwin:

I worked for them and left them the first day of January 1927. I had been in that department a year prior to that time. I have had various business' since that time. When I worked for them on the street I was a messenger. I have been in the engineering department of Stone & Webster. I have had business of my own and also worked for Thomas Bloom. I left Stone & Webster in the summer of 1928. I went with the Thomas Bloom Company in December 1928, and left in 1932. I bought and sold paper for them. They were a stationery concern. I worked as a general laborer in the Street Department of the town of Hull, Mass., not as a street cleaner, but you may put it that way. I was with them seven or eight months. I went down to Rowley, Mass. and took over a filling station there for myself. I had it up until July, 1935. It was in the center of town and used to be called the Ray Grady Station before I had it. When I left it it was called the American Oil Company, operated by me.

192

(Testimony of Thomas Burke Ryan)

THOMAS BURKE RYAN

called as a witness in his own behalf, having been duly
sworn, testified as follows:

DIRECT EXAMINATION

BY MR. O'HANNESON:

My name is Thomas Burke Ryan. I am one of the
defendants in this case. I know the defendant Ryman
and first met him at Phoenix, Arizona sometime in October, or possibly in September of 1935. I met him on several occasions. The last time I met him in Phoenix was
about the 15th of October. At that time I had a conversation with him. The first few times he came into the
place he seemed to be curious regarding those marble machines and diggers, etc. I had various different kinds and
he was interested in the operation of them. I was in
business in Phoenix, operating machines in other people's
stores. My Ryman came in there from time to time and
he rode around two or three places with me and acted as
though he was interested in that particular type of machine. He asked how much money they made and what
would be the best kind to buy. He made various trips like
that and finally one day he told me that he would be interested in purchasing some of those machines if I knew
where I could buy them. I told him there wasn't any
question in my mind about buying them, because I knew
I could buy them for half price. Then he told me he had
a little income, it was not very much, and he also had
some securities and if I knew of any place where he could
dispose of them, he would like to buy some of the machines. So I asked him concerning the securities and he

(Testimony of Thomas Burke Ryan)

told me they were different kinds of bonds. Not being familiar with bonds, I didn't know just what it was at that time, but there were several kinds of bonds. Then, the next day or two he came down town and wanted to know if I could sell any. I said that I didn't know; that I haven't anybody in mind, but that I am familiar—well acquainted in the city and I knew a few people and if I happened to see anyone that had a little money and wanted to tie it up in some bonds, I would let him know. I told him to call back in the next day or two. So he called back in a day or two and that particular time I hadn't seen anyone that would buy the bonds. I told him to come back in another day or two. He came back a few days later and I said, "Yes, I have a buyer for those bonds, providing they could be discounted." So, he says, "Well, when does he want them?" I said, "He will take them now if you can get them, providing he can discount them and make a little money." He says, "I will have to go and get them. I don't have them with me." I said, "I was under the impression you had the bonds." He said, "Well, I have, but I don't have them here. I will have to go after them." I asked him how long it would require him to go get the bonds and he told me that it would take several days. He didn't say exactly how long it would take, but it would take several days. He said, "Before I go after the bonds I would like to have you be positive that you have a purchaser for them." I told him there was no question in my mind in having a purchaser for the bonds, if the bonds were not counterfeit or were not hot. If the bonds were all right I had a purchaser for them. "All right," he said, "I will go get them." When I said

(Testimony of Thomas Burke Ryan)

that I had a purchaser for them if they were not counterfeit or hot, he said he would go get the bonds. He said
it would take him several days to get them; that he wished
to be positive, because there would be some expense in
going after them and he would have to do some repair to
his automobile.

The next time I saw Mr. Ryman was in Los Angeles.
Mr. Ryman never told me at any time that these bonds
were stolen bonds or what is sometimes known as hot
bonds. I don't remember the day when I came to Los
Angeles, but it was the day that these Hotels said I was
registered in there. I came to Los Angeles for two reasons. One was to buy slot machines and one was to help
Eddie sell bonds. The occasion that I first met Mr.
Ryman in Los Angeles was due to a message left for me
at the Avalon Cafe. When he started for these bonds,
after telling me it would take him several days to get
them, I told him that due to the fact of the length of time
it would take him to get them, that the purchaser I had
in view would not be in Phoenix at that time, but that it
was my understanding he was going to Los Angeles for
a vacation. Therefore, I told him that he would have to
meet me in Los Angeles and that I would look up this
party here. Mr. Ryman never told me where he was getting the bonds, nor he never told me that they were
stolen. The bond which one witness testified was found
in my room in one of the drawers was Mr. Ryman's bond.
That was Government's Exhibit No. 29. The reason I
say that that was Mr. Ryman's bond was, in the first
place, the bond belonged to him, and in the second place,
he claimed it. At the time Mr. Ryman claimed owner-

(Testimony of Thomas Burke Ryan)

ship of that particular bond, Mr. Sisk, the Government's Special Agent, Mr. McInerney. Special Agent in San Antonio, Texas, Mr. Olum, City Detective of Houston, and Mr. Martindale, were present. They were in the Houston Police Station being investigated by the Houston Police staff and the Government Agents. It was during that investigation that Mr. Ryman, in the presence of the gentlemen I have mentioned, admitted ownership of that particular bond. I had the bond one day and carried it up and down San Jacinto Street—Automobile Row—in Houston. I had possession of that bond and also another bond which Mr. Ryman gave me to trade for automobiles or slot machines—either one that I saw that I could get a fair deal on. I did not trade this one. The other one I had taken to an automobile man there. He had looked at the automobile, a Cadillac '32' sport coupe and had taken two demonstration rides in this car and had agreed to buy it after the bond cleared the bank. I presume the Government Agent still has the bond that was found in the drawer. The occasion that it came to be in my dresser drawer was that it was laying up on the dresser and Eddie came in and he said to put it in my shirts for the reason that I might go out and leave it and that later somebody might pick it up. There was no secret about the bonds being displayed in Houston, Texas. I had no reason to hide them and I had shown them in various places up and down the street. I have lived in Houston for twenty years. I had some of the bonds given to me by Mr. Ryman and I had shown them to various merchants. There didn't seem to be much of a market for the particular bond they found in my dresser. It was a German government bond and it was

(Testimony of Thomas Burke Ryan)

only worth about $35.00 on a hundred, or something like that. This other bond that was claimed by Mr. Ryman was for an automobile for him. 'He was introduced to a merchant.

DIRECT EXAMINATION

BY MR. OSTROM:

I discussed these bonds with John F. Muyres in Arizona about a week or two, I should judge, or three weeks, before we came over here. I was sent to Mr. Muyres and asked him if he had any surplus money that he wished to put in bonds, and he said he might buy some bonds, providing he could buy them at a discount. Well, I asked him, if I would get him the numbers of the bonds, if that would be satisfactory, and he said no, that he wished to look at the bonds, for two reasons. One of them was to be positive that they were not counterfeit, and one that they were not hot. He wished to check the bonds. The first time that I broached the subject of bonds to Mr. Woolsey was in the Avalon Buffet. I think I asked him if he knew of anyone that would be interested in buying any bonds. I think that I referred to them as "gambling bonds." I said nothing about their being hot bonds. I was short of information. I didn't know where the bonds were coming from, or what kind of bonds they were, and I referred to them in that manner, not knowing the type of bonds they were. I used the word "gambling" not any more than I would use any other word. I was not positive what type of bonds they were or where they were coming from and I was never informed.

(Testimony of John F. Muyres)

JOHN F. MUYRES

called as a witness in his own behalf, having been first
duly sworn, testified as follows:

DIRECT EXAMINATION

BY MR. OSTROM:

I reside at 19th Avenue and Madison Streets, Phoenix,
Arizona. I operate a Drive-In Sandwich and Drink
stand. It is called the Twin Barrels. It is a fair-sized
place. I have operated it for four years and a half. I
have been in business in Phoenix four years and a half.
Before that, I was in Los Angeles for about 15 years. I
was in business here, running a garage and service station.
I had this service station on Whittier Boulevard.

I have known Ham Woolsey about three and a half
years. He worked for me for about two years in '33 and
'34· Then he has worked for me after that. I had programs there twice a week and he did the announcing.
That was just about two hours twice a week—I mean a
radio program.

I have known the defendant Ryan since about August,
1935. He has one of the little grabbing machines in my
place of business. He would come there practically every
other day to collect the money and to fix the machines.

About the 3rd or 4th of October Woolsey came over
to my place of business one day and he says, "There was
a fellow in to see me who had some bonds." And I said
to him, "What kind of bonds?" "Well," he says, "I don't
know much about them, but I will find out some more and
I will let you know." That was all that was said at that
time. Then I would see Woolsey and his family—they

(Testimony of John F. Muyres)

used to come out to my place of business, and he—but
we never talked any more about bonds until the 14th of
October, when I happened to go from town in my car and
I parked in there, and Mr. Woolsey and his wife and little
boy were sitting at my place of business. I went over
there and sat with them then. I must have sat there ten
or fifteen minutes, and in a casual conversation I said that
I was going to Los Angeles in the morning, mother and
I—that is, my mother-in-law, and then when they had finished lunch he got up and told his wife to go into the car
and he followed me around the back of the building and
he said, "I saw that fellow with the bonds. They are a
couple of bonds and they won these bonds gambling.
"However," he says, "I don't know much about them,
but," he says, "While you are in Los Angeles inquire
whether you can dispose of them." I told him I didn't
know anything about bonds and that was all that was said.

On the 15th of October I came to Los Angeles and my
purpose for coming to Los Angeles was to buy uniforms
for these girls. I have from six to fifteen girls there, it
depends on the different times of the season. At that time
I had eight or nine. I came to Los Angeles with my
mother-in-law and stayed at her home, 3418 Amethyst
Street. I went back here on the 22nd of October. While
I was here in Los Angeles on that trip from the 15th to
the 22nd of October I had different businesses that I at-
tended to. I bought uniforms for the girls at the May
Company and I intended to trade my car for another car.
I owned a lot on Canto Drive, right off of Mission Road,
and on the 15th of October, in the evening I called George
Muyres—I always get in touch with him when I am in

(Testimony of John F. Muyres)

Los Angeles—he is in the insurance business. I asked George if he didn't know where I could trade a vacant lot and my car on a Chrysler. He said he would find out and let me know. He asked me where he could get me and I told him I would be at Jack's Service Station at 4801 Whittier Boulevard, between six and eight tomorrow night. That was a telephone conversation. The following day, which was October 16th, George Muyres came out there about seven o'clock and gave me a man's card and told me he would be over to see me the following day between twelve and one, in regards to a trade on our automobile. While we was talking there I finally asked George—I says, "George, do you know anything about bonds, or do you know any bondsmen?" He says, "No." And that's all that was said in regards to bonds at that time.

On the 18th of October George Muyres called me and he said, "You remember you said something about bonds the other night." "Well," he says, "a friend of mine that I have been playing squash with and whom I have known for a long time, is in the bond business. So, if you have anyone in the line of bonds, give him the business. That was all that was said in regards to bonds to George Muyres.

Between the 18th and 22nd of October I couldn't make a trade on the car, so I had it worked on and got new tires, got part of the uniforms and left here in the morning of the 22nd of October, around eight o'clock. My mother-in-law went back to Phoenix with me. She lives there with me. When we got back to Phoenix I walked in the kitchen and my cook says, "Ham wants to see you as soon

(Testimony of John F. Muyres)

as you get back." So I looked at my watch and it was just 6:30. There was quite a sand-storm going back, so I went in the house and cleaned up and went to see Ham Woolsey at his residence. Just Ham and myself were present. I got there between seven and eight o'clock. Ham Woolsey said these bonds he spoke to me about was in California. I said, "Now, Ham, are you sure that these bonds are all right and we are not going to get in trouble and they are not stolen?" He says, "They was won in gambling." "Now, I don't want to get in no trouble. If you think there was anything wrong with those bonds, or stolen, I don't want to have anything to do with them." He says, "Why, you know gamblers. They are liable to put us in jail." I said, "I think we ought to go back now." He said, "Just a minute Wait. I'll see George Mutchins." That is his boss. He said, "I'll tell him I won't be back until Saturday and we'll go back now." We left Phoenix about nine o'clock on the 22nd. That was on a Tuesday. It took us about eight hours to drive from Phoenix to here. During that time we talked about the bonds then and he told me the same thing— that the bonds was won in gambling. He told me that I knew Ryan, one of the fellows. At that time we never knew Ryan's last name. We always called him Tom. I didn't say anything to that. We arrived here pretty early, between four and five o'clock on the 23rd, and went to bed at 3418 Amethyst Street. That is my mother-in-law's house. That was on Wednesday the 23rd of October. After Ham and I got some sleep, we got up and went down to that service station on 4801 Whittier Boulevard, and while we was there we ate breakfast. There is a restaurant there connected with the service station. I got

(Testimony of John F. Muyres)

a telephone call, which I answered, and told Ham that that was Tom. He wanted us to meet him at the U. S. Hotel. We finished our breakfast and met him in front of the U. S. Hotel. Then we went up in his room and he said, "Those bonds are here." While Ham and I were driving over on the night of the 22nd or the early morning of October 23, he said—the first thing I heard when I come back—he says, "The bonds are in California now," and I says, "Why are the bonds in California?" "Well," he says, "I told Ryan that you was over there." Woolsey and I met Ryan in front of the U. S. Hotel and went up to his room. I asked Ryan then, "What about these bonds and where did they come from?" and I asked him how he got them. He says, "They won them in gambling." I said, "These bonds are not stolen?" He says, "No." "Well," I said, "I'll find out and see what we can do with them." So I left them. That was all that was said. I did not see any bonds and did not have any numbers at that time. Then I called George. I told him that these bonds was here, I told him to see what he could do. He said he would not have—he asked me what kind of bonds they were and I said that I didn't know. So he says, "You ought to get some samples of the bonds and I will take them to this broker." Which I did. This conversation with George was on the telephone. I called him at the Automobile Club.

I went back to the U. S. Hotel and told Ryan—that was on Wednesday, October 23rd, around four o'clock, and he gave me four samples. Woolsey was the only other person present. Woolsey didn't say anything, and Ryan says, "All right, I'll give you some samples. You

(Testimony of John F. Muyres)

will have to wait a few minutes." I did so, he was gone ten or fifteen minutes. He came back with four samples. That was a Kansas State Power and Light bond, $1000.00, and a German bond of $1000.00, an Austrian bond of $1000.00 and a Home Owners Loan of $100.00. That's when I asked them where they got those bonds. He says, "They won them in gambling." Up to this time I had not met Ryman. I took these four samples and gave them to George Muyres, whom I met at the Automobile Club, at about five o'clock. I told George here were four of those bonds and he would take them and show them to the broker and let me know. From the Automobile Club I went back out to that service station. Woolsey did not go with me. As near as I can recall now he stayed with Ryan. Nothing else occurred on the 23rd in regard to the bonds. I saw Ryan on Thursday the 24th at the U. S. Hotel. George hadn't told me anything the night before. I told Ryan that George had taken the bonds and said he would let me know. In the morning of the 24th I heard from George by telephone. He said the broker didn't want the bonds, but wanted the serial numbers on what bonds we had. That was all he said. He didn't say why the broker wanted the serial numbers. Then I went back to the U. S. Hotel at about 10:00 or 10:30 in the morning. I saw Ryan downstairs in the bar. Woolsey was present. I told Ryan that these men wanted the serial numbers. Ryan says, "All right, I'll get some for you." I met Ryan later on, between one and two o'clock. This meeting took place in the room. There were present Ryan, Woolsey and myself. Ryan said he would get me the serial numbers. The conversation in regard to the serial numbers took place about ten o'clock

(Testimony of John F. Muyres)

in the morning, and he told me that he would have the
serial numbers at one or two o'clock in the afternoon.
That conversation was with Ryan in Woolsey's presence
in the morning, in that room. Then I saw him in the
room at 1:30 or two o'clock. Woolsey and Ryan were
present. There wasn't anything said; he just give me a
list of the numbers and told me to copy them, which I
did. I do not recognize Government's Exhibit 3. I had
a list similar to this to copy from. It was in an envelope.
I copied the numbers at the window. There was no conversation had at that time. A man came in during that
time whom I subsequently found out was Ryan. I was
sitting at the window, the door was here, I was facing
that way, copying these, and while I was copying, I heard
the door open and I looked around and saw a man go
out. Now, I didn't know who he was, but Ham said,
"That was Ryan's partner." This other man just come
in and walked out. I just saw his back going out the
door. There was no other conversation that I recall during the time I was in Ryan's room copying serial numbers.
I finished copying the serial numbers, but Ryan said he
did not have them all. He said he would have to get them
before he could give them to me. That was all that happened that day, which was Thursday, the 24th.

About eight o'clock in the morning, Ham and I went
to the United States Hotel. We met Eddie Ryman, and
Ham introduced him to me. That was the first time I
had met him to be introduced to him. We were going up
to the room, and Ryman said to Ham, "I got the bonds
and the serial numbers right here", so I told him I did
not want any bonds, I just wanted the serial numbers.

204

Then he gave me the serial numbers, and he had some coupons. The numbers were made out on a list. It is not the list that is now shown me. This was on Friday morning, October, the 25th. He said he had all the bonds and the serial numbers, and I told him I did not want any bonds. I also told him the broker wanted these serial numbers to check up on these bonds, and he said "Well, what about these coupons? Maybe they can sell them." I said I will go and find out. I did not say then how the broker wanted to check. He then gave me the coupons.

I next went over to see George at the Southern California Automobile Club. I went alone, and arrived there around nine o'clock. I saw George. No one else was present. I told George that here was the serial numbers and the coupons—to find out whether he could sell them. He said the broker wanted these serials numbers to check on these bonds to be sure they were not stolen bonds, and that the bonds were alright, and that it would take them three or four days to check on them. I says, "You keep this. I will go back and tell them if that is agreeable, and will come back and tell you".

Then I went back to the United States Hotel. That was still in the morning. I did not see anybody at the hotel, but I met the three of them in the parking lot, right in back of the United States Hotel. That is, I met Ryman, Ryan and Woolsey I was in the car and Ryman came out and talked to me, but the others were not in hearing distance. I told Ryman why he wanted the serial numbers; that he wanted to check on them to see if the bonds were alright, and that it would take three or four days. If that was agreeable to him, I would let him know.

(Testimony of John F. Muyres)

He said that that was agreeable. He asked me, "How about the coupons?" I said. "I don't know", I said that I would find out when I got back. I had left the coupons with George. And, then, pretty close to noon, I went back to the Automobile Club alone. I saw George, and had a conversation with him No one else was present. I told George it was agreeable for him to check on the bonds. Then George gave me those four sample bonds that I gave him the day before, some coupons and three hundred eight and some-odd dollars. It was on the 24th that I gave the four samples bonds to George. He said he would take them to the broker. That is, when George called me up and told me he wanted the serial numbers and when I met him the second time on Friday, October 25th, he then gave me back these four sample bonds, some of the coupons and some three hundred eighty dollars. He said they had the serial numbers and that is all they needed. They did not want any bonds until they found the bonds were alright He said he sold the Home Owners Loan Coupons; that the other could not be sold until somebody claimed ownership. Somebody had to sign ownership—something to that effect. I don't really remember what it was. I think the coupons that I got back were on the Austrian and German bonds, but I never looked at them.

Then, I went back to the Hotel; the second time that I went over there to tell George, Eddie Ryman drove with me. I left him a ways from the Automobile Club. I left him some distance. I went in and had this conversation with George when he gave me back the four samples, some of the coupons and three hundred eighty dollars. Then

(Testimony of John F. Muyres)

I left George and came on out, and re-joined Ryman. I gave Ryman this envelope with the coupons and with some money in it, and I said, "I ought to have some expense money", and he gave me two twenty-dollar bills and a five-dollar bill. I told him that somebody would have to sign ownership to those coupons before they could be sold. I told him that the man did not want the bonds, but that he wanted the serial numbers so that he could check on them. We had no further conversation in regard to the bonds. We then went back to that parking lot adjacent to the United States Hotel. Then, I met Ham and I said, "Ham, you might just as well go home. There is nothing for you to do here, and as soon as I find out that the bonds are alright, that they are going to sell them, I am going to come home, too." Ham says, "I think I will do that. I am going to buy the wife a present. I think I will take the bus home", so I said, "Ham, I have some sweaters at the May Company. Take them along with you". So Ham and I left Ryman at the parking lot and went over there to the May Company. When I told Ham he had better go back home, he said he might; that he would be on duty Saturday night. When we got to the May Company, I went up and got the sweaters. I think there were six of them for my employees. The man I bought the sweaters from said, "You don't have to take them", he said, "we will ship them to you; it will cost you nothing extra". He said, "that is a good idea. They will get there before I do anyway". We got to the May Company about 1:30 or 2:00 o'clock.

Ham and I had walked to the May Company; then we walked back to the lot adjacent to the United States Hotel.

(Testimony of John F. Muyres)

Ham said, "I don't think I will go home. I owe myself a vacation. I might as well stay until you do." I suggested then that we go to Murietta Springs over Saturday and Sunday.

I don't know what became of this $380.00 in the envelope. When I came back and left Eddie out and parked my car, and by that time I came and they had been up to the room together. That was before we went to the May Company. After Eddie Ryman and I came back from the Automobile Club, I let him out and then I went and parked my car, and did not notice where Ryman went. Then I came back, and Ham rejoined me at the parking lot. I parked my car down the street a ways, where I usually always do. Ham told me he received $68.00 from the $380.00. That was after he said he wanted a vacation, instead of going back. It was agreeable to Ham that we go to Murietta Hot Springs. The reason for my suggestion was to pass the week-end. Ham told him we was going, so they decided to go, too.

Nothing else happened relative to the bonds on Friday, the 25th. We went to Murietta Springs on Saturday night. Nothing happened Saturday morning. We left for Murietta about seven or eight o'clock. I guess the others had gone ahead.

After I had returned from the May Company on Friday, October, the 25th, I had no conversation with Ryman, Ryan or Woolsey relative to the bonds, on Friday, October the 25th, nor Saturday, Sunday or Monday, and we stayed at Murietta Springs until Monday morning. We got back here about nine o'clock in the morning. I don't believe I saw Ryman, or Ryan on Monday, October 28th.

208

I heard from them that day. They left word at the service station they had changed rooms then. I did not contact either of them that day. I did not have a conversation with Woolsey on the 28th relative to the bonds. I did not communicate with George Muyres on Monday, October 28th, relative to the bonds, nor on any other subject.

During this time Woolsey was living with me at my mother-in-law's house on Amathyst Street, and Ryan and Ryman were together by this time at the hotel. I saw Ryman and Ryam on Tuesday, October 29th, about ten o'clock in the street in front of their hotel on Whittier Boulevard. I don't remember the name of the hotel, but it was, I should say, in the 4400 block. That is as near as I can place it. I saw them at their hotel. Woolsey was with me. That was on Tuesday, October 29th. Woolsey got out and he was talking to Ryan a little ways off. Eddie Ryman said, "I got the bonds". "Well", I said, "I have not seen those men at all". "Well", he said, "you had better take those bonds and give them to him", he says, "if they are alright. They have got them." So, he went up and got the bonds and gave me the bonds. Then he went into the hotel and came out and gave me a package wrapped up in a newspaper. He said, "here is the bonds". I took the bonds and gave them to George. When he gave me the bonds, no one said what I was to do with the bonds. He knew what I was going to do with the bonds, to give them to him to sell them. At that time, nothing was said by any one relative to a report on the serial numbers. Then I went to the Automobile Club and saw George. He is usually there around noon.

(Testimony of Irvin G. Taplin—Henry Michael Guenser)

IRVIN G. TAPLIN,

called as a witness on behalf of the defendant George J. Muyres, having first duly sworn, testified as follows:

DIRECT EXAMINATION

By Mr. Graham:

I am a judge of the Municipal Court of the City of Los Angeles, County of Los Angeles, State of California. I am acquainted with the defendant George J. Muyres, and have known him for about ten years at least. I know quite a few of the people he associates with in a business way, and socially, in this community. I am acquainted with his general reputation for honesty and integrity. That reputation is good.

HENRY MICHAEL GUENSER,

called as a witness in behalf of the defendant John F. Muyres, having been first duly sworn, testified as follows:

DIRECT EXAMINATION

By Mr. OSTROM:

I am a manufacturer of brick. I have known the defendant John F. Muyres for about 25 or 40 years. I have known the defendant in Shasta, Minnesota and here in Los Angeles. I have not been to Phoenix, but I have known him since he was there. The reputation of John F. Muyres for truth, honesty and veracity when he lived here in Los Angeles and when he lived in Minnesotta was good.

(Testimony of Ralph Reynolds)

RALPH REYNOLDS,

called as a witness on behalf of George J. Muyres, having been duly sworn, testified as follows:

DIRECT EXAMINATION:

By Mr. Graham:

I reside in Pasadena. I am Assistant Secretary of the Automobile Club of Southern California, and am in charge of the Insurance Division of said Club. I am acquainted with the defendant George J. Muyres, and have known him for approximately twenty years. He has been employed at the Automobile Club approximately all of that time, except for about a year or two around 1920. The work he has been engaged in down there is some service, but mainly selling insurance and some memberships. I am acquainted with a great many automobile dealers and accessory men who he has contacted, as well as our own members. I am acquainted to some extent with the people with whom he associates socially. We are members of the same golf club, and we have been members of other clubs since. I know his general reputation in this community for honesty and integrity. It is good.

CROSS-EXAMINATION:

BY MR. IRWIN:

George Muyres is mainly a salesman of insurance and memberships, although he does render some service. I have known him approximately twenty years. I have met his father and mother. He is a good, a very good salesman.

(Testimony of John F. Muyres)

JOHN F. MUYRES,

recalled as a witness in his own behalf, further testified as follows:

DIRECT EXAMINATION: (Continued)
BY MR. OSTROM:

I do not remember any more of that conversation with Ryman when he gave me the bonds. That was about all. I took the bonds to George Muyres that same day, between 9 and 10 o'clock that same morning. I did not see him at the Automobile Club or anywhere else that day. That was Tuesday, the 29th, when I took them to George and gave them to him. George said they wanted more time. He did not see the broker yet, but he figured they wanted more time to investigate the serial numbers of the bonds, so I told George to investigate the bonds, and if they were alright, to sell them, and if they were not, to take them back. I had no more conversation with him that day. I saw Woolsey that evening. I did not see either Ryman or Ryan any further that day. I told Woolsey that if the bonds were alright, we would go home. I expected a report the next day. I saw nobody on Wednesday, October 30th, in regard to the bonds. I saw Woolsey, and I might have seen Ryman, but I had no conversation with him. Nothing happened on Wednesday, the 30th. On Thursday, October 31st, I called George in the morning and asked him how things were coming, and he said he would find out and see me Thursday evening. I communicated that message to Ryman and Woolsey. I saw them at the hotel in the 4400 block on Whittier Boulevard. Before I saw George Muyres, on Thursday, October 30th, Eddie

(Testimony of John F. Muyres)

Ryman gave me two one thousand dollar Home Owners
Loans Bonds to turn them in, too. That was in the afternoon. I kept my appointment with George Muyres at the
Automobile Club at five o'clock that afternoon. No one
was present except George and me. No one went to the
Automobile Club with me. George Muyres said the broker
asked him if he was sure the bonds weren't stolen. I
said "George, I have met both of the fellows now, and I
am going to pin them down and find out". That was all
that was said, and I gave him the two one thousand Home
Owners Loan Bonds. Then I came back in my machine.
I went there to pick up Ham Woolsey. When I got there
in front of the hotel, Ham Woolsey and Eddie Ryman
were standing on the sidewalk, and I opened the door, and
Ham was going to come in, and I said "Wait a minute,
Eddie, get in the car. I want to talk to you". And he
got in the car, and I drove around on a side street and
stopped the car, and I turned around in the car, like this,
and I said: "Eddie, just where did you get these bonds?"
He said "I stole them". Well, I was not able to talk for
five minutes. I just sat there before I could start my car.
Finally, I started my car, then went back to the hotel and
let them out. He kept on talking. I guess————if
some one had hit me with a base ball bat, it would not
have hurt me more. I went back to the hotel and let him
out of the car, and then got Ham in the car, and when
I got out a ways, I said "Ham, that son-of-a-bitch
stole them bonds". He said "I know it. He told me all
about it this afternoon". Then I tried to get hold of
George on the telephone. I did not get him. The next
morning, I called the Automobile Club at nine o'clock.
George was not there, and I left word for him to call me

(Testimony of John F. Muyres)

at the Whittier Station. He did not call me. I called him
again that night at the Club, but could not get him. Then,
I called him at a residence and got hold of him. This
was on Friday evening about seven or seven-thirty. During that day I did not contact Ryman, Ryan or Woolsey.
Woolsey was staying with me. When I reached George
at a residence on Friday evening, on November 1st, about
seven o'clock, I told George to get those bonds back by all
means, that there something wrong. George said "I will
get them back the first thing in the morning", and he says:
"If I get them, where will I meet you?" I said, "Meet
me in front of Maier's Brewery", and he said "As soon
as I get them back, I will call you". He called me the
next morning. On Saturday, November 2nd, George
called me about 10 or 10:30, and told me that he had the
bonds. I asked him again to meet me in front of the
Brewery. He met me there and gave me the bonds and
around $2,000.00 in money, and he told me that there was
all the bonds he could get; that the rest had been sent to
New York to be sold. I also told him by all means to
try to get them back and not let them be sold if he could
help it. That is the time I told him that those bonds were
stolen. He sat there awhile and then he said "John, you
got me worried", and I said "I know it — we are liable to
get into serious trouble on account of this". That was
all the conversation. He gave me back a package containing bonds, but I could not say how many. The money
was in cash in a big envelope. I then went to the hotel
on Whittier Boulevard., the other one further down, I
think it was in the 4200 block. I went into the room and
threw the envelope on the bed. Woolsey, Ryan and Ry-

(Testimony of John F. Muyres)

man were there: I threw the envelope on the bed, money
and all. Eddie Ryman picked it up and figured up the
split, and he told Woolsey and Ryan to go out of the
room, and they went out of the room for a minute, and
he said "Will you take bonds, instead of money?" I said
"Yes", and he said "I will give you a Home Owner's Loan
and an Austrian". I said "That is all right".

I took these bonds and went up to my motherinlaw's
house. I had some one else's car. I was having something done on my own car, and I went up to the house and
met Ham, and we went Home. I took the bonds to my
motherinlaw's house, and left them there.

After I got back from Phoenix – I made a return trip
to Los Angeles. I told George I would be back next week
sometime, and see what happens. I would come back on
Thursday, November 7th. When I came back on the 7th,
I called George at the Automobile Club, and he was there,
and I told him I would be right out to see him, and George
returned to me then five bonds and a check for either
$2,100.00 or $2,300.00, which I refused to take. And I
did not want the bonds either. I said "You might as well
keep the bonds. I don't know what to do with them".
He said, "I don't want the bonds. What will I do with
the money?" I said, "Put it in the bank and forget about
it". I took the bonds. That made five one-thousand dollar bonds that I got from George on the 7th, and I had two
before, which made seven. I took those bonds, these five
bonds that George gave me were in a big envelope, and
I put the two in there, and put them up on that shelf.
Then – I did not want to leave them in the house, so I took
and put them under the house, and was packing my clothes

(Testimony of John F. Muyres)

getting ready to go home. The fact is, I was already packed, and had the door locked, and decided I had better take them along, and so I went under the house again and got them and started home. Finally, I decided I would not take them along home, that I would better bury them, which I did, out on Beverly Boulevard and San Gabriel. *The,* I went on home. I did not bury these bonds on the 8th when I saw George -- that was the following Tuesday. I did not make a trip back. I stayed here at that time.

I saw in the Phoenix paper that Ryman and Ryan had been apprehended in Texas. It was on November 27th, the day before Thanksgiving, that Officers Small and Whitson, of the Federal Department of Justice, came to see me. Mr. Whitson said, "Hello, John". I said, "How do you do?" He said, "You are John Muyres, aren't you?" I said, "Yes, sir". He said "I want to talk to you", and I said, "Just a minute. I want to wash my hands". I went back into the kitchen and washed my hands, and had just finished eating, and then came back in the front and nobody was there, and I walked back in the back. Whitson was there, and he said "I want to talk to you, John", and I said "Alright". Then, he pulled out a badge and said "Department of Justice. You know what that is?" I said, "alright, what have you got to say?" He said, "Let us go up to the office". Then we went to the office, and Small was out in front. We had a conversation there. There was not much said. They asked me whether I had a brother in Los Angeles; that I had a nice place; whether I wanted to sell it; how business was, and that was practically all the conversation

216

(Testimony of John F. Muyres)

there was. I was put in jail. Neither Small nor Whitson told me for what I was put in jail, but the other gentleman there asked me if I knew why I was there, and I said I did, I knew I was there on account of the bonds.

About 10 or 10:30 o'clock on Thursday, Small and Whitson took me out of the cell into the finger-print room. Officer Small walked ahead of me, and then Whitson behind me————just as I got inside Whitson closed the door, and Mr. Small turned around and said: "Jack, God damn it. Come clean, or we will close that God Damn place of yours up." I had a very bad cold, and I told them that I would like to have some medicine, and Whitson said he would get some, and he did, and then I told Mr. Small that I would tell him everything as well as I knew, all about this deal, which I did. I was there in the office where this statement (Government "Exhibit Number 19") was being written in longhand, from around ten o'clock to about nine or nine-thirty at night. Part of the statement was read to me, and part of it I read myself.

With reference to that last paragraph which reads, "It is my intention to plead guilty for what I have done in this case, and throw myself on the mercy of the Court, so I can get this matter disposed of as soon as possible, and get it off and over with as quickly as permissible", I did not know what the charges were, and where I made a mistake, and I said it and knew it then, was when the man told me these bonds were stolen, I should have reported them to the authorities, the evening of October 31st, when I took Ryman for the automobile ride alone around the corner and asked him "Where did you get those bonds?" and he said "I stole them" is the first I ever knew of the bonds being stolen.

(Testimony of John F. Muyres)

I did not enter into any agreement of any kind with Woolsey, Ryan or Ryman, or any of them, to transport bonds from Arizona to California, and I never knew that these bonds was in any other place than California. As near as I knew, they might have been here all the time, for when I got back to Arizona, Ham said that the bonds were in California, and I did not know whether they had been there all the time, or how they got there, or where they came from.

Neither officers, Small or Whitson, or any other officer, informed me that I was under arrest for transporting stolen bonds or that I was under arrest for conspiring to transport stolen bonds.

Referring to Government's "Exhibit Number 19", this statement in longhand, signed by me, at the end of this long statement that took so many hours, I was hurried into the final execution of this instrument.

WHEREUPON, the following questions and answers were given and made:

THE COURT: Well, at this time, you were wondering whether the bonds had been stolen or not?

THE WITNESS: I was told they weren't stolen.

THE COURT: But you had made inquiry?

THE WITNESS: (pause)

THE COURT: You were up to that very time hesitating about selling the bonds for fear they might be stolen, is not that true?

THE WITNESS: On Friday?

THE COURT: At the time you cashed these coupons.

THE WITNESS: Well, I gave him the coupons and the serial numbers.

(Testimony of John F. Muyres)

THE COURT: Yes.

THE WITNESS: When I came back he gave me the money and part of the coupons back.

THE COURT: Yes, but at that very time he was questioning you as to whether or not the bonds were stolen, wasn't he?

THE WITNESS: Who, your honor?

THE COURT: What?

THE WITNESS: Who was questioning me?

THE COURT: Your nephew.

THE WITNESS: No.

THE COURT: You were questioning the other people as to whether or not the bonds had been stolen, were you not?

THE WITNESS: I did on the first day of November.

I did right to start with from Mr. Woolsey, but nevertheless, I first cashed these coupons and divided up the money, and after that my nephew said the broker asked him whether he was sure the bonds weren't stolen. This was after he had cashed the coupons. I am forty-seven years old. I made a mistake when I did not notify some officer when I discovered that those bonds had been stolen:

THE COURT: Yes, the Court co-incides in that opinion, but that does not answer the question, why didn't you do it?

THE WITNESS: I did not know; I was not in position to.

THE COURT: You didn't know?

(Testimony of Robert Lyle Kelly)

The WITNESS: I was not in position to, I did not think – I could not talk when the man told me that for ten minutes.

For two weeks afterwards, whenever I thought of it a chill would come over me. My nephew gave me more than five of these bonds after he knew they had been stolen, and I knew they had been stolen.

DIRECT EXAMINATION

By MR. Ohanneson:

I did not give Mr. Ryan any of the money secured from these coupons to be divided. I gave Mr. Ryman all the money.

ROBERT LYLE KELLY

called as a witness on behalf of the defendant John F. Muyres, having been first duly sworn testified as follows:

DIRECT EXAMINATION

By Mr. Ostrom:

I am an insurance agent in Pasadena. I know the defendant John F. Muyres. He is a neighbor of mine on New York Avenue in Pasadena. I have known him about four or five years when he was here in Los Angeles. I know the reputation he had in the community for honesty and integrity. It was good.

CROSS EXAMINATION

by Mr. Irwin

I never wrote any insurance for Mr. Muyres nor for any business he was engaged in.

(Testimony of Albert G. Brouwers—Thomas E. Fairchild)

ALBERT G. BROUWERS

called as a witness on behalf of the defendant John F. Muyres having been first duly sworn testified as follows:

DIRECT EXAMINATION

By Mr. Ostrom:

I am a retired business man, on compulsion because of the depression. I was in the garage business. I have known the defendant John F. Muyres for 12 or 14 years here in Los Angeles. I know his reputation for truth, honesty and integrity in the community in which he resides. It is very good.

CROSS EXAMINATION

By Mr. Irwin:

I have been retired since 1929. I saw Mr. Muyres last fall. I do not know whether it was on one of his trips here from Arizona; I do not know when he made the trips. It must have been probably September or before that, or during the summer when I saw him, I could not recollect. I have never had any business with him during the past year. He never discussed bonds with me.

THOMAS E. FAIRCHILD

called as a witness on behalf of the defendant John F. Muyres having been first duly sworn, testified as follows:

DIRECT EXAMINATION

By Mr. Ostrom:

I am a clothing salesman here in Los Angeles. I have known him only socially. I know his reputation for truth, honesty and integrity in the community in which he resided. It was good, I would say.

(Testimony of John Carlisle Lee)

CROSS EXAMINATION

By Mr. Irwin:

I met him at his home in Altadena, when he lived in Los Angeles. I only see him when he comes to Los Angeles. I do not know anything about his activities since he moved to Arizona; nothing other than the place of business over there; that he is in this line of business. I have known him socially. I have known his wife and mother-in-law I guess for 35 years. We came to California in 1930 and that is when I met him. We had been in the city, I would say, probably a week when we looked them up. As a matter of fact when we came here we wired home for the address to look them up. It was in the afternoon when we went out to the house. As a matter of fact we never were at his mother-in-law's home. We went by there according to the address we had and he had just driven up to pick up his mother-in-law to go to Altadena so we drove to Altadena to his home.

JOHN CARLISLE LEE

called as a witness on behalf of the defendant John F. Muyres having been first duly sworn testified as follows:

DIRECT EXAMINATION

By Mr. Ostrom:

I had a conversation with Mrs. Woolsey in Phoenix some time the early part of this month. I do not remember the date but it was in the neighborhood of March 7th. At the first conversation I do not think anyone was present except Mrs. Woolsey's mother or mother-in-law, I do not know which one myself. Then I had another

(Testimony of Walter D. Dunham)

conversation with Mrs. Woolsey; It was the day following the first conversation but I do not remember the date. It was this month. It was at Mrs. Woolsey's residence at 1105 South 1st Avenue, Phoenix, Ariz. I think Mrs. Woolsey's mother or mother-in-law, whichever it was, was in and out of the room while I talked with Mrs. Woolsey. Two little children were also present; I do not believe any other person was present, although I do not recall now. My best recollection is that it was between 11 and 12 o'clock in the morning. I do not believe I am privileged to recite the entire conversation because of Mr. Woolsey's request.

WALTER D. DUNHAM

called as a witness on behalf of the defendant George J. Muyers, being first duly sworn testified as follows:

DIRECT EXAMINATION

By Mr. Graham:

I reside in Los Angeles and have lived here about 50 years. I am a Ford Dealer and have been such for about 20 years. I am acquainted with the defendant, George J. Muyers. I have known him for about ten years. I have known him in his capacity as insurance salesman for the Automobile Club of Southern California and have transacted business of this nature with him. I am acquainted with other people in Los Angeles with whom he has done business of that kind—other automobile dealers. I know his general reputation in this community for honesty and integrity. That reputation is good.

(Testimony of Milton L. Sutter)

CROSS EXAMINATION

By Mr. Irwin:

My concern obtains its license plates for cars that are registered in its name with the Automobile Club, and he has in his capacity been dealing with me for the Automobile Club in some of my transactions with them. He was engaged in such dealings between my company and the Automobile Club during the fall of last year.

MILTON L. SUTTER

called as a witness for the defendant George J. Muyres, having been first duly sworn, testified as follows:

DIRECT EXAMINATION

By Mr. Graham:

I have lived in Los Angeles about 20 years. I am an Insurance Solicitor with the Automobile Club. I am acquainted with defendant George J. Muyres and have known him about 20 years; ever since I have been with the Club. I know lots of people with whom he associates and with whom he does business. I know his general reputation in the community for honesty and integrity; it is good.

Whereupon the defendants rested.

EXCEPTION NO. 8

Mr. Graham:

At this time then I renew the motion which I made on behalf of defendant George J. Muyres at the close of the presentation of the evidence on the part of the Government that the Court instruct the jury to bring in a verdict of Not guilty on the ground that the evidence in general is insufficient to warrant a verdict of guilty, because of the fact that there is no evidence which will show that George J. Muyres had any connection with the transportation or with any conspiracy to transport the bonds from Arizona to Huntington Park.

THE COURT: Denied

To which denial the defendant George J. Muyres duly excepted.

Mr. Ostrom:

On behalf of this defendant John F. Muyres I make the same motion.

THE COURT: denied

Whereupon, counsel for the plaintiff and for each of the defendants on trial argued the case to the jury.

Whereupon the court instructed the jury as follows:

"COURT'S INSTRUCTIONS TO THE JURY

THE COURT: Gentlemen of the jury, it is the function, the office, of the Court to instruct as to the law of the case that is being tried before you. Whatever the Court gives you as the law, you are bound to regard as the settled law; because, if that were not so, you might easily conceive that there might be twelve different views of what the law is.

Now, it is within the power, and privilege, and very often the duty, of the Court to discuss and comment upon the evidence; but whatever the Court might say, or does say, that differs radically in its effects, as far as the evidence is concerned, from the instruction of what the law is, because you are not bound to regard the Court's view that might be expressed; for to the jury exclusively is given the power and duty of passing upon the facts of the case.

The Court is at liberty to comment upon the evidence, but that is for your advice and guidance only; and if the Court does, in this case, comment upon this evidence you will understand that that is the purpose, and though I may not repeat it, you will understand that the Court's comments upon the evidence are not controlling upon the jury.

The indictment in this case has been returned, and in and of itself it is, of course, no evidence of guilt at all. It is merely one of the steps of the law laid down which shall be taken in the ascertainment of the guilt or innocence of people charged with crime; and no presumption must be indulged against the defendants, or any of them, on account of the filing of the indictment.

It is charged in the indictment that these defendants transported in interstate commerce—that is to say, across the state line—from Arizona to California bonds worth at least $5,000 that had been stolen, and with the knowledge on the part of the defendants that the bonds had been stolen.

In the second count of the indictment it is charged that the defendants conspired to do that thing; and I think I explained to you in the beginning of this case (I frequently do) that the defendants may be punished for what is known as the substantative crime. That is, the offense itself, and also in addition thereto, and as a separate and distinct offense, were agreeing to do it; such is the law of the United States. That will be more fully explained as we go along.

Now, I shall read, because it is very plain, the law that controls, and the violation of which is the offense charged against these defendants:

'Whoever shall transport or cause to be transported in interstate or foreign commerce any goods, wares, or merchandise, securities, or money, of the value of $5,000 or more theretofore stolen or taken feloniously by fraud or with intent to steal or purloin, knowing the same to have been so stolen or taken, shall be punished'—in a certain way.

There are some other sections of the law that are important for your consideration. One is this:

'That whoever directly commits any act constituting an offense defined in any law of the United States, or who aids, abets, counsels, commands, induces, or procures its commission, is a principal, and to be dealt with in the same way, of course, as the principal himself.'

There is another law of the United States, and it is very simple, and very short, and I shall read it to you. It governs this matter of conspiracy:

'If two or more persons conspire either to commit an offense against the United States, or to defraud the United States in any manner or any purpose; and one or more of such parties do any act to affect the objects of the conspiracy, each of the parties to such conspiracy shall be dealt with'—in a certain way.

Now, let me point out, gentlemen, what may be an important distinction in this matter. I don't think you really need to have it pointed out, but it is this: A great deal of evidence has been introduced here relative to what has been done by these various defendants in the marketing or sale of these bonds.

Well, I might say that the Defendant John F. Muyres upon the witness stand admitted that; but denies guilty knowledge that the bonds had been stolen. Now, the defendants are not on trial for anything in the nature of an offense committed here in the State of California, with reference to those bonds after they were brought here. The offense, if any offense was committed, was completed when the transportation in interstate commerce—that is, across the state line—was completed. You will see that readily, of course.

The offense in this case was completed, if such offense was established, by the evidence at the time the bonds were taken out of the office of the American Express Company; and whatever place it was—Huntington Beach, or somewhere—to which they were consigned by this Mr. Ryman, to begin with; and they could not be convicted—withdraw that statement.

The conspiracy was ended then and there, because the conspiracy charges that unlawful bringing into the state. Now, no matter how, in your judgment, heinous might be the offense committed by any of the defendants, if you find such offense was committed, no matter how much you may think they are deserving of punishment, you must bear in mind you are not here to punish them for unlawfully selling these bonds to the various banks and under the various pretexts and excuses that have been testified to, and which you may or may not find to be the fact; not for having divided this money four ways, as testified by some of the defendants, however reprehensible those actions are, we are not concerned with that; but before you can convict any of the defendants you must feel beyond a reasonable doubt, as far as he was concerned, that he either transported the bonds himself, aided and abetted, assisted, or counseled, or advised in the transportation, in order to be convicted of the first offense; or that he conspired, that he agreed to do the transporting.

I feel it advisable to call your attention to that, because there might be some confusion about it; but you will at once see what I have told you.

Every defendant on trial, and that is in all cases, is presumed to be innocent of crime or wrong; but not all defendants who are on trial are innocent. That is an indisputable presumption, and may be removed by evidence sufficient to convince you of his guilt beyond a reasonable doubt.

The burden is upon the Government to prove the guilt of the defendants beyond a reasonable doubt. The 'beyond a reasonable doubt' is something that is very often used. It is the haven and refuge for the defendant; and nearly every case that I or you have ever heard or tried—every criminal case—however, it is an important thing to know about.

To justify you in returning a verdict of guilty, the evidence must be of such a character as to satisfy your judgment to the exclusion of every reasonable doubt. If, therefore, you can reconcile the evidence with any reasonable hypotehsis consistent with the defendant's innocence, it is your duty to do so, and in that case find the defendant not guilty. That is to say, if all the evidence in the case is consistent with the conduct of innocence in the part of the defendant equally with that of his guilt, then it is your business to acquit the defendant.

And if, after weighing all the proofs and looking only to the proofs, you impartially and honestly entertain the belief that the defendant may be innocent of the offenses charged against him, he is entitled to the benefit of that doubt and you should acquit him.

It is not meant by this that the proof should establish his guilt to an absolute certainty, but merely that you should not convict him unless, from all the evidence, you believe him *builty* beyond a reasonable doubt. Speculative notions or possibilities resting upon mere conjecture not arising or deducible from the proof, or the want of it, should not be confounded with a reasonable *dbout*. A doubt suggested by the ingenuity of counsel, or by your own ingenuity, not legitimately warranted by the evidence or the want of it, or one born of a merciful inclination to permit the defendant to escape the penalty of the law, or one prompted by sympathy for him, or those connected with him, is not what is meant by a reasonable doubt.

A reasonable doubt, as that term is employed in the administration of the criminal law, is an honest, substantial misgiving, generated by the proof or want of it. It is such a state of the proof as fail to convince your judgment and conscience, and satisfy your reason of the guilt of the accused. If the whole evidence, when carefully examined, weighed, compared and considered produces in your mind a settled conviction or belief of the defendant's guilt—such an abiding conviction as you would be willing to act upon in the most weighty and important affairs of your life—you may be said to be free from any reasonable doubt, and should find a verdict in accordance with that conviction or belief.

I have discussed the matter of the circumstantial evidence against the defendants. That is to say, and explained to you that if it is consistent with innocence, you are to adopt that theory. If, however, it is inconsistent with innocence, and consistent with guilt, you are equally bound to adopt that theory; and will bring in your verdict accordingly.

The Court expects you to use judgment, intelligence in this verdict, but the Court also expects that if you are convinced of the guilt of these defendants beyond a reasonable doubt, you have no hesitancy in saying so promptly.

Evidence has been introduced here as to the good reputation of some of these defendants. Now, that is introduced on the theory that a person of good character, as established by his good reputation, is not likely to commit an offense. In other words, a person of good character is not likely to commit crime.

Such a possession is inconsistent with guilt. That is its purpose.

The good character of a person accused of crime, when proven, is itself a fact in the case. It is a circumstance tending, in a greater or less degree, to establish his innocence. It must be considered in connection with all the other facts and circumstances of the case, and may be sufficient, when so considered in itself, to raise a reasonable doubt of defendant's guilt. But if, after a full consideration of all the evidence adduced, the jury believes the defendant to be guilty of the crime charged, they should so find, notwithstanding proof of good character or reputation.

All witnesses are presumed, as a matter of law, to speak the truth when they are on the witness stand. That presumption may, however, be repealed by the manner that they assume, bear, upon the witness stand by their demeanor, or by their appearance, by evidence affecting their character; oftentimes by the intelligence of the witness himself, because many times men of perfectly good intentions do not state facts accordingly, although they mean to; oftentimes by the opportunities to know the things whereof the witness is speaking, and one of the principal ones is the sympathy of the witness.

Witnesses oftentimes seem to be affected by the side which subpoenaes them, brings them on the witness stand. They feel bound, more or less, to testify according to their sympathy with that side.

Now, all of these things must be taken into consideration. The defendants—some of the defendants—one of them—has taken the witness stand, and his testimony is to be judged by the rule laid down for the testimony of all witnesses. He is to be treated just exactly like every other witness, and judged by the same standards. You are at liberty to consider how he would be affected by the verdict, and the motives that might induce him to testify the way he does. The same may be said of the witnesses for the Government, the men who have pleaded guilty to the same offense.

Now, objection was made to the suggestion by one of the counsel that they might be influenced by what might happen to them afterwards. Now, it seems to me an entirely logical view to take. So they might be. However, this case is entirely devoid of any evidence of that sort, tending to indicate, or to support, the belief or the supposition that they are going to receive any consideration because of their testimony.

Another principal governing the testimony of witnesses is that a witness who is intentionally false in a material part of his testimony is to be distrusted with respect to the remainder, even to the extent that the jury may in such reject the entire testimony of such a witness. So two witnesses here have testified, and the evidence is, that they have been guilty of the same thing. They were accomplices, in other words.

Now, an accomplice is defined to be one concerned with others in the commission of a crime. It is a settled rule in this country that even accomplices in the commission of a crime are competent witnesses, and that the Government has the right to admit their testimony, and that of the jury to consider it. The testimony of accomplices, however, os to be received with caution and weighed with great care, and while it is true that the jury may convict on such testimony alone, yet the jury should not rely on it unsupported for a conviction, unless it produces in their minds a positive conviction of its truth. If it does, the jury should act upon it.

Referring to the testimony of those two defendants, Mr. Ryman and Mr. Woolsey, this case begins with the testimony of Mr. Ryman; that he conceived this idea. That, I take it, is uncontradicted. You are at liberty to believe that. I would think that no one could justly, properly disbelieve that. However, understand, gentlemen, what I said to you in the beginning: That you may believe or disbelieve any witness in the case, and the Court has no control over that at all.

Next, he speaks to Mr. Ryan. This is the testimony. He says he can locate these bonds. Mr. Ryman is a man, as far as the evidence shows, of no particular permanent moorings anywhere. There is nothing—I don't mean to reflect upon him at all, but he is not supposed to be a man of any property, at least.

He speaks to Mr. Ryan. Mr. Ryan, apparently an industrious man, but not likely to come into possession of any large quantity of bonds, according to the testimony which you are at liberty to believe or not to believe, speaks to Mr. Woolsey. Mr. Woolsey speaks to Mr. Jack Muyres about it.

Now, Mr. Jack Muyres, I think I am safe in saying, admits that Woolsey, or somebody, spoke to him about these bonds; but Jack Muyres, you will remember, denies knowledge that they were stolen bonds.

Now, you are at liberty to believe that or not to believe it. You may, it seems to me, properly consider the proposition as to a man of Jack Muyres' situation, finding these gentlemen of the type that I mentioned. That is, I have no reflection upon them, and least of all because they haven't got money or property, or anything of that sort; and up to this point they appear to be, as far as the evidence shows, entirely respectable and honorable men.

But would not Jack Muyres be likely to inquire about the possession of such a quantity of bonds, $30,000 or $40,000? Would not a man in such a situation be strongly suspicious that these bonds were taken?

Well, I suggest that merely as a thing properly to be considered in your determination.

The admitted fact is that Mr. Jack Muyres comes to Los Angeles. It has been testified to, I recall, by someone that he came in somewhat of a hurry; that is, he returned from Los Angeles on one night, and that same night or, rather, the next morning in a very short time left again.

Now, the theory of the Government is that he consulted Mr. George Muyres over here, and Mr. George Muyres, according to the Government's theory, agreed that he would try to dispose of the bonds. There is no direct evidence, as suggested by the Government counsel himself, of that.

You must, in passing upon that, take into consideration all of the evidence in this case, gentlemen, including the good reputation of George Muyres before that. However, you must also not fail to consider the testimony here as to the actions of Mr. George Muyres after the receipt of the bonds; and action of both the defendants—of those two defendants after knowledge of the theft of the bonds was communicated to them. Then the offense apparently —or, at least, the blame, I will say—did not cease. It did not cease to the extent that Jack Muyres went and buried the bonds in that bottle afterwards.

Now, Jack Muyres, when questioned by the Court, you will remember, said he was excited and he was—I don't remember the expression he used, but indicated he was so excited, so agitated, that he did not—and made mistakes, and did not act rationally.

Now, you must consider all of that, gentlemen, in the consideration of this case; and whether that is reasonable. To refer to one specific circumstance only, the testimony of some man from the bank over here, at the time George Muyres came in to engotiate the bonds. All of those things should be considered by you in passing upon the guilt or innocence of the defendants, and their motives.

Now, let me make one qualification with respect to this, and it is important: I told you a while ago that this conspiracy ceased with the receipt of the bonds here; and that is true. Therefore, anything said or done after that conspiracy ceased is not to be taken as evidence against anyone other than the person making the statement. The evidence as to what any of these defendants did after the receipt of those bonds can be taken only as evidence, only against him, and not as evidence against the others in support of the charges of the conspiracy.

It is the right of any defendant not to take the witness stand, and the jury is prohibited by indulging in any presumption against the defendant for failure to testify.

I shall read you some instructions on the proposition of conspiracy itself:

'In order to establish the crime charged, it is necessary, first, that the conspiracy or agreement to commit the particular offense against the United States as alleged in the indictment be established, and secondly, to prove further that one or more of the parties engaging in the conspiracy has committed some act to effect the object thereof.

'To constitute a conspiracy it is not necessary that two or more persons should meet together and enter into an express or formal agreement for the unlawful venture or scheme, or that they should directly, by words or in writing, state between themselves or otherwise what the unlawful plan or scheme is to be, or the details thereof, or the means by which the unlawful combination is to be made effective. It is sufficient if two or more persons, in any manner, or through any contrivance, positively or tacitly come to a mutual understanding to accomplish a common and unlawful design. In other words, when an unlawful end is sought to be effected, and two or more persons, actuated by the common purpose of accomplishing that end, work together in any way in furtherance of the unlawful scheme, every one of said persons becomes a member of the conspiracy. The success or failure of the conspiracy is immaterial, but before the defendants may be found guilty of the charge it must appear beyond a reasonable doubt that a conspiracy was formed as alleged in the indictment, and that the defendants were active parties thereto, and that some one of the overt acts charged in the indictment was committed.

'But each party must be actuated by an intent to promote the common design. If persons pursue by the acts the same unlawful object, one performing one act, and a second another act, all with a view to the attainment of the object they are pursuing, the conclusion is warranted that they are engaged in a conspiracy to effect that object. Cooperation in some form must be shown.'

Now, to illustrate, the situation of the Defendant George Muyres, who admittedly didn't have anything to do with the taking of the bonds, or was not in Phoenix, Arizona. If you believe from the evidence beyond a reasonable doubt that he was consulted by his uncle, and that he knew or was told by his uncle what the plan was, that mere knowledge wouldn't be enough to convict him; but he must do something in furtherance of the common design, and you must find from the evidence that what he did, or agreed to do, was in furtherance of the common design.

If, for instance, he said 'Yes, I can take care of the bonds over here and sell them,' then you are at liberty to find that that was part of the conspiracy, because that was an act in promotion of the conspiracy itself. That is, the bringing of the bonds in for the unlawful purpose.

'Where the existence of a criminal conspiracy has been shown, every act or declaration of each member of such conspiracy, done or made thereafter pursuant to the concerted plan and in furtherance of the common object, is considered the act and declaration of all the conspirators and is evidence against each of them. On the other hand, after a conspiracy has come to an end, either by the accomplishment of the common design, or by the parties abandoning the same, evidence of acts or declarations thereafter made by any of the conspirators can be considered only as against the person doing such acts or making such statements. The declaration or act of a conspirator not in execution of the common design is not evidence against any of the parties other than the one making such declaration.'

Each of these defendants is entitled to your separate judgment with respect to each of the counts of the indictment; each one to be considered separately.

You will remember that while you are not to disregard the argument of counsel in the case, you are to depend upon your own recollection of what the evidence is. You are not to consider evidence that may be stricken from the record; or evidence that was offered, and refused.

You understand, of course, that your business is to choose, when you retire, a foreman, through whom you will make any communications you have to make to the Court. You are at liberty to have whatever of the exhibits you may want with you, when you are retired.

'Are there exceptions to the instructions on behalf of the Government?

MR. IRWIN: There are not, your Honor.

THE COURT: On behalf of the defendants?

MR. GRAHAM: Very few, your Honor, but I think they ought to be straightened out.'

EXCEPTION NO. 9

Mr. Graham:

I call your attention to instruction—proposed instruction—No. 4, and I believe that was all covered except that last paragraph. I take an exception to the failure of the Court to charge the jury that nothing done after the conspiracy charged was at an end could have been in furtherance of, or to the effect the object of the conspiracy—

MR. IRWIN (Interrupting): Just a minute. Just a minute. Since that is in writing, O object to him reading it.

MR. GRAHAM: That is the only way you can take an exception, according to the Circuit Court of Appeals.

THE COURT: You are mentioning the last paragraph?

MR. GRAHAM: Yes, your Honor.

THE COURT: They have been fully instructed on that feature. Go ahead. Anything else?

MR. GRAHAM: I think I will have to take my exception by stating the substance, that nothing done after the conspiracy charged was at an end could have been in furtherance of, or to effect, the object of the conspiracy; that no defendant who joined with the conspiracy, if a conspiracy existed, for the purpose of selling these said securities, after the transportation to Huntington Park, which was the object of the conspiracy, may be convicted of the offense charged in the second count.

THE COURT: The jury have been fully instructed on this subject.

EXCEPTION NO. 10

MR. GRAHAM: I think there is only one more.

No, there are two more.

Calling your attention to No. 11, requested by the Defendant George Muyres, that—I shall let your Honor look at it, perhaps—

THE COURT (Interrupting): That is covered in the instructions, I believe. I read that.

MR. GRAHAM: If it was, I overlooked the portion of it that deals with that.

THE COURT: Yes.

MR. GRAHAM: It is to the effect that—I think I had better take my exception, to the effect (Instruction 11) that in order to establish the existence of a conspiracy there must be proof outside of the statements and declarations of an alleged conspirator; hence the extra judicial declarations or statements of any defendant in this case standing alone and of themselves, if any such were made, are not sufficient to show the existence of a conspiracy.

EXCEPTION no. 11

MR. GRAHAM: The Defendant George Muyres excepts to the failure of the Court to instruct the jury on that, namely, that an inference may be drawn from a fact proven by evidence. It may not be based upon another inference."

Whereupon the jury retired to deliberate upon their verdict.

Thereafter, at 10:05 o'clock, A. M., on March 26, 1936, the jury returned into the said Court a verdict as follows:

"We, the jury in the above-entitled case, find the Defendant John F. Muyres guilty as charged in the first count of the indictment; and is guilty as charged in the second count of the indictment.

The Defendant George J. Muyres is not guilty as charged in the first count of the indictment, and is guilty as charged in the second count of the indictment.

The Defendant Thomas Burke Ryan is guilty as charged in the first count of the indictment, and is guilty as charged in the second count of the indictment.

Dated: Los Angeles, California, March 26, 1936, 1:00 a. m.

I am H. R. Hilton, Foreman of the Jury."

EXCEPTION NO. 12

"MR. GRAHAM: If the Court please, may the record show an exception on behalf of the Defendant George J. Muyres to the verdict to the second count."

BE IT REMEMBERED FURTHER: That the foregoing is all of the evidence received in said cause, and the defendants George J. Muyres and John F. Muyres pray that the same may be allowed, settled, filed and sealed by the Honorable Judge Cosgrave, before whom the ca*s*ue was tried as the Bill of Exceptions in this cause.

IN THE DISTRICT COURT OF THE UNITED
STATES FOR THE SOUTHERN DISTRICT
OF CALIFORNIA CENTRAL
DIVISION

United States of America,	)	STIPULATION
Plaintiff	)	re Order Settling Bill
-vs-	)	of Exceptions.
Edward Harold Ryman, et al,	)	No. 126198
Defendants	)	Criminal

It is hereby stipulated and agreed by and between the above named plaintiff and the defendants George J. Muyres and John F. Muyres, on appeal herein to the United States District Court of Appeals, in and for the Ninth Circuit, has been duly presented within the time allowed by the law and the rules and orders of this court duly and legally made, and the same is in proper form and conforms to the truth and sets forth all the evidence and all of the proceedings relating to the trial in the above entitled cause, and that it may be settled, allowed, signed and authenticated by this Court as the true bill of exceptions herein on behalf of said defendants, and that it may be made a part of the records of this cause.

Dated at Los Angeles, California, this 8th day of June, 1936.

PIERSON M. HALL
U. S. Attorney
By John J. Irwin
Asst. U. S. Attorney.
Attorneys for Plaintiff
Russell Graham
Atty. for George J. Muyres
Harry Graham Balter
L. A. Bloom
Atty. for John F. Muyres

IN THE DISTRICT COURT OF THE UNITED
STATES FOR THE SOUTHERN DISTRICT
OF CALIFORNIA CENTRAL
DIVISION

United States of America,	)	ORDER SETTLING AND ALLOWING BILL OF EXCEP-
Plaintiff	)	TIONS AND
-vs-	)	MAKING SAME
	)	PART OF THE
Edward Harold Ryman, et al,	)	RECORD
	)	
Defendants	)	Case No.........
		Criminal

The foregoing Bill of Exceptions duly posted by the
defendants George J. Muyres and John F. Muyres, and
duly agreed upon by the respective parties hereto, having
been duly presented to the Court within the time allowed
and required by law, and by the rules and orders of this
Court, is hereby settled, allowed and authenticated as in
proper form and as conforming to the truth and as containing all of the evidence and as all of the proceedings
relating to the trial of the above entitled cause, and as the
true bill of exceptions herein, and same is hereby made a
part of the record of this cause.

Geo. Cosgrave

Judge

[Endorsed]: Filed Jun 8 - 1936 R. S. Zimmerman,
Clerk By J. M. Horn Deputy Clerk. Docketed No. 8179
United States Circuit Court of Appeals for the Ninth
Circuit Filed Jun 11 1936 Paul P. O'Brien, Clerk

At a stated term, to-wit: The February Term, A. D. 1936, of the District Court of the United States of America, within and for the Central Division of the Southern District of California, held at the Court Room thereof, in the City of Los Angeles on Thursday the 4th day of June, in the year of our Lord one thousand nine hundred and thirty-six.

Present: The Honorable: GEO. COSGRAVE District Judge.

United States of America,   ｜

            Plaintiff,   )

         vs.   )   No. 12619-C   Crim.

John F. Muyres,   )

           Defendant.   )

This cause coming before the court for hearing to determine if John F. Muyres shall be admitted to bail; Jack Irwin, Assistant U. S. Attorney, appearing as counsel for the government, and Harry Graham Balter, Esq., appearing for the defendant, who is present;

H. G. Balter, Esq. makes a statement, and states he is satisfied Court cannot make an order staying execution, but suggests a thirty day stay;

J. Irwin, Esq., argues in opposition to stay, and the Court makes a statement, whereupon

It is by the Court ordered that the oral motion of Harry Graham Balter, Esq. to have defendant John F. Muyres granted permission to leave the jurisdiction of the Court on the bond posted on May 25, 1936, is denied; and the motion of the U. S. Attorney to vacate said appeal bond of May 25, 1936; is granted; the said bond is exonerated, and defendant is remanded to the custody of the U. S. Marshal.

At 10:22 o'clock a. m. recess is declared to Monday, June 8, 1936.

244

[Title of Court and Cause.]

ORDER

Good cause appearing, on motion of Harry Graham Balter and L. A. Bloom, attorneys for defendant, John F. Muyres,

IT IS ORDERED that for the purpose of effecting a bond on appeal in the sum of $5,000.00 heretofore set by this Court, any United States Commissioner in the State of Arizona may examine any resident of the State of Arizona as to requisite property qualifications to justify as sureties on said bond and may approve said sureties if they own the requisite amount in real property even though the same be located in the State of Arizona.

DATED this 17th day of April, 1936.

Wm. P. James
JUDGE OF THE UNITED STATES
DISTRICT COURT.

[Endorsed]: Filed Apr 17 1936 R. S. Zimmerman, Clerk, By J. M. Horn, Deputy Clerk.

At a stated term, to wit: The October Term, A. D. 1935 of the United States Circuit Court of Appeals for the Ninth Circuit held in the court room thereof, in the City and County of San Francisco in the State of California on Monday the twenty-fourth day of August in the year of our Lord one thousand nine hundred and thirty-six.

PRESENT: THE Honorable FRANCIS A. GARRECHT, Circuit Judge, Presiding.

Honorable WILLIAM DENMAN, Circuit Judge,

Honorable CLIFTON MATHEWS, Circuit Judge.

JOHN F. MUYRES,

Appellant)

vs.)   No. 8179.

)

UNITED STATES OF AMERICA,)

)

Appellee.)

ORDER GRANTING PETITION FOR ADMISSION
TO BAIL PENDING APPEAL.

Upon consideration of the petition of appellant for admission to bail, and of the oral argument on said motion made by the respective counsel, and good cause therefor appearing,

IT IS ORDERED that the said petition be, and hereby is granted, and that appellant John F. Muyres be admitted to bail pending appeal upon furnishing bail bond in the sum of $5,000 with good and sufficient security, surety or sureties thereon to justify before a United States Commissioner, the said bond to be approved by the Trial Judge, or a Judge of the District Court for the Southern District of California, and thereafter filed with the clerk of said District Court.

I HEREBY CERTIFY that the foregoing is a full, true, and correct copy of an original Order made and entered in the within-entitled cause.

ATTEST my hand and the seal of the United States Circuit Court of Appeals for the Ninth Circuit, at the City of San Francisco, in the State of California, this 24th day of August, A. D. 1936.

[Seal]   Paul P. O'Brien,
Clerk, U. S. Circuit Court of Appeals for the Ninth
    District.

[Endorsed]: Filed Aug 25 1936 R. S. Zimmerman, Clerk, By B. B. Hansen, Deputy Clerk.

[TITLE OF COURT AND CAUSE.]

NOTICE OF APPEAL.
No. 12,619-C

Name and Address of Appellant:

JOHN F. MUYRES, Los Angeles County Jail.

Name and Address of Appellant's Attorneys:

Harry Graham Balter, 440 Van Nuys Bldg., Los Angeles, California.

L. A. Bloom, 124 West 4th Street, Los Angeles, California.

OFFENSE:

Violation of Section 415 and Section 88 of Title 18, United States Code.

DATE OF JUDGMENT:

April 7, 1936.

BRIEF DESCRIPTION OF JUDGMENT OR SENTENCE:

On Count 1, sentenced to 5 years in such a penitentiary as may be designated by the Attorney General and fined $1,000.00.

On Count 2, sentenced to 2 years in such a penitentiary as may be designated by the Attorney General.

Sentences on both Counts to run consecutively and not concurrently.

NAME OF PRISON WHERE NOW CONFINED IF NOT ON BAIL:

Los Angeles County Jail.

I, the above named appellant hereby appeal to the United States Circuit Court of Appeals for the Ninth Circuit from the judgment above mentioned on the grounds set forth below.

John F. Muyres
John F. Muyres

April 13th, 1936.

GROUNDS OF APPEAL:

1. That the Court erred in denying the motion for a directed verdict requested by the defendant John F. Muyres:

2. That the Court gave erroneous and prejudicial instructions to the jury;

3. That the Court erred in denying certain requested instructions on behalf of the defendant John F. Muyres;

4. That the evidence was legally insufficient to sustain the verdict of the jury.

[Endorsed]: Received copy of the within Notice of Appeal this 13th day of April, 1936. Jack L. Powell Attorney for U. S. A. Filed Apr. 13, 1936 R. S. Zimmerman, Clerk By J. M. Horn, Deputy Clerk.

[TITLE OF COURT AND CAUSE.]

NOTICE OF APPEAL.
No. 12619 S-Crim.

Name and address of appellant:

George J. Muyres, 712 South Wilton Place, Los Angeles, California.

Name and address of appellant's attorney:

Russell Graham, 812 C. C. Chapman Building, 756 South Broadway, Los Angeles, California.

Offense:

Conspiracy to transport stolen bonds in interstate commerce.

Date of judgment:

April 7, 1936.

Brief description of judgment or sentence:

Imprisonment for two years in a penitentiary and a fine of One Thousand Dollars.

I, the above-named Appellant, hereby appeal to the United States Circuit Court of Appeals for the Ninth Circuit from the judgment above-mentioned on the grounds set forth below.

Russell Graham

APPELLANT'S Attorney

George J. Muyres

APPELLANT

DATED: This 7 day of APRIL, 1936.

Grounds of appeal:

1. That the evidence was insufficient to support the verdict of guilty.

2. That the Court erred in denying Appellant's motion for a new trial.

3. That the Court misdirected the jury in matters of law.

4. That the Court erred in refusing to instruct the jury as requested by appellant.

[Endorsed]: Filed Apr. 7, 1936   R. S. Zimmerman, Clerk By J. M. Horn, Deputy Clerk.

IN THE DISTRICT COURT OF THE UNITED
STATES, SOUTHERN DISTRICT OF CALI-
FORNIA, CENTRAL DIVISION.

UNITED STATES OF AMERICA,	)	NO. 12619-S Criminal
	)	
Plaintiff,	)	ASSIGNMENT OF
	)	ERRORS ON
vs.	)	BEHALF OF
	)	DEFENDANT
JOHN F. MUYRES, et al.,	)	JOHN F. MUYRES.
	)	
Defendants.	)	

COMES NOW John F. Muyres, one of the defendants
in the above entitled cause and in connection with his appeal herein, says that in the record and proceedings during the trial of the above entitled cause in said District
Court, error has intervened to his prejudice, and makes
the following Assignment of Errors, which he, the said
defendant, avers occurred in the trial of said cause, and
upon which he will rely upon the presentation of his appeal of the above entitled cause, to-wit:

I.

The Court erred in overruling the objection of defendant John F. Muyres to the admission of the following
testimony:

"BY MR. IRWIN:

"Q. I will ask you what was said by Mr. Lee or yourself or Mr. Muyres when Mr. Muyres was present on this

occasion, the 7th of March, concerning the coming trial of this case?

"MR. OHANNESON:

"This is only against Mr. Muyres.

"MR. IRWIN:

"John F. Muyres.

"MR. OSTROM:

"To which we object, if your Honor please, as being incompetent, irrelevant and immaterial and not tending to prove or disprove any of the points involved in this case.

"THE COURT:

"I cannot say, as it might be a statement against interest and if so it would be admissible.

"MR. IRWIN:

"It is so offered.

"THE COURT:

"Overruled.

"MR. OSTROM.

"Exception, your Honor."

II.

That the Court erred in denying the motion of defendant John F. Muyres for an instructed verdict of "Not Guilty" made at the conclusion of all of the evidence on the ground that the evidence was insufficient to warrant a conviction of the defendant John F. Muyres on either count of the indictment.

III.

That the Court erred in failing and refusing to give to the jury instruction number 4, requested by the defendant John F. Muyres, which said instruction is as follows:

"The second count of the indictment charges that the defendants conspired to transport the securities described in the first count, in interstate commerce, from Arizona to Los Angeles County, California, knowing the said securities to have been theretofore stolen and that, in furtherance of, and to effect the object of, the said conspiracy, the overt acts charged in the second count were performed.

"You are instructed that after the bonds had arrived at Huntington Park, California, and had been taken from the express office at Huntington Park, the object of the conspiracy charged had been completely attained and the conspiracy charged was therefore at an end.

"Nothing done, after the conspiracy charged was at an end, could have been in furtherance of, or to effect the object of the conspiracy. No defendant who joined with the conspirators, if a conspiracy existed, for the purpose of selling the said securities, after the transportation to Huntington Park, which was the object of the conspiracy, may be convicted of the offense charged in the second count."

IV.

That the Court erred in failing and refusing to give to the jury instruction number 13 as requested by the defendant John F. Muyres, which said instruction is as follows:

"An inference may be drawn from a fact proved by evidence. It may not be based upon another inference."

WHEREFORE, the defendant John F. Muyres by reason of the foregoing Assignment of Errors and upon the record in said case, prays that the verdict and judgment, and each of them rendered herein, may be reversed and held for naught.

Harry Graham Balter

And L. A. Bloom

Attorneys for defendant, John F. Muyres.

[Endorsed]: Received copy of the within Assignment of Errors this 8th day of June, 1936. Pierson M. Hall by Hal Hughes, Asst. U. S. Dist. Atty. Attorney for Plaintiff. Filed Jun. 8, 1936 R. S. Zimmerman, Clerk, By J. M. Horn, Deputy Clerk.

IN THE DISTRICT COURT OF THE UNITED
STATES, SOUTHERN DISTRICT OF CALI-
FORNIA, CENTRAL DIVISION.

UNITED STATES OF AMERICA,	)))	No. 12619-S Criminal
Plaintiff,	))	ASSIGNMENT OF ERRORS ON
vs.	))	BEHALF OF DEFENDANT
JOHN F. MUYRES, ET AL.,	))	GEORGE J. MUYRES
Defendants.	)	

Comes now George J. Muyres, one of the defendants
in the above entitled cause, and in connection with his
appeal herein, says that in the record and proceedings during the trial of the above entitled cause in said District
Court, error has intervened to his prejudice, and makes
the following Assignment of Errors, which he, the said
defendant, avers occurred in the trial of said cause, and
upon which he will rely upon the prosecution of his Appeal of the above entitled cause, to-wit:

I.

That the Trial Court erred in overruling the Exception
of defendant George J. Muyres to the admission of the
following testimony:

"Q. Was that general agreement entered into at the
outset, as to the split of all bonds?

MR. GRAHAM: Pardon me. I object to that as calling for a conclusion of the witness.

THE COURT: Objection sustained.

MR. IRWIN: All right. We will go around the long way.

Q. Did you have any conversation when you first got together after you had come to Los Angeles with the bonds with anybody about what would be done with the proceeds of the sale of any bonds that might be sold?

A. It was supposed to have been divided equally among us, and after it was evenly divided, 20% of each one was to go to me.

MR. GRAHAM: (Interrupting) Just a minute. That is the same thing. I have no objection to stating any conversation that he had with them.

MR. IRWIN: If you will just wait a minute, I prefer to examine my witness myself.

Q. When you say "us", who do you mean by "us"?

A. I and Mr. Muyres—as a matter of fact, it was agreed by all four of us that were present at that time.

THE COURT: When you say "all agreed", just what do you mean?

THE WITNESS: Well, it was between I and Mr. Ryan—it was agreed between I and Mr. Ryan.

THE COURT (interrupting): Tell us just what was said.

MR. GRAHAM: If the Court please, I have another objection to this conversation: On the ground that it is immaterial, and that it could have no tendency to prove or disprove transportation of bonds in interstate commerce, a transportation which had already taken place; it could have no tendency to prove or disporve a conspiracy to transport bonds, the transportation having been completed, so the conspiracy, if any, was therefore completed.

THE COURT: What do you think about that, Mr. Irwin?

MR. IRWIN: The answer to that is this, your Honor: One of the elements that must be proved is the knowledge that they were knowingly transported, and knowing that the same were stolen. The materiality of showing the split, since it has been shown here the Home Owners Loan bonds were negotiable bonds, if we show that, and the witness has testified that 30 per cent went to the man who cashed a thousand dollar bond and a five hundred dollar bond, with 70 per cent coming back to the four of them, Uncle Muyres, this man, and a other two, why, it is material to show the knowledge of the group in cashing that bond. If a bond is on the up-and-up, you don't discount it 30 per cent, a bond of the United States Government which is negotiable.

MR. GRAHAM: The answer to that, your Honor, is that he is trying to prove knowledge after the crime was complete instead of before.

MR. IRWIN: Which is entirely

THE COURT (Interrupting): Of course, all the surrounding facts and circumstances could be shown.

The objection is overruled. I think the evidence itself is admissible.

I think, though, the witness should give a more—show the time and place of this conversation, and that should be definitely fixed. We cannot leave it in saying that it was understood, et cetera.

Strike out all of the statement of this witness as to what was understood, with reference to the distribution of these bonds.

Now, put this witness down to the time, place and persons present in the regular and customary way.

MR. IRWIN: Very well, your Honor.

MR. GRAHAM: And an exception noted?

THE COURT: Yes."

II.

That the Trial Court erred in overruling the objection of the defendant George J. Muyres to the admission of the following testimony:

"MR. GRAHAM: That is objected to as entirely irrelevant and immaterial for this reason: Ryman had apparently registered in that hotel. The offense charged in each count of this indictment had been fully completed, and the man whom it concerned is not on trial. Neither of those documents, nor any of this testimony, could have the slightest tendency to show that any of the defendants who are on trial either aided or abetted Ryman in transporting these bonds to Los Angeles County, or that they conspired with him to do so.

"THE COURT: Ocerruled. I think that the mere—

"MR. GRAHAM: (Interrupting) Exception

"THE COURT: (Continuing) – testimony to the effect that he was at this hotel on this day, whatever it is, would itself be admissible, in corroboration of the other testimony.

"THE COURT: Overruled.

"MR. GRAHAM: Exception."

III.

That the Court erred in overruling the objection of the defendant George J. Muyres to the following testimony:

"THE WITNESS CONTINUING: The payment was apparently made on October 23rd, 1935.

"MR. IRWIN: I offer the card and ledger sheet as Government's Exhibit next in order in corroboration of the testimony of the witness Ryman as to the time he arrived in Los Angeles.

"MR. GRAHAM: To which I make the objection, the same objection, as the last objection made.

"THE COURT: Overruled.

"MR. GRAHAM: Exception."

IV.

That the Court erred in overruling the objection of the defendant George J. Muyres to the admission of the following testimony, to-wit:

"Whereupon, it was stipulated by counsel for the defendants that there was registered at the hotel a person giving his name as T. B. Ryan and another person giving his name as E. Roberts and it was stipulated that one of these names is that of the defendant Ryan, excepting that an objection was made by the counsel for the defendant George Muyres on the ground that this testimony was entirely immaterial as to him. The objection being overruled, an exception was noted.

V.

That the Court erred in denying the Motion of defendant George J. Muyres to strike out the following testimony of the Witness, Daymond Curtis Bassett:

"After I took down these numbers, Mr. Muyres said that he had already done that, and checked them, and I went down town to a brokerage company and talked to some friends. I waited around and investigated and decided not to handle the bonds."

VI.

That the Court erred in denying the motion of the defendant George J. Muyres for an instructed verdict of "not guilty" made at the conclusion of the evidence introduced on behalf of the plaintiff on the ground that the evidence was insufficient to warrant a conviction of the defendant George J. Muyres on either count of the indictment.

VII.

That the Court erred in denying the Motion of the defendant George J. Muyres for an instructed verdict of "not guilty" made at the conclusion of all of the evidence on the grounds that the evidence was insufficient to warrant a conviction of the defendant George J. Muyres on either count of the indictment.

VIII.

That the Court erred in failing and refusing to give to the Jury Instruction Number 4, requested by defendant George J. Muyres, which said instruction is as follows:

"The second count of the indictment charges that the defendants conspired to transport the securities described in the first count, in interstate commerce, from Arizona to Los Angeles County, California, knowing the said securities to have been theretofore stolen and that, in furtherance of, and to effect the object of, the said conspiracy, the overt acts charged in the second count were performed.

You are instructed that after the bonds had arrived at Huntington Park, California, and had been taken from the express office at Huntington Park, the object of the conspiracy charged had been completely attained and the conspiracy charged was therefore at an end.

Nothing done, after the conspiracy charged was at an end, could have been in furtherance of, or to effect the object of the conspiracy. No defendant who joined with the conspiractors, if a conspiracy existed, for the purpose of selling the said securities, after the transportation to Huntington Park, which was the object of the conspiracy, may be convicted of the offense charged in the second count."

IX.

That the Court erred in failing and refusing to give to the Jury Instruction Number 11, requested by the defendant George J. Muyres, which said requested instruction is as follows:

"In order to establish the existence of a conspiracy there must be proof outside of the statements and declarations of an alleged conspirator; hence the extra judicial declarations or statements of any defendant in this case standing alone and of themselves, if any such were made, are not sufficient to show the existence of a conspiracy."

X.

That the Court erred in failing and refusing to give to the Jury Instruction Number 13, as requested by the defendant, which requested instruction is as follows:

"An inference may be drawn from a fact proved by evidence. It may not be based upon another inference."

WHEREFORE, the defendant, GEORGE J. MUY-RES, by reason of the foregoing Assignment of Errors and upon the record in said cause, prays that the verdict and judgment, and each of them rendered herein, may be reversed and held for naught.

Russell Graham

RUSSELL GRAHAM

Attorney for defendant George J. Muyres.

[Endorsed]: Received copy of the within Assignment of Errors this 8th day of June, 1936. John J Irwin Asst. U. S. Attorney, attorney for plf. Filed Jun. 8, 1936. R. S. Zimmerman Clerk By J. M. Horn, Deputy Clerk.

[TITLE OF COURT AND CAUSE.]

STIPULATION.

IT IS HEREBY STIPULATED by and between the United States of America, plaintiff and appellee, through its counsel, Peirson M. Hall, United States Attorney for the Southern District of California, and John J. Irwin, Assistant United States Attorney for said District, and John F. Muyres and George J. Muyres, defendants and appellants, through their respective counsel, Harry Graham Balter and Russell Graham, that the exhibits received in evidence in the trial of the above entitled case and, where photostatic copies of said exhibits have been made by order of the Court and received in lieu of the originals, said photostatic copies thereof shall be sent by the Clerk of the District Court to the Clerk of the Ninth Circuit Court of Appeals, where they may be considered and used in connection with the pending appeal.

DATED: This 14 day of September, 1936.

PEIRSON M. HALL,
United States Attorney,
By John J. Irwin
JOHN J. IRWIN,
Assistant U. S. Attorney,
Attorneys for Plaintiff.

Harry Graham Balter
HARRY GRAHAM BALTER,
Attorney for John F. Muyres.
Russell Graham
RUSSELL GRAHAM,
Attorney for George J. Muyres.

[Endorsed]: Filed Sep. 18, 1936. R. S. Zimmerman, Clerk By J. M. Horn Deputy Clerk.

264

[Title of Court and Cause.]

BAIL BOND ON APPEAL
No. 12,619-S. Criminal

KNOW ALL MEN BY THESE PRESENTS:

That we, John F. Muyres of the City of Phoenix, Arizona, as principal and Western Surety Company, a corporation, as surety, are jointly and severally held firmly bound unto the United States of America in the sum of $5,000.00 for the payment of which said sum we and each of us bind ourselves, our heirs, executors, administrators and assigns.

The condition of the foregoing obligation is as follows:

WHEREAS, later, to-wit, on the 7th day of April, 1936, at a term of the District Court of the United States, in and for the Southern District of California, Central Division, in an action pending in said Court in which the United States of America was plaintiff and John F. Muyres was defendant, a judgment and sentence was made, given, rendered and entered against the said John F. Muyres, in the above entitled action, whereas he was convicted as charged in the first and second counts of the indictment in said action.

WHEREAS, in said judgment and sentence, so made, given, rendered and entered against said John F. Muyres, he was by said judgment sentenced on the first count to imprisonment for five years in the penitentiary to be designated by the Attorney General, and sentenced on the second count to imprisonment for two years in a penitentiary to be designated by the Attorney General and to pay a fine of $1,000.00 and stand committed until paid, said sentences on the first and second counts to run consecutively.

WHEREAS, the said John F. Muyres has filed a notice of appeal from the said conviction and from the said judgment and sentence, appealing to the United States Circuit Court of Appeals for the Ninth Circuit; and

WHEREAS, the said John F. Muyres has been admitted to bail pending the decision upon said appeal, in the sum of $5000.00.

NOW, THEREFORE, the conditions of this obligation are such that if said John F. Muyres shall appear in person, or by his attorney, in the United States Circuit Court of Appeals for the Ninth Circuit on such day or days as may be appointed for the hearing of said cause in said court and prosecute his appeal; and if the said John F. Muyres shall abide by and obey all orders made by the said United States Circuit Court of Appeals for the Ninth Circuit and if said John F. Muyres shall surrender himself in execution of said judgment and sentence, if the judgment and sentence be affirmed by the said United States Circuit Court of Appeals for the Ninth Circuit; and if the said John F. Muyres will appear for trial in the District Court of the United States, in and for the Southern District of California, Central Division, on such day or days as may be appointed for retrial by said District Court, if the said judgment and sentence against him be reversed,

Then this obligation shall be null and void; otherwise to remain in full force and effect.

> John F. Muyres
> PRINCIPAL
> 1838 W. Madison St.
> Address
> Phoenix, Arizona

[Seal]   WESTERN SURETY COMPANY,
a South Dakota Corporation
By P. F. Kirby
Vice-President and Attorney-in-Fact.

STATE OF CALIFORNIA,)

                           : ss.

County of Los Angeles   )

On This 25th day of August, A. D., 1936, before me, A. L. Sands, a Notary Public in and for the said County and State, personally appeared P. F. KIRBY, known to me to be the person whose name is subscribed to the within Instrument, as the Vice-President and Attorney-in-Fact of WESTERN SURETY COMPANY, A South Dakota Corporation and acknowledged to me that he subscribed the name of WESTERN SURETY COMPANY, A South Dakota Corporation thereto as principal and his own name as Attorney-in-Fact, and Vice-President.

IN WITNESS WHEREOF, I have hereunto set my hand and affixed my official seal the day and year in this certificate first above written.

[Seal]   A. L. Sands

       Notary Public in and for said County and State.

My Commission Expires April 1, 1940

Approves as to form.

PEIRSON M. HALL,
United States Attorney

Clyde Thomas
Asst. United States Attorney

I hereby certify that I have examined the within bond and that in my opinion the form hereof is correct and surety thereon is qualified.

Harry Graham Balter
Attorney for defendant and appellant

The foregoing bond is approved this 25 day of Aug., 1936.

Albert Lee Stephens
United States District Judge.

I hereby certify that I have examined the foregoing bond and find the surety thereon good and sufficient.

[Seal]   David B. Head
U. S. Commissioner.

Aug. 25-1936

[Endorsed]: Filed Aug 25 1936 R. S. Zimmerman, Clerk By B. B. Hansen Deputy Clerk

[TITLE OF COURT AND CAUSE.]

BOND OF GEORGE J. MUYRES PENDING DECISION ON APPEAL

12,619-S-Crim

KNOW ALL MEN BY THESE PRESENTS: That we, GEORGE J. MUYRES, of the City of Los Angeles, County of Los Angeles, State of California, as principal, and Clinton L. Clark and F. *H.* Hansen, both of Los Angeles, California, as sureties, are jointly and severally held and firmly bound unto the United States of America in the sum of Three Thousand Five Hundred ($3500.00) for the payment of which said sum we and each of us bind ourselves, our heirs, executors, administrators and assigns.

Signed and dated this 7 day of APRIL, 1936.

The condition of the foregoing obligation is as follows:

WHEREAS, later, to-wit, on the 7 day of April, 1936, at a term of the District Court of the United States in and for the Southern District of California, Central Division, in an action pending in said court in which the United States of America was plaintiff and George J. Muyres was defendant, a judgment and sentence was made, given, rendered and entered against the said George J. Muyres in the above entitled action, wherein he was acquitted as charged in the first count of the indictment in said action, and convicted as charged in the second count in said indictment in said action.

WHEREAS, in said judgment and sentence so made, given, rendered and entered against said George J. Muyres, he was by said judgment, sentenced to imprisonment for two years in a penetentiary to be designated by the Attorney General and to pay a fine of One Thousand Dollars ($1000.00) on the said second count of the said indictment.

WHEREAS, the said George J. Muyres has filed a notice of appeal from the said conviction and from the said judgment and sentence, appealing to the United States Circuit Court of Appeals for the Ninth Circuit for the purpose of reversing said judgment and sentence.

WHEREAS, said George J. Muyres has been admitted to bail pending the decision upon said appeal in the sum of Three Thousand Five Hundred Dollars ($3500.00).

NOW, THEREFORE, the conditions of this obligation are such that if the said George J. Muyres shall appear in person, or by his attorney, in the United States Circuit Court of Appeals for the Ninth Circuit on such day or days as may be appointed for the hearing of said cause in said court and prosecute his appeal; and if the said George J. Muyres shall abide by and obey all orders made by the United States Circuit Court of Appeals for the Ninth Circuit in said cause, and if the said George J. Muyres shall surrender himself in execution of said judgment and sentence if the said judgment and sentence be affirmed by the said United States Circuit Court of Appeals for the Ninth Circuit; and if the said George J. Muyres shall appear for trial in the District Court of the United States in and for the Southern District of California, Central Division, on such day or days as may be appointed for retrial by said District Court if the said judgment and sentence against him be reversed.

Then this obligation shall be null and void, otherwise to remain in full force and effect.

Geo. J. Muyres

Clinton L. Clark

FIRST SURETY

F. W. Hansen

SECOND SURETY

UNITED STATES OF AMERICA)
SOUTHEN DISTRICT OF CALIFORNIA) SS.
CENTRAL DIVISION)
COUNTY OF LOS ANGELES)

Clinton L. Clark and F. *H.* Hansen, being duly sworn, each for himself, deposes and says:

That he is a house holder in the district aforesaid and is worth the sum of $3500.00 over and above all debts and liabilities, exclusive of property exempt from execution, and is the owner of the property listed below under schedule of assets, which schedule is made a part of this affidavit; that the said property is not encumbered except as below listed and that the property is reasonably of the value below listed, and further, that he is not receiving or accepting compensation for acting as surety herein and is not surety upon any outstanding penal bonds except as disclosed in the schedule below.

Clinton L. Clark

FIRST SURETY

F. W. Hansen

SECOND SURETY

Subscribed and sworn to before me this 7 day of APRIL, 1936.

[Seal]   David B. Head

UNITED STATES COMMISSIONER

for the Southern District of California.

SCHEDULE OF ASSETS

First Surety: √ Clark

(1)   S. E. ¼ of Sec. 21 T 8 N. R 12 W L. A. County value $5000—clear

(2)   Lots 136-137-138 Clark and Bryants Lone Star Tract—value $100,000 clear L. A. County

(3)   Lot 3 Blk 9 L. M. Van Nuys—value 5,000

(4)   Lot A, Tr. 7109 L. A. County value 10,000

(5)   Lot 99. Tr. 6388 "   "   "   10,000

(6)   Lot 100. Tr. 8320 "   "   "   25,000

Parcels 2 to 6 inclusive mortgaged to extent of about $50,000

Second Surety:

Lot 11 R. Torrey's Grand Ave Tract value $8,000—clear. 4311 S. Grand.

I hereby certify that I have examined the sureties upon the within Bond and find them good and sufficient.

[Seal]   David B. Head

UNITED STATES COMMISSIONER

for the Southern District of California.

APPROVED AS TO FORM

PIERSON M. HALL

UNITED STATES ATTORNEY

By John J. Irwin

ASSISTANT UNITED STATES ATTORNEY

I hereby certify that I have examined the within Bond and that in my opinion the form thereof is correct and the sureties thereon are qualified.

Russell Graham

ATTORNEY FOR DEFENDANT

AND APPELLANT.

The foregoing Bond is hereby approved this 7 day of APRIL, 1936.

Geo Cosgrave

UNITED STATES DISTRICT JUDGE.

[Endorsed]: Filed Apr. 8, 1936 R. S. Zimmerman, Clerk By J. M. Horn Deputy Clerk.

[TITLE OF COURT AND CAUSE.]

PRAECIPE

To the Clerk of Said Court:

Sir:

Please issue Transcript of Record on Appeal, including:

1. The indictment;
2. The pleas of the defendants to the indictment;
3. The minutes of the trial;
4. The Bill of Exceptions;
5. The Assignments of Errors;
6. The Notices of Appeal;
7. The Orders fixing bond;
8. The Stipulations and Orders on preparation of Record on Appeal;
9. The Verdicts;
10. The Sentences and Judgments;
11. The bail bonds on appeal;
12. A Copy of this praecipe.

Harry Graham Balter

ATTORNEY FOR DEFENDANT,

JOHN F. MUYRES

Russell Graham

ATTORNEY FOR DEFENDANT,

GEORGE J. MUYRES

PEIRSON M. HALL

United States Attorney

By John J. Irwin

ASSISTANT UNITED STATES

ATTORNEY

September 11, 1936

[Endorsed]: Filed Sep. 12 1936 R. S. Zimmerman, Clerk By J. M. Horn, Deputy Clerk.

[Title of Court and Cause.]

CLERK'S CERTIFICATE.

I, R. S. Zimmerman, clerk of the United States District Court for the Southern District of California, do hereby crtify the foregoing volume containing 273 pages, numbered from 1 to 273, inclusive, to be the Transcript of Record on Appeal in the above entitled cause, as printed by the appellant, and presented to me for comparison and certification, and that the same has been compared and corrected by me and contains a full, true and correct copy of the statement of docket entries, Case No. 12,619-C Criminal; statement of docket entries, Case No. 12619-(S)-C-Crim.; indictment; minutes of December 16 and December 23, 1935; minutes of trials of March 18, March 19, March 20, March 24, March 25, March 26 and April 7, 1936; engrossed bill of exceptions; stipulation re order settling bill of exceptions; order settling and allowing bill of exceptions; minutes of June 4, 1936; order of April 17, 1936, allowing investigation of sureties on bond; order of August 24, 1936, granting petition for admission to bail, pending appeal; notice of appeal of John F. Muyres; notice of appeal of George J. Muyres; assignment of errors on behalf of John F. Muyres; assignment of errors on behalf of George J. Muyres; stipulation on exhibits in lieu of originals used in connection with pending appeal; bail bond on appeal; bond of George J. Muyres pending decision on appeal, and praecipe.

I DO FURTHER CERTIFY that the amount paid for printing the foregoing record on appeal is $ and that said amount has been paid the printer by the appellant herein and a receipted bill is herewith enclosed, also that the fees of the Clerk for comparing, correcting and certifying the foregoing Record on Appeal amount to............ and that said amount has been paid me by the appellant herein.

IN TESTIMONY WHEREOF, I have hereunto set my hand and affixed the Seal of the District Court of the United States of America, in and for the Southern District of California, Central Division, this 31st day of October, in the year of Our Lord One Thousand Nine Hundred and Thirty-six and of our Independence the One Hundred and Sixty-first.

R. S. ZIMMERMAN,

Clerk of the District Court of the United States of America, in and for the Southern District of California.

By

Deputy.

SUBJECT INDEX

INDEX—*Continued*

CITATIONS AND AUTHORITIES

JOHN F. MUYRES and GEORGE J.
MUYRES,
  Appellants,

  vs.

UNITED STATES OF AMERICA,
  Appellee.

BRIEF OF APPELLANT JOHN F. MUYRES

I.

Preliminary Statement

On December 16th, 1935, an indictment was returned in the Southern District of California, Central Division, against Harold Edward Ryman, Thomas Burke Ryan, Franklin Dolph Le Sieur, Karl L. Woolsey, John F. Muyres, George J. Muyres and John Murray Cheney, the First Count of which indictment charged that in violation of Title 18, Section 415, *United States Code Annotated,* the defendants "on or about the 22nd day of October, 1935, did knowingly, willfully, unlawfully and feloniously transport and cause to be transported in interstate commerce from the State of Arizona to Huntington Park, County of Los Angeles, State of California * * * certain securities of the value of more than $5,000.00, to-wit, of the value of $42,500.00, to-wit, (herein follows detailed description of the bonds) * * * all of said securities being then and there the property of Nellie P. Covert and having been theretofore stolen from the said Nellie P. Covert, the said defendants and each of them then and there well knowing said securities to have been stolen."

The Second Count of the indictment charged that in violation of Title 18, Section 88, *United States Code Annotated,* the same defendants "did knowingly, wilfully, unlawfully, corruptly and feloniously conspire, combine, confederate, arrange and agree together and with each other, and with divers other persons whose names are to the grand jurors unknown, to commit an offense against the United States of America and the laws thereof, the offense being to knowingly, wilfully, unlawfully and feloniously transport and cause to be transported in interstate commerce from the State of Arizona to the County of Los Angeles, California, certain securities of the value of more than Five Thousand Dollars ($5000.00), to-wit: those securities described in count one of this indictment, all of said securities being then and there the property of Nellie P. Covert, and having been theretofore stolen from the said Nellie P. Covert, as the defendants well knew." (Tr. of Rec., pp. 4 to 11.)

The defendant Franklin Dolph Le Sieur was never brought to trial.

On March 18th, 1936, the case was called for trial before the Honorable Geo. Cosgrave, Judge of the United States District Court, Southern District of California.

The Government dismissed the case as against the defendant John Murray Cheney.

Defendants Edward Harold Ryman and Karl L. Woolsey had changed their pleas from "Not Guilty" to "Guilty".

A trial by jury proceeded against the defendants Thomas Burke Ryan, John F. Muyres, appellant herein, and George J. Muyres.

The jury returned a verdict of "Guilty" as against the defendant Thomas Burke Ryan on both counts of the indictment, as against the defendant John F. Muyres on both counts of the indictment, and as against the defendant George J. Muyres on only the second count of the indictment, the count charging conspiracy. (Tr. of Rec., p. 47.)

On April 7th, 1936, the following sentences were meted out:

(1) The defendant George J. Muyres was sentenced to two years in a Federal Penitentiary together with a fine of $1,000.00.

(2) Defendant Edward Harold Ryman was sentenced to eight years on Count I and two years on Count II to run concurrently.

(3) Defendant Thomas Burke Ryan was sentenced to three years on Count I and two years on Count II to run concurrently.

(4) Defendant Karl L. Woolsey was granted probation on both Counts.

(5) Defendant John F. Muyres, appellant herein, was sentenced to imprisonment in a Federal Penitentiary for five years upon the first count and to imprisonment in a Federal Penitentiary for two years on the second count, the sentences to run consecutively, totaling a seven year penitentiary term, and in addition thereto, a fine of $1,000.00 upon the second count. (Tr. of Rec., pp. 49 to 52.)

On April 13th, 1936, John F. Muyres filed a written notice of appeal from the conviction, setting out as his grounds for appeal the following:

"1. That the Court erred in denying the motion for a directed verdict requested by the defendant John F. Muyres;

"2. That the Court gave erroneous and prejudicial instructions to the jury;

"3. That the Court erred in denying certain requested instructions on behalf of the defendant John F. Muyres;

"4. That the evidence was legally insufficient to sustain the verdict of the jury." (Tr. of Rec., p. 248.)

Assignments of error were filed on behalf of John F. Muyres setting out substantially the same grounds. (Tr. of Rec., p. 251.)

II.

Specification of Errors Relied Upon

John F. Muyres believes that the conviction as against him must be reversed because of the following errors committed at the time of the trial, and upon which he now relies:

(1) The Court erred in denying the motion of John F. Muyres for an instructed verdict of "Not Guilty" made at the conclusion of all the evidence on the ground that there was no substantial evidence in the record proving that John F. Muyres knew that the bonds were stolen before the transportation or the conspiracy to transport took place.

(2) The Court erred in denying the motion of John F. Muyres for an instructed verdict of "Not Guilty" made at the conclusion of all the evidence on the ground that there was no substantial evidence in the record proving that John F. Muyres knew that the bonds had been stolen in the State of Arizona or in any other state or territory other than the State of California.

(3) In view of the nature of the Government's case, it was error to allow the introduction into evidence of the testimony of Mrs. Woolsey, wife of a co-defendant who had pleaded guilty and had testified for the Government in the following respect, to-wit:

"By Mr. Irwin:

"Q. I will ask you what was said by Mr. Lee or yourself or Mr. Muyres when Mr. Muyres was present on this occasion, the 7th of March, concerning the coming trial of this case?

"Mr. Ohanneson:

"This is only against Mr. Muyres.

"Mr. Irwin:
"John F. Muyres.

"Mr. Ostrom:
"To which we object, if your Honor please, as being incompetent, irrelevant and immaterial and not tending to prove or disprove any of the points involved in this case.

"The Court:
"I cannot say, as it might be a statement against interest and if so it would be admissible.

"Mr. Irwin:
"It is so offered.

"The Court:
"Overruled.

"Mr. Ostrom:
"Exception, your Honor." (Tr. of Rec., pp. 251 and 252.)

(5) In view of the nature of the Government's case, it was error for the trial judge to refuse to grant Instruction No. 13 requested by appellant John F. Muyres and which was as follows:

"An inference may be drawn from a fact proved by evidence. It may not be based upon another inference." (Tr. of Rec., pp. 253 and 254.)

III.

ARGUMENT

A.

The Court Erred in Denying the Motion of John F. Muyres for an Instructed Verdict of "Not Guilty" Made at the Conclusion of All the Evidence on the Ground That There Was No Substantial Evidence in the Record Proving That John F. Muyres Knew That the Bonds Were Stolen Before the Transportation or the Conspiracy to Transport Took Place.

No useful purpose can be served by making a detailed recital of the entire evidence at this point. Instead, we shall refer to pertinent parts of the testimony as various phases of the case are analyzed.

Count I of the Indictment in substance charges as follows:

That the defendants on or about the 22nd day of October, 1935, "did knowingly, willfully and feloniously transport and cause to be transported in interstate commerce from the State of Arizona to Huntington Park, County of Los Angeles, State of California," certain therein described securities, being the property of a named individual, having theretofore been stolen from said individual "the said defendants and each of them then and there well knowing said securities to have been stolen."

Count II of the Indictment charges a conspiracy between the same defendants to transport these same bonds from the State of Arizona to the State of California.

Section 415 of Title 18, *U. S. Code,* upon which the substantive offense is based, provides as follows:

"§415. Same; transportation of stolen or feloniously taken goods, securities or money.

"Whoever shall transport or cause to be transported in interstate or foreign commerce any goods, wares, or merchandise, securities, or money, of the value of $5,000 or more theretofore stolen or taken feloniously by fraud or with intent to steal or purloin, knowing the same to have been so stolen or taken, shall be punished by a fine of not more than $10,000 or by imprisonment for not more than ten years, or both."

It is apparent that the conviction of the appellant John F. Muyres under either Count I or Count II of the Indictment cannot stand *unless there is substantial evidence to prove not only that he participated in the transportation of the bonds, but even if this were proved, that at the time of his participation in the transaction, he knew that the bonds which would be or were the subject of the interstate transportation, were stolen bonds.*

We realize, of course, that we cannot ask this Court to pass upon conflicting evidence presented to the jury; nor will this Court be asked to interfere with the verdict of the jury if there is *substantial* evidence in the record to sustain the charges; on the other hand, it is well established that there must be *substantial proof* in order to sustain a jury's verdict, slight proof not being sufficient.

Nicole v: United States, 72 F. (2d) 780:

"Where all substantial evidence is as consistent with innocence as with guilt, Appellate Court must reverse conviction."

Rossi v. United States, 49 F. (2d) 1:

"Conviction cannot be sustained on appeal unless charge laid in indictment is supported by some substantial evidence."

There is no substantial evidence proving that John· F. Muyres knew at the time of the alleged transportation· that the bonds were stolen bonds.

Apart from the statements to officers made by various defendants, which will be alluded to later, the only witnesses for the Government who could in any way link the appellant John F. Muyres with knowledge *at the time of the transportation* that the bonds were stolen, were Ryman, a co-defendant who actually stole the bonds and who pleaded guilty, and "Ham" Woolsey, a co-defendant who also pleaded guilty, and both of whom testified for the Government.

A very careful analysis of the testimony of Ryman fails to show any evidence that John F. Muyres knew before the transportation took place that the bonds were stolen. It should be recalled here that the theory of the Government's case was that Ryman knew where these bonds could be stolen, that he first approached the defendant Ryan, and asked him if he knew where he could sell these bonds, that Ryan asked Woolsey if he could sell them, that Woolsey in turn asked appellant John F. Muyres if he could sell them, and that appellant John F. Muyres told Woolsey that he thought he could sell them in Los Angeles.

Ryman is unequivocal in his testimony that he never knew appellant in Arizona, never discussed with him the prospect of stealing the bonds, never discussed with him the matter of transporting the bonds from Arizona to California, and never discussed with him while in Arizona anything to do with selling the bonds in California or with disposing of the proceeds.

> "I got in through the window and I went to the box where the bonds were kept. I opened the box and took out the bonds. Then I carried the bonds and put them in the car and I drove to St. Mary's hospital and I buried some of the bonds, because I didn't know what these fellows that I had made the agreement with might cheat me out of them, and I would have some left for me, anyway, if they did. Although there was no other fellow that I had any agreement with I took it for granted that there would be other people because he told me there were other people whom he had contacted. But the only person I talked to about stealing the bonds and disposing of them before I left Arizona was Ryan." (Tr. of Rec., pp. 84 and 85.)

> "I never knew or talked to John F. Muyres until I met him in the hotel room in Los Angeles." (Tr. of Rec., p. 89.)

> "In the room I was introduced to Jack Muyres and Ham Woolsey, neither of whom I had ever known

before, although I recalled having seen Ham Woolsey bartending at the Avalon Club in Phoenix." (Tr. of Rec., p. 77.)

After the bonds were transported from Phoenix to Los Angeles, Ryman, Ryan, Woolsey and appellant John F. Muyres met at the U. S. Hotel in Los Angeles. In speaking of the list of the bonds which was discussed at this first meeting, Ryman said:

"I first met John F. Muyres in a room in the U. S. Hotel. I can't be positive of the date but I think it was a couple of days after I gave Ryan the samples, either the next day or the day after. I can't remember which. It may have been I saw him that same day that I gave Ryan the bonds and went upstairs. Anyway, I went upstairs to see what they were doing, or he was doing. This fellow was supposed to be up there. I didn't know him at that time, whoever he was, and I went upstairs to see what they were doing. They were locked in their room and Mr. Muyres and Mr. Woolsey was in the room at the time. (Whereupon, the witness identified the defendant, John F. Muyres.) I know Ham Woolsey. He was there. If I remember right, I walked in the room and Mr. Woolsey was lying on the bed there and I said, 'Hello, Ham,' like that, because I had seen him before, as he is a bartender at the Avalon Club, and I had seen him before. I did not go up to the room pursuant to Ryan's request but went on my own account. I had a conversation with John F. Muyres in the room there but I just kind of forget what he said. At the time I walked in the room, I remember distinctly Mr. Muyres was copying down a list. I think you have it there—of the bonds. I made up a list of all the bonds that I had and he was copying the list of them which I had given to Ryan. The list which is handed to me is the list of which I was speaking. It is in my writing. It is the one which Muyres was copying when I walked into the room. (The list referred to was received in evidence and marked Plaintiff's Exhibit No. 3. It is a list of the serial numbers and the denominations of the bonds which the witness testified that he stole from Mrs. Nellie P. Covert and shipped to California.) I think that list was later given back to me by Ryan. I put it in my grip. The list which I had copied contained the numbers of all the bonds which I had shipped over there. As I recall, at the time, the reason that the list was given to him, the reason I wrote the list out, was there seemed to be some doubt in their minds if the bonds had been stolen, and the idea was that I wrote the list out so they could check up and see if they were reported stolen or not. I mean, reported stolen. I think the time I first approached Ryan back in Arizona during the discussion of these bonds, I told him they were Government bonds and naturally they were negotiable. I looked at that, up in the room and John F. Muyres was making a copy of that list." (Tr. of Rec., pp. 61 to 63.)

This testimony of Ryman indicates clearly that appellant John F. Muyres did not even at that time immediately after the transportation, know that the bonds had been stolen.

Nor did Ryman ever discuss the matter of sale of the
bonds or of splitting the proceeds therefrom with anyone
but Ryan prior to the meeting of the defendants in the
U. S. Hotel in Los Angeles.

"Before I came to Los Angeles the only one I had
discussed this deal with was Ryan. Before leaving
Arizona, Ryan and I had a discussion as to what
would be done with these bonds after I reached Los
Angeles. I don't know how to say just what that
discussion was except by saying they were all to be
sold. He knew somebody else that knew somebody
else that would sell them. While we were in Arizona
it was not decided between Ryan and myself as to
what would be done with the money that might be
obtained when the bonds were sold. When I came
to Los Angeles and met Ryan and gave him the
samples there was nothing said between us as to
what would be done with the proceeds from any of
the bonds that might be sold. And later on when I
met Ryan together with Uncle Muyres and Woolsey
in Ryan's room where I saw Uncle Muyres copying
the list which I had given Ryan and there was
nothing said by anyone in the presence of the other
three concerning the proceeds from any bonds that
might be sold." (Tr. of Rec., p. 70.)

And it was not until some time after this first meeting
that Ryan told John F. Muyres that the bonds had been
stolen and not won in gambling.

"You see it all happened so unexpected, I wasn't
even to go up to the room, I just broke in there and
it all happened so unconcerned, so quick without fore-

thought, it wasn't arranged. I just broke in this room and it was all unexpected. As I remember it, it seems to me that Muyres asked me where I got them, it is all very vague in my mind. I don't think I told him. I don't remember if I did. There was nothing said whether they were stolen or not.

"I remember taking an automobile ride with Mr. Muyres the week following the week of October— ending Saturday, October the 26th.

"Q. Do you remember Mr. Muyres saying to you 'Are those bonds stolen?'

"A. Do I remember that?

"Q. Yes.

"A. I think I do.

"Q. And you admitted to him then that they were stolen?

"A. Yes.

"Q. And that is the first time you ever told Mr. Muyres that those bonds were stolen?

"A. That is the first time I had ever seen him; yes.

"Q. No, no. I mean—I am talking about an automobile ride about the following Wednesday?

"A. No. We never went for a ride on Wednesday. It was Saturday, the first automobile ride I had with Mr. Muyres. That was where we went to this street out there to Figueroa to cash the coupons. That was the first ride I ever had with him. I do not recall a ride with him the following week. I know for sure that I took one ride, that was the day we cashed the coupons, October 28th or 29th, I mean the 26th, the day we went to Murietta Hot Springs. I now recall that subsequent to our return from Murietta Hot Springs, either Wednesday or Thursday, I remember taking an automobile ride with Mr. Muyres to his home on Topaz, out there in a little house along the hill. That was the time that I was living at this hotel on Whittier Boulevard. I cannot recall whether it was practically said at that time by Mr. Muyres, 'Are those bonds stolen?', and I said 'yes'."

From Ryman's testimony, it is very clear that the only person with whom he in any way discussed the theft of the bonds or their transportation from Arizona to California was Ryan.

Ryman also testified that after he stole the bonds on October 22nd, 1935, he came to Phoenix to look for Ryan. Failing to find him, Ryman left a note telling Ryan to meet him in Los Angeles in front of the main post-office, either at noon or at 5 o'clock in the afternoon, as they had previously arranged. *Ryman then left alone for Los Angeles.* (Tr., p. 76.) *From all of this testimony, it is very plain that everything that had to do with the transportation of the bonds transpired only between Ryman and Ryan.* If appellant John F. Muyres had anything to do with the transportation feature of this case, it is inescapable that Ryman would not have left Phoenix without having looked up John F. Muyres and consulted with him before he left for Los Angeles. *Whatever part appellant may have played in this crime, it must be plain it was entirely limited to the selling phase, a crime not charged in this indictment.*

There was no incentive for Ryman to lie. He had pleaded guilty and was testifying for the Government.

Yet, there is not an iota of evidence in his lengthy testimony which would indicate that appellant John F. Muyres knew *before the transportation took place* that the bonds, in the sale of which he later participated, were stolen bonds. Nor, indeed, that he had any connection with the interstate transportation of them.

The only other Government witness whose testimony in any way related to appellant's knowledge of the stolen nature of the bonds, before transportation, was "Ham" Woolsey. He, as did Ryman, pleaded guilty. The strongest evidence in the entire record in this regard, appears in the Transcript of Record, page 108:

"The first time I talked to Muyres about them, I approached him and said 'Mr. Muyres, I have been approached by a man who says he has a bunch of hot bonds and wanted to know if I could handle it and knowing you like I do and knowing you had business contacts, what do you think about it?' He said 'hell yes, we can sell them.' In that conversation when I said 'hot bonds,' I believe I also said 'bonds that had been won on a gambling game by those men who have them.' After this conversation, Muyres and I talked frequently about the bonds. Shortly after this conversation, Muyres and his mother-in-law went to Los Angeles. I don't know how long he was gone. It was probably two or three days. When he returned, he said he had made a contact in Los Angeles and that he was positive he could dispose of them and for me to get in touch with Ryman and have him give him some bonds. Muyres made another trip to Los Angeles before the bonds were ever brought there. I can't tell you the date when I had this conversation with Muyres in which he told me he thought he could sell the bonds in Los Angeles. After this conversation, I told Ryan that the bonds could be sold. Ryan said he would send his partner after the bonds immediately. This conversation took place in Phoenix. Ryan told me his partner had to go east and get them. He never told me what town he had to go to but he said it would take some time to go and come. This conversation with Ryan was as near as I can remember about a week after Muyres told me he could sell the bonds. This conversation with Muyres after he returned from Los Angeles was the first time to my recollection that there was anything ever said that the bonds could be sold. It would be impossible for me to state how soon after October 22nd, which was the date when Ryan went to California, I had this conversation with Jack Muyres when he told me he could sell the bonds in Los Angeles."

And again in the Transcript of Record, page 110:

"I can't recall whether Ryan and Jack Muyres ever talked about these bonds in Arizona, because we negotiated over the deal so much but I don't say that they didn't have such conversations in Arizona."

And again in the Transcript of Record, page 112:

"Ryman went out and got what he called a full list and Muyres copied them all off. Muyres wanted them so that he could check to see if they were counterfeit and he told us he was going to check to see if he had learned whether the bonds had got 'hot' yet or not. Up to this time, these bonds were not referred to as 'stolen,' not to my recollection, but they were referred to as 'hot' bonds."

Even this testimony which is the only testimony the Government produced apart from inferences drawn from other inferences, does not preclude the belief that to the appellant John F. Muyres "hot" bonds meant not stolen bonds, but bonds won in gambling and, therefore, properly subject to be sold at a discount.

Ryman in his testimony stated he never told Ryan in Arizona that the bonds were stolen; yet Woolsey who according to his own testimony could only get his information from Ryan before the transportation took place, testified that it was understood by all the parties that "hot" bonds meant stolen bonds. The fact that Ryman received a sentence of eight years and Woolsey was placed on probation, might significantly point towards a genuine belief that Woolsey stretched a point in his testimony in order to bolster up this undeniably weak gap in the Government's case against John F. Muyres.

There is nothing in the sworn statement of John F. Muyres to indicate that he admitted he knew the bonds were stolen before the transportation took place; quite the contrary:

(A part of his sworn statement)

"About the middle of October, 1935, Ham Woolsey met me and told me that he knew a fellow who had a bunch of bonds and that he had asked Ham if he knew where they could be sold or disposed of. Ham asked me if I knew anybody this fellow could turn the bonds to. I told him I did not know anyone right at the time, but that I might know somebody in Los Angeles, California, who might know someone. I asked Ham at this time why the party or parties owning these bonds did not dispose of them, and Ham told me that these men were gamblers and they had got the bonds through gambling and that if they attempted to dispose of them, someone might be suspicious, that they were hot and thus destroy the deal." (Tr. of Rec., p. 132.)

Even in Woolsey's testimony, there is confirmation of appellant's contention that he did not know until he arrived in California that the bonds were stolen property.

"We came down and met him at the U. S. Hotel. Muyres said: 'Well, have you got some of the bonds?' He said no, but he said he was to meet his partner at 11 o'clock here in front of the post office. That he would have everything for him then. He came out and was gone awhile. Then he came back and he had three bonds wrapped in a newspaper. We looked them over and Muyres said 'Well, if you will get me the numbers of these bonds, I will go out and check up on them right away and some samples, so I can see whether they are bogus bonds or not.' By bogus I mean counterfeit." (Tr. of Rec., p. 100.)

"About a week or ten days after Ryan talked to me about these bonds, I first talked to Uncle Muyres about them. Before I talked to Muyres about the bonds, I have had frequent conversations with Ryan about them after the first time he mentioned them. The first time I talked to Muyres about them, I approached him and said 'Mr. Muyres, I have been approached by a man who says he has a bunch of hot bonds and wanted to know if I could handle it and knowing you like I do and knowing you have a business contact, what do you think about it?' He said 'hell yes, we can sell them.' In that conversation when I said 'hot bonds,' I believe I also said 'bonds that had been won on a gambling game by these men who have them.'" (Tr. of Rec., p. 108.)

"To the best of my recollection the first time that Ryan approached me relative to any bonds was in the early part of September. A few days after I had the first conversation with Ryan, I got in touch with Jack Muyres. Ryan approached me when I was behind the bar on duty and no one else heard the conversation that he approached me on but I presume there were other people in the building. Ryan approached me and said he had some hot bonds that he and his friend had won in a gambling game. He named the destination Kansas City and asked if I knew anyone who could dispose of the bonds and I said I would see if I could locate anybody. I am sure he used the word 'hot.'" (Tr. of Rec., p. 111.)

Some mention may be made by Government's counsel of the fact that appellant John F. Muyres in his statement to Government Officers indicated that he would plead guilty. In explaining this, appellant in his own defense had this to say:

"With reference to that last paragraph which reads, 'It is my intention to plead guilty for what I have done in this case, and throw myself on the mercy of the Court, so I can get this matter disposed of as soon as possible, and get it off and over with as quickly as permissible.' I did not know what the charges were, and where I made a mistake, and I said it and knew it then, was that the man told me these bonds were stolen, I should have reported them to the authorities, the evening of October 31st, when I took Ryman for the automobile ride alone around the corner and asked him 'Where did you get these bonds?' and he said 'I stole them' is the first I ever knew of the bonds being stolen." (Tr. of Rec., p. 216.)

While the record clearly shows that some time after appellant met the other defendants in Los Angeles, he knew that the bonds were stolen, or should have known from the actions of the other defendants, *we respectfully submit that there is no substantial evidence in the record to prove that appellant knew before the transportation of the bonds took place that the bonds were stolen property.*

B.

There is no Evidence Whatever in the Record Tending to Prove That Appellant John F. Muyres Knew That the Bonds Had Been Stolen in the State of Arizona or in Any Other State or Territory Other Than the State of California.

Although we have been unable to find any decisions under Section 415 of Title 18 of the *U. S. Code,* directly dealing with the prerequisite of proving the interstate character of the shipment, decisions under the analogous

National Motor Vehicle Theft Act (Section 408, Title 18, *U. S. Code*) indicate clearly that it is an elementary requirement that the Government must prove that the *defendant knew that the property was to be transported from one state to another.* See for example:

> *McCloud v. United States,* 75 F. (2d) 576;
> *Davidson v. United States,* 61 F. (2d) 250;
> *Loftus v. United States,* 46 F. (2d) 841.

The case of *United States v. Newhoff,* 83 F. (2d) 942, involved an indictment under Section 415, Title 18, *U. S. Code Annotated.* Although the case itself has no application to the facts at bar, the Court in speaking of the indictment under the statute said:

> "The first count of the indictment charged that the defendant Newhoff and Neuwirth conspired to receive, sell and dispose of bonds of the value upwards of $5,000 *which had been stolen while moving in interstate commerce.* The overt acts alleged were (1) receiving and selling seven Minnesota Land Bank Bonds and six Indiana Land Bank Bonds identified by numbers *which were moving in interstate commerce."* (Italics ours.)

Now again reverting to the record, the only Government witnesses who could shed any light on this question as to appellant John F. Muyres' knowledge or lack of knowledge of the interstate character of the transportation of the bonds, would be Ryman and Woolsey.

As to Ryman, we refer again to the excerpts of his testimony appearing above under point "A." Nowhere does it appear that John F. Muyres at any time knew that the bonds had been stolen in Arizona, so that interstate transportation would have to take place. *Ryman, who stole the bonds and sent them from Arizona to California, testified that he never met appellant in Arizona;* all that the record shows is that John F. Muyres knew that the bonds were in California and that he could sell them in California.

Nor does Woolsey in his testimony produce any evidence on this score. Even construing Woolsey's testimony most favorably for the Government, there is no proof whatever that John F. Muyres knew that the bonds had been stolen in Arizona; the only inference to be drawn from Woolsey's testimony *is that the bonds were to be sold in Los Angeles, California, but that is not the offense charged in either count of the indictment.*

Nor will a careful examination of John F. Muyres' own statement to the Government Officers offer any proof that he knew that they had been stolen in any other state but California.

As far as the record goes, there is nothing to contradict the statement of John F. Muyres made in his own defense that "I did not enter into any agreement of any kind with Woolsey, Ryan or Ryman, or any of them, to transport bonds from Arizona to California, and I never knew that these bonds was in any other place than California. As near as I knew, they might have been here all the time, for when I got back to Arizona, Ham said that the bonds were ·in California, and I did not know whether they had been there all the time, or how they got there, or where they came from." (Tr. of Rec., p. 217.)

It is, therefore, respectfully submitted that the verdict of guilty *on both counts must fall because of a failure of proof that appellant John F. Muyres knew that there was to be any interstate shipment of the bonds.*

C.

The Verdict of Guilty on Count I of the Indictment Must be Set Aside Because the Record Fails to Show Any Substantial Evidence Proving That as a Matter of Law Appellant Was Either a Principal or an Abettor to the Interstate Transportation of the Bonds.

Let us concentrate for a moment upon the first count of the indictment, that which charges the interstate transportation of the stolen bonds.

It is too plain to require discussion that John F. Muyres had nothing directly to do with the transportation of the bonds from Arizona to California. The only principal to that charge was Ryman, the man who stole the bonds and the man who sent them in a suitcase from Phoeniz, Arizona, to Huntington Park, California.

Appellant must have been convicted upon the first count, therefore, solely upon the theory that he was an aider and abettor to the transportation of the bonds from Arizona to California.

It is our position that under no legitimate theory of the law of aider and abettor would the evidence permit the conviction of appellant under the substantive charge of the indictment.

The "aider and abettor" statute (18 *U. S. Code Annotated,* Section 550) reads as follows:

> "Whoever directly commits an act constituting an offense defined in any law of the United States, or aids, abets, counsels, commands, induces or procures its commission, is a principal."

It is elementary that *knowledge* of the act constituting the substantive crime is a necessary part to establish one as a common law principal in the second degree as an aider and abettor, (1 *R. C. L.* 138.)

Where in the record does it appear that John F. Muyres knew that Ryman was going to transport the bonds which he would steal in Arizona, from Arizona to California? Even if we give to the Government the full benefit of the strongest interpretation of the evidence, it still only leaves us with the inference that before Ryman stole the bonds he asked Ryan if he knew where these bonds could be sold, and that Ryan then asked Woolsey and that Woolsey then asked John F. Muyres. But even if Woolsey did ask John F. Muyres if he could sell these "hot" bonds, and even if John F. Muyres did say he could sell them in Los Angeles, California, *there still must be filled in by the imagination gap after gap in the evidence to come to the necessary conclusion that before Muyres met Ryman in Los Angeles on October 23rd, that Muyres knew Ryman was going to steal the bonds in Arizona and knew that Ryman was going to send these bonds in interstate commerce from Arizona to Calfiornia.*

And far fetched as this inference would be from the record, it would still be insufficient without a strong showing that John F. Muyres in some tangible way actually assisted or aided in the act of transporting the bonds from Arizona to California.

Even if John F. Muyres told Woolsey that he could sell stolen bonds in California, which is assuming something not proved by the record, this in itself, in our opinion, would not be legally sufficient to make John F. Muyres an aider or abettor to the substantive charge of *transportation.*

While we appreciate that Courts are inclined to treat a conspiracy charge as a blanket, catch-all covering a multitude of loosely connected participants, the Court should and must require adequate legal proof before it uses the aider and abettor statute as a similar catch-all for alleged participation in a substantive charge. Otherwise, the substantive charge becomes a sham, and in practice all charges would be treated as similar to a conspiracy case. This is neither consonant with the common law principle of criminal liability nor is it a true application of the statutory prerequisites for a conviction upon a substantive charge as distinguished from a conspiracy count.

D.

In View of the Nature of the Government's Case, it Was Error to Allow the Introduction Into Evidence of the Testimony of Mrs. Woolsey, Wife of a Co-defendant Who Had Pleaded Guilty and Who Had Testified for the Government.

It must be apparent by now that the Government's case against John F. Muyres was based almost entirely upon inferences and circumstantial evidence. The more reason why the error herein assigned assumes a definite prejudicial character!

After the Government's case in chief had been about completed, the Assistant United States Attorney called as a witness in chief (not in rebuttal), a Mrs. Henrietta Woolsey, wife of the defendant "Ham" Woolsey, who had previously testified for the Government. Although when reduced to cold print, its effect is largely lost, we take the liberty of setting her testimony out in full:

"Mrs. Henrietta Woolsey,

called as a witness on behalf of the Government, having been first duly sworn, testified as follows:

"Direct Examination by Mr. Irwin:

"I am the wife of Mr. Ham Woolsey. I reside in Phoenix, Arizona. Mr. Woolsey has previously pleaded guilty in this case. I recall the time he was arrested, and after that I engaged counsel for him. In January of this year I received a communication from my husband with regard to keeping counsel I had retained. I then went to the office of that attorney. I told him what my husband had to say. That attorney was John Lee, who is in the Court Room. I know John F. Muyres. I saw him at my home since my husband was arrested. He first came to my home after he got his bond and returned to Phoenix. He came there alone. It was before Christmas. He was there in January, before the 31st, alone. He also came there in connection with the case in the month of February. At all times when he called it was in connection with the case. I was living with my mother. He was there around the 6th of February, because I was in bed then. He was alone that time and he talked to me in connection with the case. He came to my house in the month of March. On one of these visits John F. Muyres was accompanied by Mr. Lee, the attorney I had engaged for my husband. As far as I knew, Mr. Lee was then representing my husband. They were down there on the 7th of March of this year. I had just had my baby and they came down on Friday, the 6th, and mother would not let them see me and both came the next day to see me. I have been in bed. This is just two weeks today since I had my baby, since I have been up. On the 7th they talked to me about my husband, about what he was going to do and what his attitude was in this case.

("EXCEPTION No. 6)

"By Mr. Irwin:

"Q. I will ask you what was said by Mr. Lee or yourself or Mr. Muyres when Mr. Muyres was present on this occasion, the 7th of March, concerning the coming trial of this case?

"Mr. O'Hanneson:

"This is only against Mr. Muyres.

"Mr. Irwin:

"John F. Muyres.

"Mr. Ostrom:

"To which we object, if your Honor please, as being incompetent, irrelevant and immaterial and not tending to prove or disprove any of the points involved in this case.

"The Court:

"I cannot say, as it might be a statement against interest and if so it would be admissible.

"Mr. Irwin:

"It is so offered.

"The Court:

"Overruled.

"Mr. Ostrom:

"Exception, your Honor.

"Mr. Lee asked whether I wanted him to come over and defend my husband against his wishes or not, and he said that I did have the right, that if I wanted to and my husband had wrote and said he didn't want him, and I asked him what he would do since my husband had pleaded guilty, and he said there was only one thing he could do and that was to make a plea to the court to have him withdraw that plea on the allegation that my husband, being up in the jail like he has been, didn't know what he was talking about and didn't know what he had done. He wanted—I told him that I would not do anything until I talked to my sister, and after I talked to my sister I told him that I didn't want him to come over there, because my husband had said he didn't want him to and I didn't want to go against his wishes. So he told me if I wanted to come over by Tuesday, he would arrange transportation for me. When he left, after I told him that I didn't want him to go to defend my husband, why he said, 'If you change your mind by Tuesday, you can let me know and I will see that you get transportation.' I told him that I—I asked him if he was coming over anyhow, and he said yes, he thought he was, and if I wanted to come, he would see that I got transportation over. I didn't know my husband was going to change his plea. I didn't know it then, because that was before the 10th. He made his plea on the. 10th. I knew it on the 10th. I knew it then, because he made his plea on the 10th and this was after the 10th of March. That was after they came for that conversation. He had already changed his plea to guilty, and Mr. Muyres came down and that conversation was had at my house. At the time when Mr. Lee and Mr. Muyres were down there talking to me I told them I didn't have any money at all. They said there was some money over here and that if they could keep the money, the lawyers' fees would be paid out of that. They didn't say that the money would come right off from the bonds. They said that the money was tied up over here in the bank and they were not allowed to use it.

"Cross-examination by Mr. Ostrom:

"Mr. Lee and Mr. Muyres came there on the 6th, but I didn't see them. I was in bed and mother wouldn't let them in. One came first and then the other. On the 7th they came and I saw them both in the presence of each other. My mother was in and out of the room. This conversation took approximately half an hour or so. Mr. Lee told me on that occasion that Mr. Woolsey had never communicated to him the facts that would warrant a plea of guilty. Around the 7th of that month my husband had told Mr. Lee he didn't want him. I don't remember Mr. Lee making the statement to me that Mr. Woolsey had told him the facts of the case. Mr. Lee said to me in substance that from what information he, Mr. Lee, had obtained from my husband, that he, Mr. Lee, did not feel that my husband should have entered a plea of guilty. Mr. Lee on that same occasion said to me that he, Mr. Lee, did not believe that my husband was in a state of mind where he knew what he was doing when he entered his plea of guilty. Mr. Lee also told me that from what he had learned from Mr. Woolsey when he was representing my husband, that he did not believe my husband was guilty, or words to that effect.

"Re-direct examination by Mr. Irwin:

"These conversations were had on the 7th before leaving to come over here, and the day of sentence was set for March 10th. They came back when I had this conversation in that connection. When they called on March 7th, I had been in bed two days." (Tr. of Rec., pp. 149-152.)

What possible materiality would this testimony have? It does not show any guilt on the part of appellant John F. Muyres, nor any guilty conduct on the part after the commission of the offense. The "strategy" of the prosecution becomes obvious when attention is called to other parts of the record. Earlier in the case, the same Mr. Lee referred to in Mrs. Woolsey's testimony, while appearing as attorney for the defendant Ryan, attempted to cross-examine Mr. Woolsey. Mr. Woolsey objected on the ground that Mr. Lee had at one time represented him and that the communications between them remained confidential. The cross-examination was halted. (Tr. of Rec., p. 107.)

Subsequently, Mrs. Woolsey testified as outlined. Later, as part of the defense of John F. Muyres, Mr. Lee was called to testify as to the same conversation about which Mrs. Woolsey had testified as a witness for the Government. Before he concluded his testimony, however, he abruptly ended by stating "I do not believe I am privileged to recite the entire conversation because of Mr. Woolsey's request." (Tr. of Rec., pp. 221, 222.) The obvious purpose of the testimony of Mrs. Woolsey was to have the jury draw an inference that John F. Muyres and the attorney Lee had contacted Mrs. Woolsey while she was sick and in bed and attempted to coerce her into persuading her husband to change his plea back from guilty to not guilty. This testimony could have only one effect on the jury, namely, to degrade the defendant John F. Muyres before it. It must have been known to the Government prosecutor that whatever Mrs. Woolsey testified to could hardly be rebutted by Mr. Lee because of the relationship of attorney and client existing between Mr. Lee and Mr. Woolsey. It is submitted that this type of "strategy" goes far beyond legitimate bounds and is actually prejudicial towards the appellant John F.

Muyres. Particularly as in the case here where the evidence against the accused is entirely circumstantial and inferential, the accused is entitled to all legitimate safeguards, which were denied him by these tactics on behalf of the Government's prosecutor.

E.

In View of the Nature of the Government's Case, It Was Error for the Trial Judge to Refuse to Give Appellant John F. Muyres' Requested Instruction Number 13.

The appellant John F. Muyres filed a written request that the Court give an instruction to the effect that the jury may not draw inferences from other inferences but only from facts actually proved. (Requested Instruction Number 13.) The Court failed to give this instruction and failed to discuss this matter in any of the instructions which it gave. At the close of the oral instructions by the Court, the Court asked whether or not there were any objections to the instructions or any exceptions to the instructions *on behalf of the defendants.* Mr. Graham, attorney of record for the defendant George Muyres, stated that there were exceptions and then proceeded to enumerate certain exceptions including the failure to give the instruction herein noted. Practically identical instructions were requested by both the defendant John F. Muyres and the defendant George Muyres. In fact the requested instruction herein noted appears on Number 13 on behalf of both defendants. While it is true that Graham stated that he excepted on behalf of defendant George Muyres to the failure of the Court to give requested instruction Number 13, it must be obvious from the record that Graham was handling the matter of exceptions to instructions on behalf of all the defendants. While it is true that ordinarily a failure to give an instruction not specifically excepted to will not be considered by the Appellate Court, there are numerous cases to the effect that the Appellate Court may as a matter of grace, where the failure to give the instruction was a serious error, consider this matter and order a reversal, even though a specific exception was not noted.

> *United States v. Vignito,* 67 F. (2d) 329, Certiorari Denied, 290 U. S. 705;
> *United States v. Sprinkle,* 57 F. (2d) 968;
> *Smith v. United States,* 47 F. (2d) 518.

This requested instruction was more than a mere formality. There are numerous cases to the effect that the failure to give an instruction to the effect that inferences may not be drawn from other inferences but only from facts proved and in evidence, is sufficiently serious to warrant a reversal on that ground.

> *United States v. Ross,* 92 U. S. 281 at 283.

> "It is obvious that this presumption could have been made only by piling inference upon inference, and presumption upon presumption. * * * These seem to us to be nothing more than conjectures. They are not legitimate inferences, even to establish a fact; much less are they presumptions of law. They are inferences from inferences; presumptions resting on the basis of another presumption. Such a mode of

arriving at a conclusion of fact is generally, if not universally, inadmissible. No inference of fact or of law is reliable drawn from premises which are uncertain. Whenever circumstantial evidence is relied upon to prove a fact, the circumstances must be proved, and not themselves presumed. * * * It is upon this principle that courts are daily called upon to exclude evidence as too remote for the consideration of the jury. The law requires an open, visible connection between the principal and evidentiary facts and the deductions from them, and does not permit a decision to be made on remote inferences. * * *."

Gargotta v. United States, 77 F. (2d) 977 at 982.

"This Court has likewise held, and it is well settled in this circuit, that presumptions cannot be based on presumptions. * * *

Nations v. United States, 52 F. (2d) 97 at 105.

"Such double inferences are too remote to constitute evidence * * *."

Dahly v. United States, 50 F. (2d) 37;
Niderlucke v. United States, 21 F. (2d) 511;
Keen v. United States, 11 F. (2d) 260;
Wagner v. United States, 8 F. (2d) 581 at 586.

Here the Government's case as against appellant John F. Muyres was obviously based on inferences and circumstantial evidence. The appellant was certainly entitled to an instruction which would caution the jury against drawing inferences from other inferences. The failure to give this instruction was obviously of serious moment to John F. Muyres. The purpose of requiring an exception to the failure to give a requested instruction is that the Court may have an opportunity to determine whether to give the instruction. The function of an exception was actually met in this case because an exception to the failure to give the identical instruction was actually made. Therefore, the Court was given the opportunity to cover the requested instruction if it so desired. It is, therefore, not unfair to call to the attention of this Court the failure of the trial court to give this requested instruction. In view of the seriousness of the omission of this requested instruction, it is respectfully submitted that this Court should as a matter of grace if not as a matter of right, consider whether or not there was reversible error in failing to give this instruction.

IV.

Conclusion

This is not intended to be a routine appeal in a criminal case.

Appellant John F. Muyres, now in his fifties, is faced with a very severe sentence of seven years in the penitentiary, nearly six years of which he must serve before he will be eligible for parole. Ryman, the man who stole the bonds and who is responsible for the whole situation and who is guilty of transporting the bonds from one state to another, is given a maximum sentence of eight years and need serve less than three years before he is eligible for parole.

While we realize that we cannot urge this Honorable Court to interfere with the sentence though it is grossly unfair upon its face, we do feel confident that we have a right on behalf of appellant to urge a most careful weighing of the case in an effort to justly determine whether the record warrants conviction of the appellant upon each of the two counts of the indictment.

In summary, we sincerely urge that the record fails to be supported by that substantiality of evidence which is indispensable to sustain a verdict of guilty because: (.1) the court erred in denying the motion of John F. Muyres for an instructed verdict of "Not Guilty" made at the conclusion of all the evidence on the ground that there was no substantial evidence in the record proving that John F. Muyres knew that the bonds were stolen before the transportation or the conspiracy to transport took place; (2) there is no evidence whatever in the record tending to prove that appellant John F. Muyres knew that the bonds had been stolen in the State of Arizona or in any other state or territory other than the State of California; and (3) the verdict of guilty on count one of the indictment must be set aside because the record fails to show any substantial evidence proving that as a matter of law appellant was either a principal or an abettor to the interstate transportation of the bonds.

Apart from the flimsiness of the Government's case against this appellant, two errors in the conduct of the trial deprived appellant of a fair hearing: (1) In view of the nature of the Government's case, it was error to allow the introduction into evidence of the testimony of Mrs. Woolsey, wife of a co-defendant who had pleaded guilty and who had testified for the Government; and (2) in view of the nature of the Government's case, it was error for the trial judge to refuse to give appellant John F. Muyres' requested instruction Number 13.

For these reasons, it is our firm conviction that the case must be reversed.

Respectfully submitted,

HARRY GRAHAM BALTER,

L. A. BLOOM,

Attorneys for Appellant John F. Muyres.

Circuit Court of Appeals

SUBJECT INDEX

CITATIONS AND AUTHORITIES

JOHN F. MUYRES and GEORGE J. MUYRES,

Appellants,

vs.

UNITED STATES OF AMERICA,

Appellee.

Brief of Appellee

Preliminary Statement

On December 16th, 1935, an indictment was returned in the Southern District of Caliornia, Central Division, against Harold Edward Ryman, Thomas Burke Ryan, Franklin Dolph LeSieur, Karl L. Woolsey, John F. Muyres, George J. Muyres and John Murray Cheney, the First Count of which indictment charged that in violation of Title 18, Section 415, *United States Code Annotated,* the defendants "on or about the 22nd day of October, 1935, did knowingly, wilfully, unlawfully and feloniously transport and cause to be transported in interstate commerce from the State of Arizona to Huntington Park, County of Los Angeles, State of California,

* * * certain securities of the value of more than $5,000.00, to-wit, of the value of $42,500.00, to-wit, (herein follows detailed description of the bonds) * * * all of said securities being then and there the property of Nellie P. Covert and having been theretofore stolen from the said Nellie P. Covert, the said defendants and each of them then and there well knowing said securities to have been stolen."

The Second Count of the indictment charged that in violation of Title 18, Section 88, *United States Code Annotated,* the same defendants "did knowingly, wilfully, unlawfully, corruptly and feloniously conspire, combine, confederate, arrange and agree together and with each other and with divers other persons whose names are to the grand jurors unknown, to commit an offense against the United States of America and the laws thereof, the offense being to knowingly, wilfully, unlawfully and feloniously transport and cause to be transported in interstate commerce from the State of Arizona to the County of Los Angeles, California, certain securities of the value of more than Five Thousand Dollars ($5,000.00), to-wit: those securities described in count one of this indictment, all of said securities being then and there the property of Nellie P. Covert, and having been theretofore stolen from the said Nellie P. Covert, as the defendants well knew." (Tr., of Rec., pp. 4 to 11.)

The defendant Franklin Dolph LeSieur was never brought to trial.

On March 18th, 1936, the case was called for trial before the Honorable George Cosgrave, Judge of the

United States District Court, Southern District of California.

The Government dismissed the case as against the defendant John Murray Cheney.

Defendants Edward Harold Ryman and Karl L. Woolsey had changed their pleas from "Not Guilty" to "Guilty."

A trial by jury proceeded against the defendants Thomas Burke Ryan, John F. Muyres, appellant herein, and George J. Muyres.

The jury returned a verdict of "Guilty" as against the defendant Thomas Burke Ryan on both counts of the indictment, as against the defendant John F. Muyres on both counts of the indictment, and as against the defendant George J. Muyres on only the second count of the indictment, the count charging conspiracy. (Tr. of Rec., p. 47.)

On April 7th, 1936, the following sentences were meted out:

(1) The defendant George J. Muyres was sentenced to two years in a Federal Penitentiary together with a fine of $1,000.00.

(2) Defendant Edward Harold Ryman was sentenced to eight years on Count One and two years on Count Two to run concurrently.

(3) Defendant Thomas Burke Ryan was sentenced to three years on Count One and two years on Count Two to run concurrently.

(4) Defendant Karl L. Woolsey was granted probation on both Counts.

(5) Defendant John F. Muyres, appellant herein, was sentenced to imprisonment in a Federal Penitentiary for five years upon the first count and to imprisonment in a Federal Penitentiary for two years on the second count, the sentences to run consecutively, totaling a seven-year penitentiary term, and in addition thereto, a fine of $1,000.00 upon the second count. (Tr. of Rec., pp. 49 to 52.)

On April 13th, 1936, John F. Muyres filed a written notice of appeal from the conviction, setting out as his grounds for appeal the following:

"1. That the Court erred in denying the motion for a directed verdict requested by the defendant John F. Muyres;

"2. That the Court gave erroneous and prejudicial instructions to the jury;

"3. That the Court erred in denying certain requested instructions on behalf of the defendant John F. Muyres;

"4. That the evidence was legally insufficient to sustain the verdict of the jury." (Tr., of Rec., p. 248.)

Assignments of error were filed on behalf of John F. Muyres setting out substantially the same grounds. (Tr. of Rec., p. 251.)

George J. Muyres filed his notice of appeal and from the assignments of error thereafter filed by the appellant George J. Muyres it appears that his two principal grounds of appeal are the alleged insufficiency of the evidence to support the verdict of guilty as to the appel-

lant George J. Muyres and errors of the Court in denying certain requested instructions by the defendant
George J. Muyres.

I.

The Evidence Was Sufficient to Support the Verdict of Guilty Returned Against the Defendant John F. Muyres.

It was the contention of the Government at the trial
that the evidence showed that, while the bonds of Miss
Nellie Covert were stolen in Tucson, Arizona, by the
defendant Edward Ryman alone, the theft was not
attempted until the defendant Ryman was advised by
his codefendant Ryan that arrangements had been made
to dispose of the bonds in Los Angeles and that he,
Ryman, should go and get them. While there was but
slight direct evidence imputing knowledge to the appellant
John F. Muyres of the fact that the bonds were stolen
bonds prior to their arrival in California and their transportation in interstate commerce, much circumstantial
evidence was received and considered showing that the
appellant John F. Muyres' actions prior to the theft of
the bonds and during their shipment, together with his
actions in Los Angeles after the bonds' arrival here.

The direct evidence which, it is contended, establishes
that the defendant appellant John F. Muyres' knowledge
of the bonds and their stolen condition is to be found in
the testimony of the defendant Karl Woolsey. (Tr. of
Rec., pp. 94, *et seq.*)

Woolsey, it will be observed, testified in substance that
in the summer of 1935 he was employed as a bartender

at the Avalon Cafe, Phoenix, Arizona, (it appears from the testimony of defendant John F. Muyres that he was the owner of that cafe); that in the early part of September, 1935, he was approached by the defendant Ryan, who said:

"* * * he noticed I had quite a few personal friends there, leading business men of the city and he told me he had a bunch of 'hot' bonds and asked me if I thought I could dispose of them. I told him I would let him know a little later, that I would look into the thing. I asked him from what source they came and he said that he and his partner had won them through gambling and I asked him where and he said 'back in the east.' I said what part of the east, and he said 'Kansas City,' so I said 'I'll see what I can do.' * * * I talked to Jack Muyres. Owing to the fact that I had a lot of business dealings with Muyres and we had been in business together, he dawned on me as a prospect who might know of some place to place a bond. I knew he had big connections in Los Angeles so I went to him and told him that Ryan had approached me with a bunch of bonds that he called 'hot' bonds and that at the time Ryan approached me, he thought there was in the neighborhood of $74,000.00. I asked Muyres if he knew where we could dispose of them. His remark to me was 'hell yes, get me some of the bonds.' I later went back and asked Ryan for some of the bonds. He said he would have to send his partner after them. He was supposed to have gone after them and Muyres and his mother-in-law in the meantime made a trip to California on some kind of business and he said he would look into it while he was over here. He had in mind seeing some firend of .his here about it. When he returned back, he told me that friend that he had intended to see was up in Canada. * * * He told me later that he contacted his nephew at 4801 Whittier Boulevard and they talked it over.

"A. He said he had some contact with his nephew there; that him and his lady friend had met him at 4801 Whittier Boulevard, and they talked it over, and would get—and if I would get in the bonds, why, he could—he was sure he could find a sale for them.

"Q. Who could get the bonds?

"A. If I could get the bonds from Ryan, why, then, he would dispose of the bonds.

"Q. Where?

"A. He could bring them to California to sell."

" * * * That Jack Muyres' nephew and his lady friend had met him there and that if I would get him the bonds, why he was sure he could find a sale for them. He would bring them to California to sell. I went back and told Ryan that I would like to have the bonds." (Tr. of Rec., p. 98.)

"He said his partner was away for them so Muyres got in his car and returned to California and Ryan and Ryman were to come and meet him there. * * * The morning of October 22nd, Ryan came in and asked me to loan him $10.00 so that he could come to California. He said this man had left with the bonds for California and asked me where Muyres was. I said 'over there waiting for you' in California. Before Muyres left, I had talked to Muyres that he could be reached in Los Angeles at 4801 Whittier Boulevard at Jack's Filling Station by which I understood that he meant it was his station. * * * " (Tr. of Rec., pp. 98, 99.)

Thereafter Woolsey testified that on the evening of October 22nd he left word at John Muyres' house that if he returned from California he would see Woolsey immediately. Muyres came to his home about 7:30 and after being informed by Woolsey that Ryman was in California with the bonds, Muyres stated that if Woolsey would get up and keep him awake, as he was very tired, they would drive over that night. This they did. That they drove all night, arrived in Los Angeles at 4 o'clock in the morning. They arose at 7 o'clock and went to Jack's Service Station and while having breakfast, Muyres was called to the phone, returned and told Woolsey that it was Ryan and that he, Ryan, was at the U. S. Hotel and wanted to see them right away.

> "We came down and met him at the U. S. Hotel. Muyres said, 'Well, have you got some of the bonds?' He said no, but he said he was to meet his partner at 11 o'clock here in front of the post office. That he would have everything for him then. He came out and was gone awhile. Then he came back and he had three bonds wrapped in a newspaper. We looked them over and Muyres said, 'Well, if you will get me the numbers of these bonds, I will go out and check up on them right away and some samples, so I can see whether they are bogus bonds or not.' By bogus I mean counterfeit." (Tr. of Rec., p. 100.)

That Muyres and Ryan went out together and when he saw Muyres that night he told him that Ryman (the one who stole the bonds), who had come into the room at the U. S. Hotel that morning while Muyres, Ryan and Woolsey were there, had turned a bunch of the bonds over to them and he had taken them down and turned them over to his nephew. Muyres further told Woolsey that they would have to make some kind of arrangement before the bonding house would accept them. That they would take someone and make them a member of the Southern California Athletic Club and also have to deposit $100.00 in the bank so that the man would have a place of residence and so that the man who bought the bonds would have somebody to refer back to in event the bonds were illegal.

It is the contention of the defense that the defendant John F. Muyres was told simply that the bonds were won in gambling. It will be seen from the evidence just quoted that from the first these bonds were referred to as "hot" bonds but claimed that they were won in gambling. While an attempt is made to play on words and assert that the defendant and appellant Muyres believed the bonds were "hot" simply because they had been won in a gambling game. Such an assertion was for approval or rejection left to the jury. Upon the surrounding circumstances the jury was more than warranted in disbelieving the defendant John Muyres and accepting the vernacular interpretation of "hot" as stolen. First of all no business man would feel it necessary to go out of his state to assist in the sale of negotiable bonds merely because they were won in gambling, nor would he after returning from a business trip to Los Angeles in the evening at 7 o'clock return that same night again by auto upon being advised that the bonds had left for California in the custody of Ryman and Ryan that same day. It is plain from the circumstances of the first meeting in

Los Angeles in the hotel room at the U. S. Hotel that
what the defendant John F. Muyres, as a business man,
wanted to make certain of, was that the bonds were not
counterfeit but were in fact as represented, negotiable
bonds which had not yet been reported stolen. Further
strength is given this interpretation by the following
excerpt from Woolsey's testimony:

> "One of the things said back in Arizona was that
> Ryan told me 'we'll get away from the fact that they
> were won by gambling. The bonds were 'hot' enough
> but they will never be missed until the first of the
> year owing to the fact that they have all of these
> coupons on them and the party wouldn't go to them
> until the first of the year and we can sell them and
> clean up and all go before the bonds were missed."
> (Tr. of Rec. 101.)

In response to cross examination of the defendant
Ryman (the one who stole the bonds) by defendant Ryan
who for a time represented himself at the trial, Ryman
said:

> "After some conversations we discussed the mat-
> ter of bonds and I told you I knew where there
> were a lot of bonds and I think I asked you whether
> you knew where you could sell some bonds. I told
> you, first, that I would have to take them from
> somebody else's house. I didn't tell you I had them.
> If they had belonged to me I would have taken them
> to a bank. If they had belonged to me I would not
> have gone to you to have you sell them for me. * * *
> After you told me you had a buyer for the bonds
> you asked me to produce the bonds. * * * It would
> take three or four days to get them and I wanted

to be sure that you had a buyer for them and you explained to me that there wasn't any question in your mind that if the bonds were not counterfeit, were not hot, that you had a sale for them." (Tr. of Rec. 90, 91.)

Upon his re-direct examination Ryman again emphasized the purpose of giving the list of bonds he had to the defendant and appellant John F. Muyres when they met in the U. S. Hotel here in Los Angeles the same morning that the defendants Muyres and Woolsey arrived by auto from Arizona.

"The purpose of giving the list was not to see whether the bonds had been stolen but whether they had been reported stolen." (Tr. of Rec., 92.)

Further evidence, which we submit was properly considered by the jury in looking to the defendant John Muyres' intent in associating himself with the enterprise of the disposal of the bonds, completely discredits his contention that he did not know the bonds were stolen. In his testimony defendant John F. Muyres after detailing his alleged care and caution as to the source of the bonds stated that one morning about a week after they first met in Los Angeles defendant Ryman (the one who stole the bonds) told him they were stolen and that he was very much upset about it. (Tr. of Rec., 212.) But he goes on to say that the next day following this discovery he contacted his nephew who was disposing of the bonds, and his nephew, George Muyres, gave him some of the bonds back and around $2,000.00 in money, that he went back to the hotel and met Woolsey, Ryan and Ryman:

> "I threw the envelope on the bed, money and all. Eddie Ryman picked it up and figured up the split, and he told Woolsey and Ryan to go out of the room, and they went out of the room for a minute, and he said 'Will you take bonds, instead of money?' I said 'Yes,' and he said 'I will give you a Home Owners Loan and an Austrian.' I said 'That is all right.'
>
> "I took these bonds and went up to my mother-in-law's house * * * and left them there." (Tr. of Rec., 213, 214.)

There was introduced by the defendant and appellant through his counsel a longhand statement made by the defendant on the date of his arrest in Phoenix, Arizona, November 18, 1935, wherein he said in part after relating how Ham Woolsey approached him about disposing of some bonds,

> "I asked Ham at this time why the party or parties owning these bonds did not dispose of them, and Ham told me that these men were gamblers and they had got the bonds through gambling and that if they attempted to dispose of them, someone might be suspicious, that they were hot, and thus destroy the deal." (Tr. of Rec., 132.)

The task of accurately directing this Honorable Court's attention to every pertinent circumstance in the record which we contend substantially establishes defendant John F. Muyres' guilty knowledge, is a difficult one. We respectfully submit, however, that the statement of John

F. Muyres beginning on page 131 of the Transcript together with the excerpts from the testimony of the defendants Ryan and Woolsey herein quoted, show a chain of evidence both direct and circumstantial which more than justified the jury in finding that the defendant appellant John F. Muyres was guilty. Further that his knowledge of the true character of the bonds dated from the day he was first approached by his bartender Carl Woolsey in the appellant John F. Muyres' cafe in Phoenix, Arizona.

It should be noted that while the record is not clear it would appear that no exception was taken by the counsel for the defendant appellant John F. Muyres to the ruling of the Court denying the motion for directed verdict on the grounds of the insufficiency of the evidence. (Tr. of Rec., 224.)

II.

The Defendant Appellant Contends That the Jury Was Improperly Instructed.

Since the same instructions were submitted by both appellants, discussion of this point is reserved.

III.

The Evidence Is Sufficient to Sustain the Verdict of Guilty As to the Appellant George J. Muyres.

As has been pointed out, the defendant George J. Muyres was convicted on the conspiracy charge and acquitted on the substantative charge. As will be seen from the indictment, the defendants were charged with conspiracy to transport in interstate commerce certain securities and this conspiracy was formed prior to the date of the overt acts alleged in the indictment, the overt acts which are particularly applicable being overt acts No. 1 and No. 2, occurring on October 22, 1935, and October 23, 1935, respectively. In approaching a presentation of the Government's position that there was substantial evidence to go to the jury upon the question of the guilt or innocence of the appellant, it is desired to advert to several well established principles regarding the law of conspiracy. In the case of *Craig v. United States,* 81 F. (2d) 816, at page 827 (C. C. A. 9th), the Honorable Justice Garrecht said:

> "To sustain a conviction, we need not be convinced *beyond reasonable doubt* that the defendant is guilty: it is sufficient if there is in the record substantial evidence to sustain the verdict.

> "In Felder v. United States (C. C. A. 2) 9 F. (2d) 872, 875, * * * the court said:

> " 'That we cannot investigate it (the testimony) to pass on the weight of the evidence is a point too often decided to need citation; nor can we, after investigation, use such doubts as may assail us to disturb the verdict of the jury. *The reasonable doubt which often prevents conviction must be the jury's doubt, and not that of any court, either original or appellate.* (Cases cited.) Our duty is but to declare whether the jury had the right to pass on what evidence there was.' (Italics ours.)

> "The correct rule was thus tersely phrased in Humes v. United States, 170 U. S. 210, * * * :

" 'The alleged fact that the verdict was against the weight of evidence we are precluded from considering, if there was any evidence proper to go to the jury in support of the verdict.' "

It is admitted that the defendant George J. Muyres did not know any of his alleged coconspirators with the exception of his uncle, John F. Muyres. It is further admitted that the defendant George Muyres was not in Arizona at or about the time of the theft of the bonds. It is further admitted that the defendant George Muyres' participation in the conspiracy, if one existed, must have commenced before the bonds completed their transportation from Arizona to California.

It is respectfully submitted that the conspiracy to transport the bonds to California was suggested and completed by the appellant John Muyres. We have but to revert to the testimony of Karl Woolsey to establish that fact. Woolsey in substance testified that he was approached by Ryan (who had first been approached by Ryman); that Ryan told him that he had a bunch of hot bonds and he wanted Woolsey's help in disposing of them; that he thereupon talked to John Muyres and John Muyres, in response to Woolsey's inquiry if he knew where the bonds could be disposed of, said, "hell yes, get me some of the bonds;" that Woolsey went back and asked Ryan for some of the bonds and Ryan said he would have to send his partner (Ryman) after them; that John Muyres was to make a trip to Los Angeles and he said to Woolsey that he (Muyres) would look into it while he was there, that he had in mind seeing some friend in Los Angeles about it; that when John Muyres returned from Los Angeles he told Woolsey that the friend whom he had intended to see was in Canada and that he (Muyres) had contacted his nephew at 4801 Whittier Boulevard. (Tr. of Rec., pp. 95-96.)

To repeat, we submit that it was the appellant John F. Muyres who originated the conspiracy to transport the bonds to California and the agreement was made at that time. It has been our contention that in dealing with a conspiracy it is not essential that the persons act together in a formal manner ordinarily found in lawful transactions.

United States v. Wilson, 23 F. (2d) 112.

It has been repeatedly held that a person joining and participating in a conspiracy after its formation is equally guilty with the originators.

United States v. Wilson, 23 F. (2d) 112.

It is likewise the law that a defendant is responsible for the acts of his coconspirators committed before as well as after he joined the conspiracy.

Baker v. United States, 276 U. S. 621.

A conspirator is liable though he was never in the state where the overt acts were committed.

Ferracane v. United States, 29 F. (2d) 691 (C. C. A. 7th).

In applying the rules just cited to the evidence adduced and received against the appellant George Muyres, we find the following chain of circumstances: Woolsey testified that John Muyres said that the bonds should be disposed of in California. John Muyres went to California and came back and told Woolsey that he (Muyres) had talked the matter over with his nephew, that the bonds could be disposed of. Woolsey then gave the word to Ryan and Ryan in turn gave the word to Ryman, who then went and stole the bonds and shipped them to Los Angeles. (Tr. of Rec., pp. 94-95.) (It should be noted that Woolsey's testimony was not at first received against the appellant George Muyres until he had been further connected with the enterprise.)

Both John Muyres and George Muyres admitted that on the occasion of the trip to Los Angeles of John Muyres, referred to by Woolsey, he, John Muyres, called his nephew on the telephone and George Muyres came out to Jack's Service Station at 4801 Whittier Boulevard, where John Muyres discussed whether or not George Muyres knew of anybody who could dispose of some bonds. They both denied that anything was said about the bonds being hot. (Tr. of Rec., p. 199.) It should be noted in this connection that George Muyres made two statements, Government's Exhibit 27 (Tr. of Rec., pp. 168 *et seq.*) and Government's Exhibit 28 (Tr. of Rec., p. 174). In the first statement, on page 169 of the Transcript of Record, made when George Muyres was first arrested in Denver, Colorado, on November 27, 1935, he stated that John Muyres came to the Automobile Club of Southern California and told him, George Muyres, that he had some bonds and would like him to sell them; that this was on October 12th or 15th; and that the following day John Muyres called him out to the service station and gave him a couple of bonds. In the second statement, on page 174 of the Transcript of Record, made at Los Angeles, December 3, 1935, George Muyres corrected that portion of his earlier statement and said that on October 14th or 15th John Muyres phoned him at his, George Muyres' office at the Automobile Club of Southern California and asked him to come out to Jack's Service Station and during the ensuing conversation he mentioned some bonds. George Muyres stated that he did not commit himself one way or the other in regard to the disposition of such bonds mentioned. He further stated that on or about October 23rd or 24th his uncle, John Muyres, phoned him at the Automobile Club and asked him to come out to Muyres' brewery, which he did that evening; that John Muyres gave him an envelope containing four to six bonds; that the brewery was closed and his uncle handed him the bonds in front of the brewery. He denied that he was at any time given a list of bonds by his uncle.

It was argued to the jury that this statement was false because: His uncle, John Muyres, testified that the first conversation had with George Muyres relative to the bonds was in Jack's Service Station on approximately the 16th of October and that, while George Muyres at that time said he did not know anyone who had bonds, he called on the 18th and said that he had a friend with whom he played squash who was in the bond business and advised John Muyres to give him the business. (Tr. of Rec., p. 199.) Furthermore, as has been previously shown, immediately upon his return from Los Angeles to Arizona, John Muyres told Woolsey that he had seen his nephew and that the bonds could be disposed of through him at Los Angeles. It was urged that Woolsey's testimony was supported by the surrounding circumstances and that George Muyres did not state the truth as to the conversation which he had with his uncle. The surrounding circumstances, as has been previously referred to at some length in a discussion of the evidence, were that John Muyres returned to Phoenix and told Woolsey that the bonds could be sold in California; that Woolsey told Ryan; that Ryan told Ryman; and that Ryman stole the bonds on the 22d of October and shipped them by Express to Los Angeles that night and came here. John Muyres, who had during this interim again come to California to await Ryan and Ryman, returned to Phoenix on the night of October 23rd. He and Woolsey left that night by automobile and the next morning in Los Angeles were contacted on the phone by Ryan. John Muyres after being given a list of the bonds went immediately to contact George Muyres. John Muyres said that he took samples of the bonds to George Muyres at the Automobile Club that same day. (George Muyres in his statement said that he was handed the bonds in the evening outside the Muyres' brewery. Tr. of Rec., p. 175.) George Muyres said that he never had a list of the bonds nor did he ever see any list of any bonds. (Tr. of Rec., p. 175.) John Muyres said that pursuant to George Muyres' request he took the list of the bonds, went to the Automobile Club, and gave that list to his nephew, George Muyres. (Tr. of Rec., pp. 201-205.)

The witness, Ira C. Hilger, testified that he was a bond broker; that he had been advised that George Muyres had come into some money; that he called Muyres on the phone about the 23rd of October soliciting his business; that George Muyres told him the amount of bonds which Mr. Hilger had been advised George Muyres was to receive was excessive and there were instead about $48,000.00 or $49,000.00 worth of bonds; that George Muyres came to his, Hilger's, office and called on him; that George Muyres said that these bonds were from an estate of his grandparents in Holland, which had been settled, and that these bonds were George Muyres' share and that he was also going to help his uncle in selling them. Hilger testified that George Muyres asked him if the bonds could be checked as to whether anything might be the matter with them as to title; that he told Muyres that they could be checked very easily and that it could be done right then but George Muyres said that he was afraid there might be something the matter with the title because of his uncle's past reputation. George Muyres then said that he preferred not to have them check the bonds because he did not want to cause his uncle any undue trouble. (Tr. of Rec., pp. 164-165.)

On cross-examination Mr. Hilger stated that he told George Muyres that banks or large New York brokerage houses had lists of stolen bonds so that any big brokerage house could check them; that the New York brokerage houses so described included E. F. Hutton and Company; and that they had lists of bonds *which were reported as stolen.* (Italics supplied.)

On re-direct examination Hilger stated that they did not have a record of all negotiable bonds or Government bonds in circulation if there had been no report on them, that on those bonds whatever may have been their condition, if it was not reported, Hilger could not check them nor could anyone else, that if they were not reported stolen he, Hilger, would not be able to check them. (Tr. of Rec., pp. 165-166.)

The witness, John Murray Cheney, testified that he was employed as an equipment clerk in the Department of Physical Education in the gymnasium of the University of Southern California; that he knew defendant George Muyres who played squash at the gymnasium about twice a week; that George Muyres called him on the phone on the 23rd of October and asked him if he knew anyone who knew anything about bonds; that he referred Muyres to a young man by the name of Bassett who was a graduate student in the University; that he understood he had an account with E. F. Hutton and Company; that an appointment was made with Bassett for the afternoon of October 23rd; that Bassett and George Muyres came and in Cheney's presence George Muyres said that he would have some bonds for sale, that he did not have any bonds with him but *had a list of bonds he had for sale* (italics ours); that a day later George Muyres came in with some bonds and again came in later that day or the next with his uncle and it was then arranged for an account to be opened under Cheney's name with Hutton and Company; that Cheney was to sell the bonds George Muyres gave him with a five per cent commission on the face value of the bonds;

that Cheney clipped off some of the coupons, totaling $140.00, and used the money to reopen his account at the bank which had been closed for more than a year; that the face value of the bonds turned over by George Muyres to Cheney was approximately $8,000.00. (Tr. of Rec., pp. 125-127.)

Witness Arthur E. Dusenberry testified that he was employed at a bank; that he was approached by George Muyres for the purpose of ascertaining if they could sell certain bonds; that George Muyres said the bonds were given to him by his uncle who was to receive them from an estate. (Tr. of Rec., pp. 143-144.)

Witness Daymond Curtis Bassett testified in substance that he met George Muyres as related by Cheney and that George Muyres told him that he had some bonds and intimated that they came from some foreign country and part of them came from some north central state as a result of some mortgage deals up there: that George Muyres said that the reason he was not selling them was because he had domestic difficulties. Bassett further testified that George Muyres brought over some bonds and he, Bassett, took down the number, titles, and maturity date with the intention of checking the values of them; that at this time Muyres said that he *had already checked the negotiability and found it was all right and there was no claim against them;* that Muyres exhibited to him a letter from some foreign country in a foreign language and represented that it was from some relative of his: that this occurred at the time George Muyres was talking about the source of these bonds. Witness Bassett went down to a brokerage company and after talking to some friends decided not to handle the bonds. (Tr. of Rec., pp. 145-146.)

It will be recalled that earlier in this brief we pointed out that the defendant John Muyres contended and contradicted Woolsey in that he claimed he did not know the actual character of the bonds until a week after they arrived here. It is the Government's contention and it was so urged to the jury that George Muyres' actions and statements in approaching the broker Hilger and the gymnasium attendant Cheney and graduate student Bassett justified the jury in believing that on October 14th or 16th at Jack's Service Station John Muyres discussed the proposed deal fully and it was agreed to at that time by George Muyres. This contention was further strengthened by the testimony of the banker Watkins. He testified that on the morning of November 2d a Mr. Thompson called him and asked him if he could dispose of a Home Owners' Loan bond; that upon his reply,—"Yes," Mr. Thompson came into the bank about 11:30 A.M., November 2d with Mr. George Muyres and gave him the bond; that during this conversation and while the bond was being accepted and cashier's check issued George Muyres told him, Watkins, that he had a relative who died in Holland and he expected to receive a portion of the estate. (Tr. of Rec., p. 161.)

Edward Harold Ryman testified that he and Ryan left Los Angeles on November 2d. (Tr. of Rec., p. 83.) John Muyres testified that on October 31st the broker asked him if he was sure that the bonds were not stolen and he told George he would go and pin the fellows down; that he went back to his machine, found Woolsey and Ryman, and told Woolsey to wait a minute and took Eddie in his car; that it was then that Eddie Ryman admitted the bonds were stolen. John Muyres testified that he did not reach George Muyres until Friday evening (this was November 1st) and that he told George Muyres there was something wrong with the bonds and to get them back by all means. (Tr., of Rec., pp. 211-213.) Yet according to the uncontradicted testimony of the banker Watkins on the following day, November 2d George Muyres procured the cashing of a Home Owners' Loan bond and represented, as he had done before, that it was from an estate in Holland.

We submit, therefore, there was ample evidence to justify the jury in finding that the defendant George Muyres entered into the conspiracy when his uncle contacted him here in Los Angeles on October 14th and 16th; that at that time he knew the true nature of the bonds; and that this knowledge was properly concluded from the actions and statements of George Muyres after the bonds arrived here on the 23rd of October, 1935, and he undertook the disposition of them.

IV.

Defendants John F. Muyres and George F. Muyres Complain of the Failure of the Court to Give Certain Requested Instructions.

Examination of the record discloses that only counsel for defendant George Muyres took exceptions to any instructions given by the court. (Tr. of Rec., pp. 238-240.) It is therefore submitted that any claimed errors and omissions by the trial court in his charge to the jury are not here available to the appellant John F. Muyres.

Considering the exceptions taken by counsel for appellant George F. Muyres we will proceed to a discussion of the claimed failure of the Court to give requested instruction No. 4. In that connection it will be noted that counsel at the time of taking exception stated that he believed it was all covered except the last paragraph. (Tr. of Rec., p. 238.) The requested instruction is set out in full on page 26 of appellant George Muyres' brief. It is submitted that the Court fully covered the instruction requested by the appellant by the following:

"Now, let me point out, gentlemen, what may be an important distinction in this matter. I don't think you really need to have it pointed out, but it is this: A great deal of evidence has been introduced here relative to what has been done by these various defendants in the marketing or sale of these bonds.

"Well, I might say that the Defendant John F. Muyres upon the witness stand admitted that; but denies guilty knowledge that the bonds had been stolen. Now, the defendants are not on trial for anything in the nature of an offense committed here in the State of California, with reference to those bonds after they were brought here. The offense, if any offense was committed, was completed when the transportation in interstate commerce—that is, across the state line—was completed. You will see that readily, of course.

"The offense in this case was completed, if such offense was established, by the evidence at the time the bonds were taken out of the office of the American Express Company; * * * to which they were consigned by this Mr. Ryman, to begin with. * * *

"The conspiracy was ended then and there, because the conspiracy charges that unlawful bringing into the state. Now, no matter how, in your judgment, heinous might be the offense committed, no matter how much you may think they are deserving of punishment, you must bear in mind you are not here to punish them for unlawfully selling these bonds to the various banks and under the various pretexts and excuses that have been testified to, and which you may or may not find to be the fact; not for having divided this money four ways, as testified by some of the defendants, however reprehensible those actions are, we are not concerned with that; but before you can convict any of the defendants you must feel beyond a reasonable doubt, as far as he was concerned, that he either transported the bonds himself, aided and abetted, assisted, or counseled, or advised in the transportation, in order to be convicted of the first offense; or that he conspired, that he agreed to do the transporting." (Tr. of Rec., pp. 226-228.)

As to the failure of the Court to give instruction No. 11 requested by the defendant as particularly set out on page 29 of Appellant George Muyres' brief is, we submit, covered by that portion of the charge commencing with the third paragraph on page 235 of the Transcript to and including the second paragraph on page 237 of the Transcript.

The requested instruction No. 13 of the appellant George Muyres,

"An inference may be drawn from fact to prove by evidence. It may be based upon another evidence" is, we submit, covered by that portion of the charge commencing with the last paragraph of page 228 of the Transcript and concluding with the first paragraph on page 230 of the Transcript.

Apology is made for not setting forth some certain sentence or paragraph in the two elaborate references just made but a perusal of those portions of the charge discloses an interweaving which defies separation.

Conclusion

It is respectfully submitted that the judgments herein appealed from should be by this court affirmed.

Respectfully submitted,

PEIRSON M. HALL,
United States Attorney,

JOHN J. IRWIN,
Assistant United States Attorney,

Attorneys for Appellee. jo

CPSIA information can be obtained
at www.ICGtesting.com
Printed in the USA
BVHW08*1343210918
528171BV00009B/95/P